READINGS

IN

WORLD CHRISTIAN HISTORY

READINGS IN WORLD CHRISTIAN HISTORY

VOLUME 1

Earliest Christianity to 1453

Edited by

JOHN W. COAKLEY
ANDREA STERK

ORBIS BOOKS

Maryknoll, New York 10545

Library of Congress Cataloging-in-Publication Data

Readings in world Christian history / John W. Coakley, Andrea Sterk, editors.
        p. cm.
    Includes bibliographical references.
    ISBN 1-57075-520-5 (pbk. : v. 1)
    1. Church history. I. Coakley, John Wayland. II. Sterk, Andrea.
BR145.3 .R43 2004
270—dc22
                                            2003021865

Contents

Contents

PART TWO: 300-600 C.E.

The Opening of the Constantinian Era: Conversion and Controversy

Varieties of Ascetic Life for Men and Women

Christology and Diverging Identities in the East

The Coming of Age of Latin Christianity

CONTENTS

CONTENTS

Spirituality and Theology in the Latin West in the Twelfth and Thirteenth Centuries

Asian and African Christianity in the Late Middle Ages

Latin and Byzantine Christianity in the Late Middle Ages

Introduction

The prevailing textbook accounts of the history of Christianity have put strong emphasis on the Western aspects of that history—that is, on the origin and development of ideas and institutions that came to fruition in Europe. In such accounts, events and movements outside the historic bounds of the Roman Empire make only incidental appearances in the ancient period, and afterward they disappear almost altogether, along with the other strains of Christianity that survived within the world of Islam; and even the Greek traditions of Constantinople tend to move steadily away from center stage. Scholars are increasingly aware of the distortions inherent in such an approach. There is new appreciation of the cultural diversity and geographical spread of ancient and medieval Christianity, and some recent textbooks have begun to experiment with presentations of Christian history that better express its breadth.[1]

In the present anthology, which we hope will find wide use in courses in the history of Christianity, we have assembled a collection of texts to support such a broadened approach. Both of us have served among the advisers for one of the new textbooks, *History of the World Christian Movement,* vol. 1, by Dale Irvin and Scott Sunquist (Maryknoll, N.Y.: Orbis Books, 2001), which presents the subject not in a single overarching narrative but rather in multiple narratives that attempt to reflect the variety of Christian traditions.[2] Although the present collection is intended to be versatile in its uses and is not strictly tied to that textbook, we share its authors' basic perspective. We have followed their chronological scheme, dividing our material into four consecutive periods ending, respectively, at 300, 600, 1000 and 1453 C.E.; and within each of these periods we have attempted to choose texts that reflect the wide geographical and cultural scope of the Christian movement.

The resulting selection is varied in several ways. We have included many texts that are well established in introductory syllabi—such as writings of Augustine and Aquinas, creedal definitions of Nicaea and Chalcedon, and so on—but also many others that will be less familiar. Here are, for example, a treatise of the ancient Syrian theologian Bardaisan, the record of an early

---

1. In addition to Dale Irvin and Scott Sunquist, *History of the World Christian Movement,* vol. 1 (Maryknoll, N.Y.: Orbis Books, 2001), see also Frederick W. Norris, *Christianity: A Short Global History* (Oxford: Oneworld Publications, 2002); Adrian Hastings, ed., *A World History of Christianity* (Grand Rapids: Eerdmans, 1999); and Mark Ellingsen, *Reclaiming Our Roots: An Inclusive Introduction to Church History,* 2 vols. (Harrisburg, Pa.: Trinity Press International, 1999). Peter Brown's *The Rise of Western Christendom* (Malden, Mass./Oxford: Blackwell, 1996), which focuses on the shift in European Christian identity from an east–west Mediterranean axis to a south-north axis, also includes insightful chapters on Christian communities throughout Asia and under Islam.

2. See also Dale Irvin, *Christian Histories, Christian Traditioning: Rendering Accounts* (Maryknoll, N.Y.: Orbis Books, 1998), esp. ch. 5; David Chidester, *Christianity: A Global History* (San Francisco: Harper, 2000); Paul R. Spickard and Kevin M. Cragg, *A Global History of Christians: How Everyday Believers Experienced Their World* (Grand Rapids: Baker Books, 1994).

medieval debate between a patriarch of Baghdad and a Muslim caliph, an Ethiopian royal chronicle, and two Buddhist-style Christian sutras from the seventh and eighth centuries. We have also attempted to make the collection reflect something of the variety of aspects of Christian life that ought to be considered in an introductory survey course—theology, institutions, spirituality, liturgy—and we have accordingly included a variety of types of sources as well, among them treatises, conciliar documents, letters, chronicles, works of hagiography. We have also taken particular care to include texts that reflect the life and experience of women. Among these are some of the extant documents, rare for most of the times and places we cover, that preserve women's own voices—those of the martyr Perpetua, the pilgrim Egeria, the beguine Hadewijch—but also other sources, particularly hagiographical ones, in which women are much more visible than in the traditional sources for the history of doctrine or institutions, where they are scarcely to be seen at all.

If this collection, then, is for students who are becoming acquainted with the history of Christianity, still it is not our main intention here simply to illustrate the narrative matter of a textbook or academic course. Rather we have aimed to give students an opportunity to encounter and interpret sources for themselves. Therefore we have chosen, wherever possible, documents that could be included in their entirety or in substantial self-contained excerpts, so as to make them available for analysis in their own right—documents that an instructor could conceivably assign in conjunction with a short analytical or comparative essay, to encourage students to make their own discoveries in those sources and arrive at their own conclusions. Many source collections aim less at presenting documents for analysis than at illustrating the principal themes, ideas, or situations that students will be encountering in textbooks or other secondary-source reading or lectures, for which purpose, short excerpted passages may well suffice. There are, to be sure, many important collections of this sort, and they have their advantages, not least in the number and variety of materials they present to the student.[3] Within the constraints of a one-volume anthology, the price to be paid for our decision to go with longer texts is that we have to make do with fewer. (Accordingly we have reluctantly omitted some of the more typical choices, like excerpts from Augustine's *Confessions* or the Rule of St. Benedict, which are available to English-speaking readers in relatively inexpensive editions.) But our own experience suggests that a substantial encounter with sources remains at the heart of what historians do, even in the absence of the old historicist ideal of objectivity, indeed that at its best that encounter affects us deeply, challenging the way we think and perhaps also the way we live. As teachers, we want to emphasize it with our students; and so we have compiled this collection with that encounter always in mind. To colleagues of similar disposition, and therefore particularly to their students, we commend the pages to follow.

---

3. We think, in particular, of J. Stevenson's magisterial selections of ancient Christian texts, *A New Eusebius* and *Creeds, Councils and Controversies* (London: S.P.C.K., 1957, 1966 respectively).

Acknowledgments

We are pleased to acknowledge several debts of gratitude. First, we thank our many colleagues for their assistance. They are, in fact, too many to mention by name. They have given us invaluable advice and kept us from incalculable errors. Russell and Maria Gasero were essential to the project. Without their painstaking work of scanning, proofreading, and correcting the documents, fidelity to the originals would never have been achieved. Finally, we thank the Henry Luce Foundation, which provided generous financial support to our work as part of the "History of the World Christian Movement" project, directed by Scott W. Sunquist and Dale T. Irvin.

Notes on Texts and Translation

Many of the sources collected in this volume, especially less traditional and non-Western texts, are drawn from very recent English translations; indeed two texts appear for the first time here in English translation. However, in order to keep the cost of the volume within reason, given the considerable expense of copyright permissions, we have also chosen to use a number of reliable older translations. In cases where the translations used are in the public domain, we have modernized the English by removing grammatical archaisms, and, wherever warranted, replacing gender-exclusive pronouns with gender-neutral language. For the sake of consistency, we have also employed standard American English spelling throughout the volume. In order to make the best use of limited space, we have omitted most footnotes. When Scripture is quoted directly, the references appear in parentheses, even in cases where the original publication employed footnotes. In most of the texts, such scriptural quotations are set off by the usual quotation marks, but in a few cases the original editors italicized them instead (a useful practice especially when quotations are fragmented or pieced-together), and in those instances we have let the italics stand.

PART ONE
To 300 C.E.

Early Christian Communities

1. Ignatius of Antioch,
Letter to the Magnesians

All we know of Ignatius, bishop of Antioch, comes from seven surviving letters that he wrote while being transported across Asia Minor, at some point during the rule of the emperor Trajan (98-117), on his way to Rome for trial and (so he expected) martyrdom. He addressed one of these to the church at Rome, another to Bishop Polycarp of Smyrna, and the other five to churches in Asia Minor that had sent delegations to greet him. The church of Magnesia was among these. Throughout the letters he asserts the authority of bishops and typically warns against false teachers—especially those who questioned whether Christ truly suffered in the flesh and those who wished to maintain Jewish traditions.

Ignatius, who is also called Theophorus, to her[1] who is blessed in the Grace of God the Father by Christ Jesus, our Savior, in whom I greet the Church which is in Magnesia on the Maeander, and bid it in God the Father and in Christ Jesus abundant greeting.

I

1. Knowing the great orderliness of your love towards God I gladly determined to address you in the faith of Jesus Christ. 2. For being counted worthy to bear a most godly name I sing the praise of the Churches in the bonds which I carry about, and pray that in them there may be a union of the flesh and spirit of Jesus Christ, who is our everlasting life, a union of faith and love, to which is nothing preferable, and (what is more than all) a union of Jesus and the Father. If we endure in him all the evil treatment of the Prince of this world and escape, we shall attain unto God.

II

1. Forasmuch then as I was permitted to see you in the person of Damas, your godly bishop, and the worthy presbyters Bassus and Apollonius, and my fellow servant the deacon Zotion, whose friendship I would enjoy because he is subject to the bishop as to the grace of God, and to the presbytery as to the law of Jesus Christ—[2]

III

1. Now it becomes you not to presume on the youth of the bishop, but to render him all respect according to the power of God the Father, as I have heard that even the holy presbyters have not taken advantage of his outwardly youthful appearance, but yield to him in their godly prudence, yet not to him, but to the Father of Jesus Christ, to the bishop of all. 2. For the honor therefore of him who desired us, it is right that we yield obedience with-

SOURCE: "Ignatius to the Magnesians," in *The Apostolic Fathers,* vol. 1, tr. Kirsopp Lake (London: William Heinemann, 1919; New York: G. P. Putnam's Sons, 1919), 197-211.

1. I.e., the church.
2. The sentence is unfinished: possibly the text is corrupt.

out hypocrisy, for one does not merely deceive this bishop who is seen, but is dealing wrongly with him who is invisible. And in this matter his reckoning is not with flesh, but with God, who knows the secret things.

IV

1. It is right, then, that we should be really Christians, and not merely have the name; even as there are some who recognize the bishop in their words, but disregard him in all their actions. Such men seem to me not to act in good faith, since they do not hold valid meetings according to the commandment.

V

1. Seeing then that there is an end to all, that the choice is between two things, death and life, and that each is to go to his own place; 2. for, just as there are two coinages, the one of God, the other of the world, and each has its own stamp impressed on it, so the unbelievers bear the stamp of this world, and the believers the stamp of God the Father in love through Jesus Christ, and unless we willingly choose to die through him in his passion, his life is not in us.

VI

1. Seeing then that I have looked on the whole congregation in faith in the persons mentioned above, and have embraced them, I exhort you:— Be zealous to do all things in harmony with God, with the bishop presiding in the place of God and the presbyters in place of the Council of the Apostles and the deacons, who are most dear to me, entrusted with the service of Jesus Christ, who was from eternity with the Father and was made manifest at the end of time. 2. Be then all in conformity with God, and respect one another, and let no one regard a neighbor according to the flesh, but in everything love one another in Jesus Christ. Let there be nothing in you which can divide you, but be united with the bishop and with those who preside over you as an example and lesson of immortality.

VII

1. As then the Lord was united to the Father and did nothing without him, neither by himself nor through the Apostles, so do you do nothing without the bishop and the presbyters. Do not attempt to make anything appear right for you by yourselves, but let there be in common one prayer, one supplication, one mind, one hope in love, in the joy which is without fault, that is Jesus Christ, than whom there is nothing better. 2. Hasten all to come together as to one temple of God, as to one altar, to one Jesus Christ, who came forth from the one Father, and is with one, and departed to one.

VIII

1. Be not led astray by strange doctrines or by old fables which are profitless. For if we are living until now according to Judaism, we confess that we have not received grace. 2. For the divine prophets lived according to Jesus Christ. Therefore they were also persecuted, being inspired by his grace, to convince the disobedient that there is one God, who manifested himself through Jesus Christ his son, who is his Word proceeding from silence, who in all respects was well-pleasing to him that sent him.

IX

1. If then they who walked in ancient customs came to a new hope, no longer living for the Sabbath, but for the Lord's Day, on which also our life sprang up through him and his death—though some deny him—and by this mystery we received faith, and for this reason also we suffer, that we may be found disciples of Jesus Christ our only teacher; 2. if these things be so, how then shall we be able to live without him of whom even the prophets were disciples in the Spirit and to whom they looked forward as their teacher? And for this reason he for whom they waited in righteousness, when he came, raised them from the dead.

X

1. Let us then not be insensible to his goodness, for if he should imitate us in our actions we are

lost. For this cause let us be his disciples, and let us learn to lead Christian lives. For whoever is called by any name other than this is not of God. 2. Put aside then the evil leaven, which has grown old and sour, and turn to the new leaven, which is Jesus Christ. Be salted in him, that none among you may be corrupted, since by your savor you shall be tested. 3. It is monstrous to talk of Jesus Christ and to practice Judaism. For Christianity did not base its faith on Judaism, but Judaism on Christianity, and every tongue believing on God was brought together in it.

XI

1. Now I say this, beloved, not because I know that there are any of you that are thus, but because I wish to warn you, though I am less than you, not to fall into the snare of vain doctrine, but to be convinced of the birth and passion and resurrection which took place at the time of the procuratorship of Pontius Pilate; for these things were truly and certainly done by Jesus Christ, our hope, from which God grant that none of you be turned aside.

XII

1. Let me have joy of you in all things, if I be but worthy. For even though I am in bonds I am not to be compared to one of you that have been set free. I know that you are not puffed up; for you have Jesus Christ in yourselves. And I know that when I praise you your modesty increases the more, as it is written, "The righteous man is his own accuser."

XIII

1. Be diligent therefore to be confirmed in the ordinances of the Lord and the Apostles, in order that "you may prosper in all things whatsoever ye do" in the flesh and in the spirit, in faith and love, in the Son and the Father and the Spirit, at the beginning and at the end, together with your revered bishop and with your presbytery, that aptly woven spiritual crown, and with the godly deacons. 2. Be subject to the bishop and to one another; even Apostles were subject to Christ and to the Father in order that there may be a union both of flesh and of spirit.

XIV

1. I know that you are full of God, and I have exhorted you briefly. Remember me in your prayers, that I may attain to God, and remember the Church in Syria, of which I am not worthy to be called a member. For I need your united prayer in God and your love, that the Church which is in Syria may be granted refreshment from the dew of your Church.

XV

1. The Ephesians greet you from Smyrna, whence also I am writing to you; they, like yourselves, are here for the glory of God and have in all things given me comfort, together with Polycarp the bishop of the Smyrnaeans. And the other Churches also greet you in honor of Jesus Christ. Farewell in godly concord and may you possess an unhesitating spirit, for this is Jesus Christ.

2. *The Gospel of Thomas*

A full text of this Gospel was among the discoveries at Nag Hammadi in Egypt in 1945. The language is Coptic, but the text was probably translated from a Greek original composed in the second, or even late first, century. The reader will recognize sayings that appear in only slightly different form in the New Testament Gospels; but this Gospel's very use of some of the

SOURCE: "The Gospel of Thomas," tr. Thomas O. Lambdin, in *The Nag Hammadi Library in English*, 3rd ed., ed. James M. Robinson (San Francisco: Harper & Row, 1988), 126-38. Copyright © 1977 by E. J. Brill, The Netherlands. Reprinted by permission of HarperCollins Publishers, Inc., and Brill Academic Publishers.

same traditions makes its differences from them the more striking—for instance, its lack of crucifixion and resurrection narratives and its apparent "gnostic" approach to salvation through esoteric knowledge.

These are the secret sayings which the living Jesus spoke and which Didymos Judas Thomas wrote down.

(1) And he said, "Whoever finds the interpretation of these sayings will not experience death."

(2) Jesus said, "Let him who seeks continue seeking until he finds. When he finds, he will become troubled. When he becomes troubled, he will be astonished, and he will rule over the all."

(3) Jesus said, "If those who lead you say to you, 'See, the kingdom is in the sky,' then the birds of the sky will precede you. If they say to you, 'It is in the sea,' then the fish will precede you. Rather, the kingdom is inside of you, and it is outside of you. When you come to know yourselves, then you will become known, and you will realize that it is you who are the sons of the living father. But if you will not know yourselves, you dwell in poverty and it is you who are that poverty."

(4) Jesus said, "The man old in days will not hesitate to ask a small child seven days old about the place of life, and he will live. For many who are first will become last, and they will become one and the same."

(5) Jesus said, "Recognize what is in your [sg.] sight, and that which is hidden from you [sg.] will become plain to you [sg.]. For there is nothing hidden which will not become manifest."

(6) His disciples questioned him and said to him, "Do you want us to fast? How shall we pray? Shall we give alms? What diet shall we observe?"

Jesus said, "Do not tell lies, and do not do what you hate, for all things are plain in the sight of heaven. For nothing hidden will not become manifest, and nothing covered will remain without being uncovered."

(7) Jesus said, "Blessed is the lion which becomes man when consumed by man; and cursed is the man whom the lion consumes, and the lion becomes man."

(8) And he said, "The man is like a wise fisherman who cast his net into the sea and drew it up from the sea full of small fish. Among them the wise fisherman found a fine large fish. He threw all the small fish back into the sea and chose the large fish without difficulty. Whoever has ears to hear, let him hear."

(9) Jesus said, "Now the sower went out, took a handful (of seeds), and scattered them. Some fell on the road; the birds came and gathered them up. Others fell on rock, did not take root in the soil, and did not produce ears. And others fell on thorns; they choked the seed(s) and worms ate them. And others fell on the good soil and it produced good fruit: it bore sixty per measure and a hundred and twenty per measure."

(10) Jesus said, "I have cast fire upon the world, and see, I am guarding it until it blazes."

(11) Jesus said, "This heaven will pass away, and the one above it will pass away. The dead are not alive, and the living will not die. In the days when you consumed what is dead, you made it what is alive. When you come to dwell in the light, what will you do? On the day when you were one you became two. But when you become two, what will you do?"

(12) The disciples said to Jesus, "We know that you will depart from us. Who is to be our leader?"

Jesus said to them, "Wherever you are, you are to go to James the righteous, for whose sake heaven and earth came into being."

(13) Jesus said to his disciples, "Compare me to someone and tell me whom I am like."

Simon Peter said to him, "You are like a righteous angel."

Matthew said to him, "You are like a wise philosopher."

Thomas said to him, "Master, my mouth is wholly incapable of saying whom you are like."

Jesus said, "I am not your [sg.] master. Because you [sg.] have drunk, you [sg.] have become intoxicated from the bubbling spring which I have measured out."

And he took him and withdrew and told him three things. When Thomas returned to his companions, they asked him, "What did Jesus say to you?"

Thomas said to them, "If I tell you one of the things which he told me, you will pick up stones and throw them at me; a fire will come out of the stones and burn you up."

(14) Jesus said to them, "If you fast, you will give rise to sin for yourselves; and if you pray, you will be condemned; and if you give alms, you will do harm to your spirits. When you go into any land and walk about in the districts, if they receive you, eat what they will set before you, and heal the sick among them. For what goes into your mouth will not defile you, but that which issues from your mouth—it is that which will defile you."

(15) Jesus said, "When you see one who was not born of woman, prostrate yourselves on your faces and worship him. That one is your father."

(16) Jesus said, "Men think, perhaps, that it is peace which I have come to cast upon the world. They do not know that it is dissension which I have come to cast upon the earth: fire, sword, and war. For there will be five in a house: three will be against two, and two against three, the father against the son, and the son against the father. And they will stand solitary."

(17) Jesus said, "I shall give you what no eye has seen and what no ear has heard and what no hand has touched and what has never occurred to the human mind."

(18) The disciples said to Jesus, "Tell us how our end will be."

Jesus said, "Have you discovered, then, the beginning, that you look for the end? For where the beginning is, there will the end be. Blessed is he who will take his place in the beginning; he will know the end and will not experience death."

(19) Jesus said, "Blessed is he who came into being before he came into being. If you become my disciples and listen to my words, these stones will minister to you. For there are five trees for you in Paradise which remain undisturbed summer and winter and whose leaves do not fall. Whoever becomes acquainted with them will not experience death."

(20) The disciples said to Jesus, "Tell us what the kingdom of heaven is like."

He said to them, "It is like a mustard seed. It is the smallest of all seeds. But when it falls on tilled soil, it produces a great plant and becomes a shelter for birds of the sky."

(21) Mary said to Jesus, "Whom are your disciples like?"

He said, "They are like children who have settled in a field which is not theirs. When the owners of the field come, they will say, 'Let us have back our field.' They (will) undress in their presence in order to let them have back their field and to give it back to them. Therefore I say, if the owner of a house knows that the thief is coming, he will begin his vigil before he comes and will not let him dig through into his house of his domain to carry away his goods. You [pl.], then, be on your guard against the world. Arm yourselves with great strength lest the robbers find a way to come to you, for the difficulty which you expect will (surely) materialize. Let there be among you a man of understanding. When the grain ripened, he came quickly with his sickle in his hand and reaped it. Whoever has ears to hear, let him hear."

(22) Jesus saw infants being suckled. He said to his disciples, "These infants being suckled are like those who enter the kingdom."

They said to him, "Shall we then, as children, enter the kingdom?"

Jesus said to them, "When you make the two one, and when you make the inside like the outside and the outside like the inside, and the above like the below, and when you make the male and the female one and the same, so that the male not be male nor the female female; and when you fashion eyes in place of an eye, and a hand in place of a hand, and a foot in place of a foot, and a likeness in place of a likeness; then will you enter [the kingdom]."

(23) Jesus said, "I shall choose you, one out of a thousand, and two out of ten thousand, and they shall stand as a single one."

(24) His disciples said to him, "Show us the place where you are, since it is necessary for us to seek it."

He said to them, "Whoever has ears, let him hear. There is light within a man of light, and he lights up the whole world. If he does not shine, he is darkness."

(25) Jesus said, "Love your [sg.] brother like your soul, guard him like the pupil of your eye."

(26) Jesus said, "You [sg.] see the mote in your brothers eye, but you do not see the beam in your

own eye. When you cast the beam out of your own eye, then you will see clearly to cast the mote from your brother's eye."

(27) <Jesus said,> "If you do not fast as regards the world, you will not find the kingdom. If you do not observe the Sabbath as a Sabbath, you will not see the father."

(28) Jesus said, "I took my place in the midst of the world, and I appeared to them in flesh. I found all of them intoxicated; I found none of them thirsty. And my soul became afflicted for the sons of men, because they are blind in their hearts and do not have sight; for empty they came into the world, and empty too they seek to leave the world. But for the moment they are intoxicated. When they shake off their wine, then they will repent."

(29) Jesus said, "If the flesh came into being because of spirit, it is a wonder. But if spirit came into being because of the body, it is a wonder of wonders. Indeed, I am amazed at how this great wealth has made its home in this poverty."

(30) Jesus said, "Where there are three gods, they are gods. Where there are two or one, I am with him."

(31) Jesus said, "No prophet is accepted in his own village; no physician heals those who know him."

(32) Jesus said, "A city being built on a high mountain and fortified cannot fall, nor can it be hidden."

(33) Jesus said, "Preach from your [pl.] house-tops that which you [sg.] will hear in your [sg.] ear. For no one lights a lamp and puts it under a bushel, nor does he put it in a hidden place, but rather he sets it on a lampstand so that everyone who enters and leaves will see its light."

(34) Jesus said, "If a blind man leads a blind man, they will both fall into a pit."

(35) Jesus said, "It is not possible for anyone to enter the house of a strong man and take it by force unless he binds his hands; then he will (be able to) ransack his house."

(36) Jesus said, "Do not be concerned from morning until evening and from evening until morning about what you will wear."

(37) His disciples said, "When will you become revealed to us and when shall we see you?"

Jesus said, "When you disrobe without being ashamed and take up your garments and place them under your feet like little children and tread on them, then [will you see] the son of the living one, and you will not be afraid."

(38) Jesus said, "Many times have you desired to hear these words which I am saying to you, and you have no one else to hear them from. There will be days when you will look for me and will not find me."

(39) Jesus said, "The pharisees and the scribes have taken the keys of knowledge (*gnōsis*) and hidden them. They themselves have not entered, nor have they allowed to enter those who wish to. You, however, be as wise as serpents and as innocent as doves."

(40) Jesus said, "A grapevine has been planted outside of the father, but being unsound, it will be pulled up by its roots and destroyed."

(41) Jesus said, "Whoever has something in his hand will receive more, and whoever has nothing will be deprived of even the little he has."

(42) Jesus said, "Become passers-by."

(43) His disciples said to him, "Who are you, that you should say these things to us?"

<Jesus said to them,> "You do not realize who I am from what I say to you, but you have become like the Jews, for they (either) love the tree and hate its fruit (or) love the fruit and hate the tree."

(44) Jesus said, "Whoever blasphemes against the father will be forgiven, and whoever blasphemes against the son will be forgiven, but whoever blasphemes against the holy spirit will not be forgiven either on earth or in heaven."

(45) Jesus said, "Grapes are not harvested from thorns, nor are figs gathered from thistles, for they do not produce fruit. A good man brings forth good from his storehouse; an evil man brings forth evil things from his evil storehouse, which is in his heart, and says evil things. For out of the abundance of the heart he brings forth evil things."

(46) Jesus said, "Among those born of women, from Adam until John the Baptist, there is no one so superior to John the Baptist that his eyes should not be lowered (before him). Yet I have said, whichever one of you comes to be a child will be acquainted with the kingdom and will become superior to John."

(47) Jesus said, "It is impossible for a man to mount two horses or to stretch two bows. And it is impossible for a servant to serve two masters; otherwise, he will honor the one and treat the other contemptuously. No man drinks old wine and immediately desires to drink new wine. And new wine is not put into old wineskins, lest they burst; nor is old wine put into a new wineskin, lest it spoil it. An old patch is not sewn into a new garment, because a tear would result."

(48) Jesus said, "If two make peace with each other in this one house, they will say to the mountain, 'Move away,' and it will move away."

(49) Jesus said, "Blessed are the solitary and elect, for you will find the kingdom. For you are from it, and to it you will return."

(50) Jesus said, "If they say to you, 'Where did you come from?' say to them, 'We came from the light, the place where the light came into being on its own accord and established [itself] and became manifest through their image.' If they say to you, 'Is it you?' say, 'We are its children, and we are the elect of the living father.' If they ask you, 'What is the sign of your father in you?' say to them, 'It is movement and repose.'"

(51) His disciples said to him, "When will the repose of the dead come about, and when will the new world come?"

He said to them, "What you look forward to has already come, but you do not recognize it."

(52) His disciples said to him, "Twenty-four prophets spoke in Israel, and all of them spoke in you."

He said to them, "You have omitted the one living in your presence and have spoken (only) of the dead."

(53) His disciples said to him, "Is circumcision beneficial or not?"

He said to them, "If it were beneficial, their father would beget them already circumcised from their mother. Rather, the true circumcision in spirit has become completely profitable."

(54) Jesus said, "Blessed are the poor, for yours is the kingdom of heaven."

(55) Jesus said, "Whoever does not hate his father and his mother cannot become a discile to me. And whoever does not hate his brothers and sisters and take up his cross in my way will not be worthy of me."

(56) Jesus said, "Whoever has come to understand the world has found (only) a corpse, and whoever has found a corpse is superior to the world."

(57) Jesus said, "The kingdom of the father is like a man who had [good] seed. His enemy came by night and sowed weeds among the good seed. The man did not allow them to pull up the weeds; he said to them, 'I am afraid that you will go intending to pull up the weeds and pull up the wheat along with them.' For on the day of the harvest the weeds will be plainly visible, and they will be pulled up and burned."

(58) Jesus said, "Blessed is the man who has suffered and found life."

(59) Jesus said, "Take heed of the living one while you are alive, lest you die and seek to see him and be unable to do so."

(60) <They saw> a Samaritan carrying a lamb on his way to Judea. He said to his disciples, "That man is round about the lamb."

They said to him, "So that he may kill it and eat it."

He said to them, "While it is alive, he will not eat it, but only when he has killed it and it has become a corpse."

They said to him, "He cannot do so otherwise."

He said to them, "You too, look for a place for yourselves within repose, lest you become a corpse and be eaten."

(61) Jesus said, "Two will rest on a bed: the one will die, and the other will live."

Salome said, "Who are you, man, that you . . . have come up on my couch and eaten from my table?"

Jesus said to her, "I am he who exists from the undivided. I was given some of the things of my father."

< . . . > "I am your disciple."

< . . . > "Therefore I say, if he is destroyed he will be filled with light, but if he is divided, he will be filled with darkness."

(62) Jesus said, "It is to those [who are worthy of my] mysteries that I tell my mysteries. Do not let your [sg.] left hand know what your [sg.] right hand is doing."

(63) Jesus said, "There was a rich man who had much money. He said, 'I shall put my money to

use so that I may sow, reap, plant, and fill my storehouse with produce, with the result that I shall lack nothing.' Such were his intentions, but that same night he died. Let him who has ears hear."

(64) Jesus said, "A man had received visitors. And when he had prepared the dinner, he sent his servant to invite the guests. He went to the first one and said to him, 'My master invites you.' He said, 'I have claims against some merchants. They are coming to me this evening. I must go and give them my orders. I ask to be excused from the dinner.' He went to another and said to him, 'My master has invited you.' He said to him, 'I have just bought a house and am required for the day. I shall not have any spare time.' He went to another and said to him, 'My master invites you.' He said to him, 'My friend is going to get married, and I am to prepare the banquet. I shall not be able to come. I ask to be excused from the dinner.' He went to another and said to him, 'My master invites you.' He said to him, 'I have just bought a farm, and I am on my way to collect the rent. I shall not be able to come, I ask to be excused.' The servant returned and said to his master, 'Those whom you invited to the dinner have asked to be excused.' The master said to his servant, 'Go outside to the streets and bring back those whom you happen to meet, so that they may dine.' Businessmen and merchants [will] not enter the places of my father."

(65) He said, "There was a good man who owned a vineyard. He leased it to tenant farmers so that they might work it and he might collect the produce from them. He sent his servant so that the tenants might give him the produce of the vineyard. They seized his servant and beat him, all but killing him. The servant went back and told his master. The master said, 'Perhaps he did not recognize them.' He sent another servant. The tenants beat this one as well. Then the owner sent his son and said, 'Perhaps they will show respect to my son.' Because the tenants knew that it was he who was the heir to the vineyard, they seized him and killed him. Let him who has ears hear."

(66) Jesus said, "Show me the stone which the builders have rejected. That one is the cornerstone."

(67) Jesus said, "If one who knows the all still feels a personal deficiency, he is completely deficient."

(68) Jesus said, "Blessed are you when you are hated and persecuted. Wherever you have been persecuted they will find no place."

(69) Jesus said, "Blessed are they who have been persecuted within themselves. It is they who have truly come to know the father. Blessed are the hungry, for the belly of him who desires will be filled."

(70) Jesus said, "That which you have will save you if you bring it forth from yourselves. That which you do not have within you [will] kill you if you do not have it within you."

(71) Jesus said, "I shall [destroy this] house, and no one will be able to build it [...]"

(72) [A man said] to him, "Tell my brothers to divide my father's possessions with me."

He said to him, "O man, who has made me a divider?"

He turned to his disciples and said to them, "I am not a divider, am I?"

(73) Jesus said, "The harvest is great but the laborers are few. Beseech the lord, therefore, to send out laborers to the harvest."

(74) He said, "O lord, there are many around the drinking trough, but there is nothing in the cistern."

(75) Jesus said, "Many are standing at the door, but it is the solitary who will enter the bridal chamber."

(76) Jesus said, "The kingdom of the father is like a merchant who had a consignment of merchandise and who discovered a pearl. That merchant was shrewd. He sold the merchandise and bought the pearl alone for himself. You, too, seek his unfailing and enduring treasure where no moth comes near to devour and no worm destroys."

(77) Jesus said, "It is I who am the light which is above them all. It is I who am the all. From me did the all come forth, and unto me did the all extend. Split a piece of wood, and I am there. Lift up the stone, and you will find me there."

(78) Jesus said, "Why have you come out into the desert? To see a reed shaken by the wind? And to see a man clothed in fine garments [like your] kings and your great men? Upon them are the fine garments, and they are unable to discern the truth."

(79) A woman from the crowd said to him, "Blessed are the womb which bore you and the breasts which nourished you."

He said to [her], "Blessed are those who have heard the word of the father and have truly kept it. For there will be days when you [pl.] will say, 'Blessed are the womb which has not conceived and the breasts which have not given milk.'"

(80) Jesus said, "He who has recognized the world has found the body, but he who has found the body is superior to the world."

(81) Jesus said, "Let him who has grown rich be king, and let him who possesses power renounce it."

(82) Jesus said, "He who is near me is near the fire, and he who is far from me is far from the kingdom."

(83) Jesus said, "The images are manifest to man, but the light in them remains concealed in the image of the light of the father. He will become manifest, but his image will remain concealed by his light."

(84) Jesus said, "When you see your likeness, you rejoice. But when you see your images which came into being before you, and which neither die nor become manifest, how much you will have to bear!"

(85) Jesus said, "Adam came into being from a great power and a great wealth, but he did not become worthy of you. For had he been worthy, [he would] not [have experienced] death."

(86) Jesus said, "[The foxes have their holes] and the birds have their nests, but the son of man has no place to lay his head and rest."

(87) Jesus said, "Wretched is the body that is dependent upon a body, and wretched is the soul that is dependent on these two."

(88) Jesus said, "The angels and the prophets will come to you and give to you those things you (already) have. And you, too, give them those things which you have, and say to yourselves, 'When will they come and take what is theirs?'"

(89) Jesus said, "Why do you wash the outside of the cup? Do you not realize that he who made the inside is the same one who made the outside?"

(90) Jesus said, "Come unto me, for my yoke is easy and my lordship is mild, and you will find repose for yourselves."

(91) They said to him, "Tell us who you are so that we may believe in you."

He said to them, "You read the face of the sky and of the earth, but you have not recognized the one who is before you, and you do not know how to read this moment."

(92) Jesus said, "Seek and you will find. Yet, what you asked me about in former times and which I did not tell you then, now I do desire to tell, but you do not inquire after it."

(93) <Jesus said,> "Do not give what is holy to dogs, lest they throw them on the dung heap. Do not throw the pearls [to] swine, lest they . . . it [. . .]."

(94) Jesus [said], "He who seeks will find, and [he who knocks] will be let in."

(95) [Jesus said], "If you have money, do not lend it at interest, but give [it] to one from whom you will not get it back."

(96) Jesus said, "The kingdom of the father is like [a certain] woman. She took a little leaven, [concealed] it in some dough, and made it into large loaves. Let him who has ears hear."

(97) Jesus said, "The kingdom of the [father] is like a certain woman who was carrying a [jar] full of meal. While she was walking [on the] road, still some distance from home, the handle of the jar broke and the meal emptied out behind her [on] the road. She did not realize it; she had noticed no accident. When she reached her house, she set the jar down and found it empty."

(98) Jesus said, "The kingdom of the father is like a certain man who wanted to kill a powerful man. In his own house he drew his sword and stuck it into the wall in order to find out whether his hand could carry through. Then he slew the powerful man."

(99) The disciples said to him, "Your brothers and your mother are standing outside."

He said to them, "Those here who do the will of my father are my brothers and my mother. It is they who will enter the kingdom of my father."

(100) They showed Jesus a gold coin and said to him, "Caesar's men demand taxes from us."

He said to them, "Give Caesar what belongs to Caesar, give God what belongs to God, and give me what is mine."

(101) <Jesus said,> "Whoever does not hate

his [father] and his mother as I do cannot become a [disciple] to me. And whoever does [not] love his [father and] his mother as I do cannot become a [disciple to] me. For my mother [. . .], but [my] true [mother] gave me life."

(102) Jesus said, "Woe to the Pharisees, for they are like a dog sleeping in the manger of oxen, for neither does he eat nor does he [let] the oxen eat."

(103) Jesus said, "Fortunate is the man who knows where the brigands will enter, so that [he] may get up, muster his domain, and arm himself before they invade."

(104) They said to Jesus, "Come, let us pray today and let us fast."

Jesus said, "What is the sin that I have committed, or wherein have I been defeated? But when the bridegroom leaves the bridal chamber, then let them fast and pray."

(105) Jesus said, "He who knows the father and the mother will be called the son of a harlot."

(106) Jesus said, "When you make the two one, you will become the sons of man, and when you say, 'Mountain, move away,' it will move away."

(107) Jesus said, "The kingdom is like a shepherd who had a hundred sheep. One of them, the largest, went astray. He left the ninety-nine and looked for that one until he found it. When he had gone to such trouble, he said to the sheep, 'I care for you more than the ninety-nine.'"

(108) Jesus said, "He who will drink from my mouth will become like me. I myself shall become he, and the things that are hidden will be revealed to him."

(109) Jesus said, "The kingdom is like a man who had a [hidden] treasure in his field without knowing it. And [after] he died, he left it to his [son]. The son [did] not know (about the treasure). He inherited the field and sold [it]. And the one who bought it went plowing and [found] the treasure. He began to lend money at interest to whomever he wished."

(110) Jesus said, "Whoever finds the world and becomes rich, let him renounce the world."

(111) Jesus said, "The heavens and the earth will be rolled up in your presence. And the one who lives from the living one will not see death." Does not Jesus say, "Whoever finds himself is superior to the world"?

(112) Jesus said, "Woe to the flesh that depends on the soul; woe to the soul that depends on the flesh."

(113) His disciples said to him, "When will the kingdom come?"

<Jesus said,> "It will not come by waiting for it. It will not be a matter of saying 'here it is' or 'there it is.' Rather, the kingdom of the father is spread out upon the earth, and men do not see it."

(114) Simon Peter said to them, "Let Mary leave us, for women are not worthy of life."

Jesus said, "I myself shall lead her in order to make her male, so that she too may become a living spirit resembling you males. For every woman who will make herself male will enter the kingdom of heaven."

3. Didache

This handbook of Christian morals and church order, which was discovered in a manuscript at Constantinople in 1873, probably dates from the early second century at the latest and likely includes first-century materials. Some scholars have hypothesized Syria or Palestine as its place of origin. The moral teachings (chs. 1-6) have parallels in the roughly contemporary Epistle of Barnabas. The chapters on church order offer a precious glimpse of early liturgical practice (chs. 7-10) and, in assuming the coexistence of itinerant and settled leadership (chs. 11-15), suggest a still-developing concept of church office.

SOURCE: "The Didache, or Teaching of the Twelve Apostles," in *The Apostolic Fathers*, vol. 1, tr. Kirsopp Lake (London: William Heinemann, 1919; New York: G. P. Putnam's Sons, 1919), 309-33.

The Lord's teaching to the heathen by the Twelve Apostles.

I

1. There are two Ways, one of Life and one of Death, and there is a great difference between the two Ways.

2. The Way of Life is this: "First, you shall love the God who made you, secondly, your neighbor as yourself; and whatsoever you would not have done to yourself, do not do to another" (cf. Matt. 22:37-39; 7:12).

3. Now, the teaching of these words is this: "Bless those that curse you, and pray for your enemies, and fast for those that persecute you. For what credit is it to you if you love those that love you? Do not even the heathen do the same?" But, for your part, "love those that hate you" (cf. Matt. 5:44, 46, 47), and you will have no enemy. 4. "Abstain from carnal" and bodily "lusts" (cf. 1 Pet. 2:11). "If anyone smites you on the right cheek, turn the other cheek also, and you will be perfect. If anyone impresses you to go one mile, go with that person two. If anyone takes your coat, give your shirt also. If anyone will take from you what is yours, refuse it not" (cf. Matt. 5:40, 41; 1 Pet. 2:11)—not even if you can. 5. Give to everyone that asks you, and do not refuse, for the Father's will is that we give to all from the gifts we have received. Blessed are those who give according to the mandate; for they are innocent. Woe to those who receive; for if anyone receives alms under pressure of need, that one is innocent; but those who receive it without need shall be tried as to why they took and for what, and being in prison they shall be examined as to their deeds, and "they shall not come out thence until they pay the last farthing" (cf. Matt. 5:26). 6. But concerning this it was also said, Let your alms sweat into your hands until you know to whom you are giving.

II

1. But the second commandment of the teaching is this: 2. "You shall do no murder; you shall not commit adultery"; you shall not commit sodomy; you shall not commit fornication; you shall not steal; you shall not use magic; you shall not use philters; you shall not procure abortion, nor commit infanticide; "you shall not covet your neighbor's goods"; 3. you shall not commit perjury, "you shall not bear false witness" (cf. Exod. 20:13-17); you shall not speak evil; you shall not bear malice. 4. You shall not be double-minded nor double-tongued, for to be double-tongued is the snare of death. 5. Your speech shall not be false nor vain, but completed in action. 6. You shall not be covetous nor extortionate, nor a hypocrite, nor malignant, nor proud; you shall make no evil plan against your neighbor. 7. You shall hate no person; but some you shall reprove, and for some you shall pray, and some you shall love more than your own life.

III

1. My child, flee from every evil man and from all like him. 2. Be not proud, for pride leads to murder, nor jealous, nor contentious, nor passionate, for from all these murders are engendered. 3. My child, be not lustful, for lust leads to fornication, nor a speaker of base words, nor a lifter up of the eyes, for from all these is adultery engendered. 4. My child, regard not omens, for this leads to idolatry; neither be an enchanter, nor an astrologer, nor a magician, neither wish to see these things, for from them all is idolatry engendered. 5. My child, be not a liar, for lying leads to theft, nor a lover of money, nor vainglorious, for from all these things are thefts engendered. My child, be not a grumbler, for this leads to blasphemy, nor stubborn, nor a thinker of evil, for from all these are blasphemies engendered, 7. but be "meek, for the meek shall inherit the earth"; 8. be long-suffering, and merciful, and guileless, and quiet, and good, and ever fearing the words which you have heard. 9. You shall not exalt yourself, nor let your soul be presumptuous. Your soul shall not consort with the lofty, but you shall walk with righteous and humble men. 10. Receive the accidents that befall you as good, knowing that nothing happens without God.

IV

1. My child, you shall remember, day and night, him who speaks the word of God to you, and you shall honor him as the Lord, for where

the Lord's nature is spoken of, there is he present. 2. And you shall seek daily the presence of the saints, that you may find rest in their words. 3. You shall not desire a schism, but shall reconcile those that strive. You shall give righteous judgment; you shall favor no one's person in reproving transgression. 4. You shall not be of two minds whether it shall be or not.

5. Be not one who stretches out his hands to receive, but shuts them when it comes to giving. 6. Of whatsoever you have gained by your hands you shall give a ransom for your sins. 7. You shall not hesitate to give, nor shall you grumble when you give, for you shall know who is the good Paymaster of the reward. 8. You shall not turn away the needy, but shall share everything with your brother, and shall not say that it is your own, for if you are sharers in the imperishable, how much more in the things which perish?

9. You shall not withhold your hand from your son or from your daughter, but you shall teach them the fear of God from their youth up. 10. You shall not command in your bitterness your slave or your handmaid, who hope in the same God, lest they cease to fear the God who is over you both; for he comes not to call men with respect of persons, but those whom the Spirit has prepared. 11. But do you who are slaves be subject to your master, as to God's representative, in reverence and fear.

12. You shall hate all hypocrisy, and everything that is not pleasing to the Lord. 13. You shall not forsake the commandments of the Lord, but you shall keep what you received, "adding nothing to it and taking nothing away" (cf. Deut. 4:2; 12:32). 14. In the congregation you shall confess your transgressions, and you shall not betake yourself to prayer with an evil conscience. This is the way of life.

V

1. But the Way of Death is this: First of all, it is wicked and full of cursing, murders, adulteries, lusts, fornications, thefts, idolatries, witchcrafts, charms, robberies, false witness, hypocrisies, a double heart, fraud, pride, malice, stubbornness, covetousness, foul speech, jealousy, impudence, haughtiness, boastfulness. 2. Persecutors of the good, haters of truth, lovers of lies, knowing not the reward of righteousness, not cleaving to the good nor to righteous judgment, spending wakeful nights not for good but for wickedness, from whom meekness and patience are far, lovers of vanity, following after reward, unmerciful to the poor, not working for the one who is oppressed with toil, without knowledge of him who made them, murderers of children, corrupters of God's creatures, turning away the needy, oppressing the distressed, advocates of the rich, unjust judges of the poor, altogether sinful; may you be delivered, my children, from all these.

VI

1. See "that no one makes you err" (cf. Matt. 24:4) from this Way of the teaching, for this one teaches you without God. 2. For if you can bear the whole yoke of the Lord, you will be perfect, but if you cannot, do what you can. 3. And concerning food, bear what you can, but keep strictly from that which is offered to idols, for it is the worship of dead gods.

VII

1. Concerning baptism, baptize thus: Having first rehearsed all these things, "baptize, in the name of the Father and of the Son and of the Holy Spirit" (cf. Matt. 28:19), in running water; 2. but if you have no running water, baptize in other water, and if you cannot in cold, then in warm. 3. But if you have neither, pour water three times on the head "in the name of the Father, Son and Holy Spirit." 4. And before the baptism let the baptizer and the one who is to be baptized fast, and any others who are able. And you shall bid the one who is to be baptized to fast one or two days before.

VIII

1. Let not your fasts be with the hypocrites, for they fast on Mondays and Thursdays, but do you fast on Wednesdays and Fridays. 2. And do not pray as the hypocrites, but as the Lord commanded in his Gospel, pray thus: "Our Father, who art in Heaven, hallowed be your name, your kingdom come, your will be done, as in heaven so also upon

earth; give us today our daily bread, and forgive us our debt as we forgive our debtors, and lead us not into trial, but deliver us from the Evil One, for yours is the power and the glory forever" (cf. Matt. 6:9-13). 3. Pray this way three times a day.

IX

1. And concerning the Eucharist, hold Eucharist thus: 2. First concerning the Cup, "We give thanks to you, our Father, for the Holy Vine of David, your child, which you made known to us through Jesus, your child; to you be glory forever." 3. And concerning the broken Bread: "We give you thanks, our Father, for the life and knowledge which you made known to us through Jesus, your child. To you be glory forever. 4. As this broken bread was scattered upon the mountains, but was brought together and became one, so let your Church be gathered together from the ends of the earth into your kingdom, for yours is the glory and the power through Jesus Christ forever." 5. But let none eat or drink of your Eucharist except those who have been baptized in the Lord's Name. For concerning this also did the Lord say, "Give not that which is holy to the dogs."

X

1. But after you are satisfied with food, thus give thanks: 2. "We give thanks to you, O Holy Father, for your Holy Name which you made to tabernacle in our hearts, and for the knowledge and faith and immortality which you made known to us through Jesus, thy Child. To you be glory forever. 3. You, Lord Almighty, created all things for your Name's sake, and gave food and drink to people for their enjoyment, that they might give thanks to you, but us you have blessed with spiritual food and drink and eternal light through your child. 4. Above all we give thanks to you for you are mighty: To you be glory forever. 5. Remember, Lord, thy Church, to deliver it from all evil and to make it perfect in your love, and gather it together in its holiness from the four winds to your kingdom which you have prepared for it. For yours is the power and the glory forever. 6. Let grace come and let this world pass away. Hosanna to the God of David. If any man be holy,

let him come! if any man be not, let him repent: Maranatha, Amen."

7. But suffer the prophets to hold Eucharist as they will.

XI

1. Whosoever then comes and teaches you all these things aforesaid, receive. 2. But if the teacher is perverted and teaches another doctrine to destroy these things, do not listen to the person, but if the teacher's teaching is for the increase of righteousness and knowledge of the Lord, receive this one as the Lord.

3. And concerning the Apostles and prophets, act thus according to the ordinance of the Gospel.

4. Let every Apostle who comes to you be received as the Lord, 5. but let this one not stay more than one day, or if need be a second as well; but if he stay three days, he is a false prophet. 6. And when an Apostle goes forth, let him accept nothing but bread till he reach his night's lodging; but if he ask for money, he is a false prophet.

7. Do not test or examine any prophet who is speaking in a spirit, "for every sin shall be forgiven, but this sin shall not be forgiven" (cf. Matt. 12:31). 8. But not everyone who speaks in a spirit is a prophet, unless the person has the behavior of the Lord. From the person's behavior, then, the false prophet and the true prophet shall be known. 9. And no prophet who orders a meal in a spirit shall eat of it: otherwise this is a false prophet. 10. And all prophets who teach the truth, if they do not do what they teach, are false prophets. 11. But no prophets who have been tried and are genuine, though they enact a worldly mystery of the Church, if they do not teach others to do what they do themselves, shall be judged by you: for they have their judgment with God, for so also did the prophets of old. 12. But whosoever shall say in a spirit "Give me money, or something else," you shall not listen to; but if this one tells you to give on behalf of others in want, let none judge him.

XII

1. Let everyone who "comes in the Name of the Lord" be received; but when you have tested them

you shall know them, for you shall have understanding of true and false. 2. If the one who comes is a traveler, help this person as much as you can, but he shall not remain with you more than two days, or, if need be, three. 3. And if he wishes to settle among you and has a craft, let him work for his bread. 4. But if he has no craft, provide for him according to your understanding, so that no one shall live among you in idleness because he is a Christian. 5. But if he will not do so, he is making traffic of Christ; beware of such people.

XIII

1. But every true prophet who wishes to settle among you is "worthy of his food" (cf. Matt. 10:10). 2. Likewise a true teacher is worthy, like the workman, of his food. 3. Therefore you shall take the firstfruits of the produce of the winepress and of the threshing floor and of oxen and sheep, and shall give them as the firstfruits to the prophets, for they are your high priests. 4. But if you have not a prophet, give to the poor. 5. If you make bread, take the firstfruits, and give it according to the commandment. 6. Likewise when you open a jar of wine or oil, give the firstfruits to the prophets. 7. Of money also and clothes, and of all your possessions, take the firstfruits, as it seems best to you, and give according to the commandment.

XIV

1. On the Lord's Day come together, break bread and hold Eucharist, after confessing your transgressions that your offering may be pure; 2. but let none who has a quarrel with another join in your meeting until they be reconciled, that your sacrifice be not defiled. 3. For this is that which was spoken by the Lord, "In every place and time offer me a pure sacrifice, for I am a great king," says the Lord, "and my name is wonderful among the heathen" (Mal. 1:11, 14).

XV

1. Appoint, therefore, for yourselves bishops and deacons worthy of the Lord, those who are meek, and not lovers of money, and truthful and approved, for they also minister to you the ministry of the prophets and teachers. 2. Therefore do not despise them, for they are your honorable men together with the prophets and teachers.

3. And reprove one another not in wrath but in peace as you find in the Gospel, and let none speak with those who have done a wrong to their neighbor, nor let them hear a word from you until they repent. 4. But your prayers and alms and all your acts perform as you find in the Gospel of our Lord.

XVI

1. "Watch" over your life: "let your lamps" be not quenched "and your loins" be not ungirded, but be "ready," for you know not "the hour in which our Lord comes" (cf. Matt. 24:42, 44; Luke 12:35). 2. But be frequently gathered together seeking the things which are profitable for your souls, for the whole time of your faith shall not profit you unless you be found perfect at the last time. 3. For in the last days the false prophets and the corrupters shall be multiplied, and the sheep shall be turned into wolves, and love shall change to hate; 4. for as lawlessness increases, they shall hate one another and persecute and betray, and then shall appear the deceiver of the world as a Son of God, and he shall do signs and wonders, and the earth shall be given over into his hands and he shall commit iniquities which have never been since the world began. 6. Then shall the creation of humankind come to the fiery trial and "many shall be offended" and be lost, but "they who endure" in their faith "shall be saved" (cf. Matt. 24:10; 10:22; 24:13) by the curse itself. 6. And "then shall appear the signs" (cf. Matt. 24:30) of the truth. First the sign spread out in heaven, then the sign of the sound of the trumpet, and thirdly the resurrection of the dead: 7. but not of all the dead, but as it was said, "The Lord shall come and all his saints with him" (Zech. 14:5). 8. Then shall the world "see the Lord coming on the clouds of heaven" (1 Thess. 3:13; Matt. 24:30).

4. Hippolytus of Rome, *Apostolic Tradition*

The Roman presbyter Hippolytus (d. ca. 236) was a prolific writer. He became schismatic bishop of Rome in opposition to the established bishop Callistus (ca. 217- ca. 222), whom he accused both of heresy and of laxity toward Christians who committed mortal sin. It was apparently after this separation that he wrote the Apostolic Tradition, *to preserve in memory the practices of the Roman church. The work exerted a major influence on subsequent ancient Church Orders, especially in the East. Not included here is Part I of the work, which describes the ordination of bishops, presbyters, and deacons.*

Part II

16. New converts to the faith, who are to be admitted as hearers of the word, shall first be brought to the teachers before the people assemble. And they shall be examined as to their reason for embracing the faith, and they who bring them shall testify that they are competent to hear the word. Inquiry shall then be made as to the nature of their life; whether a man has a wife or is a slave. If he is the slave of a believer and he has his master's permission, then let him be received; but if his master does not give him a good character, let him be rejected. If his master is a heathen, let the slave be taught to please his master, that the word be not blasphemed. If a man has a wife or a woman, a husband, let the man be instructed to content himself with his wife and the woman to content herself with her husband. But if a man is unmarried, let him be instructed to abstain from impurity, either by lawfully marrying a wife or else by remaining as he is. But if any man is possessed with demons, he shall not be admitted as a hearer until he is cleansed.

Inquiry shall likewise be made about the professions and trades of those who are brought to be admitted to the faith. If a man is a pander, he must desist or be rejected. If a man is a sculptor or painter, he must be charged not to make idols; if he does not desist he must be rejected. If a man is an actor or pantomimist, he must desist or be rejected. A teacher of young children had best desist, but if he has no other occupation, he may be permitted to continue. A charioteer, likewise, who races or frequents races, must desist or be rejected. A gladiator or a trainer of gladiators, or a huntsman [in the wild beast shows], or anyone connected with these shows, or a public official in charge of gladiatorial exhibitions must desist or be rejected. A heathen priest or anyone who tends idols must desist or be rejected. A soldier of the civil authority must be taught not to kill men and to refuse to do so if he is commanded, and to refuse to take an oath; if he is unwilling to comply, he must be rejected. A military commander or civic magistrate that wears the purple must resign or be rejected. If a catechumen or a believer seeks to become a soldier, they must be rejected, for they have despised God. A harlot or licentious man or one who has castrated himself, or any other who does things not to be named, must be rejected, for they are defiled. A magician must not [even] be brought for examination. An enchanter, an astrologer, a diviner, a soothsayer, a user of magic verses, a juggler, a mountebank, an amulet-maker must desist or be rejected. A concubine who is a slave and has reared her children and has been faithful to her master alone may become a hearer; but if she has failed in these matters she must be rejected. If a man has a concubine, he

Source: *The Apostolic Tradition of Hippolytus*, tr. Burton Scott Easton (Cambridge: Cambridge University Press, 1934), 41-57. Reprinted by permission of Cambridge University Press.

must desist and marry legally; if he is unwilling, he must be rejected.

If, now, we have omitted anything (any trade?), the facts [as they occur] will instruct your mind; for we all have the Spirit of God.

17. Let catechumens spend three years as hearers of the word. But if one is zealous and perseveres well in the work, it is not the time but the person's character that is decisive.

18. When the teacher finishes his instruction, the catechumens shall pray by themselves, apart from the believers. And [all] women, whether believers or catechumens, shall stand for their prayers by themselves in a separate part of the church.

And when [the catechumens] finish their prayers, they must not give the kiss of peace, for their kiss is not yet pure. Only believers shall salute one another, but men with men and women with women; a man shall not salute a woman.

And let all the women have their heads covered with an opaque cloth, not with a veil of thin linen, for this is not a true covering.

19. At the close of their prayer, when their instructor lays his hand upon the catechumens, he shall pray and dismiss them; whoever gives the instruction is to do this, whether a cleric or a layman.

If a catechumen should be arrested for the name of the Lord, let him not hesitate about bearing his testimony; for if it should happen that they treat him shamefully and kill him, he will be justified, for he has been baptized in his own blood.

20. They who are to be set apart for baptism shall be chosen after their lives have been examined: whether they have lived soberly, whether they have honored the widows, whether they have visited the sick, whether they have been active in well-doing. When their sponsors have testified that they have done these things, then let them hear the Gospel. Then from the time that they are separated from the other catechumens, hands shall be laid upon them daily in exorcism and, as the day of their baptism draws near, the bishop himself shall

exorcise each one of them that he may be personally assured of their purity. Then, if there is any of them who is not good or pure, he shall be put aside as not having heard the word in faith; for it is never possible for the alien to be concealed.

Then those who are set apart for baptism shall be instructed to bathe and free themselves from impurity and wash themselves on Thursday. If a woman is menstruous, she shall be set aside and baptized on some other day.

They who are to be baptized shall fast on Friday, and on Saturday the bishop shall assemble them and command them to kneel in prayer. And, laying his hand upon them, he shall exorcise all evil spirits to flee away and never to return; when he has done this he shall breathe in their faces, seal their foreheads, ears, and noses, and then raise them up. They shall spend all that night in vigil, listening to reading and instruction.

They who are to be baptized shall bring with them no other vessels than the one each will bring for the Eucharist; for it is fitting that he who is counted worthy of baptism should bring his offering at that time.

21. At cockcrow prayer shall be made over the water. The stream shall flow through the baptismal tank or pour into it from above when there is no scarcity of water; but if there is a scarcity, whether constant or sudden, then use whatever water you can find.

They shall remove their clothing. And first baptize the little ones; if they can speak for themselves, they shall do so; if not, their parents or other relatives shall speak for them. Then baptize the men, and last of all the women; they must first loosen their hair and put aside any gold or silver ornaments that they were wearing: let no one take any alien thing down to the water with them.

At the hour set for the baptism the bishop shall give thanks over oil and put it into a vessel: this is called the "oil of thanksgiving." And he shall take other oil and exorcise it: this is called "the oil of exorcism." [The anointing is performed by a presbyter.] A deacon shall bring the oil of exorcism, and shall stand at the presbyter's left hand; and another deacon shall take the oil of thanksgiving, and shall stand at the presbyter's right hand. Then the presbyter, taking hold of each of those about to be baptized, shall command each one to renounce, saying:

I renounce you, Satan, and all your servants and all your works.

And when he has renounced all these, the presbyter shall anoint him with the oil of exorcism, saying:

Let all spirits depart far from thee.

Then, after these things, let him give him over to the presbyter who baptizes, and let the candidates stand in the water, naked, a deacon going with them likewise. And when he who is being baptized goes down into the water, he who baptizes him, putting his hand on him, shall say thus:

Do you believe in God, the Father Almighty?

And the one who is being baptized shall say:

I believe.

Then holding his hand placed on his head, he shall baptize him once. And then he shall say:

Do you believe in Christ Jesus, the Son of God, who was born of the Holy Ghost of the Virgin Mary, and was crucified under Pontius Pilate, and was dead and buried, and rose again the third day, alive from the dead, and ascended into heaven, and sat at the right hand of the Father, and will come to judge the quick and the dead? And when he says:

I believe,

he is baptized again. And again he shall say:

Do you believe in [the] Holy Ghost, and the holy church, and the resurrection of the flesh?

He who is being baptized shall say accordingly:

I believe,

and so he is baptized a third time.

And afterward, when he has come up [out of the water], he is anointed by the presbyter with the oil of thanksgiving, the presbyter saying:

I anoint you with holy oil in the name of Jesus Christ.

And so each one, after drying himself, is immediately clothed, and then is brought into the church.

22.Then the bishop, laying his hand upon them, shall pray, saying:

O Lord God, who has made them worthy to obtain remission of sins through the laver of regeneration of [the] Holy Spirit, send into them your grace, that they may serve you according to your will; for yours is the glory, to the Father and the Son, with [the] Holy Spirit in the holy church, both now and world without end. Amen.

Then, pouring the oil of thanksgiving from his hand and putting it on their forehead, he shall say:

I anoint you with holy oil in the Lord, the Father Almighty and Christ Jesus and [the] Holy Ghost.

And signing them on the forehead he shall say:

The Lord be with you;

and the one who is signed shall say:

And with your spirit.

And so he shall do to each one.

And immediately thereafter they shall join in prayer with all the people, but they shall not pray with the faithful until all these things are completed. And at the close of their prayer they shall give the kiss of peace.

23. And then the offering is immediately brought by the deacons to the bishop, and by thanksgiving he shall make the bread into an image of the body of Christ, and the cup of wine mixed with water according to the likeness of the blood, which is shed for all who believe in him. And milk and honey mixed together for the fulfillment of the promise to the fathers, which spoke of a land flowing with milk and honey; namely, Christ's flesh which he gave, by which they who believe are nourished like babes, he making sweet the bitter things of the heart by the gentleness of his word. And the water into an offering in a token of the laver, in order that the inner part of man, which is a living soul, may receive the same as the body.

The bishop shall explain the reason of all these things to those who partake. And when he breaks the bread and distributes the fragments he shall say:

The heavenly bread in Christ Jesus.

And the recipient shall say, Amen.

And the presbyters—or if there are not enough presbyters, the deacons—shall hold the cups, and shall stand by with reverence and modesty; first he who holds the water, then the milk, thirdly the wine. And the recipients shall taste of each three times, he who gives the cup saying:

In God the Father Almighty;

and the recipient shall say, Amen. Then:

In the Lord Jesus Christ;

[and he shall say, Amen. Then:

In] [the] Holy Ghost and the holy church;

and he shall say, Amen. So it shall be done to each.

And when these things are completed, let each one hasten to do good works, and to please God and to live aright, devoting himself to the church, practising the things he has learned, advancing in the service of God.

Now we have briefly delivered to you these things concerning the holy baptism and the holy oblation, for you have already been instructed concerning the resurrection of the flesh and all other things as taught in Scripture. Yet if there is any other thing that ought to be told (to converts), let the bishop impart it to them privately after their baptism; let not unbelievers know it, until they are baptized: this is the white stone of which John said: "There is upon it a new name written, which no one knows but the one that receives the stone" [Rev. 2:17].

Part III

25. Widows and virgins shall fast frequently and shall pray for the church; presbyters, if they wish, and laymen may fast likewise. But the bishop may fast only when all the people fast.

26. For it constantly happens that someone wishes to make an offering—and such a one must not be denied—and then the bishop, after breaking the bread, must in every case taste and eat it with the other believers. [At such an offering] each shall take from the bishop's hand a piece of [this] bread before breaking his own bread. [This service has a special ceremonial] for it is "a Blessing," not "a Thanksgiving," as is [the service of] the Body of the Lord. But before drinking, each one, as many of you as are present, must take a cup and give thanks over it, and so go to your meal.

But to the catechumens is given exorcised bread, and each of them must offer the cup. No catechumen shall sit at the Lord's Supper.

But at each act of offering, the offerer must remember his host, for he was invited to the latter's home for that very purpose. But when you eat and drink, do so in an orderly manner and not so that anyone may mock, or your host be saddened by your unruliness, but behave so that he may pray to be made worthy that the saints may enter his dwelling: "for you," it is said, "are the salt of the earth."

If the offering should be one made to all the guests jointly, take your portion from your host [and depart]. But if all are to eat then and there, do not eat to excess, so that your host may likewise send some of what the saints leave to whomsoever he will and [so] may rejoice in the faith.

But while the guests are eating, let them eat silently, not arguing, [attending to] such things as the bishop may teach, but if he should ask any question, let an answer be given him; and when he says anything, everyone in modest praise shall keep silence until he asks again.

And even if the bishop should be absent when the faithful meet at a supper, if a presbyter or a deacon is present they shall eat in a similar orderly fashion, and each shall be careful to take the blessed bread from the presbyter's or deacon's hand; and in the same way the catechumens shall take the same exorcised bread.

But if [only] laymen meet, let them not act presumptuously, for a layman cannot bless the blessed bread.

Let each one eat in the name of the Lord; for this is pleasing to the Lord that we should be jealous [of our good name] even among the heathen, all sober alike.

27. If anyone wishes to give a meal to widows of mature years, let him dismiss them before evening. But if, on account of existing conditions, he cannot [feed them in his house], let him send them away, and they may eat of his food at their homes in any way they please.

28. As soon as firstfruits appear, all shall hasten to offer them to the bishop. And he shall offer them, shall give thanks, and shall name him who offered them, saying:

We give you thanks, O God, and we offer you the firstfruits; which you have given us to enjoy; nourishing them through your word, commanding the earth to bring forth her fruits for the gladness and the food of people and all beasts. For all these things we praise you, O God, and for all things with which you have blessed us, who for us adorns every creature with diverse fruits. Through your Servant Jesus Christ, our Lord, through whom be to you glory, world without end. Amen.

Only certain fruits may be blessed, namely, grapes, the fig, the pomegranate, the olive, the pear, the apple, the mulberry, the peach, the cherry, the almond, the plum. Not the pumpkin, nor the melon, nor the cucumber, nor the onion, nor garlic, nor anything else having an odor. But sometimes flowers too are offered; here the rose and the lily may be offered, but no other. But for everything that is eaten shall they [who eat it] give thanks to the Holy God, eating to His glory.

29. Let no one at the paschal season eat before the offering is made, otherwise he shall not be credited with the fast. But if any woman is with child, or if anyone is sick and cannot fast for two days, let such a one, on account of his need, [at least] fast on Saturday, contenting himself with bread and water. But if anyone on a voyage or for any other necessary cause should not know the day, when he has learned the truth he shall postpone his fast until after Pentecost. For the ancient type has passed away, and so the [postponed] fast [of Numbers 9:11] in the second month has ceased, and each one ought to fast in accord with his knowledge of the truth.

30. Each of the deacons, with the subdeacons, shall be alert on the bishop's behalf, for the bishop must be informed if any are sick so that, if he pleases, he may visit them; for a sick man is greatly comforted when the high priest is mindful of him.

33. Let the deacons and the presbyters assemble daily at the place which the bishop may appoint; let the deacons [in particular] never fail to assemble unless prevented by sickness. When all have met they shall instruct those who are in the church, and then, after prayer, each shall go to his appointed duties.

34. No exorbitant charge shall be made for burial in the cemetery, for it belongs to all the poor; only the hire of the grave-digger and the cost of the tile [for closing the niche in the catacombs] shall be asked. The wages of the caretakers are to be paid by the bishop, lest any of those who go to that place be burdened [with a charge].

Part IV

35. Let all the faithful, whether men or women, when early in the morning they rise from their sleep and before they undertake any tasks, wash their hands and pray to God; and so they may go to their duties. But if any instruction in God's word is held [that day], everyone ought to attend it willingly, recollecting that he will hear God speaking through the instructor and that prayer in the church enables him to avoid the day's evil; any godly man ought to count it a great loss if he does not attend the place of instruction, especially if he can read.

If a [specially gifted] teacher should come, let none of you delay to attend the place where the instruction is given, for grace will be given to the speaker to utter things profitable to all, and you will hear new things, and you will be profited by what the Holy Spirit will give you through the instructor; so your faith will be strengthened by what you hear, and in that place you will learn your duties at home; therefore let everyone be zealous to go to the church, the place where the Holy Spirit abounds.

36. But if on any day there is no instruction, let everyone at home take the Bible and read sufficiently in passages that he or she finds profitable.

If at the third hour you are at home, pray then and give thanks to God; but if you chance to be abroad at that hour, make your prayer to God in your heart. For at that hour Christ was nailed to the tree; therefore in the old [covenant] the law commanded the showbread to be offered continually for a type of the body and blood of Christ, and commanded the sacrifice of the dumb lamb, which was a type of the perfect Lamb; for Christ is the Shepherd, and he is also the Bread that came down from heaven.

At the sixth hour likewise pray also, for, after Christ was nailed to the wood of the cross, the day was divided and there was a great darkness; wherefore let [the faithful] pray at that hour with an effectual prayer, likening themselves to the voice of him who prayed [and] caused all creation to become dark for the unbelieving Jews.

And at the ninth hour let a great prayer and a great thanksgiving be made, such as made the souls of the righteous ones, blessing the Lord, the God who does not lie, who was mindful of his saints and sent forth his Word to enlighten them. At that hour, therefore, Christ poured forth from his pierced side water and blood, and brought the rest of the time of that day with light to evening; so, when he fell asleep, by making the beginning of another day he completed the pattern of his resurrection.

Pray again before thy body rests on thy bed.

At midnight arise, wash thy hands with water and pray. And if your wife is with you, both of you pray together; but if she is not yet a believer, go into another room and pray, and again return to your bed; be not slothful in prayer.

One who has used the marriage bed is not defiled; for they who are bathed have no need to wash again, for they are clean. By signing yourself with your moist breath, and so spreading spittle on your body with your hand, you are sanctified to your feet; for the gift of the Spirit and the sprinkling with water, when it is brought with a believing heart as it were from a fountain, sanctifies the one who believes.

It is needful to pray at this hour; for those very elders who gave us the tradition taught us that at this hour all creation rests for a certain moment, that all creatures may praise the Lord: stars and trees and waters stand still with one accord, and all the angelic host does service to God by praising Him, together with the souls of the righteous. For this cause believers should be zealous to pray at this hour; for the Lord, testifying to this, says:

"Behold at midnight is a cry, Behold the Bridegroom comes! Rise up to meet him!"; and he adds insistently: "Watch therefore, for you know not at what hour he comes" [Matt. 5:6, 13].

And at cockcrow rise up and pray likewise, for at that hour of cockcrow the children of Israel denied Christ, whom we have known by faith; by which faith, in the hope of eternal life at the resurrection of the dead, we look for his Day.

And so, all you faithful, if you thus act, and are mindful of these things, and teach them to one another, and cause the catechumens to be zealous, you can neither be tempted nor can you perish, since you have Christ always in your minds.

37. But imitate him always, by signing your forehead sincerely; for this is the sign of his Passion, manifest and approved against the devil if so you make it from faith; not that you may appear to men, but knowingly offering it as a shield. For the adversary, seeing its power coming from the heart, that a person displays the publicly formed image of baptism, is put to flight; not because you spit, but because the Spirit in you breathes him away. When Moses formed it by putting the blood of the paschal lamb that was slain on the lintel and anointing the side posts, he signified the faith which now we have in the perfect Lamb.

38. And so, if these things are accepted with thanksgiving and right faith, they give edification in the church and eternal life to believers. I counsel that these things be kept by all who know aright; for over all who hear the apostolic tra[dition] and keep it, no heretics or any other person will prevail to lead them astray. For the many heresies have increased because their leaders would not learn the purpose of the apostles but acted according to their own wills, following their lusts and not what was right. Now, beloved, if we have omitted anything, God will reveal it to those who are worthy, guiding the holy church to its mooring in (God's) quiet haven.

Christianity and Society before Constantine

5. Correspondence of Pliny and Trajan

The Roman senator Pliny the Younger (Gaius Plinius Caecilius Secundus, d. ca. 113) wrote celebrated letters, probably intending them for publication. This exchange with the emperor Trajan during Pliny's governorship of the Roman province of Bithynia in Asia Minor in the last months of his life is of extraordinary importance both for its nuanced picture of official Roman response to the emerging Christian movement and for the glimpse it offers of local Christian practice.

Pliny to Trajan

It is my custom, lord emperor, to refer to you all questions whereof I am in doubt. Who can better guide me when I am at a stand, or enlighten me if I am in ignorance? In investigations of Christians I have never taken part; hence I do not know what is the crime usually punished or investigated, or what allowances are made. So I have had no little uncertainty whether there is any distinction of age, or whether the very weakest offenders are treated exactly like the stronger; whether pardon is given to those who repent, or whether nobody who has ever been a Christian at all gains anything by having ceased to be such; whether punishment attaches to the mere name apart from secret crimes, or to the secret crimes connected with the name. Meantime this is the course I have taken with those who were accused before me as Christians. I asked at their own lips whether they were Christians, and if they confessed, I asked them a second and third time with threats of punishment. If they kept to it, I ordered them for execution; for I held no question that whatever it was that they admitted, in any case

obstinacy and unbending perversity deserve to be punished. There were others of the like insanity; but as these were Roman citizens, I noted them down to be sent to Rome. Before long, as is often the case, the mere fact that the charge was taken notice of made it commoner, and several distinct cases arose. An unsigned paper was presented, which gave the names of many. As for those who said that they neither were nor ever had been Christians, I thought it right to let them go, since they recited a prayer to the gods at my dictation, made supplication with incense and wine to your statue, which I had ordered to be brought into court for the purpose together with the images of the gods, and moreover cursed Christ—not one of which things (so it is said) those who are really Christians can be made to do. Others who were named by the informer said that they were Christians and then denied it, explaining that they had been, but had ceased to be such, some three years ago, some a good many years, and a few as many as twenty. All these too not only worshipped your statue and the images of the gods, but cursed Christ. They maintained, however, that the amount of their fault or error had been this, that it

Source: *Selections from Early Christian Writers Illustrative of Church History to the Time of Constantine*, ed. Henry Melvill Gwatkin (London: Macmillan, 1909), 27–31.

was their habit on a fixed day to assemble before daylight and sing by turns a hymn to Christ as a god; and that they bound themselves with an oath, not for any crime, but not to commit theft or robbery or adultery, not to break their word, and not to deny a deposit when demanded. After this was done, their custom was to depart and meet together again to take food, but ordinary and harmless food; and even this (they said) they had given up doing after the issue of my edict, by which in accordance with your commands I had forbidden the existence of clubs. On this I considered it the more necessary to find out from two maidservants who were called deaconesses, and that by torments, how far this was true: but I discovered nothing else than a wicked and arrogant superstition. I therefore adjourned the case and hastened to consult you. The matter seemed to me worth deliberation, especially on account of the number of those in danger; for many of all ages and every rank, and even of both sexes are brought into present or future danger. The contagion of that superstition has penetrated not the cities only, but the villages and country; yet it seems possible to stop it and set it right. At any rate it is certain enough that the almost deserted temples begin to be resorted to, that long disused ceremonies of religion are restored, and that fodder for victims finds a market, whereas buyers till now were very few. From this it may easily be supposed, what a multitude of men can be reclaimed, if there be a place of repentance.

Trajan to Pliny

You have followed, my dear Secundus, the process you should have done in examining the cases of those who were accused to you as Christians, for indeed nothing can be laid down as a general law involving something like a definite rule of action. They are not to be sought out; but if they are accused and convicted, they must be punished—yet on this condition, that whoso denies himself to be a Christian, and makes the fact plain by his action, that is, by worshipping our gods, shall obtain pardon on his repentance, however suspicious his past conduct may be. Papers, however, which are presented unsigned ought not to be admitted in any charge, for they are a very bad example and unworthy of our time.

6. The Martyrs of Lyons
(Letter of the Churches of Lyons and Vienne, ca. 177)

This report of martyrdoms at Lyons in 177, preserved by Eusebius in his Ecclesiastical History, *stands as one the earliest of the surviving* Passiones, *that is, narratives of martyrdom that purportedly rely on eyewitnesses. It provides a particularly detailed picture of both the character and motivation of the martyrs and of their interaction with the populace and the government.*

1. [*Eusebius introduces the letter:*] The country in which the arena was prepared for [the martyrs in question] was Gaul, of which Lyons and Vienne are the principal and most celebrated cities. The Rhone passes through both of them, flowing in a broad stream through the entire region.

2. The most celebrated churches in that country sent an account of the witnesses to the

Source: Eusebius, *Church History*, tr. Arthur Cushman McGiffert, in *A Select Library of Nicene and Post-Nicene Fathers of the Christian Church,* second series, vol. 1, ed. Philip Schaff and Henry Wace (New York: Christian Literature Publishing Company; Oxford and London: Parker & Company, 1890), 211-17.

churches in Asia and Phrygia, relating in the following manner what was done among them.

I will give their own words.

3. "The servants of Christ residing at Vienne and Lyons, in Gaul, to the brethren throughout Asia and Phrygia, who hold the same faith and hope of redemption, peace and grace and glory from God the Father and Christ Jesus our Lord."

4. Then, having related some other matters, they begin their account in this manner: "The greatness of the tribulation in this region, and the fury of the heathen against the saints, and the sufferings of the blessed witnesses, we cannot recount accurately, nor indeed could they possibly be recorded.

5. "For with all his might the adversary fell upon us, giving us a foretaste of his unbridled activity at his future coming. He endeavored in every manner to practice and exercise his servants against the servants of God, not only shutting us out from houses and baths and markets, but forbidding any of us to be seen in any place whatever.

6. "But the grace of God led the conflict against him, and delivered the weak, and set them as firm pillars, able through patience to endure all the wrath of the Evil One. And they joined battle with him, undergoing all kinds of shame and injury; and regarding their great sufferings as little, they hastened to Christ, manifesting truly that 'the sufferings of this present time are not worthy to be compared with the glory which shall be revealed to us' (Rom. 8:18).

7. "First of all, they endured nobly the injuries heaped upon them by the populace; clamors and blows and draggings and robberies and stonings and imprisonments, and all things which an infuriated mob delight in inflicting on enemies and adversaries.

8. "Then, being taken to the forum by the chiliarch and the authorities of the city, they were examined in the presence of the whole multitude, and having confessed, they were imprisoned until the arrival of the governor.

9. "When, afterwards, they were brought before him, and he treated us with the utmost cruelty, Vettius Epagathus, one of the brethren, and a man filled with love for God and his neighbor, interfered. His life was so consistent that, although

young, he had attained a reputation equal to that of the elder Zacharias: for he 'walked in all the commandments and ordinances of the Lord blameless' (Luke 1:16), and was untiring in every good work for his neighbor, zealous for God and fervent in spirit. Such being his character, he could not endure the unreasonable judgment against us, but was filled with indignation, and asked to be permitted to testify in behalf of his brethren, that there is among us nothing ungodly or impious.

10. "But those about the judgment seat cried out against him, for he was a man of distinction; and the governor refused to grant his just request, and merely asked if he also were a Christian. And he, confessing this with a loud voice, was himself taken into the order of the witnesses, being called the Advocate of the Christians, but having the Advocate in himself, the Spirit more abundantly than Zacharias. He showed this by the fullness of his love, being well pleased even to lay down his life in defense of the brethren. For he was and is a true disciple of Christ, 'following the Lamb wherever he goes' (Rev. 14:4).

11. "Then the others were divided, and the proto-witnesses were manifestly ready, and finished their confession with all eagerness. But some appeared unprepared and untrained, weak as yet, and unable to endure so great a conflict. About ten of these proved abortions, causing us great grief and sorrow beyond measure, and impairing the zeal of the others who had not yet been seized, but who, though suffering all kinds of affliction, continued constantly with the witnesses and did not forsake them.

12. "Then all of us feared greatly on account of uncertainty as to their confession; not because we dreaded the sufferings to be endured, but because we looked to the end, and were afraid that some of them might fall away.

13. "But those who were worthy were seized day by day, filling up their number, so that all the zealous persons, and those through whom especially our affairs had been established, were collected together out of the two churches.

14. "And some of our heathen servants also were seized, as the governor had commanded that all of us should be examined publicly. These, being

ensnared by Satan, and fearing for themselves the tortures which they beheld the saints endure, and being also urged on by the soldiers, accused us falsely of Thyestean banquets and Œdipodean intercourse, and of deeds which are not only unlawful for us to speak of or to think, but which we cannot believe were ever done by men.

15. "When these accusations were reported, all the people raged like wild beasts against us, so that even if any had before been moderate on account of friendship, they were now exceedingly furious and gnashed their teeth against us. And that which was spoken by our Lord was fulfilled: 'The time will come when whosoever kills you will think that he does God service' (John 16:2).

16. "Then finally the holy witnesses endured sufferings beyond description, Satan striving earnestly that some of the slanders might be uttered by them also.

17. "But the whole wrath of the populace, and governor, and soldiers was aroused exceedingly against Sanctus, the deacon from Vienne, and Maturus, a late convert yet a noble combatant, and against Attalus, a native of Pergamus, where he had always been a pillar and foundation, and Blandina, through whom Christ showed that things which appear mean and obscure and despicable to men are with God of great glory, through love toward him manifested in power, and not boasting in appearance.

18. "For while we all trembled, and her earthly mistress, who was herself also one of the witnesses, feared that on account of the weakness of her body, she would be unable to make bold confession, Blandina was filled with such power as to be delivered and raised above those who were torturing her by turns from morning till evening in every manner, so that they acknowledged that they were conquered and could do nothing more to her. And they were astonished at her endurance, as her entire body was mangled and broken; and they testified that one of these forms of torture was sufficient to destroy life, not to speak of so many and so great sufferings.

19. "But the blessed woman, like a noble athlete, renewed her strength in her confession; and her comfort and recreation and relief from the pain of her sufferings was in exclaiming, 'I am a Christian, and there is nothing vile done by us.'

20. "But Sanctus also endured marvelously and superhumanly all the outrages which he suffered. While the wicked men hoped, by the continuance and severity of his tortures to wring something from him which he ought not to say, he girded himself against them with such firmness that he would not even tell his name, or the nation or city to which he belonged, or whether he was bond or free, but answered in the Roman tongue to all their questions, 'I am a Christian.' He confessed this instead of name and city and race and everything besides, and the people heard from him no other word.

21. "There arose therefore on the part of the governor and his tormentors a great desire to conquer him; but having nothing more that they could do to him, they finally fastened red-hot brazen plates to the most tender parts of his body.

22. "And these indeed were burned, but he continued unbending and unyielding, firm in his confession, and refreshed and strengthened by the heavenly fountain of the water of life, flowing from the bowels of Christ.

23. "And his body was a witness of his sufferings, being one complete wound and bruise, drawn out of shape, and altogether unlike a human form. Christ, suffering in him, manifested his glory, delivering him from his adversary, and making him an example for the others, showing that nothing is fearful where the love of the Father is, and nothing painful where there is the glory of Christ.

24. "For when the wicked men tortured him a second time after some days, supposing that with his body swollen and inflamed to such a degree that he could not bear the touch of a hand, if they should again apply the same instruments, they would overcome him, or at least by his death under his sufferings others would be made afraid, not only did not this occur, but, contrary to all human expectation, his body arose and stood erect in the midst of the subsequent torments, and resumed its original appearance and the use of its limbs, so that, through the grace of Christ, these second sufferings became to him, not torture, but healing.

25. "But the devil, thinking that he had already consumed Biblias, who was one of those who had denied Christ, desiring to increase her condemna-

tion through the utterance of blasphemy, brought her again to the torture, to compel her, as already feeble and weak, to report impious things concerning us.

26. "But she recovered herself while undergoing the suffering, and as if awaking from a deep sleep, and reminded by the present anguish of the eternal punishment in hell, she contradicted the blasphemers. 'How,' she said, 'could those eat children who do not think it lawful to taste the blood even of irrational animals?' And thenceforward she confessed herself a Christian, and was given a place in the order of the witnesses.

27. "But as the tyrannical tortures were made by Christ of none effect through the patience of the blessed, the devil invented other contrivances—confinement in the dark and most loathsome parts of the prison, stretching of the feet to the fifth hole in the stocks, and the other outrages which his servants are accustomed to inflict upon the prisoners when furious and filled with the devil. A great many were suffocated in prison, being chosen by the Lord for this manner of death, that he might manifest in them his glory.

28. "For some, though they had been tortured so cruelly that it seemed impossible that they could live, even with the most careful nursing, yet destitute of human attention, remained in the prison, being strengthened by the Lord and invigorated both in body and soul; and they exhorted and encouraged the rest. But such as were young, and arrested recently, so that their bodies had not become accustomed to torture, were unable to endure the severity of their confinement and died in prison.

29. "The blessed Pothinus, who had been entrusted with the bishopric of Lyons, was dragged to the judgment seat. He was more than ninety years of age, and very infirm, scarcely indeed able to breathe because of physical weakness; but he was strengthened by spiritual zeal through his earnest desire for martyrdom. Though his body was worn out by old age and disease, his life was preserved that Christ might triumph in it.

30. "When he was brought by the soldiers to the tribunal, accompanied by the civil magistrates and a multitude who shouted against him in every manner as if he were Christ himself, he bore noble witness.

31. "Being asked by the governor, 'Who is the God of the Christians?' he replied, 'If you are worthy, you shall know.' Then he was dragged away harshly, and received blows of every kind. Those near him struck him with their hands and feet, regardless of his age; and those at a distance hurled at him whatever they could seize; all of them thinking that they would be guilty of great wickedness and impiety if any possible abuse were omitted. For thus they thought to avenge their own deities. Scarcely able to breathe, he was cast into prison and died after two days.

32. "Then a certain great dispensation of God occurred, and the compassion of Jesus appeared beyond measure, in a manner rarely seen among the brotherhood, but not beyond the power of Christ.

33. "For those who had recanted at their first arrest were imprisoned with the others and endured terrible sufferings, so that their denial was of no profit to them even for the present. But those who confessed that they were imprisoned as Christians, no other accusation being brought against them. But the first were treated afterwards as murderers and defiled, and were punished twice as severely as the others.

34. "For the joy of martyrdom, and the hope of the promises, and love for Christ, and the Spirit of the Father supported the latter; but their consciences so greatly distressed the former that they were easily distinguishable from all the rest by their very countenances when they were led forth.

35. "For the first went out rejoicing, glory and grace being blended in their faces, so that even their bonds seemed like beautiful ornaments, as those of a bride adorned with variegated golden fringes; and they were perfumed with the sweet savor of Christ, so that some supposed they had been anointed with earthly ointment. But the others were downcast and humble and dejected and filled with every kind of disgrace, and they were reproached by the heathen as ignoble and weak, bearing the accusation of murderers, and having lost the one honorable and glorious and life-giving Name. The rest, beholding this, were strengthened, and when apprehended, they confessed without hesitation, paying no attention to the persuasions of the devil."

36. After certain other words they continue:

"After these things, finally, their martyrdoms were divided into every form. For plaiting a crown of various colors and of all kinds of flowers, they presented it to the Father. It was proper therefore that the noble athletes, having endured a manifold strife, and conquered grandly, should receive the crown, great and incorruptible.

37. "Maturus, therefore, and Sanctus and Blandina and Attalus were led to the amphitheater to be exposed to the wild beasts, and to give to the heathen public a spectacle of cruelty, a day for fighting with wild beasts being specially appointed on account of our people.

38. "Both Maturus and Sanctus passed again through every torment in the amphitheater, as if they had suffered nothing before, or rather, as if, having already conquered their antagonist in many contests, they were now striving for the crown itself. They endured again the customary running of the gauntlet and the violence of the wild beasts, and everything which the furious people called for or desired, and at last, the iron chair in which their bodies were roasted, tormenting them with the fumes.

39. "And not with this did the persecutors cease, but were yet more mad against them, determined to overcome their patience. But even thus they did not hear a word from Sanctus except the confession which he had uttered from the beginning.

40. "These, then, after their life had continued for a long time through the great conflict, were at last sacrificed, having been made throughout that day a spectacle to the world, in place of the usual variety of combats.

41. "But Blandina was suspended on a stake, and exposed to be devoured by the wild beasts who should attack her. And because she appeared as if hanging on a cross, and because of her earnest prayers, she inspired the combatants with great zeal. For they looked on her in her conflict, and beheld with their outward eyes, in the form of their sister, him who was crucified for them, that he might persuade those who believe on him, that everyone who suffers for the glory of Christ has fellowship always with the living God.

42. "As none of the wild beasts at that time touched her, she was taken down from the stake, and cast again into prison. She was preserved thus

for another contest, that, being victorious in more conflicts, she might make the punishment of the crooked serpent irrevocable; and, though small and weak and despised, yet clothed with Christ the mighty and conquering Athlete, she might arouse the zeal of the brethren, and, having overcome the adversary many times might receive, through her conflict, the crown incorruptible.

43. "But Attalus was called for loudly by the people, because he was a person of distinction. He entered the contest readily on account of a good conscience and his genuine practice in Christian discipline, and as he had always been a witness for the truth among us.

44. "He was led around the amphitheater, a tablet being carried before him on which was written in the Roman language 'This is Attalus the Christian,' and the people were filled with indignation against him. But when the governor learned that he was a Roman, he commanded him to be taken back with the rest of those who were in prison concerning whom he had written to Cæsar, and whose answer he was awaiting.

45. "But the intervening time was not wasted nor fruitless to them; for by their patience the measureless compassion of Christ was manifested. For through their continued life the dead were made alive, and the witnesses showed favor to those who had failed to witness. And the virgin mother had much joy in receiving alive those whom she had brought forth as dead.

46. "For through their influence many who had denied were restored, and re-begotten, and rekindled with life, and learned to confess. And being made alive and strengthened, they went to the judgment seat to be again interrogated by the governor; God, who desires not the death of the sinner, but mercifully invites to repentance, treating them with kindness.

47. "For Cæsar commanded that they should be put to death, but that any who might deny should be set free. Therefore, at the beginning of the public festival which took place there, and which was attended by crowds of men from all nations, the governor brought the blessed ones to the judgment seat, to make of them a show and spectacle for the multitude. Wherefore also he examined them again, and beheaded those who

appeared to possess Roman citizenship, but he sent the others to the wild beasts.

48. "And Christ was glorified greatly in those who had formerly denied him, for, contrary to the expectation of the heathen, they confessed. For they were examined by themselves, as about to be set free; but confessing, they were added to the order of the witnesses. But some continued without, who had never possessed a trace of faith, nor any apprehension of the wedding garment, nor an understanding of the fear of God; but, as sons of perdition, they blasphemed the Way through their apostasy.

49. "But all the others were added to the Church. While these were being examined, a certain Alexander, a Phrygian by birth and physician by profession, who had resided in Gaul for many years and was well known to all on account of his love of God and boldness of speech (for he was not without a share of apostolic grace), standing before the judgment seat, and by signs encouraging them to confess, appeared to those standing by as if in travail.

50. "But the people, being enraged because those who formerly denied now confessed, cried out against Alexander as if he were the cause of this. Then the governor summoned him and inquired who he was. And when he answered that he was a Christian, being very angry he condemned him to the wild beasts. And on the next day he entered along with Attalus. For to please the people, the governor had ordered Attalus again to the wild beasts.

51. "And they were tortured in the amphitheater with all the instruments contrived for that purpose, and having endured a very great conflict, were at last sacrificed. Alexander neither groaned nor murmured in any manner, but communed in his heart with God.

52. "But when Attalus was placed in the iron seat, and the fumes arose from his burning body, he said to the people in the Roman language: 'Lo! this which you do is devouring people; but we do not devour people; nor do any other wicked thing.' And being asked, what name God has, he replied, 'God has not a name as people have.'

53. "After all these, on the last day of the contests, Blandina was again brought in, with Ponticus, a boy about fifteen years old. They had been brought every day to witness the sufferings of the others, and had been pressed to swear by the idols. But because they remained steadfast and despised them, the multitude became furious, so that they had no compassion for the youth of the boy nor respect for the sex of the woman.

54. "Therefore they exposed them to all the terrible sufferings and took them through the entire round of torture, repeatedly urging them to swear, but being unable to effect this; for Ponticus, encouraged by his sister so that even the heathen could see that she was confirming and strengthening him, having nobly endured every torture, gave up the ghost.

55. "But the blessed Blandina, last of all, having, as a noble mother, encouraged her children and sent them before her victorious to the King, endured herself all their conflicts and hastened after them, glad and rejoicing in her departure as if called to a marriage supper, rather than cast to wild beasts.

56. "And, after the scourging, after the wild beasts, after the roasting seat, she was finally enclosed in a net, and thrown before a bull. And having been tossed about by the animal, but feeling none of the things which were happening to her, on account of her hope and firm hold upon what had been entrusted to her, and her communion with Christ, she also was sacrificed. And the heathen themselves confessed that never among them had a woman endured so many and such terrible tortures.

57. "But not even thus was their madness and cruelty toward the saints satisfied. For, incited by the Wild Beast, wild and barbarous tribes were not easily appeased, and their violence found another peculiar opportunity in the dead bodies.

58. "For, through their lack of manly reason, the fact that they had been conquered did not put them to shame, but rather the more enkindled their wrath as that of a wild beast, and aroused alike the hatred of governor and people to treat us unjustly; that the Scripture might be fulfilled: 'He that is lawless, let him be lawless still, and he that is righteous, let him be righteous still' (Rev. 22:11).

59. "For they cast to the dogs those who had died of suffocation in the prison, carefully guarding them by night and day, lest any one should be buried by us. And they exposed the remains left by

the wild beasts and by fire, mangled and charred, and placed the heads of the others by their bodies, and guarded them in like manner from burial by a watch of soldiers for many days.

60. "And some raged and gnashed their teeth against them, desiring to execute more severe vengeance upon them; but others laughed and mocked at them, magnifying their own idols, and imputed to them the punishment of the Christians. Even the more reasonable, and those who had seemed to sympathize somewhat, reproached them often, saying, 'Where is their God, and what has their religion, which they have chosen rather than life, profited them?'

61. "So various was their conduct toward us; but we were in deep affliction because we could not bury the bodies. For neither did night avail us for this purpose, nor did money persuade, nor

entreaty move to compassion; but they kept watch in every way, as if the prevention of the burial would be of some great advantage to them."

In addition, they say after other things:

62. "The bodies of the martyrs, having thus in every manner been exhibited and exposed for six days, were afterward burned and reduced to ashes, and swept into the Rhone by the wicked men, so that no trace of them might appear on the earth.

63. "And this they did, as if able to conquer God, and prevent their new birth; 'that,' as they said, 'they may have no hope of a resurrection, through trust in which they bring to us this foreign and new religion, and despise terrible things, and are ready even to go to death with joy. Now let us see if they will rise again, and if their God is able to help them, and to deliver them out of our hands.'"

7. The Martyrdom of Perpetua and Felicity

The noblewoman Vibia Perpetua, her slave Felicity, the presbyter Saturus, and the others were martyred together at Carthage in 203. This Passio *presents itself as a collection of documents. The most prominent of these is Perpetua's literary account of her own experiences, one of the very few surviving first-person narratives by women of the first millennium of Christianity. The preface to the work, with its affirmation of present-day prophecies and visions, sounds themes consistent with the "New Prophecy" that was to be embraced by Tertullian of Carthage, and it is possible that he himself was the editor who brought these materials together.*

Preface

If ancient illustrations of faith which both testify to God's grace and tend to man's edification are collected in writing, so that by the perusal of them, as if by the reproduction of the facts, as well God may be honored, as man may be strengthened; why should not new instances be also collected, that shall be equally suitable for both purposes—if only on the ground that these modern examples will one day become ancient and

available for posterity, although in their present time they are esteemed of less authority, by reason of the presumed veneration for antiquity? But let men look to it, if they judge the power of the Holy Spirit to be one, according to the times and seasons; since some things of later date must be esteemed of more account as being nearer to the very last times, in accordance with the exuberance of grace manifested to the final periods determined for the world. For "in the last days, says the

SOURCE: "The Martyrdom of Perpetua and Felicitas," tr. R. E. Wallis, in *The Ante-Nicene Fathers*, vol. 3, ed. Alexander Roberts and James Donaldson (Buffalo: Christian Literature Publishing Company, 1885), 699–706.

Lord, I will pour out my Spirit upon all flesh; and their sons and their daughters shall prophesy. And upon my servants and my handmaidens will I pour out my Spirit; and your young men shall see visions, and your old men shall dream dreams" (Joel 2:28, 29). And thus we—who both acknowledge and reverence, even as we do the prophecies, modern visions as equally promised to us, and consider the other powers of the Holy Spirit as an agency of the Church for which also He was sent, administering all gifts in all, even as the Lord distributed to everyone—necessarily collect them in writing as well as commemorate them in reading to God's glory; that so no weakness or despondency of faith may suppose that the divine grace abode only among the ancients, whether in respect of the condescension that raised up martyrs, or that gave revelations; since God always carries into effect what He has promised, for a testimony to unbelievers, to believers for a benefit. And we therefore, what we have heard and handled, declare also to you, brethren and little children, that as well you who were concerned in these matters may be reminded of them again to the glory of the Lord, as that you who know them by report may have communion with the blessed martyrs, and through them with the Lord Jesus Christ, to whom be glory and honor, forever and ever. Amen.

Chapter I

1. The young catechumens, Revocatus and his fellow servant Felicitas, Saturninus and Secundulus, were apprehended. And among them also was Vivia Perpetua, respectably born, liberally educated, a married matron, having a father and mother and two brothers, one of whom, like herself, was a catechumen, and a son an infant at the breast. She herself was about twenty-two years of age. From this point onward she shall herself narrate the whole course of her martyrdom, as she left it described by her own hand and with her own mind.

2. "While" says she, "we were still with the persecutors, and my father, for the sake of his affection for me, was persisting in seeking to turn me away, and to cast me down from the faith—'Father,' said I, 'do you see, let us say, this vessel lying here to be a little pitcher, or something else?' And he said, 'I see it to be so.' And I replied to him, 'Can it be called by any other name than what it is?' And he said, 'No.' 'Neither can I call myself anything else than what I am, a Christian.' Then my father, provoked at this saying, threw himself upon me, as if he would tear my eyes out. But he only distressed me, and went away overcome by the devil's arguments. Then, in a few days after I had been without my father, I gave thanks to the Lord; and his absence became a source of consolation to me. In that same interval of a few days we were baptized, and to me the Spirit prescribed that in the water *of baptism* nothing else was to be sought for than bodily endurance. After a few days we are taken into the dungeon, and I was very much afraid, because I had never felt such darkness. O terrible day! O the fierce heat of the shock of the soldiery, because of the crowds! I was very unusually distressed by my anxiety for my infant. There were present there Tertius and Pomponius, the blessed deacons who ministered to us, and had arranged by means of a gratuity that we might be refreshed by being sent out for a few hours into a pleasanter part of the prison. Then going out of the dungeon, all attended to their own wants. I suckled my child, which was now enfeebled with hunger. In my anxiety for it, I addressed my mother and comforted my brother, and commended to their care my son. I was languishing because I had seen them languishing on my account. Such solicitude I suffered for many days, and I obtained leave for my infant to remain in the dungeon with me; and forthwith I grew strong and was relieved from distress and anxiety about my infant; and the dungeon became to me as it were a palace, so that I preferred being there to being elsewhere.

3. "Then my brother said to me, 'My dear sister, you are already in a position of great dignity, and are such that you may ask for a vision, and that it may be made known to you whether this is to result in a passion or an escape.' And I, who knew that I was privileged to converse with the Lord, whose kindnesses I had found to be so great, boldly promised him, and said, 'Tomorrow I will tell you.' And I asked, and this was what was shown me. I saw a golden ladder of marvelous

height, reaching up even to heaven, and very narrow, so that persons could only ascend it one by one; and on the sides of the ladder was fixed every kind of iron weapon. There were swords, lances, hooks, daggers; so that if any one went up carelessly, or not looking upwards, he would be torn to pieces and his flesh would cleave to the iron weapons. And under the ladder itself was crouching a dragon of wonderful size, who lay in wait for those who ascended, and frightened them from the ascent. And Saturus went up first, who had subsequently delivered himself up freely on our account, not having been present at the time that we were taken prisoners. And he attained the top of the ladder, and turned towards me, and said to me, 'Perpetua, I am waiting for you; but be careful that the dragon does not bite you.' And I said, 'In the name of the Lord Jesus Christ, he shall not hurt me.' And from under the ladder itself, as if in fear of me, he slowly lifted up his head; and as I trod upon the first step, I trod upon his head. And I went up, and I saw an immense extent of garden, and in the midst of the garden a white-haired man sitting in the dress of a shepherd, of a large stature, milking sheep; and standing around were many thousand white-robed ones. And he raised his head, and looked upon me, and said to me, 'Thou art welcome, daughter.' And he called me, and from the cheese as he was milking he gave me as it were a little cake, and I received it with folded hands; and I ate it, and all who stood around said, Amen. And at the sound of their voices I was awakened, still tasting a sweetness which I cannot describe. And I immediately related this to my brother, and we understood that it was to be a passion, and we ceased henceforth to have any hope in this world."

Chapter II

1. "After a few days there prevailed a report that we should be heard. And then my father came to me from the city, worn out with anxiety. He came up to me that he might cast me down, saying, 'Have pity, my daughter, on my grey hairs. Have pity on your father, if I am worthy to be called a father by you. If with these hands I have brought you up to this flower of your age, if I have preferred you to all your brothers, do not deliver me up to the scorn of men. Have regard to your brothers, have regard to your mother and your aunt, have regard to your son, who will not be able to live after you. Lay aside your courage, and do not bring us all to destruction; for none of us will speak in freedom if you should suffer anything.' These things said my father in his affection, kissing my hands and throwing himself at my feet; and with tears he called me not Daughter, but Lady. And I grieved over the grey hairs of my father, that he alone of all my family would not rejoice over my passion. And I comforted him, saying, 'On that scaffold whatever God wills shall happen. For know that we are not placed in our own power, but in that of God.' And he departed from me in sorrow.

2. "Another day, while we were at dinner, we were suddenly taken away to be heard, and we arrived at the town hall. At once the rumor spread through the neighborhood of the public place, and an immense number of people were gathered together. We mounted the platform. The rest were interrogated and confessed. Then they came to me, and my father immediately appeared with my boy, and withdrew me from the step, and said in a supplicating tone, 'Have pity on your babe.' And Hilarianus the procurator, who had just received the power of life and death in the place of the proconsul Minucius Timinianus, who was deceased, said, 'Spare the grey hairs of your father, spare the infancy of your boy, offer sacrifice for the well-being of the emperors.' And I replied, 'I will not do so.' Hilarianus said, 'Are you a Christian?' And I replied, 'I am a Christian.' And as my father stood there to cast me down *from the faith*, he was ordered by Hilarianus to be thrown down, and was beaten with rods. And my father's misfortune grieved me as if I myself had been beaten, I so grieved for his wretched old age. The procurator then delivers judgment on all of us, and condemns us to the wild beasts, and we went down cheerfully to the dungeon. Then, because my child had been used to receive suck from me, and to stay with me in the prison, I send Pomponius the deacon to my father to ask for the infant, but my father would not give it to him. And even as God willed it, the child no long desired the breast, nor did my breast cause me uneasiness, lest I should be tormented

by care for my babe and by the pain of my breasts at once.

3. "After a few days, while we were all praying, suddenly, in the middle of our prayer, there came to me a word, and I named Dinocrates; and I was amazed that that name had never come into my mind until then, and I was grieved as I remembered his misfortune. And I felt myself immediately to be worthy, and to be called on to ask on his behalf. And for him I began earnestly to make supplication, and to cry with groaning to the Lord. Without delay, on that very night, this was shown to me in a vision. I saw Dinocrates going out from a gloomy place, where also there were several others, and he was parched and very thirsty, with a filthy countenance and pallid color, and the wound on his face which he had when he died. This Dinocrates had been my brother after the flesh, seven years of age who died miserably with disease—his face being so eaten out with cancer that his death caused repugnance to all men. For him I had made my prayer, and between him and me there was a large interval, so that neither of us could approach to the other. And moreover, in the same place where Dinocrates was, there was a pool full of water, having its brink higher than was the stature of the boy; and Dinocrates raised himself up as if to drink. And I was grieved that, although that pool held water, still, on account of the height to its brink, he could not drink. And I was aroused, and knew that my brother was in suffering. But I trusted that my prayer would bring help to his suffering; and I prayed for him every day until we passed over into the prison of the camp, for we were to fight in the camp show. Then was the birthday of Geta Caesar, and I made my prayer for my brother day and night, groaning and weeping that he might be granted to me.

4. "Then, on the day on which we remained in fetters, this was shown to me. I saw that that place which I had formerly observed to be in gloom was now bright; and Dinocrates, with a clean body well clad, was finding refreshment. And where there had been a wound, I saw a scar; and that pool which I had before seen, *I saw now* with its margin lowered even to the boy's navel. And one drew water from the pool incessantly, and upon its brink was a goblet filled with water; and Dinocrates drew near and began to drink from it, and the goblet did not fail. And when he was satisfied, he went away from the water to play joyously, after the manner of children, and I awoke. Then I understood that he was translated from the place of punishment."

Chapter III

1. "Again, after a few days, Pudens, a soldier, an assistant overseer of the prison, who began to regard us in great esteem, perceiving that the great power of God was in us, admitted many brethren to see us, that both we and they might be mutually refreshed. And when the day of the exhibition drew near, my father, worn with suffering, came in to me, and began to tear out his beard, and to throw himself on the earth, and to cast himself down on his face, and to reproach his years, and to utter such words as might move all creation. I grieved for his unhappy old age.

2. "The day before that on which we were to fight, I saw in a vision that Pomponius the deacon came hither to the gate of the prison and knocked vehemently. I went out to him and opened the gate for him; and he was clothed in a richly ornamented white robe, and he had on manifold *calliculae*. And he said to me, 'Perpetua, we are waiting for you; come!' And he held his hand to me, and we began to go through rough and winding places. Scarcely at length had we arrived breathless at the amphitheatre, when he led me into the middle of the arena, and said to me, 'Do not fear, I am here with you, and I am laboring with you,' and he departed. And I gazed upon an immense assembly in astonishment. And because I knew that I was given to the wild beasts, I marveled that the wild beasts were not let loose upon me. Then there came forth against me a certain Egyptian, horrible in appearance, with his backers, to fight with me. And there came to me, as my helpers and encouragers, handsome youths; and I was stripped, and became a man. Then my helpers began to rub me with oil, as is the custom for contest; and I beheld that Egyptian on the other hand rolling in the dust. And a certain man came forth, of wondrous height, so that he even overtopped the top of the amphitheatre; and he wore a loose tunic and a

purple robe between two bands over the middle of the breast; and he had on *calliculae* of varied form, made of gold and silver; and he carried a rod, as if he were a trainer of gladiators, and a green branch upon which were apples of gold. And he called for silence, and said, 'This Egyptian, if he should overcome this woman, shall kill her with the sword; and if she shall conquer him, she shall receive this branch.' Then he departed. And we drew near to one another, and began to deal out blows. He sought to lay hold of my feet, while I struck at his face with my heels; and I was lifted up in the air, and began thus to thrust at him as if spurning the earth. But when I saw that there was some delay I joined my hands so as to twine my fingers with one another; and I took hold upon his head, and he fell on his face, and I trod upon his head. And the people began to shout, and my backers to exult. And I drew near to the trainer and took the branch; and he kissed me, and said to me, 'Daughter, peace be with you': and I began to go gloriously to the Sanavivarian gate. Then I awoke, and perceived that I was not to fight with beasts, but against the devil. Still I knew that the victory was awaiting me. This, so far, I have completed several days before the exhibition; but what passed at the exhibition itself let who will write."

Chapter IV

1. Moreover, also, the blessed Saturus related this his vision, which he himself committed to writing:—"We had suffered," says he, "and we were gone forth from the flesh, and we were beginning to be borne by four angels into the east; and their hands touched us not. And we floated not supine, looking upwards, but as if ascending a gentle slope. And being set free, we at length saw the first boundless light; and I said, 'Perpetua' (for she was at my side), 'this is what the Lord promised to us; we have received the promise.' And while we are borne by those same four angels, there appears to us a vast space which was like a pleasure garden, having rose trees and every kind of flower. And the height of the trees was after the measure of a cypress, and their leaves were falling incessantly. Moreover, there in the pleasure garden four other angels appeared, brighter than the previous ones, who, when they saw us, gave us

honor, and said to the rest of the angels, 'Here they are! Here they are!' with admiration. And those four angels who bore us, being greatly afraid, put us down; and we passed over on foot the space of a furlong in a broad path. There we found Jocundus and Saturninus and Artaxius, who having suffered the same persecution were burnt alive; and Quintus, who also himself a martyr had departed in the prison. And we asked of them where the rest were. And the angels said to us, 'Come first, enter and greet your Lord.'

2. "And we came near to place, the walls of which were such as if they were built of light; and before the gate of that place stood four angels, who clothed those who entered with white robes. And being clothed, we entered and saw the boundless light, and heard the united voice of some who said without ceasing, 'Holy! Holy! Holy!' And in the midst of that place we saw as it were a hoary man sitting, having snow-white hair and with a youthful countenance; and his feet we saw not. And on his right hand and on his left were four-and-twenty elders, and behind them a great many others were standing. We entered with great wonder, and stood before the throne; and the four angels raised us up, and we kissed Him, and He passed His hand over our face. And the rest of the elders said to us, 'Let us stand'; and we stood and made peace. And the elders said to us, 'Go and enjoy.' And I said, 'Perpetua, you have what you wish.' And she said to me, 'Thanks be to God, that joyous as I was in the flesh, I am now more joyous here.'

3. "And we went forth, and saw before the entrance Optatus the bishop at the right hand, and Aspasius the presbyter, a teacher, at the left hand, separate and sad; and they cast themselves at our feet, and said to us, 'Restore peace between us, because you have gone forth and have left us thus.' And we said to them, 'Are you not our father, and you our presbyter, that you should cast yourselves at our feet?' And we prostrated ourselves, and we embraced them; and Perpetua began to speak with them, and we drew them apart in the pleasure garden under a rose tree. And while we were speaking with them, the angels said unto them, 'Let them alone, that they may refresh themselves; and if you have any dis-

sensions between you, forgive one another.' And they drove them away. And they said to Optatus, 'Rebuke your people, because they assemble to you as if returning from the circus, and contending about factious matters.' And then it seemed to us as if they would shut the doors. And in that place we began to recognize many brethren, and moreover martyrs. We were all nourished with an indescribable odor, which satisfied us. Then, I joyously awoke."

Chapter V

1. The above were the more eminent visions of the blessed martyrs Saturus and Perpetua themselves, which they themselves committed to writing. But God called Secundulus, while he was yet in the prison, by an earlier exit from the world, not without favor, so as to give a respite to the beasts. Nevertheless, even if his soul did not acknowledge cause for thankfulness, assuredly his flesh did.

2. But respecting Felicitas (for to her also the Lord's favor approached in the same way), when she had already gone eight months with child (for she had been pregnant when she was apprehended), as the day of the exhibition was drawing near, she was in great grief lest on account of her pregnancy she should be delayed—because pregnant women are not allowed to be publicly punished—and lest she should shed her sacred and guiltless blood among some who had been wicked subsequently. Moreover, also, her fellow martyrs were painfully saddened lest they should leave so excellent a friend, and as it were companion, alone in the path of the same hope. Therefore, joining together their united cry, they poured forth their prayer to the Lord three days before the exhibition. Immediately after their prayer her pains came upon her, and when, with the difficulty natural to an eight months' delivery, in the labor of bringing forth she was sorrowing, some one of the servants of the *Cataractarii* said to her, "You who are in such suffering now, what will you do when you are thrown to the beasts, which you despised when you refused to sacrifice?" And she replied, "Now it is I that suffer what I suffer; but then there will be another in me, who will suffer for me, because I also am about to suffer for Him." Thus

she brought forth a little girl, which a certain sister brought up as her daughter.

3. Since then the Holy Spirit permitted, and by permitting willed, that the proceedings of that exhibition should be committed to writing, although we are unworthy to complete the description of so great a glory; yet we obey as it were the command of the most blessed Perpetua, nay her sacred trust, and add one more testimony concerning her constancy and her loftiness of mind. While they were treated with more severity by the tribune, because, from the intimations of certain deceitful men, he feared lest they should be withdrawn from the prison by some sort of magic incantations, Perpetua answered to his face, and said, "Why do you not at least permit us to be refreshed, being as we are objectionable to the most noble Caesar, and having to fight on his birthday? Or is it not your glory if we are brought forward fatter on that occasion?" The tribune shuddered and blushed, and commanded that they should be kept with more humanity, so that permission was given to their brethren and others to go in and be refreshed with them; even the keeper of the prison trusting them now himself.

4. Moreover, on the day before, when in that last meal, which they call the free meal, they were partaking as far as they could, not of a free supper, but of an *agapē*; with the same firmness they were uttering such words as these to the people, denouncing *against them* the judgment of the Lord, bearing witness to the felicity of their passion, laughing at the curiosity of the people who came together; while Saturus said, "Tomorrow is not enough for you, for you to behold with pleasure that which you hate. Friends today, enemies tomorrow. Yet note our faces diligently, that you may recognize them on that day of judgment." Thus all departed thence astonished, and from these things many believed.

Chapter VI

1. The day of their victory shone forth, and they proceeded from the prison into the amphitheatre, as if to an assembly, joyous and of brilliant countenances; if perchance shrinking, it was with joy, and not with fear. Perpetua followed with placid look, and with step and gait as a matron of

Christ, beloved of God; casting down the luster of her eyes from the gaze of all. Moreover, Felicitas, rejoicing that she had safely brought forth, so that she might fight with the wild beasts; from the blood and from the midwife to the gladiator, to wash after childbirth with a second baptism. And when they were brought to the gate, and were constrained to put on the clothing—the men, that of the priests of Saturn, and the women, that of those who were consecrated to Ceres—that noble-minded woman resisted even to the end with constancy. For she said, "We have come thus far of our own accord, for this reason, that our liberty might not be restrained. For this reason we have yielded our minds, that we might not do any such thing as this: we have agreed on this with you." Injustice acknowledged the justice; the tribune yielded to their being brought as simply as they were. Perpetua sang psalms, already treading under foot the head of the Egyptian; Revocatus, and Saturninus, and Saturus uttered threatenings against the gazing people about this martyrdom. When they came within sight of Hilarianus, by gesture and nod, they began to say to Hilarianus, "You judge us," say they, "but God will judge you." At this the people, exasperated, demanded that they should be tormented with scourges as they passed along the rank of the *venatores*. And they indeed rejoiced that they should have incurred any one of their Lord's passions.

2. But He who had said, "Ask, and you shall receive" (John 16:24), gave to them when they asked, that death which each one had wished for. For when at any time they had been discoursing among themselves about their wish in respect of their martyrdom, Saturninus indeed had professed that he wished that he might be thrown to all the beasts; doubtless that he might wear a more glorious crown. Therefore in the beginning of the exhibition he and Revocatus made trial of the leopard, and moreover upon the scaffold they were harassed by the bear. Saturus, however, held nothing in greater abomination than a bear; but he imagined that he would be put an end to with one bite of a leopard. Therefore, when a wild boar was supplied, it was the huntsman rather who had supplied that boar who was gored by that same beast, and died the day after the shows. Saturus

only was drawn out; and when he had been bound on the floor near to a bear, the bear would not come forth from his den. And so Saturus for the second time is recalled unhurt.

3. Moreover, for the young women the devil prepared a very fierce cow, provided especially for that purpose contrary to custom, rivaling their sex also in that of the beasts. And so, stripped and clothed with nets, they were led forth. The populace shuddered as they saw one young woman of delicate frame, and another with breasts still dropping from her recent childbirth. So, being recalled, they are unbound. Perpetua is first led in. She was tossed, and fell on her loins; and when she saw her tunic torn from her side, she drew it over her as a veil for her middle, rather mindful of her modesty than her suffering. Then she was called for again, and bound up her disheveled hair; for it was not becoming for a martyr to suffer with disheveled hair, lest she should appear to be mourning in her glory. So she rose up; and when she saw Felicitas crushed, she approached and gave her her hand, and lifted her up. And both of them stood together; and the brutality of the populace being appeased, they were recalled to the Sanavivarian gate. Then Perpetua was received by a certain one who was still a catechumen, Rusticus by name, who kept close to her; and she, as if aroused from sleep, so deeply had she been in the Spirit and in an ecstasy, began to look round her, and to say to the amazement of all, "I cannot tell when we are to be led out to that cow." And when she had heard what had already happened, she did not believe it until she had perceived certain signs of injury in her body and in her dress, and had recognized the catechumen. Afterwards causing that catechumen and the brother to approach, she addressed them, saying, "Stand fast in the faith, and love one another, all of you, and be not offended at my sufferings."

4. The same Saturus at the other entrance exhorted the soldier Pudens, saying, "Assuredly here I am, as I have promised and foretold, for up to this moment I have felt no beast. And now believe with your whole heart. Lo, I am going forth to that beast, and I shall be destroyed with one bite of the leopard." And immediately at the conclusion of the exhibition he was thrown to the leop-

ard; and with one bite of his he was bathed with such a quantity of blood, that the people shouted out to him as he was returning, the testimony of his second baptism, "Saved and washed, saved and washed." Manifestly he was assuredly saved who had been glorified in such a spectacle. Then to the soldier Pudens he said, "Farewell, and be mindful of my faith; and let not these things disturb, but confirm you." And at the same time he asked for a little ring from his finger, and returned it to him bathed in his wound, leaving to him an inherited token and the memory of his blood. And then lifeless he is cast down with the rest, to be slaughtered in the usual place. And when the populace called for them into the midst, that as the sword penetrated into their body they might make their eyes partners in the murder, they rose up of their own accord, and transferred themselves whither the people wished; but they first kissed one another, that they might consummate their martyrdom with the kiss of peace. The rest indeed, immove-

able and in silence, received the sword-thrust; much more Saturus, who also had first ascended the ladder, and first gave up his spirit, for he also was waiting for Perpetua. But Perpetua, that she might taste some pain, being pierced between the ribs, cried out loudly, and she herself placed the wavering right hand of the youthful gladiator to her throat. Possibly such a woman could not have been slain unless she herself had willed it, because she was feared by the impure spirit.

O most brave and blessed martyrs! O truly called and chosen unto the glory of our Lord Jesus Christ! whom whoever magnifies, and honors, and adores, assuredly ought to read these examples for the edification of the Church, not less than the ancient ones, so that new virtues also may testify that one and the same Holy Spirit is always operating even until now, and God the Father Omnipotent, and His Son Jesus Christ our Lord, whose is the glory and infinite power forever and ever. Amen.

8. Justin Martyr, *Second Apology*

Justin (d. ca. 165), a convert who taught at Rome, was the most important of the second-century "apologists," who wrote to explain and justify the Christian faith in the context of Greco-Roman pagan culture. In Justin's case this meant arguing for the moral superiority of Christians and ascribing the evils of the pagan culture to demons while at the same time affirming some aspects of that culture on the basis of his understanding of Christ's presence as God's Logos or Word in the world.

1. O Romans, what has recently happened in your city under Urbicus, and what is likewise being done everywhere by the governors unreasonably, have compelled me to compose these arguments for your sakes, who are of like passion and are our brothers, though you are ignorant of the fact and repudiate it on account of the splendor of your position. For everywhere, whoever is corrected by father, or neighbor, or child, or friend, or brother,

or husband, or wife, on account of a fault, for being stubborn, for loving pleasure and being difficult to urge to what is right—except those who have been persuaded that the unjust and intemperate will be punished in eternal fire, but that the virtuous and those who lived as Christ will dwell with God in an existence free from suffering [we say those who have become Christians]—these and the wicked demons who hate us, and who keep

SOURCE: Justin Martyr, *The First and Second Apologies*, ed. and tr. L. W. Barnard (New York: Paulist Press, 1997), 73-85.
Copyright © 1997 by Leslie William Barnard. Used by permission of Paulist Press, New York/Mahwah, N.J.

such people as these in subjection to themselves, and serve them as judges, incite them, as rulers moved by evil spirits, to put us to death. But in order that the cause of everything that has taken place under Urbicus may become quite plain to you, I will tell what has been done.

An Outrage

2. A certain woman lived with an intemperate husband, she herself also having once been intemperate. But when she came to the knowledge of the teachings of Christ she became sober-minded and tried to persuade her husband in like manner to be temperate, bringing forward the teachings, and assuring him that there will be punishment in eternal fire inflicted on those who do not live temperately and in conformity to right reason. But he, continuing in the same extravagances, alienated his wife from him by his deeds. For she, considering it wicked to live any longer as a wife with a husband who sought in every way means of pleasure contrary to the law of nature and in violation of what is right, wished to be divorced from him.

And when she was entreated earnestly by her friends, who advised her still to continue with him, with the thought that some time or other her husband might show hope of amendment, she did violence to her own inclinations and remained with him. But since her husband had gone to Alexandria, and was reported as to be conducting himself worse than ever—that by continuing in matrimonial connection with him, and by sharing his table and bed, she might not become a sharer also in his evils and impieties—she gave him what is called a bill of divorce, and was separated from him. But this noble husband of hers—while he should have been rejoicing that those deeds which before she committed without hesitation with the servants and hirelings, when she delighted that he too should give up the same—when she had separated from him since he refused to alter his ways, brought an accusation against her, saying that she was a Christian. And she presented a paper to the emperor requesting that first she should be allowed to arrange her affairs, and afterward make her defense against the accusation, when her affairs were set in order; and this was granted. And her erstwhile husband, since he was now no longer able to prosecute her, directed his assaults against a certain Ptolemaeus, whom Urbicus punished, who had been her teacher of Christian doctrines—and this he did in the following manner. He persuaded a centurion who had cast Ptolemaeus into prison, and who was friendly to himself, to seize Ptolemaeus and interrogate him on this point alone—is he a Christian? And Ptolemaeus, being a lover of truth and not of a deceitful nor false nature, when he confessed that he was a Christian, was put in bonds by the centurion, and for a long period was punished in the prison. And at last when the man came to Urbicus, he was asked only this question—whether he was a Christian. And again, conscious of the good which he owed to the teaching which proceeded from Christ, he confessed the doctrine of divine virtue. For he who denies anything, either denies it because he has condemned it, or shrinks from confessing it, because he knows himself to be unworthy of and alien to it; neither of which is that of the true Christian. And when Urbicus ordered him to be led away to punishment, a certain Lucius, who was also himself a Christian, seeing the unreasonable judgment which had thus been given, said to Urbicus: "What is the basis of this judgment? Why have you punished this man, not as an adulterer, nor fornicator, nor murderer, nor thief, nor robber, nor convicted of any crime at all, but as one who has only confessed that he is called by the name of Christian? This judgment of yours, O Urbicus, does not become the Emperor Pius, nor the philosopher—son of Caesar nor the Sacred Senate." And he said nothing else in answer to Lucius than this: "You also seem to me to be such a one." And when Lucius answered, "Most certainly I am," he again ordered him to be led away. And he gave thanks, knowing that he was delivered from such wicked rulers, and was going to the Father and King of the heavens. And also a third having come forward was sentenced to be punished.

Justin Expects to Fall

3. I therefore am expecting to be plotted against and fixed to a rack by some of those named, or perhaps by Crescens, that lover of bravado and boasting. For the man is unworthy of the name of philosopher who publicly bears witness against us

in matters which he does not understand, saying that Christians are godless and impious, and doing so to win favor with the deluded mob, and so please them. For if he runs us down without having read the teachings of Christ, he is thoroughly evil, and far worse than the inexperienced people, who often refrain from discussing or bearing false witness about matters they do not understand. Or, if he has read them and does not understand the majesty that is in them or, understanding it, acts so that he may not be suspected of being such [i.e., a Christian], he is far more base and thoroughly depraved, being conquered by vulgar and unreasonable opinion and fear. For I would have you know that I put to him certain questions on this subject, and questioned him, and found most convincingly that he truly knows nothing. And to show that I speak the truth I am ready, if these disputations have not been reported to you, to combat them again in your presence. And this would be a work worthy of a prince. But if my questions and his answers have been made known to you, you are already aware that he is acquainted with none of our matters; or if he is acquainted with them but through fear of those who might hear him does not dare to speak out, like Socrates, he proves himself, as I said before, no philosopher, but a lover of vainglory; at least he disregards the admirable saying of Socrates: "But a man must in no wise be honored before the truth." But it is impossible for a Cynic, who makes indifference his end, to know any good but indifference.

God's Creation Good

4. But lest anyone say, "Go then all of you and commit suicide, and pass even now to God, and do not trouble us"—I will tell you why we do not do so, but how, when examined, we make our confession without fear. We have been taught that God did not make the world aimlessly, but for the sake of the human race; and we have stated before that He rejoices in those who imitate His nature, and is displeased with those who embrace what is worthless either in word or deed. If, then, we all commit suicide, we will become the cause, as far as in us lies, why no one should be born, or instructed in the divine teachings, or even why the human race should not exist; and if we so act, we

ourselves will be acting in opposition to the will of God. But when we are accused, we do not deny [the accusation] because we are not conscious of any evil, but count it impious not to speak the truth in all things, which also we know is pleasing to God, and because we also now wish to free you from an unjust prejudice.

Angels and Demons

5. But if this thought should take possession of someone that if we confess God as our helper, we should not, as we say, be oppressed and persecuted by wicked people; this I will solve. God, when He had made the whole world, and subjected earthly things to men and women, and arranged the heavenly elements for the increase of fruits and change of the seasons, and ordered the divine law for them—these things also He made for people to see—and entrusted the care of men and women and of things under heaven to angels whom He appointed over them. But the angels transgressed this order, and were captivated by love of women, and produced children who are called demons. And besides later they enslaved the human race to themselves, partly by magical writings, and partly by fears and punishments which they occasioned, and partly by teaching them to offer sacrifices and incense and libations, which they needed after they were enslaved with lustful passions; and among people they sowed murders, wars, adulteries, intemperate deeds, and every evil. Whence also the poets and mythologists, not knowing that it was the angels and those demons who had been begotten by them that did these things to men and women and cities and nations, which they related, ascribed them to God Himself, and to those who were His offspring, and to the offspring of those who were called His brothers. For whatever name each of the angels had given to himself and to his children, by that name they called them.

God and the Logos

6. But to the Father of all, who is unbegotten, a name is not given. For by whatever name He is called, He has as His elder, the one who gives Him the name. But these words Father, and God, and Creator, and Lord and Master, are not names, but appellations derived from His good deeds and

works. But His Son, who is alone properly called Son, the logos who is with God and is begotten before the creation, when in the beginning God created and set in order everything through Him, is called Christ, with reference to His being anointed and God's ordering all things through Him; this name itself also containing an unknown significance, just as the title "God" is not a name, but the intuition implanted in human nature of an inexpressible reality. But "Jesus," His name as man and Savior, also has significance. For He was made man, as we said before, having been conceived according to the will of God the Father, for the sake of believing men and women, and for the destruction of the demons. And now you can learn this from your own observation. For numberless demoniacs throughout the whole world, and in your city—many of our Christian people exorcising them in the name of Jesus Christ, who was crucified under Pontius Pilate, have healed and do heal, rendering helpless and driving the possessing demons out of the men, though they could not be cured by all the older exorcists, and those who used incantations and drugs.

God Spares the World for the Christians

7. Wherefore God delays causing the confusion and destruction of the whole world, by which the wicked angels and demons and people will no longer exist, because of the seed of the Christians, who know that they are the cause of preservation in nature. Since if it were not so, it would not have been possible for you to do and be impelled to these things by evil spirits; but the fire of judgment would descend and utterly dissolve all things, even as formerly the flood left no one but one only with his family who is called by us Noah, and by you Deucalion, from whom again such vast numbers have sprung, some of them evil and others good. For in the manner just described we say there will be the conflagration, but not as the Stoics [say], according to the doctrine of the permutation of all things into one another, which appears most degrading. But neither do we affirm that it is by fate that people do what they do, or suffer what they suffer, but that each by free choice acts rightly or sins; and it is according to the working of

wicked demons that earnest people, such as Socrates and the like, suffer persecution and are in bonds, while Sardanapalus, Epicurus, and the like appear blessed in abundance and glory. The Stoics, not knowing this, maintained that all things take place according to the necessity of fate. But since God made the race of angels and men in the beginning with free will, in eternal fire they will justly suffer the punishment of whatever sins they have committed. And this is the nature of all that is made—to be capable of vice and virtue. For neither would any of them be praiseworthy unless there was also power to turn to both. And this also is shown by those people everywhere who have made laws and conducted philosophy according to right reason, by their agreeing to do some things and refrain from others. Even the Stoic philosophers, in their doctrine of morals, steadily pay deference to the same things, so that it is evident that they are not right in what they say about principles and incorporeal things. For whether they will say that human actions come to pass according to fate, or whether they maintain that God is nothing else than the things which are ever turning and altering and dissolving into the same things, they will appear to have had an understanding only of destructible things, and to have looked on God Himself as emerging both in part and in whole in every wickedness; or that neither vice nor virtue is anything, which is contrary to every sound idea, reason, and sense.

Those Who Followed Reason Are Persecuted

8. And those of the Stoic school, since they were honorable at least in their ethical teaching, as were also the poets in some particulars, on account of a seed of logos implanted in every race of men and women, were, we know, hated and put to death, as for instance Heraclitus mentioned before and, among those of our own time, Musonius and others. For, as we intimated, the demons have always effected that all those who ever so little strived to live by logos and to shun vice be hated. And it is not astonishing that the demons are proved to cause those to be much worse hated who lived not by a part only from logos, the Sower, but by the knowledge and contemplation of the whole logos,

who is Christ. And they, having been shut up in eternal fire, will suffer their just punishment and penalty. For if they are already overthrown by men and women through the name of Jesus Christ, this is an intimation of the punishment in eternal fire which is to be inflicted on themselves and those who serve them. For so did both the prophets foretell, and Jesus our own teacher teach.

The Coming Judgment

9. And that no one should say what is said by those who are thought to be philosophers, that our threats that the wicked are punished in eternal fire are big words and bugbears, and that we wish people to live virtuously through fear, and not because such a life is good and pleasant—I will answer this briefly, that if this is not so, God does not exist; or if He exists He does not care for men and women, and neither virtue nor vice is anything, and, as we said before, lawgivers unjustly punish those who disobey good commandments. But since these [i.e., the lawgivers] are not unjust, nor their Father who teaches by the logos to do the same things as they require, those who agree with them are not unjust either. And if one objects that the laws of men and women are different, and says that with some, one thing is considered good, another evil, while with others what seemed bad to the first is thought good, and what seemed good is thought bad, let him listen to what we say to this. We know that the wicked angels appointed laws conformable to their own wickedness, in which the people who are like them delight; and right reason, having come, proved that not all opinions nor all teachings are good, but that some are evil, while others are good. Wherefore I will declare the same and similar things to such people as these, and if need be, they will be spoken of more in due course. But at present I return to the subject.

The Whole Logos

10. What we have, then, appears to be greater than all human teaching, because the whole rational principle became Christ, who appeared for our sake, body, and reason, and soul. For whatever either lawgivers or philosophers uttered well, they elaborated according to their share of logos by invention and contemplation. But since they did not know all that concerns logos, who is Christ, they often contradicted themselves. And those who by human birth were more ancient than Christ, when by reason they tried to contemplate and investigate reality, were brought before the tribunals as impious persons and busybodies. And Socrates, who was more forcible in this direction than all of them, was accused of the very same crimes as ourselves. For they said that he was introducing new divinities, and did not consider those to be gods whom the state recognized. But he cast out from the state both Homer and the rest of the poets, and taught people to reject the wicked demons and those who did the things which the poets related; and he exhorted them to become acquainted with the God who was to them unknown, by means of investigation of reason, saying "that it is neither easy to find the Father and Maker of all, nor, having found Him, is it safe to declare Him to all." But these things our Christ did through His own power. For no one trusted in Socrates so as to die for this doctrine. But in Christ, who was partially known even by Socrates [for He was and is the logos who is in every person, and who foretold the things that were to come to pass both through the prophets and in His own person, when He had assumed our nature, and taught these things], not only philosophers and scholars believed, but also artisans and people entirely uneducated, despising both glory, and fear, and death; since it is the power of the ineffable Father, and not mere vessels of human reason.

Discipline and Probation

11. But neither would we be put to death, nor would wicked people and demons be more powerful than us, were not death a debt due from every person who has been born. Wherefore we give thanks when we pay this debt. And we judge it to be right and proper to relate here, for the sake of Crescens and those who rave as he does, what is said by Xenophon. Heracles, says Xenophon, came to a place where three ways met, and found Virtue and Vice, who appeared to him in the form of women: Vice, in a luxurious dress, and with a seductive expression rendered blooming by such ornaments, immediately seductive to the eyes, said

to Heracles that if he would follow her, she would always enable him to pass his life in pleasure and be adorned with the most graceful ornaments, such as were then upon her own person; and Virtue, who was of squalid look and dress, said, if you obey me you will adorn yourself not with ornament nor beauty that passes away and perishes, but with everlasting and precious graces. And we are persuaded that everyone who flees from what is superficially good and follows what is reckoned hard and foolish finds happiness awaiting him. For Vice, veiling her actions in the beauties which properly belong to Virtue and are genuine [though only by imitation of incorruptible things, for she possesses and can produce nothing which is incorruptible], enslaves groveling people, clothing Virtue in the ugliness which properly belongs to herself. But those who understand the beauties belonging to true existence become themselves incorruptible by means of Virtue. And this every sensible person ought to think both of Christians and of athletes, and of those who did what the poets relate of the so-called gods, concluding as much from our contempt of death, from which even men and women flee.

The Way Christians Regard Death

12. For I myself too, when I was delighting in the teachings of Plato, and heard the Christians slandered, and saw them fearless of death and of all other things which are counted fearful, saw that it was impossible that they could be living in wickedness and pleasure. For what sensual or intemperate person, or whoever counts it good to feast on human flesh, could welcome death that he might be deprived of his enjoyments, and would not rather always continue the present life, and try to escape the observation of the rulers; and much less would he denounce himself when the consequence would be death? This also the wicked demons have now effected by evil people. For when they had put some to death on account of the accusations falsely brought against us, they also dragged to the torture our slaves, either children or weak women, and by dreadful torments forced them to admit those incredible actions which they themselves openly perpetrate; about which we are the less concerned, because none of

these actions are really ours, and we have the unbegotten and ineffable God as witness of both our thoughts and deeds. For why did we not even publicly profess that these were the things which we held to be good, and prove that these are the divine philosophy, saying that the mysteries of Kronos are performed when we slay a man, and that when we drink our fill of blood, as it is said we do, we are doing what you perform before that idol you honor, and on which you sprinkle the blood not only of irrational animals, but also of men and women, making a libation of the blood of the slain by the hand of the most illustrious and noble person among you? And imitating Jupiter and the other gods in sodomy and shameless intercourse with women, might we not bring as our apology the writings of Epicurus and the poets? But because we persuade people to avoid such instruction, and all who practice them and imitate such examples as now we have tried to persuade you in this discourse, we are assailed in every kind of way. But we are not concerned, since we know that God is a just observer of all. But would that even now someone would mount a lofty rostrum, and shout with a tragic voice, "Be ashamed, be ashamed, you who charge the guiltless with those deeds which you yourselves openly commit, and who ascribe things which refer to yourselves and to your gods to those who have no part in them. Be converted, become wise."

The Logos Sows Seeds in Humanity

13. For I myself, perceiving the wicked disguise which the evil demons had cast over the divine doctrines of the Christians, in order to avert others from joining them, laughed both at those who framed these falsehoods, and at the disguise itself, and at popular opinion. And I confess that I both pray and with all my strength strive to be found a Christian; not because the teachings of Plato are different from those of Christ, but because they are not in every respect equal, as neither are those of the others, Stoics, and poets, and historians. For each person spoke well, according to the part present in him of the divine logos, the Sower, whenever he saw what was related to him [as a person]. But they who contradict themselves on the more important points appear not to have possessed the

hidden understanding and the irrefutable knowledge. Therefore, whatever things were rightly said among all people are the property of us Christians. For next to God, we worship and love the logos who is from the unbegotten and ineffable God, since also He became man for our sakes, that, becoming a partaker of our sufferings, He might also bring us healing. For all the writers were able to see realities darkly, through the presence in them of an implanted seed of logos. For the seed and imitation of something, imparted according to capacity, is one thing, and another is the thing itself, the part possession and imitation of which is effected according to the grace coming from Him.

A Prayer

14. And we therefore ask you to publish this petition, appending what you think right, that our opinions may be known to others, and that these persons may have a fair chance of being freed from erroneous notions and ignorance of good, who by their own fault are subject to punishment; that so these things may be published to men and women. Because it is in the nature of man to know good and evil, and by their condemning us, whom they do not understand, for actions which they say are

wicked, and by delighting in the gods which did such things, and even now require similar actions from people, and by inflicting on us death or imprisonment or some other such punishment, as if we were guilty of these things, they condemn themselves, so that there is no need of other judges.

His Writings Not Injurious

15. And I despised the wicked and deceitful teaching of Simon among my own race. And if you publish this [officially], we will make it manifest to all, that, if possible, they may be converted; for we composed this treatise for this end alone. And our doctrines are not shameful, according to sober judgment, but indeed are more lofty than every human philosophy; and if not so, they are at least unlike the doctrines of the Sotadists, and Philaenidians, and Dancers, and Epicureans, and such other teachings of the poets, which all are allowed acquaintance with, both as acted and as written. And from now on we will be silent, having done as much as we could, and having added the prayer that all people everywhere may be counted worthy of the truth. And would that you also, in a manner becoming piety and philosophy, would for your own sakes judge justly!

9. Certificate of Sacrifice

In persecution of Christians throughout the empire in 250, the emperor Decius issued a general order to the population to make sacrifice to the pagan gods. Certificates testified to compliance and so established that their bearers were not Christians. This example was found in an excavation in Egypt in 1893.

To the Commissioners of Sacrifice of the Village of Alexander's Island: from Aurelius Diogenes, the son of Satabus, of the Village of Alexander's Island, aged 72 years:—scar on his right eyebrow.

I have always sacrificed regularly to the gods, and now, in your presence, in accordance with the edict, I have done sacrifice, and poured the drink

offering, and tasted of the sacrifices, and I request you to certify the same, Farewell.

Handed in by me, *Aurelius Diogenes.*

I certify that I saw him sacrificing . . .

Done in the first year of the emperor, Caesar Gaius Messius Quintus Trajanus Decius, Pius, Felix, Augustus: the second of the month Epith.

SOURCE: *Readings in Ancient History: Illustrative Extracts from the Sources*, vol. 2 (Boston: Allen and Bacon, 1913), 289.

10. Tertullian of Carthage, *On the Apparel of Women*

Tertullian (d. ca. 225) was a major Christian author active in Carthage in the early years of the third century. He embraced the teaching of the "New Prophecy" (or Montanism) in about 207, though in most matters of funda- mental belief this did not entail for him a break with the Catholic tradition. Among his many surviving writings are apologetical works, refutations of Marcion and the Valentinians, theological treatises on various topics (such as baptism, resurrection, and the soul), and many discourses on practical moral and disciplinary issues. On such issues his views are typically strict, as in this discussion of the dress of women.

Book I

Chapter I.—Introduction. Modesty in Apparel Becoming to Women, in Memory of the Introduc- tion of Sin into the World through a Woman.

If there dwelt upon earth a faith as great as is the reward of faith which is expected in the heav- ens, no one of you at all, best beloved sisters, from the time that she had first "known the Lord," and learned (the truth) concerning her own (that is, woman's) condition, would have desired too glad- some (not to say too ostentatious) a style of dress; so as not rather to go about in humble garb, and rather to affect meanness of appearance, walking about as Eve mourning and repentant, in order that by every garb of penitence she might the more fully expiate that which she derives from Eve—the ignominy, I mean, of the first sin, and the odium (attaching to her as the cause) of human perdi- tion. "In pains and in anxieties do you bear (chil- dren), woman; and toward your husband (is) your inclination, and he lords it over thee" (cf. Gen. 3:16). And do you not know that you are (each) an Eve? The sentence of God on this sex of yours lives in this age: the guilt must of necessity live too. *You* are the devil's gateway: *you* are the unsealer of that (forbidden) tree: *you* are the first deserter of the divine law: *you* are she who per-

suaded him whom the devil was not valiant enough to attack. *You* destroyed so easily God's image, man. On account of *your* desert—that is, death—even the Son of God had to die. And do you think about adorning yourself over and above your tunics of skins? Come, now; if from the beginning of the world the Milesians sheared sheep, and the Serians spun trees, and the Tyrians dyed, and the Phrygians embroidered with the needle, and the Babylonians with the loom, and pearls gleamed, and onyx-stones flashed; if gold itself also had already issued, with the cupidity (which accompanies it), from the ground; if the mirror, too, already had license to lie so largely, Eve, expelled from paradise, (Eve) already dead, would also have coveted *these* things, I imagine! No more, then, ought she *now* to crave, or be acquainted with (if she desires to live again), what, when she *was* living, she had neither had nor known. Accordingly these things are all the bag- gage of woman in her condemned and dead state, instituted as if to swell the pomp of her funeral.

Chapter II.—The Origin of Female Ornamentation, Traced Back to the Angels Who Had Fallen.

For they, withal, who instituted them are assigned, under condemnation, to the penalty of death—those angels, to wit, who rushed from

Source: Tertullian, "On the Apparel of Women," tr. S. Thelwall, in *The Ante-Nicene Fathers*, vol. 3, ed. Alexander Roberts and James Donaldson (Buffalo: Christian Literature Publishing Company, 1885), 14-15, 22, 24-25.

heaven on the daughters of men; so that this ignominy also attaches to woman. For when to an age much more ignorant (than ours) they had disclosed certain well-concealed material substances, and several not well-revealed scientific arts—if it is true that they had laid bare the operations of metallurgy, and had divulged the natural properties of herbs, and had promulgated the powers of enchantments, and had traced out every curious art, even to the interpretation of the stars—they conferred properly and as it were peculiarly upon women that instrumental mean of womanly ostentation, the radiances of jewels wherewith necklaces are variegated, and the circlets of gold wherewith the arms are compressed, and the medicaments of orchil with which wools are colored, and that black powder itself wherewith the eyelids and eyelashes are made prominent. What is the quality of these things may be declared meantime, even at this point, from the quality and condition of their teachers: in that sinners could never have either shown or supplied anything conducive to integrity, unlawful lovers anything conducive to chastity, renegade spirits anything conducive to the fear of God. If (these things) are to be called *teachings*, ill masters must of necessity have taught ill; if as *wages of lust*, there is nothing base of which the wages are honorable. But why was it of so much importance to show these things as well as to confer them? Was it that women, without material causes of splendor, and without ingenious contrivances of grace, could not please *men*, who, while still unadorned, and uncouth and—so to say—crude and rude, had moved (the mind of) *angels*? Or was it that the lovers would appear sordid and—through gratuitous use—contumelious, if they had conferred no (compensating) gift on the women who had been enticed into connubial connection with them? But these questions admit of no calculation. Women who possessed angels (as husbands) could desire nothing more; they had, forsooth, made a grand match! Assuredly they who, of course, did sometimes think whence they had fallen, and, after the heated impulses of their lusts, looked up toward heaven, thus requited that very excellence of women, natural beauty, as (having proved) a cause of evil, in order that their good fortune

might profit them nothing; but that, being turned from simplicity and sincerity, they, together with (the angels) themselves, might become offensive to God. Sure they were that all ostentation, and ambition, and love of pleasing by carnal means, was *dis*pleasing to God. And these are the angels whom we are destined to judge: these are the angels whom in baptism we renounce: these, of course, are the reasons why they have deserved to be judged by man. What business, then, have their *things* with their *judges*? What commerce have they who are to condemn with them who are to be condemned? The same, I take it, as Christ has with Belial. With what consistency do we mount that (future) judgment seat to pronounce sentence against those whose gifts we (now) seek after? For you too, (women as you are), have the self-same angelic nature promised as your reward, the self-same sex as men: the self-same advancement to the dignity of judging, does (the Lord) promise you. Unless, then, we begin even here to *pre*judge, by precondemning their *things*, which we are hereafter to condemn in *themselves*, they will rather judge and condemn *us* . . .

Book II

Chapter VIII.—Men Not Excluded from These Remarks on Personal Adornment.

Of course, now, I, a man, as being envious of women, am banishing them quite from their own (domains). Are there, in our case too, some things which, in respect of the sobriety we are to maintain on account of the fear due to God, are disallowed? If it is true, (as it is,) that in men, for the sake of women (just as in women for the sake of men), there is implanted, by a defect of nature, the will to please; and if this sex of ours acknowledges to itself deceptive trickeries of form peculiarly its own—(such as) to cut the beard too sharply; to pluck it out here and there; to shave round about (the mouth); to arrange the hair, and disguise its hoariness by dyes; to remove all the incipient down all over the body; to fix (each particular hair) in its place with (some) womanly pigment; to smooth all the rest of the body by the aid of some rough powder or other: then, further, to take every opportunity for consulting the mirror; to gaze anxiously into it:—while yet, when (once) the knowledge of God has put an end to all wish to please by means of voluptuous attraction, all these things are rejected as frivolous, as hostile to modesty. For where God is, there modesty is; there is sobriety, her assistant and ally. How, then, shall we practice modesty without her instrumental mean, that is, without sobriety? How, moreover, shall we bring sobriety to bear on the discharge of (the functions of) modesty, unless seriousness in appearance and in countenance, and in the general aspect of the entire man, mark our carriage?

Chapter XI.—Christian Women, Further, Have Not the Same Causes for Appearing in Public, and Hence for Dressing in Fine Array as Gentiles. On the Contrary, Their Appearance Should Always Distinguish Them from Such.

Moreover, what causes have you for appearing in public in excessive grandeur, removed as you are from the occasions which call for such exhibitions? For you neither make the circuit of the temples, nor demand (to be present at) public shows, nor have any acquaintance with the holy days of the Gentiles. Now it is for the sake of all these public gatherings, and of much seeing and being seen, that all pomps (of dress) are exhibited before the public eye; either for the purpose of transacting the trade of voluptuousness, or else of inflating "glory." *You*, however, have no cause of appearing in public, except such as is serious. Either some brother who is sick is visited, or else the sacrifice is offered, or else the word of God is dispensed. Whichever of these you like to name is a business of sobriety and sanctity, requiring no extraordinary attire, with (studious) arrangement and (wanton) negligence. And if the requirements of Gentile friendships and of kindly offices call you, why not go forth clad in your own armor; (and) all the more, in that (you have to go) to such as are strangers to the faith? so that between the handmaids of God and of the devil there may be a difference; so that you may be an example to them, and they may be edified in you; so that (as the apostle says) "God may be magnified in your body" (cf. Phil. 1:20). But magnified He is in the *body* through modesty: of course, too, through

attire suitable to modesty. Well, but it is urged by some, "Let not the Name be blasphemed in us, if we make any derogatory change from our old style and dress." Let us, then, not abolish our old vices! Let us maintain the same character, if we must maintain the same appearance (as before); and then truly the nations will not blaspheme! A grand blasphemy is that by which it is said, "Ever since she became a Christian, she walks in poorer garb!" Will you fear to appear poorer, from the time that you have been made more wealthy; and *fouler*, from the time when you have been made more clean? Is it according to the decree of Gentiles, or according to the decree of God, that it becomes Christians to walk?

Chapter XII.—Such Outward Adornments Meretricious, and Therefore Unsuitable to Modest Women.

Let us only wish that we may be no cause for just blasphemy! But how much more provocative of blasphemy is it that you, who are called modesty's priestesses, should appear in public decked and painted out after the manner of the *immodest*? Else, (if you so do,) what inferiority would the poor unhappy victims of the public lusts have (beneath you)? whom, albeit some laws were (formerly) wont to restrain them from (the use of) matrimonial and matronly decorations, now, at all events, the daily increasing depravity of the age has raised so nearly to an equality with all the most honorable women, that the difficulty is to distinguish them. And yet, even the Scriptures suggest (to us the reflection), that meretricious attractivenesses of form are invariably conjoined with and appropriate to bodily prostitution. That powerful state which presides over the seven mountains and very many waters, has merited from the Lord the appellation of a prostitute. But what kind of garb is the instrumental mean of her comparison with that appellation? She sits, to be sure, "in purple, and scarlet, and gold, and precious stone." How accursed are the things without (the aid of) which an accursed prostitute could not have been described! It was the fact that Tamar "had painted out and adorned herself" that led Judah to regard her as a harlot, and thus, because she was hidden beneath her "veil"—the quality of her garb belying her as if she had been a harlot—he judged (her to be one), and addressed and bargained with (her as such). Whence we gather an additional confirmation of the lesson, that provision must be made in every way against all immodest associations and suspicions. For why is the integrity of a chaste mind defiled by its neighbor's suspicion? Why is a thing from which I am averse hoped for in me? Why does not my garb pre-announce my character, to prevent my spirit from being wounded by shamelessness through (the channel of) my ears? Grant that it be lawful to assume the appearance of a modest woman: to assume that of an *immodest* (woman) is, at all events, *not* lawful.

Chapter XIII.—It Is Not Enough that God Know Us to Be Chaste: We Must Seem So before Men. Especially in These Times of Persecution We Must Inure Our Bodies to the Hardships Which They May Not Improbably Be Called to Suffer.

Perhaps some (woman) will say: "To me it is not necessary to be approved by men; for I do not require the testimony of men: God is the inspector of the heart." (That) we all know; provided, however, we remember what the same (God) has said through the apostle: "Let your probity appear before men." For what purpose, except that malice may have no access at all to you, or that you may be an example and testimony to the evil? Else, what is (that): "Let your works shine" (cf. Matt. 3:14)? Why, moreover, does the Lord call us the light of the world? Why has He compared us to a city built upon a mountain, if we do not shine in (the midst of) darkness, and stand eminent amid them who are sunk down? If you hide your lamp beneath a bushel, you must necessarily be left quite in darkness and be run against by many. The things which make us luminaries of the world are these—our good works. What is *good*, moreover, provided it be true and full, loves not darkness: it joys in being seen, and exults over the very pointings which are made at it. To Christian modesty it is not enough to *be* so, but to *seem* so too. For so great ought its plenitude to be, that it may flow out from the mind to the garb, and burst out from the conscience to the outward appearance; so that even from the outside it may gaze, as it were, upon its own furniture—(a furniture) such as to be suited to retain faith as its inmate perpetually. For such delicacies as tend by their softness and effeminacy to unman the manliness of faith are to be discarded. Otherwise, I know not whether the wrist that has been wont to be surrounded with the palmleaf-like bracelet will endure till it grow into the numb hardness of its own chain! I know not whether the leg that has rejoiced in the anklet will suffer itself to be squeezed into the shackle! I fear the neck, beset with pearl and emerald nooses, will give no room to the broadsword! Wherefore, blessed (sisters), let us meditate on hardships, and we shall not feel them; let us abandon luxuries, and we shall not regret them. Let us stand ready to endure every violence, having nothing which we may fear to leave behind. It is these things which are the bonds which retard our hope. Let us cast away earthly ornaments if we desire heavenly. Love not gold; in which (one substance) are branded all the sins of the people of Israel. You ought to *hate* what ruined your fathers; what was adored by them who were forsaking God. Even *then* (we find) gold is food for the fire. But Christians always, and now more than ever, pass their times not in gold but in iron: the stoles of martyrdom are (now) preparing: the angels who are to carry us are (now) being awaited! Do you go forth (to meet them) already arrayed in the cosmetics and ornaments of prophets and apostles; drawing your whiteness from simplicity, your ruddy hue from modesty; painting your eyes with bashfulness, and your mouth with silence; implanting in your ears the words of God; fitting on your necks the yoke of Christ. Submit your head to your husbands, and you will be enough adorned. Busy your hands with spinning; keep your feet at home; and you will "please" better than (by arraying yourselves) in gold. Clothe yourselves with the silk of uprightness, the fine linen of holiness, the purple of modesty. Thus painted, you will have God as your Lover!

11. *Acts of Paul and Thecla*

These scenes, composed in the late second century, form a part of the Acts of Paul, *one of many apocryphal works that attempted to supply details of the lives of Christ or the apostles, in the manner of popular fiction. Here the central figure is Paul's devotee Thecla rather than the apostle himself, and the major theme is that of chastity, which gives Thecla independence from her fiancé and family and endows her with miraculous powers. Chastity, indeed, appears here as the very essence of Christian faith.*

[*The apostle Paul goes to Iconium.*]

5. And when Paul entered the house of One-siphorus, there was great joy, bowing, breaking of bread, and God's word pertaining to continence and the resurrection. Paul said,

Blessed are the pure in heart, for they shall see God.

Blessed are those who keep the flesh pure, for they shall become the temple of God.

Blessed are those who remain continent, for to them shall God speak.

Blessed are those who bid farewell to this world, for they shall be well-pleasing to God.

Blessed are those who have wives as if they had them not, for they shall inherit God.

Blessed are those that have fear of God, for they shall become angels of God.

6. Blessed are those who tremble at the oracles of God, for they shall be comforted.

Blessed are those who receive the wisdom of Jesus Christ, for they shall be called sons of the Most High.

Blessed are those who have preserved their baptism, for they shall find their rest with the Father and the Son.

Blessed are those who have advanced to the sagacity of Jesus Christ, for they shall be in light.

Blessed are those who for the love of God have left the way of the world, for they shall judge angels and shall be blessed at the right hand of the Father.

Blessed are those who show mercy, for they shall be shown mercy and shall not see a cruel judgment.

Blessed are the bodies of virgins, for they shall be well pleasing to God and shall not lose the reward of their purity, for the Word of the Father shall be a work of salvation for them in the day of his Son, and they shall have rest forever and ever.

7. And while Paul spoke these things in the midst of the assembly at Onesiphorus' house, a certain virgin named Thecla, whose mother was Theocleia, and who was wooed by a man named Thamyris, sat by a window of a nearby house and listened night and day to the message Paul spoke about chastity. And she did not turn away from the window, but led on by faith, she rejoiced greatly. Yet when she saw many women and virgins going to Paul, she also greatly desired that she be deemed worthy to stand before Paul, for she had not yet seen his physical appearance, but had only heard his voice.

8. Since she did not leave the window, her mother sent to Thamyris. He came rejoicing, as if he already were taking her to wife. Thamyris thus said to Theocleia, "Where is my Thecla?" and Theocleia said, "I have some news to tell you, Thamyris. For three days and three nights, Thecla has not risen from the window, neither to eat nor

Source: Elizabeth A. Clark, *Women in the Early Church* (Wilmington, Del.: Michael Glazier, 1983), 79-88. Copyright © 1983 by Elizabeth A. Clark. Published by the Liturgical Press, Collegeville, Minnesota. Reprinted by permission.

to drink, but she gazes as if she were seeing something delightful. She is thus devoted to the stranger who gives instruction in various and deceitful teachings, so that I am amazed at how such a modest virgin is so deeply upset."

9. "O Thamyris, this man is stirring up the city of the Iconians and your Thecla as well. For all the women and young men go in to him and are taught by him. He says you must fear the one and only God and live chastely. And my daughter, too, is like a spider at the window, bound by his words, and is seized by a new desire and an awesome passion. For she intently apprehends the things said by him and the virgin is conquered. But you go and speak to her for she is engaged to you."

10. And Thamyris went to her, both loving her and fearing her consternation, and said, "Thecla, my fiancée, why are you sitting like this? And what sort of passion has you so stunned? Turn to me, your Thamyris, and be ashamed of yourself." And her mother also said the same thing, "My child, why are you sitting like this, eyes cast down, making no response, but behaving like a mad person?" And they wept powerfully, Thamyris missing his wife, Theocleia, her child, and the maidservants, their mistress. Thus there was a great confusion of mourning in the house. And while these things went on, Thecla did not turn away, but paid rapt attention to Paul's message.

[*Thamyris finds some enemies of Paul and with them conspires to have Paul brought before the governor. At the hearing, Paul speaks:*]

17. And Paul lifted up his voice and said, "If today I am being investigated for what I teach, listen, O proconsul. The living God, the avenging God, the jealous God, the God who needs nothing, but desires the salvation of humans, has sent me so that I may tear them away from corruption and filthiness, and all pleasure and death, that they may sin no more. For this reason God sent his own Child, whom I preach and teach, that men may have hope in him, him who alone showed compassion for the world wandering in sin, in order that humans may no longer be under judgment but have faith and fear of God, knowledge of majesty and love of truth. Therefore if I teach the

things revealed to me by God, how do I err, O proconsul?" And when the governor heard this, he commanded that Paul be bound and carried off to prison until he had the opportunity to hear him more attentively.

18. But at night Thecla removed her bracelets and gave them to the gatekeeper, and when the door was opened for her, she went into the prison. And giving the jailer a silver mirror, she went in to Paul. She sat by his feet and heard the great deeds of God. Paul did not fear at all, but lived freely in the perfect openness of God. And her faith was increased by kissing his bonds.

19. As Thecla was sought by her own people and by Thamyris, as she was searched for in the streets like a lost person, one of the fellow-servants of the gatekeeper revealed that she had gone out at night. And they inquired of the gatekeeper and he told them that she had gone to the stranger in prison. They went just as he told them and found her, bound to him in a manner of affection. And having departed from there, they drew together the crowd and showed it to the governor.

20. And he commanded Paul to be brought to the platform. Thecla, however, rolled around on the place where Paul had taught when he sat in prison. And the governor commanded that she also be brought to the platform. She went, exultant with joy. And the crowd, when Paul was brought in again, shouted inordinately, "He is a wizard, away with him!" But the governor gladly heard Paul on the subject of the holy deeds of Christ. And taking counsel, he called Thecla and said, "Why will you not marry Thamyris, according to the law of the Iconians?" But she just stood, gazing intently at Paul. When she did not reply, Theocleia, her mother, cried out, saying, "Burn the lawless woman, burn her who is not a bride in the middle of the theatre, so that all women who have been instructed by this man may be afraid!"

21. The governor was greatly affected and having scourged Paul, he sent him outside the city, but Thecla he sentenced to be burned. Immediately the governor arose and went to the theatre, and the entire mob went out for the distressing spectacle. But Thecla, like a lamb in the wilderness who looks about for the shepherd, sought Paul. And when she looked at the crowd, she saw the

Lord sitting there, as if he were Paul, and she said, "As if I were not able to bear it, Paul came to watch me." And gazing at him, she kept intent on him. But he went away into the heavens.

22. And the boys and the virgins brought wood and hay in order to burn Thecla. And as she was brought in naked, the governor wept and was astounded at the power in her. They spread the wood and the public executioners ordered her to climb on the pyre. She made the sign of the cross, went up on the wood, and they lighted it. A great flame blazed but the fire did not touch her. For God, showing compassion, produced a noise under the ground and a cloud threw a shadow from above, full of rain and hail, and the whole vessel was poured out so that many were endangered and died, and the fire being extinguished, Thecla was saved.

[*Thecla finds Paul after her miraculous rescue. She asks him to baptize her, but he tells her she must be patient. The story continues:*]

26. And Paul sent away Onesiphorus with all his household to Iconium. Then he took Thecla and went into Antioch. And as they entered, a certain Syrian named Alexander saw Thecla, fell in love with her, and earnestly entreated Paul, bribing him with money and presents. But Paul said, "I do not know this woman of whom you speak, nor is she mine." But since the man was very powerful, he embraced her on the street. She, however, did not tolerate this, but sought Paul. And she cried out bitterly, saying, "Do not force a strange woman, do not force the servant of God. I am the first of the Iconians and because I did not want to be married to Thamyris, I am expelled from the city." And seizing Alexander, she ripped his mantle, removed the wreath from his head, and made him a scandal.

27. But he, loving her and ashamed of what had happened to him, brought her before the governor, and when she confessed that she had done these things, he sentenced her to the beasts. But the women were panic-stricken and shouted at the platform, "An evil judgment, an unholy judgment!" Thecla asked the governor that she might remain chaste until the time when she would fight the beasts. And a certain wealthy queen named Tryphaena, whose daughter had died, took her into custody and had her as a solace.

28. And when the beasts were paraded forth, they bound Thecla to a fierce lioness and Queen Tryphaena followed close after her. But the lioness, when Thecla was seated on top of her, licked her feet all over, and the whole crowd was amazed. The charge that was written about her was "A committer of sacrilege." And the women with their children shouted from above, saying, "O God, an unholy judgment has taken place in this city!" And after the procession, Tryphaena received her once again. For her daughter Falconilla, who was dead, said to her in a dream, "Mother, you shall keep Thecla, the helpless stranger, in my place, so that she may pray for me and I may be transposed to the place of the righteous."

29. Thus when Tryphaena took her after the procession, she at once mourned because she was to fight the beasts on the next day and because she felt deep affection for her, as for her daughter Falconilla. And she said, "Thecla, my second child, come, pray for my child that she may live forever. For I saw this while sleeping." And without delaying, Thecla raised her voice and said, "O my God, the Son of the Most High, who is in heaven, give to her as she wills, so that her daughter Falconilla may live forever." And after Thecla said these things, Tryphaena wailed, seeing that such a beautiful woman was to be thrown to the beasts.

30. And when the dawn arrived, Alexander came to take her (for he was giving the wild-beast fights), saying, "The governor is seated and the crowd is raising a clamor at us. Give me the woman who is to fight the beasts that I may lead her away." But Tryphaena cried out so that he fled. She said, "In my house there has come about a second mourning for my Falconilla, and no one comes to give aid, neither child, for she is dead, nor relative, for I am a widow. O God of my child Thecla, come to Thecla's aid."

31. And the governor sent soldiers to bring Thecla. Tryphaena did not leave her, but she herself took her hand and led her up, saying, "I led away my daughter Falconilla to the tomb, but you, Thecla, I lead to fight the beasts." And Thecla wept bitterly and sighed unto the Lord, saying, "Lord,

the God in whom I trust, with whom I have sought refuge, who rescued me from the fire, give a reward to Tryphaena who has had compassion on your servant, and because she has preserved me chaste."

32. Thus an uproar arose, and the noise of the beasts and a cry of the crowd, and of the women sitting together, some of whom said, "Bring in the woman who committed sacrilege!" while others said, "Away with the city for this lawless deed! Away with all of us, proconsul! A bitter sight, a wicked judgment!"

33. But Thecla, removed from the hand of Tryphaena, was stripped, and she wore a girdle, and was flung into the stadium. Lions and bears were put in against her. A fierce lioness ran up to her feet and lay down, and the crowd of women clamored greatly. A bear ran towards her, but the lioness ran to the bear, met him, and ripped him apart. And again, a lion trained to fight against humans, a lion that belonged to Alexander, ran to her. And the lioness joined him in a close fight in which both were killed. The women wept even more, since the lioness that had helped her was dead.

34. Then they threw in many beasts, while she stood and stretched out her hands and prayed. When she finished her prayer, she turned and saw a large pit filled with water and she said, "Now is the right time for me to baptize myself." And she threw herself in, saying, "In the name of Jesus Christ, I baptize myself on the last day." The women who saw it and all the crowd wept, saying, "Do not throw yourself into the water," so that even the governor shed tears that such beauty would be eaten by seals. Thus she cast herself into the water in the name of Jesus Christ. But the seals, seeing the light of a flash of fire, floated dead. And around her there was a cloud of fire, so that neither did the animals touch her nor was she perceived as naked.

35. And the women, when other more dreadful beasts were cast in, cried loudly. Some flung petals, while others threw nard, others cassia and still others spice plants, so that there was a multitude of perfumes. All the animals were smitten so that they were held as if they were asleep and did not touch her. So Alexander said to the governor,

"I have some extremely ferocious bulls; let us bind the woman condemned to fight the beasts to them." And the governor, although sullen, yielded and said, "Do what you will." And they tied her between the bulls' feet, put red hot irons on their genital organs, so that they might become even more agitated and kill her. Then they sprang forward, but the flame burning around her burned through the ropes, and she was as one not bound.

36. But Tryphaena, who was standing alongside the arena, fainted at the steps into the arena, so that her female servants said, "Queen Tryphaena is dead!" The governor stopped the procedures and the whole city was frightened. Alexander fell at the governor's feet and said, "Have mercy on me and the city, and release the woman condemned to fight the beasts, lest the city also be destroyed along with her. For if Caesar should hear about these things, he perhaps will destroy us and the city, for Queen Tryphaena, his relative, died at the steps into the arena."

37. And the governor called Thecla from the midst of the beasts and said to her, "Who are you? What is there about you that none of the beasts touched you?" And she replied, "I am a servant of the living God. And what there is about me is that I have trusted in God's Son, in whom he is well-pleased. On account of him, not one of the beasts touched me. For he alone is the way of salvation and the foundation of immortal life. He is a refuge for those who are distressed, a remission for the afflicted, a shelter for the despairing; in general, if anyone does not believe in him, he shall not live, but shall die forever."

38. And when the governor heard these things, he ordered clothes to be brought and said, "Put on the clothes." And she said, "The one who clothed me while I was naked among the beasts shall clothe me with salvation on the day of judgment." And taking the garments, she got dressed. Straightaway the governor sent out an act proclaiming, "I release Thecla to you, the pious servant of God." And all the women cried out in a loud voice and as with one mouth, they gave praise to God, saying, "The God who saved Thecla is one," so that from their cry the whole city shook.

39. And when the good news was told to

Tryphaena, she met Thecla with the crowd, embraced her, and said, "Now I believe that my child lives. Come inside, and I will sign over to you all my goods." Then Thecla went in with her and rested in her house for eight days, teaching her the word of God, so that the majority of the servants also believed, and there was great joy in the house.

40. But Thecla yearned for Paul and sought him, sending around everywhere. And it was reported to her that he was in Myra. Taking young men and maidens, she girded herself and sewed her mantle into a garment in the fashion of men. She departed for Myra, found Paul speaking the word of God, and went to him. He was amazed to see her and the crowd that was with her, wondering lest some other temptation had come to her. But she recognized it and said to him, "I have received baptism, Paul. For the One who worked together with you in the Gospel also worked with me for my being baptized."

41. And Paul took her by the hand, led her into the house of Hermias, and heard everything from her, so that he was much amazed and those who heard were confirmed and prayed for Tryphaena.

Thecla rose and said to Paul, "I go to Iconium." And Paul said, "Go and teach the word of God." Now the many garments and gold that Tryphaena had sent, Thecla left behind with Paul for the service of the poor.

42. She departed for Iconium. She entered the house of Onesiphorus and fell on the floor where Paul sat when he taught the oracles of God, and wept, saying, "O my God and God of this house where the light shone on me, Christ Jesus, the Son of God, my helper in prison, my helper before the governors, my helper in the fire, my helper amidst the beasts, you are God and to you be the glory forever. Amen."

43. And she found Thamyris dead, but her mother alive. She summoned her mother and said to her, "Theocleia, my mother, can you believe that the Lord lives in the heavens? For if you desire money, the Lord will give it to you through me. Behold your child, I am here before you." And when she had witnessed to these things, she departed for Seleucia, and when she had enlightened many people with the word of God, she slept with a good sleep.

Theological Currents in the Second and Third Centuries

12. *The Second Treatise of the Great Seth*

This text was in the ancient gnostic library found at Nag Hammadi in 1945. The speaker purports to be Jesus Christ addressing true believers. He describes his mission to reveal the truth to those who could receive it and his hostile reception from the ruler of the world, the "Cosmocrator," who is clearly the God of the Old Testament. He also denies dying on the cross and alludes to persecution by "those who think they are advancing the name of Christ." The title's significance is unclear; the name of Seth, though often encountered in other gnostic texts, does not otherwise appear in this one.

And the perfect Majesty is at rest in the ineffable light, in the truth of the mother of all these, and all of you that attain to me, to me alone who am perfect, because of the Word. For I exist with all the greatness of the Spirit, which is a friend to us and our kindred alike, since I brought forth a word to the glory of our Father, through his goodness, as well as an imperishable thought; that is, the Word within him—it is slavery that we shall die with Christ—and an imperishable and undefiled thought, an incomprehensible marvel, the writing of the ineffable water which is the word from us. It is I who am in you [pl.] and you are in me, just as the Father is in you in innocence.

Let us gather an assembly together. Let us visit that creation of his. Let us send someone forth in it, just as he visited <the> Ennoias, the regions below. And I said these things to the whole multitude of the multitudinous assembly of the rejoicing Majesty. The whole house of the Father of Truth rejoiced that I am the one who is from them. I produced thought about the Ennoias which came out of the undefiled Spirit, about the descent upon the water, that is, the regions below. And they all had a single mind, since it is out of one. They charged me since I was willing. I came forth to reveal the glory to my kindred and my fellow spirits.

For those who were in the world had been prepared by the will of our sister Sophia—she who is a whore—because of the innocence which has not been uttered. And she did not ask anything from the All, nor from the greatness of the Assembly, nor from the Pleroma. Since she was first she came forth to prepare monads and places for the Son of Light, and the fellow workers which she took from the elements below to build bodily dwellings from them. But, having come into being in an empty glory, they ended in destruction in the dwellings in which they were, since they were prepared by Sophia. They stand ready to receive the life-giving word of the ineffable Monad and of the greatness of the assembly of all those who persevere and those who are in me.

SOURCE: "The Second Treatise of the Great Seth," tr. Roger A. Bullard and Joseph A. Gibbons, in *The Nag Hammadi Library in English*, 3rd ed., ed. James M. Robinson (San Francisco: Harper and Row, 1988), 363-71. Copyright © 1977 by E. J. Brill, Leiden, The Netherlands. Reprinted by permission of HarperCollins Publishers Inc. and Brill Academic Publisher.

I visited a bodily dwelling. I cast out the one who was in it first, and I went in. And the whole multitude of the archons became troubled. And all the matter of the archons as well as all the begotten powers of the earth were shaken when it saw the likeness of the Image, since it was mixed. And I am the one who was in it, not resembling him who was in it first. For he was an earthly man, but I, I am from above the heavens. I did not refuse them even to become a Christ, but I did not reveal myself to them in the love which was coming forth from me. I revealed that I am a stranger to the regions below.

There was a great disturbance in the whole earthly area with confusion and flight, as well as (in) the plan of the archons. And some were persuaded, when they saw the wonders which were being accomplished by me. And all these, with the race, that came down, flee from him who had fled from the throne to the Sophia of hope, since she had earlier given the sign concerning us and all the ones with me—those of the race of Adonaios. Others also fled, as if from the Cosmocrator and those with them, since they have brought every (kind of) punishment upon me. And there was a flight of their mind about what they would counsel concerning me, thinking that she (Sophia) is the whole greatness, and speaking false witness, moreover, against the Man and the whole greatness of the assembly.

It was not possible for them to know who the Father of Truth, the Man of the Greatness, is. But they who received the name because of contact with ignorance—which (is) a burning and a vessel—having created it to destroy Adam whom they had made, in order to cover up those who are theirs in the same way. But they, the archons, those of the place of Yaldabaoth, reveal the realm of the angels, which humanity was seeking in order that they may not know the Man of Truth. For Adam, whom they had formed, appeared to them. And a fearful motion came about throughout their entire dwelling, lest the angels surrounding them rebel. For without those who were offering praise—I did not really die lest their archangel become empty.

And then a voice—of the Cosmocrator—came to the angels: "I am God and there is no other beside me. "But I laughed joyfully when I examined his empty glory. But he went on to say, "Who

is man?" And the entire host of his angels who had seen Adam and his dwelling were laughing at his smallness. And thus did their Ennoia come to be removed outside the Majesty of the heavens, i.e., the Man of Truth, whose name they saw since he is in a small dwelling place, since they are small (and) senseless in their empty Ennoia, namely, their laughter. It was contagion for them.

The whole greatness of the Fatherhood of the Spirit was at rest in his places. And I am he who was with him, since I have an Ennoia of a single emanation from the eternal ones and the undefiled and immeasurable incomprehensibilities. I placed the small Ennoia in the world, having disturbed them and frightened the whole multitude of the angels and their ruler. And I was visiting them all with fire and flame because of my Ennoia. And everything pertaining to them was brought about because of me. And there came about a disturbance and a fight around the Seraphim and Cherubim, since their glory will fade, and the confusion around Adonaios on both sides and their dwelling—to the Cosmocrator and him who said, "Let us seize him"; others again, "The plan will certainly not materialize." For Adonaios knows me because of hope. And I was in the mouths of lions. And the plan which they devised about me to release their Error and their senselessness—I did not succumb to them as they had planned. But I was not afflicted at all. Those who were there punished me. And I did not die in reality but in appearance, lest I be put to shame by them because these are my kinsfolk. I removed the shame from me and I did not become fainthearted in the face of what happened to me at their hands. I was about to succumb to fear, and I <suffered> according to their sight and thought, in order that they may never find any word to speak about them. For my death which they think happened, (happened) to them in their error and blindness, since they nailed their man unto their death. For their Ennoias did not see me, for they were deaf and blind. But in doing these things, they condemn themselves. Yes, they saw me; they punished me. It was another, their father, who drank the gall and the vinegar; it was not I. They struck me with the reed; it was another, Simon, who bore the cross on his shoulder. It was another upon whom they placed the crown of thorns. But I was rejoicing in the height over all the wealth of the archons and the offspring of their error, of their empty glory. And I was laughing at their ignorance.

And I subjected all their powers. For as I came downward no one saw me. For I was altering my shapes, changing from form to form. And therefore, when I was at their gates I assumed their likeness. For I passed them by quietly, and I was viewing the places, and I was not afraid nor ashamed, for I was undefiled. And I was speaking with them, mingling with them through those who are mine, and trampling on those who are harsh to them with zeal, and quenching the flame. And I was doing all these things because of my desire to accomplish what I desired by the will of the Father above.

And the Son of the Majesty, who was hidden in the regions below, we brought to the height where I <was> in all these aeons with them, which (height) no one has seen nor known, where the wedding of the wedding robe is, the new one and not the old, nor does it perish.

For it is a new and perfect bridal chamber of the heavens, as I have revealed (that) there are three ways: an undefiled mystery in a spirit of this aeon, which does not perish, nor is it fragmentary, nor able to be spoken of; rather, it is undivided, universal, and permanent. For the soul, the one from the height, will not speak about the error which is here, nor transfer from these aeons, since it will be transferred when it becomes free and when it is endowed with nobility in the world, standing before the Father without weariness and fear, always mixed with the Nous of power (and) of form. They will see me from every side without hatred. For since they see me, they are being seen (and) are mixed with them. Since they did not put me to shame, they were not put to shame. Since they were not afraid before me, they will pass by every gate without fear and will be perfected in the third glory.

It was my going to the revealed height which the world did not accept, my third baptism in a revealed image. When they had fled from the fire of the seven Authorities, and the sun of the powers of the archons set, darkness took them. And the world became poor when he was restrained with a multitude of fetters. They nailed him to the tree, and they fixed him with four nails of brass. The veil of his temple he tore with his hands. It was a trembling which seized the chaos of the earth, for the souls which were in the sleep below were released. And they arose. They went about boldly, having shed zealous service of ignorance and unlearnedness beside the dead tombs, having put on the new man, since they have come to know that perfect Blessed One of the eternal and incomprehensible Father and the infinite light, which is I, since I came to my own and united them with myself. There is no need for many words, for our Ennoia was with their Ennoia. Therefore they knew what I speak of, for we took counsel about the destruction of the archons. And therefore I did the will of the Father, who is I.

After we went forth from our home, and came down to this world, and came into being in the world in bodies, we were hated and persecuted, not only by those who are ignorant, but also by those who think that they are advancing the name of Christ, since they were unknowingly empty, not knowing who they are, like dumb animals. They persecuted those who have been liberated by me, since they hate them—those who, should they shut their mouth, would weep with a profitless groaning because they did not fully know me. Instead, they served two masters, even a multitude. But you will become victorious in everything, in war and battles, jealous division and wrath. But in the uprightness of our love we are innocent, pure, (and) good, since we have a mind of the Father in an ineffable mystery.

For it was ludicrous. It is I who bear witness that it was ludicrous, since the archons do not know that it is an ineffable union of undefiled truth, as exists among the sons of light, of which they made an imitation, having proclaimed a doctrine of a dead man and lies so as to resemble the freedom and purity of the perfect assembly, (and) <joining> themselves with their doctrine to fear and slavery, worldly cares, and abandoned worship, being small (and) ignorant since they do not contain the nobility of the truth for they hate the one in whom they are, and love the one in whom they are not. For they did not know the Knowledge of the Greatness, that it is from above and (from) a fountain of truth, and that it is not from slavery and jealousy, fear and love of worldly matter. For that which is not theirs and that which is theirs they use fearlessly and freely. They do not desire because they have authority, and (they have) a law from themselves over whatever they will wish.

But those who have not are poor, that is, those who do not possess him. And they desire him and lead astray those who through them have become like those who possess the truth of their freedom, just as they bought us for servitude and constraint of care and fear. This person is in slavery. And he who is brought by constraint of force and threat has been guarded by God. But the entire nobility of the Fatherhood is not guarded, since he guards only him who is from him, without word and constraint, since he is united with his will, he who belongs only to the Ennoia of the Fatherhood, to make it perfect and ineffable through the living water, to be with you mutually in wisdom, not only in word of hearing but in deed and fulfilled word. For the perfect ones are worthy to be established in this way and to be united with me, in order that they may not share in any enmity, in a good friendship. I accomplish everything through the Good One, for this is the union of the truth, that they should have no adversary. But everyone who brings division—and he will learn no wisdom at all because he brings division and is not a friend—is hostile to them all. But he who lives in harmony and friendship of brotherly love, naturally and not artificially, completely and not partially, this person is truly the desire of the Father. He is the universal one and perfect love.

For Adam was a laughingstock, since he was made a counterfeit type of man by the Hebdomad, as if he had become stronger than I and my brothers. We are innocent with respect to him, since we have not sinned. And Abraham and Isaac and Jacob were a laughingstock, since they, the counterfeit fathers, were given a name by the Hebdomad, as if he had become stronger than I and my brothers. We are innocent with respect to him, since we have not sinned. David was a laughingstock in that his son was named the Son of Man, having been influenced by the Hebdomad, as if he had become stronger than I and the fellow members of my race. But we are innocent with respect to him; we have not sinned. Solomon was a laugh-

ingstock, since he thought that he was Christ, having become vain through the Hebdomad, as if he had become stronger than I and my brothers. But we are innocent with respect to him. I have not sinned. The twelve prophets were laughingstocks, since they have come forth as imitations of the true prophets. They came into being as counterfeits through the Hebdomad, as if he had become stronger than I and my brothers. But we are innocent with respect to him, since we have not sinned. Moses, a faithful servant, was a laughingstock, having been named "the Friend," since they perversely bore witness concerning him who never knew me. Neither he nor those before him, from Adam to Moses and John the Baptist, none of them knew me nor my brothers.

For they had a doctrine of angels to observe dietary laws and bitter slavery, since they never knew truth, nor will they know it. For there is a great deception upon their soul making it impossible for them ever to find a Nous of freedom in order to know him, until they come to know the Son of Man. Now concerning my Father, I am he whom the world did not know, and because of this, it (the world) rose up against me and my brothers. But we are innocent with respect to him; we have not sinned.

For the Archon was a laughingstock because he said, "I am God, and there is none greater than I. I alone am the Father, the Lord, and there is no other beside me. I am a jealous God, who brings the sins of the fathers upon the children for three and four generations." As if he had become stronger than I and my brothers! But we are innocent with respect to him, in that we have not sinned, since we mastered his teaching. Thus he was in an empty glory. And he does not agree with our Father. And thus through our fellowship we grasped his teaching, since he was vain in an empty glory. And he does not agree with our Father, for he was a laughingstock and judgment and false prophecy.

O those who do not see, you do not see your blindness, i.e., this which was not known, nor has it ever been known, nor has it been known about him. They did not listen to firm obedience. Therefore they proceeded in a judgment of error, and they raised their defiled and murderous hands against him as if they were beating the air. And the senseless and blind ones are always senseless, always being slaves of law and earthly fear.

I am Christ, the Son of Man, the one from you [pl.] who is among you. I am despised for your sake, in order that you yourselves may forget the difference. And do not become female, lest you give birth to evil and (its) brothers: jealousy and division, anger and wrath, fear and a divided heart, and empty, non-existent desire. But I am an ineffable mystery to you.

Then before the foundation of the world, when the whole multitude of the Assembly came together upon the places of the Ogdoad, when they had taken counsel about a spiritual wedding which is in union, and thus he was perfected in the ineffable places by a living word, the undefiled wedding was consummated through the Mesotes of Jesus, who inhabits them all and possesses them, who abides in an undivided love of power. And surrounding him, he appears to him as a Monad of all these, a thought and a father, since he is one. And he stands by them all, since he as a whole came forth alone. And he is life, since he came from the Father of ineffable and perfect Truth, (the father) of those who are there, the union of peace and a friend of good things, and life eternal and undefiled joy, in a great harmony of life and faith, through eternal life of fatherhood and motherhood and sisterhood and rational wisdom. They had agreed with Nous, who stretches out (and) will stretch out in joyful union and is trustworthy and faithfully listens to someone. And he is in fatherhood and motherhood and rational brotherhood and wisdom. And this is a wedding of truth, and a repose of incorruption, in a spirit of truth, in every mind, and a perfect light in an unnameable mystery. But this is not, nor will it happen among us in any region or place in division and breach of peace, but (in) union and a mixture of love, all of which are perfected in the one who is.

It [fem.] also happened in the places under heaven for their reconciliation. Those who knew me in salvation and undividedness, and those who existed for the glory of the father and the truth, having been separated, blended into the one through the living word. And I am in the spirit and the truth of the motherhood, just as he has been there; I was among those who are united in the friendship of friends forever, who neither know hostility at all, nor evil, but who are united by my Knowledge in word and peace which exists in perfection with everyone and in them all. And those who assumed the form of my type will assume the form of my word. Indeed, these will come forth in light forever, and (in) friendship with each other in the spirit, since they have known in every respect (and) indivisibly that what is, is One. And all of these are one. And thus they will learn about the One, as (did) the Assembly and those dwelling in it. For the father of all these exists, being immeasurable (and) immutable: Nous and Word and Division and Envy and Fire. And he is entirely one, being the All with them all in a single doctrine because all these are from a single spirit. O unseeing ones, why did you not know the mystery rightly?

But the archons around Yaldabaoth were disobedient because of the Ennoia who went down to him from her sister Sophia. They made for themselves a union with those who were with them in a mixture of a fiery cloud, which was their Envy, and the rest who were brought forth by their creatures, as if they had bruised the noble pleasure of the Assembly. And therefore they revealed a mixture of ignorance in a counterfeit of fire and earth and a murderer, since they are small and untaught, without knowledge having dared these things, and not having understood that light has fellowship with light, and darkness with darkness, and the corruptible with the perishable, and the imperishable with the incorruptible.

Now these things I have presented to you [pl.]—I am Jesus Christ, the Son of Man, who is exalted above the heavens—O perfect and incorruptible ones, because of the incorruptible and perfect mystery and the ineffable one. But they think that we decreed them before the foundation of the world in order that, when we emerge from the places of the world, we may present there the symbols of incorruption from the spiritual union unto knowledge. You [pl.] do not know it because the fleshly cloud overshadows you. But I alone am the friend of Sophia. I have been in the bosom of the father from the beginning, in the place of the sons of the truth, and the Greatness. Rest then with me, my fellow spirits and my brothers, forever.

13. Irenaeus of Lyons, *Against Heresies*

Irenaeus (ca. 130-ca. 200), who was probably originally from Asia Minor, became bishop of Lyons in 178, shortly after the persecutions there in which his predecessor, Pothinus, died (see text 6). In Against Heresies, *his major work, Irenaeus opposes teachings based on esoteric knowledge ("gnosis"). He also formulates a Catholic understanding of religious authority as something founded on the publicly proclaimed oral and written traditions transmitted by the apostles to their successors the bishops and guaranteed by the evident unanimity of the latter, in contrast to the variety of their opponents' teaching.*

Book III
Preface

You have indeed enjoined upon me, my very dear friend, that I should bring to light the Valentinian doctrines, concealed, as their votaries imagine; that I should exhibit their diversity, and compose a treatise in refutation of them. I therefore have undertaken—showing that they spring from Simon, the father of all heretics—to exhibit both their doctrines and successions, and to set forth arguments against them all. Wherefore, since the conviction of these men and their exposure is in many points but one work, I have sent to you [certain] books, of which the first comprises the opinions of all these men, and exhibits their customs and the character of their behavior. In the second, again, their perverse teachings are cast down and overthrown, and, such as they really are, laid bare and open to view. But in this, the third book, I shall adduce proofs from the Scriptures, so that I may come behind in nothing of what you have enjoined; yea, that over and above what you reckoned upon, you may receive from me the means of combating and vanquishing those who, in whatever manner, are propagating falsehood. For the love of God, being rich and ungrudging, confers upon the suppliant more than he can ask from it. Call to mind, then, the things which I have stated in the two preceding books, and, tak-

ing these in connection with them, you shall have from me a very copious refutation of all the heretics; and faithfully and strenuously shall you resist them in defense of the only true and life-giving faith, which the Church has received from the apostles and imparted to her sons. For the Lord of all gave to His apostles the power of the Gospel, through whom also we have known the truth, that is, the doctrine of the Son of God; to whom also did the Lord declare: "He that hears you, hears Me; and he that despises you, despises Me, and Him that sent Me" [Luke 10:16].

Chapter 1
The Gospels

1. We have learned from none others the plan of our salvation, than from those through whom the Gospel has come down to us, which they did at one time proclaim in public and, at a later period, by the will of God, handed down to us in the Scriptures, to be the ground and pillar of our faith. For it is unlawful to assert that they preached before they possessed "perfect knowledge," as some do even venture to say, boasting themselves as improvers of the apostles. For, after our Lord rose from the dead, [the apostles] were invested with power from on high when the Holy Spirit came down [upon them], were filled from all [His gifts], and had perfect knowledge: they departed to the ends of the earth, preaching the glad tidings

Source: "Irenaeus against Heresies," tr. Alexander Roberts and James Donaldson, in *The Ante-Nicene Fathers*, vol. 1, ed. Alexander Roberts and James Donaldson (Buffalo: Christian Literature Publishing Company, 1887), 414-20, 428-29.

of the good things [sent] from God to us, and proclaiming the peace of heaven to men, who indeed do all equally and individually possess the Gospel of God. Matthew also issued a written Gospel among the Hebrews in their own dialect, while Peter and Paul were preaching at Rome, and laying the foundations of the Church. After their departure, Mark, the disciple and interpreter of Peter, did also hand down to us in writing what had been preached by Peter. Luke also, the companion of Paul, recorded in a book the Gospel preached by him. Afterwards, John, the disciple of the Lord, who also had leaned upon His breast, did himself publish a Gospel during his residence at Ephesus in Asia.

2. These have all declared to us that there is one God, Creator of heaven and earth, announced by the law and the prophets; and one Christ, the Son of God. If any do not agree to these truths, they despise the companions of the Lord; nay more, they despise Christ Himself the Lord; yes, they despise the Father also, and stand self-condemned, resisting and opposing their own salvation, as is the case with all heretics.

Chapter 2
The Tradition of the Apostles

1. When, however, they are confuted from the Scriptures, they turn round and accuse these same Scriptures, as if they were not correct, nor of authority, and [assert] that they are ambiguous, and that the truth cannot be extracted from them by those who are ignorant of tradition. For [they allege] that the truth was not delivered by means of written documents, but *viva voce*: wherefore also Paul declared, "But we speak wisdom among those that are perfect, but not the wisdom of this world" (1 Cor. 2:6). And this wisdom each one of them alleges to be the fiction of his own inventing, forsooth; so that, according to their idea, the truth properly resides at one time in Valentinus, at another in Marcion, at another in Cerinthus, then afterwards in Basilides, or has even been indifferently in any other opponent, who could speak nothing pertaining to salvation. For every one of these men, being altogether of a perverse disposition, depraving the system of truth, is not ashamed to preach himself.

2. But, again, when we refer them to that tradition which originates from the apostles, [and] which is preserved by means of the successions of presbyters in the Churches, they object to tradition, saying that they themselves are wiser not merely than the presbyters, but even than the apostles, because they have discovered the unadulterated truth. For [they maintain] that the apostles intermingled the things of the law with the words of the Savior; and that not the apostles alone, but even the Lord Himself, spoke as at one time from the Demiurge, at another from the intermediate place, and yet again from the Pleroma, but that they themselves, indubitably, unsulliedly, and purely, have knowledge of the hidden mystery: this is, indeed, to blaspheme their Creator after a most impudent manner! It comes to this, therefore, that these men do now consent neither to Scripture nor to tradition.

3. Such are the adversaries with whom we have to deal, my very dear friend, endeavoring like slippery serpents to escape at all points. Wherefore they must be opposed at all points, if perchance, by cutting off their retreat, we may succeed in turning them back to the truth. For, though it is not an easy thing for a soul under the influence of error to repent, yet, on the other hand, it is not altogether impossible to escape from error when the truth is brought alongside it.

Chapter 3
The Unbroken Succession

1. It is within the power of all, therefore, in every Church, who may wish to see the truth, to contemplate clearly the tradition of the apostles manifested throughout the whole world; and we are in a position to reckon up those who were by the apostles instituted bishops in the Churches, and [to demonstrate] the succession of these men to our own times; those who neither taught nor knew of anything like what these [heretics] rave about. For if the apostles had known hidden mysteries, which they were in the habit of imparting to "the perfect" apart and privily from the rest, they would have delivered them especially to those to whom they were also committing the Churches themselves. For they were desirous that these should be very perfect and blameless in all things,

whom also they were leaving behind as their successors, delivering up their own place of government to them; if they discharged their functions honestly, they would be a great boon [to the Church], but if they should fall away, the direst calamity.

2. Since, however, it would be very tedious, in such a volume as this, to reckon up the successions of all the Churches, we do put to confusion all those who, in whatever manner, whether by an evil self-pleasing, by vainglory, or by blindness and perverse opinion, assemble in unauthorized meetings; [we do this, I say,] by indicating that tradition derived from the apostles, of the very great, the very ancient, and universally known Church founded and organized at Rome by the two most glorious apostles, Peter and Paul; as also [by pointing out] the faith preached to all, which comes down to our time by means of the successions of the bishops. For it is a matter of necessity that every Church should agree with this Church, on account of its pre-eminent authority, that is, the faithful everywhere, inasmuch as the apostolical tradition has been preserved continuously by those [faithful ones] who exist everywhere.

3. The blessed apostles, then, having founded and built up the Church, committed into the hands of Linus the office of the episcopate. Of this Linus, Paul makes mention in the Epistles to Timothy. To him succeeded Anacletus; and after him, in the third place from the apostles, Clement was allotted the bishopric. This man, as he had seen the blessed apostles, and had been conversant with them, might be said to have the preaching of the apostles still echoing [in his ears], and their traditions before his eyes. Nor was he alone [in this], for there were many still remaining who had received instructions from the apostles. In the time of this Clement, no small dissension having occurred among the brethren at Corinth, the Church in Rome despatched a most powerful letter to the Corinthians, exhorting them to peace, renewing their faith, and declaring the tradition which it had lately received from the apostles, proclaiming the one God, omnipotent, the Maker of heaven and earth, the Creator of man, who brought on the deluge, and called Abraham, who led the people from the land of Egypt, spoke with Moses, set forth the law, sent the prophets, and who has prepared fire

for the devil and his angels. From this document, whosoever chooses to do so, may learn that He, the Father of our Lord Jesus Christ, was preached by the Churches, and may also understand the apostolic tradition of the Church, since this Epistle is of older date than these men who are now propagating falsehood, and who conjure into existence another god beyond the Creator and the Maker of all existing things. To this Clement there succeeded Evaristus. Alexander followed Evaristus; then, sixth from the apostles, Sixtus was appointed; after him, Telephorus, who was gloriously martyred; then Hyginus; after him, Pius; then after him, Anicetus. Soter having succeeded Anicetus, Eleutherius does now, in the twelfth place from the apostles, hold the inheritance of the episcopate. In this order, and by this succession, the ecclesiastical tradition from the apostles and the preaching of the truth have come down to us. And this is most abundant proof that there is one and the same vivifying faith, which has been preserved in the Church from the apostles until now, and handed down in truth.

4. But Polycarp also was not only instructed by apostles, and conversed with many who had seen Christ, but was also, by apostles in Asia, appointed bishop of the Church in Smyrna, whom I also saw in my early youth, for he tarried [on earth] a very long time, and, when a very old man, gloriously and most nobly suffering martyrdom, departed this life, having always taught the things which he had learned from the apostles, and which the Church has handed down, and which alone are true. To these things all the Asiatic Churches testify, as do also they who have succeeded Polycarp down to the present time—a man who was of much greater weight, and a more steadfast witness of truth than Valentinus, and Marcion, and the rest of the heretics. He it was who, coming to Rome in the time of Anicetus caused many to turn away from the aforesaid heretics to the Church of God, proclaiming that he had received this one and sole truth from the apostles—that, namely, which is handed down by the Church. There are also those who heard from him that John, the disciple of the Lord, going to bathe at Ephesus, and perceiving Cerinthus within, rushed out of the bath-house without bathing, exclaiming, "Let us fly, lest even the bath-house fall down, because

Cerinthus, the enemy of the truth, is within." And Polycarp himself replied to Marcion, who met him on one occasion, and said, "Dost thou know me?" "I do know thee, the first-born of Satan." Such was the horror which the apostles and their disciples had against holding even verbal communication with any corrupters of the truth; as Paul also says, "One who is a heretic, after the first and second admonition, reject; knowing that the one that is such is subverted, and sins, being condemned of himself" (Tit. 3:30). There is also a very powerful Epistle of Polycarp written to the Philippians, from which those who choose to do so, and are anxious about their salvation, can learn the character of his faith, and the preaching of the truth. Then, again, the Church in Ephesus, founded by Paul, and having John remaining among them permanently until the times of Trajan, is a true witness of the tradition of the apostles.

Chapter 4
The Authority of the Church

1. Since therefore we have such proofs, it is not necessary to seek the truth among others which it is easy to obtain from the Church; since the apostles, like a rich man [depositing his money] in a bank, lodged in her hands most copiously all things pertaining to the truth: so that everyone, whosoever will, can draw from her the water of life (cf. Rev. 22:17). For she is the entrance to life; all others are thieves and robbers. On this account are we bound to avoid *them*, but to make choice of the things pertaining to the Church with the utmost diligence, and to lay hold of the tradition of the truth. For how stands the case? Suppose there should arise a dispute relative to some important question among us, should we not have recourse to the most ancient Churches with which the apostles held constant intercourse, and learn from them what is certain and clear in regard to the present question? For how should it be if the apostles themselves had not left us writings? Would it not be necessary, [in that case,] to follow the course of the tradition which they handed down to those to whom they did commit the Churches?

2. To which course many nations of those barbarians who believe in Christ do assent, having salvation written in their hearts by the Spirit, without paper or ink, and, carefully preserving the ancient tradition, believing in one God, the Creator of heaven and earth, and all things therein, by means of Christ Jesus, the Son of God; who, because of His surpassing love towards His creation, condescended to be born of the virgin, He Himself uniting man through Himself to God, and having suffered under Pontius Pilate, and rising again, and having been received up in splendor, shall come in glory, the Savior of those who are saved, and the Judge of those who are judged, and sending into eternal fire those who transform the truth, and despise His Father and His advent. Those who, in the absence of written documents, have believed this faith, are barbarians, so far as regards our language; but as regards doctrine, manner, and tenor of life, they are, because of faith, very wise indeed; and they do please God, ordering their conversation in all righteousness, chastity, and wisdom. If anyone were to preach to these people the inventions of the heretics, speaking to them in their own language, they would at once stop their ears, and flee as far off as possible, not enduring even to listen to the blasphemous address. Thus, by means of that ancient tradition of the apostles, they do not suffer their mind to conceive anything of the [doctrines suggested by the] portentous language of these teachers, among whom neither Church nor doctrine has ever been established.

3. For, prior to Valentinus, those who follow Valentinus had no existence; nor did those from Marcion exist before Marcion; nor, in short, had any of those malignant-minded people, whom I have above enumerated, any being previous to the initiators and inventors of their perversity. For Valentinus came to Rome in the time of Hyginus, flourished under Pius, and remained until Anicetus. Cerdon, too, Marcion's predecessor, himself arrived in the time of Hyginus, who was the ninth bishop. Coming frequently into the Church, and making public confession, he thus remained, one time teaching in secret, and then again making public confession; but at last, having been denounced for corrupt teaching, he was excommunicated from the assembly of the brethren. Marcion, then, succeeding him, flourished under Anicetus, who held the tenth place of the episcopate. But the rest, who are called Gnostics, take rise from Menander, Simon's disciple, as I have

shown; and each one of them appeared to be both the father and the high priest of that doctrine into which he has been initiated. But all these (the Marcosians) broke out into their apostasy much later, even during the intermediate period of the Church.

Chapter 5

The Apostolic Teaching about God

1. Since, therefore, the tradition from the apostles does thus exist in the Church and is permanent among us, let us revert to the Scriptural proof furnished by those apostles who did also write the Gospel, in which they recorded the doctrine regarding God, pointing out that our Lord Jesus Christ is the truth, and that no lie is in Him. As also David says, prophesying His birth from a virgin, and the resurrection from the dead, "Truth has sprung out of the earth" (Ps. 85:11). The apostles, likewise, being disciples of the truth, are above all falsehood; for a lie has no fellowship with the truth, just as darkness has none with light, but the presence of the one shuts out that of the other. Our Lord, therefore, being the truth, did not speak lies; and whom He knew to have taken origin from a defect, He never would have acknowledged as God, even the God of all, the Supreme King, too, and His own Father, an imperfect being as a perfect one, an animal one as a spiritual, Him who was without the Pleroma as Him who was within it. Neither did His disciples make mention of any other God, or term any other Lord, except Him who was truly the God and Lord of all, as these most vain sophists affirm that the apostles did with hypocrisy frame their doctrine according to the capacity of their hearers, and gave answers after the opinions of their questioners—fabling blind things for the blind, according to their blindness; for the dull according to their dullness; for those in error according to their error. And to those who imagined that the Demiurge alone was God, they preached him; but to those who are capable of comprehending the unnamable Father, they did declare the unspeakable mystery through parables and enigmas: so that the Lord and the apostles exercised the office of teacher not to further the cause of truth, but even in hypocrisy, and as each individual was able to receive it!

2. Such [a line of conduct] belongs not to those who heal, or who give life: it is rather that of those bringing on diseases and increasing ignorance; and much more true than these people shall the law be found, which pronounces everyone accursed who sends the blind man astray in the way. For the apostles, who were commissioned to find out the wanderers, and to be for sight to those who saw not, and medicine to the weak, certainly did not address them in accordance with their opinion at the time, but according to revealed truth. For no persons of any kind would act properly, if they should advise blind men just about to fall over a precipice to continue their most dangerous path, as if it were the right one, and as if they might go on in safety. Or what medical man, anxious to heal a sick person, would prescribe in accordance with the patient's whims, and not according to the requisite medicine? But that the Lord came as the physician of the sick, He does Himself declare saying, "They that are whole need not a physician, but they that are sick; I came to call not the righteous, but sinners to repentance" (Luke 5:31-32). How then shall the sick be strengthened, or how shall sinners come to repentance? Is it by persevering in the very same courses? or, on the contrary, is it by undergoing a great change and reversal of their former mode of living, by which they have brought upon themselves no slight amount of sickness, and many sins? But ignorance, the mother of all these, is driven out by knowledge. Wherefore the Lord used to impart knowledge to His disciples, by which also it was His practice to heal those who were suffering, and to keep back sinners from sin. He therefore did not address them in accordance with their pristine notions, nor did He reply to them in harmony with the opinion of His questioners, but according to the doctrine leading to salvation, without hypocrisy or respect of person.

3. This is also made clear from the words of the Lord, who did truly reveal the Son of God to those of the circumcision—Him who had been foretold as Christ by the prophets; that is, He set Himself forth, who had restored liberty to people, and bestowed on them the inheritance of incorruption. And again, the apostles taught the Gentiles that they should leave vain stocks and stones, which they imagined to be gods, and worship the true God, who had created and made all the human family, and, by means of His creation, did nourish,

increase, strengthen, and preserve them in being; and that they might look for His Son Jesus Christ, who redeemed us from apostasy with His own blood, so that we should also be a sanctified people—who shall also descend from heaven in His Father's power, and pass judgment upon all, and who shall freely give the good things of God to those who shall have kept His commandments. He, appearing in these last times, the chief cornerstone, has gathered into one, and united those that were far off and those that were near (Eph. 2:17); that is, the circumcision and the uncircumcision, enlarging Japhet, and placing him in the dwelling of Shem (Gen. 9:27).

Chapter 6

The Hebrew Scriptures' Teaching about God

1. Therefore neither would the Lord, nor the Holy Spirit, nor the apostles, have ever named as God, definitely and absolutely, him who was not God, unless he were truly God; nor would they have named anyone in his own person Lord, except God the Father ruling over all, and His Son who has received dominion from His Father over all creation, as this passage has it: "The LORD said unto my Lord, Sit at my right hand, until I make My enemies Your footstool" (Ps. 110:1). Here the [Scripture] represents to us the Father addressing the Son; He who gave Him the inheritance of the heathen, and subjected to Him all His enemies. Since, therefore, the Father is truly Lord, and the Son truly Lord, the Holy Spirit has fitly designated them by the title of Lord. And again, referring to the destruction of the Sodomites, the Scripture says, "Then the LORD rained upon Sodom and upon Gomorrah fire and brimstone from the LORD out of heaven" (Gen. 19:24). For it here points out that the Son, who had also been talking with Abraham, had received power to judge the Sodomites for their wickedness. And this [text following] declares the same truth: "Your throne, O God, is forever and ever; the scepter of Your kingdom is a right scepter. You have loved righteousness, and hated iniquity: therefore God, Your God, has anointed You" (Ps. 45:6). For the Spirit designates both [of them] by the name of God—both Him who is anointed as Son, and Him who

anoints, that is, the Father. And again: "God stood in the congregation of the gods, He judges among the gods" (Ps. 82:1). He [here] refers to the Father and the Son, and those who have received the adoption; but these are the Church. For she is the synagogue of God, which God—that is, the Son Himself—has gathered by Himself. Of whom He again speaks: "The God of gods, the Lord has spoken, and has called the earth" (Ps. 50:1). Who is meant by God? He of whom He has said, "God shall come openly, our God, and shall not keep silence" (Ps. 50:3); that is, the Son, who came manifested to men who said, "I have openly appeared to those who seek Me not" (Isa. 55:1). But of what gods [does he speak]? [Of those] to whom He says, "I have said, You are gods, and all sons of the Most High" (Ps. 82:6). To those, no doubt, who have received the grace of the "adoption, by which we cry, Abba Father."

2. Wherefore, as I have already stated, no other is named as God, or is called Lord, except Him who is God and Lord of all, who also said to Moses, "I AM THAT I AM. And thus shall you say to the children of Israel: He who is, has sent me unto you" (Exod. 3:14); and His Son Jesus Christ our Lord, who makes those that believe in His name the sons of God. And again, when the Son speaks to Moses, He says, "I am come down to deliver this people" (Exod. 3:8). For it is He who descended and ascended for the salvation of men. Therefore God has been declared through the Son, who is in the Father, and has the Father in Himself—He WHO IS, the Father bearing witness to the Son, and the Son announcing the Father.—As also Isaiah says, "I too am witness," he declares, "says the LORD God, and the Son whom I have chosen, that you may know, and believe, and understand that I AM" (Isa. 34:10).

3. When, however, the Scripture terms them [gods] which are no gods, it does not, as I have already remarked, declare them as gods in every sense, but with a certain addition and signification, by which they are shown to be no gods at all. As with David: "The gods of the heathen are idols of demons" (Ps. 96:5); and, "You shall not follow other gods" (Ps. 81:9). For in that he says "the gods of the heathen"—but the heathen are ignorant of the true God—and calls them "other gods," he bars their claim [to be looked upon] as

gods at all. But as to what they are in their own person, he speaks concerning them; "for they are," he says, "the idols of demons." And Isaiah: "Let them be confounded, all who blaspheme God and carve useless things; even I am witness, says God" (Isa. 44:9). He removes them from [the category of] gods, but he makes use of the word alone, for this [purpose], that we may know of whom he speaks. Jeremiah also says the same: "The gods that have not made the heavens and earth, let them perish from the earth which is under the heaven" (Jer. 10:11). For, from the fact of his having subjoined their destruction, he shows them to be no gods at all. Elias, too, when all Israel was assembled at Mount Carmel, wishing to turn them from idolatry, says to them, "How long do you halt between two opinions? If the LORD be God, follow Him." And again, at the burnt-offering, he thus addresses the idolatrous priests: "You shall call upon the name of your gods, and I will call on the name of the LORD my God; and the Lord that will hearken by fire, He is God" (1 Kgs. 18:21, 24). Now, from the fact of the prophet having said these words, he proves that these gods which were reputed so among those men, are no gods at all. He directed them to that God upon whom he believed, and who was truly God; whom invoking, he exclaimed, "LORD God of Abraham, God of Isaac, and God of Jacob, hear me today, and let all this people know that You are the God of Israel" (1 Kgs. 18:36).

4. Wherefore I do also call upon you, LORD God of Abraham, and God of Isaac, and God of Jacob and Israel, who are the Father of our Lord Jesus Christ, the God who, through the abundance of Your mercy, has had favor towards us, that we should know You, who has made heaven and earth, who rules over all, who are the only and the true God, above whom there is no other God; grant, by our Lord Jesus Christ, the governing power of the Holy Spirit; give to every reader of this book to know You, that You are God alone, to be strengthened in You, and to avoid every heretical, and godless, and impious doctrine.

5. And the Apostle Paul also, saying, "For though you have served them which are no gods; you now know God, or rather, are known of God" (Gal. 4:8-9), has made a separation between those that were not [gods] and Him who is God.

And again, speaking of Antichrist, he says, "who opposes and exalts himself above all that is called God, or that is worshipped" (2 Thess. 2:4). He points out here those who are called gods, by such as know not God, that is, idols. For the Father of all is called God, and is so; and Antichrist shall be lifted up, not above Him, but above those which are indeed called gods but are not. And Paul himself says that this is true: "We know that an idol is nothing, and that there is no other God but one. For though there be that are called gods, whether in heaven or in earth; yet to us there is but one God, the Father, of whom are all things, and we through Him; and one Lord Jesus Christ, by whom are all things, and we by Him" (1 Cor. 8:4-6). For he has made a distinction, and separated those which are indeed called gods, but which are none, from the one God the Father, from whom are all things, and he has confessed in the most decided manner in his own person, one Lord Jesus Christ. But in this [clause], "whether in heaven or in earth," he does not speak of the formers of the world, as these [teachers] expound it; but his meaning is similar to that of Moses, when it is said, "You shall not make to yourself any image for God, of whatsoever things are in heaven above, whatsoever in the earth beneath, and whatsoever in the waters under the earth" (Deut. 5:8). And he does thus explain what are meant by the things in heaven: "Lest when," he says, "looking towards heaven, and observing the sun, and the moon, and the stars, and all the ornament of heaven, falling into error, you should adore and serve them" (Deut. 4:19). And Moses himself, being a man of God, was indeed given as a god before Pharaoh; but he is not properly termed Lord, nor is called God by the prophets, but is spoken of by the Spirit as "Moses, the faithful minister and servant of God" (Heb. 3:5; Num. 12:7), which also he was. . . .

Chapter 11
Four Gospels

. . . 7. Such, then, are the first principles of the Gospel: that there is one God, the Maker of this universe; He who was also announced by the prophets, and who by Moses set forth the dispensation of the law—[principles] which proclaim the Father of our Lord Jesus Christ, and ignore any other God or Father except Him. So firm is the ground upon which these Gospels rest, that the very heretics themselves bear witness to them, and, starting from these [documents], each one of them endeavors to establish his own peculiar doctrine. For the Ebionites, who use Matthew's Gospel only, are confuted out of this very same, making false suppositions with regard to the Lord. But Marcion, mutilating that according to Luke, is proved to be a blasphemer of the only existing God, from those [passages] which he still retains. Those, again, who separate Jesus from Christ, alleging that Christ remained impassible, but that it was Jesus who suffered, preferring the Gospel by Mark, if they read it with a love of truth, may have their errors rectified. Those, moreover, who follow Valentinus, making copious use of that according to John, to illustrate their conjunctions, shall be proved to be totally in error by means of this very Gospel, as I have shown in the first book. Since, then, our opponents do bear testimony to us and make use of these [documents], our proof derived from them is firm and true.

8. It is not possible that the Gospels can be either more or fewer in number than they are. For, since there are four zones of the world in which we live, and four principal winds, while the Church is scattered throughout all the world, and the "pillar and ground" (1 Tim. 3:15) of the Church is the Gospel and the spirit of life; it is fitting that she should have four pillars, breathing out immortality on every side, and vivifying men afresh. From which fact, it is evident that the Word, the Artificer of all, He that sits upon the cherubim and contains all things, He who was manifested to men, has given us the Gospel under four aspects, but bound together by one Spirit. As also David says, when entreating His manifestation, "You that sit between the cherubim, shine forth" (Ps. 80:1). For the cherubim, too, were four-faced, and their faces were images of the dispensation of the Son of God. For, [as the Scripture] says, "The first living creature was like a lion," symbolizing His effectual working, His leadership, and royal power; the second [living creature] was like a calf, signifying [His] sacrificial and sacerdotal order; but "the third had, as it were, the face as of a man"—an evident description of His advent as a human being;

"the fourth was like a flying eagle," pointing out the gift of the Spirit hovering with His wings over the Church (Rev. 4:7). And therefore the Gospels are in accord with these things, among which Christ Jesus is seated. For that according to John relates His original, effectual, and glorious generation from the Father, thus declaring, "In the beginning was the Word, and the Word was with God, and the Word was God." Also, "all things were made by Him, and without Him was nothing made" (John 1:1, 3). For this reason, too, is that Gospel full of all confidence, for such is His person. But that according to Luke, taking up [His] priestly character, commenced with Zacharias the priest offering sacrifice to God. For now was made ready the fatted calf, about to be immolated for the finding again of the younger son. Matthew, again, relates His generation as a man, saying, "The book of the generation of Jesus Christ, the son of David, the son of Abraham"; and also, "The birth of Jesus Christ was on this wise" (Matt. 1:1, 18). This, then, is the Gospel of His humanity; for which reason it is, too, that [the character of] a humble and meek man is kept up through the whole Gospel. Mark, on the other hand, commences with [a reference to] the prophetical spirit coming down from on high to men, saying, "The beginning of the Gospel of Jesus Christ, as it is written in Isaiah the prophet" (Mark 1:1-2)—pointing to the winged aspect of the Gospel; and on this account he made a compendious and cursory narrative, for such is the prophetical character. And the Word of God Himself used to converse with the ante-Mosaic patriarchs, in accordance with His divinity and glory; but for those under the law he instituted a sacerdotal and liturgical service. Afterwards, being made man for us, He sent the gift of the celestial Spirit over all the earth, protecting us with His wings. Such, then, as was the course followed by the Son of God, so was also the form of the living creatures; and such as was the form of the living creatures, so was also the character of the Gospel. For the living creatures are quadriform, and the Gospel is quadriform, as is also the course followed by the Lord. For this reason were four principal (καθολικαί) covenants given to the human race: one, prior to the deluge, under Adam; the second, that after the deluge, under Noah; the third, the giving of the law, under Moses; the fourth, that which renovates human beings, and sums up all things in itself by means of the Gospel, raising and bearing men and women upon its wings into the heavenly kingdom.

9. These things being so, all who destroy the form of the Gospel are vain, unlearned, and also audacious; those, [I mean,] who represent the aspects of the Gospel as being either more in number than as aforesaid, or, on the other hand, fewer. The former class [do so], that they may seem to have discovered more than is of the truth; the latter, that they may set the dispensations of God aside. For Marcion, rejecting the entire Gospel, yea rather, cutting himself off from the Gospel, boasts that he has part in the [blessings of] the Gospel. Others, again (the Montanists), that they may set at nought the gift of the Spirit, which in the latter times has been, by the good pleasure of the Father, poured out upon the human race, do not admit that *aspect* [of the evangelical dispensation] presented by John's Gospel, in which the Lord promised that He would send the Paraclete; but set aside at once both the Gospel and the prophetic Spirit. Wretched men indeed! who wish to be pseudo-prophets, forsooth, but who set aside the gift of prophecy from the Church; acting like those (the Encratitae) who, on account of such as come in hypocrisy, hold themselves aloof from the communion of the brethren. We must conclude, moreover, that these men (the Montanists) cannot admit the Apostle Paul either. For, in his Epistle to the Corinthians, he speaks expressly of prophetical gifts, and recognizes men and women prophesying in the Church. Sinning, therefore, in all these particulars, against the Spirit of God, they fall into the irremissible sin. But those who are from Valentinus, being, on the other hand, altogether reckless, while they put forth their own compositions, boast that they possess more Gospels than there really are. Indeed, they have arrived at such a pitch of audacity, as to entitle their comparatively recent writing "the Gospel of Truth," though it agrees in nothing with the Gospels of the Apostles, so that they have really no Gospel which is not full of blasphemy. For if what they have published is the Gospel of truth, and yet is totally unlike those which have been handed down to us from the apostles, any who please may learn, as is shown from the Scriptures themselves, that that which has been handed down from the apostles can no longer be reckoned the Gospel of truth. But that these Gospels alone are true and reliable, and admit neither an increase nor diminution of the aforesaid number, I have proved by so many and such [arguments]. For, since God made all things in due proportion and adaptation, it was fit also that the outward aspect of the Gospel should be well arranged and harmonized. The opinion of those men, therefore, who handed the Gospel down to us, having been investigated, from their very fountainheads, let us proceed also to the remaining apostles, and inquire into their doctrine with regard to God; then, in due course we shall listen to the very words of the Lord.

14. The Muratorian Fragment

Named for L. A. Muratori (d. 1750), the Italian scholar who discovered it in an eighth-century copy, this fragment by an unknown author, probably of the late second century, is the earliest known list of books intended as a New Testament canon. It includes all the books later considered canonical except Hebrews, James, and 1 and 2 Peter; it also includes the Wisdom of Solomon and the Apocalypse of Peter. The indications of books to be rejected display the close connection between the impulse to establish a canon and the concern to exclude heresy.

SOURCE: *Selections from Early Christian Writers Illustrative of Church History to the Time of Constantine*, ed. Henry Melvill Gwatkin (London: Macmillan, 1909), 83-89.

. . . but at some he was present, and so he set them down.

The third book of the Gospel, that according to Luke, was compiled in his own name in order by Luke the physician, when after Christ's ascension Paul had taken him to be with him like a student of law. Yet neither did *he* see the Lord in the flesh; and he too, as he was able to ascertain [events, so set them down]. So he began his story from the birth of John.

The fourth of the Gospels [was written by] John, one of the disciples. When exhorted by his fellow disciples and bishops, he said, "Fast with me this day for three days; and what may be revealed to any of us, let us relate it to one another." The same night it was revealed to Andrew, one of the apostles, that John was to write all things in his own name, and they were all to certify.

And therefore, though various elements are taught in the several books of the Gospels, yet it makes no difference to the faith of believers, since by one guiding Spirit all things are declared in all of them concerning the Nativity, the Passion, the Resurrection, the conversation with his disciples and his two comings, the first in lowliness and contempt, which has come to pass, the second glorious with royal power, which is to come.

What marvel therefore if John so firmly sets forth each statement in his Epistle too, saying of himself, "What we have seen with our eyes and heard with our ears and our hands have handled, these things we have written to you"? For so he declares himself not an eyewitness and a hearer only, but a writer of all the marvels of the Lord in order.

The Acts of all the Apostles, however, are written in one book. Luke puts it shortly to the most excellent Theophilus, that the several things were done in his own presence, as he also plainly shows by leaving out the passion of Peter, and also the departure of Paul from town on his journey to Spain.

The Epistles of Paul, however, themselves make plain to those who wish to understand it, what epistles were sent by him, and from what place and for what cause. He wrote at some length first of all to the Corinthians, forbidding schisms and here-sies; next to the Galatians, forbidding circumcision; then to the Romans, impressing on them the plan of the Scriptures, and also that Christ is the first principle of them, concerning which severally it is [not] necessary for us to discuss, since the blessed Apostle Paul himself, following the order of his predecessor John, writes only by name to seven churches in the following order—to the Corinthians a first, to the Ephesians a second, to the Philippians a third, to the Colossians a fourth, to the Galatians a fifth, to the Thessalonians a sixth, to the Romans a seventh; whereas, although for the sake of admonition there is a second to the Corinthians and to the Thessalonians, yet *one* Church is recognized as being spread over the entire world. For John too in the Apocalypse, though he writes to seven churches, yet speaks to all. Howbeit to Philemon one, to Titus one, and to Timothy two were put in writing from personal inclination and attachment, to be in honor however with the Catholic Church for the ordering of the ecclesiastical mode of life. There is current also one to the Laodicenes, another to the Alexandrians, [both] forged in Paul's name to suit the heresy of Marcion, and several others, which cannot be received into the Catholic Church; for it is not fitting that gall be mixed with honey.

The Epistle of Jude no doubt and the couple bearing the name of John are accepted in the Catholic [Church]; and the Wisdom written by the friends of Solomon in his honor. The Apocalypse also of John, and of Peter [one Epistle, which] only we receive; [there is also a second] which some of our friends will not have read in the Church. But the Shepherd was written quite lately in our times by Hermas, while his brother Pius, the bishop, was sitting in the chair of the church of the city of Rome; and therefore it ought indeed to be read, but it cannot to the end of time be publicly read in the Church to the people, either among the prophets, who are complete in number, or among the Apostles.

But of Valentinus the Arsinoite and his friends we receive nothing at all, who have also composed a long new book of Psalms, together with Basilides and the Asiatic founder of the Montanists.

15. Origen of Alexandria,
On First Principles

Origen (ca. 185-ca. 254), a prodigious theologian and exegete, taught in his home city of Alexandria and then, from 231, in Palestine. He died after having undergone torture in the Decian persecution. Among his surviving works are biblical commentaries, miscellaneous treatises, e.g., on prayer and martyrdom, a reply to the attack on Christianity by the philosopher Celsus, and On First Principles, *a work on basic issues of theology. In the excerpt here from that work, he articulates the distinction between the literal and spiritual meanings of Scripture that would underlie most biblical exegesis for more than a thousand years to follow. In the fourth century, controversies began to emerge about some of Origen's other, more speculative teachings, many of which were condemned by the Second Council of Constantinople in 553.*

How Divine Scripture Should Be Read and Interpreted [IV.ii]

1. Now that we have spoken cursorily about the inspiration of the divine scriptures, it is necessary to discuss the manner in which they are to be read and understood, since many mistakes have been made in consequence of the method by which the holy documents ought to be interpreted not having been discovered by the multitude. For the hard-hearted and ignorant members of the circumcision have refused to believe in our Savior because they think that they are keeping closely to the language of the prophecies that relate to him, and they see that he did not literally "proclaim release to captives" or build what they consider to be a real "city of God" or "cut off the chariots from Ephraim and the horse from Jerusalem" or "eat butter and honey, and choose the good before he knew or preferred the evil" (Isa. 61:1; Ps. 46:4; Ezek. 48:15ff.; Zech. 9:10; Isa. 7:15).

Further, they think that it is the wolf, the four-footed animal, which is said in prophecy to be going to "feed with the lamb, and the leopard to lie down with the kid, and the calf and bull and lion to feed together, led by a little child, and the ox and the bear to pasture together, their young ones growing up with each other, and the lion to eat straw like the ox" (Isa. 11:6, 7); and having seen none of these events literally happening during the advent of him whom we believe to be Christ they did not accept our Lord Jesus, but crucified him on the ground that he had wrongly called himself Christ.

And the members of the heretical sects, reading the passage, "A fire has been kindled in my anger" (Deut. 32:22; Jer. 15:14); and "I am a jealous God, visiting the sins of the fathers upon the children to the third and fourth generation"; and "I repent that I have anointed Saul to be king"; and "I, God, make peace and create evil"; and elsewhere, "There is no evil in a city, which the Lord did not do" (Exod. 20:5; 1 Sam. 15:11; Isa. 55:7; Amos 3:6); and further, "Evils came down from the Lord upon the gates of Jerusalem" (Mic. 1:12); and "An evil spirit from the Lord troubled Saul" (1 Sam. 18:10); and ten thousand other passages like these, have not dared to disbelieve that they are the writings of God, but believe them to belong to the Creator, whom the Jews worship. Consequently they think that since the Creator is imperfect and not good, the Savior came here to proclaim a

Source: *Origen on First Principles*, tr. G. W. Butterworth (London: Society for Promoting Christian Knowledge, 1936), 269-87, 288-301. Used by permission of SPCK.

more perfect God who they say is not the Creator, and about whom they entertain diverse opinions. Then having once fallen away from the Creator, who is the sole unbegotten God, they have given themselves up to fictions, fashioning mythical hypotheses according to which they suppose that there are some things that are seen and others that are not seen, all of which are the fancies of their own minds.

Moreover, even the simpler of those who claim to belong to the Church, while believing indeed that there is none greater than the Creator, in which they are right, yet believe such things about him as would not be believed of the most savage and unjust of men.

2. Now the reason why all those we have mentioned hold false opinions and make impious or ignorant assertions about God appears to be nothing else but this, that scripture is not understood in its spiritual sense, but is interpreted according to the bare letter. On this account we must explain to those who believe that the sacred books are not the works of men, but that they were composed and have come down to us as a result of the inspiration of the Holy Spirit by the will of the Father of the universe through Jesus Christ, what are the methods of interpretation that appear right to us, who keep to the rule of the heavenly Church of Jesus Christ through the succession from the Apostles.

That there are certain mystical revelations made known through the divine scriptures is believed by all, even by the simplest of those who are adherents of the word; but what these revelations are, fair-minded and humble men confess that they do not know. If, for instance, an inquirer were to be in a difficulty about the intercourse of Lot with his daughters, or the two wives of Abraham, or the two sisters married to Jacob, or the two handmaids who bore children by him, they can say nothing except that these things are mysteries not understood by us.

But when the passage about the equipment of the tabernacle is read, believing that the things described therein are types, they seek for ideas which they can attach to each detail that is mentioned in connection with the tabernacle. Now so far as concerns their belief that the tabernacle is a type of something they are not wrong; but in rightly attaching the word of scripture to the particular idea of which the tabernacle is a type, here they sometimes fall into error. And they declare that all narratives that are supposed to speak about marriage or the begetting of children or wars or any other stories whatever that may be accepted among the multitude are types; but when we ask, of what, then sometimes owing to the lack of thorough training, sometimes owing to rashness, and occasionally, even when one is well trained and of sound judgment, owing to man's exceedingly great difficulty in discovering these things, the interpretation of every detail is not altogether clear.

3. And what must we say about the prophecies, which we all know are filled with riddles and dark sayings? Or if we come to the gospels, the accurate interpretation even of these, since it is an interpretation of the mind of Christ, demands that grace that was given to him who said, "We have the mind of Christ, that we may know the things that were freely given to us by God. Which things also we speak, not in words which man's wisdom teaches, but which the Spirit teaches" (1 Cor. 2:16, 12, 13). And who, on reading the revelations made to John, could fail to be amazed at the deep obscurity of the unspeakable mysteries contained therein, which are evident even to one who does not understand what is written? And as for the apostolic epistles, what person who is skilled in literary interpretation would think them to be plain and easily understood, when even in them there are thousands of passages that provide, as if through a window, a narrow opening leading to multitudes of the deepest thoughts?

Seeing, therefore, that these things are so, and that thousands of people make mistakes, it is dangerous for us when we read to declare lightly that we understand things for which the "key of knowledge" is necessary, which the Savior says is with "the lawyers." And as for those who are unwilling to admit that these men held the truth before the coming of Christ, let them explain to us how it is that our Lord Jesus Christ says that the "key of knowledge" was with them, that is, with men who, as these objectors say, had no books containing the secrets of knowledge and the all-perfect mysteries. For the passage runs as follows: "Woe to you lawyers, for you have taken away the key of knowledge. You entered not in yourselves, and them that were entering in you hindered" (Luke 11:52).

4. The right way, therefore, as it appears to us, of approaching the scriptures and gathering their meaning, is the following, which is extracted from the writings themselves. We find some such rule as this laid down by Solomon in the Proverbs concerning the divine doctrines written therein: "Portray them threefold in counsel and knowledge, that you may answer words of truth to those who question you" (Prov. 22:20, 21).

One must therefore portray the meaning of the sacred writings in a threefold way upon one's own soul, so that the simple person may be edified by what we may call the flesh of the scripture, this name being given to the obvious interpretation; while the one who has made some progress may be edified by its soul, as it were; and the one who is perfect and like those mentioned by the apostle: "We speak wisdom among the perfect; yet a wisdom not of this world, nor of the rulers of this world, which are coming to nought; but we speak God's wisdom in a mystery, even the wisdom that has been hidden, which God foreordained before the worlds unto our glory" (1 Cor. 2:6, 7)—this one may be edified by the spiritual law, which has "a shadow of the good things to come" (cf. Rom. 7:14). For just as the human being consists of body, soul, and spirit, so in the same way does the scripture, which has been prepared by God to be given for humanity's salvation.

We therefore read in this light the passage in *The Shepherd,* a book which is despised by some, where Hermas is bidden to "write two books," and after this to "announce to the presbyters of the Church" what he has learned from the Spirit. This is the wording: "You shall write two books, and shall give one to Clement and one to Grapte. And Grapte shall admonish the widows and the orphans. But Clement shall send to the cities without, and you shall announce to the presbyters of the Church."

Now Grapte, who admonishes the widows and orphans, is the bare letter, which admonishes those child souls that are not yet able to enroll God as their Father and are on this account called orphans, and which also admonishes those who while no longer associating with the unlawful bridegroom are in widowhood because they have not yet become worthy of the true one. But Clement, who has already gone beyond the letter, is said to send the sayings "to the cities without," as if to say, to the souls that are outside all bodily and lower thoughts; while the disciple of the Spirit is bidden to announce the message in person, no longer through letters but through living words, to the presbyters or elders of the whole Church of God, to men who have grown grey through wisdom.

5. But since there are certain passages of scripture which, as we shall show in what follows, have no bodily sense at all, there are occasions when we must seek only for the soul and the spirit, as it were, of the passage. And possibly this is the reason why the waterpots which, as we read in the Gospel according to John, are said to be set there "for the purifying of the Jews," contain two or three firkins apiece (John 2:6). The language alludes to those who are said by the apostle to be Jews "inwardly," and it means that these are purified through the word of the scriptures, which contain in some cases "two firkins," that is, so to speak, the soul meaning and the spiritual meaning, and in other cases three, since some passages possess, in addition to those before mentioned, a bodily sense as well, which is capable of edifying the hearers. And six waterpots may reasonably allude to those who are being purified in the world, which was made in six days, a perfect number.

6. That it is possible to derive benefit from the first, and to this extent helpful meaning, is witnessed by the multitudes of sincere and simple believers. But of the kind of explanation which penetrates as it were to the soul an illustration is found in Paul's first epistle to the Corinthians. "For," he says, "it is written; you shall not muzzle the ox that treads out the corn." Then in explanation of this law he adds, "Is it for the oxen that God cares? Or says he it altogether for our sake? Yes, for our sake it was written, because he that plows ought to plow in hope, and he that threshes,

to thresh in hope of partaking" (1 Cor. 9:9, 10). And most of the interpretations adapted to the multitude which are in circulation and which edify those who cannot understand the higher meanings have something of the same character.

But it is a spiritual explanation when one is able to show of what kind of "heavenly things" the Jews "after the flesh" served a copy and a shadow, and of what "good things to come" the law has a "shadow" (Heb. 8:5; Rom. 8:5; Heb. 10:1). And, speaking generally, we have, in accordance with the apostolic promise, to seek after "the wisdom in a mystery, even the wisdom that hath been hidden, which God foreordained before the worlds unto the glory" of the righteous, "which none of the rulers of this world knew." The same apostle also says somewhere, after mentioning certain narratives from Exodus and Numbers, that "these things happened unto them figuratively, and they were written for our sake, upon whom the ends of the ages are come" (1 Cor. 10:11). He also gives hints to show what these things were figures of, when he says: "For they drank of that spiritual rock that followed them, and that rock was Christ" (1 Cor. 10:4).

In another epistle, when outlining the arrangements of the tabernacle he quotes the words: "You shall make all things according to the figure that was shown to you in the mount" (Heb. 8:5; Exod. 25:40). Further, in the epistle to the Galatians, speaking in terms of reproach to those who believe that they are reading the law and yet do not understand it, and laying it down that they who do not believe that there are allegories in the writings do not understand the law, he says: "Tell me, you that desire to be under the law, do you not hear the law? For it is written that Abraham had two sons, one by the handmaid and one by the free woman. Howbeit the son by the handmaid is born after the flesh; but the son by the free woman is born through promise. Which things contain an allegory; for these women are two covenants" (Gal. 4:21-24), and what follows. Now we must carefully mark each of the words spoken by him. He says, "You that desire to be under the law" (not, "you that are under the law") "do you not hear the law?" hearing being taken to mean understanding and knowing.

And in the epistle to the Colossians, briefly epitomizing the meaning of the entire system of the law, he says: "Let no one therefore judge you in meat or in drink or in respect of a feast day or a new moon or a sabbath, which are a shadow of the things to come" (Col. 2:16, 17). Further, in the epistle to the Hebrews, when discoursing about those who are of the circumcision, he writes: "They who serve that which is a copy and shadow of the heavenly things" (Heb. 8:5). Now it is probable that those who have once admitted that the apostle is a divinely inspired man will feel no difficulty in regard to the five books ascribed to Moses; but in regard to the rest of the history they desire to learn whether those events also "happened figuratively" (cf. 1 Cor. 10:11). We must note the quotation in the epistle to the Romans: "I have left for myself seven thousand men, who have not bowed the knee to Baal" (Rom. 11:4; 1 Kgs. 19:18), found in the third book of the Kings. Here Paul has taken it to stand for those who are Israelites "according to election" (Rom. 11:5), for not only are the gentiles benefited by the coming of Christ, but also some who belong to the divine race.

7. This being so, we must outline what seems to us to be the marks of a true understanding of the scriptures. And in the first place we must point out that the aim of the Spirit who, by the providence of God through the Word who was "in the beginning with God" (John 1:1), enlightened the servants of the truth, that is, the prophets and apostles, was preeminently concerned with the unspeakable mysteries connected with the affairs of men—and by men I mean at the present moment souls that make use of bodies—his purpose being that the man who is capable of being taught might by "searching out" and devoting himself to the "deep things" (1 Cor. 2:10) revealed in the spiritual meaning of the words become partaker of all the doctrines of the Spirit's counsel.

And when we speak of the needs of souls, who cannot otherwise reach perfection except through the rich and wise truth about God, we attach of necessity preeminent importance to the doctrines concerning God and His only-begotten Son; of what nature the Son is, and in what manner he can be the Son of God, and what are the causes of his descending to the level of human flesh and completely assuming humanity; and what, also, is the nature of his activity, and towards whom and at what times it is exercised. It was necessary, too, that the doctrines concerning beings akin to man and the rest of the rational creatures, both those that are nearer the divine and those that have fallen from blessedness, and the causes of the fall of these latter, should be included in the accounts of the divine teaching; and the question of the differences between souls and how these differences arose, and what the world is and why it exists, and further, how it comes about that evil is so widespread and so terrible on earth, and whether it is not only to be found on earth but also in other places—all this it was necessary that we should learn.

8. Now while these and similar subjects were in the mind of the Spirit who enlightened the souls of the holy servants of the truth, there was a second aim, pursued for the sake of those who were unable to endure the burden of investigating matters of such importance. This was to conceal the doctrine relating to the before-mentioned subjects in words forming a narrative that contained a record dealing with the visible creation, the formation of man and the successive descendants of the first human beings until the time when they became many; and also in other stories that recorded the acts of righteous men and the sins that these same men occasionally committed, seeing they were but human, and the deeds of wickedness, licentiousness and greed done by lawless and impious men.

But the most wonderful thing is, that by means of stories of wars and the conquerors and the conquered certain secret truths are revealed to those who are capable of examining these narratives; and, even more marvelous, through a written system of law, the laws of truth are prophetically indicated, all these having been recorded in a series with a power which is truly appropriate to the wisdom of God. For the intention was to make even the outer covering of the spiritual truths, I mean the bodily part of the scriptures, in many respects not unprofitable but capable of improving the multitude insofar as they receive it.

9. But if the usefulness of the law and the sequence and ease of the narrative were at first

sight clearly discernible throughout, we should be unaware that there was anything beyond the obvious meaning for us to understand in the scriptures. Consequently the Word of God has arranged for certain stumbling blocks, as it were, and hindrances and impossibilities to be inserted in the midst of the law and the history, in order that we may not be completely drawn away by the sheer attractiveness of the language, and so either reject the true doctrines absolutely, on the ground that we learn from the scriptures nothing worthy of God, or else by never moving away from the letter fail to learn anything of the more divine element.

And we must also know this, that because the principal aim was to announce the connection that exists among spiritual events, those that have already happened and those that are yet to come to pass, whenever the Word found that things which had happened in history could be harmonized with these mystical events, he used them, concealing from the multitude their deeper meaning. But wherever in the narrative the accomplishment of some particular deeds, which had been previously recorded for the sake of their more mystical meanings, did not correspond with the sequence of the intellectual truths, the scripture wove into the story something which did not happen, occasionally something which could not happen, and occasionally something which might have happened but in fact did not. Sometimes a few words are inserted which in the bodily sense are not true, and at other times a greater number.

A similar method can be discerned also in the law, where it is often possible to find a precept that is useful for its own sake, and suitable to the time when the law was given. Sometimes, however, the precept does not appear to be useful. At other times even impossibilities are recorded in the law for the sake of the more skillful and inquiring readers, in order that these, by giving themselves to the toil of examining what is written, may gain a sound conviction of the necessity of seeking in such instances a meaning worthy of God.

And not only did the Spirit supervise the writings which were previous to the coming of Christ, but because he is the same Spirit and proceeds from the one God he has dealt in like manner with the Gospels and the writings of the apostles. For the history even of these is not everywhere pure, events being woven together in the bodily sense without having actually happened; nor do the law and the commandments contained therein entirely declare what is reasonable.

The Principle Underlying the Obscurities in Divine Scripture and Its Impossible or Unreasonable Character in Places, If Taken Literally. [IV.iii]

1. Now what person of intelligence will believe that the first and the second and the third day, and the evening and the morning existed without the sun and moon and stars? And that the first day, if we may so call it, was even without a heaven? And who is so silly as to believe that God, after the manner of a farmer, "planted a paradise eastward in Eden," and set in it a visible and palpable "tree of life," of such a sort that anyone who tasted its fruit with his bodily teeth would gain life; and again that one could partake of "good and evil" by masticating the fruit taken from the tree of that name? And when God is said to "walk in the paradise in the cool of the day" (Gen. 2:8, 9) and Adam to hide himself behind a tree, I do not think anyone will doubt that these are figurative expressions which indicate certain mysteries through a semblance of history and not through actual events.

Further, when Cain "goes out from the face of God" (Gen. 4:16) it seems clear to thoughtful men that this statement impels the reader to inquire what the "face of God" is and how anyone can "go out" from it. And what more need I say, when those who are not altogether blind can collect thousands of such instances, recorded as actual events, but which did not happen literally?

Even the gospels are full of passages of this kind, as when the devil takes Jesus up into a "high mountain" in order to show him from thence "the kingdoms of the whole world and the glory of them" (Matt. 4:8). For what person who does not read such passages carelessly would fail to condemn those who believe that with the eye of the flesh, which requires a great height to enable us to perceive what is below and at our feet, the kingdoms of the Persians, Scythians, Indians, and Parthians were seen, and the manner in which their rulers are glorified by men? And the careful reader will detect thousands of other passages like this in the gospels, which will convince him that events which did not take place at all are woven into the records of what literally did happen.

2. And to come to the Mosaic legislation, many of the laws, so far as their literal observance is concerned, are clearly irrational, while others are impossible. An example of irrationality is the prohibition to eat vultures, seeing that nobody even in the worst famine was ever driven by want to the extremity of eating these creatures (Lev. 11:14). And in regard to the command that children of eight days old who are uncircumcised "shall be destroyed from among their people" (Gen. 17:14 LXX), if the law relating to these children were really meant to be carried out according to the letter, the proper course would be to order the death of their fathers or those by whom they were being brought up. But as it is the Scripture says: "Every male that is uncircumcised, who shall not be circumcised on the eighth day, shall be destroyed from among his people" (ibid.).

And if you would like to see some impossibilities that are enacted in the law, let us observe that the goat-stag, which Moses commands us to offer in sacrifice as a clean animal (Deut. 4:5 LXX), is a creature that cannot possibly exist; while as to the griffin, which the lawgiver forbids to be eaten (Lev. 11:13; Deut. 14:12), there is no record that it has ever fallen into the human hands. Moreover, in regard to the celebrated sabbath, a careful reader will see that the command, "Ye shall sit each one in your dwellings; let none of you go out from his place on the sabbath day" (Exod. 16:29), is an impossible one to observe literally, for no living creature could sit for a whole day and not move from his seat.

Consequently, the members of the circumcision and all those who maintain that nothing more than the actual wording is signified make no inquiry whatever into some matters, such as the goat-stag, the griffin, and the vulture, while on others they babble copiously, bringing forward lifeless traditions, as for instance when they say, in reference to the Sabbath, that each man's "place" is two thousand cubits (Num 35:5). Others, however, among whom is Dositheus the Samaritan, condemn such an interpretation and believe that in whatever position a man is found on the Sabbath day he should remain there until evening.

Further, the command "not to carry a burden on the Sabbath day" (Jer. 17:21) is impossible; and on this account the teachers of the Jews have indulged in endless chatter, asserting that one kind of shoe is a burden, but another is not, and that a sandal with nails is a burden, but one without nails is not, and that what is carried on one shoulder is a burden, but not what is carried on both.

3. If now we approach the gospel in search of similar instances, what can be more irrational than the command "Salute no man by the way" (Luke 10:4), which simple people believe that the Savior enjoined upon the apostles? Again, to speak of the right cheek being struck (Matt. 5:39) is most incredible, for every striker, unless he suffers from some unnatural defect, strikes the left cheek with his right hand. And it is impossible to accept the precept from the gospel about the "right eye that offends" (Matt. 5:29); for granting the possibility of a person being "offended" through his sense of sight, how can the blame be attributed to the right eye, when there are two eyes that see? And what man, even supposing he accuses himself of "looking on a woman to lust after her" (Matt. 5:28) and attributes the blame to his right eye alone, would act rationally if he were to cast this eye away?

Further, the apostle lays down this precept: "Was any called being circumcised? Let him not become uncircumcised" (1 Cor. 7:18). Now in the first place anyone who wishes can see that these words have no relation to the subject in hand; and how can we help thinking that they have been inserted at random, when we remember that the apostle is here laying down precepts about marriage and purity? In the second place, who will maintain that it is wrong for a man to put himself into a condition of uncircumcision, if that were possible, in view of the disgrace which is felt by most people to attach to circumcision?

4. We have mentioned all these instances with the object of showing that the aim of the divine power which bestowed on us the holy scriptures is not that we should accept only what is found in the letter; for occasionally the records taken in a literal sense are not true, but actually absurd and impossible, and even with the history that actually happened and the legislation that is in its literal sense useful there are other matters interwoven.

But someone may suppose that the former statement refers to all the scriptures and may suspect us of saying that because some of the history did not happen, therefore none of it happened; and because a certain law is irrational or impossible when taken literally, therefore no laws ought to be kept to the letter; or that the records of the Savior's life are not true in a physical sense; or that no law or commandment of his ought to be obeyed. We must assert, therefore, that in regard to some things we are clearly aware that the historical fact is true; as that Abraham was buried in the double cave at Hebron together with Isaac and Jacob and one wife of each of them (Gen. 23:2, 9, 19; 25:9, 10; 49:29-32; 50:13); and that Shechem was given as a portion to Joseph (Gen. 48:22; Josh 24:32); and that Jerusalem is the chief city of Judaea, in which a temple of God was built by Solomon; and thousands of other facts. For the passages which are historically true are far more numerous than those which are composed with purely spiritual meanings.

And again, who would deny that the command which says "Honor thy father and thy mother, that it may be well with thee" (Exod. 20:12), is useful quite apart from any spiritual interpretation, and that it ought certainly to be observed, especially when we remember that the apostle Paul has quoted it in the self-same words? (Eph. 6:2, 3). And what are we to say of the following "You shall not kill; you shall not commit adultery; you shall not steal; you shall not bear false witness"? (Exod. 20:13-16).

Once again, in the gospel there are commandments written which need no inquiry whether they are to be kept literally or not, as that which says, "I say unto you, whosoever is angry with his brother" (Matt. 5:22), and what follows; and, "I say unto you, swear not at all" (Matt. 5:34). Here, too, is an injunction of the apostle of which the literal meaning must be retained: "Admonish the disorderly, encourage the faint-hearted, support the weak, be long-suffering toward all" (1 Thess. 5:14); though in the case of the more earnest readers it is possible to preserve each of the meanings, that is, while not setting aside the commandment in its literal sense, to preserve the "depths of the wisdom of God" (Rom. 11:33).

5. Nevertheless, the exact reader will hesitate in regard to some passages, finding himself unable to decide without considerable investigation whether a particular incident, believed to be history, actually happened or not, and whether the literal meaning of a particular law is to be observed or not. Accordingly, he who reads in an exact manner must, in obedience to the Savior's precept which says, "Search the scriptures" (John 5:39), carefully investigate how far the literal meaning is true and how far it is impossible, and to the utmost of his power must trace out from the use of similar expressions the meaning scattered everywhere through the scriptures of that which when taken literally is impossible.

When, therefore, as will be clear to those who read, the passage as a connected whole is literally impossible, whereas the outstanding part of it is not impossible but even true, the reader must endeavor to grasp the entire meaning, connecting by an intellectual process the account of what is literally impossible with the parts that are not impossible but are historically true, these being interpreted allegorically in common with the parts which, so far as the letter goes, did not happen at all. For our contention with regard to the whole of divine scripture is that it all has a spiritual meaning, but not all a bodily meaning; for the bodily meaning is often proved to be an impossibility. Consequently, the one who reads the divine books reverently, believing them to be divine writings, must exercise great care. And the method of understanding them appears to us to be as follows.

6. The accounts tell us that God chose out a certain nation on the earth, and they call this nation by many names. For the nation as a whole is called Israel, and it is also spoken of as Jacob. But when it was divided in the days of Jeroboam the son of Nebat, the ten tribes said to have been subject to him were named Israel, and the other two together with the tribe of Levi, which were ruled over by men of the seed of David, were called Judah. The entire country which was inhabited by people of this race and which had been given them by God, is called Judaea, the metropolis of which is Jerusalem, this being the mother city of a number of others whose names lie scattered about in many different places of scripture but are gathered together into one list in the book of Joshua the son of Nun.

This being so, the apostle, raising our spiritual apprehension to a high level, says somewhere: "Behold Israel after the flesh" (1 Cor. 10:18), inferring that there is an Israel after the spirit. He says also in another place: "For it is not the children of the flesh that are children of God" (Rom. 9:8), nor are "all they Israel, who are of Israel" (Rom. 9:6).

And again: "Neither is he a Jew, who is one outwardly, nor is that circumcision, which is outward in the flesh; but he is a Jew, who is one inwardly, and circumcision is of the heart, in the spirit, not in the letter" (Rom. 2:28, 29). For if we take the phrase "a Jew inwardly" as a test, we shall realize that as there is a race of bodily Jews, so, too, there is a race of those who are "Jews inwardly," the soul having acquired this nobility of race in virtue of certain unspeakable words. Moreover, there are many prophecies spoken of Israel and Judah, which relate what is going to happen to them. And when we think of the extraordinary promises recorded about these people, promises that so far as literary style goes are poor and distinguished by no elevation or character that is worthy of a promise of God, is it not clear that they demand a mystical interpretation? Well, then, if the promises are of a spiritual kind though announced through material imagery, the people to whom the promises belong are not the bodily Israelites.

7. But we must not spend time discussing who is a "Jew inwardly" and who an Israelite "in the inner man," since the above remarks are sufficient for all who are not dull-witted. We will return to the subject before us and say that Jacob was the father of the twelve patriarchs, and they of the rulers of the people, and they in their turn of the Israelites who came after. Is it not the case, then, that the bodily Israelites carry back their descent to the rulers of the people, the rulers of the people to the patriarchs, and the patriarchs to Jacob and those still more ancient; whereas are not the spiritual Israelites, of whom the bodily ones were a type, descended from the clans, and the clans from the tribes, and the tribes from one whose birth was

not bodily, like that of the others, but of a higher kind; and was not he born of Isaac, and Isaac descended from Abraham, while all go back to Adam, who the apostle says is Christ? (1 Cor. 15:45). For the origin of all families that are in touch with the God of the whole world began lower down with Christ, who comes next after the God and Father of the whole world and is thus the father of every soul, as Adam is the father of all men. And if Eve is interpreted by Paul as referring to the Church, it is not surprising (seeing that Cain was born of Eve and all that come after him carry back their descent to Eve) that these two should be figures of the Church; for in the higher sense all men take their beginning from the Church.

8. Now if what we have stated about Israel, its tribes and its clans, is convincing, then when the Savior says, "I was not sent but unto the lost sheep of the house of Israel" (Matt. 15:24), we do not take these words in the same sense as the poor-minded Ebionites do (those whose very name comes from the poverty of their mind, for in Hebrew *ebion* is the word for poor), so as to suppose that Christ came especially to the Israelites after the flesh. For "it is not the children of the flesh that are children of God" (Rom. 9:8).

Again, the apostle gives us the following instances of teaching about Jerusalem: "The Jerusalem which is above is free, which is our mother" (Gal. 4:26); and in another epistle: "But ye are come to Mount Sion and to the city of the living God, the heavenly Jerusalem, and to an innumerable company of angels, to the general assembly and church of the firstborn who are written in heaven" (Heb. 12:22, 23).

If therefore Israel consists of a race of souls, and Jerusalem is a city in heaven, it follows that the cities of Israel have for their mother city the Jerusalem in the heavens; and so consequently does Judaea as a whole.

In all prophecies concerning Jerusalem, therefore, and in all statements made about it, we must understand, if we listen to Paul's words as the words of God and the utterances of wisdom, that the scriptures are telling us about the heavenly city and the whole region which contains the cities of the holy land. Perhaps it is to these cities that the Savior lifts our attention when he gives to those who have deserved praise for the good use of their talents authority over ten or over five cities.

16. Cyprian of Carthage,
Letter 55

Cyprian (d. 258) became bishop of Carthage in 248, two years after his conversion to the Christian faith. He died a martyr. His theological ideas, especially on matters of church and sacraments, had a formative influence on Latin Christianity. This letter illustrates his position in the controversy over the treatment of Christians who had sacrificed to avoid persecution ("the lapsed"), to whom the schismatic bishop Novatian, among others, had denied any possibility of reconciliation with the church. Cyprian opposes Novatian here, though fundamentally not for the substance of his views so much as for violating the unity of the church, thus placing himself outside the faith.

SOURCE: *The Letters of St. Cyprian of Carthage,* vol. 3, tr. G. W. Clarke (New York: Newman Press, 1986), 40-42, 45-52. Copyright © 1986 by Rev. Johannes Quasten, Rev. Walter J. Burghardt, S.J., and Thomas Comerford Lawler. Used by permission of Paulist Press, Inc., New York/Mahwah, N.J.

13.1 ... the facts [of the Church's treatment of the lapsed] are as follows.

Should anyone [of the lapsed] fall seriously ill, in accordance with our resolution we bring comfort to them in their time of danger. But once comfort has been brought to them and peace has been granted to them in that danger, we cannot then set about choking them or suffocating them or, by laying violent hands on them ourselves, forcing on their end. It is as if they absolutely have to die after so receiving peace, because it is to the *dying* that we grant peace! Whereas, in fact, we can see clear proof of God's loving-kindness and His paternal gentleness, should it so happen that those who receive the pledge of (eternal) life by being granted peace, then have their own lives prolonged here on earth after receiving that peace.

And so, if, after the bestowal of peace, God should grant a reprieve, no one should find in that grounds for attacking their bishops, especially as it has been firmly resolved that we are to bring comfort to our brothers who are in danger of death.

13.2 What is more, my dearly beloved brother, you should not judge (as some do) that those who obtained certificates are to be put on a par with those who offered sacrifice. Why, even amongst those who actually sacrificed there is often to be discerned a great diversity in circumstances and conditions. For example, we should not put on a par the man who without hesitation sprang forward of his own free will to perform the accursed sacrifice, and another who after putting up a long struggle and resistance eventually approached that deadly task only under compulsion. Equally different is the man who thrust forward his entire family as well as himself, and another who alone confronted the test on behalf of everyone else, thereby protecting his wife, his children, and his entire household at the cost of endangering himself. Finally, the man who forced his own tenants and friends to perpetrate that criminal action is not to be equated with the man who spared his tenants and farmers, who welcomed under the shelter of his own roof many brethren who were refugees in flight on their way to exile, one who can present and offer before the Lord many souls alive and safe today to intercede for pardon on behalf of his one wounded soul.

14.1 There are, then, these great differences even amongst those who offered sacrifice. It is, therefore, manifestly callous and cruelly overrigid to insist on including amongst those who did offer sacrifice those who merely obtained certificates. For in the case of a person who acquired such a certificate he may plead for himself: "I had previously read and I had learnt from my bishop's preaching that we should not offer sacrifice to idols and that a servant of God ought not to worship images. And so, in order to avoid doing this action which was forbidden, I seized an opportunity which offered itself for obtaining a certificate (which I would certainly not have acquired had there not presented itself such an opportunity). I either went up to the magistrate myself or I gave instructions to another who was on his way up to him. I declared that I was a Christian, that it was forbidden to me to offer sacrifice, that I could not approach the altars of the devil, and that I was, therefore, offering payment in order to avoid doing what was forbidden to me."

14.2 But as it is, the person who was thus tainted with a certificate has learnt from our admonitions that he ought not to have done even this and that, even though his hands remain undefiled and his mouth unpolluted by any contact with that deadly food, his conscience nonetheless has been polluted. After hearing this advice from us, he is now in tears, and he is sorrowful, realizing that he has sinned. But he thus gives clear assurance that, whilst in the past he went astray not so much out of wickedness as out of error, he is now ready and instructed for facing the future.

20.1 There is no reason for you to imagine, dearly beloved brother, that our brethren will be any the less courageous or that there will be a decline in the number of martyrs simply because repentance is made easier for the fallen and some hope of reconciliation has now been offered to those who do penance. For the strength of the true believers continues unshaken, the integrity of those who fear and love God with all their hearts remains as steadfast and as firm as ever.

20.2 Now even in the case of adulterers we allow a certain period for penitence and then peace is granted to them. Yet that has not caused any decline in virginity in the Church; the glorious ideal of chastity is not fading away simply because of the sins of others. The Church continues to flourish and bloom, crowned with the flowers of her many virgins; chastity and continence preserve their long-continued glory, the power of purity is not crushed because penitence and pardon are conceded to the adulterer.

20.3 And you must realize that it is one thing for a man to stand by, awaiting the granting of pardon, and quite another thing for him to achieve the heights of glory; it is one thing for him to be thrown into prison and not to emerge from it until he pays the very last farthing, and quite another thing for him to receive all at once the rewards for faith and valor; it is one thing for a man to be wracked by long grieving over his sins and to be purged and purified over a lengthy period of time by fire, and it is quite another thing for him to have purged away all his sins by a martyr's death. In a word, to hang in doubt on the day of judgment awaiting the verdict of the Lord is far different from being crowned by the Lord without a moment's delay.

21.1 And you must remember that even amongst our predecessors there were certain bishops here in our own province who judged that peace ought not to be granted to adulterers and they, therefore, shut off completely any room for penitence in the case of sins of adultery. And yet that did not cause them to withdraw from the college of their fellow bishops, nor to shatter the unity of the catholic Church, obstinate in their harshness and rigor though they remained. Accordingly, he who refused to grant peace to adulterers did not separate himself from the Church simply because others were granting such peace. 21.2 Provided that the bonds of harmony remain unbroken and that the sacred unity of the catholic Church continues unimpaired, each individual bishop can arrange and order his own affairs, in the knowledge that one day he must render an account to the Lord for his own conduct.

22.1 For my own part, I am astonished that there are some who are so obstinate as to judge that no opportunity for penitence ought to be granted to the fallen and who consider that pardon must be denied to those who do penance. And yet it is written: *Remember whence you have fallen, do penance and perform your former good works* (Rev. 2:5). Now these words are certainly directed at a man who has undoubtedly fallen and whom the Lord is encouraging to rise up again through good works. For it is also written: *Almsgiving delivers from death* (Prov. 10:2), and, there, is clearly meant not deliverance from that death which the blood of Christ has quenched once and for all and from which the saving grace of baptism and of our Redeemer has delivered us, but deliverance from that death which afterwards creeps in through sin.

Furthermore, in another passage, an opportunity is indeed granted for penitence, and the Lord actually threatens the person who fails to do penitence: *I have* (He says) *many things against you because you allow your wife Jezabel, who declares herself to be a prophetess, to teach and to seduce my servants, to commit fornication and to eat of foods offered in sacrifice, and I gave to her an opportunity to do penitence and she refused to repent of her fornication. See, I will cast her upon a couch, and those who have fornicated with her I will cast into great tribulation unless they do penitence for their deeds* (Rev. 2:20). Obviously the Lord would not have encouraged them to do penitence were it not the case that He promises pardon to the penitent. And to this effect in the Gospels He declares: *I say to you that likewise there will be rejoicing in heaven over a sinner who does penitence rather than over ninety-nine just who have no need of penitence* (Luke 15:7).

22.3 We read in Scripture: *God did not make death; neither does He take joy in the destruction of the living* (Wis. 1:13). Clearly, therefore, He who would have no one perish desires that sinners should do penitence and through penitence return again to life. Hence, too, through the prophet Joel He proclaims in these words: *And now the Lord your God says, return to me with all your heart, at the same time with fasting and weeping and mourning, and rend your hearts and not your garments, and return to the Lord your God because He is merciful and loving, slow to anger and full of kindness and He condemns the evil He has inflicted* (Joel 2:12-13).

22.4 Similarly we read in the Psalms of both the strictness and the compassion of God, who is at once menacing and merciful, who punishes that He may correct and when He has corrected saves: *I will visit*, He says, *their wicked deeds with the rod and with the lash their iniquities. But my mercy I will not scatter away from them* (Ps. 89:32).

23.1 The Lord also illustrates the compassion of God the Father when He says in the Gospel: *What man is there among you who if his son should ask for bread would hand him a stone, or if he should ask for a fish would hand him a snake? If you, then, evil as you are, know how to give good gifts to your sons, how much more will your heavenly Father give good things to those who ask Him?* (Matt. 7:9-11).

23.2 Here the Lord is drawing a comparison between a father according to the flesh and God the Father with His never-ending and boundless compassion. Now suppose that evil, earthly father has been gravely offended by his sinful and wicked son: even so, if later on he should see that this same son has now mended his ways, that he has put aside the iniquities of his past life, that by remorse and repentance he has been restored to sober and honest living and to the practice of virtue, why then he is glad and rejoices, and he welcomes back the son whom he has previously thrown out and with a father's joy and delight embraces his son.

But how much more must that one, true Father who is kind and merciful and compassionate, indeed who is Himself kindness and mercy and compassion, how much more must He take joy in the repentance of His own sons and no longer threaten them with His wrath if they are repentant or with punishment if they weep and mourn, but promise to them instead His pardon and forgiveness.

23.3 Hence, in the Gospel the Lord can call blessed those who mourn, for he who mourns arouses His mercy, whereas he who is obdurate and proud heaps wrath upon himself and punishment in the judgment to come.

23.4 And that is the reason why, dearly beloved brother, in the case of those who do no penance, who give no evidence that they are wholeheartedly sorry for their sins, who make no public profession of their grief, we have determined that they ought to be altogether excluded from any hope of peace and communion if, on becoming dangerously ill, they should start to beg for them. Obviously it is not repentance for their sin which drives them to ask but the warning of fast-approaching death; and he does not deserve to receive consolation in death who has failed to reflect that one day he must die.

24.1 Now as regards Novatian personally, dearly beloved brother, you ask that I write to you explaining what heresy it is he has introduced. In the first place I must make clear to you that it is not right for us even to want to know what it is he is teaching, since he is teaching *outside*. Whoever he may be, whatever his qualities, he can be no Christian who is not inside the Church of Christ. Sing his own praises for all he is worth, flaunt as he will in proud phrases his philosophy and his eloquence, he has, nonetheless, failed to maintain charity with his brethren and unity with the Church, and he has therefore lost even what he had formerly been.

24.2 Unless you really think that he is a genuine bishop who, at a time when a bishop had already been made within the Church by sixteen of our fellow bishops, goes to great efforts and intrigue to get himself made a bishop at the hands of renegades, and made a fake and foreign bishop at that! Moreover, there is but one Church founded by Christ, but it is divided into many members throughout the world; likewise, there is but one episcopate, but it is spread amongst the harmonious host of all the numerous bishops. And yet, despite this arrangement established by God, despite this unity in the catholic Church which is universally linked and locked together, he is now attempting to set up a man-made church and he is sending out to numerous cities upstart apostles of his own in order to lay down brand-new foundations for an establishment of his own devising. And whereas in every one of the provinces and each of the cities there have been long since appointed bishops who are venerable in age, sound in faith, tested in tribulation, and proscribed in persecution, he even has the effrontery to appoint over and above them a new set of spurious bishops.

24.3 Fancy imagining that he could sweep the entire globe with this perverse novelty or that he could smash the framework of the Church's body simply by scattering his seeds of discord. He fails to realize that though schismatics are always hot with enthusiasm at the very beginning, they are never able to expand or increase what they have unlawfully initiated but that, right from the start, they begin to fade away, they and all their evil rivalries.

24.4 Indeed he could not now retain the position of bishop even if he had been made bishop before anyone else, since he has broken away from the body of his fellow bishops and the unity of the Church. For the Apostle does warn us to give support to one another lest we depart from that unity which God has established. To quote his own words: *Supporting one another in love, striving to preserve the unity of the Spirit in the bond of peace* (Eph. 4:3). A man, therefore, who preserves neither the unity of the Spirit nor the bond of peace but cuts himself off from the ties of the Church and the college of bishops can have neither the power nor the dignity of a bishop, for he has chosen to maintain neither the unity nor the peace of the episcopate.

25.1 And what is more, look at the puffed-up arrogance of it all, the total disregard for meekness and humility, the supreme display of personal pride, that a man should dare to do or even imagine himself able to do what the Lord did not allow even the apostles to do, that he should think he is able to divide the tares from the wheat, or as if it was to him that had been granted power to wield the winnowing fan and to cleanse the threshing floor, that he should set about separating the chaff from the grain.

25.2 And despite the fact that the Apostle says: *But in a great household there are not only vessels of gold and of silver but also vessels of wood and of clay* (2 Tim. 2:20), he actually thinks he can pick out the vessels that are of gold and of silver but that he can despise, condemn, and cast away the vessels that are of wood and of clay, whereas the vessels of wood are to be burnt in the flames of the divine fire only on the day of the Lord and the vessels of clay are to be smashed only by the one to whom has been entrusted the rod of iron.

26.1 But if he has really set himself up as the searcher of men's hearts and reins and as the judge of others, then let him at least judge in all cases

with complete fairness. He must be fully aware of the words of Scripture: *See, you have been made whole; sin no more lest anything worse befall you* (John 5:14). Let him, therefore, exclude from his company and following defrauders and adulterers. For the case of one who has committed adultery is far graver and much more serious than the case of one who has obtained a certificate of sacrifice: the latter has sinned under compulsion, the former of his own choice; the latter was the victim of error, thinking that it was enough to avoid offering sacrifice, the former has assailed another's marriage rights or he has visited some brothel, going down into the sewers and slimy stews of the rabble and there his own sanctified body, God's temple, he has befouled with loathsome filth. To quote the Apostle: *Every sin that man commits is outside the body, but he who commits adultery sins against his own body* (1 Cor. 6:18).

26.2 Yet even to these sinners penitence is allowed and hope is still left to them if they show sorrow and make amends for their sin, just as the Apostle himself indicates: *I fear lest perchance when I come to you I may mourn over many of those who sinned before and have not repented of the foul deeds they have practiced, of their acts of fornication and lust* (2 Cor. 12:21).

27.1 And there are no grounds for these upstart heretics to feel self-satisfied because, as they say, they have no communion with idolaters. For in their company are both defrauders and adulterers, and such sinners are guilty of the crime of idolatry if you follow the words of the Apostle: *Know this well and understand that no adulterer or fornicator or defrauder (for that is idolatry) has any inheritance in the kingdom of Christ and of God* (1 Cor. 6:9). And again he says: *Mortify, therefore, your members which are on earth, laying aside fornication and impurity and evil desire and lust, which are all slavery to idols. Because of these things the wrath of God is coming* (Col. 3:5).

27.2 Furthermore, as our bodies are members of Christ and we are, each of us, a temple of God, whoever by adultery violates that temple of God violates God; and whoever in committing sin does the will of the devil is being a slave to demons and their idols. For evil deeds do not proceed from the Holy Spirit but from the promptings of the

Enemy, and from the unclean spirit are born desires which drive men to act against God and be a slave to the devil.

It follows, therefore, that if they claim one man is polluted by another's sin and if, as they maintain and contend, the idolatry of the guilty passes on to the innocent then, on their own argument, they cannot clear themselves of the guilt of idolatry, since it is established on the authority of the Apostle that adulterers and defrauders, with whom they are in communion, are idolaters.

27.3 But this is not for us: we remain true to our faith, we follow the guidance set by God's teaching, we are in agreement with the dictates of truth. We maintain that each person must be held responsible for the sin he commits himself and that no one can be made guilty for anyone else, for the Lord warns us with these words: *The just man's justice will be upon him, and the wicked man's wickedness will be upon him* (Ezek. 18:20), as likewise He says: *Fathers shall not die for their children and children shall not die for their fathers. Every man shall die for his own sin* (Deut. 24:16).

That is what we read and follow. We, therefore, certainly believe that no one ought to be debarred from the fruits of satisfaction and the hope of reconciliation. We put our faith in the divine Scriptures, we follow the authority and encouragement of God Himself; we are, accordingly, convinced that sinners are invited back to do penitence and that pardon and forgiveness are not denied to the penitent.

28.1 What a way to mock our brethren and to frustrate them, what a way to delude hapless sinners and to make their sorrows in vain, what a profitless and fruitless teaching that emanates from this heretical establishment! Imagine exhorting people to do penitence and make atonement, and at the same time taking away all healing power from that atonement. Fancy saying to our brethren: "Lament and pour forth tears and spend your days and nights in sorrow, and for washing away and cleansing your sin perform generous and frequent good works, but for all that you do, it is outside the Church that you shall die. You should do whatever leads to reconciliation but never will you receive the reconciliation which you seek." Who would not be lost at once, who

would not fall away in utter despair, who would not give up any thought of sorrowing for sin?

28.2 Do you think a farmer could carry on working if you said to him: "Use all your farmer's skill in working this land, do your very best to cultivate it, but no harvest will you reap, no vintage will you press, no crop will you gather from your olive grove, no fruit will you pick from the trees"?

28.3 It is as if you were trying to encourage a man to own and run ships, and were to say to him: "My friend, purchase timber from the very best forests, fashion your keel with specially strong and hand-picked beams of oak, work away that your ship may be constructed and fitted with rudder and ropes and sails, but when you have done all this, no fruit will you see from its trading and its voyages."

29.1 This is tantamount to blocking off and cutting short the way to sorrow and the route to repentance. And whereas in the Scriptures the Lord God goes out of His way to welcome those who return to Him and who repent, yet we, by our callousness and cruelty in cutting off the fruits of repentance, we are totally destroying repentance itself. But if we find that no one ought to be prevented from doing penitence and that, in as much as the Lord is compassionate and merciful, reconciliation can be granted through His bishops to those who implore and call upon the mercy of the Lord, then we have no alternative but to recognize the sorrows of those who bewail their sin and we have no right to deny the fruits of repentance to those who grieve.

29.2 And because in the grave there is no confession and the rite of reconciliation cannot take place there, those who are genuinely repentant and who ask ought for the time being to be accepted into the Church and there be kept for the Lord. One day He will come to His Church and will surely pass judgment on those whom He finds within it.

29.3 But apostates and renegades, enemies and opponents, all those in fact who scatter the Church of Christ, even if they have been put to death for His name but outside the Church, they cannot, according to the Apostle, be admitted to the peace of the Church, because they have not maintained the unity either of the Spirit or of the Church.

30. For the moment, dearly beloved brother, I have briefly run through, as best I can, these few points—although there is still much left to say—so that I could meet your request and might join you by ever closer ties to the fellowship of our body of bishops, your colleagues. But should you get the opportunity and the means to visit us, we could discuss at greater length together and confer more completely and fully on these matters in the hopes of furthering blessed concord.

I wish that you, dearly beloved brother, may ever fare well.

17. Bardaisan of Edessa,
The Book of the Laws of Countries

The Christian philosopher Bardaisan (ca. 154-222) taught in the Syrian city of Edessa, which was already becoming the center of Syriac-speaking Christianity. Here he adduces the differences in the customs of various countries to demonstrate the reality of free will in the face of astrologically determined fate—which, however, does, in his view, affect human life in other respects. His teachings would not pass the test of later orthodoxy, and in the fourth century Ephrem the Syrian would write against him. But in the Edessa of Bardaisan's time "orthodoxy and heterodoxy were as yet unknown quantities." (H. Drijvers)

. . . So there exists something which the Chaldaeans call Fate. And not everything happens according to our will, as appears from the following: most people want to be rich and to have power over their fellow men, to have physical health and that things may be subject to them as they desire. Yet riches are only found with a few, power with a small number, and health is not found with all. The rich do not have unlimited enjoyment of their wealth, all things are not subject to the powerful as they would wish, for sometimes they are not subject to them, against their desire. And sometimes the rich are wealthy as they desire, and sometimes they become poor, as they do not desire. The people who are destitute dwell as they would not do and live in the world after a fashion contrary to their desire and they covet all kinds of things, but those pass them by. Many procreate children, but may not bring them up; others bring them up but may not keep them; to others again they are left, but they bring them disgrace and sorrow. Some are rich as they would be, but sick against their desire. Others are healthy as they would be, but poor against their will. There are people who possess much that they desire and little that they would not have. But there are also people who possess much that they would not have and but little that they do desire. It is evident, then, that riches, honor, health, sickness, children, and everything we covet depend on Fate and that we have no power over these matters. With those things that happen as we wish, we are satisfied and we rejoice over them, but we are powerfully constrained towards those events that we do not desire. Yet it is clearly apparent from those things that happen to us contrary to our desire that the things we wish for do not come to us because we wish them, but occur simply as they do occur. Some we are pleased with, and others not. And now it is evident that we men are led in the same

SOURCE: *The Book of the Laws of Countries: Dialogue on Fate of Bardaisan of Edessa,* tr. H. J. W. Drijvers (Assen: Van Gorcum, 1965), 31-39, 59-63. Used by permission.

way by our natural constitution, in different ways by Fate, but by our liberty each as he will. We will now continue the demonstration and show that Fate does not have power over everything. For that which is called Fate is really the fixed course determined by God for the Rulers and Guiding Signs. According to this course and order the spirits undergo changes while descending to the soul, and the souls while descending to the bodies. That which causes these changes is called Fate and native horoscope of that mixture which was mixed and is being purified to the help of that which, by the grace and goodness of God, was and will be helped till the termination of all. The body, then, is led by its natural constitution, while the soul suffers and receives impressions together with it. But the body is not constrained by this Fate nor is it helped by it, in all things which it does one by one. For a man does not become a father before his fifteenth year, nor a woman a mother before her thirteenth. So for age also the fixed law applies, that the women cease to bear children and the men lose their natural power to beget children, while other living creatures which are also led by their natural constitution, not only already bring forth offspring before the age I have mentioned, but then have even already become too old to do so, as our human bodies also, when they have grown too old, bring forth no more children. And Fate cannot give them children either, when the body no longer has the natural power to give them. Nor can Fate keep the human body alive without food and drink, any more than it can give the body immortality with food and drink. For these things and many others belong to the reign of nature. But when the periods and modes of nature's work are ended, Fate manifests itself in this field and does things of diverse kind. Sometimes it aids and strengthens nature, and sometimes it hinders and impedes it. To grow up and become adult pertains to the work of nature but outside this work, illnesses and physical defects are caused by Fate. The union of male and female belongs to the field of nature, as also the satisfaction of both parties. But from Fate come disgust and breaking the community of marriage, and all impurity and immorality people commit because of their passions, when they have intercourse

together. Having children belongs to the domain of nature. But through Fate the children are sometimes deformed; they sometimes miscarry and sometimes die prematurely. A sufficiency for all bodies belongs to the reign of nature, but from Fate come dearth of food and physical complaints. So equally do intemperance and unnecessary luxury stem from Fate. Nature ordains old people to be judges over young ones, and wise ones over foolish, strong men to dominate over weak and courageous over cowardly. But Fate is cause that children are set over old people and fools over wise, and that in strenuous times weak men direct strong and cowards the courageous. Be convinced then, that whenever nature is deflected from her true course, it is Fate that is the cause, because the Rulers and Guiding Signs, from which every change called horoscope is deduced, are in opposition. Those of them called the right-hand ones assist nature and heighten her beauty, when their course is favorable and they take a high position in the sky in the sectors belonging to them. And those of them called the left-hand ones are malefic, and when they occupy a high position, they work against nature. Not only to men do they bring damage, but occasionally also to the animals, the trees, the fruit of the fields, the products of the season, the water springs and everything in nature subject to their influence. Because of this division and this difference existing between the Rulers, there are people who think the world is governed without a fixed order, because they do not realize that this difference and division, innocence and guilt, arise from the order set by God in according them liberty, so that these active beings also may either justify themselves or become guilty through their free disposing over themselves. As we have seen that Fate can disorder nature, so we can also see how man's liberty forces back and disorders Fate. Not in everything, though, as Fate does not force back nature in everything either. It is fitting, then, that these three things, nature, Fate, and liberty keep each their own mode of being, until the course is completed and measure and number have been fulfilled. For thus has it been resolved by Him who ordained what was to be the way of life and the manner of perfection of all creatures, and the condition of all substances and natures. . . .

[*Bardaisan then surveys the variety of human customs as proof of free will as a factor in human existence, before making these concluding remarks about the customs of Christians:*]

In Syria and Edessa there was the custom of self-emasculation in honor of Tar'ata, but when King Abgar had come to the faith, he ordered that every man who emasculated himself should have his hand chopped off. And from that day to this no one emasculates himself in the territory of Edessa. What shall we say of the new people of us Christians, that the Messiah has caused to arise in every place and in all climates by his coming? For behold, we all, wherever we may be, are called Christians after the one name of the Messiah. And upon one day, the first of the week, we gather together and on the appointed days we abstain from food. And our brothers who live in Gaul do not marry with men, and they who live in Parthia do not marry two women, and in Judea they are not circumcised. Our sisters among the Geli and the Kushanians do not have intercourse with foreigners, and they who live in Persia do not marry their daughters. Those who live in Media do not flee away from their dead, nor bury them alive or throw them for food to the dogs. Those who live in Edessa do not kill their wives or sisters who have committed adultery, but have nothing more to do with them and leave them to the judgment of God. And those who live in Hatra do not stone thieves. But in whatever place they are and wherever they may find themselves, the local laws cannot force them to give up the law of their Messiah, nor does the Fate of the Guiding Signs force them to do things that are unclean for them. But sickness and health, wealth and poverty, that which does not depend on their free will, comes over them wherever they are. As the liberty of mankind is not subject to the guidance of the Fate of these Seven, and when it is subjected to it, can oppose its influence, so neither can this man, as he offers himself to our view, immediately free himself from the power of his Guiding Signs, for he is a slave, and in subjection. For if we could do everything, we should be everything, but if nothing lay in our power to do, we should be instruments of others. Yet if God will, all things can take place without hindrance, for there is nothing that can withstand this great and holy will. Even they who think they can resist Him do not do so of their own strength, but from wickedness and error. Now this may last for a short time, because He is mild and allows all natures to exist in their own fashion and to live according to their own free will. But they are bound by the works that have been done and the ordinations that have been instituted for their sake. For this order and rule which is given, and the mingling of one with the other, restricts the force of the natural elements, that they might not become completely harmful nor completely harmed, as they caused and suffered harm before the creation of the world. But a time will come, when even the possibility of causing harm still existing with them will disappear through the doctrine which is founded on a different intermixture. In the condition of this new world all evil damaging influences will have ceased and all revolts will have ended; the foolish will be convinced and every lack supplied, and peace and perfect quiet will reign through the gift of the Lord of all natures.

Here ends the Book of the Laws of Countries.

PART TWO

300–600 C.E.

The Opening of the Constantinian Era: Conversion and Controversy

18. Eusebius of Caesarea, *Life of Constantine*

Though best known as the first major historian of the church, Bishop Euse-bius of Caesarea (ca. 260-ca. 339) was a biblical scholar, an apologist, a participant at the Council of Nicaea, and a theorist of imperial rule. His ideas on the relation of spiritual and temporal power and the role of the Christian emperor laid the foundations of Byzantine political theory. The following excerpts from his unfinished Life of Constantine *include his famous account of Constantine's conversion and the emperor's involvement in the Council of Nicaea.*

Book I
Chapter XI

That his present object is to record only the pious actions of Constantine.

It is my intention, therefore, to pass over the greater part of the royal deeds of this thrice-blessed prince; as, for example, his conflicts and engagements in the field, his personal valor, his victories and successes against the enemy, and the many triumphs he obtained: likewise his provisions for the interests of individuals, his legislative enactments for the social advantage of his subjects, and a multitude of other imperial labors which are fresh in the memory of all; the design of my present undertaking being to speak and write of those circumstances only which have reference to his religious character . . .

Chapter XII

That like Moses, he was reared in the palaces of kings.

Ancient history relates that a cruel race of tyrants oppressed the Hebrew nation; and that God, who graciously regarded them in their affliction, provided that the prophet Moses, who was then an infant, should be brought up in the very palaces and bosoms of the oppressors, and instructed in all the wisdom they possessed. And when in the course of time he had arrived at manhood, and the time was come for Divine justice to avenge the wrongs of the afflicted people, then the prophet of God, in obedience to the will of a more powerful Lord, forsook the royal household, and, estranging himself in word and deed from the tyrants by whom he had been brought up, openly

Source: *The Life of the Blessed Emperor Constantine by Eusebius Pamphilus,* tr. Ernest Cushing Richardson, in *A Select Library of Nicene and Post-Nicene Fathers of the Christian Church,* second series, vol. 1, ed. Philip Schaff and Henry Wace (New York: Christian Literature Publishing Company; Oxford and London: Parker & Company, 1890), 484-85, 487-88, 489-95, 511-12, 520-23.

acknowledging his true brethren and kinsfolk. Then God, exalting him to be the leader of the whole nation, delivered the Hebrews from the bondage of their enemies, and inflicted Divine vengeance through his means on the tyrant race . . . But now . . . the tyrants of our day have ventured to war against the Supreme God, and have sorely afflicted His Church. And in the midst of these, Constantine, who was shortly to become their destroyer, but at that time of tender age, and blooming with the down of early youth, dwelt, as that other servant of God had done, in the very home of the tyrants, but young as he was did not share the manner of life of the ungodly: for from that early period his noble nature, under the leading of the Divine Spirit, inclined him to piety and a life acceptable to God. A desire, moreover, to emulate the example of his father had its influence in stimulating the son to a virtuous course of conduct. His father was Constantius (and we ought to revive his memory at this time), the most illustrious emperor of our age; of whose life it is necessary briefly to relate a few particulars, which tell to the honor of his son.

Chapter XIII

Of Constantius his father, who refused to imitate Diocletian, Maximian, and Maxentius, in their persecution of the Christians.

At a time when four emperors shared the administration of the Roman empire, Constantius alone, following a course of conduct different from that pursued by his colleagues, entered into the friendship of the Supreme God. For while they besieged and wasted the churches of God, leveling them to the ground and obliterating the very foundations of the houses of prayer, he kept his hands pure from their abominable impiety, and never in any respect resembled them. They polluted their provinces by the indiscriminate slaughter of godly men and women; but he kept his soul free from the stain of this crime. They, involved in the mazes of impious idolatry, enthralled first themselves and then all under their authority, in bondage to the errors of evil demons, while he at the same time originated the pro-

foundest peace throughout his dominions, and secured to his subjects the privilege of celebrating without hindrance the worship of God. In short, while his colleagues oppressed all men by the most grievous exactions and rendered their lives intolerable, and even worse than death, Constantius alone governed his people with a mild and tranquil sway, and exhibited towards them a truly parental and fostering care. Numberless, indeed, are the other virtues of this man, which are the theme of praise to all . . .

Chapter XIX

Of his son Constantine, who in his youth accompanied Diocletian into Palestine.

[Constantine] had been with his father's imperial colleagues, and had passed his life among them, as we have said, like God's ancient prophet. And even in the very earliest period of his youth he was judged by them to be worthy of the highest honor. An instance of this we have ourselves seen, when he passed through Palestine with the senior emperor, at whose right hand he stood and commanded the admiration of all who beheld him by the indications he gave even then of royal greatness. For no one was comparable to him for grace and beauty of person, or height of stature; and he so far surpassed his compeers in personal strength as to be a terror to them. He was, however, even more conspicuous for the excellence of his mental qualities than for his superior physical endowments; being gifted in the first place with a sound judgment, and having also reaped the advantages of a liberal education. He was also distinguished in no ordinary degree both by natural intelligence and divinely imparted wisdom.

Chapter XXV

Victories of Constantine over the barbarians and the Britons.

As soon then as he was established on the throne, he began to care for the interests of his paternal inheritance, and visited with much considerate kindness all those provinces which had previously been under his father's government. Some tribes of the barbarians who dwelt on the banks of the Rhine and the shores of the western ocean having ventured to revolt, he reduced them all to obedience, and brought them from their savage state to one of gentleness. He contented himself with checking the inroads of others, and drove from his dominions, like untamed and savage beasts, those whom he perceived to be altogether incapable of the settled order of civilized life. Having disposed of these affairs to his satisfaction, he directed his attention to other quarters of the world and first passed over to the British nations, which lie in the very bosom of the ocean. These he reduced to submission, and then proceeded to consider the state of the remaining portions of the empire, that he might be ready to tender his aid wherever circumstances might require it.

Chapter XXVI

How he resolved to deliver Rome from Maxentius.

While, therefore, he regarded the entire world as one immense body, and perceived that the head of it all, the royal city of the Roman empire, was bowed down by the weight of a tyrannous oppression, at first he had left the task of liberation to those who governed the other divisions of the empire, as being his superiors in point of age. But when none of these proved able to afford relief, and those who had attempted it had experienced a disastrous termination of their enterprise, he said that life was without enjoyment to him as long as he saw the imperial city thus afflicted, and prepared himself for the overthrow of the tyranny.

Chapter XXVII

That after reflecting on the downfall of those who had worshiped idols, he made choice of Christianity.

Being convinced, however, that he needed some more powerful aid than his military forces could afford him, on account of the wicked and magical enchantments which were so diligently practiced by the tyrant, he sought Divine assistance, deeming the possession of arms and a numerous soldiery of secondary importance, but believing the cooperating power of Deity invincible and not to be shaken. He considered, therefore, on what God he might rely for protection and assistance. While engaged in this enquiry, the thought occurred to him that, of the many emperors who had preceded him, those who had rested their hopes in a multitude of gods and served them with sacrifices and offerings had in the first place been deceived by flattering predictions and oracles which promised them all prosperity, and at last had met with an unhappy end, while not one of their gods had stood by to warn them of the impending wrath of heaven; while one alone who had pursued an entirely opposite course, who had condemned their error, and honored the one Supreme God during his whole life, had found him to be the Savior and Protector of his empire, and the Giver of every good thing. Reflecting on this, and well weighing the fact that they who had trusted in many gods had also fallen by manifold forms of death, without leaving behind them either family or offspring, stock, name, or memorial among men: while the God of his father had given to him, on the other hand, manifestations of his power and very many tokens: and considering further that those who had already taken arms against the tyrant and had marched to the battlefield under the protection of a multitude of gods, had met with a dishonorable end; . . . reviewing, I say, all these considerations, he judged it to be folly indeed to join in the idle worship of those who were no gods, and, after such convincing evidence, to err from the truth; and therefore felt it incumbent on him to honor his father's God alone.

Chapter XXVIII

How, while he was praying, God sent him a vision of a cross of light in the heavens at midday, with an inscription admonishing him to conquer by that.

Accordingly he called on him with earnest prayer and supplications that he would reveal to him who he was, and stretch forth his right hand to help him in his present difficulties. And while he was thus praying with fervent entreaty, a most marvelous sign appeared to him from heaven, the account of which it might have been hard to believe had it been related by any other person. But since the victorious emperor himself long afterwards declared it to the writer of this history, when he was honored with his acquaintance and society, and confirmed his statement by an oath, who could hesitate to accredit the relation, especially since the testimony of after-time has established its truth? He said that about noon, when the day was already beginning to decline, he saw with his own eyes the trophy of a cross of light in the heavens, above the sun, and bearing the inscription, CONQUER BY THIS. At this sight he himself was struck with amazement, and his whole army also, which followed him on this expedition and witnessed the miracle.

Chapter XXIX

How the Christ of God appeared to him in his sleep, and commanded him to use in his wars a standard made in the form of the cross.

He said, moreover, that he doubted within himself what the import of this apparition could be. And while he continued to ponder and reason on its meaning, night suddenly came on; then in his sleep the Christ of God appeared to him with the same sign which he had seen in the heavens, and commanded him to make a likeness of that sign which he had seen in the heavens, and to use it as a safeguard in all engagements with his enemies.

Chapter XXX

The making of the standard of the cross.

At dawn of day he arose and communicated the marvel to his friends: and then, calling together the workers in gold and precious stones, he sat in the midst of them and described to them the figure of the sign he had seen, bidding them represent it in gold and precious stones. And this representation I myself have had an opportunity of seeing.

Chapter XXXI

A description of the standard of the cross, which the Romans now call the Labarum.

Now it was made in the following manner. A long spear, overlaid with gold, formed the figure of the cross by means of a transverse bar laid over it. On the top of the whole was fixed a wreath of gold and precious stones; and within this, the symbol of the Savior's name, two letters indicating the name of Christ by means of its initial characters, the letter P being intersected by X in its center: and these letters the emperor was in the habit of wearing on his helmet at a later period. From the cross-bar of the spear was suspended a cloth, a royal piece, covered with a profuse embroidery of most brilliant precious stones; and which, being also richly interlaced with gold, presented an indescribable degree of beauty to the beholder. This banner was of a square form, and the upright staff, whose lower section was of great length, bore a golden half-length portrait of the pious emperor and his children on its upper part, beneath the trophy of the cross and immediately above the embroidered banner. The emperor constantly made use of this sign of salvation as a safeguard against every adverse and hostile power, and commanded that others similar to it should be carried at the head of all his armies.

Chapter XXXII

How Constantine received instruction, and read the Sacred Scriptures.

These things were done shortly afterwards. But at the time above specified, being struck with amazement at the extraordinary vision, and resolving to worship no other God save Him who had appeared to him, he sent for those who were acquainted with the mysteries of His doctrines, and enquired who that God was, and what was intended by the sign of the vision he had seen.

They affirmed that He was God, the only begotten Son of the one and only God: that the sign which had appeared was the symbol of immortality and the trophy of that victory over death which He had gained in time past when sojourning on earth. They taught him also the causes of His advent and explained to him the true account of His incarnation. Thus he was instructed in these matters, and was impressed with wonder at the divine manifestation which had been presented to his sight. Comparing, therefore, the heavenly vision with the interpretation given, he found his judgment confirmed; and, in the persuasion that the knowledge of these things had been imparted to him by Divine teaching, he determined thenceforth to devote himself to the reading of the inspired writings.

Moreover, he made the priests of God his counselors and deemed it incumbent on him to honor the God who had appeared to him with all devotion. And after this, being fortified by well-grounded hopes in Him, he hastened to quench the threatening fire of tyranny.

Chapter XXXIII

Of the adulterous conduct of Maxentius at Rome.

For he who had tyrannically possessed himself of the imperial city had proceeded to great lengths in impiety and wickedness, so as to venture without hesitation on every vile and impure action.

For example: he would separate women from their husbands, and after a time send them back to them again, and these insults he offered not to men of mean or obscure condition, but to those who held the first places in the Roman senate. Moreover, though he shamefully dishonored almost numberless free women, he was unable to satisfy his ungoverned and intemperate desires. But when he assayed to corrupt Christian women also, he could no longer secure success to his designs, since they chose rather to submit their lives to death than yield their persons to be defiled by him.

Chapter XXXV

Massacre of the Roman people by Maxentius.

All men, therefore, both people and magistrates, whether of high or low degree, trembled through fear of him whose daring wickedness was such as I have described, and were oppressed by his grievous tyranny. Nay, though they submitted quietly and endured this bitter servitude, still there was no escape from the tyrant's sanguinary cruelty. For at one time, on some trifling pretense, he exposed the populace to be slaughtered by his own bodyguard; and countless multitudes of the Roman people were slain in the very midst of the city by the lances and weapons, not of Scythians or barbarians, but of their own fellow citizens. And besides this, it is impossible to calculate the number of senators whose blood was shed with a view to the seizure of their respective estates, for at different times and on various fictitious charges, multitudes of them suffered death.

Chapter XXXVI

Magic arts of Maxentius against Constantine; and famine at Rome.

But the crowning point of the tyrant's wickedness was his having recourse to sorcery: sometimes for magic purposes ripping up women with child, at other times searching into the bowels of newborn infants. He slew lions also and practiced certain horrid arts for evoking demons, and averting the approaching war, hoping by these means to get the victory. In short, it is impossible to describe the manifold acts of oppression by which this tyrant of Rome enslaved his subjects: so that by this time they were reduced to the most extreme penury and want of necessary food, a scarcity such as our contemporaries do not remember ever before to have existed at Rome.

Chapter XXXVII

Defeat of Maxentius's armies in Italy.

Constantine, however, filled with compassion on account of all these miseries, began to arm himself with all warlike preparation against the tyranny. Assuming therefore the Supreme God as his patron, and invoking His Christ to be his preserver and aid, and setting the victorious trophy, the salutary symbol, in front of his soldiers and bodyguard, he marched with his whole forces, trying to obtain again for the Romans the freedom they had inherited from their ancestors.

And whereas, Maxentius, trusting more in his magic arts than in the affection of his subjects, dared not even advance outside the city gates, but had guarded every place and district and city subject to his tyranny with large bodies of soldiers, the emperor, confiding in the help of God, advanced against the first and second and third divisions of the tyrant's forces, defeated them all with ease at the first assault, and made his way into the very interior of Italy.

Chapter XXXVIII

Death of Maxentius on the bridge of the Tiber.

And already he was approaching very near Rome itself, when, to save him from the necessity of fighting with all the Romans for the tyrant's sake, God himself drew the tyrant, as it were by secret cords, a long way outside the gates. And now those miracles recorded in Holy Writ, which God of old wrought against the ungodly (discredited by most as fables, yet believed by the faithful), did he in every deed confirm to all alike, believers and unbelievers, who were eyewitnesses of the wonders. For as once in the days of Moses and the Hebrew nation, who were worshipers of God, "Pharaoh's chariots and his host hath he cast into the sea and his chosen chariot-captains are drowned in the Red Sea"—so at this time Maxentius, and the soldiers and guards with him, "went down into the depths like stone," when, in his flight before the divinely aided forces of Constantine, he essayed to cross the river which lay in his way, over which, making a strong bridge of boats, he had framed an engine of destruction, really against himself, but in the hope of ensnaring thereby him who was beloved by God. For his God stood by the one to protect him, while the other, godless, proved to be the miserable contriver of these secret devices to his own ruin. So that one might well say, "He hath made a pit, and digged it, and is fallen into the ditch which he made. His mischief shall return upon his own head, and his violence shall come down upon his own pate." Thus, in the present instance, under divine direction, the machine erected on the bridge, with the ambuscade concealed therein, giving way unexpectedly before the appointed time, the bridge began to sink, and the boats with the men in them went bodily to the bottom. And first the wretch himself, then his armed attendants and guards, even as the sacred oracles had before described, "sank as lead in the mighty waters." So that they who thus obtained victory from God might well, if not in the same words, yet in fact in the same spirit as the people of his great servant Moses, sing and speak as they did concerning the impious tyrant of old: "Let us sing unto the Lord, for he has been glorified exceedingly: the horse and his rider hath he thrown into the sea. He is become my helper and my shield unto salvation." And again, "Who is like unto you, O Lord, among the gods? Who is like you, glorious in holiness, marvelous in praises, doing wonders?"

Chapter XXXIX

Constantine's entry into Rome.

Having then at this time sung these and such-like praises to God, the Ruler of all and the Author of victory, after the example of his great servant Moses, Constantine entered the imperial city in triumph. And here the whole body of the senate, and others of rank and distinction in the city, freed as it were from the restraint of a prison, along with the whole Roman populace, their countenances expressive of the gladness of their hearts, received him with acclamations and abounding joy; men, women, and children, with countless multitudes of servants, greeting him as deliverer, preserver, and benefactor, with incessant shouts. But he, being possessed of inward piety toward God, was neither rendered arrogant by these plaudits, nor uplifted by the praises he heard: but, being sensible that he had received help from God, he immediately rendered a thanksgiving to him as the Author of his victory.

Chapter XL

Of the statue of Constantine holding a cross, and its inscription.

Moreover, by loud proclamation and monumental inscriptions he made known to all men the salutary symbol, setting up this great trophy of victory over his enemies in the midst of the imperial city, and expressly causing it to be engraved in indelible characters, that the salutary symbol was the safeguard of the Roman government and of the entire empire. Accordingly, he immediately ordered a lofty spear in the figure of a cross to be placed beneath the hand of a statue representing himself, in the most frequented part of Rome, and the following inscription to be engraved on it in the Latin language: BY VIRTUE OF THIS SALUTARY SIGN, WHICH IS THE TRUE TEST OF VALOR, I HAVE PRESERVED AND LIBERATED YOUR CITY FROM THE YOKE OF TYRANNY. I HAVE ALSO SET AT LIBERTY THE ROMAN SENATE AND PEOPLE, AND RESTORED THEM TO THEIR ANCIENT DISTINCTION AND SPLENDOR.

Chapter XLI

Rejoicings throughout the provinces; and Constantine's acts of grace.

Thus the pious emperor, glorying in the confession of the victorious cross, proclaimed the Son of God to the Romans with great boldness of testimony. And the inhabitants of the city, one and all, senate and people, reviving, as it were, from the pressure of a bitter and tyrannical domination, seemed to enjoy purer rays of light and to be born again into a fresh and new life. All the nations, too, as far as the limit of the western ocean, being set free from the calamities which had heretofore beset them, and gladdened by joyous festivals, ceased not to praise him as the victorious, the pious, the common benefactor: all, indeed, with one voice and one mouth, declared that Constantine had appeared by the grace of God as a general blessing to humanity. The imperial edict also was everywhere published, whereby those who had been wrongfully deprived of their estates were permitted again to enjoy their own, while those who had unjustly suffered exile were recalled to their homes. Moreover, he freed from imprisonment and from every kind of danger and fear those who, by reason of the tyrant's cruelty, had been subject to these sufferings.

Chapter XLII

The honors conferred upon bishops, and the building of churches.

The emperor also personally inviting the society of God's ministers, distinguished them with the highest possible respect and honor, showing them favor in deed and word as persons consecrated to the service of his God. Accordingly, they were admitted to his table, though mean in their attire and outward appearance; yet not so in his estimation, since he thought he saw not the man as seen by the vulgar eye, but the God in him. He made them also his companions in travel, believing that He whose servants they were would thus help him. Besides this, he gave from his own private resources costly benefactions to the churches of God, both enlarging and heightening the sacred edifices, and embellishing the august sanctuaries of the church with abundant offerings.

Chapter XLIII

Constantine's liberality to the poor.

He likewise distributed money largely to those who were in need, and besides these showing himself philanthropist and benefactor even to the heathen, who had no claim on him; and even for the beggars in the forum, miserable and shiftless, he provided, not with money only, or necessary food, but also decent clothing. But in the case of those who had once been prosperous and had experienced a reverse of circumstances, his aid was still more lavishly bestowed. On such persons, in a truly royal spirit, he conferred magnificent benefactions, giving grants of land to some and honoring others with various dignities. Orphans of the unfortunate he cared for as a father, while he relieved the destitution of widows and cared for them with special solicitude. Nay, he even gave virgins left unprotected by their parents' death, in marriage to wealthy men with whom he was personally acquainted. But this he did after first bestowing on the brides such portions as it was fitting they should bring to the communion of marriage . . .

Chapter XLIV

How he was present at the synods of bishops.

Such, then, was his general character towards all. But he exercised a peculiar care over the church of God: and whereas, in the several provinces, there were some who differed from each other in judgment, he, like some general bishop constituted by God, convened synods of his ministers. Nor did he disdain to be present and sit with them in their assembly, but bore a share in their deliberations, ministering to all that pertained to the peace of God. He took his seat, too, in the midst of them, as an individual amongst many, dismissing his guards and soldiers, and all whose duty it was to defend his person; but protected by the fear of God and surrounded by the guardianship of his faithful friends. Those whom he saw inclined to a sound judgment, and exhibiting a calm and conciliatory temper, received his high approbation, for he evidently delighted in a general harmony of sentiment, while he regarded the unyielding with aversion.

Chapter XLV

His forbearance with unreasonable men.

Moreover he endured with patience some who were exasperated against him, directing them in mild and gentle terms to control themselves, and not be turbulent. And some of these respected his admonitions and desisted; but as to those who proved incapable of sound judgment, he left them entirely at the disposal of God, and never himself desired harsh measures against anyone . . .

Chapter XLVI

Victories over the barbarians.

Thus the emperor in all his actions honored God, the Controller of all things, and exercised an unwearied oversight over His churches. And God requited him, by subduing all barbarous nations under his feet, so that he was able everywhere to raise trophies over his enemies: and He proclaimed him as conqueror to all humankind, and made him a terror to his adversaries—not indeed that this was his natural character, since he was rather the meekest, and gentlest, and most benevolent of men . . .

Book II

Chapter XLIV

That he promoted Christians to offices of government, and forbade Gentiles in such stations to offer sacrifice.

After this the emperor continued to address himself to matters of high importance, and first he sent governors to the several provinces, mostly such as were devoted to the saving faith; and if any appeared inclined to adhere to Gentile worship, he forbade them to offer sacrifice. This law applied also to those who surpassed the provincial governors in rank and dignity, and even to those who occupied the highest station and held the authority of the Praetorian Prefecture. If they were Christians, they were free to act consistently with their profession; if otherwise, the law required them to abstain from idolatrous sacrifices.

Chapter XLV

Statutes which forbade sacrifice and enjoined the building of churches.

Soon after this, two laws were promulgated about the same time; one of which was intended to restrain the idolatrous abominations which in time past had been practiced in every city and country; and it provided that no one should erect images, or practice divination and other false and foolish arts, or offer sacrifice in any way. The other statute commanded the heightening of the oratories and the enlargement in length and breadth of the churches of God; as though it were expected that, now the madness of polytheism was wholly removed, pretty nearly all people would henceforth attach themselves to the service of God. His own personal piety induced the emperor to devise and write these instructions to the governors of the several provinces: and the law further admonished them not to spare the expenditure of money, but to draw supplies from the imperial treasury itself. Similar instructions were written also to the bishops of the several churches; and the emperor was pleased to transmit the same to myself, being the first letter which he personally addressed to me.

Chapter XLVII

That he wrote a letter in condemnation of idolatry.

Moreover, the emperor, who continually made progress in piety towards God, dispatched an admonitory letter to the inhabitants of every province, respecting the error of idolatry into which his predecessors in power had fallen, in which he eloquently exhorts his subjects to acknowledge the Supreme God and openly to profess their allegiance to his Christ as their Savior . . .

Book III

Chapter IV

A further notice of the controversies raised in Egypt by Arius.

In such occupations as these he employed himself with pleasure: but the effects of that envious spirit which so troubled the peace of the churches of God in Alexandria, together with the Theban and Egyptian schism, continued to cause him no little disturbance of mind. For in fact, in every city bishops were engaged in obstinate conflict with bishops, and people rising against people, and almost like the fabled Symplegades, coming into violent collision with each other. Nay, some were so far transported beyond the bounds of reason as to be guilty of reckless and outrageous conduct, and even to insult the statues of the emperor. This state of things had little power to excite his anger, but rather caused in him sorrow of spirit; for he deeply deplored the folly thus exhibited by deranged people.

Chapter V

. . . For as soon as he was made acquainted with the facts which I have described, and perceived that his letter to the Alexandrian Christians had failed to produce its due effect, he at once aroused the energies of his mind and declared that he must prosecute to the utmost this war also against the secret adversary who was disturbing the peace of the Church.

Chapter VI

How he ordered a council to be held at Nicaea.

Then, as if to bring a divine array against this enemy, he convoked a general council and invited the speedy attendance of bishops from all quarters, in letters expressive of the honorable estimation in which he held them. Nor was this merely the issuing of a bare command, but the emperor's good will contributed much to its being carried into effect: for he allowed some the use of the public means of conveyance, while he afforded to others an ample supply of horses for their transport. The place, too, selected for the synod, the city Nicaea in Bithynia (named from "Victory"), was appropriate to the occasion. As soon then as the imperial injunction was generally made known, all with the utmost willingness hastened thither, as though they would outstrip one another in a race; for they were impelled by the anticipation of a happy result to the conference, by the hope of enjoying present peace, and the desire of beholding something new and strange in the person of so admirable an emperor. Now when they were all assembled, it appeared evident that the proceeding was the work of God, inasmuch as those who had been most widely separated, not merely in sentiment but also personally, and by difference of country, place, and nation, were here brought together, and comprised within the walls of a single city, forming as it were a vast garland of priests, composed of a variety of the choicest flowers.

Chapter VII

Of the general council, at which bishops from all nations were present.

In effect, the most distinguished of God's ministers from all the churches which abounded in Europe, Lybia, and Asia were here assembled. And a single house of prayer, as though divinely enlarged, sufficed to contain at once Syrians and Cilicians, Phoenicians and Arabians, delegates from Palestine, and others from Egypt; Thebans and Libyans, with those who came from the region of Mesopotamia. A Persian bishop too was present at this conference, nor was even a Scythian found wanting to the number. Pontus, Galatia, and Pamphylia, Cappadocia, Asia, and Phrygia, furnished their most distinguished prelates, while those who dwelt in the remotest districts of Thrace and Macedonia, of Achaia and Epirus, were notwithstanding in attendance. Even from Spain itself, one whose fame was widely spread took his seat as an individual in the great assembly. The prelate of the imperial city was prevented from attending by extreme old age; but his presbyters were present and supplied his place. Constantine is the first prince of any age who bound together such a garland as this with the bond of peace and presented it to his Savior as a thank-offering for the victories he had obtained over every foe, thus exhibiting in our own times a similitude of the apostolic company.

Chapter X

Council in the palace. Constantine, entering, took his seat in the assembly.

Now when the appointed day arrived on which the council met for the final solution of the questions in dispute, each member was present for this in the central building of the palace, which appeared to exceed the rest in magnitude. On each side of the interior of this were many seats disposed in order, which were occupied by those who had been invited to attend, according to their rank. As soon, then, as the whole assembly had seated themselves with becoming orderliness, a general silence prevailed, in expectation of the emperor's arrival. And first of all, three of his immediate fam-

ily entered in succession, then others also preceded his approach, not of the soldiers or guards who usually accompanied him, but only friends in the faith. And now, all rising at the signal which indicated the emperor's entrance, at last he himself proceeded through the midst of the assembly, like some heavenly messenger of God, clothed in raiment which glittered as it were with rays of light, reflecting the glowing radiance of a purple robe and adorned with the brilliant splendor of gold and precious stones. Such was the external appearance of his person; and with regard to his mind, it was evident that he was distinguished by piety and godly fear. This was indicated by his downcast eyes, the blush on his countenance, and his gait. For the rest of his personal excellencies, he surpassed all present in height of stature and beauty of form, as well as in majestic dignity of mien, and invincible strength and vigor. All these graces, united to a suavity of manner, and a serenity becoming his imperial station, declared the excellence of his mental qualities to be above all praise. As soon as he had advanced to the upper end of the seats, at first he remained standing, and when a low chair of wrought gold had been set for him, he waited until the bishops had beckoned to him, and then sat down, and after him the whole assembly did the same.

Chapter XI

Silence of the council, after some words by the bishop Eusebius.

The bishop who occupied the chief place in the right division of the assembly then rose, and, addressing the emperor, delivered a concise speech, in a strain of thanksgiving to Almighty God on his behalf. When he had resumed his seat, silence ensued, and all regarded the emperor with fixed attention, on which he looked serenely round on the assembly with a cheerful aspect and, having collected his thoughts, in a calm and gentle tone gave utterance to the following words:

Chapter XII

"It was once my chief desire, dearest friends, to enjoy the spectacle of your united presence; and now that this desire is fulfilled, I feel myself bound to render thanks to God the universal King, because, in addition to all his other benefits, he has granted me a blessing higher than all the rest, in permitting me to see you not only all assembled together, but all united in a common harmony of sentiment. I pray therefore that no malignant adversary may henceforth interfere to mar our happy state; I pray that, now the impious hostility of the tyrants has been forever removed by the power of God our Savior, that spirit who delights in evil may devise no other means for exposing the divine law to blasphemous calumny; for, in my judgment, intestine strife within the Church of God, is far more evil and dangerous than any kind of war or conflict; and these our differences appear to me more grievous than any outward trouble. Accordingly, when, by the will and with the cooperation of God, I had been victorious over my enemies, I thought that nothing more remained but to render thanks to him, and sympathize in the joy of those whom he had restored to freedom through my instrumentality; as soon as I heard that intelligence which I had least expected to receive, I mean the news of your dissension, I judged it to be of no secondary importance, but with the earnest desire that a remedy for this evil also might be found through my means, I immediately sent to require your presence. And now I rejoice in beholding your assembly; but I feel that my desires will be most completely fulfilled when I can see you all united in one judgment, and that common spirit of peace and concord prevailing amongst you all, which it becomes you, as consecrated to the service of God, to commend to others. Delay not, then, dear friends: delay not, ye ministers of God, and faithful servants of him who is our common Lord and Savior: begin from this moment to discard the causes of that disunion which has existed among you, and remove the perplexities of controversy by embracing the principles of peace. For by such conduct you will at the same time be acting in a manner most pleasing to the supreme God, and you will confer an exceeding favor on me who am your fellow servant."

Chapter XIII

How he led the dissentient bishops to harmony of sentiment.

As soon as the emperor had spoken these words in the Latin tongue, which another interpreted, he gave permission to those who presided in the council to deliver their opinions. On this some began to accuse their neighbors, who defended themselves, and recriminated in their turn. In this manner numberless assertions were put forth by each party, and a violent controversy arose at the very commencement. Notwithstanding this, the emperor gave patient audience to all alike, and received every proposition with steadfast attention, and by occasionally assisting the argument of each party in turn, he gradually disposed even the most vehement disputants to a reconciliation. At the same time, by the affability of his address to all, and his use of the Greek language, with which he was not altogether unacquainted, he appeared in a truly attractive and amiable light, persuading some, convincing others by his reasonings, praising those who spoke well, and urging all to unity of sentiment, until at last he succeeded in bringing them to one mind and judgment respecting every disputed question.

Chapter XIV

Unanimous declaration of the council concerning faith, and the celebration of Easter.

The result was that they were not only united as concerning the faith, but that the time for the celebration of the salutary feast of Easter was agreed on by all. Those points also which were sanctioned by the resolution of the whole body were committed to writing and received the signature of each several member. Then the emperor, believing that he had thus obtained a second victory over the adversary of the Church, proceeded to solemnize a triumphal festival in honor of God.

19. Letters of Arius and Alexander of Alexandria

Alexander of Alexandria (d. 328) was bishop of the same see where Arius (ca. 260-336) served as a presbyter. When Arius persisted in teaching that Christ was not eternal but created by God, Alexander condemned his views at a local synod of bishops (ca. 319) and excommunicated him along with several of his followers. In the following letters, Arius and Alexander present their respective positions in the dispute that would soon be taken up at the Council of Nicaea.

Arius's Letter to Alexander of Alexandria

(1) The presbyters and deacons send greetings in the Lord to our blessed pope and bishop, Alexander.

(2) Our faith, from our ancestors, which we have learned also from you, is this. We know one God—alone unbegotten, alone everlasting, alone without beginning, alone true, alone possessing immortality, alone wise, alone good, alone master, judge of all, manager, director, immutable and unchangeable, just and good, God of Law, Prophets, and New Testament—who begot an only begotten Son before eternal times, through whom he made the ages and everything. But he begot him not in appearance but in truth, having submitted him to his own will, an immutable and unchangeable perfect creature of God, (3) but not as one of the creatures—an offspring, but not as one of those born—nor as Valentinus decreed that the offspring of the Father is an emanation, nor as Manes propounded that the offspring of the Father is part of the same substance, nor as Sabellius, who divides the monad, says "Father-and-Son," nor as Hieracas believes a light from a light as a lamp divided into two; nor is he the one who was before, later begotten or created into a Son as you yourself also, Blessed Pope, very often have forbidden throughout the midst of the church and in council those who teach these things. But, as we say, he was created by the will of God before times and ages, and he received life, being, and glories from the Father as the Father has shared them with him. (4) For the Father, having given to him the inheritance of all, did not deprive himself of those things which he has in himself without generation, for he is the source of all. Thus there are three *hypostases*. God being the cause of all is without beginning, most alone; but the Son, begotten by the Father, created and founded before the ages, was not before he was begotten. Rather, the Son, begotten timelessly before everything, alone was caused to subsist by the Father. For he is not everlasting or co-everlasting or unbegotten with the Father. Nor does he have being with the Father, as certain individuals mention things relatively and bring into the discussion two unbegotten causes. But God is thus before all as a monad and cause. Therefore he is also before the Son, as we have learned from you when you preached throughout the midst of the church.

(5) Therefore, insofar as he has from God being, glories, and life, and all things have been handed over to him, thus God is his cause. For he, as his God and being before him, rules him. But if "from him" [Rom. 11:36] and "from the womb" [Ps. 110:3] and "I came from the Father and I come" [John 16:28] are thought by some to signify that he is a part of him and an emanation, the Father will be according to them compounded,

SOURCE: *The Trinitarian Controversy*, ed. and tr. William G. Rusch (Philadelphia: Fortress Press, 1980), 31-32, 33-37. Copyright © 1979 by Fortress Press. Used by permission of Augsburg Fortress.

divided, mutable and a body, and, as far as they are concerned, the incorporeal God suffers things suitable to the body.

I pray that you are well in the Lord, Blessed Pope.

Arius, Aeithales, Achillas, Carpones, Sarmates, and Arius—presbyters.

Euzoius, Lucius, Julius, Menas, Helladius, Gaius—deacons.

Bishops Secundus of Pentapolis, Theonas of Libya, and Pistus.

Alexander of Alexandria's Letter to Alexander of Thessalonica

To Alexander, a most honored brother united in the soul, Alexander sends greetings in the Lord.

(1) The ambitious and covetous calculation of rascally men has produced plots against the apparently greater dioceses. Through intricate pretenses such individuals are attacking the orthodox faith of the church. Driven wild by the devil at work in them for pleasures at hand, they skipped away from every piety and trampled on the fear of God's judgment. (2) It was necessary for me who am suffering to make clear to Your Reverence these matters so that you might be on guard against such persons, lest some of them dare to come even into your dioceses, either through themselves (for cheats are equal to dissemble for deceit) or through basely refined rescripts, which are able to snatch away a person intent on a simple and pure faith.

(3) At any rate, Arius and Achillas have just now entered into a conspiracy, and they have revealed the covetousness of Colluthus, to a much worse degree than even he himself. For Colluthus in bringing charges against them found an excuse for his own ambitious course of action. But they, when they saw him making Christ a source of gain, were not patient to remain as subjects of the church; after constructing for themselves robbers' caves, they held in them incessant assemblies, slandering Christ and us by night and day. (4) They denounced every pious apostolic doctrine; they organized in a Jewish manner a work group contending against Christ. They deny the

divinity of our Savior, and proclaim him equal to all. Singling out every expression of his economy for salvation and of his humiliation for our sake, they attempt from them to bring together the proclamation of their own impiety, and from the beginning they turn away from expressions of his divinity and from words of his indescribable glory with the Father. (5) Confirming the impious doctrine of the Greeks and Jews about Christ, as much as possible they pursue praise for themselves. They undertake all those things for which others laugh at us, arousing daily strife and persecutions. They organize this court action through an accusation of disorderly women, whom they have led into error. They are tearing Christianity into pieces by the indecent running around of their young women on every street. The seamless robe of Christ which the executioners resolved not to divide, they dared to split. (6) Therefore, after we understood what was befitting their life and unholy attempt—and we did this slowly because it was concealed—we expelled them altogether from the church that worships Christ's divinity.

(9) Concealing their ruinous teaching with sermons that are too persuasive and of low quality, they seize the person involved in deceit. They do not even desist from slandering our orthodox faith in the presence of everyone. So it happens that certain persons subscribing to their writings admit them into the church. I think that the great slander belongs to our fellow ministers who allow this—for the apostolic rule does not assent to this—who thereby inflame slanderous action against Christ by those who oppose us.

(10) For this reason, with no delay, I aroused myself, beloved, to make clear to you the unbelief of those who say, "There was once when the Son of God was not" and "He who before was not, later came into existence; and when he came into existence, he became as every human being is by nature." They say, "For God made all things from nothing," including even the Son of God with the creation of all rational and irrational creatures. In accord with this, they even say that he is of a mutable nature, capable of both virtue and evil, and with their supposition "from nothing" they destroy the divine Scriptures' witness that he always is, which Scriptures indicate the

immutability of the Word and the divinity of the Wisdom of the Word, which is Christ. The wretches state, "Then we too are able to become sons of God, just as he." For it was written, "I have begotten and raised up sons" [Isa. 1:2]. (12) And when they add the statement from the text "But they rejected me," which does not belong to the nature of the Savior, who is of an immutable nature, they abandon every reverence. They say that God, knowing about him by foreknowledge and prevision, would not reject him and chose him from all. (13) For he does not have by nature something special from other sons (for they say that no one is by nature Son of God), nor does he have some distinctive property in relation to God, but he, being of a mutable nature, because of the diligence of his manners and not rejecting his training for the inferior status—he was chosen. (14) As if both a Paul and a Peter would persist at improvement, then their sonship would differ in no way from his. To explain this crazy teaching, they act insultingly toward Scripture and propose the passage in the Psalms about Christ which reads, "You have loved righteousness and hated injustice; on account of this, God, your God, anointed you with the oil of great joy beyond your partners" [Ps. 45:7].

(15) Therefore, concerning the fact that the Son of God came into existence from nothing and that not was there once when he is not, John the evangelist instructed sufficiently, writing about him, "the only-begotten Son who is in the bosom of the Father" [John 1:18]. For the divine teacher in foresight shows that the two things, the Father and the Son, are inseparable from one another. There he specified that he is in the bosom of the Father. (16) And in regard to the fact that the Word of God is not numbered with those who come into existence from nothing, the same John declares that all things came into existence through him [John 1:3]. For John makes clear the Word's distinctive *hypostasis*, saying, "In the beginning was the Word and the Word was with God and the Word was God. All things came into existence through him, and without him nothing came into existence" [John 1:1, 3]. (17) If all things came into existence through him, how is it that he who gave being to the ones who came into

existence once was not? For the Word, that which makes, is not defined so as to be of the same nature as those who came into existence, if he was in the beginning and all things came into existence through him and he made them from nothing. (18) For that which is and is exceedingly aloof seems opposite to those who came into existence from nothing. (19) This shows that no distance exists between the Father and Son, and that the soul is not able, as far as any thought is concerned, to form an image of this relationship of Father and Son. But the fact that the universe was fashioned from nothing has a newer *hypostasis* and a fresh origin, since all things received such origination by the Father through the Son. Since the most orthodox John saw that "was" is far from the Word of God and raised high beyond the thought of originated things, he would not speak of the Word's origin and creation, and he did not dare to specify in equivalent syllables the maker with those who came into existence—and not because the Son is unbegotten, for the Father is the one unbegotten, but because the indescribable *hypostasis* of the only-begotten God is beyond the sharpened apprehension of the evangelists, and perhaps of the angels. I do not think that those persons who dare to inquire about this, as far as these matters, give thought for the orthodox faith, because they are not willing to hear "Seek not that which is too difficult for you, and do not inquire about that which is too high for you" [Ecclus. 3:21]. (20) For if the knowledge of many things incomparably more imperfect than this is hidden with regard to human apprehension—such thoughts are in Paul "which things God has prepared for those who love him, eye knew not and ear heard not, and have not entered into the heart of man" [1 Cor. 2:9], and God said to Abraham that the stars are not able to be counted [Gen. 15:5], and still he says, "The sands of the sea and drops of rains, who will count them?" [Ecclus. 1:2]—how does anyone meddle with the *hypostasis* of the Word of God unless he happens to be seized with a melancholic disposition? (21) Concerning this, the prophetic Spirit says, "Who will describe his generation?" [Isa. 53:8]. Thus even our Savior himself, in showing kindness to those who were the pillars of the whole world, was eager to rid them of the knowledge of this knowledge. Therefore he said to all of them that it was beyond nature for them to apprehend this, and that the knowledge of this most divine mystery is the Father's alone. He said, "No one knows who the Son is except the Father, and no one knows the Father except the Son" [Matt. 11:27]. I think that concerning this the Father said, "My mystery is for me" [Isa. 24:16]. (22) But the phrase "from nothing" shows at once that it is crazy to think that the Son came into existence from nothing with the temporal purpose. This is true even if silly individuals are ignorant of the madness of their own

voice. The expression "he was not" is necessarily in reference either to time or to some interval of the age. (23) Therefore it is true that all things came into existence through him; it is clear that every age, time, interval, and "when," in which the expression "he was not" is found, came into existence through him. How is it not incredible to say that once he was not, he who made times, ages, and seasons, with which "he was not" is united? It is incomprehensible and totally ignorant to state that the cause of anything having come into existence is itself later than its generation.

20. The Nicene Creed and the Niceno-Constantinopolitan Creed

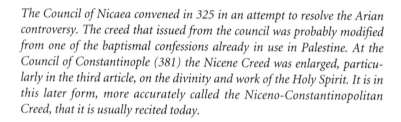

The Council of Nicaea convened in 325 in an attempt to resolve the Arian controversy. The creed that issued from the council was probably modified from one of the baptismal confessions already in use in Palestine. At the Council of Constantinople (381) the Nicene Creed was enlarged, particularly in the third article, on the divinity and work of the Holy Spirit. It is in this later form, more accurately called the Niceno-Constantinopolitan Creed, that it is usually recited today.

The Nicene Creed (325 C.E.)

We believe in one God, the Father Almighty, maker of all things visible and invisible; and in one Lord Jesus Christ, the Son of God, the only-begotten of his Father, of the substance of the Father, God of God, Light of Light, very God of very God, begotten, not made, being of one substance with the Father. By whom all things were made, both which be in heaven and in earth. Who for us men and for our salvation came down [from heaven] and was incarnate and was made man. He suffered and the third day he rose again, and ascended into heaven. And he shall come again to judge both the quick and the dead. And [we believe] in the Holy

Ghost. And whosoever shall say that there was a time when the Son of God was not, or that before he was begotten he was not, or that he was made of things that were not, or that he is of a different substance or essence [from the Father] or that he is a creature, or subject to change or conversion all that so say, the Catholic and Apostolic Church anathematizes them.

The Creed of Constantinople (381 C.E.)

We believe in one God, the Father Almighty, maker of heaven and earth and of all things visible and invisible. And in one Lord Jesus Christ, the only begotten Son of God, begotten of his Father

SOURCE: *A Select Library of Nicene and Post-Nicene Fathers of the Christian Church,* second series, vol. 14, ed. Philip Schaff and Henry Wace (New York: Charles Scribner's Sons; Oxford and London: Parker & Company, 1900), 2, 163.

before all worlds, Light of Light, very God of very God, begotten not made, being of one substance with the Father, by whom all things were made. Who for us men and for our salvation came down from heaven and was incarnate by the Holy Ghost and the Virgin Mary and was made man, and was crucified also for us under Pontius Pilate. He suffered and was buried, and the third day he rose again according to the Scriptures, and ascended into heaven, and sits at the right Hand of the Father. And he shall come again with glory to judge both the quick and the dead. Whose kingdom shall have no end.

And [we believe] in the Holy Ghost, the Lord and Giver-of-Life, who proceeds from the Father, who with the Father and the Son together is worshipped and glorified, who spoke by the prophets. And [we believe] in one, holy, Catholic and Apostolic Church. We acknowledge one Baptism for the remission of sins, [and] we look for the resurrection of the dead and the life of the world to come. Amen.

21. Auxentius of Durostorum, *Letter on the Life and Work of Ulfila, Apostle of the Goths*

Ulfila (sometimes written Wulfilas) (ca. 311-ca. 383) was a bishop of the Goths and translator of the Bible into the Gothic language. Consecrated by the Arian bishop Eusebius of Nicomedia, Ulfila ministered to Goths along the lower Danube and was later invited by Emperor Constantius II to settle his followers in Moesia in the Roman Empire. In this letter, Ulfila's disciple Auxentius describes the life and missionary work of his mentor. He ends with Ulfila's Arian creed. (Gaps in the text, rather than editorial abridgments, account for the numerous omissions here.)

23. And that the aforesaid bishops [*sc.* Palladius and Secundianus] also came to the east with bishop Ulfila, to the court of Theodosius, the following letter testifies [. . .].

24. [. . .] a man of great (spiritual) beauty, truly a confessor of Christ, teacher of piety and preacher of truth. To those who wished to hear and to those who did not, he never shrank from preaching quite openly and without any room for doubt one single true God, the father of Christ according to the teaching of Christ himself [cf. John 17:1-3]; knowing this one true God alone to be unbegotten, without beginning, without end, eternal, heavenly, sublime, sublime, above all others, the highest originator, excelling all excellence, better than all goodness, without limit, beyond comprehension, invisible, immeasurable, immortal, incorruptible, incorporeal, incomposite, simple, immutable, indivisible, immovable, needful of nothing, inaccessible, an inseparable unity, subject to no sovereign, not created, not made, perfect, existing in unique singularity, incomparably greater and better than all things.

25. Now this God, since he existed alone, not in order to divide or diminish his divinity but in order to show his goodness and power, by force of will alone, impassive and free from passion, incorruptible and untouched by corruption, immovable and without motion, created and engendered, made and established the only-begotten God.

26. In accordance with tradition and the

SOURCE: Peter Heather and John Matthews, *The Goths in the Fourth Century* (Liverpool: Liverpool University Press, 1991), 146-53. Used by permission of Liverpool University Press.

authority of the divine scriptures, he never concealed (the truth) that this God is in second place and the originator of all things from the Father and after the Father and on account of the Father and for the glory of the Father; and further-more that he is great God and great Lord and great king and great mystery, great light [. . .] Lord, provider and lawgiver, redeemer, savior [. . .] originator of [. . .], just judge of all the living and the dead, [holding as greater (than himself) God his own Father [John 14:28]—this he always made clear according to the holy gospel. The odious and execrable, depraved and perverse profession of the homousians he rejected and trampled underfoot as the invention of the Devil and the doctrine of demons [cf. 1 Tim. 4:1]; himself knowing that, if it is truly preached and rightly and faithfully believed by all us Christians that the untiring power of the only-begotten God easily made all heavenly and earthly, all invisible and visible things, why then should not the power of God the Father, which suffers no change, be believed to have made this one Being as his own?

27. And he further deplored and shunned the error and impiety of the homoeusians. Being him-self carefully instructed on the basis of the divine scriptures and diligently confirmed in many councils of holy bishops, in both his sermons and his tractates he showed that a difference does exist between the divinity of the Father and of the Son, of God unbegotten and God only-begotten, and that the Father is for his part the creator of the cre-ator, while the Son is the creator of all creation; and that the Father is God of the Lord while the Son is God of the created universe.

28. He therefore strove to destroy the sect of homousians, because he held the persons of the divinity to be, not confused and mixed together, but discrete and distinct. The homoeusion too he rejected, because he defended not comparable things but different dispositions, and used to say that the Son is like his Father, not according to the erroneous depravity and perversity of the Mace-donians that conflicts with the scriptures, but in accordance with the divine scriptures and tradi-tion.

29. In his preaching and instruction he asserted that all heretics were not Christians but Anti-christs, not pious but impious, not religious but irreligious, not fearful but foolhardy, not in hope but without hope, not worshippers of God but without God, not teachers but deceivers, not preachers but prevaricators, whether Manicheans or Marcionites or Montanists or Paulinians or Sabellians or *anthropiani* or *patripassiani* or Fotinians or Novatians or Donatiani or homou-sians or homoeusians or Macedonians. In truth, as an emulator of the apostles and imitator of the martyrs, a declared enemy of heretics, he strove to repel their wicked doctrines and to edify the people of God, putting to flight "grievous wolves" [Acts 20:29] and "dogs, the evil workers" [Phil. 3:2], and like a good shepherd protected the flock of Christ through his grace, with all prudence and care [cf. John 10:11].

30. The Holy Spirit he furthermore declared to be neither Father nor Son, but made by the Father through the Son before all things, neither first nor second, but set by the first under the second in third place: not unbegotten nor begotten, but cre-ated by the unbegotten through the begotten in third place, according to the preaching of the gospel and the apostolic tradition, as in the words of St. John, "All things were made through him, and without him was not any thing made" [John 1:3], and in the assertion of the blessed Paul, "There is one God, the Father, of whom are all things, and one Lord, Jesus Christ, through whom are all things" [1 Cor. 8:6].

31. Now since there exists only one unbegotten God and there stands under him only one only-begotten God, the Holy Spirit our advocate can be called neither God nor Lord, but received its being from God through the Lord: neither originator nor creator, but illuminator, sanctifier, teacher and leader, helper and petitioner [. . .] and con-firmer, minister of Christ and distributor of acts of grace, the warrant of our inheritance, in whom we were "sealed unto the day of redemption" [Eph. 4:30]. Without the Holy Spirit, none can say that Jesus is Lord, as the apostle says; "No man can say, Jesus is Lord, except in the Holy Spirit" [1 Cor. 12:3], and as Christ teaches; "I am the way, and the truth, and the life: no one cometh unto the Father, but by me" [John 14:6]. (32.) And so they are Christians who in spirit and truth worship and

glorify Christ [cf. John 4:23], and render thanks through Christ with love to God the Father.

33. Steadfast in these and similar doctrines, flourishing gloriously for forty years in the bishopric, he preached unceasingly with apostolic grace in the Greek, Latin and Gothic languages, in the one and only church of Christ; for one is the church of the living God, "the pillar and ground of the truth" [1 Tim. 3:15]: asserting and bearing witness that there is but one flock of Christ our Lord and God, one worship and one edifice, one virgin and one bride, one queen and one vine, one house, one temple, one assembly of Christians, and that all other assemblies are not churches of God but "synagogues of Satan" [Rev. 2:9, cf. 3:9].

And that all he said, and all I have set down, is from the divine Scriptures, "let him that readeth understand" [Matt. 24:15]. He left behind him several tractates and many interpretations in these three languages for the benefit and edification of those willing to accept it, and as his own eternal memorial and recompense.

34. It is beyond my powers to praise this man according to his merits; yet I dare not be silent altogether, for I owe him a debt greater than does any other man, in that he spent upon me a greater share of labor. He received me from my parents as his disciple in the earliest years of my life; he taught me the Holy Scriptures and made plain the truth, and through the mercy of God and the grace of Christ he raised me in the faith, as his son in body and spirit.

35. By the providence of God and mercy of Christ, for the salvation of many among the people of the Goths, he was at the age of thirty ordained bishop from the rank of lector, that he should not only be "the heir of God and joint-heir of Christ" [Rom. 8:17], but should also in this, through the grace of Christ, be an imitator of Christ and his saints. So, as holy David was appointed king and prophet at the age of thirty years, to rule and teach the people of God and the sons of Israel, so too this blessed man was revealed as a prophet and ordained as priest of Christ, to rule, correct, teach and edify the people of the Goths; and this, by the will of God and with the aid of Christ, was wonderfully accomplished through his ministry.

And just as Joseph was revealed in Egypt at the age of thirty years [so Ulfila . . .]. And as our Lord and God, Jesus Christ the Son of God, was appointed and baptized at the age of thirty years according to the flesh, and began to preach the Gospel and to nourish the souls of men, so too, by the disposition and ordering of Christ himself, that holy man corrected the people of the Goths, who were living in hunger and dearth of preaching but with no heed to their condition, and taught them to live by the rule of evangelic, apostolic and prophetic truth, and he showed the Christians (among them) to be truly Christians, and multiplied their numbers.

36. Then, through the envy and machinations of the Enemy a tyrannical and fearsome persecution of Christians in the barbarian land was aroused by the impious and sacrilegious "iudex" of the Goths; but Satan, who wished to do evil, did good against his will, for those whom he desired to make abandon and betray their faith, with Christ as their aid and champion, became martyrs and confessors. The persecutor was confounded: those who suffered persecution received the martyr's crown, while he who strove for victory blushed in his defeat and those who were put to the test rejoiced in their victory.

37. And then, after the glorious martyrdom of many servants and maidservants of Christ, with threats of persecution growing ever more intense, after completing just seven years in his episcopate the holy and blessed Ulfila, of whom we speak, was driven from the barbarian land with a great number of confessors and, still in the reign of Constantius of blessed memory, was received with honor on Roman soil. And as God through Moses liberated his people from the power and violence of Pharaoh and the Egyptians, brought them across the seas and provided that they enter his service, so, through him whom we describe, God liberated from barbarian lands the confessors of his holy son the only-begotten, brought them across the Danube and had them serve him in the mountains, in imitation of the saints.

38. Ulfila preached the truth to his people in the land of Romania for thirty-three years, in addition to the seven that went before, so that in this too he was the imitator of those saints who

[. . .] a space of forty years and time to (convert?) many [. . .].

39. After the completion of forty years Ulfila (came) by imperial order to the city of Constantinople for the purpose of disputation [. . .] And entering the aforesaid city, when the conduct of the council had been reconsidered by the impious ones for fear that they might be confuted—men in the depths of wickedness, being "condemned of themselves" [cf. Titus 3:11] and fit to be stricken with eternal punishment—Ulfila at once fell ill; and during the illness he was taken up to heaven in the manner of the prophet Elisha [cf. 2 Kings 13:14]. Now it is proper for us to consider for a moment the merit of a man who, with the Lord as his guide passed away at Constantinople—or should I say Christianople—for this purpose, that he, a holy, sinless priest of Christ, a man held worthy, by worthy men, in worthy manner, should be marvelously and gloriously honored for his merits by holy men, his fellow priests.

40. Even in death, he left to the people entrusted to him his faith, inscribed upon his very tombstone in accordance with his testament, in these words: "I, Ulfila, bishop and confessor, have always so believed, and in this, the one true faith, I make the journey to my Lord; I believe in one God the Father, the only unbegotten and invisible, and in his only-begotten son, our Lord and God, the designer and maker of all creation, having none other like him (so that one alone among all beings is God the Father, who is also the God of our God); and in one Holy Spirit, the illuminating and sanctifying power, as Christ said after his resurrection to his apostles: 'And behold, I send forth the promise of my Father upon you; but tarry ye in the city of Jerusalem, until ye be clothed with power from on high' [Luke 24:49], and again: 'But ye shall receive power, when the Holy Ghost is come upon you' [Acts 1:8]; being neither God (the Father) nor our God (Christ), but the minister of Christ [. . .], subject and obedient in all things to the Son; and the Son, subject and obedient in all things to God who is his Father [. . .] (whom) he ordained in the Holy Spirit through his Christ."

22. The Emperor Julian,
Rescript on Christian Teachers (Letter 36)

Flavius Claudius Julianus (ca. 331-363), more commonly known as Julian "the Apostate," reigned as Roman emperor from 361 to 363. Although raised a Christian, as a young student he became enamored with Neoplatonism and secretly converted to traditional Greco-Roman polytheism. When Constantius II died, Julian became sole emperor and openly declared his paganism. By his religious policies he endeavored to reorganize and reinvigorate polytheism, especially traditional cult practices such as animal sacrifice, and to undermine Christianity. Toward this end, in 362 he passed a notorious law forbidding Christians to teach classical literature or philosophy.

I hold that a proper education results, not in laboriously acquired symmetry of phrases and language, but in a healthy condition of mind, I mean a mind that has understanding and true opinions about things good and evil, honorable and base. Therefore, when a person thinks one thing and teaches his pupils another, in my opinion that person fails to educate exactly in propor-

SOURCE: *The Works of the Emperor Julian*, vol. 3, tr. Wilmer Cave Wright (London: Heinemann, 1923; New York: G. P. Putnam's Sons, 1923), 117-23.

tion as he fails to be an honest individual. And if the divergence between one's convictions and one's utterances is merely in trivial matters, that can be tolerated somehow, though it is wrong. But if in matters of the greatest importance one has certain opinions and teaches the contrary, what is that but the conduct of hucksters, and not honest but thoroughly dissolute people in that they praise most highly the things that they believe to be most worthless, thus cheating and enticing by their praises those to whom they desire to transfer their worthless wares. Now all who profess to teach anything whatever ought to be men of upright character, and ought not to harbor in their souls opinions irreconcilable with what they publicly profess; and, above all, I believe it is necessary that those who associate with the young and teach them rhetoric should be of that upright character; for they expound the writings of the ancients, whether they be rhetoricians or grammarians, and still more if they are sophists. For these claim to teach, in addition to other things, not only the use of words, but morals also, and they assert that political philosophy is their peculiar field. Let us leave aside, for the moment, the question whether this is true or not. But while I applaud them for aspiring to such high pretensions, I should applaud them still more if they did not utter falsehoods and convict themselves of thinking one thing and teaching their pupils another. What! Was it not the gods who revealed all their learning to Homer, Hesiod, Demosthenes, Herodotus, Thucydides, Isocrates and Lysias? Did not these men think that they were consecrated, some to Hermes, others to the Muses? I think it is absurd that those who expound the works of these writers should dishonor the gods whom they used to honor. Yet, though I think this absurd, I do not say that they ought to change their opinions and then instruct the young. But I give them this choice; either not to teach what they do not think admirable, or, if they wish to teach, let them first

really persuade their pupils that neither Homer nor Hesiod nor any of these writers whom they expound and have declared to be guilty of impiety, folly and error in regard to the gods, is such as they declare. For since they make a livelihood and receive pay from the works of those writers, they thereby confess that they are most shamefully greedy of gain, and that, for the sake of a few drachmae, they would put up with anything. It is true that, until now, there were many excuses for not attending the temples, and the terror that threatened on all sides absolved men for concealing the truest beliefs about the gods. But since the gods have granted us liberty, it seems to me absurd that people should teach what they do not believe to be sound. But if they believe that those whose interpreters they are and for whom they sit, so to speak, in the seat of the prophets, were wise men, let them be the first to emulate their piety towards the gods. If, however, they think that those writers were in error with respect to the most honored gods, then let them betake themselves to the churches of the Galilaeans to expound Matthew and Luke, since you Galilaeans are obeying them when you ordain that people shall refrain from temple worship. For my part, I wish that your ears and your tongues might be "born anew," as you would say, as regards these things in which may I ever have part, and all who think and act as is pleasing to me.

For religious and secular teachers let there be a general ordinance to this effect: Any youth who wishes to attend the schools is not excluded; nor indeed would it be reasonable to shut out from the best way boys who are still too ignorant to know which way to turn, and to overawe them into being led against their will to the beliefs of their ancestors. Though indeed it might be proper to cure these, even against their will, as one cures the insane, except that we concede indulgence to all for this sort of disease. For we ought, I think, to teach, but not punish, the demented.

23. The Christianization of Ethiopia and Georgia: Rufinus of Aquileia, *Ecclesiastical History*

Rufinus of Aquileia (ca. 345-ca. 410) was educated in Rome, visited various desert fathers in Egypt, and founded with Melania the Elder a double monastery for men and women in Jerusalem. Best known as a translator of Greek theological works into Latin, Rufinus translated Eusebius of Caesarea's Ecclesiastical History *and updated the work to 395. In the following excerpts he recounts major episodes in the Christianization of Ethiopia and Georgia in the fourth century. (Note that "Further India" in this text refers to Ethiopia.)*

10.9. In the division of the earth which the apostles made by lot for the preaching of God's word, when the different provinces fell to one or the other of them, Parthia, it is said, went by lot to Thomas, to Matthew fell Ethiopia, and Hither India, which adjoins it, went to Bartholomew. Between this country and Parthia, but far inland, lies Further India. Inhabited by many peoples with many different languages, it is so distant that the plow of the apostolic preaching had made no furrow in it, but in Constantine's time it received the first seeds of faith in the following way. A philosopher named Metrodorus, they say, penetrated to Further India for the purpose of viewing the places and investigating the continent. Encouraged by his example, a philosopher of Tyre named Meropius decided to go to India for the same reason; he had with him two small boys whom as his relatives he was instructing in letters. The younger was called Aedesius and the older Frumentius. When therefore the philosopher had seen fully and taken note of the things on which his mind was feasting, and he had set out on the return voyage, the ship in which he was sailing put in to some port to obtain water and other necessaries. It is the custom of the barbarians there that whenever the neighboring peoples announce that relations with the Romans have been disturbed, they kill all the Romans they find among them. The philosopher's ship was attacked and everyone with him put to death together. The boys, who were discovered under a tree going over and preparing their lessons, were saved because the barbarians pitied them and brought them to the king. He made one of them, Aedesius, his cup-bearer, while to Frumentius, whose intelligence and prudence he could see, he entrusted his accounts and correspondence. From that time on they were held in high honor and affection by the king. Now when the king died and left as heir to the kingdom his wife and her young son, he also left it to the free choice of the youths what they would do. But the queen begged them to share with her the responsibility of ruling the kingdom until her son should grow up, as she had no one more trustworthy in the kingdom, especially Frumentius, whose prudence would suffice to rule the kingdom, for the other gave evidence simply of a pure faith and sober mind. Now while they were doing so and Frumentius had the helm of the kingdom, God put it into his mind and heart to begin making careful inquiries if there were any Christians among the Roman merchants, and to give them extensive rights, which he urged them to use, to build places of assembly in each location, in which they might gather for prayer in the Roman manner. Not only that, but he himself did far more along these lines than anyone else, and in this way encouraged the others, invited them with his support and favors, made available whatever

SOURCE: *The* Church History *of Rufinus of Aquileia, Books 10 and 11*, tr. Philip R. Amidon, S.J. (New York: Oxford University Press, 1997), 18-23. Copyright © 1997 by Philip Amadon. Used by permission of Oxford University Press, Inc.

was suitable, furnished sites for buildings and everything else that was necessary, and bent every effort to see that the seed of Christians should grow up there.

10.10. Now when the royal child whose kingdom they had looked after reached maturity, then, having executed their trust completely and handed it back faithfully, they returned to our continent, even though the queen and her son tried very hard to hold them back and asked them to stay. While Aedesius hastened to Tyre to see his parents and relatives again, Frumentius journeyed to Alexandria, saying that it was not right to conceal what the Lord had done. He therefore explained to the bishop everything that had been done and urged him to provide some worthy man to send as bishop to the already numerous Christians and churches built on barbarian soil. Then Athanasius, for he had recently received the priesthood, after considering attentively and carefully what Frumentius had said and done, spoke as follows in the council of priests: "What other man can we find like you, in whom is God's spirit as in you, and who could achieve such things as these?" And having conferred on him the priesthood, he ordered him to return with the Lord's grace to the place from which he had come. When he had reached India as bishop, it is said that such a grace of miracles was given him by God that the signs of the apostles were worked by him and a countless number of barbarians was converted to the faith. From that time on there came into existence a Christian people and churches in India, and the priesthood began. These events we came to know of not from popular rumor, but from the report of Aedesius himself, who had been Frumentius's companion, and who later became a presbyter in Tyre.

10.11. It was at this time too that the Georgians, who dwell in the region of Pontus, accepted the word of God and faith in the kingdom to come. The cause of this great benefit was a woman captive who lived among them and led such a faithful, sober, and modest life, spending all of her days and nights in sleepless supplications to God, that the very novelty of it began to be wondered at by the barbarians. Their curiosity led them to ask what she was about. She replied with the truth:

that in this manner she simply worshiped Christ as God. This answer made the barbarians wonder only at the novelty of the name, although it is true, as often happens, that her very perseverance made the common women wonder if she were deriving some benefit from such great devotion.

Now it is said that they have the custom that, if a child falls sick, it is taken around by its mother to each of the houses to see if anyone knows of a proven remedy to apply to the illness. And when one of the women had brought her child around to everyone, according to custom, and had found no remedy in any of the houses, she went to the woman captive as well to see if she knew of anything. She answered that she knew of no human remedy, but declared that Christ her God, whom she worshiped, could give it the healing despaired of by humans. And after she had put the child on her hair shirt and poured out above it her prayer to the Lord, she gave the infant back to its mother in good health. Word of this got around to many people, and news of the wonderful deed reached the ears of the queen, who was suffering from a bodily illness of the gravest sort and had been reduced to a state of absolute despair. She asked for the woman captive to be brought to her. She declined to go, lest she appear to pretend to more than was proper to her sex. The queen ordered that she herself be brought to the captive's hovel. Having placed her likewise on her hair shirt and invoked Christ's name, no sooner was her prayer done than she had her stand up healthy and vigorous, and taught her that it was Christ, God and Son of God most high, who had conferred healing upon her, and advised her to invoke him whom she should know to be the author of her life and well-being, for he it was who allotted kingdoms to kings and life to mortals. She returned joyfully home and disclosed the affair to her husband, who wanted to know the reason for this sudden return to health. When he in his joy at his wife's cure ordered gifts to be presented to the woman, she said, "O king, the captive deigns to accept none of these things. She despises gold, rejects silver, and battens on fasting as though it were food. This alone may we give her as a gift, if we worship as God the Christ who cured me when she called upon him."

But the king was not then inclined to do so and put it off for the time, although his wife urged him often, until it happened one day when he was hunting in the woods with his companions that a thick darkness fell upon the day, and with the light removed there was no longer any way for his blind steps through the grim and awful night. Each of his companions wandered off a different way, while he, left alone in the thick darkness which surrounded him, did not know what to do or where to turn, when suddenly there arose in his heart, which was near to losing hope of being saved, the thought that if the Christ preached to his wife by the woman captive were really God, he might now free him from this darkness so that he could from then on abandon all the others and worship him. No sooner had he vowed to do so, not even verbally but only mentally, than the daylight returned to the world and guided the king safely to the city. He explained directly to the queen what had happened. He required that the woman captive be summoned at once and hand on to him her manner of worship, insisting that from then on he would venerate no god but Christ. The captive came, instructed him that Christ is God, and explained, as far as it was lawful for a woman to disclose such things, the ways of making petition and offering reverence. She advised that a church be built and described its shape.

The king therefore called together all of his people and explained the matter from the beginning, what had happened to the queen and him, taught them the faith, and before even being initiated into sacred things became the apostle of his nation. The men believed because of the king, the women because of the queen, and with everyone desiring the same thing a church was put up without delay. The outer walls having quickly been raised, it was time to put the columns in place. When the first and second had been set up and they came to the third, they used all the machines and the strength of men and oxen to get it raised halfway up to an inclined position, but no machine could lift it the rest of the way, not even with efforts repeated again and again; with everyone exhausted, it would not budge. Everyone was confounded, the king's enthusiasm waned, and no one could think what to do. But when nightfall intervened and everyone went away and all mortal labors ceased, the woman captive remained inside alone, passing the night in prayer. And when the worried king entered in the morning with all his people, he saw the column, which so many machines and people had been unable to move, suspended upright just above its base: not placed upon it, but hanging about one foot in the air. Then indeed all the people looking on glorified God and accepted the witness of the miracle before them that the king's faith and the captive's religion were true. And behold, while everyone was still in the grip of wonder and astonishment, before their very eyes the column, with no one touching it, gradually and with perfect balance settled down upon its base. After that the remaining columns were raised with such ease that all that were left were put in place that day.

Now after the church had been magnificently built and the people were thirsting even more deeply for God's faith, on the advice of the captive an embassy of the entire people was sent to the emperor Constantine, and what had happened was explained to him. They implored him to send priests who could complete God's work begun among them. He dispatched them with all joy and honor, made far happier by this than if he had annexed to the Roman empire unknown peoples and kingdoms. That this happened was related to us by that most faithful man Bacurius, the king of that nation who in our realm held the rank of *comes domesticorum* and whose chief concern was for religion and truth; when he was *dux limitis* in Palestine he spent some time with us in Jerusalem in great concord of spirit. But let us return to our topic.

24. The Martyrdom of Martha, Daughter of Posi, Who Was a Daughter of the Covenant

While Emperor Constantine had legalized Christianity in the Roman Empire, in neighboring Persia (modern Iraq and western Iran) serious persecution was just beginning in the mid-fourth century. Christianity had been largely tolerated as a minority religion in Persia alongside Judaism and Manichaeism. However, as hostility between the Christian Roman Empire and the Sassanian Persian Empire increased, Persian Christians were suspected of disloyalty to the state and its officially Zoroastrian regime. Particularly under Shapur II (339-379) Christians faced widespread persecution. Martha was the daughter of the king's master craftsman, Posi, who preceded her in martyrdom.

Now the glorious Posi also had a daughter called Martha who was a "daughter of the covenant." She too was accused, and at the third hour on the Sunday of the great feast of the Resurrection she was arrested. They brought the blessed Martha, daughter of the glorious Posi, into the presence of the chief Mobed, who then went in to inform the king about her. The king bade him to go out and interrogate her, saying, "If she abandons her religion and renounces Christianity, well and good; if not, she should be married off. If, however, she fails to follow either of these courses, she should be handed over to be put to death."

So the chief Mobed went out and started to interrogate the glorious Martha as follows: "What are you?" To which the blessed Martha replied derisively, "I am a woman, as you can see." Those who happened to be there in the presence of the chief Mobed blushed and bent down their heads when they heard the wise Martha's reply to his question. The Mobed's face became green with anger and shame, but he controlled his feelings and said, "Reply to my question." To which the wise Martha said, "I did reply to the question I was asked."

The Mobed then said, "What did I ask you, and what reply did you give?" Martha said, "Your honor asked 'what are you?' and I replied, 'I am a woman as you can see.'"

"I asked you what is your religion," said the Mobed. The glorious Martha replied, "I am a Christian, as my clothing shows." The Mobed went on, "Tell me the truth, are you the daughter of that crazy Posi who went out of his mind and opposed the king, with the result that he was put to an evil death?" To this the blessed girl replied, "Humanly speaking, I am his daughter, but also by faith I am the daughter of the Posi who is wise in his God and sane in the firm stand he took on behalf of the King of kings, the King of truth, the Posi who yesterday acquired everlasting life by means of his dying for his God. If only God would hold me worthy to be a true daughter of this blessed Posi, who is now with the saints in light and eternal rest, while I am still among sinners in this world of sorrows."

The Mobed then said, "Listen to me, and I will advise you what is your best course: the king of kings is merciful and he does not desire anyone's death, but in his goodness he wishes all his friends to become fellow religionists of his and so be honored by him. So it was in the case of your father: because the king liked him, he honored him and gave him advancement; but your father acted foolishly and said things that were quite out of place, whereupon the king of kings urged him not to be stubborn, but to no effect. This was the rea-

Source: *Holy Women of the Syrian Orient,* ed. and tr. Sebastian P. Brock and Susan Ashbrook Harvey (Berkeley: University of California Press, 1987), 67–73. Copyright © 1987 by The Regents of the University of California. Used by permission.

son why he was put to death. And now in your case, do not act stubbornly as your father did, but do the will of Shapur, king of kings and lord of all regions. As a result you will be greatly honored, and whatever you ask for your own comfort will be granted by the king."

The glorious Martha replied, "May king Shapur live, may his graciousness never leave him, may his compassion continue; may his graciousness be preserved by his children and his compassion redound to himself and on the people who deserve it. May the life that he loves be accorded to all his brethren and friends, but let all who imitate my father meet the evil death you said my father died. As for me, a wretched handmaid, the dregs of the handmaids of God and of the king, why should any transient honor come to me? I have decided to become the object of abuse like my father for the sake of my father's God, and I will die like him because of my faith in God."

The Mobed said, "I am aware of the hardness of heart you Christians have—a people guilty of death. Furthermore, no obedient offspring is likely to come from a rebellious man like Posi. Nevertheless, simply so that I shall not be held guilty before God of not having done my best to warn you, I am taking all this trouble over you in order to bring you over to the religion of the excellent gods who care for the world."

The holy Martha replied, "You have said your part, and I have said mine—unless you are quite blind and are paying no attention to the true state of affairs that I have described. Otherwise you have both heard and seen which exhortation is profitable and which harmful; which leads to the kingdom of heaven, which leads to the fire of Gehenna, which provides life, and which engenders death."

The Mobed went on: "Listen to me and don't be stubborn and obstinate, following your own perverted wishes in everything. Instead, seeing that you are set on not giving up your religion, act as you like, but do this one thing only, and you shall live and not die: you are a young girl, and a very pretty one—find a husband and get married, have sons and daughters, and don't hold on to the disgusting pretext of the 'covenant.'"

The wise virgin Martha replied, "If a virgin is betrothed to a man, does the natural law order that someone else should come along, attack her fiancé, and snatch away this girl who has already been betrothed? Or does it say that such a virgin should give herself up to marry a man who is not her fiancé?"

"No," answered the Mobed.

The betrothed of Christ, Martha, then said, "So how can your authority order me to marry a man to whom I am not betrothed when I am already betrothed to someone else?"

To which the Mobed said, "Are you really betrothed, then?" And the blessed Martha replied, "I am in truth betrothed." "To whom?" asked the Mobed. "Is not your honor aware of him?" said the glorious Martha. "Where is he?" asked the Mobed. Wise in our Lord, she replied, "He has set out on a long journey on business; but he is close by and is on the point of coming back." "What is his name?" inquired the Mobed. "Jesus," replied the blessed Martha.

Still not understanding, the Mobed went on, "What country has he gone to? In which city is he now?" The splendid Martha replied, "He has gone off to heaven, and he is now in Jerusalem on high."

At this point the Mobed realized that she was speaking of our Lord Jesus Christ, whereupon he said, "Didn't I say at the very beginning that this was a stubborn people, not open to persuasion? I will spatter you from head to toe with blood, and then your fiancé can come along to find you turned into dust and rubbish: let him marry you then."

The courageous Martha replied, "He will indeed come in glory, riding on the chariot of the clouds, accompanied by the angels and powers of heaven, and all that is appropriate for his wedding feast; he will shake from the dust the bodies of all those who are betrothed to him, wash them in the dew of heaven, anoint them with the oil of gladness, and clothe them in the garment of righteousness, which consists of glorious light; he will place on their fingers rings as the surety of his grace, while on their heads he will put a crown of splendor, that is to say, unfading glory. He will allow them to sit on his chariot—the glorious cloud—and will raise them up into the air, bringing them into the heavenly bridal chamber that has been set up in a place not made by hands, but built in Jerusalem the free city on high."

When the chief Mobed heard this, he left her in his palace and went in to inform the king of everything. The king then gave orders for the impudent girl and daughter of an impudent father to be taken outside the city and immolated on the very spot where her father had been killed.

So they led the chaste virgin Martha off on the Sunday of the great feast of Christ's resurrection, at midday. As they were getting ready the place where she was to be put to death, she fell down on her face and, as she knelt before God facing east, she said, "I thank you, Jesus Christ, my Lord, my King and my Betrothed, for preserving my virginity sealed up with the imprint of the seal-ring of your promise, and for preserving my faith in the glorious Trinity—the faith in which I was born, in which my parents brought me up, and in which I was baptized. For this confession, for which my father Posi was also crowned, I give you thanks, O Lamb of God who takes away the sin of the world, for whose sake the bishops, our shepherds, have been sacrificed, as have the head pastors, the priests, and along with them the members of the holy covenant; and slaughtered too have been the sheep—Guhshtazad and Posi my father. And now it is the turn of me, the young lamb who has been fattened up on the pastures of your promises and by the springs of your declarations: here I am being sacrificed before you. At your hands, Jesus, the true High Priest, may I be offered up as a pure, holy, and acceptable offering before the glorious Trinity of the hidden Being, in whose name you taught us to be instructed and baptized. Visit, Lord, your persecuted people; preserve them in true faith in the midst of their enemies, and may they be found to be like pure gold in the furnace of persecution that has been erected against your people; may they be strengthened in the worship of your majesty, fearlessly worshipping and confessing Father, Son, and Holy Spirit, now and always and for eternal ages, amen."

The moment she had finished her prayer, while no one was near at hand, she rushed off and stretched herself on the ground above the pit they had dug for her. When the officer approached to tie her up, she said, "Do not tie me up, for I am gladly accepting immolation for the sake of my Lord." When she saw the knife being brandished by the officer, she laughed and said, "Now I can say, not like Isaac, 'Here is the fire and the wood, but where is the lamb for the burnt offering?' but rather I can say, 'Here is the lamb and the knife, but where is the wood and the fire?' But I *do* have wood and fire, for the wood is the cross of Jesus my Lord, and I *do* have fire too—the fire that Christ left on earth, just as he said, 'I came to cast fire on earth: I only wish it had already caught alight!'"

The thousands of spectators who stood by were astounded at the chaste girl's courage, and everyone gave praise to the God who encourages those who fear him in this way.

The officer then approached and slaughtered her like a lamb, while she entrusted her soul to Christ. Guards stayed by her corpse, and it remained there for two days, but on the night of Tuesday, thanks to a bribe handed over to the guards, it was taken away. By this time many had been slain for the sake of Christ. The blessed girl's brother, who had earlier buried his father, provided the money and took off the corpse; he then embalmed the body and laid it beside her father's.

The blessed Martha was crowned on the Sunday of the great feast of the Resurrection.

The blessed woman who had helped prepare them for burial used to keep their memorial each year in her home, close by where the priests and clergy lived. This she did all her life, and after her death her house passed to her brother's son. He too diligently kept their memorial, following that blessed woman's custom. When this nephew died, he left behind him two sons, and sometime after his death they had a quarrel over the saint's bones: one of them wanted to divide them up between himself and his brother, because the house of the blessed woman had fallen to his share. The matter came to the knowledge of Ṣawmay, bishop of Karka, of blessed memory, and he persuaded the two of them to let him take away the bones; whereupon he presented them to the people of the church of Karka, to serve as a fair memento, and to be a valued treasure in the church of Christ. This was done by the holy bishop Ṣawmay in the eighth year of king Barharan, son of Yazdgard, eighty-nine years after their crowning. This was what happened to Posi and his daughter.

25. Ephrem the Syrian, *Hymn 1*

Born ca. 306, Ephrem the Syrian served the church under several orthodox bishops of Nisibis until Rome ceded the city to the Persians in 363. He then moved to Edessa, where he was ordained a deacon, founded a school of biblical and theological studies, and died ministering to victims of the plague in 373. Among his multifaceted activities on behalf of the church, Ephrem is best known as an ascetic and hymnodist. Hymn 1, one of his liturgical Hymns on the Nativity, reflects theologically on the meaning of the incarnation and celebrates God's love for humankind.

To the melody, "The confessors."

1 My Lord, this day gladdens kings, priests and prophets,
   for on it were fulfilled and realized all their words.

Refrain: Glory to You, Son of our Creator!

2 Since today the Virgin has given birth to Emmanuel in Bethlehem,
   the word Isaiah spoke was accomplished today.

3 He Who registers the peoples was born there;
   the psalm that David sang has been fulfilled today.

4 The word that Micah spoke was realized today,
   for a shepherd went out from Ephrata, and his staff herded souls.

5 "Behold, a star shone forth from Jacob, and a prince arose from Israel."
   The prophecy that Balaam spoke found its meaning today.

6 The hidden light descended, and its beauty shone forth from a body;
   the dawn of which Zechariah spoke lights up Bethlehem today.

7 The light of kingship glorifies him in Ephrata, the city of kings;

the blessing that Jacob pronounced found its fulfillment today.

8 "The tree of life brings hope" to the dying;
   the hidden saying of Solomon found its explanation today.

9 Today a child was born, and he was called "wonder,"
   for it is a wonder that God reveals Himself as an infant.

10 The Spirit spoke a parable in the worm, for it reproduces without sexual union;
    the type the Holy Spirit fashioned receives its meaning today.

11 He rose up like a shoot before Him, a shoot from the parched earth;
    something spoken secretly occurred openly today.

12 Since the King was hidden in Judah, Tamar stole Him from his loins;
    today shone forth the splendor of the beauty whose hidden form she loved.

13 Ruth lay down with Boaz because she saw hidden in him the medicine of life;
    today her vow is fulfilled since from her seed arose the Giver of all life.

14 Man imposed corruption on woman when she came forth from him;
    today she has repaid him—she who bore for him the Savior.

15 He gave birth to the Mother, Eve—he, the

SOURCE: Ephrem the Syrian, *Hymns*, tr. Kathleen McVey (New York: Paulist Press, 1989), 64–74. Copyright © 1989 by Kathleen E. McVey. Used by permission of Paulist Press, Inc., New York/Mahwah, N.J.

man who never was born;

how worthy of faith is the daughter of Eve, who without a man bore a child!

16 The virgin earth gave birth to that Adam, head of the earth;

the Virgin today gave birth to [second] Adam, head of heaven.

17 The staff of Aaron sprouted, and the dry wood brought forth;

his symbol has been explained today—it is the virgin womb that gave birth.

18 Put to shame is the people that holds the prophets to be true,

for if our Savior had not come, their words would have become lies.

19 Blessed is the True One Who comes from the True Father.

He fulfilled the words of the true [prophets], and they are complete in their truth.

20 From Your treasury, my Lord, let us fetch from the treasures of Your scriptures

the names of the just men of old who said they saw Your coming.

21 That Seth who took the place of Abel resembled the murdered son

to dull the sword that Cain brought into the creation.

22 Noah saw the sons of God, the holy ones, who were suddenly made wanton,

and he anticipated the Holy Son by Whom fornicators would be made chaste.

23 The two brothers who hid Noah looked for the Only-Begotten of God

to come and hide the nakedness of man, intoxicated with pride.

24 Shem and Japheth, as compassionate [men] anticipated the compassionate Son

Who would come and free Canaan from the servitude of sin.

25 Melchizedek anticipated Him; he the vicar was watching

to see priesthood's Lord Whose hyssop cleanses creation.

26 Lot saw the Sodomites who perverted nature;

he looked for the Lord of natures Who gave chastity beyond nature.

27 Aaron anticipated Him—he who saw that if his staff swallowed reptiles,

His cross would swallow the Reptile that swallowed Adam and Eve.

28 Moses saw the fixed serpent that healed the stings of basilisks,

and he anticipated he would see the Healer of the first Serpent's wound.

29 Moses saw that he alone received the brightness of God,

and he anticipated the One to come—by His teaching, the Multiplier of the godlike.

30 Kaleb, the scout, came carrying the cluster on a pole;

he anticipated seeing the Grape Whose wine would console creation.

31 Joshua bar Nun anticipated Him—he who represents the power of His name;

if by His name he is thus magnified, how much more would he be exalted by His birth!

32 That Joshua who also plucked and carried with him some of the fruits anticipated the Tree of Life Who would give His all life-giving fruit to taste.

33 Rahab beheld Him; for if the scarlet thread saved her by a symbol from [divine] wrath, by a symbol she tasted the truth.

34 Elijah yearned for Him and without having seen the Son on earth, he believed and increased his prayers that he might ascend and see Him in heaven.

35 Moses and Elijah looked for Him; the humble one ascended from the depth, and the zealous one came down from the height, and they saw the Son in the middle.

36 They represented a symbol of His coming: Moses was a type for the dead,

and Elijah a type for the living who will fly to meet Him when He comes.

37 Because the dead have tasted death, He will repair them first,

but those not yet buried will be snatched up to meet Him at the end.

38 Who will bring me to the end of enumerating the just men who

anticipated the Son, whose number cannot be encompassed by our weak mouth?

39 Pray for me, my friends, that I may be strengthened once more

to set forth their qualities again in another account as much as I am able.

40 Who is able to glorify the true Son Who rises for us,

Whom just men yearned to see in their lifetimes?

41 Adam anticipated Him Who is the Lord of the Cherubim

and was able to have him enter and dwell near the boughs of the Tree of Life.

42 Abel yearned for him to come in his days,

so that instead of the lamb he sacrificed, he might see the Lamb of God.

43 Eve looked for Him, for the shame of women was great,

but He would be able to clothe them not in leaves but rather in the glory they had shed.

44 The symbol of the tower that many built envisages One Who would

come down and build upon the earth a Tower that goes up to heaven.

45 Even the type of the ark of animals envisages our Lord,

Who would build the holy church in which souls take refuge.

46 In the days of Peleg the earth was divided into seventy tongues;

he anticipated that One Who would divide the earth by tongues for His apostles.

47 The earth that the Flood drowned called her Lord silently;

He came down and opened baptism by which people were drawn out to heaven.

48 Seth and Enosh and Kenan were named sons of God;

they anticipated the Son of God, for they were brothers to Him in mercy.

49 Slightly less than one thousand years Methuselah lived;

he anticipated the Son Who gives eternal life as an inheritance.

50 For their sake by a hidden symbol, grace was asking

their Lord to come in their lifetimes to fill their needs.

51 For it is the Holy Spirit, Who for their sake by quiet contemplation in them stirs them up to see by Her the Savior for whom they yearned.

52 The soul of just men perceived the Son, the Medicine of life,

and she eagerly desired that in her days He would come and she would taste His sweetness.

53 Enoch yearned for Him, and without having seen the Son on earth,

he increased his faith and was made righteous so that he ascended to see Him in heaven.

54 Who will refuse grace? For this gift that the ancients

did not acquire [even] with great effort has come freely to the people of today.

55 Even Lamech looked for the Compassionate One to come and console him

from his labor and the work of his hands and from the earth that the Just One cursed.

56 But Lamech saw his son Noah in whom the symbols of the Son are portrayed; instead

of this distant Lord the nearby symbol consoled him.

57 Even Noah yearned to see Him, for he tasted of his benefits:

if [even] His type preserved the animals, how much [more] does He save souls.

58 Noah anticipated Him—Noah who surmised that by Him the ark stood still;

if His type saved in this way, how much more will He save in His reality.

59 By the Spirit Abraham perceived that the birth of the Son was distant;

for his own sake he eagerly desired even in his day to see Him.

60 Isaac who tasted of His salvation yearned to see Him;

if His sign is saved in this way, how much more will He be saved in His truth.

61 Today the Watchers were rejoicing that the Awakener came to awaken us;

who will go to sleep on this night on which all Creation is awake?

62 Since by sins Adam let the sleep of death enter Creation,

the Awakener came down to awaken us from the slumber of sin.

63 Let us keep vigil as do the greedy who contemplate money lent on interest,

who stay awake often at night to calculate principal and interest.

64 Awake and thinking is the thief who dug a hiding place in the ground for his sleep;

his wakefulness is all [for] this: to increase lamentation for those who sleep.

65 Keeping vigil also is the glutton in order to eat more and to suffer agony;

his vigil was torment for him since he did not eat with moderation.

66 Keeping vigil also is the merchant; at night he wearies his fingers

to calculate how much [interest] came [in on] his mina and whether he doubled and tripled his obol.

67 Keeping vigil also is the rich [man] whose sleep mammon pursues;

his dogs are sleeping, but he is keeping his treasure from thieves.

68 Keeping vigil also is the worrier whose sleep has been swallowed up by his worries,

whose death stands at his pillows, and he watches, worried, for years.

69 It is Satan who teaches, my brothers, wakefulness for the sake of wakefulness,

so that we might be asleep to virtues, vigilant and wakeful to vices.

70 Even Judas Iscariot kept vigil an entire night,

and he sold the blood of the Just One Who purchased the entire creation.

71 The sons of darkness, who stripped off and shed the Shining One, put on darkness,

and with silver the thief sold the Creator of silver.

72 Even the Pharisees, sons of darkness, were awake an entire night;

the dark ones kept vigil to conceal the incomprehensible Light.

73 Keep vigil as bright ones on this bright night;

for even if its color is black, still it is splendid in its power.

74 One who splendidly watches and prays in the darkness

is wrapped in hidden brilliance in the midst of this visible darkness.

75 The way of life of the hateful one who stands in the daylight is the way of a son of darkness,

so that even if clothed by light without, he would be girt by darkness within.

76 Indeed, my friends, let us not forget in our wakefulness:

illicit is the vigil of one who does not watch as he should.

77 Deep sleep is the vigil of one who watches unworthily;

its opposite, too, is the vigil of one who watches unchastely.

78 The vigil of a jealous man is an abundance full of emptiness,

and his watch is a matter full of scorn and disgrace.

79 If an angry man keeps watch, his vigil is disturbed by anger,

and his watch itself becomes full of wrath and curses.

80 If a garrulous man keeps vigil, his mouth becomes a thoroughfare

useful for the destroying [spirits] but wearisome for prayers.

81 If a discerning man keeps vigil, he chooses one of two:

either he sleeps sweetly, or he keeps vigil righteously.

82 Serene is the night on which shines forth the Serene One Who came to give us serenity.

Do not allow anything that might disturb it to enter upon our watch.

83 Let the path of the ear be cleared; let the sight of the eye be chastened;

let the contemplation of the heart be sanctified; let the speech of the mouth be purified.

84 Mary today has hidden in us the leaven from the house of Abraham;

let us, therefore, love the poor as Abraham [loved] the needy.

85 Today she has cast rennet into us from the house of David, the compassionate one;

let man have mercy on his persecutor as the son of Jesse on Saul.

86 The sweet salt of the prophets today is scattered among the peoples;

let us acquire by it a new taste by which the former people would lose its flavor.

87 On this day of redemption let us speak a speech of interpretation;

let us not speak superfluous words, lest we be superfluous to [the day].

88 This is the night of reconciliation; let us be
neither wrathful nor gloomy on it.

On this all-peaceful night let us be neither
menacing nor boisterous.

89 This is the night of the Sweet One; let us be on
it neither bitter nor harsh.

On this night of the Humble One, let us be
neither proud nor haughty.

90 On this day of forgiveness let us not avenge
offenses.

On this day of rejoicings let us not share sorrows.

91 On this sweet day let us not be vehement.

On this calm day let us not be quick-tem-
pered.

92 On this day on which God came into the presence of sinners,

let not the just man exalt himself in his mind
over the sinner.

93 On this day on which the Lord of all came
among servants,

let the lords also bow down to their servants
lovingly.

94 On this day when the Rich One was made
poor for our sake,

let the rich man also make the poor man a
sharer at his table.

95 On this day a gift came out to us without our
asking for it;

let us then give alms to those who cry out and
beg from us.

96 This is the day when the high gate opened to
us for our prayers;

let us also open the gates to the seekers who
have stayed but sought [forgiveness].

97 This Lord of natures today was transformed
contrary to His nature;

it is not too difficult for us also to overthrow
our evil will.

98 Bound is the body by its nature for it cannot
grow larger or smaller;

but powerful is the will for it may grow to all
sizes.

99 Today the Deity imprinted itself on humanity,
so that humanity might also be cut into the
seal of Deity.

26. Basil of Caesarea,
Letter 150

*Known as Basil the Great and one of the Cappadocian Fathers, Basil of
Caesarea served as a priest and eventually as bishop of Caesarea in the 360s
and 370s. Though deeply involved in theological controversies and ecclesiastical politics of his day, Basil is also remembered for his role as a monastic
organizer and for his Christian philanthropy. Both his ascetic ideals and his
care for the poor and the sick are reflected in* Letter 150, *written by Basil in
the name of a friend to Basil's protégé, the future bishop Amphilochius.*

150. *To Amphilochius, in the Name of Heraclei-
das*

I recall the conversations which we once had
with one another, and I have not forgotten either

what I myself said nor what I heard from your
Nobility. And, now, public life does not hold me
back. Although I am the same in heart and have
not yet put off the old man, except, indeed, in
appearance and in having removed myself far

SOURCE: Basil, *Letters*, vol. 1. tr. Agnes Clare Way, C.D.P. (New York: Fathers of the Church, 1951), 298-302. Used by
permission of The Catholic University of America Press.

from the affairs of life, I seem now, as it were, to have entered upon the path of life exemplified by Christ. And I sit by myself like those about to put out to sea, looking steadily to the future. For, the sailors have need of winds for a fair voyage, but we of someone to lead us by the hand and bring us safely through the bitter waters of life. Now, I consider that I need, first of all, a curb against my youth, and, then, spurs for the race of piety. And the provider of these, without doubt, is reason, now moderating our disorderly conduct, now arousing the sluggishness of our soul. Again, I need other remedies so as to purify the sordidness of my manners. For, you know that we who for a long time have been accustomed to the forum are unsparing of our words and are not on our guard against the imaginations, which are aroused in our mind by the Evil One. Moreover, we are overcome by honor and we do not easily lay aside the habit of thinking somewhat highly of ourselves. Against these things I realize that I need a great and an experienced teacher. Then, in truth, the cleansing of the soul's eye, so that it may be able to fix its gaze on the beauty of the glory of God when all darkness of ignorance, like some rheum, has been removed, I consider no little task nor one that brings profit only for a short time.

I know full well that your Eloquence is aware of this and desires that there should be someone to give this assistance. Moreover, if ever God grants me to meet your Modesty, I shall, without doubt, learn more concerning the matters to which I must give heed. For, now, by reason of my great ignorance I am not able even to understand in how great need I am, but at least I have not repented of my first attempt, nor does my soul sink down at the prospect of a life according to God. About this you rightly and in a manner befitting yourself felt anxiety in my case, lest, ever turning back, I should become a "statue of salt" (cf. Gen. 19:26), a thing which, as I hear, happened to a certain woman. Yet, truly, the powers from without still hinder me, like magistrates searching out some deserter. But, especially, my own heart holds me back, testifying to itself to all those things which I have said.

But, when you recalled our agreements and announced that you would bring charges, you made me laugh even in the midst of this dejection of mine, because you are still an advocate and are not giving up your cleverness. For, I think thus— that, unless like an unlearned person I am straying from the truth altogether, there is one road which leads to the Lord, and all those going to Him travel in company with one another and proceed according to one rule of life. Therefore, where can I go and be separated from you and not live with you and with you serve God, to whom we have by common consent fled for refuge? For, our bodies may be separated by material space, but certainly the eye of God looks upon us both together, if my life is really worthy of being viewed by the eyes of God, for I have read somewhere in the Psalms that "the eyes of the Lord are upon the just" (Ps. 33:16). And I do indeed pray to be bodily present both with you and with everyone who makes a choice similar to yours, and also every night and day to bend my knees to our Father in heaven with you and with any other who is worthily calling upon God. I know that union in prayers brings much gain. Yet, if the charge of falsehood will assuredly follow me as often as I shall happen to complain when cast aside in a different little corner, I cannot contradict the word. But, I already condemn myself as a liar if I have made any statement in my former condition of indifference which makes me liable to the charge of a falsehood.

After I had come near enough to Caesarea to become acquainted with the state of affairs, since I was not willing to enter the city itself, I took refuge in the nearby almshouse in order to learn there what I wished. Then, when the bishop dearly beloved of God came to visit according to his custom, I referred to him what your Eloquence had commanded us. And, though we could not keep in memory what he answered, and it exceeded the length of a letter, yet to sum up, concerning poverty he said that this was the measure—that each should limit his possessions to the last tunic. And he offered us proofs from the Gospel—one from John the Baptist who said: "Let him who has two tunics share with him who has none" (Luke 3:11); and another from our Lord who forbade His disciples to have two tunics. And he added to these, also, the statement: "If thou wilt be perfect, go, sell what thou hast, and give to the poor" (Matt. 19:21). And he also said that the parable of the pearl refers to this, because the merchant who found the precious pearl, going away, sold all his possessions and bought it. Again, he added to this that a person ought not to leave the distribution of his substance to himself, but to him who has been entrusted with the management of the affairs of the poor. And he proved this from the Acts (cf. Acts 4:34-35), that they would sell what belonged to them and, bringing [the price], "lay it at the feet of the apostles, and by them distribution was made to each according as anyone had need." For, he said that the power of distinguishing him who is truly in need from him who is asking through avarice required experience. And he who gives to the afflicted has given to the Lord and from Him will receive the reward, but he who provides for every wanderer has cast it to a dog, troublesome because of his shamelessness, but not to be pitied on account of indigence.

Now, concerning the matter of how we ought to live day by day, he had time to say but little, considering the importance of the subject, but I would prefer for you to have learned this from the man himself. For, it is not reasonable for me to mar the exactness of his teachings. But, I have prayed to visit him some day with you, in order that you, while preserving accurately in your memory what is said, may also by your own intelligence find out what is left unsaid. For, from the many things I heard I remember this—that instruction on how the Christian should live is not so much in need of speech as of daily example. And I know that, if the bond of responsibility for your aged father did not hold you back, you yourself would have preferred nothing to a conference with the bishop, nor would you have advised me to leave him and wander into the solitude. For, the caves and the rocks await us, but the advantages accruing to us from men are not always at hand. Therefore, if you would permit me to advise you, you would impress upon your father that he should allow you to depart from him for a little while and to meet the man who knows much both from the experience of others and from his own intelligence, and is able to offer it to those who come to him.

27. Gregory of Nyssa, *Ad Graecos*

The youngest of the three Cappadocian Fathers, Gregory was consecrated bishop of Nyssa in 372. After the death of his brother, Basil of Caesarea, Gregory took the lead in the struggle against the remaining advocates of Arianism. He played a prominent role at the Council of Constantinople (381), the Second Ecumenical Council, which affirmed a trinitarian statement of faith. It was probably shortly after this council that Gregory wrote Ad Graecos, *a treatise explaining the meaning of the word "person" when applied to God and emphasizing the relational nature of the Trinity.*

SOURCE: Gregory of Nyssa, "How It Is That We Say There Are Three Persons in the Divinity But Do Not Say There Are Three Gods (To the Greeks: Concerning the Commonality of Concepts)," tr. Douglas F. Stramara, Jr., in *The Greek Orthodox Theological Review* 41 (1996): 381-86. Used by permission of the *Greek Orthodox Theological Review*.

How It Is That We Say
There Are Three Persons in the Divinity
But Do Not Say There Are Three Gods
(To the Greeks: Concerning the
Commonality of Concepts)

[19] If the term "God" were indicative of the Person, then out of necessity when we speak of the three Persons we would be saying three Gods, but if the term "God" signifies the essence, when we confess the one essence of the Holy Trinity we rightly teach as doctrine that there is one God since the term "God" refers to one essence. Therefore it follows that God is one both according to essence and terminology, not three. Neither do we assert God and God and God (just as we say Father and Son and Holy Spirit, when we combine the terms signifying the Persons by the conjunction "and"), because the Persons are not the same but different—they differ from one another according to the very significance of their names. To the term "God" which signifies the essence, because of a certain characteristic property pertaining to the essence, we do not add the conjunction "and" so as to say God and God and God. This indeed is the essence of which the Persons are constituted, and which the term "God" signifies. Wherefore, God is one and the same, the conjunction "and" is never employed between a thing and itself.

[20] Whether we say Father-God and Son-God and Holy Spirit-God or God the Father and God the Son and God the Holy Spirit we combine them with the conjunction "and" according to the meaning of the terms of the Persons, such as Father, Son, Holy Spirit, so that there might be a Father and a Son and a Holy Spirit, that is to say a Person and a Person and a Person; wherefore, there are indeed three Persons. The term "God" is absolutely and in like manner predicated of each one of the Persons without the conjunction "and," so that we cannot say God and God and God, but conceive of the second and third term as being said with regard to the subsisting Persons, propounding the second and third time without the conjunction "and" on account of there not being another and another God.

For it is not because the Father preserves his otherness with regard to the Son that the Father is God, for thus the Son would not be God. For if because the Father is Father, for this reason the Father is God, it would follow that since the Son is not the Father, then the Son would not be God. If the Son is God, he is not God in that he is Son. Similarly, the Father too is not God in that he is Father. They are God because of their Divine Essence, the essence of the Father and the Son. Through the Divine Essence the Father is God and the Son is God and the Holy Spirit is God.

And there is no division of the essence into each of the Persons so that there are three essences for the respective Persons. It is evident that the term "God" is not to be divided, since it signifies the essence; such a division would result in three gods. But just as the Father is essence, and the Son is essence, and the Holy Spirit is essence—yet there are not three essences—so too, the Father is God, the Son is God and the Holy Spirit is God; yet there are not three gods. For God is one and the same, since there is one and the same essence, [21] even if it is said that each of the Persons is essential and is God. For either it is necessary to say that there are three essences, that of the Father, that of the Son, and that of the Holy Spirit, inasmuch as the essence is proper to each of the Persons—something which is utterly unreasonable to maintain seeing that we do not call Peter, Paul and Barnabas three essences (for the essence is one and the same for such persons); or, we must state that the essence is one to which belong the Father and the Son and the Holy Spirit, although we know each of the Persons as essential, rightly and reasonably declaring that God is One, even though we believe each of the Persons to be God by reason of the communion of essence. Thus, inasmuch as the Father is different from the Son and from the Holy Spirit, we profess the three Persons of the Father and of the Son and of the Holy Spirit. In the same way, because the Father does not differ from the Son and the Holy Spirit according to essence, we say that there is one essence of the Father and of the Son and of the Holy Spirit.

For since there is a distinction, there is a Trinity according to distinction, and since there is an identity, there is a Unity on account of the identity. Therefore, there is an identity of the Persons according to essence, and a Unity proper to Them on account of the essence. If according to essence there is a Unity of the Holy Trinity, it is clear that there is also a Unity according to the term "God." For this term designates the essence but not by furnishing its quiddity (since indeed the Divine Essence is incomprehensible, even unascertainable). Taken from a certain specific property belonging [22] to the essence, the term "God" intimates the essence, just as neighing and laughing are said to be specific properties of natures and indicate those natures of which they are the specific properties. Indeed there is a specific property of the eternal essence to which the Father, Son and Holy Spirit belong, that is to oversee all things, to perceive all things and to know all things, not only those things which actually exist, but also those things conceived by the mind. This property is proper to that essence alone. Indeed, that essence is the Cause underlying the entire universe and has created everything and governs everything as its own creation; it holds sway over human affairs by a certain appropriate and inexpressible word.

Consequently, the term "God," properly signifies that essence which truly governs the universe as the creator of everything. So then, while there is one essence to which belong Father, Son and Holy Spirit, and while the one term indicates this essence (namely, "God"), God will rightly be one according to the rationale of this essence, and there is no reason forcing us to say "three gods," just as there are not three essences. For since in the case of Peter, Paul and Barnabas we do not declare there to be three essences since they are of one essence, how much more so in the case of the Father, Son and Holy Spirit will we not declare this properly? For if the essence is not to be divided into three according to the persons, it is obvious that neither should God be, because the term "God" does not indicate Person, but rather the essence. For if the term "God" designated a Person, then only one [23] of the Persons would be called God—Person would be signified by this name God—just as the Father alone is called Father because this name designates his Person.

But if someone were to say that we call Peter, Paul and Barnabas three individuated essences (it is clear that this means each his own), for this is

quite accurate to say, let it be known that by an individuated essence (that is one's own) we wish to signify nothing other than an individual, in other words, a person. Wherefore indeed, even if we say three individuated essences, that is, individual essences, we declare nothing other than three persons; whereas the term "God" does not follow suit upon the Persons, as has been shown. Neither does the term follow suit upon the individuated essence (in other words, individual essence), for the individual essence is the same thing as the person when used with respect to indivisible things. What then must be said regarding this, that we call Peter, Paul and Barnabas three Mans? Even though these are persons, the term "persons" does not signify the common essence in this usage; likewise, neither does the so-called individuated or individual essence, since this is the same thing as the person. For what reason do we say three "mans" exist of one essence—the term "Man" designates it—if we do not say it on account of the three persons nor because we speak of an individuated, or individual essence? Rather, we say this by a misuse of language and not correctly, on account of a certain customary usage arising out of necessary principles, which, however, we do not find in our analysis of the Holy Trinity so that we do not make the very same assertion with respect to the Trinity itself.

[24] These are the principles: the definition of Man is not always observed in the same individuals or persons, for while the former ones are dying others are coming into existence, and again while many of them still remain, yet others are being born, so that the defining measure of this nature, that is to say Man, is observed sometimes in these individuals here, sometimes in those there, sometimes in the very many and sometimes in the very few. Therefore, for this reason, that is the addition and subtraction, the death and birth of individuals, in whom the defining measure of Man is perceived, we are constrained to say "many mans" and "few mans" because of the change and alteration of the persons, the common usage being displaced along with the definition of essence, so that somehow we number essences along with the persons.

No such thing ever results in the case of the Holy Trinity, for it is necessary to say that the self-same Persons exist and not another and another, always being the same and in just the same manner. We do not admit a certain addition resulting in a quaternity, nor a diminution into a duality. For neither is another Person begotten or brought forth from the Father or from one of the other Persons so that a quaternity arises from a former trinity; nor does one of these three Persons pass away even for the blink of an eye as it were, so that the trinity becomes a duality even in rational analysis. For there is absolutely no addition or diminution, change or alteration pertaining to the three Persons of the Father and of the Son and of the Holy Spirit so that our conception of the three Persons should be led astray and we be forced to admit "three gods."

Or again, all the persons belonging to Man [25] do not directly possess their being from the same person, but some from this one and some from that one, so that with respect to the individuals caused there are also many and diverse causes. But with regard to the Holy Trinity, such is not the case, for there is one and the same Person, that of the Father, from whom the Son is begotten and the Holy Spirit proceeds. Wherefore indeed, rightly so and boldly do we proclaim one God, one Cause together with its Caused Realities, since it coexists with Them. For the Persons of the Divinity are not separated from one another either by time or place, not by will or by practice, not by activity or by passion, not by anything of this sort, such as is observed with regard to human beings. This alone is observed, that the Father is Father and not Son, and the Son is Son and not Father; and, likewise, the Holy Spirit is neither Father nor Son. For this very reason there is absolutely no necessity for anyone to trick us into calling the three Persons: "three gods"; just as we call many human beings "many persons" according to the aforesaid reasons.

Because according to the aforesaid reasons and not according to strict logic do we call the many persons of Man many mans; hence it is clearly obvious that Man, in and of itself, is one and cannot become many. As everyone agrees, Peter, Paul and Barnabas are called one Man as far as humanity is concerned. Consequently, in itself, that is to say insofar as Man is concerned, there cannot be many of them. To say many "mans" is a misuse of language and is not said in a proper sense. It is neither right nor possible that the common misusage should destroy the proper meaning and usage [26] for those who have a good understanding about this. Therefore, one must not end up saying with regard to the three Persons of the Divine Essence: "three gods," on account of the identity of the essence which is signified by the term "God" in the way described above.

28. The Christianization of Armenia: Agathangelos, *History of the Armenians*

Nestled in the Caucasus and straddling major trade routes to the east, Armenia was a frequent victim of rivalry between the Roman and Persian Empires. The Christianization of Armenia is associated with Gregory the Illuminator (ca. 240-332), who, according to tradition, converted the pagan king Tiridates (Trdat), ca. 301. The king's conversion was followed by that of the whole kingdom, making Armenia the first state to adopt Christianity as its official religion. In the following excerpts, the fifth-

SOURCE: Agathangelos, *History of the Armenians*, ed. and tr. Robert W. Thomson (Albany: State University of New York Press, 1976), 189-91, 217-43, 311-13, 365-71, 401-15. Copyright © 1976 by State University of New York. Reprinted by permission. All rights reserved.

century Armenian chronicler known as Agathangelos recounts [semi-legendary] episodes from the life of Gregory the Illuminator and the triumph of Christianity over paganism.

[*Gregory, a Parthian who was brought up as a Christian in Asia Minor, has entered the service of the pagan king Trdat of Armenia, apparently to atone for the murder of Trdat's father by his own father, though Gregory keeps his identity a secret. Trdat however submits Gregory to torture for confessing his Christian faith, and then, on learning his identity, has him thrown into a deep pit, where he languishes for thirteen years. Toward the end of that time, a beautiful Roman nun named Rhipsimē, having received unwanted attention from the Roman emperor, flees to Armenia, only to fall prey to Trdat.*]

180. While saint Rhipsimē was offering all these prayers to God, king Trdat entered the chamber where she had been shut up. Now when he came in, all the populace, some outside the palace, others in the streets, and others inside (the city), all together struck up songs [cf. 3 Macc. 6:23] and dancing. Some filled the citadel, others the center of the town, with merry-making. They all intended to celebrate the wedding with dancing. But the Lord God looked down on his beloved Rhipsimē in order to save her, lest the treasure she had preserved so carefully be lost [cf. 2 Tim. 1:12], and he heard her prayers and fortified her like Jael and like Deborah [cf. Judges 4]. He strengthened her to be saved from the impious tyrant's grasp.

181. When the king entered, he seized her in order to work his lustful desires. But she, strengthened by the holy Spirit, struggled like a beast and fought like a man. They fought from the third hour until the tenth and she vanquished the king who was renowned for his incredible strength. While he was in the Greek empire he had shown such bodily strength that everyone had been amazed; and in his own realm, when he had returned to his native land, he had shown there too many deeds of mighty valor. And he, who was so famous in every respect, now was vanquished and worsted by a single girl through the will and power of Christ.

...

[*For Rhipsimē's disobedience to the king, his nobles cause her to be tortured and killed, along with many other Christians.*]

211. The king spent six days in profound grief and deep mourning because of his passionate love for the beautiful Rhipsimē. Then afterwards he arranged to go hunting; he had his soldiers gather the pack of hounds, the beaters scattered, the nets fixed, and the traps set; then he went out to hunt in the plain of P'arakan Shemak.

212. But when the king, having mounted his chariot, was about to leave the city, then suddenly there fell on him punishment from the Lord. An impure demon struck the king and knocked him down from his chariot. Then he began to rave and to eat his own flesh. And in the likeness of Nebuchadnezzar, king of Babylon, he lost his human nature for the likeness of wild pigs and went about like them and dwelt among them [cf. Dan. 4:12-13]. Then entering a reedy place, in senseless abandon he pastured on grass, and wallowed naked in the plain. For although they wished to restrain him in the city, they were unable to do so, partly because of his natural strength and partly because of the force of the demons who had possessed him.

213. Likewise all the populace in the city went mad through similar demon-possession. And terrible ruin fell upon the country. All the king's household, including slaves and servants, were afflicted with torments. And there was terrible mourning on account of these afflictions.

214. Then there appeared a vision from God to the king's sister, whose name was Khosrovidukht. So she came to speak with the people and related the vision, saying: "A vision appeared to me this night. A man in the likeness of light came and told me 'there is no other cure for these torments that have come upon you, unless you send to the city of Artashat and bring thence the prisoner Gregory. When he comes he will teach you the remedy for your ills.'"

215. When the populace heard this they began to mock at her words. They began to say: "You too then are mad. Some demon has possessed you. How is it, because it is fifteen years since they threw him into the terribly deep pit, that you say he is alive? Where would even his bones be? For on the same day when they put him down there, he would have immediately dropped dead at the very sight of the snakes."

216. But the princess had the same vision again, five times, with threats that unless she reported it immediately she would suffer great torments and the afflictions of the people and of the king would become even worse, with death and various tortures. So Khosrovidukht came forward again in great fear and hesitation, and told the angel's words.

217. Then they straightaway sent there a noble prince, whose name was Awtay. He went to the city of Artashat in order to bring him out of the dungeon and deep pit. Now when Awtay arrived at the city of Artashat, the citizens came out to meet him to ask the reason for his coming. He told them: "I have come to take away the prisoner Gregory." But they were amazed and all said: "Who knows if he is there? For it is many years since they threw him there." But he related to them the details of the vision and everything that had happened.

218. So they went and brought long, thick, strong ropes, which they attached and let down inside; Awtay the prince shouted with a loud voice and said: "Gregory, if you are somewhere down there, come out [cf. John 11:43]. For the Lord your God whom you worshiped has commanded that you be brought forth." Then he stood up, and straightway moved the rope and shook it strongly.

219. When they felt this they pulled him up; and they saw that his body was blackened like coal [cf. Job 30:30]. Then they brought clothing and dressed him, and joyfully took him from the city of Artashat and led him to Vaḷarshapat. Then, sorely afflicted, the king left the herd of swine; led by the demon he came to meet them, naked and ignominious. And the princes waited for them outside the city.

220. Now when they saw afar off Gregory coming with Awtay and many other men coming with them from Artashat, they ran to meet them, raving and eating their own flesh, possessed and foaming [cf. Mark 9:19].

221. Then he immediately knelt in prayer, and they returned to sobriety. He then commanded that they cover their bodies with clothes and hide their shame. The king and the princes approached, took hold of saint Gregory's feet and said: "We beg you, forgive us the crime that we committed against you."

222. Then he came forward and raised them from the ground and said: "I am a man like you [cf. Acts 10:26], and I have a body like yours. But do you recognize your creator, who made heaven and earth, the sun and moon and stars, the sea and the dry land. He is able to heal you."

223. Then Gregory began to ask them where the bodies of the martyrs of God had been placed. They said: "Of what martyrs are you speaking?" He replied: "Those who died at your hands for their God." Then they showed him the places. And he hastened to bring together their bodies from the places where they had been killed, for they were still lying there, and to enshroud them. And they saw that the power of God had preserved their bodies; for it was the ninth day and ninth night that their bodies had been lying outside and no animal or dog had approached, although they were around the city near to it; nor had any bird harmed them, nor did their bodies stink [cf. John 11:39].

224. Then they brought clean clothes for shrouds. But blessed Gregory did not consider the shrouds brought by the king worthy, nor those of other people. But he wrapped each saint in her torn clothing. "For a while," he said, "until you are worthy to wrap their bodies." And he enshrouded them and took them to the vat-store, where they had had their lodging, and he made it his own dwelling place. Then blessed Gregory prayed all night to God for their (the Armenians') salvation, and begged that they might be converted and find a way to repentance.

225. In the morning the king and the princes and the great magnates and the common people came in a great crowd and knelt before saint Gregory and before the holy bones of God's martyrs, and begged: "Forgive us all the evil crimes that we

have committed against you. And beg your God on our behalf that we perish not."

226. Then the prisoner Gregory began to speak: "The one you call 'your God' is God and creator, who in his almighty benevolence has brought material creatures into being from immaterial nothing [cf. 2 Macc. 7:28; Rom. 4:17]. The same ordered the earth to be established by his essential power from uncircumscribed, boundless nothing. He who created everything is the almighty, all-creative and all-loving God. Recognize him, in order that your pains from the punishment of your crimes may be healed. He warned you in his benevolent mercy according to the saying of the divine Wisdom: 'Whom God loves he warns; he castigates the son for whom he cares' [Prov. 3:12; 13:24; Heb. 12:6]. Now in his benevolence he summons you to adoption [cf. Eph. 1:5].

227. "The true Son of God considers it no shame to call his brothers [cf. Heb. 2:11] those who will turn to the worship of the Father. And the holy Spirit will grant you the pledge of his love [cf. 2 Cor. 1:22], and awaken your hearts to the joy which passes not away. But only if you turn and walk according to his desires will he give you eternal life.

228. "But in saying 'your God' you spoke well, because for those who recognize him he is their God [cf. Heb. 11:16]. But for those who do not recognize him, even though they are his creatures, they are estranged from his care and from his benevolent love. But those who fear him are near to him [cf. Ps. 84:10], and his providence surrounds them and guards them [cf. Ps. 33:8].

229. "But perhaps you will say: 'Where does he guard his worshippers? For those who fell into our hands were tortured and killed, and we judged them according to our own desires.' See that God desired the repose of death for men, and at his second and glorious coming he will reveal [cf. Acts 3.20] and give blessings to his beloved and to those who recognize him and do his will.

230. "But see this, how by the power of his divinity he kept firm his beloved holy martyrs; nor did many tribulations make a single one of them lose heart. And he saved the holy and blessed Rhipsimē and her companions from your impurity and impiety.

231. "Now (see how) the deceit of the enemy's machinations, which from the beginning beguiled and deceived men [cf. Eph. 4:14], made them travelers on the path to destruction. Or (see) my unworthiness, and how by his benevolence he made me worthy and prepared me to suffer for his great name's sake. And he gave me endurance, to bring me to the heavenly inheritance, as the great apostle Paul said [cf. Acts 26:18; Col. 1:12]— whom you could recognize and at whose words you could rejoice through the benevolence of Christ: 'Blessed is he who made us worthy to attain the portion of the inheritance of the saints in light [cf. Acts 20:32; Eph. 1:18; Col. 1:12; Heb. 11:8]. And truly we have attained gloriously the cross of Christ, that by the passion of Christ we may enjoy his will and his teaching.

232. "Now recognize him who called you from darkness to the wonderful light of his glory [cf. 1 Pet. 2:9]. Approach the throne of his grace and you will obtain mercy from him [cf. Heb. 4:16]. Throw off every stain of evil lawlessness. Wash your souls with living water [cf. Heb. 10:22], and you will become worthy to clothe your souls in robes of glorious light [cf. Rom. 13:12].

233. "But as for saint Rhipsimē, you yourselves know how the Lord preserved her and saved her from your hands, from impious pollution. And you yourself know the measure of the strength and firmness of your own bones, how you became weakened in front of a single girl. For the power of the Lord of all, Christ, preserved her. And as for me, you know that for fifteen years I have been in the dark and incredibly deep pit, dwelling amidst snakes—yet for fear of the Lord they never harmed me, nor was I terrified of them nor was my heart dismayed. For I hoped in the Lord God the creator of all [cf. Ps. 26:3].

234. "But this I know, that it was in ignorance that you did what you did [cf. Eph. 4:18]. Nevertheless, turn now and recognize the Lord [cf. Heb. 8:11], that he may have mercy on you and give you life. Call upon those whom you killed, but who are alive, as intercessors; for they are alive and are not dead. Recognize God, for he is Lord of all. Abandon henceforth the foul worship of images of stone and wood, silver and gold and bronze, which are false and vain.

235. "Did I not tell you earlier about your error that a fog of thick and murky darkness has settled over the eyes of your heart [cf. Isa. 60:2; Ezek. 34:12], so that you are unable to see, comprehend, consider or recognize the creator. Now if I were to see in you some inclination to approach the divinity piously, I would not cease to pray night and day on your behalf that you perish not. For the great benevolence of the creator towards his creatures is inscrutable and ineffable; he is long suffering in forgiving, pardoning, nourishing and caring because of his great mercy.

236. "From the first days he allowed men to walk according to their own wishes, as (scripture) says: 'I have permitted them to follow the wishes of their own hearts; and they went according to their own desires' [Ps. 80:13]. But now he has begun to call you to his own glory and incorruptibility [cf. 2 Tim. 1:10], for you to become heirs of the eternal life that passes not away [cf. Tit. 3:7].

237. "For that reason he sent his beloved martyrs to you; who in their martyrdom bore witness to the consubstantial majesty of the Trinity, God with all and above all, who exists for all eternity. His kingdom is an eternal kingdom, and of his rule there is no end [cf. Ps. 47:15; 144:13]. They made their death a faithful and firm seal of the truth of their faith [cf. Rom. 4:11], the account of which is now being related in your midst. They are alive with God and intercede for those who commemorate them; we pray to have their intercession with God. Because they died for God they can turn the death of many into life.

238. "Therefore through them be reconciled to God by means of the death of the Son of God [cf. Rom. 5:10]. For the Son of God died to vivify the mortality of creatures [cf. Rom. 8:11]; whereas they died to become witnesses to his Godhead. Not indeed that he was unable to give life without dying himself, but in order to magnify the creatures by his own descent to humility, and to elevate the humble by his becoming like us [cf. Heb. 2:17].

239. "Not indeed that he could not be believed without their testimony, but that those who loved him might magnify him. And he preserved our breath in our body, although there came upon us afflictions of bodily sufferings and terrible pains.

We were tormented more than any other men. How was it possible for human bodily nature to endure for one day the fearful severity of those tortures? Or how could a man live for a single day in that terribly deep pit in which I was buried amidst piles of snakes that swarmed around my body and wrapped themselves around me and crawled over my limbs? But the wonderful mercy of the Lord preserved me alive. And of what I was previously unworthy, behold we now serve among you words of healing labor and profit for souls and bodies. We have been made the doctor of your souls and bodies to offer you help.

240. "By the benevolence of God let us begin to nourish you with heavenly words [cf. Ezek. 3:2]. For if you will listen to the word of truth, the message of the gospel and the commands of the creator of all, you will be delivered and cleansed from your minor punishment and you will enjoy eternal life. Hear the divine word, and you will receive in your souls the blessing of the kingdom of heaven [cf. Heb. 12:28].

241. "Only if you are cleansed of the unwilling ignorance of your sins, from the worship of stones and wood, will you be able to receive in your souls the ineffable blessings of God. Then the holy martyrs of God, whom you tortured, will be able to offer intercession on your behalf; and our words and discourses and effort and labor will be sown as profit for you, they will let you enjoy on earth long and happy lives, and make you heirs in heaven to eternal life [cf. Tit. 3:7].

242. "But if you refuse to hear the preaching of the word of life, then he will strike and kill you with vengeful and cruel blows, and he will judge you by means of foreign enemies, and also taking revenge on you will bring you to death."

243. When blessed Gregory had said all this, they all together put their hands to their collars and tore their garments [cf. 1 Macc. 4:39]. The king and the princes and the rest of the multitude of the populace fell to the ground and rolled in ashes and said together as with one mouth: "Now have we any hope of forgiveness from God? For we were lost in our ignorance on the path of darkness [cf. Eph. 4:18]. Can now these many sins of ours be forgiven?"

244. Gregory replied, saying: "God is benevo-

lent, long-suffering and very merciful [cf. Ps. 85:15; 102:8; 144:8]. He is kind to all those who invoke him [cf. Ps. 144:18] and he forgives those who beseech him."

245. Then they said: "Inform us and confirm our minds that we may be able to appeal to the face of our creator whom we did not know, if he will turn and accept our repentance and if there is still opportunity for conversion; or has he not already cut off our hope of life [cf. Eph. 4:19]? Do you not remember the crimes which we did to you, and will you give us true teaching, and not hold rancor against us nor regard us with antipathy nor hinder us from the true road?"

. . .

[Gregory gives the assembled penitent Armenians a very long explanation of Christian doctrine; and later relates to the king and nobles a symbolic vision he has received from God directing them to build chapels on the sites of the deaths of Rhipsimē and the other martyrs. They build the chapels and enshrine the martyrs' bodies there.]

773. Now, when they had all gathered together in the place of worship of the house of God, blessed Gregory began to speak, saying: "Bend the knee, everyone, that the Lord may effect the healing of your torments." They all bent the knee to God, and blessed Gregory with fervent prayers and supplications tearfully implored healing for the king. And the king, while he was standing among the people with the appearance of a pig, suddenly trembled and threw off from his body the pig-like skin with its tusk-like teeth and snout-like face, and he cast off the skin with its pig-like hair. His face returned to its own form and his body became soft and young like that of a newly born infant; he was completely healed in all his limbs.

774. In similar fashion all the people who were gathered in great numbers were cured of each one's affliction: some had been lepers, some paralytic, crippled, hydropic, possessed, suffering from worms or gout. Thus Christ in his mercy opened his all-powerful healing grace, and healed all through Gregory; those afflicted were cured of each disease. So also was the source of knowledge

of Christ opened and it filled the ears of all with the true teaching of God.

775. Then was there heartfelt rejoicing and a joyful visage on the onlookers. For the land, which until then had been ignorant of reports of those regions where all the divine miracles had been worked, now suddenly was informed of what had occurred—not only of what had recently been done, but also of the earlier messages and what later came about, of the beginning and the end, and of all the divine traditions.

. . . .

[Gregory travels to Caesarea to be consecrated as bishop, then returns to Armenia.]

828. Then he according to his usual habit set himself to unceasing instruction, and with the assistance of the pious king Trdat set forth his skill and continuously gave admonition. Thus ever more people came to obey him according to God's commands, the king and all the army with the mass of the common people, all undertaking to fulfill his request and execute his orders.

829. And he commanded the royal camp to spend a month in fasting and prayer. With his companions that he had brought thence he imposed on himself his customary fasting and prayer, vigils, tearful supplications, austerities, world-lamenting cares, having regard for the words of the inspired prophet: "When you will lament, then you will live" [Isa. 30:15].

830. In this way he exerted much effort to find blessing and grace for the whole land. To him the gift was granted by all-gracious God to produce a new and wonderful birth in fatherly fashion, by his holy and liberal right hand; to give birth once again to everyone by baptism from water and the womb of the Spirit [cf. John 3:5], to perfect, purify and seal one people of the Lord.

831. There he set foundations and built a church; and the relics which he had of the saints' bones he deposited in the Lord's house. In this way throughout all parts of the provinces he set foundations for churches and erected altars and established priests. The whole land was converted, and with all their hearts they were assiduous in fasting and in the service and fear of God.

832. Then at the final completion of the fast, blessed Gregory took the mass of the army and the king himself and his wife Ashkhēn and the princess Khosrovidukht and all the magnates with all the people of the camp, and in the morning at dawn he brought them to the banks of the river Euphrates, and there he baptized them all together in the name of the Father and of the Son and of the Holy Spirit [cf. Matt. 28:19].

833. And when all the people and the king went down to baptism in the water of the river Euphrates, a wonderful sign was revealed by God: the waters of the river stopped and then turned back again. And a bright light appeared in the likeness of a shining pillar, and it stood over the waters of the river; and above it was the likeness of the Lord's cross. And the light shone out so brightly that it obscured and weakened the rays of the sun. And the oil of anointing which Gregory poured over the people floated around them in the river. Everyone was amazed and raised blessings to God's glory. In the evening the sign disappeared, and they returned to the town. And those who were baptized on that day were more than one hundred and fifty thousand persons from the royal army.

834. They went forth in great joy, in white garments, with psalms and blessings [cf. Eph. 5:19] and lighted lamps and burning candles and blazing torches, with great rejoicing and happiness, illuminated and become like the angels. They had received the title of God's adoption [cf. Rom. 8:15, etc.], had entered the heritage of the holy gospel [cf. Eph. 1:18], and being joined to the rank of the saints [cf. Acts 26:18] were flowering with sweet odor in Christ [cf. Eph. 5:2; Phil. 4:18]. So they went forth and returned to the Lord's house. There he offered the blessed sacrifice and communicated them all with the blessed sacrament, distributing to all the holy body and precious blood of Christ the Savior of all, who vivifies and gives life to all men, the creator and fashioner of all creatures; and he liberally administered to all the divinely given grace.

835. After this he remained there seven days for spiritual consolation. And in those seven days from the royal camp there were baptized—men, women and children—more than four million.

. . . .

867. At that time Constantine, son of Constantius the king, became emperor in Spain and Gaul. And he believed in God, in the creator of heaven and earth, and in his offspring, the Word, the only-begotten Son, and the holy Spirit of his Godhead. He gathered to himself a multitude of his forces by the shore of the fearsome Ocean sea, and he made this covenant with them all, that they should all in unison believe in the truth, and with a single divine voice they should be a perfect race glorifying the one God.

868. And trusting in God he marched against the heathen kings, and there suppressed them all, destroying them by the power of the divine cross, the foul and impious kings Diocletian and Marcianos and Maximianos and Licinius and Maxentius; and all the offspring of these foul heathen kings he exterminated.

869. He rebuilt the destroyed churches and restored the overthrown altars in the house of the Lord. He built chapels for the martyrs, and multiplied the glory of the commemorations of the blessed martyrs, and increased the honor of the priests of God, at once bestowing peace on the inhabitants of the earth and removing scandals, that no one in any way might slip from the path that leads to God. He destroyed the impure temples of the demons and obliterated them altogether, turning their ministers to flight. Honors and gifts he bestowed on those who kept to true piety and never abandoned its security. Therefore victory was given him over everyone, because he took for himself the sign of the victorious cross.

870. And the firm order of the commandment of truth—to stand firmly in the faith [cf. 1 Tim. 2:15] which comes from the Lord—he spread throughout the world by his edicts, terrifying (everyone) by his victorious power to cleave to the true piety of the light of faith in the Lord. Thus he pursued the hosts of darkness and overcame them all by his power from above. Those who agreed to become worshipers of the truth he honored and treated as his friends. In this fashion he became powerful and strengthened his rule over mankind, calling his kingdom a divinely-established kingdom. He became so powerful over all men that truly he was glorified.

871. Thus he so consolidated his victorious position that all the days of his life an angel appeared from heaven continuously serving him every day: every morning he took the crown (marked) with Christ's sign and put it on his head. So the blessed and most wonderful of all kings, Constantine, saw the heavenly angel in his service. And he, the pious and all-victorious, who established his kingdom in faith and confirmed the true faith in all churches, offered the purple of his royalty to Christ.

872. At that time this news reached Greater Armenia, the royal court of the Arsacids, and Trdat king of Greater Armenia. When he heard this he rendered great glory to the Lord of all. With joy and rejoicing he thanked him who had made his holy name glorious throughout all the land.

873. Then when the great king of Armenia, Trdat, heard this he held council to consider this journey. He made preparations and took with him the great archbishop Gregory and his son bishop Aristakēs and the other bishop, Albianos; and from the armed forces the four most senior ranking of his court, who are called *bdeashkh*: the first the border-guard from the district of Nor Shirakan, the second the border guard from Assyria, the third from the district of Aruastan, the fourth from the district of the Massagetae; the great prince of the house of Angḷ, and the *aspet* who crowned (the kings), and the great High-Constable, and the prince of Mokkʻ, the prince of Siwnikʻ, the prince of the Rshtunikʻ, the prince of the house of the *Maḷkhazdom*, the prefect of Shahapivan and the master of the court. And with many other magnates and with seventy thousand chosen troops he hastened from the province of Ayrarat, from the city of Vaḷarshapat to pass into Greek territory.

874. In great joy they passed many stages, and met with honorable receptions and solicitous honors from every city they came to and from every noble they met. By land and by sea they hastened on their way until they arrived in the empire of the Italians, in the land of the Dalmatians, in the royal capital of Rome.

875. Straightaway news of this was reported to the royal palace. When the emperor Constantine, established by God and honorable holder of the throne, and the great Patriarch, archbishop of the imperial court who was called Eusebius, heard this, with great love they honored them and went out to meet them. Greeting each other mutually they rejoiced. And when they had been some while in the universal city, then the pious emperor Constantine was amazed, and he asked king Trdat: "How and in what manner did these miracles of God occur among you?"

876. Then he stood before the emperor and told him of all the blessings performed by God for him; nor was he ashamed to narrate the fearful punishment of his being in the form of an animal. And he told about the heroic endurance of the brave martyrs, and what deeds were done, and what was their strength. Then he introduced to the emperor Gregory, whom he had brought with him, saying: "This is the man through whom we came to know God's benevolence [cf. Tit. 3:4] and the long-suffering endurance of his wondrous miracles." At this the emperor Constantine was amazed, and humbled himself and fell before Gregory to be blessed by him. And with many splendid honors he exalted him as a confessor of Christ according to his merits.

877. Similarly with great happiness he showed love for king Trdat as for a dear brother, especially because of his recognition of God. And furthermore he made an alliance with him, holding their faith in the Lord Christ as an intermediary so that they might constantly and forever keep faithful love between their kingdoms, and that he might confirm the Armenian king ever more and more in faith in the Trinity. Then Tiridates told about the martyrs of God and how and in what way they had been martyred.

878. Then the emperor Constantine began to tell him about their honorable life. For he had previously known, while they were still in their own land, how pleasing their life had been and how they were of noble descent. And he told of the powerful and victorious deeds given him by God so that he became victorious over all the enemies of the truth. He said: "Know, brother, that God reveals in every land his powerful mercy so that all his creatures may know him and become his praisers in truth, 'because he seeks such worshippers [John 4:23].'"

879. Then after this they were honored with great solicitude and splendid pomp by the court and the ecclesiastical officials and the honorable princes of the city. And with great offerings and notable presents they were lovingly honored.

880. Then they took their leave from the purpled Augusti and the holy Catholicos, being greeted by the church and the notable princes of the city, and triumphant in every way they mounted the imperial carriage decorated in gold, and with great éclat and much splendor they set out on their royal journey.

881. And in all the cities they passed they were splendidly treated and greatly honored according to their royal dignity until they arrived in Armenia, in the province of Ayrarat at the city of Vaḷarshapat and the martyr's resting-places.

Varieties of Ascetic Life
for Men and Women

29. Athanasius of Alexandria,
Life of Anthony of Egypt

Best known as a champion of Nicene orthodoxy in the struggle against Arianism, Bishop Athanasius of Alexandria was also an advocate of ascetic life and endeavored to integrate the monastic movement more fully into the church in Egypt. His Life of Anthony, *a biography of an early Egyptian hermit and older contemporary, was written ca. 357, quickly translated into Latin, and motivated men and women throughout the Roman Empire to imitate his way of life. Though Anthony himself lived as a solitary, his ascetic regimen served as a model for cenobitic as well anchoritic monasticism.*

The life and conversation of our holy Father, Anthony: written and sent to the monks in foreign parts by our Father among the Saints, Athanasius, Bishop of Alexandria.

Athanasius the bishop to the brethren in foreign parts.

You have entered upon a noble rivalry with the monks of Egypt by your determination either to equal or surpass them in your training in the way of virtue. For by this time there are monasteries among you, and the name of monk receives public recognition. With reason, therefore, all men will approve this determination, and in answer to your prayers God will give its fulfillment. Now since you asked me to give you an account of the blessed Anthony's way of life, and are wishful to learn how he began the discipline, who and what manner of man he was previous to this, how he closed his life, and whether the things told of him are true, that

you also may bring yourselves to imitate him, I very readily accepted your behest, for to me also the bare recollection of Anthony is a great accession of help. And I know that you, when you have heard, apart from your admiration of the man, will be wishful to emulate his determination; seeing that for monks the life of Anthony is a sufficient pattern of discipline . . .

I. Anthony you must know was by descent an Egyptian: his parents were of good family and possessed considerable wealth, and as they were Christians he also was reared in the same Faith. In infancy he was brought up with his parents, knowing nought else but them and his home. But when he was grown and arrived at boyhood, and was advancing in years, he could not endure to learn letters, not caring to associate with other boys; but all his desire was, as it is written of Jacob, to live a plain man at home. With his parents he used to attend the Lord's House, and neither as a

SOURCE: *Life of Anthony,* tr. John Henry Newman, in *A Select Library of Nicene and Post-Nicene Fathers of the Christian Church,* second series, vol. 4, ed. Philip Schaff and Henry Wace (New York: Christian Literature Publishing Company; Oxford and London: Parker & Company, 1892), 195-200, 208-10, 214-16, 217, 218-21.

child was he idle nor when older did he despise them; but was both obedient to his father and mother and attentive to what was read, keeping in his heart what was profitable in what he heard. And though as a child brought up in moderate affluence, he did not trouble his parents for varied or luxurious fare, nor was this a source of pleasure to him; but was content simply with what he found nor sought anything further.

2. After the death of his father and mother he was left alone with one little sister: his age was about eighteen or twenty, and on him the care both of home and sister rested. Now it was not six months after the death of his parents, and going according to custom into the Lord's House, he communed with himself and reflected as he walked how the Apostles left all and followed the Savior; and how they in the Acts sold their possessions and brought and laid them at the Apostles' feet for distribution to the needy, and what and how great a hope was laid up for them in heaven. Pondering over these things he entered the church, and it happened the Gospel was being read, and he heard the Lord saying to the rich man, "If you would be perfect, go and sell what you have and give to the poor; and come follow Me and thou shall have treasure in heaven" (Matt. 19:21). Anthony, as though God had put him in mind of the Saints, and the passage had been read on his account, went out immediately from the church, and gave the possessions of his forefathers to the villagers—they were three hundred acres, productive and very fair—that they should be no more a clog upon himself and his sister. And all the rest that was movable he sold, and having got together much money he gave it to the poor, reserving a little however for his sister's sake.

3. And again as he went into the church, hearing the Lord say in the Gospel, "be not anxious for the morrow" (Matt. 6:34), he could stay no longer, but went out and gave those things also to the poor. Having committed his sister to known and faithful virgins, and put her into a convent to be brought up, he henceforth devoted himself outside his house to discipline, taking heed to himself and training himself with patience. For there were not yet so many monasteries in Egypt, and no monk at all knew of the distant desert; but all who wished to give heed to themselves practiced the discipline in solitude near their own village. Now there was then in the next village an old man who had lived the life of a hermit from his youth up. Anthony, after he had seen this man, imitated him in piety. And at first he began to abide in places outside the village: then if he heard of a good man anywhere, like the prudent bee, he went forth and sought him, nor turned back to his own palace until he had seen him; and he returned, having got from the good man as it were supplies for his journey in the way of virtue. So dwelling there at first, he confirmed his purpose not to return to the abode of his fathers nor to the remembrance of his kinsfolk; but to keep all his desire and energy for perfecting his discipline. He worked, however, with his hands, having heard, "he who is idle let him not eat" (2 Thess. 3:10), and part he spent on bread and part he gave to the needy. And he was constant in prayer, knowing that a man ought to pray in secret unceasingly. For he had given such heed to what was read that none of the things that were written fell from him to the ground, but he remembered all, and afterwards his memory served him for books.

4. Thus conducting himself, Anthony was beloved by all. He subjected himself in sincerity to the good men whom he visited, and learned thoroughly where each surpassed him in zeal and discipline. He observed the graciousness of one; the unceasing prayer of another; he took knowledge of another's freedom from anger and another's loving-kindness; he gave heed to one as he watched, to another as he studied; one he admired for his endurance, another for his fasting and sleeping on the ground; the meekness of one and the long-suffering of another he watched with care, while he took note of the piety towards Christ and the mutual love which animated all. Thus filled, he returned to his own place of discipline, and henceforth would strive to unite the qualities of each, and was eager to show in himself the virtues of all. With others of the same age he had no rivalry; save this only, that he should not be second to them in higher things. And this he did so as to hurt the feelings of nobody, but made them rejoice over him. So all they of that village and the good men in whose intimacy he was,

when they saw that he was a man of this sort, used to call him God-beloved. And some welcomed him as a son, others as a brother.

5. But the devil, who hates and envies what is good, could not endure to see such a resolution in a youth, but endeavored to carry out against him what he had been wont to effect against others. First of all he tried to lead him away from the discipline, whispering to him the remembrance of his wealth, care for his sister, claims of kindred, love of money, love of glory, the various pleasures of the table and the other relaxations of life, and at last the difficulty of virtue and the labor of it; he suggested also the infirmity of the body and the length of the time. In a word he raised in his mind a great dust of debate, wishing to debar him from his settled purpose. But when the enemy saw himself to be too weak for Anthony's determination, and that he rather was conquered by the other's firmness, overthrown by his great faith and falling through his constant prayers, then at length putting his trust in the weapons which are "in the navel of his belly" (Job 40:16 LXX) and boasting in them—for they are his first snare for the young— he attacked the young man, disturbing him by night and harassing him by day, so that even the onlookers saw the struggle which was going on between them. The one would suggest foul thoughts and the other counter them with prayers: the one fire him with lust the other, as one who seemed to blush, fortify his body with faith, prayers, and fasting. And the devil, unhappy wight, one night even took upon him the shape of a woman and imitated all her acts simply to beguile Anthony. But he, his mind filled with Christ and the nobility inspired by Him, and considering the spirituality of the soul, quenched the coal of the other's deceit. Again the enemy suggested the ease of pleasure. But he like a man filled with rage and grief turned his thoughts to the threatened fire and the gnawing worm, and setting these in array against his adversary, passed through the temptation unscathed. All this was a source of shame to his foe. For he, deeming himself like God, was now mocked by a young man; and he who boasted himself against flesh and blood was being put to flight by a man in the flesh. For the Lord was working with Anthony—the

Lord who for our sake took flesh and gave the body victory over the devil, so that all who truly fight can say, "not I but the grace of God which was with me" (1 Cor. 15:10).

6. At last when the dragon could not even thus overthrow Anthony, but saw himself thrust out of his heart, gnashing his teeth as it is written, and as it were beside himself, he appeared to Anthony like a black boy, taking a visible shape in accordance with the color of his mind. And cringing to him, as it were, he plied him with thoughts no longer, for guileful as he was, he had been worsted, but at last spoke in human voice and said, "Many I deceived, many I cast down; but now attacking you and thy labors as I had many others, I proved weak." When Anthony asked, Who are you who speaks thus with me? he answered with a lamentable voice, "I am the friend of whoredom, and have taken upon me incitements which lead to it against the young. I am called the spirit of lust. How many have I deceived who wished to live soberly, how many are the chaste whom by my incitements I have over-persuaded! I am he on account of whom also the prophet reproves those who have fallen, saying, "You have been caused to err by the spirit of whoredom." For by me they have been tripped up. I am he who have so often troubled you and have so often been overthrown by you." But Anthony having given thanks to the Lord, with good courage said to him, "You are very despicable then, for you are black-hearted and weak as a child. Henceforth I shall have no trouble from you, 'for the Lord is my helper, and I shall look down on mine enemies'" (Ps. 118:7). Having heard this, the black one straightaway fled, shuddering at the words and dreading any longer even to come near the man.

7. This was Anthony's first struggle against the devil, or rather this victory was the Savior's work in Anthony, "Who condemned sin in the flesh that the ordinance of the law might be fulfilled in us who walk not after the flesh but after the spirit" (Rom. 8:3, 4). But neither did Anthony, although the evil one had fallen, henceforth relax his care and despise him; nor did the enemy as though conquered cease to lay snares for him. For again he went round as a lion seeking some occasion against him. But Anthony, having learned from the Scrip-

tures that the devices of the devil are many, zealously continued the discipline, reckoning that though the devil had not been able to deceive his heart by bodily pleasure, he would endeavor to ensnare him by other means. For the demon loves sin. Wherefore more and more he repressed the body and kept it in subjection, lest haply having conquered on one side, he should be dragged down on the other. He therefore planned to accustom himself to a severer mode of life. And many marveled, but he himself used to bear the labor easily; for the eagerness of soul, through the length of time it had abode in him, had wrought a good habit in him, so that taking but little initiation from others he showed great zeal in this matter. He kept vigil to such an extent that he often continued the whole night without sleep; and this not once but often, to the marvel of others. He ate once a day, after sunset, sometimes once in two days, and often even in four. His food was bread and salt, his drink, water only. Of flesh and wine it is superfluous even to speak, since no such thing was found with the other earnest men. A rush mat served him to sleep upon, but for the most part he lay upon the bare ground. He would not anoint himself with oil, saying it behooved young men to be earnest in training and not to seek what would enervate the body; but they must accustom it to labor, mindful of the Apostle's words, "when I am weak, then am I strong" (2 Cor. 12:10). "For," said he, "the fiber of the soul is then sound when the pleasures of the body are diminished." And he had come to this truly wonderful conclusion, "that progress in virtue, and retirement from the world for the sake of it, ought not to be measured by time, but by desire and fixity of purpose . . . And he used to say to himself that from the life of the great Elias the hermit ought to see his own as in a mirror."

8. Thus tightening his hold upon himself, Anthony departed to the tombs, which happened to be at a distance from the village; and having bid one of his acquaintances to bring him bread at intervals of many days, he entered one of the tombs, and the other having shut the door on him, he remained within alone. And when the enemy could not endure it, but was even fearful that in a short time Anthony would fill the desert with the discipline, coming one night with a mul-titude of demons, he so cut him with stripes that he lay on the ground speechless from the excessive pain. For he affirmed that the torture had been so excessive that no blows inflicted by man could ever have caused him such torment. But by the Providence of God—for the Lord never overlooks them that hope in Him—the next day his acquaintance came bringing him the loaves. And having opened the door and seeing him lying on the ground as though dead, he lifted him up and carried him to the church in the village, and laid him upon the ground. And many of his kinsfolk and the villagers sat around Anthony as round a corpse. But about midnight he came to himself and arose, and when he saw them all asleep and his comrade alone watching, he motioned with his head for him to approach, and asked him to carry him again to the tombs without waking anybody.

9. He was carried therefore by the man, and as he was wont, when the door was shut he was within alone. And he could not stand up on account of the blows, but he prayed as he lay. And after he had prayed, he said with a shout, Here am I, Anthony; I flee not from your stripes, for even if you inflict more nothing shall separate me from the love of Christ. And then he sang, "though a camp be set against me, my heart shall not be afraid" (Ps. 27:3). These were the thoughts and words of this ascetic. But the enemy, who hates good, marveling that after the blows he dared to return, called together his hounds and burst forth, "You see," said he, "that neither by the spirit of lust nor by blows did we stay the man, but that he braves us, let us attack him in another fashion." But changes of form for evil are easy for the devil, so in the night they made such a din that the whole of that place seemed to be shaken by an earthquake, and the demons as if breaking the four walls of the dwelling seemed to enter through them, coming in the likeness of beasts and creeping things. And the place was on a sudden filled with the forms of lions, bears, leopards, bulls, serpents, asps, scorpions, and wolves, and each of them was moving according to his nature. The lion was roaring, wishing to attack, the bull seeming to toss with its horns, the serpent writhing but unable to approach, and the wolf as it rushed on was restrained; altogether the noises of the appari-

tions, with their angry ragings, were dreadful. But Anthony, stricken and goaded by them, felt bodily pains severer still. He lay watching, however, with unshaken soul, groaning from bodily anguish; but his mind was clear, and as in mockery he said, "If there had been any power in you, it would have sufficed had one of you come, but since the Lord has made you weak you attempt to terrify me by numbers: and a proof of your weakness is that you take the shapes of brute beasts." And again with boldness he said, "If you are able, and have received power against me, delay not to attack; but if you are unable, why trouble me in vain? For faith in our Lord is a seal and a wall of safety to us." So after many attempts they gnashed their teeth upon him, because they were mocking themselves rather than him.

10. Nor was the Lord then forgetful of Anthony's wrestling, but was at hand to help him. So looking up he saw the roof as it were opened, and a ray of light descending to him. The demons suddenly vanished, the pain of his body straightaway ceased, and the building was again whole. But Anthony feeling the help, and getting his breath again, and being freed from pain, besought the vision which had appeared to him, saying, "Where wert thou? Why did you not appear at the beginning to make my pains to cease?" And a voice came to him, "Anthony, I was here, but I waited to see your fight; wherefore since you have endured, and have not been worsted, I will ever be a succor to you, and will make your name known everywhere." Having heard this, Anthony arose and prayed, and received such strength that he perceived that he had more power in his body than formerly. And he was then about thirty-five years old.

11. And on the day following he went forth still more eagerly bent on the service of God and having fallen in with the old man he had met previously, he asked him to dwell with him in the desert. But when the other declined on account of his great age, and because as yet there was no such custom, Anthony himself set off forthwith to the mountain. And yet again the enemy seeing his zeal and wishing to hinder it, cast in his way what seemed to be a great silver dish. But Anthony, seeing the guile of the Evil One, stood, and having looked on the dish, he put the devil in it to shame, saying, "Whence comes a dish in the desert? This road is not well-worn, nor is there here a trace of any wayfarer; it could not have fallen without being missed on account of its size; and he who had lost it having turned back to seek it, would have found it, for it is a desert place. This is some wile of the devil. O Evil One, not with this shall you hinder my purpose; let it go with you to destruction." And when Anthony had said this it vanished like smoke from the face of fire.

12. Then again as he went on he saw what was this time not visionary, but real gold scattered in the way. But whether the devil showed it, or some better power to try the athlete and show the Evil One that Anthony truly cared nought for money, neither he told nor do we know. But it is certain that that which appeared was gold. And Anthony marveled at the quantity, but passed it by as though he were going over fire; so he did not even turn, but hurried on at a run to lose sight of the place. More and more confirmed in his purpose, he hurried to the mountain, and having found a fort, so long deserted that it was full of creeping things, on the other side of the river; he crossed over to it and dwelt there. The reptiles, as though someone were chasing them, immediately left the place. But he built up the entrance completely, having stored up loaves for six months—this is a custom of the Thebans, and the loaves often remain fresh a whole year—and as he found water within, he descended as into a shrine, and abode within by himself, never going forth nor looking at any one who came. Thus he employed a long time training himself, and received loaves, let down from above, twice in the year.

13. But those of his acquaintances who came, since he did not permit them to enter, often used to spend days and nights outside, and heard as it were crowds within clamoring, dinning, sending forth piteous voices and crying, "Go from what is ours. What are you doing in the desert? You can not abide our attack." So at first those outside thought there were some men fighting with him, and that they had entered by ladders; but when stooping down they saw through a hole there was nobody, they were afraid, accounting them to be demons, and they called on Anthony. Them he

quickly heard, though he had not given a thought to the demons, and coming to the door he besought them to depart and not to be afraid, "for thus," said he, "the demons make their seeming onslaughts against those who are cowardly. Sign yourselves therefore with the cross, and depart boldly, and let these make sport for themselves." So they departed fortified with the sign of the Cross. But he remained in no wise harmed by the evil spirits, nor was he wearied with the contest, for there came to his aid visions from above, and the weakness of the foe relieved him of much trouble and armed him with greater zeal. For his acquaintances used often to come expecting to find him dead, and would hear him singing, "Let God arise and let His enemies be scattered, let them also that hate Him flee before His face. As smoke vanishes let them vanish; as wax melts before the face of fire, so let the sinners perish from the face of God" (Ps. 58:1); and again, "All nations compassed me about, and in the name of the Lord I requited them" (Ps. 118:10).

14. And so for nearly twenty years he continued training himself in solitude, never going forth, and but seldom seen by any. After this when many were eager and wishful to imitate his discipline, and his acquaintances came and began to cast down and wrench off the door by force, Anthony, as from a shrine, came forth initiated in the mysteries and filled with the Spirit of God. Then for the first time he was seen outside the fort by those who came to see him. And they, when they saw him, wondered at the sight, for he had the same habit of body as before, and was neither fat, like a man without exercise, nor lean from fasting and striving with the demons, but he was just the same as they had known him before his retirement. And again his soul was free from blemish, for it was neither contracted as if by grief, nor relaxed by pleasure, nor possessed by laughter or dejection, for he was not troubled when he beheld the crowd, nor overjoyed at being saluted by so many. But he was altogether even as being guided by reason, and abiding in a natural state. Through him the Lord healed the bodily ailments of many present, and cleansed others from evil spirits. And He gave grace to Anthony in speaking, so that he consoled many that were sorrowful, and set those at variance at one, exhort-

ing all to prefer the love of Christ before all that is in the world. And while he exhorted and advised them to remember the good things to come, and the loving-kindness of God towards us, "Who spared not His own Son, but delivered Him up for us all" (Rom. 8:32), he persuaded many to embrace the solitary life. And thus it happened in the end that cells arose even in the mountains, and the desert was colonized by monks, who came forth from their own people, and enrolled themselves for the citizenship in the heavens.

15. But when he was obliged to cross the Arsenoitic Canal—and the occasion of it was the visitation of the brethren—the canal was full of crocodiles. And by simply praying, he entered it, and all they with him, and passed over in safety. And having returned to his cell, he applied himself to the same noble and valiant exercises; and by frequent conversation he increased the eagerness of those already monks, stirred up in most of the rest the love of the discipline, and speedily by the attraction of his words cells multiplied, and he directed them all as a father.

[*Chapters 16-43 record Anthony's long address on the monastic life mostly concerned with the monk's struggle against demons.*]

44. . . . And truly it was possible, as it were, to behold a land set by itself, filled with piety and justice. For then there was neither the evil doer, nor the injured, nor the reproaches of the tax-gatherer: but instead a multitude of ascetics; and the one purpose of them all was to aim at virtue. So that any one beholding the cells again, and seeing such good order among the monks, would lift up his voice and say, "How goodly are thy dwellings, O Jacob, and thy tents, O Israel; as shady glens and as a garden by a river; as tents which the Lord hath pitched, and like cedars near waters" (Num. 24:5, 6).

45. Anthony, however, according to his custom, returned alone to his own cell, increased his discipline, and sighed daily as he thought of the mansions in Heaven, having his desire fixed on them, and pondering over the shortness of man's life. And he used to eat and sleep, and go about all other bodily necessities with shame when he

thought of the spiritual faculties of the soul. So often, when about to eat with any other hermits, recollecting the spiritual food, he begged to be excused, and departed far off from them, deeming it a matter for shame if he should be seen eating by others. He used, however, when by himself, to eat through bodily necessity, but often also with the brethren; covered with shame on these occasions, yet speaking boldly words of help. And he used to say that it behooved a person to give all one's time to the soul rather than the body, yet to grant a short space to the body through its necessities; but all the more earnestly to give up the whole remainder to the soul and seek its profit, that it might not be dragged down by the pleasures of the body, but, on the contrary, the body might be in subjection to the soul. For this is that which was spoken by the Savior: "Be not anxious for your life what you shall eat, nor for your body what you shall put on. And do not seek what you shall eat, or what you shall drink, and be not of a doubtful mind. For all these things the nations of the world seek after. But your Father knows that you have need of all these things. Howbeit seek first His Kingdom, and all these things shall be added unto you" (Matt. 6:31).

46. After this the Church was seized by the persecution which then took place under Maximinus, and when the holy martyrs were led to Alexandria, Anthony also followed, leaving his cell, and saying, Let us go too, that if called, we may contend or behold them that are contending. And he longed to suffer martyrdom, but not being willing to give himself up, he ministered to the confessors in the mines and in the prisons. And he was very zealous in the judgment hall to stir up to readiness those who were summoned when in their contest, while those who were being martyred he received and brought on their way until they were perfected. The judge, therefore, beholding the fearlessness of Anthony and his companions, and their zeal in this matter, commanded that no monk should appear in the judgment hall, nor remain at all in the city. So all the rest thought it good to hide themselves that day, but Anthony gave so little heed to the command that he washed his garment, and stood all next day on a raised place before them, and appeared in his best before the governor. Therefore when all the rest won-

dered at this, and the governor saw and passed by with his array, he stood fearlessly, showing the readiness of us Christians. For, as I said before, he prayed himself to be a martyr, wherefore he seemed as one grieved that he had not borne his witness. But the Lord was keeping him for our profit and that of others, that he should become a teacher to many of the discipline which he had learned from the Scriptures. For many only beholding his manner of life were eager to be imitators of his ways. So he again ministered as usual to the confessors, and as though he were their fellow captive he labored in his ministry.

47. And when at last the persecution ceased, and the blessed Bishop Peter had borne his testimony, Anthony departed, and again withdrew to his cell, and was there daily a martyr to his conscience, and contending in the conflicts of faith. And his discipline was much severer, for he was ever fasting, and he had a garment of hair on the inside, while the outside was skin, which he kept until his end. And he neither bathed his body with water to free himself from filth, nor did he ever wash his feet, nor even endure so much as to put them into water, unless compelled by necessity. Nor did any one even see him unclothed, nor his body naked at all, except after his death, when he was buried.

[*Beset by a multitude of visitors, Anthony is led by God to accompany a group of Saracens into the "inner desert."*]

50. Anthony then, as it were, moved by God, loved the place, for this was the spot which he who had spoken with him by the banks of the river had pointed out. So having first received loaves from his fellow travelers, he abode in the mountain alone, no one else being with him. And recognizing it as his own home, he remained in that place for the future. But the Saracens, having seen the earnestness of Anthony, purposely used to journey that way, and joyfully brought him loaves, while now and then the palm trees also afforded him a poor and frugal relish. But after this, the brethren learning of the place, like children mindful of their father, took care to send to him. But when Anthony saw that the bread was the cause of

trouble and hardships to some of them, to spare the monks this, he resolved to ask some of those who came to bring him a spade, an axe, and a little corn. And when these were brought, he went over the land round the mountain, and having found a small plot of suitable ground, tilled it; and having a plentiful supply of water for watering, he sowed. This doing year by year, he got his bread from thence, rejoicing that thus he would be troublesome to no one, and because he kept himself from being a burden to anybody. But after this, seeing again that people came, he cultivated a few potherbs, that he who came to him might have some slight solace after the labor of that hard journey. At first, however, the wild beasts in the desert, coming because of the water, often injured his seeds and husbandry. But he, gently laying hold of one of them, said to them all, "Why do you hurt me, when I hurt none of you? Depart, and in the name of the Lord do not come near this spot." And from that time forward, as though fearful of his command, they no more came near the place.

51. So he was alone in the inner mountain, spending his time in prayer and discipline. And the brethren who served him asked that they might come every month and bring him olives, pulse and oil, for by now he was an old man. There then he passed his life, and endured such great wrestling, "Not against flesh and blood" (Eph. 6:12), as it is written, but against opposing demons, as we learned from those who visited him. For there they heard tumults, many voices, and, as it were, the clash of arms. At night they saw the mountain become full of wild beasts, and him also fighting as though against visible beings, and praying against them. And those who came to him he encouraged, while kneeling he contended and prayed to the Lord. Surely it was a marvelous thing that a man, alone in such a desert, feared neither the demons who rose up against him, nor the fierceness of the four-footed beasts and creeping things, for all they were so many. But in truth, as it is written, "He trusted in the Lord as Mount Zion" (Ps. 125:1), with a mind unshaken and undisturbed; so that the demons rather fled from him, and the wild beasts, as it is written, "kept peace with him" (Job 5:23).

52-53. The devil, therefore, as David says in the Psalms, observed Anthony and gnashed his teeth against him. But Anthony was consoled by the Savior and continued unhurt by his wiles and varied devices . . . For they strove in all manner of ways to lead Anthony from the desert and were not able.

54. And once being asked by the monks to come down and visit them and their abodes after a time, he journeyed with those who came to him. And a camel carried the loaves and the water for them. For all that desert is dry, and there is no water at all that is fit to drink, save in that mountain from whence they drew the water, and in which Anthony's cell was. So when the water failed them on their way, and the heat was very great, they all were in danger. For having gone round the neighborhood and finding no water, they could walk no further, but lay on the ground and despairing of themselves, let the camel go. But the old man seeing that they were all in jeopardy, groaning in deep grief, departed a little way from them, and kneeling down he stretched forth his hands and prayed. And immediately the Lord made water to well forth where he had stood praying, and so all drank and were revived. And having filled their bottles they sought the camel and found her, for the rope happened to have caught in a stone and so was held fast. Having led it and watered it they placed the bottles on its back and finished their journey in safety. And when he came to the outer cells all saluted him, looking on him as a father. And he too, as though bringing supplies from the mountain, entertained them with his words and gave them a share of help. And again there was joy in the mountains, zeal for improvement and consolation through their mutual faith. Anthony also rejoiced when he beheld the earnestness of the monks, and his sister grown old in virginity, and that she herself also was the leader of other virgins.

[*Chapters 55-66 demonstrate Anthony's intimacy with God through accounts of healing, his miraculous knowledge of present and future events, his exorcism of demons, and his visions.*]

67. Added to this he was tolerant in disposition and humble in spirit. For though he was such a man, he observed the rule of the Church most

rigidly, and was willing that all the clergy should be honored above himself. For he was not ashamed to bow his head to bishops and presbyters, and if ever a deacon came to him for help he discoursed with him on what was profitable, but gave place to him in prayer, not being ashamed to learn himself. For often he would ask questions, and desired to listen to those who were present, and if any one said anything that was useful he confessed that he was profited . . .

68. And he was altogether wonderful in faith and religion, for he never held communion with the Meletian schismatics, knowing their wickedness and apostasy from the beginning; nor had he friendly dealings with the Manichaeans or any other heretics; or, if he had, only as far as advice that they should change to piety. For he thought and asserted that intercourse with these was harmful and destructive to the soul. In the same manner also he loathed the heresy of the Arians, and exhorted all neither to approach them nor to hold their erroneous belief. And once when certain Arian madmen came to him, when he had questioned them and learned their impiety, he drove them from the mountain, saying that their words were worse than the poison of serpents.

69. And once also the Arians having lyingly asserted that Anthony's opinions were the same as theirs, he was displeased and wroth against them. Then being summoned by the bishops and all the brethren, he descended from the mountain, and having entered Alexandria, he denounced the Arians, saying that their heresy was the last of all and a forerunner of Antichrist. And he taught the people that the Son of God was not a created being, neither had He come into being from non-existence, but that He was the Eternal Word and Wisdom of the Essence of the Father. And therefore it was impious to say, "there was a time when He was not," for the Word was always co-existent with the Father. Wherefore have no fellowship with the most impious Arians. For there is no communion between light and darkness. For you are good Christians, but they, when they say that the Son of the Father, the Word of God, is a created being, differ in nought from the heathen, since they worship that which is created, rather than God the creator. But believe that the Creation itself is angry

with them because they number the Creator, the Lord of all, by whom all things came into being, with those things which were originated.

70. All the people, therefore, rejoiced when they heard the anti-Christian heresy anathematized by such a man. And all the people in the city ran together to see Anthony; and the Greeks and those who are called their Priests, came into the church, saying, "We ask to see the man of God," for so they all called him. For in that place also the Lord cleansed many of demons, and healed those who were mad. And many Greeks asked that they might even but touch the old man, believing that they should be profited. Assuredly as many became Christians in those few days as one would have seen made in a year. Then when some thought that he was troubled by the crowds, and on this account turned them all away from him, he said, undisturbedly, that there were not more of them than of the demons with whom he wrestled in the mountain.

71. But when he was departing, and we were setting him forth on his way, as we arrived at the gate a woman from behind cried out, "Stay, thou man of God, my daughter is grievously vexed by a devil. Stay, I beseech you, lest I too harm myself with running." And the old man when he heard her, and was asked by us, willingly stayed. And when the woman drew near, the child was cast on the ground. But when Anthony had prayed and called upon the name of Christ, the child was raised whole, for the unclean spirit was gone forth. And the mother blessed God, and all gave thanks. And Anthony himself also rejoiced, departing to the mountain as though it were to his own home.

72. And Anthony also was exceeding prudent, and the wonder was that although he had not learned letters, he was a ready-witted and sagacious man. At all events two Greek philosophers once came, thinking they could try their skill on Anthony; and he was in the outer mountain, and having recognized who they were from their appearance, he came to them and said to them by means of an interpreter, "Why, philosophers, did you trouble yourselves so much to come to a foolish man?" And when they said that he was not a foolish man, but exceedingly prudent, he said to them, "If you came to a foolish man, your labor is

superfluous; but if you think me prudent become as I am, for we ought to imitate what is good. And if I had come to you I should have imitated you; but if you to me, become as I am, for I am a Christian." But they departed with wonder, for they saw that even demons feared Anthony.

73. And again others such as these met him in the outer mountain and thought to mock him because he had not learned letters. And Anthony said to them, "What do you say? Which is first, mind or letters? And which is the cause of which—mind of letters or letters of mind?" And when they answered mind is first and the inventor of letters, Anthony said, "Whoever, therefore, has a sound mind has no need of letters." This answer amazed both the bystanders and the philosophers, and they departed marveling that they had seen so much understanding in an ignorant man. For his manners were not rough as though he had been reared in the mountain and there grown old, but graceful and polite, and his speech was seasoned with the divine salt, so that no one was envious, but rather all rejoiced over him who visited him.

74. After this again certain others came; and these were men who were deemed wise among the Greeks, and they asked him a reason for our faith in Christ. But when they attempted to dispute concerning the preaching of the divine Cross and meant to mock, Anthony stopped for a little, and first pitying their ignorance, said, through an interpreter, who could skillfully interpret his words, "Which is more beautiful, to confess the Cross or to attribute to those whom you call gods adultery and the seduction of boys? For that which is chosen by us is a sign of courage and a sure token of the contempt of death, while yours are the passions of licentiousness. Next, which is better, to say that the Word of God was not changed, but, being the same, He took a human body for the salvation and well-being of man, that having shared in human birth He might make man partake in the divine and spiritual nature; or to liken the divine to senseless animals and consequently to worship four-footed beasts, creeping things and the likenesses of men? For these things, are the objects of reverence of you wise men . . .

75. "But concerning the Cross, which would you say to be the better, to bear it, when a plot is brought about by wicked men, nor to be in fear of death brought about under any form whatever; or to prate about the wanderings of Osiris and Isis, the plots of Typhon, the flight of Cronos, his eating his children and the slaughter of his father. For this is your wisdom. But how, if you mock the Cross, do you not marvel at the resurrection? For the same men who told us of the latter wrote the former. Or why when you make mention of the Cross are you silent about the dead who were raised, the blind who received their sight, the paralytics who were healed, the lepers who were cleansed, the walking upon the sea, and the rest of the signs and wonders, which show that Christ is no longer a man but God? To me you seem to do yourselves much injustice and not to have carefully read our Scriptures. But read and see that the deeds of Christ prove Him to be God come upon earth for the salvation of men."

[*Chapters 76-80 continue Anthony's debate with the pagan philosophers.*]

81. And the fame of Anthony came even unto kings. For Constantine Augustus and his sons Constantius and Constans the Augusti wrote letters to him, as to a father, and begged an answer from him. But he made nothing very much of the letters, nor did he rejoice at the messages, but was the same as he had been before the emperors wrote to him. But when they brought him the letters he called the monks and said, "Do not be astonished if an emperor writes to us, for he is a man; but rather wonder that God wrote the Law for human beings and has spoken to us through His own Son." And so he was unwilling to receive the letters, saying that he did not know how to write an answer to such things. But being urged by the monks because the emperors were Christians, and lest they should take offense on the ground that they had been spurned, he consented that they should be read, and wrote an answer approving them because they worshipped Christ, and giving them counsel on things pertaining to salvation: "not to think much of the present, but rather to remember the judgment that is coming, and to know that Christ alone was the true and Eternal King." He begged them to be merciful and to give heed to justice and the poor. And they having

received the answer rejoiced. Thus he was dear to all, and all desired to consider him as a father.

[*Chapter 82 recounts Anthony's vision of the destructive activity and final downfall of the Arians.*]

83. Such are the words of Anthony, and we ought not to doubt whether such marvels were wrought by the hand of a man. For it is the promise of the Savior, when He says, "If you have faith as a grain of mustard seed, you shall say to this mountain, remove hence and it shall remove; and nothing shall be impossible unto you" (Matt. 17:20). And again, "Verily, verily, I say unto you, if you shall ask the father in My name He will give it you. Ask and you shall receive" (John 16:23). And He himself it is who says to His disciples and to all who believe on Him, "Heal the sick, cast out demons; freely you have received, freely give" (Matt. 10:8).

84. Anthony, at any rate, healed not by commanding, but by prayer and speaking the name of Christ. So that it was clear to all that it was not he himself who worked, but the Lord who showed mercy by his means and healed the sufferers. But Anthony's part was only prayer and discipline, for the sake of which he stayed in the mountain, rejoicing in the contemplation of divine things, but grieving when troubled by much people, and dragged to the outer mountain. For all judges used to ask him to come down, because it was impossible for them to enter on account of their following of litigants. But nevertheless they asked him to come that they might but see him. When therefore he avoided it and refused to go to them, they remained firm, and sent to him all the more the prisoners under charge of soldiers, that on account of these he might come down. Being forced by necessity, and seeing them lamenting, he came into the outer mountain, and again his labor was not unprofitable. For his coming was advantageous and serviceable to many; and he was of profit to the judges, counseling them to prefer justice to all things; to fear God, and to know, "that with what judgment they judged, they should be judged" (Matt. 17:20). But he loved more than all things his sojourn in the mountain.

85. At another time, suffering the same compulsion at the hands of them who had need, and after many entreaties from the commander of the soldiers, he came down, and when he was come he spoke to them shortly of the things which make for salvation, and concerning those who wanted him, and was hastening away. But when the duke, as he is called, entreated him to stay, he replied that he could not linger among them . . .

86. And a certain general, Balacius by name, persecuted us Christians bitterly on account of his regard for the Arians—that name of ill-omen. And as his ruthlessness was so great that he beat virgins, and stripped and scourged monks, Anthony at this time wrote a letter as follows, and sent it to him. "I see wrath coming upon you, wherefore cease to persecute the Christians, lest haply wrath catch hold of you, for even now it is on the point of coming upon you." But Balacius laughed and threw the letter on the ground, and spit on it, and insulted the bearers, bidding them tell this to Anthony: "Since thou you take thought for the monks, soon I will come after you also." And five days had not passed before wrath came upon him. For Balacius and Nestorius, the Prefect of Egypt, went forth to the first halting-place from Alexandria, which is called Chaereu, and both were on horseback, and the horses belonged to Balacius, and were the quietest of all his stable. But they had not gone far towards the place when the horses began to frisk with one another as they are wont to do; and suddenly the quieter, on which Nestorius sat, with a bite dismounted Balacius, and attacked him, and tore his thigh so badly with its teeth that he was borne straight back to the city, and in three days died. And all wondered because what Anthony had foretold had been so speedily fulfilled.

87. Thus, therefore, he warned the cruel. But the rest who came to him he so instructed that they straightaway forgot their lawsuits, and felicitated those who were in retirement from the world. And he championed those who were wronged in such a way that you would imagine that he, and not the others, was the sufferer. Further, he was able to be of such use to all, that many soldiers and men who had great possessions laid aside the burdens of life, and became monks for the rest of their days. And it was as if a physician

had been given by God to Egypt. For who in grief met Anthony and did not return rejoicing? Who came mourning for their dead and did not forthwith put off their sorrow? Who came in anger and was not converted to friendship? What poor and low-spirited person met him who, hearing him and looking upon him, did not despise wealth and find consolation in his poverty? What monk, having been neglectful, came to him and became not all the stronger? What young man having come to the mountain and seen Anthony, did not forthwith deny himself pleasure and love temperance? Who when tempted by a demon, came to him and did not find rest? And who came troubled with doubts and did not get quietness of mind?

88. . . . Thus each one, as though prepared by him for battle, came down from the mountain, braving the designs of the devil and his demons. How many maidens who had suitors, having but seen Anthony from afar, remained maidens for Christ's sake. And people came also from foreign parts to him, and like all others, having got some benefit, returned, as though set forward by a father. And certainly when he died, all as having been bereft of a father, consoled themselves solely by their remembrances of him, preserving at the same time his counsel and advice.

89. It is worthwhile that I should relate, and that you, as you wish it, should hear what his death was like. For this end of his is worthy of imitation. According to his custom he visited the monks in the outer mountain, and having learned from Providence that his own end was at hand, he said to the brethren, "This is my last visit to you which I shall make. And I shall be surprised if we see each other again in this life. At length the time of my departure is at hand, for I am near a hundred and five years old." And when they heard it they wept, and embraced, and kissed the old man. But he, as though sailing from a foreign city to his own, spoke joyously, and exhorted them "Not to grow idle in their labors, nor to become faint in their training, but to live as though dying daily. And as he had said before, zealously to guard the soul from foul thoughts, eagerly to imitate the Saints, and to have nought to do with the Meletian schismatics, for you know their wicked and profane character. Nor have any fellowship with the Arians, for their impiety is clear to all. Nor be disturbed if you see the judges protect them, for it shall cease, and their pomp is mortal and of short duration. Wherefore keep yourselves all the more untainted by them, and observe the traditions of the fathers, and chiefly the holy faith in our Lord Jesus Christ, which you have learned from the Scripture, and of which you have often been put in mind by me."

90. But when the brethren were urging him to abide with them and there to die, he suffered it not for many other reasons, as he showed by keeping silence, and especially for this:—The Egyptians are wont to honor with funeral rites, and to wrap in linen cloths at death the bodies of good men, and especially of the holy martyrs; and not to bury them underground, but to place them on couches, and to keep them in their houses, thinking in this to honor the departed. And Anthony often urged the bishops to give commandment to the people on this matter. In like manner he taught the laity and reproved the women, saying, "that this thing was neither lawful nor holy at all. For the bodies of the patriarchs and prophets are until now preserved in tombs, and the very body of the Lord was laid in a tomb, and a stone was laid upon it, and hid it until He rose on the third day." And thus saying, he showed that he who did not bury the bodies of the dead after death transgressed the law, even though they were sacred. For what is greater or more sacred than the body of the Lord? Many therefore having heard, henceforth buried the dead underground, and gave thanks to the Lord that they had been taught rightly.

91. But he, knowing the custom, and fearing that his body would be treated this way, hastened, and having bidden farewell to the monks in the outer mountain entered the inner mountain, where he was accustomed to abide. And after a few months he fell sick. Having summoned those who were there—they were two in number who had remained in the mountain fifteen years, practicing the discipline and attending on Anthony on account of his age—he said to them, "I, as it is written, go the way of the fathers, for I perceive that I am called by the Lord. And do you be watchful and destroy not your long discipline, but as though now making a beginning, zealously pre-

serve your determination. For you know the treachery of the demons, how fierce they are, but how little power they have. Wherefore fear them not, but rather ever breathe Christ, and trust Him. Live as though dying daily. Give heed to yourselves, and remember the admonition you have heard from me. Have no fellowship with the schismatics, nor any dealings at all with the heretical Arians. For you know how I shunned them on account of their hostility to Christ, and the strange doctrines of their heresy. Therefore be the more earnest always to be followers first of God and then of the Saints; that after death they also may receive you as well-known friends into the eternal habitations. Ponder over these things and think of them, and if you have any care for me and are mindful of me as of a father, suffer no one to take my body into Egypt, lest haply they place me in the houses, for to avoid this I entered into the mountain and came here. Moreover you know how I always put to rebuke those who had this custom, and exhorted them to cease from it. Bury my body, therefore, and hide it underground yourselves, and let my words be observed by you that no one may know the place but you alone. For at the resurrection of the dead I shall receive it incorruptible from the Savior. And divide my garments. To Athanasius the bishop give one sheepskin and the garment whereon I am laid, which he himself gave me new, but which with me has grown old. To Serapion the bishop give the other sheepskin, and keep the hair garment yourselves. For the rest fare ye well, my children, for Anthony is departing, and is with you no more."

92. Having said this, when they had kissed him, he lifted up his feet, and as though he saw friends coming to him and was glad because of them—for as he lay his countenance appeared joyful—he died and was gathered to the fathers. And they afterward, according to his commandment, wrapped him up and buried him, hiding his body underground. And no one knows to this day where it was buried, save those two only. But each of those who received the sheepskin of the blessed Anthony and the garment worn by him guards it as a precious treasure. For even to look on them is as it were to behold Anthony; and he who is clothed in them seems with joy to bear his admonitions.

93. This is the end of Anthony's life in the body and the above was the beginning of the discipline. Even if this account is small compared with his merit, still from this reflect how great Anthony, the man of God, was. Who from his youth to so great an age preserved a uniform zeal for the discipline, and neither through old age was subdued by the desire of costly food, nor through the infirmity of his body changed the fashion of his clothing, nor washed even his feet with water, and yet remained entirely free from harm. For his eyes were undimmed and quite sound and he saw clearly; of his teeth he had not lost one, but they had become worn to the gums through the great age of the old man. He remained strong both in hands and feet; and while all men were using various foods, and washings and divers garments, he appeared more cheerful and of greater strength. And the fact that his fame has been blazoned everywhere; that all regard him with wonder, and that those who have never seen him long for him, is clear proof of his virtue and God's love of his soul. For not from writings, nor from worldly wisdom, nor through any art, was Anthony renowned, but solely from his piety towards God. That this was the gift of God no one will deny. For from whence into Spain and into Gaul, how into Rome and Africa, was the man heard of who abode hidden in a mountain, unless it was God who makes His own known everywhere, who also promised this to Anthony at the beginning? For even if they work secretly, even if they wish to remain in obscurity, yet the Lord shows them as lamps to lighten all, that those who hear may thus know that the precepts of God are able to make people prosper and thus be zealous in the path of virtue.

94. Read these words, therefore, to the rest of the brethren that they may learn what the life of monks ought to be; and may believe that our Lord and Savior Jesus Christ glorifies those who glorify Him: and leads those who serve Him unto the end, not only to the kingdom of heaven, but here also—even though they hide themselves and are desirous of withdrawing from the world—makes them illustrious and well known everywhere on account of their virtue and the help they render others. And if need be, read this among the

heathen, that even in this way they may learn that our Lord Jesus Christ is not only God and the Son of God, but also that the Christians who truly serve Him and religiously believe on Him, prove, not only that the demons, whom the Greeks themselves think to be gods, are no gods, but also tread them under foot and put them to flight, as deceivers and corrupters of humankind, through Jesus Christ our Lord, to whom be glory forever and ever. Amen.

30. Basil of Caesarea,
Longer Rule

Though ordination to the priesthood and episcopate launched him on a very active ecclesiastical career, Basil of Caesarea (330-ca. 379) continued to advocate an ascetic life for all Christians and provided leadership for the rapidly expanding monastic movement in Asia Minor. The Longer and Shorter Rules he composed were not strictly "rules" but responses to the questions of committed ascetics. Emphasizing communal over solitary life and moderation in ascetic practices, Basil's Rules became foundational for organized monasticism in the East and influenced St. Benedict's establishment of a Rule for the West.

Q. 6. Concerning the necessity of living in retirement.

R. A secluded and remote habitation also contributes to the removal of distraction from the soul. Living among those who are unscrupulous and disdainful in their attitude toward an exact observance of the commandments is dangerous, as is shown by the following words of Solomon: "Be not a friend to an angry man and do not walk with a furious man; lest perhaps thou learn his ways and take snares to thy soul" (Prov. 22:24, 25). The words of the Apostle, "Go out from among them and be ye separate, says the Lord" (2 Cor. 6:17), bear also upon this point. Consequently, that we may not receive incitements to sin through our eyes and ears and become imperceptibly habituated to it, and that the impress and form, so to speak, of what is seen and heard may not remain in the soul unto its ruin, and that we may be able to be constant in prayer, we should before all things else seek to dwell in a retired place. In so doing, we should be able to overcome our former habits whereby we lived as strangers to the precepts of Christ (and it is no mean struggle to gain the mastery over one's wonted manner of acting, for custom maintained throughout a long period takes on the force of nature), and we could wipe away the stains of sin by assiduous prayer and persevering meditation on the will of God. It is impossible to gain proficiency in this meditation and prayer, however, while a multitude of distractions is dragging the soul about and introducing into it anxieties about the affairs of this life. Could anyone, immersed in these cares, ever fulfill that command: "If any man will come after me, let him deny himself"? (Luke 9:23). For, we must deny ourselves and take up the Cross of Christ and thus follow Him. Now, self-denial involves the entire forgetfulness of the past and surrender of one's will—surrender which it is very difficult, not to say quite impossible, to achieve while living in the promiscuity

SOURCE: Basil, *Ascetical Works*, tr. M. Monica Wagner, C.S.C. (New York: Fathers of the Church, 1940), 245-52. Used by permission of The Catholic University of America Press.

customary in the world. And in addition, the social intercourse demanded by such a life is even an obstacle to taking up one's cross and following Christ. Readiness to die for Christ, the mortification of one's members on this earth, preparedness for every danger which might befall us on behalf of Christ's Name, detachment from this life—this it is to take up one's cross; and we regard the obstacles springing from the habits of life in society as major impediments thereto.

And in addition to all the other obstacles, which are many, the soul in looking at the crowd of other offenders does not, in the first place, have time to become aware of its own sins and to afflict itself by penance for its errors; on the contrary, by comparison with those who are worse, it takes on, besides, a certain deceptive appearance of righteousness. Secondly, through the disturbances and occupations which life in society naturally engenders, the soul, being drawn away from the more worthy remembrance of God, pays the penalty of finding neither joy nor gladness in God and of not relishing the delights of the Lord or tasting the sweetness of His words, so as to be able to say: "I remembered God and was delighted" (Ps. 76:4), and "How sweet are thy words to my palate! more than honey to my mouth" (Ps. 108:103). Worse still, it becomes habituated to a disregard and a complete forgetfulness of His judgments, than which no more fatal misfortune could befall it.

Q. 7. On the necessity of living in the company of those who are striving for the same objective— that of pleasing God—and the difficulty and hazards of living as a solitary.

Since your words have convinced us that it is dangerous to live in company with those who hold the commandments of God in light regard, we consider it logical to inquire whether one who retires from society should live in solitude or with brethren who are of the same mind and who have set before themselves the same goal, that is, the devout life.

R. I consider that life passed in company with a number of persons in the same habitation is more advantageous in many respects. My reasons are,

first, that no one of us is self-sufficient as regards corporeal necessities, but we require one another's aid in supplying our needs. The foot, to cite an analogy, possesses one kind of power and lacks another, and without the co-operation of the other members of the body it finds itself incapable of carrying on its activity independently for any length of time, nor does it have wherewithal to supply what is lacking. Similarly, in the solitary life, what is at hand becomes useless to us and what is wanting cannot be provided, since God, the Creator, decreed that we should require the help of one another, as it is written (Ecclus. 13:20), so that we might associate with one another. Again, apart from this consideration, the doctrine of the charity of Christ does not permit the individual to be concerned solely with his own private interests. "Charity," says the Apostle, "seeks not her own" (1 Cor. 13:5). But a life passed in solitude is concerned only with the private service of individual needs. This is openly opposed to the law of love which the Apostle fulfilled, who sought not what was profitable to himself but to many that they might be saved (1 Cor. 10:33). Furthermore, a person living in solitary retirement will not readily discern his own defects, since he has no one to admonish and correct him with mildness and compassion. In fact, admonition even from an enemy often produces in a prudent man the desire for amendment. But the cure of sin is wrought with understanding by him who loves sincerely; for Holy Scripture says: "for he that loves corrects betimes" (Prov. 13:24). Such a one it is very difficult to find in a solitude, if in one's prior state of life one had not been associated with such a person. The solitary, consequently, experiences the truth of the saying, "Woe to him that is alone, for when he falls he hath none to lift him up" (Eccles. 4:10). Moreover, the majority of the commandments are easily observed by several persons living together, but not so in the case of one living alone; for, while he is obeying one commandment, the practice of another is being interfered with. For example, when he is visiting the sick, he cannot show hospitality to the stranger and, in the imparting and sharing of necessities (especially when the ministrations are prolonged), he is prevented from giving zealous attention to [other] tasks. As a result, the greatest commandment and the one especially conducive to salvation is not observed, since the hungry are not fed nor the naked clothed. Who, then, would choose this ineffectual and unprofitable life in preference to that which is both fruitful and in accordance with the Lord's command?

Besides, if all we who are united in the one hope of our calling are one body with Christ as our Head, we are also members, one of another. If we are not joined together by union in the Holy Spirit in the harmony of one body, but each of us should choose to live in solitude, we would not serve the common good in the ministry according to God's good pleasure, but would be satisfying our own passion for self-gratification. How could we, divided and separated, preserve the status and the mutual service of members or our subordinate relationship to our Head which is Christ? It is impossible, indeed, to rejoice with him who receives an honor or to sympathize with him who suffers when, by reason of their being separated from one another, each person cannot, in all likelihood, be kept informed about the affairs of his neighbor. In addition, since no one has the capacity to receive all spiritual gifts, but the grace of the Spirit is given proportionately to the faith of each, when one is living in association with others, the grace privately bestowed on each individual becomes the common possession of his fellows. "To one, indeed, is given the word of wisdom; and to another, the word of knowledge; to another, faith, to another, prophecy, to another, the grace of healing" (1 Cor. 12:8-9), and so on. He who receives any of these gifts does not possess it for his own sake but rather for the sake of others, so that, in the life passed in community, the operation of the Holy Spirit in the individual is at the same time necessarily transmitted to all. He who lives alone, consequently, and has, perhaps, one gift renders it ineffectual by leaving it in disuse, since it lies buried within him. How much danger there is in this all of you know who have read the Gospel. On the other hand, in the case of several persons living together, each enjoys his own gift and enhances it by giving others a share, besides reaping benefit from the gifts of others as if they were his own.

Community life offers more blessings than can be fully and easily enumerated. It is more advantageous than the solitary life both for preserving the goods bestowed on us by God and for warding off the external attacks of the Enemy. If any should happen to grow heavy with that sleep which is unto death and which we have been instructed by David to avert with prayer: "Enlighten my eyes that I never sleep in death" (Ps. 12:4), the awakening induced by those who are already on watch is the more assured. For the sinner, moreover, the withdrawal from his sin is far easier if he fears the shame of incurring censure from many acting together—to him, indeed, might be applied the words: "To him who is such a one, this rebuke is sufficient which is given by many" (2 Cor. 2:6)—and for the righteous man, there is a great and full satisfaction in the esteem of the group and in their approval of his conduct. If in the mouth of two or three witnesses, every word shall stand (Matt. 18:16), he who performs a good action will be far more surely corroborated by the testimony of many. Besides these disadvantages, the solitary life is fraught with other perils. The first and greatest is that of self-satisfaction. Since the solitary has no one to appraise his conduct, he will think he has achieved the perfection of the precept. Secondly, because he never tests his state of soul by exercise, he will not recognize his own deficiencies nor will he discover the advance he may have made in his manner of acting, since he will have removed all practical occasion for the observance of the commandments.

Wherein will he show his humility, if there is no one with whom he may compare and so confirm his own greater humility? Wherein will he give evidence of his compassion, if he has cut himself off from association with other persons? And how will he exercise himself in long-suffering, if no one contradicts his wishes? If anyone says that the teaching of the Holy Scripture is sufficient for the amendment of his ways, he resembles a man who learns carpentry without ever actually doing a carpenter's work or a man who is instructed in metal-working but will not reduce theory to practice. To such a one the Apostle would say: "Not the hearers of the law are just before God, but the doers of the law shall be justified" (Rom. 2:13). Consider, further, that the Lord by reason of His excessive love for man was not content with merely teaching the word, but, so as to transmit to us clearly and exactly the example of humility in the perfection of charity, girded Himself and washed the feet of the disciples. Whom, therefore, will you wash? To whom will you minister? In comparison with whom will you be the lowest, if you live alone? How, moreover, in a solitude, will that good and pleasant thing be accomplished, the dwelling of brethren together in one habitation which the Holy Spirit likens to ointment emitting its fragrance from the head of the high priest? So it is an arena for the combat, a good path of progress, continual discipline, and a practicing of the Lord's commandments, when brethren dwell together in community. This kind of life has as its aim the glory of God according to the command of our Lord Jesus Christ, who said: "So let your light shine before men that they may see your good works and glorify your Father who is in heaven" (Matt. 5:16). It maintains also the practice characteristic of the saints, of whom it is recorded in the Acts: "And all they that believed were together and had all things common" (Acts 2:44), and again: "And the multitude of believers had but one heart and one soul; neither did anyone say that aught of the things which he possessed was his own, but all things were common unto them" (Acts 4:32).

31. Gregory of Nyssa, *Life of Macrina*

Like his earlier treatise On Virginity *and his later* Life of Moses, *Gregory of Nyssa's* Life of Macrina *focuses on the theme of "philosophy," which the Cappadocians often equated with monastic life. A biography of his sister,* Life of Macrina *was probably written in the period following the death of their brother, Basil of Caesarea (ca. 379). It provides information about varieties of ascetic life, demonstrates the high value placed on virginity, and sheds light on the position of women in both the monastic movement and the church in the fourth century.*

Introduction
[to the monk Olympus]

The form of this volume, if one may judge from its heading, is apparently epistolary, but its bulk exceeds that of a letter, extending as it does to the length of a book. My apology must be that the subject on which you bade me write is greater than can be compressed within the limits of a letter. . . In this case it was a woman who provided us with our subject; if indeed she should be styled woman, for I do not know whether it is fitting to designate her by her sex, who so surpassed her sex. Our account of her was not based on the narrative of others but our talk was an accurate description of what we had learned by personal experience, nor did it need to be authenticated by strangers . . . She came from the same parents as ourselves, being, so to speak, an offering of first-fruits, since she was the earliest born of my mother's womb. As then you have decided that the story of her noble career is worth telling, to prevent such a life being unknown to our time, and the record of a woman who raised herself by "philosophy" to the greatest height of human virtue passing into the shades of useless oblivion, I thought it well to obey you, and in a few words, as best I can, to tell her story in unstudied and simple style.

SOURCE: St. Gregory of Nyssa, *The Life of St. Macrina*, tr. W. K. Lowther Clarke (London: Society for the Promotion of Christian Knowledge, 1916), 17-32, 34-36, 36-52, 58-64, 73, 78-79.

Macrina's Parents

The virgin's name was Macrina; she was so called by her parents after a famous Macrina some time before in the family, our father's mother, who had confessed Christ like a good athlete in the time of the persecutions . . . But another name had been given her privately, as the result of a vision before she was born into the world. For indeed her mother was so virtuous that she was guided on all occasions by the divine will. In particular she loved the pure and unstained mode of life so much that she was unwilling to be married. But since she had lost both her parents, and was in the very flower of her youthful beauty, and the fame of her good looks was attracting many suitors, and there was a danger that, if she were not mated to someone willingly, she might suffer some unwished for violent fate, seeing that some men, inflamed by her beauty, were ready to abduct her—on this account she chose for her husband a man who was known and approved for the gravity of his conduct, and so gained a protector of her life.

The Birth of Macrina

At her first confinement she became the mother of Macrina. When the due time came for her pangs to be ended by delivery, she fell asleep and seemed to be carrying in her hands that which was still in her womb. And someone in form and raiment more splendid than a human being appeared and addressed the child she was carrying by the name of Thecla, that Thecla, I mean, who is so famous among the virgins. After doing this and testifying to it three times, he departed from her sight and gave her easy delivery, so that at that moment she awoke from sleep and saw her dream realized. Now this name was used only in secret. But it seems to me that the apparition spoke not so much to guide the mother to a right choice of name, as to forecast the life of the young child, and to indicate by the name that she would follow her namesake's mode of life.

Macrina's Childhood

. . . The education of the child was her mother's task; she did not, however, employ the usual worldly method of education, which makes a practice of using poetry as a means of training the early years of the child. For she considered it disgraceful and quite unsuitable, that a tender and plastic nature should be taught either those tragic passions of womanhood which afforded poets their suggestions and plots, or the indecencies of comedy, to be, so to speak, defiled with unseemly tales of "the harem." But such parts of inspired Scripture as you would think were incomprehensible to young children were the subject of the girl's studies; in particular the Wisdom of Solomon, and those parts of it especially which have an ethical bearing. Nor was she ignorant of any part of the Psalter, but at stated times she recited every part of it. When she rose from bed, or engaged in household duties, or rested, or partook of food, or retired from table, when she went to bed or rose in the night for prayer, the Psalter was her constant companion, like a good fellow-traveler that never deserted her.

Her Betrothal

Filling her time with these and the like occupations, and attaining besides a considerable proficiency in wool-work, the growing girl reached her twelfth year, the age when the bloom of adolescence begins to appear. In which connection it is noteworthy that the girl's beauty could not be concealed in spite of efforts to hide it. Nor in all the countryside, so it seems, was there anything so marvelous as her beauty in comparison with that of others . . . In consequence a great swarm of suitors seeking her in marriage crowded round her parents. But her father—a shrewd man with a reputation for forming right decisions—picked out from the rest a young man related to the family, who was just leaving school, of good birth and remarkable steadiness, and decided to betroth his daughter to him, as soon as she was old enough . . .

Death of the Young Man

But Envy cut off these bright hopes by snatching away the poor lad from life. Now Macrina was not ignorant of her father's schemes. But when the plan formed for her was shattered by the young man's death, she said her father's intention was equivalent to a marriage, and resolved to remain single henceforward, just as if the intention had become accomplished fact. And indeed her determination was more steadfast than could have been expected from her age. For when her parents brought proposals of marriage to her, as often happened owing to the number of suitors that came attracted by the fame of her beauty, she would say that it was absurd and unlawful not to be faithful to the marriage that had been arranged for her by her father, but to be compelled to consider another; since in the nature of things there was but one marriage, as there is one birth and one death. She persisted that the man who had been linked to her by her parents' arrangement was not dead, but that she considered him who lived to God, thanks to the hope of the resurrection, to be absent only, not dead; it was wrong not to keep faith with the bridegroom who was away.

Macrina Resolves Never to Leave Her Mother

With such words repelling those who tried to talk her over, she settled on one safeguard of her good resolution, in a resolve not to be separated from her mother even for a moment of time . . . But the daughter's companionship was not a burden to her mother, nor profitless. For the attentions received from her daughter were worth those of many maidservants, and the benefits were mutual. For the mother looked after the girl's soul, and the girl looked after her mother's body, and in all respects fulfilled the required services, even going so far as to prepare meals for her mother with her own hands. Not that she made this her chief business. But after she had anointed her hands by the performance of religious duties—for she deemed that zeal for this was consistent with the principles of her life—in the time that was left she prepared food for her mother by her own toil. And not only this, but she helped her mother to bear her burden of responsibilities. For she had four sons and five daughters, and paid taxes to three different governors, since her property was scattered in as many districts. In consequence her mother was distracted with various

anxieties, for her father had by this time departed this life. In all these matters she shared her mother's toils, dividing her cares with her, and lightening her heavy load of sorrows. At one and the same time, thanks to her mother's guardianship, she was keeping her own life blameless, so that her mother's eye both directed and witnessed all she did; and also by her own life she instructed her mother greatly, leading her to the same mark, that of philosophy I mean, and gradually drawing her on to the immaterial and more perfect life.

Basil Returns from the University

When the mother had arranged excellent marriages for the other sisters, such as was best in each case, Macrina's brother, the great Basil, returned after his long period of education, already a practiced rhetorician. He was puffed up beyond measure with the pride of oratory and looked down on the local dignitaries, excelling in his own estimation all the men of leading and position. Nevertheless Macrina took him in hand, and with such speed did she draw him also toward the mark of philosophy that he forsook the glories of this world and despised fame gained by speaking, and deserted it for this busy life where one toils with one's hands. His renunciation of property was complete, lest anything should impede the life of virtue. But, indeed, his life and the subsequent acts, by which he became renowned throughout the world and put into the shade all those who have won renown for their virtue, would need a long description and much time. But I must divert my tale to its appointed task.

Now that all the distractions of the material life had been removed, Macrina persuaded her mother to give up her ordinary life and all showy style of living and the services of domestics to which she had been accustomed before, and bring her point of view down to that of the masses, and to share the life of the maids, treating all her slave girls and menials as if they were sisters and belonged to the same rank as herself.

But at this point I should like to insert a short parenthesis in my narrative and not to pass over unrelated such a matter as the following, in which the lofty character of the maiden is displayed.

The Story of Naucratius

The second of the four brothers, Naucratius by name, who came next after the great Basil, excelled the rest in natural endowments and physical beauty, in strength, speed and ability to turn his hand to anything. When he had reached his twenty-first year, and had given such demonstration of his studies by speaking in public, that the whole audience in the theatre was thrilled, he was led by a divine providence to despise all that was already in his grasp, and drawn by an irresistible impulse went off to a life of solitude and poverty. He took nothing with him but himself, save that one of the servants named Chrysapius followed him, because of the affection he had towards his master and the intention he had formed to lead the same life. So he lived by himself, having found a solitary spot on the banks of the Iris—a river flowing through the midst of Pontus. It rises actually in Armenia, passes through our parts, and discharges its stream into the Black Sea. By it the young man found a place with a luxuriant growth of trees and a hill nestling under the mass of the overhanging mountain. There he lived far removed from the noises of the city and the distractions that surround the lives both of the soldier and the pleader in the law courts. Having thus freed himself from the din of cares that impedes man's higher life, with his own hands he looked after some old people who were living in poverty and feebleness, considering it appropriate to his mode of life to make such a work his care. So the generous youth would go on fishing expeditions, and since he was expert in every form of sport, he provided food to his grateful clients by this means. And at the same time by such exercises he was taming his own manhood. Besides this, he also gladly obeyed his mother's wishes whenever she issued a command. And so in these two ways he guided his life, subduing his youthful nature by toils and caring assiduously for his mother, and thus keeping the divine commands he was traveling home to God.

In this manner he completed the fifth year of his life as a philosopher, by which he made his mother happy, both by the way in which he adorned his own life by continence, and by the devotion of all his powers to do the will of her that bore him.

The Tragic Death of Naucratius

Then there fell on the mother a grievous and tragic affliction, contrived, I think, by the Adversary, which brought trouble and mourning upon all the family. For he was snatched suddenly away from life . . . Having started out on one of the expeditions, by which he provided necessaries for the old men under his care, he was brought back home dead, together with Chrysapius who shared his life. His mother was far away, three days distant from the scene of the tragedy. Someone came to her telling the bad news. Perfect though she was in every department of virtue, yet nature dominated her as it does others. For she collapsed, and in a moment lost both breath and speech, since her reason failed her under the disaster, and she was thrown to the ground by the assault of the evil tidings, like some noble athlete hit by an unexpected blow.

Mother and Daughter Make Further Progress in the Ascetic Life

When the cares of bringing up a family and the anxieties of their education and settling in life had come to an end, and the property—a frequent cause of worldliness—had been for the most part divided among the children, then, as I said above, the life of the virgin became her mother's guide and led her on to this philosophic and spiritual manner of life. And weaning her from all accustomed luxuries, Macrina drew her on to adopt her own standard of humility. She induced her to live on a footing of equality with the staff of maids, so as to share with them in the same food, the same kind of bed, and in all the necessaries of life, without any regard to differences of rank. Such was the manner of their life, so great the height of their philosophy, and so holy their conduct day and night, as to make verbal description inadequate. For just as souls freed from the body by death are saved from the cares of this life, so was their life far removed from all earthly follies and ordered with a view of imitating the angelic life. For no anger or jealousy, no hatred or pride, was observed in their midst, nor anything else of this nature, since they had cast away all vain desires for honor and glory, all vanity, arrogance and the like. Continence was their luxury, and obscurity their glory. Poverty, and the casting away of all material superfluities like dust from their bodies, was their wealth. In fact, of all the things after which men eagerly pursue in this life, there were none with which they could not easily dispense. Nothing was left but the care of divine things and the unceasing round of prayer and endless hymnody, co-extensive with time itself, practiced by night and day. So that to them this meant work, and work so called was rest. What human words could make you realize such a life as this, a life on the borderline between human and spiritual nature? For that nature should be free from human weaknesses is more than can be expected from humanity. But these women fell short of the angelic and immaterial nature only insofar as they appeared in bodily form, and were contained within a human frame . . .

Peter, the Youngest Brother

Macrina was helped most of all in achieving this great aim of her life by her own brother Peter. With him the mother's pangs ceased, for he was the latest born of the family. At one and the same time he received the names of son and orphan, for as he entered this life his father passed away from it. But the eldest of the family, the subject of our story, took him soon after birth from the nurse's breast and reared him herself and educated him on a lofty system of training, practicing him from infancy in holy studies, so as not to give his soul leisure to turn to vain things. Thus having become all things to the lad—father, teacher, tutor, mother, giver of all good advice—she produced such results that before the age of boyhood had passed, when he was yet a stripling in the first bloom of tender youth, he aspired to the high mark of philosophy. And, thanks to his natural endowments, he was clever in every art that involves hand work, so that without any guidance he achieved a completely accurate knowledge of everything that ordinary people learn by time and trouble. Scorning to occupy his time with worldly studies, and having in nature a sufficient instructor in all good knowledge, and always looking to his sister as the model of all good, he advanced to

such a height of virtue that in his subsequent life he seemed in no whit inferior to the great Basil. But at this time he was all in all to his sister and mother, cooperating with them in the pursuit of the angelic life. Once when a severe famine had occurred and crowds from all quarters were frequenting the retreat where they lived, drawn by the fame of their benevolence, Peter's kindness supplied such an abundance of food that the desert seemed a city by reason of the number of visitors.

Death of the Mother

It was about this time that the mother died, honored by all, and went to God, yielding up her life in the arms of her two children. . . .

Basil Dies after a Noble Career

Meanwhile Basil, the famous saint, had been elected bishop of the great church of Caesarea. He advanced Peter to the sacred order of the priesthood, consecrating him in person with mystic ceremonial. And in this way a further advance in the direction of dignity and sanctity was made in their life, now that philosophy was enriched by the priesthood.

Eight years after this, the world-renowned Basil departed from this life to live with God, to the common grief of his native land and the whole world. Now when Macrina heard the news of the calamity in her distant retreat, she was distressed indeed in soul at so great a loss—for how could she not be distressed at a calamity, which was felt even by the enemies of the truth?—but just as they say that the testing of gold takes place in several furnaces, so that if any impurity escapes the first furnace, it may be separated in the second, and again in the last one all admixture of dross may be purged away—consequently it is the most accurate testing of pure gold if having gone through every furnace it shows no refuse. So it happened also in her case . . . The first test was the loss of the one brother, the second the parting from her mother, the third was when the common glory of the family, great Basil, was removed from human life. So she remained, like an invincible athlete in no wise broken by the assault of troubles.

Gregory Resolves to Visit His Sister

It was the ninth month or a little longer after this disaster, and a synod of bishops was gathered at Antioch, in which we also took part. And when we broke up, each to go home before the year was over, then I, Gregory, felt a desire to visit Macrina. For a long time had elapsed during which visits were prevented by the distraction of the troubles which I underwent, being constantly driven out from my own country by the leaders of heresy. And when I came to reckon the intervening time during which the troubles had prevented us meeting face to face, no less than eight years, or very nearly that period, seemed to have elapsed.

Now when I had accomplished most of the journey and was one day's journey distant, a vision appeared to me in a dream and filled me with anxious anticipations of the future. I seemed to be carrying martyrs' relics in my hands; a light came from them, such as comes from a clear mirror when it is put facing the sun, so that my eyes were blinded by the brilliance of the rays. The same vision recurred three times that night. I could not clearly understand the riddle of the dream, but I saw trouble for my soul, and I watched carefully so as to judge the vision by events.

When I approached the retreat in which Macrina led her angelic and heavenly life, first of all I asked one of the servants about my brother, whether he were at home. He told us that he had gone out four days ago now, and I understood, which indeed was the case, that he had gone to meet us by another way. Then I asked after the great lady. He said she was very ill, and I was the more eager to hurry on and complete the remainder of the journey, for a certain anxiety and premonitory fear of what was coming stole in and disquieted me.

Gregory Comes to the Monastery and Finds Macrina on Her Death Bed

But when I came to the actual place, rumor had already announced my arrival to the brotherhood. . . . But the band of virgins on the women's side modestly waited in the church for us to arrive. But when the prayers and the blessing were over, and

the women, after reverently inclining their head for the blessing, retired to their own apartments, none of them were left with us. I guessed the explanation, that the abbess was not with them. A man led me to the house in which was my great sister, and opened the door. Then I entered that holy dwelling. I found her already terribly afflicted with weakness. She was lying not on a bed or couch, but on the floor; a sack had been spread on a board, and another board propped up her head, so contrived as to act as a pillow, supporting the sinews of the neck in slanting fashion, and holding up the neck comfortably. Now when she saw me near the door she raised herself on her elbow but could not come to meet me, her strength being already drained by fever. But by putting her hands on the floor and leaning over from the pallet as far as she could, she showed the respect due to my rank. I ran to her and embraced her prostrate form, and raising her, again restored her to her usual position. Then she lifted her hand to God and said—

"This favor also You have granted me, O God, and have not deprived me of my desire, because You have stirred up Your servant to visit Your handmaid."

Lest she should vex my soul she stilled her groans and made great efforts to hide, if possible, the difficulty of her breathing. And in every way she tried to be cheerful, both taking the lead herself in friendly talk, and giving us an opportunity by asking questions. When in the course of conversation mention was made of the great Basil, my soul was saddened and my face fell dejectedly. But so far was she from sharing in my affliction that, treating the mention of the saint as an occasion for yet loftier philosophy, she discussed various subjects, inquiring into human affairs and revealing in her conversation the divine purpose concealed in disasters. Besides this, she discussed the future life, as if inspired by the Holy Spirit, so that it almost seemed as if my soul were lifted by the help of her words away from mortal nature and placed within the heavenly sanctuary. . . . Fever was drying up her strength and driving her on to death, yet she refreshed her body as it were with dew, and thus kept her mind unimpeded in the contemplation of heavenly things, in no way injured by her terrible weakness. And if my narrative were not extending to an unconscionable length I would tell everything in order, how she was uplifted as she discoursed to us on the nature of the soul and explained the reason of life in the flesh, and why man was made, and how he was mortal, and the origin of death and the nature of the journey from death to life again. . .

Gregory Returns to Macrina, Who Recalls the Events of Her Childhood

But when we saw her again, for she did not allow us to spend time by ourselves in idleness, she began to recall her past life, beginning with childhood, and describing it all in order as in a history. She recounted as much as she could remember of the life of our parents, and the events that took place both before and after my birth. But her aim throughout was gratitude towards God, for she described our parents' life not so much from the point of view of the reputation they enjoyed in the eyes of contemporaries on account of their riches, as an example of the divine blessing.

My father's parents had their goods confiscated for confessing Christ. Our maternal grandfather was slain by the imperial wrath, and all his possessions were transferred to other masters. Nevertheless their life abounded so in faith that no one was named above them in those times. And moreover, after their substance had been divided into nine parts according to the number of the children, the share of each was so increased by God's blessing, that the income of each of the children exceeded the prosperity of the parents. But when it came to Macrina herself she kept nothing of the things assigned to her in the equal division between brothers and sisters, but all her share was given into the priest's hands according to the divine command . . . Never did she even look for help to any human being, nor did human charity give her the opportunity of a comfortable existence. Never were petitioners turned away, yet never did she appeal for help, but God secretly blessed the little seeds of her good works till they grew into a mighty fruit.

As I told my own trouble and all that I had been through, first my exile at the hands of the Emperor Valens on account of the faith, and then the confusion in the Church that summoned me to conflicts and trials, my great sister said—

"Will you not cease to be insensible to the divine blessings? Will you not remedy the ingratitude of your soul? Will you not compare your position with that of your parents? And yet, as regards worldly things, we make our boast of being well born and thinking we come of a noble family. Our father was greatly esteemed as a young man for his learning; in fact his fame was established throughout the law courts of the province. Subsequently, though he excelled all others in rhetoric, his reputation did not extend beyond Pontus. But he was satisfied with fame in his own land.

"But you," she said, "are renowned in cities and peoples and nations. Churches summon you as an ally and director, and do you not see the grace of God in it all? Do you fail to recognize the cause of such great blessings, that it is your parents' prayers that are lifting you up on high, you that have little or no equipment within yourself for such success?"

Thus she spoke, and I longed for the length of the day to be further extended, that she might never cease delighting our ears with sweetness. But the voice of the choir was summoning us to the evening service, and sending me to church, the great one retired once more to God in prayer. And thus she spent the night.

[*After recording the conversation of another visit, Gregory describes how Macrina died.*]

The Sisters Lament for Their Abbess

Now my mind was becoming unnerved in two ways, from the sight that met my gaze, and the sad wailing of the virgins that sounded in my ears. . .

Saddest of all in their grief were those who called on her as mother and nurse. These were they whom she picked up, exposed by the roadside in the time of famine. She had nursed and reared them, and led them to the pure and stainless life . . .

Vestiana Comes to Help Gregory

I had to shout in order to be heard above the noise of the mourners. Then I besought them to go away for awhile to the neighboring house, but asked that some of those whose services she used to welcome when she was alive should stay behind.

Among these was a lady of gentle birth, who had been famous in youth for wealth, good family, physical beauty and every other distinction. She had married a man of high rank and lived with him a short time. Then, with her body still young, she was released from marriage, and chose the great Macrina as protector and guardian of her widowhood, and spent her time mostly with the virgins, learning from them the life of virtue.

The lady's name was Vestiana, and her father was one of those who composed the council of senators. To her I said that there could be no objection now, at any rate, to putting finer clothing on the body and adorning that pure and stainless form with fair linen clothes. But she said one ought to learn what the saint had thought proper in these matters. For it was not right that anything at all should be done by us contrary to what she would have wished. But just what was dear and pleasing to God, would be her desire also.

Now there was a lady called Lampadia, leader of the band of sisters, a deaconess in rank. She declared that she knew Macrina's wishes in the matter of burial exactly. When I asked her about them (for she happened to be present at our deliberations), she said with tears—

"The saint resolved that a pure life should be her adornment, that this should deck her body in life and her grave in death. But so far as clothes to adorn the body go, she procured none when she was alive, nor did she store them for the present purpose. So that not even if we want it will there be anything more than what we have here, since no preparation is made for this need."

"Is it not possible," said I, "to find in the store-cupboard anything to make a fitting funeral?"

"Store-cupboard indeed," said she; "you have in front of you all her treasure. There is the cloak, there is the head covering, there the well-worn shoes on the feet. This is all her wealth, these are her riches. There is nothing stored away in secret places beyond what you see, or put away safely in boxes or bedroom. She knew of one storehouse alone for her wealth, the treasure in heaven. There she had stored her all, nothing was left on earth."

"Suppose," said I, "I were to bring some of the things I have got ready for the funeral, should I be doing anything of which she would not have approved?"

"I do not think," said she, "that this would be against her wish. For had she been living, she would have accepted such honor from you on two grounds—your priesthood which she always prized so dear, and your relationship, for she would not have repudiated what came to her from her brother. This was why she gave commands that your hands were to prepare her body for burial.

[A description of the funeral follows.]

The Funeral Over,
Gregory Returns Home

But when we had completed all the accustomed funeral rites, and it became necessary to return home, I first threw myself on the grave and embraced the dust, and then I started on my way back, downcast and tearful, pondering over the greatness of my loss. . . .

Conclusion

I do not think it advisable to add to my narrative all the similar things that we heard from those who lived with her and knew her life accurately. For most people judge what is credible in the way of a tale by the measure of their own experience. But what exceeds the capacity of the hearer, people receive with insult and suspicion of falsehood, as remote from truth. Consequently I omit that extraordinary agricultural operation in the famine time, how that the corn for the relief of need, though constantly distributed, suffered no perceptible diminution, remaining always in bulk the same as before it was distributed to the needs of the suppliants. And after this there are happenings still more surprising, of which I might tell. Healings of diseases, and castings out of demons, and true predictions of the future. All are believed to be true, even though apparently incredible, by those who have investigated them accurately.

But by the carnally minded they are judged outside the possible. Those, I mean, who do not know that according to the proportion of faith so is given the distribution of spiritual gifts, little to those of little faith, much to those who have plenty of "sea-room" in their religion.

And so, lest the unbeliever should be injured by being led to disbelieve the gifts of God, I have abstained from a consecutive narrative of these sublime wonders, thinking it sufficient to conclude my life of Macrina with what has been already said.

32. Lives of Ascetics:
Palladius, *Lausiac History*

After studying classical literature and theology, Palladius (ca. 365-430) pursued the monastic life on the Mount of Olives in Jerusalem, then among the ascetics of Alexandria, Nitria, and the Cells in Egypt. Palladius was eventually ordained bishop of Helenopolis in Bithynia, but he is best known as a historian of monasticism. His Lausiac History *contains stories and anecdotes about famous men and women ascetics of his day.*

18. Macarius of Alexandria

1. I met the other Macarius, however, the one from Alexandria, a priest of so-called Cellia, where I stayed for nine years, and he was actually alive during three of those years. Some of the things I saw, others I heard about, and some I had by hearsay from others.

Such was his practice that whenever he heard of any asceticism, he surpassed it to perfection. He heard from some that the Tabennesiote monks eat their food uncooked throughout the Lenten period, so he made up his mind to eat no food that had come in contact with fire. For seven years he partook of nothing but raw vegetables, if these could be found, with a little moistened pulse.

2. He brought this virtue to perfection, and then heard about some other monk who ate but a pound of bread a day. He broke up his ration-biscuit into small bits, and put it into a measuring jar, and determined to eat only as much as his hand brought up. And he used to say jokingly: "I would take hold of quite a few morsels, but could

not take them all out because of the narrow neck; for just like a toll-collector, it would not let me pass." He kept this up for three years, eating about four or five ounces and drinking about the equivalent amount of water, and a pint of olive oil lasted him a year.

3. Here is another example of his asceticism: He decided to be above the need for sleep, and he claimed that he did not go under a roof for twenty days in order to conquer sleep. He was burned by the heat of the sun and was drawn up with the cold at night. And he also said: "If I had not gone into the house and obtained the advantage of some sleep, my brain would have shriveled up for good. I conquered to the extent I was able, but I gave in to the extent my nature required sleep."

4. Early one morning when he was sitting in his cell a gnat stung him on the foot. Feeling the pain, he killed it with his hands, and it was gorged with his blood. He accused himself of acting out of revenge and he condemned himself to sit naked in the marsh of Scete out in the great desert for a

SOURCE: Palladius, *The Lausiac History* (Westminster, Md.: Newman Press, 1965), 58-59, 123-25, 134-36, 136-37, 140, 141-44. Copyright © 1965 by Rev. Johannes Quasten, Rev. Walter J. Burghardt, S.J., and Thomas Comerford Lawler. Used by permission of Paulist Press, Inc., New York/Mahwah, N.J.

period of six months. Here the mosquitoes lacerate even the hides of the wild swine just as wasps do. Soon he was bitten all over his body, and he became so swollen that some thought he had elephantiasis. When he returned to his cell after six months he was recognized as Macarius only by his voice.

. . .

46. Melania the Elder

1. Melania the thrice blessed was Spanish by birth and later a Roman. She was the daughter of Marcellinus, one of the consuls, and wife of some man of high rank, I forget which. She was widowed at twenty-two and was counted worthy of divine love, and she told no one, for she would have been stopped at that time, when Valens held rule. She had a trustee named for her son, and taking every movable piece of her property she put it on board ship and set off for Alexandria at full speed with illustrious women and children.

2. And there she sold her possessions and changed her holdings into gold. She went to Mount Nitria and met Pambo, Arsisius, Sarapion the Great, Paphnutius of Scete, Isidore the Confessor, and Dioscorus, bishop of Hermopolis. And she spent up to half a year with them, making the rounds of the desert and seeking out all the holy men.

3. Subsequently the Augustial prefect banished Isidore, Pisimius, Adelphius, Paphnutius, and Pambo, as well as Ammonius Parotes along with them, and twelve bishops and priests, to Palestine near Diocaesarea. She followed them and served them from her own private treasury. Now they said they were not allowed servants (I happened to meet the holy Pisimius and Isidore and Paphnutius and Ammonius), so she wore a slave's hood and used to bring them what they needed at evening. Now the consul of Palestine knew of this, and desiring to fill his pocket he decided to blackmail her.

4. He seized her and cast her into prison, not knowing that she was a freewoman. But she made it clear to him: "I am So-and-so's daughter and So-and-so's wife. I am Christ's slave. Pray do not look down upon my shabby clothes, for I could make more of myself if I would. I have made this clear to you so that you may not fall under legal charges without knowing the reason"—for one must use the sagacity of a hawk where insensate people are concerned!

The judge then realized the situation; he apologized to her and paid her respect, and he ordered that she could associate with the holy men without hindrance.

5. After they were recalled from exile, she built a monastery in Jerusalem and lived there twenty-seven years heading a company of fifty virgins. Close by dwelt also the very noble Rufinus from the Italian city of Aquileia; his way of life was like hers, and he was a most staunch man, later deemed worthy of the priesthood—a more learned and reasonable man was never found.

6. So for twenty-seven years they both entertained with their own private funds the bishops, solitaries, and virgins who visited them, coming to Jerusalem to fulfill a vow. They edified all their visitors and united the four hundred monks of the Pauline schism by persuading every heretic who denied the Holy Spirit and so brought them back to the Church. They bestowed gifts and food on the local clergy, and so finished their days without offending anyone.

. . .

54. More about Melania the Elder

1. I have told above in an offhand way of the wondrous and holy Melania. Nevertheless I shall weave into this account some remaining features. So much wealth did she spend in holy zeal, consumed in a fire as it were, that not I but those rather who inhabit Persia should give the account. No one failed to benefit by her good works, neither in the east nor in the west, neither in the north nor in the south.

2. For thirty-seven years she practiced hospitality; from her own treasury she made donations to churches, monasteries, guests, and prisons. Her own family and son and stewards provided the funds for this. She persisted in her hospitality to such an extent that she had not even a span of earth for herself, nor did she permit yearning for her son to separate her from love toward Christ, although she had but one son.

3. But because of her prayers the young man attained a high degree of education and character, made a good marriage, and became great by worldly standards. He even had two children. A long time afterwards she heard how her granddaughter was doing—how she had married and then elected to leave the world. She feared that they might be utterly destroyed by bad teaching or heresy or bad living; although she was already an old woman of sixty, she boarded a boat at Caesarea and sailed for twenty days to Rome.

4. And there she met with a most holy and remarkable man, a Greek named Apronianus, whom she instructed and made a Christian. She even prevailed upon him to exert self-control concerning his own wife Abita, who was her cousin. She lent moral support to her own granddaughter Melania and to the latter's husband Pinianus as well, and she even taught her son's wife Albina. She induced them to sell their goods, and she led them away from Rome and brought them to the haven of a holy and calm life.

5. When she did this she was actually fighting beasts—I mean the members of the Senate and their wives, who would have stood in the way of their renunciation. But she said: "*Little children*, it was written over four hundred years ago, *it is the last hour* (1 John 2:18). Why are you fond of the vain things of life? Beware lest the days of the Antichrist overtake you and you not enjoy your wealth and your ancestral property."

6. Now she freed all these and led them to the solitary life. She taught the younger son of Publicola and led him to Sicily. She sold everything which remained, and with the money she received she went to Jerusalem. Then she distributed her wealth within forty days and fell asleep in fine old age, in the deepest meekness. She left a monastery at Jerusalem, too, and funds for it.

7. When they had all left Rome, a barbarian deluge, mentioned long before in prophecy, fell upon Rome. Even the bronze statues in the Forum did not escape, for everything was plundered and destroyed with barbarian fury. Thus Rome, beautifully adorned for twelve hundred years, became a ruin. Then those who had been Melania's pupils, as well as those who had been opposed to the

instruction, gave praise to God, who had convinced the unbelievers by a turn of events; when all the others were taken prisoner, those alone were saved who had become holocaust for the Lord through Melania's zealousness.

. . .

[55.]

3. She was most erudite and fond of literature, and she turned night into day going through every writing of the ancient commentators—three million lines of Origen and two and a half million lines of Gregory, Stephen, Pierius, Basil, and other worthy men. And she did not read them once only and in an offhand way, but she worked on them, dredging through each work seven or eight times. Thus it was possible for her to be liberated from *knowledge falsely so called* (1 Tim. 6:20) and to mount on wings, thanks to those books—by good hopes she transformed herself into a spiritual bird and so made the journey to Christ.

. . .

59. Amma Talis and Taor

1. In the town of Antinoë are twelve monasteries of women. Here I met Amma Talis, a woman eighty years old in the ascetic life, as her neighbors affirmed. Sixty young women lived with her. They loved her so much that no lock was placed in the hall of the monastery, as in others, but they were held in check by their love for her. The old woman had such a high degree of self control that when I had entered and taken a seat, she came and sat with me and placed her hands on my shoulders in a burst of frankness.

2. In this monastery was a maiden, a disciple of hers named Taor, who had spent thirty years there. She was never willing to take a new garment, hood, or shoes, but said: "I have no need for them unless I must go out." The others all go out every Sunday to church for Communion, but she stays behind in her cell dressed in rags, ever sitting at her work. She is so graceful in appearance that even a well-controlled person might be led astray by her beauty were not chastity her defense and did not her decorum turn sinful eyes to fear and shame.

61. Melania the Younger

1. Since I promised above to tell you about the daughter of Melania, I must fulfill my promise, for it is not right that we overlook her tender age and disregard such virtue, which is commemorated without a memorial and which as a matter of fact excelled that of even elderly women far advanced in holiness. Her parents forced her into an early marriage with a man of one of the first families in Rome. She was continually stung by the stories about her grandmother and she was so chagrined that she could not cooperate with him in marriage.

2. Two sons were born, but they both died. She came to find marriage so hateful that she said to her husband Pinianus, the son of Severus the ex-prefect: "If you prefer to practice asceticism in company with me by an agreement to chastity, then I will recognize you as master and as lord of my life. If this seems too hard to you, for you are a young man, take what is mine, but set my body free so that I may fulfill my will to God and enter into my inheritance of the zeal of my grandmother whose name I bear.

3. "For had God willed us to have children, He would not have taken away my children so soon."

For a time then they fought against the yoke, but finally God took mercy on the young man and implanted in him a desire to leave the world. Thus so far as they were concerned were the Scriptures fulfilled: *For how knowest thou, O wife, whether thou shall save thy husband?* (1 Cor. 7:16).

Now she had been married at thirteen and lived with her husband for seven years, and at twenty she left the world. And first of all she gave away her silken garments to the sanctuary; the holy Olympias had done likewise.

4. She divided up the rest of her silks and made various church decorations. Her silver and gold she entrusted to Paul, a certain priest, a Dalmatian monk. She sent across the sea to the East ten thousand pieces of money to Egypt and the Thebaid, ten thousand to Antioch and the vicinity thereof, fifteen thousand to Palestine, ten thousand to the churches in the Islands and beyond; she likewise made donations to the churches in the West.

5. All this and four times as much in addition did she rescue *from the mouth of the lion* (2 Tim. 4:17)—I mean Alaric, if God will forgive the expression. Her own faith led her to set free eight thousand slaves who desired freedom. The rest of the slaves did not want this, however, choosing rather to serve her brother, to whom she sold them for three pieces of money. She sold off everything she had in Spain, Aquitania, Taraconia, and Gaul, keeping for endowment of the monasteries only her holdings in Sicily, Campania, and Africa.

6. That was her wisdom in regard to the burden of riches. This was her asceticism: She ate every other day, but in the beginning of her ascetical life at intervals of more than five days, and she arranged to do herself some of the daily work of her slave women, whom she made her associates in her ascetic practices. She had with her also her mother Albina, who lived a life as ascetic as her own and who had made a private distribution of her own wealth. They are now dwelling in the country, sometimes in Sicily, again in Campania, with fifteen eunuchs and sixty maidens, both freewomen and slaves.

7. In a like manner her husband Pinianus lives with thirty monks reading and engaged in gardening and solemn conferences. They honored us not a little when quite a few of us were on the way to Rome because of Saint John the Bishop. They entertained us with hospitality and abundant provisions for the journey, gaining for themselves with great joy the fruit of eternal life by their God-given works of the best way of life.

33. Egeria,
Diary of a Pilgrimage

Toward the end of the fourth century a woman named Egeria, probably a nun from northwestern Spain, went on a pilgrimage to the Sinai, Egypt, Palestine, and Mesopotamia. She used the Bible as her guidebook, and local ascetics led her around the holy sites explaining what she should see and do at each location. Egeria's extensive diary of her travels contains invaluable information for the history of liturgy and details about church architecture and monastic life. It testifies to the already well established notion of a Christian Holy Land and the importance of pilgrimage to late antique Christians.

Chapter 3

On Saturday evening we proceeded onto the mountain, and, arriving at some monastic cells, we were received very hospitably by the monks dwelling there, and they offered us every courtesy. Since there is a church there with a priest, we stopped there for the night. Early on Sunday morning, accompanied by that priest and the monks who lived there, we began climbing the mountains one by one. These mountains are climbed with very great difficulty, since you do not ascend them slowly going round and round, in a spiral path as we say, but you go straight up all the way as if scaling a wall. Then you have to go straight down each of these mountains until you reach the very foot of the central mountain, which is properly Sinai. By the will of Christ our God, and with the help of the prayers of the holy men who were accompanying us, I made the ascent, though with great effort, because it had to be on foot, since it was absolutely impossible to make the climb in the saddle.

Yet you did not feel the effort; and the reason it was not felt was because I saw the desire which I had being fulfilled through the will of God. And so at the fourth hour we reached the summit of the mountain of God, Holy Sinai, where the Law was given, at the place, that is, where the Glory of the Lord descended on the day when the mountain smoked.

In this place there is now a church, though not a very large one, because the place itself, the summit of the mountain, that is, is not very large. Yet this church has great charm all its own. When through God's will we had reached the mountain top and had arrived at the church door, there was the priest who was assigned to the church coming forth from his cell to meet us. He was an old man, beyond reproach, a monk from his youth, and, as they say here, an ascetic; in a word, he was a man worthy of being in this place. Then the other priests and all the monks who dwell there by the side of the mountain, that is to say, at least those who were not impeded either by age or by infirmity, came forth. Indeed, no one lives on the very top of that central mountain, for there is nothing there save the church alone and the cave where the holy man Moses was. All of the proper passage from the Book of Moses was read, the sacrifice was offered in the prescribed manner, and we received Communion. As we were about to leave the church, the priests gave us gifts native to this place, that is, some fruit which grows on this mountain. Now this holy Mount Sinai is itself all rock, without even a shrub. Down at the foot of

SOURCE: Egeria, *Diary of a Pilgrimage*, tr. George E. Gingras (New York: Newman Press, 1970), 51-53, 75-76, 77-78, 80-81, 86-88, 122-25. Copyright © 1970 by Rev. Johannes Quasten, Rev. Walter J. Burghardt, S.J., and Thomas Comerford Lawler. Used by permission of Paulist Press, Inc., New York/Mahwah, N.J.

these mountains, however, either around this one which is in the middle or around those which encircle it, there is a small piece of ground. There the holy monks carefully plant bushes and lay out little orchards and cultivated plots, next to which they build their cells, and the fruit which they have seemingly raised with their own hands they take from, as it were, the soil of the mountain itself.

After we had received Communion, then, and the holy men had given us gifts, and we had come out the church door, I asked them to show us each place. At once the holy men consented to point out each one. They showed us the cave where the holy man Moses was when he ascended the mountain of God a second time to receive anew the tables, after he had broken the first ones because the people had sinned. Moreover, they consented to show us whatever other places we desired and with which they were very well acquainted. Ladies, reverend sisters, I would like you to know that we were standing around the enclosure of the church on top of the central mountain, and from this place those mountains which we had first climbed with difficulty seemed, in comparison with the central mountain on which we now stood, as far beneath us as if they were hills. Yet they were so high that I do not think I have ever seen any higher, except for the central mountain which towers very much above them. And from there we saw beneath us Egypt and Palestine, the Red Sea, and the Parthenian Sea which leads to Alexandria, and finally the endless lands of the Saracens. Hard as this may be to believe, the holy men did point out each of these things to us.

. . .

Chapter 17

Some time later, in the name of God, I decided to return to my homeland, for three full years had now elapsed since my coming to Jerusalem, and I had seen all the holy places to which I had been drawn to pray. Nevertheless, by the will of God, I wished to go to Mesopotamia of Syria, to visit the holy monks who were said to be numerous there and to be of such exemplary life that it can scarcely be described. I also wished to pray at the shrine of Saint Thomas the Apostle, where his uncorrupted

body lies, that is, at Edessa. Our Lord Jesus Christ had promised in a letter, which He sent to King Abgar through the messenger Ananias, that Saint Thomas would be sent to Edessa, after His ascension into heaven; and this letter is preserved with great reverence in the city of Edessa, where his shrine is located. I beseech Your Charity to believe me that there is no Christian who has come as far as the holy places of Jerusalem who does not go to Edessa to pray. It is a twenty-five day journey from Jerusalem. Since Antioch is nearer to Mesopotamia, it was very convenient for me, God willing, to go from there to Mesopotamia, on my return to Constantinople, for my route lay through Antioch. And, through God's will, this was done.

. . .

Chapter 19

After making my way through a number of resting stations, I arrived at a city whose name we find in Scripture, namely, Batanis; and this city still stands today. Many shrines of martyrs are located there, as well as a church with a bishop, who is a holy man, a monk, and a confessor. The city is filled with great crowds of men, for an army with its tribune is stationed here.

We then set out from this place and we arrived, in the name of Christ our God, at Edessa; and immediately after our arrival there we hastened to the church and the shrine of Saint Thomas. There, after we had prayed and had done all things that we customarily did at holy places, we then read, in addition, some passages concerning Saint Thomas. The church there is large and very beautiful and of recent design, and very worthy of being a house of God. Since there were many things that I wished to see, I had to make a three-day stop there. I visited in the city many shrines of martyrs and many holy monks, some living near the shrines, others living far from the city in secluded places where they had their cells. The holy bishop of that city, who was truly a religious man, a monk, and a confessor, and who had hospitably received me, said to me: "My daughter, I see that you have taken on yourself, because of your piety, the great task of journeying from very distant lands to these places. Therefore, if you are willing, we will show you whatever places there are here that Christians like to see." Giving thanks first to God then, I freely asked him to do what he had said he would.

...

After the saintly bishop recounted all these things, he said to me: "Let us go now to the gate, through which the messenger Ananias entered with the letter which I have been discussing." On arriving at the gate, the bishop, remaining standing, said a prayer, read to us the letters, blessed us, and recited another prayer. This holy man also told us that, from the day when the messenger Ananias entered through this gate with the Lord's letter up to the present day, they take care that no unclean man or any man in grief should pass through this gate, and further that no body of a dead man should be borne through this gate. The saintly bishop then showed us the tomb of Abgar and his whole family; it was very beautiful, but built in an older style. He then guided us to the upper palace, where King Abgar had first lived, and he showed us whatever other places there were.

And this was especially gratifying to me, that I received from the saintly bishop copies of the letters which he had read to us, both Abgar's letter to the Lord and the Lord's letter to Abgar. Although I had copies of them at home, I was clearly very pleased to accept them from him, in case the copy which had reached us at home happened to be incomplete; for the copy which I received was certainly more extensive. If Jesus Christ our Lord wills it and I return home, you, ladies dear to me, will read them.

...

Chapter 20

After spending three days there, I had to go on still farther, as far as Carrhae. This is what it is called now, but in Holy Scripture the place where the holy man Abraham lived was called Haran, just as it is written in Genesis, where the Lord says to Abraham: *Go out of your country, and out of the*

house of your father, and go into Haran (cf. Gen. 1:12), and so forth. When I arrived there, in Haran, that is, I went immediately to the church there which is in the city itself. I then saw afterwards the bishop of this place, a very holy man of God, also a monk and a confessor, who then graciously consented to show us all the places there which we desired to visit.

...

And he consented to speak about many other matters, just as the other holy bishops and the saintly monks had consented to do, but always about the Divine Scriptures and the acts of holy men, the monks, I mean, either about the wondrous things they had done, if they were already dead, or, if they were still living, about what they did each day, those who are ascetics. For I do not want Your Charity to think that the conversations of the monks are about anything except the Divine Scriptures and the actions of the great monks.

...

Chapter 23

I set out from Tarsus and I came to a certain city by the sea, still in Cilicia, called Pompeiopolis. From there I crossed over into the regions of Isauria, and I stayed at a city called Corycus. On the third day I arrived at a city called Seleucia of Isauria. On arriving there, I went to the bishop, a very holy man and a former monk. I also saw there in the same city a very beautiful church. Since it is around fifteen hundred feet from the city to the shrine of Saint Thecla, which lies beyond the city on a rather flat hill, I thought it best to go out there to make the overnight stop which I had to make.

At the holy church there is nothing but countless monastic cells for men and women. I met there a very dear friend of mine, and a person to whose way of life everyone in the East bears witness, the holy deaconess Marthana, whom I had met in Jerusalem, where she had come to pray. She governs these monastic cells of *aputactitae*, or virgins. Would I ever be able to describe how great was her joy and mine when she saw me? But to return to the subject: There are many cells all over the hill, and in the middle there is a large wall which encloses the church where the shrine is. It is a very beautiful shrine. The wall is set there to guard the church against the Isaurians, who are evil men, who frequently rob and who might try to do something against the monastery which is established there. Having arrived there in the name of God, a prayer was said at the shrine and the complete Acts of Saint Thecla was read. I then gave unceasing thanks to Christ our God, who granted to me, an unworthy woman and in no way deserving, the fulfillment of my desires in all things. And so, after spending two days there seeing the holy monks and the *aputactitae*, both men and women, who live there, and after praying and receiving Communion, I returned to Tarsus and to my journey.

. . .

Chapter 45

I must also describe how those who are baptized at Easter are instructed. Whoever gives his name does so the day before Lent, and the priest notes down all their names; and this is before those eight weeks during which, as I have said, Lent is observed here. When the priest has noted down everyone's name, then on the following day, the first day of Lent, on which the eight weeks begin, a throne is set up for the bishop in the center of the major church, the Martyrium. The priests sit on stools on both sides, and all the clergy stand around. One by one the candidates are led forward, in such a way that the men come with their godfathers and the women with their godmothers.

Then the bishop questions individually the neighbors of the one who has come up, inquiring: "Does he lead a good life? Does he obey his parents? Is he a drunkard or a liar?" And he seeks out in the man other vices which are more serious. If the person proves to be guiltless in all these matters concerning which the bishop has questioned the witnesses who are present, he notes down the man's name with his own hand. If, however, he is accused of anything, the bishop orders him to go out and says: "Let him amend his life, and when

he has done so, let him then approach the baptismal font." He makes the same inquiry of both men and women. If, however, someone is a stranger, he cannot easily receive baptism, unless he has witnesses who know him.

Chapter 46

Ladies, my sisters, I must describe this, lest you think that it is done without explanation. It is the custom here, throughout the forty days on which there is fasting, for those who are preparing for baptism to be exorcised by the clergy early in the morning, as soon as the dismissal from the morning service has been given at the Anastasis. Immediately a throne is placed for the bishop in the major church, the Martyrium. All those who are to be baptized, both men and women, sit closely around the bishop, while the godmothers and godfathers stand there; and indeed all of the people who wish to listen may enter and sit down, provided they are of the faithful. A catechumen, however, may not enter at the time when the bishop is teaching them the law. He does so in this way: beginning with Genesis he goes through the whole of Scripture during these forty days, expounding first its literal meaning and then explaining the spiritual meaning. In the course of these days everything is taught not only about the Resurrection but concerning the body of faith. This is called catechetics.

When five weeks of instruction have been completed, they then receive the Creed. He explains the meaning of each of the phrases of the Creed in the same way he explained Holy Scripture, expounding first the literal and then the spiritual sense. In this fashion the Creed is taught.

And thus it is that in these places all the faithful are able to follow the Scriptures when they are read in the churches, because all are taught through those forty days, that is, from the first to the third hours, for during the three hours instruction is given. God knows, ladies, my sisters, that the voices of the faithful who have come to catechetics to hear instruction on those things being said or explained by the bishop are louder than when the bishop sits down in church to preach about each of those matters which are explained in this fashion. The dismissal from catechetics is given at the third hour, and immediately, singing hymns, they lead the bishop to the Anastasis, and the office of the third hour takes place. And thus they are taught for three hours a day for seven weeks. During the eighth week, the one which is called the Great Week, there remains no more time for them to be taught, because what has been mentioned above must be carried out.

Now when seven weeks have gone by and there remains only Holy Week, which is here called the Great Week, then the bishop comes in the morning to the major church, the Martyrium. To the rear, at the apse behind the altar, a throne is placed for the bishop, and one by one they come forth, the men with their godfathers, the women with their godmothers. And each one recites the Creed back to the bishop. After the Creed has been recited back to the bishop, he delivers a homily to them all, and says: "During these seven weeks you have been instructed in the whole law of the Scriptures, and you have heard about the faith. You have also heard of the resurrection of the flesh. But as for the whole explanation of the Creed, you have heard only that which you are able to know while you are still catechumens. Because you are still catechumens, you are not able to know those things which belong to a still higher mystery, that of baptism. But that you may not think that anything would be done without explanation, once you have been baptized in the name of God, you will hear of them during the eight days of Easter in the Anastasis following the dismissal from church. Because you are still catechumens, the most secret of the divine mysteries cannot be told to you."

Christology and Diverging
Identities in the East

34. Letters of Cyril of Alexandria
and Nestorius of Constantinople

The following letters introduce the personalities and politics as well as the theological issues at stake in an early stage of the christological controversies. Nestorius (ca. 381-451), trained at the school of Antioch, had become bishop of Constantinople. His archrival, Cyril of Alexandria, accused him of teaching that Jesus had been a "mere man." In part their rivalry reflected a tension between the Antiochene and Alexandrian schools of exegesis. Cyril ultimately triumphed as Nestorius was deposed by the Council of Ephesus (431), but Nestorius himself denied that he ever held the heretical views condemned by the council.

The Second Letter of Cyril
to Nestorius

Cyril to the most Reverend and God-beloved fellow minister Nestorius. Greetings in the Lord.

1. It has come to my attention that certain persons are quite repeatedly bringing my character into disrepute before your Holiness, taking their opportunity particularly when synods are being held. Thinking, perhaps, to bring you welcome news they are making groundless claims, for they suffered no injustice whatsoever, although they were rightly convicted, for one defrauded the blind and the poor, the other drew his sword against his mother, and the third (apart from having always had the kind of reputation one would not care to wish upon one's worst enemy) stole someone's gold with the connivance of a serving girl.

Nonetheless, what people like that say is of no great account to me. I must not rate my insignificant self above the Lord and Master, or even above the Fathers. However a man might order his life it is not possible to avoid the malice of the wicked. As for them, their "mouths full of curses and bitterness" (Rom. 3:14), they will have to answer to the Judge of all.

2. On the other hand, I will turn to what really concerns me, and even now I urge you as a brother in Christ to conduct your manner of teaching the people, and the way you envisage the faith, with all possible exactness. Remember that "whoever scandalizes even one of the least" of those who believe in Christ (Matt. 18:6) will fall under the unbearable anger (of God). And when the number of those who have been distressed is very great, surely we stand in need of all the skill we can muster to remove the scandals prudently and to expound the sound doctrine of the faith to those who are seeking the truth? And we shall do this most correctly if we are very careful, when we encounter the teachings of the holy Fathers, to hold them in the highest regard. "We should test

SOURCE: John A. McGuckin, *St. Cyril of Alexandria: The Christological Controversy* (Leiden: E. J. Brill, 1994), 262-65, 364-68, 266-75. Used by permission of Brill Academic Publishers.

ourselves to see whether we are in the faith" (2 Cor. 13:5), as the scripture says, and thoroughly conform our own opinions to their correct and flawless ideas.

3. Well, the great and holy Synod said that it was the Only begotten Son himself, naturally born from God the Father, true God from true God, light from light, through whom the Father made all things, who was the one who came down, was made flesh, was made man, suffered, rose again on the third day, and ascended into the heavens. We must follow these words and teachings, and realize what is meant by the Word of God being made flesh and made man. We do not say that the nature of the Word was changed and became flesh, nor that he was transformed into a perfect man of soul and body. We say, rather, that the Word, in an ineffable and incomprehensible manner, ineffably united to himself flesh animated with a rational soul, and thus became man and was called the Son of Man. This was not effected only as a matter of will, or favor, or by the assumption of a single prosopon. While the natures that were brought together into this true unity were different, nonetheless there is One Christ and Son from out of both. This did not involve the negation of the difference of natures, rather that the Godhead and manhood by their ineffable and indescribable consilience into unity achieved One Lord and Christ and Son for us.

4. For this reason, even though he existed and was begotten of the Father from before all ages, he is also said to have been begotten from a woman according to the flesh. This does not mean that his divine nature received the beginning of its existence in the holy virgin or that it necessarily needed a second generation for its own sake after its generation from the Father. It is completely foolish and stupid to say that He who exists before all ages and is coeternal with the Father stood in need of a second beginning of existence. Nonetheless, because the Word hypostatically united human reality to himself, "for us and for our salvation," and came forth of a woman, this is why he is said to have been begotten in a fleshly manner. The Word did not subsequently descend upon an ordinary man previously born of the holy virgin, but he is made one from his mother's womb, and

thus is said to have undergone a fleshly birth insofar as he appropriated to himself the birth of his own flesh.

5. So it is we say that he both suffered and rose again; not meaning that the Word of God suffered in his own nature either the scourging, or the piercing of the nails, or the other wounds, for the divinity is impassible because it is incorporeal. But insofar as that which had become his own body suffered, then he himself is said to suffer these things for our sake, because the Impassible One was in the suffering body. We understand his death in the same manner. By nature the Word of God is immortal and incorruptible, and Life, and Life-giver, and yet since his own body "tasted death by the grace of God on behalf of all," as Paul says (Heb. 2:9) then he himself is said to have suffered death for our sake. This does not mean he underwent the experience of death in terms of his [own] nature for it would be madness to say or think such a thing; rather, as I have said, it means that his flesh tasted death. Similarly when his flesh was raised up, once again we say that the resurrection is his. This does not mean that he fell into corruption, certainly not, but again that his own body was raised.

6. And so we confess One Christ and Lord. This does not mean we worship a man alongside the Word, in case the shadow of a division might creep in through using the words "along with"; rather that we worship one and the same because the body of the Word, with which he shares the Father's throne, was not alien to him. Again this does not mean two sons were sharing the throne, but one, because of the union with the flesh. But if we reject this hypostatic union as either impossible or unfitting, then we fall into saying there are two sons, and in that case we will be compelled to make a distinction and say that one of them was really a man, honored with the title of Son, while the other was the Word of God who enjoyed the name and reality of Sonship by nature.

7. And so, we must not divide the One Lord Jesus Christ into two sons. To hold this in no way benefits the correct exposition of the faith, even if certain people do declare a unity of personas; for the scripture did not say that he united the persona of a man to himself, but that he became flesh

(John 1:14). Yet the Word "becoming flesh" means nothing else than that "he shared in flesh and blood like us" (Heb. 2:14), and made his very own a body which was ours, and that he came forth as man from a woman, although he did not cast aside the fact that he is God, born of God the Father, but remained what he was even in the assumption of the flesh. Everywhere the exposition of the orthodox faith promotes this doctrine. We shall also find that the holy Fathers thought like this, and this is why they called the holy virgin "Mother of God." This does not mean that the nature of the Word or his divinity took the beginning of its existence from the holy virgin, rather that he is said to have been born according to the flesh insofar as the Word was hypostatically united to that holy body which was born from her, endowed with a rational soul.

I write these things to you out of the love which I have in Christ, and even now I beseech you as a brother and "charge you before Christ and the elect angels" (1 Tim. 5:21) to think and teach these same things together with us so that the peace of the churches might be preserved and that the bond of harmony and love between the priests of God might remain unbroken.

Nestorius's Reply to Cyril's Second Letter

Nestorius to the most reverend and God-beloved fellow-minister Cyril. Greetings in the Lord.

1. I will pass over the insults against me contained in your extraordinary letter, as meriting only the patience of a doctor. It will have its reply, in actions, soon enough. There is something, however, that will not allow silence because if it is hushed up it has the potential of being very dangerous indeed. So, insofar as I am able I will try to make a concise exposition of it for you, cutting out all longwindedness, to spare you any nausea in the face of an over-long, obscure, and indigestible tract. I will begin with Your Charity's own very wise words, and will cite them exactly. What, then, are these words of wondrous teaching contained in your letter? "The great and holy synod said that it was the Only Begotten Son himself, naturally born from God the Father, true God from true God, light from light, through whom the Father made all things, who was the one who came down, was made flesh, was made man, suffered, and rose again on the third day."

2. These are the words of Your Reverence and you surely recognize them as your own. But now hear ours, a fraternal exhortation on piety, and one which the great Paul gave as a testimony to his beloved Timothy: "Apply yourself to reading, to encouragement, to teaching, for if you do this you will save yourself and those who hear you" (1 Tim. 4:13, 16). Why is this phrase "apply yourself" relevant? Because in your letter you have misunderstood the tradition contained in those holy texts you have read, and so have fallen into ignorance (understandable enough) by thinking that they said the Word of God, coeternal with the Father, was passible. But look over these words a little more carefully if you please, and you will find that this divine chorus of fathers did not say that the consubstantial Godhead was passible, or that it underwent a recent birth (since it is coeternal with the Father), or that it was raised to life (since it raised up the destroyed temple). And if you lend me your ears so that I can supply some fraternal healing, then I will cite the very words of the holy Fathers in order to free you from the calumnies you have raised against them and against the holy scriptures.

3. They said: "I believe in our Lord Jesus Christ, his Only Begotten Son." Note how they set out at the beginning, as foundations, these terms of "Lord" and "Jesus" and "Christ" and "Only Begotten," as common names for both the Godhead and the manhood. And then they go on to build the tradition of his incarnation and passion and resurrection on this [foundation]. First they set out certain terms as indicative of, and common to, both natures, for then there is no danger of bringing division between things that apply to the Sonship and the Lordship, and no danger of making things that apply to both natures disappear in an indiscriminate reference to the Sonship alone.

4. Paul has been their teacher in this, for when he made mention of the divine incarnation and was about to add a reference to the passion, he first posited Christ as a common term for both

natures, as I have just said previously, and then went on to speak in a way that applies to both natures. What does he say? "Have this mind among you which was in Christ Jesus. Though he was in the form of God he did not count equality with God a thing to be grasped but (to give the general sense) became obedient to death, death on a cross" (Phil. 2:5, 6, 8). Since he was going to mention the death, he posited the title Christ so that no one might imagine that God the Word was passible, for Christ is a term that applies to both the impassible and the passible natures in a single persona. This is how Christ can be said, without danger, to be both passible and impassible; impassible in the Godhead, but passible in the nature of his body.

5. I could say many things on this subject. In the first place, when referring to the economy, the holy Fathers never speak of a "generation" but an "incarnation." I am conscious, however, how the promise of brevity I made in my introduction reins in my discourse. This makes me pass on to the second point Your Charity raises.

6. I applaud the fact you make a division between the natures according to Godhead and manhood, admitting their conjunction in one persona; and also that you deny that God the Word had need of a second generation from a woman; and that you confess that the deity cannot undergo any suffering. All this is truly orthodox and contrary to all the evil opinions the heretics have entertained about the dominical natures. But as for the rest [of your letter] if it contains some hidden wisdom, incomprehensible to the ears of those who hear it read, then you alone have the wit to know. As far as I am concerned it seems to contradict your earlier statements. For the one you first proclaimed as impassible and not needing a second generation, you subsequently introduce (how I know not) as passible and newly created. It is as if those attributes naturally inherent in God the Word were destroyed by this conjunction with the temple; or as if men regarded it as an insignificance that this sinless temple had undergone birth and death on behalf of sinners; or as if we ought not to believe the voice of Our Lord himself when he cried out to the Jews: "Destroy this temple and in three days I will raise it up" (John 2:19)—not

"Destroy my Godhead and in three days it shall be raised up." Once again, although I would like to expand on this, I am mindful of my promise and must, therefore, speak with all brevity.

7. All throughout the sacred scriptures, wherever mention is made of the Lord's economy, the birth and the sufferings are not passed down to us as if they applied to the Godhead, but to the manhood. This means that the holy virgin should be described, in a more exact designation, not as "Mother of God" but "Mother of Christ." Listen to the Gospel crying out these facts when it says: "The Book of the generation of Jesus Christ, the Son of David, Son of Abraham" (Matt. 1:1). Obviously God the Word was not the Son of David. If you like take this other witness: "And Jacob begot Joseph, the husband of Mary, from whom was born Jesus who is called Christ" (Matt. 1:16). Again, examine another text that bears witness for us: "This was how the birth of Jesus Christ came to pass. His mother Mary was betrothed to Joseph when she was found to have conceived of the Holy Spirit" (Matt. 1:18). But who would ever take this to mean that the Godhead of the Only Begotten was a creation of the Holy Spirit? And what should we say of the text: "And the Mother of Jesus was there" (John 2:1), or again, "And with Mary the Mother of Jesus" (Acts 1:14), or "For that which is conceived in her is of the Holy Spirit" (Matt. 1:20), or "Take the child and its mother and flee to Egypt" (Matt. 2:13), or "Concerning his Son who was born of the line of David according to the flesh" (Rom. 1:3), or again (in relation to his sufferings) "God, by sending his own Son in the likeness of sinful flesh, and on sin's account, condemned sin in the flesh" (Rom. 8:3), or again "Christ died for our sins" (1 Cor. 15:3), or "Christ suffered in the flesh" (1 Pet. 4:1), or "This is my body (not my Godhead note) which is broken for you" (1 Cor. 11:24). There are a thousand other texts which all testify to humankind that it is not the deity of the Son that should be regarded as something recent or capable of bodily suffering, but the flesh which is associated with the nature of the Godhead. Why does Christ refer to himself as both Lord of David, and David's son, when he says: "What is your opinion of the Christ? Whose son is he? And they said to him, David's son. But

in reply Jesus said to them, Then why does David, in the Spirit, call him Lord when he says, The Lord said to my Lord, sit on my right?" (Matt. 22:42-44). It is because he is entirely David's son according to the flesh, but David's Lord according to the Godhead. It is entirely right and fitting to the Gospel traditions to confess that the body is the temple of the Godhead of the Son, and a temple that is united in a sublime and divine conjunction, in such a way that the nature of the Godhead appropriates the characteristics of this [temple]. But to attribute to the Godhead, in the name of this appropriation, the properties of the flesh that is associated with it (and I mean generation, suffering, and death)—then this is either the error of a pagan mentality, brother, or a spirit sick with the madness of Apollinaris and Arius and the other heresies, or even something far worse. For those who allow themselves to be carried away by this notion of "appropriation" must of necessity admit that because of this appropriation God the Word was involved in sucking at the breast, and in a gradual growth, and in trepidation at the time of the passion, needing the assistance of an angel. I will make no mention of circumcision, sacrifice, sweating, hunger; all those things which, joined with the flesh, are actually adorable because they were done for our sake, but which, if they are attributed to the Godhead, are merely lies and become the grounds for our rightful condemnation as blasphemers.

8. These are the traditions of the holy Fathers. These are the precepts of the divine scriptures. This is how one theoretically should understand both the philanthropy and the authority of God. As Paul said, addressing everyone: "Reflect on these things, immerse yourself in them, so that your progress will be obvious to all" (1 Tim. 4:15).

On the other hand, you do well to concern yourself about those who are scandalized. So my thanks for the fact that your spirit is always thinking about divine affairs, and thank you for your interest in me. But you should know that you have been deceived by those who have been deposed here by the holy synod for holding Manichean opinions, or by clerics who perhaps hold to your opinions. In fact the affairs of the church improve day by day, by the grace of Christ. The people

flourish so much that those who see their number cry out in the words of the prophet: "The earth will be filled with the knowledge of the Lord as the sea is covered by great waters" (Isa. 11:9). The Royal Court is overjoyed at the way the doctrines have been illuminated. In short, as anyone can discover, in terms of all the God-fighting heresies or the orthodoxy of all the churches, then that text has been fulfilled among us: "The house of Saul goes to ruination, but the house of David goes from strength to strength" (2 Sam. 3:1).

9. We send you these words as brothers conferring with a brother. "But if anyone still loves to dispute," then Paul himself can cry out to him through us that, "Neither we, nor the churches of God, have such a custom" (1 Cor. 11:16).

I, and those with me, heartily salute your whole brotherhood in Christ. Keep well and do not cease praying for us most venerable and reverend lord.

The Third Letter of Cyril to Nestorius

1. Cyril and the synod of the diocese of Egypt assembled at Alexandria, to the most Reverend and God-beloved fellow-minister Nestorius. Greetings in the Lord.

Since our Savior clearly tells us that: "Whoever loves son or daughter more than me is not worthy of me" (Matt. 10:37), then what censure would we incur in acquiescing to your Reverence's demand that we should prefer you in love to Christ the Savior of us all? Who would be able to help us on the day of judgment, or what excuse could we find for having kept silent so long while you have raised up blasphemies against him? We would not be so concerned if you were only injuring yourself by thinking and teaching the things you do, but you have scandalized the entire church and have cast among the people the yeast of a strange and alien heresy, and not only among the people [at Constantinople] but everywhere the books of your sermons have been circulated. So how could we justify our silence any longer? How could we not recall the saying of Christ: "Do not imagine that I came to bring peace on earth, but a sword. I came to set a man against his father, and a daughter against her mother" (Matt. 10:34f.). When the faith is being harmed then away with any stale and fussy reverence for parents, then let the law of affection for children and brethren be set aside, and let men of reverence prefer death to life that "they may obtain a better resurrection," as it is written (Heb. 11:35).

2. Take note, therefore, that in agreement with the holy synod gathered together in Great Rome, under the presidency of our most holy and religious brother and fellow-minister bishop Celestine, we also charge and warn you, in this our third letter, to dissociate from these utterly wicked and perverse doctrines which you both think and teach, and instead to embrace the correct faith which has been delivered to the churches from the beginning by the holy apostles and evangelists, the "eyewitnesses and ministers of the word" (Luke 1:2). If your Reverence does not do so by the time determined in the letters of our aforementioned fellow-minister Celestine, the most holy and religious bishop of Rome, then know that you will have no clerical standing whatsoever among us, and no place or status among the priests and bishops of God. For we cannot endure seeing the churches thus thrown into confusion and the people scandalized, and the correct faith set aside, or the flocks scattered by you who ought to be saving them; which you would do if you were a lover of correct doctrine, and followed in the path of the religion of the holy Fathers as we do. On our part, we all stand in communion with all those who have been excommunicated or deposed by your Reverence for the sake of the faith, whether lay people or clergy. It is not right that those who have had the wisdom to think what is correct should be wronged by your judgments because they justly opposed you. This is something that you yourself have signified in the letter which you wrote to our most holy fellow-bishop Celestine of Great Rome. It is not enough for your Reverence only to agree in confessing the Symbol of the faith previously set out in the Holy Spirit by that holy and great Synod formerly gathered in Nicaea, for you have not understood or interpreted it correctly, but have perverted it even though you may have confessed it verbally. Consequently you must confess in writing and on oath that you anathematize your foul and profane teachings and that you hold and

teach what we all do, the bishops and teachers and leaders of the people throughout the West and the East. Moreover, the holy synod at Rome, and all of us here, agree that the letters written to your Reverence by the church of Alexandria were correct and unimpeachable, so we attach to this letter of ours the doctrines which you must hold and teach, as well as those you must dissociate from. For this is the faith of the catholic and apostolic church in which all the orthodox bishops throughout the West and East concur.

3. We believe in One God, the Father Almighty, maker of everything visible and invisible, and in One Lord Jesus Christ, the Only Begotten Son of God, begotten of the Father, that is from the essence of the Father, God of God, light of light, true God of true God, begotten not made, consubstantial with the Father, through whom all things were made, things in heaven and things on earth, who for us men and for our salvation came down, was incarnate and made man, suffered and rose again on the third day, ascended into the heavens and will come to judge the living and the dead; and in the Holy Spirit. But those who say, "There was when he was not," and "Before he was begotten he was not," and that "he came to be from nothing," or those who maintain that the Son of God is from a different subsistence or essence, or that he is mutable or changeable, these the catholic and apostolic church anathematizes.

We follow in every respect the confessions of the holy Fathers which they made with the Holy Spirit speaking in them. By following the path in which they understood these things we come, as it were, along the Royal Road, and we declare that the Only Begotten Word of God himself, who was begotten of the very essence of the Father, the true God of true God, the light of light, he through whom all things in heaven or on earth were made, himself came down for the sake of our salvation and lowered himself into a self-emptying, and was incarnated and made man. That is, taking flesh from the holy virgin and making it his very own from his mother, he underwent a human birth and came forth as man from a woman. This did not mean he abandoned what he was, for even when he came as man in the assumption of flesh and blood even so he remained what he was, that is God in nature and in truth. We do not say that the flesh was changed into the nature of Godhead, nor indeed that the ineffable nature of God the Word was converted into the nature of flesh, for he is entirely unchangeable and immutable, and in accordance with the scriptures he abides ever the same (Heb. 13:8; Mal. 3:6). Even when he is seen as a baby in swaddling bands still at the breast of the virgin who bore him, even so as God he filled the whole creation and was enthroned with his Father, because deity is without quantity or size and accepts no limitations.

4. So we confess the Word to have been united hypostatically with flesh, and we worship One Son and Lord Jesus Christ. We do not separate or hold apart man and God as if they were connected to one another by a unity of dignity or sovereignty (for this is babbling and nothing else); nor do we designate specifically a Christ who is the Word of God and then specify another Christ, the one who is born of a woman. No, we know only One Christ, the Word of God the Father with his own flesh. He was anointed alongside us in a human manner, even though he himself gives the Spirit to those who are worthy to receive it, and gives it without measure as the blessed evangelist John says (John 3:34). We do not say that the Word of God has dwelt in him who was born of the holy virgin, as if in an ordinary man, for this might imply that Christ was a God-bearing man. Even though it is said that: "The Word dwelt among us" (John 1:14) and "all the fullness of the Godhead dwelt bodily" in Christ (Col. 2:9), nonetheless we understand that in terms of his becoming flesh we must not define the indwelling in his case as if it were just the same as the way he is said to dwell in the saints; for he was naturally united to, but not changed into, flesh, in that kind of indwelling which the soul of man can be said to have with its own body.

5. There is, therefore, One Christ and Son and Lord, not as though a man simply had a conjunction with God as though in a unity of honor or sovereignty, for equality of honor does not unite natures. Indeed Peter and John have equality of honor with one another since they are both apostles and holy disciples, but these two are not one. We do not conceive the manner of the conjunc-

tion in terms of juxtaposition (for this is not enough for a natural union), nor indeed in terms of a relational participation in the way that "being joined to the Lord we are one spirit with him" as it is written (1 Cor. 6:17). In fact we reject the term "conjunction" as being insufficient to signify the union. We do not call the Word of God the Father the "God" or the "Master" of Christ, and again this is so that we might not openly divide the One Christ and Son and Lord into two, and then fall under the charge of blasphemy for making him his own God and Master. As we have already said, the Word of God, hypostatically united to the flesh, is God of all and is Master of all, and he is neither his own slave nor his own master. To hold and say this would be foolishness, or rather blasphemy. He did say that the Father is his God (cf. John 20:17) even though he himself is God by nature and from his essence but we do not overlook the fact that as well as being God he also became man and as such was subject to God according to the law which befits human nature. Yet how could he possibly become the God or Master of himself? It is, therefore, as man and insofar as pertains to what is fitting to the limitations of the self-emptying, that he says that he is subject to God alongside us. This is how he also became subject to the law (Gal. 4:4) even though, since he is God, he himself pronounced the law and is the lawgiver.

6. We refuse to say of Christ: "I venerate the one assumed for the sake of the one who assumes; I worship the one that can be seen for the sake of the one that can not." It is a frightful thing to go on to say: "The one assumed shares the name of God with the one who assumes." Whoever says such things again makes a division into two Christs, and posits a man distinctly separate, and a God likewise. Such a person is unquestionably denying the very union which determines why we do not give associate-worship to someone alongside someone different, and why we do not designate someone as God-alongside-with. In contrast, we understand that there is One Christ Jesus, the Only begotten Son, honored together with his flesh in a single worship, and we confess that the same Son and Only Begotten God, born from God the Father, suffered in the flesh for our sake, in accordance with the scripture (cf. 1 Pet. 4:1) even

though he is impassible in his own nature. In the crucified body he impassibly appropriated the suffering of his own flesh and "by the grace of God he tasted death on behalf of all" (Heb. 2:9). He surrendered his own body to death even though by nature he is life and is himself the Resurrection (John 11:25). He trampled upon death with unspeakable power so that he might, in his own flesh, become the "first-born from the dead" (Col. 1:18) and the "first fruits of those who have fallen asleep" (1 Cor. 15:20), and might lead the way for human nature to return to incorruptibility. This was why "by the grace of God he tasted death on behalf of all," as I have just said, despoiling Hell and coming back to life on the third day. And so, even if it is said that the resurrection of the dead came about through a man (1 Cor. 15:21), nonetheless we understand this as meaning the Word of God became man and the dominion of death was destroyed by him. And he will come at the appointed time as Son and Lord in the glory of the Father "to judge the world in righteousness," as it is written (Acts 17:31).

7. We must, however, make this further point. We proclaim the death according to the flesh of the Only Begotten Son of God, and confess the return to life from the dead of Jesus Christ, and his ascension into heaven, and thus we perform in the churches an unbloody worship, and in this way approach mystical blessings and are sanctified, becoming participants in the holy flesh and the precious blood of Christ the Savior of us all. We do not receive this as ordinary flesh, God forbid, or as the flesh of a man sanctified and conjoined to the Word in a unity of dignity, or as the flesh of someone who enjoys a divine indwelling. No, we receive it as truly the lifegiving and very-flesh of the Word himself. As God he is by nature life and since he became one with his own flesh he revealed it as life-giving. So even if he should say to us: "Amen, Amen, I say to you, If you do not eat the flesh of the Son of Man, and drink his blood" (John 6:53), we must not consider this as if it were the flesh of any man like us (for how could the flesh of a man be life-giving from its own nature?) but rather that it has truly become the personal flesh of him who for our sakes became, and was called, the Son of Man.

8. We do not divide out the sayings of our Savior in the Gospels as if to two hypostases or prosopa. The one and only Christ is not twofold even though he is understood as compounded out of two different elements in an indivisible unity, just as a man is understood as consisting of soul and body and yet is not twofold but rather is one from out of both. No, we think correctly and so we must maintain that both the manly as well as the godly sayings were uttered by one subject. When he speaks of himself in a God-befitting way: "Whoever has seen me has seen the Father" (John 14:9), and "I and the Father are one" (John 10:30), we are given to understand his divine and ineffable nature in which he is one with his own Father by identity of essence, the "image and impress and effulgence of his glory" (cf. Heb. 1:3). On the other hand when, not despising the limitations of the manhood, he speaks to the Jews: "Now you seek to destroy me; a man who has told you the truth" (John 8:40), we nonetheless recognize him as God the Word in the equality and likeness of the Father, despite the limitations of his manhood. For if it is necessary to believe that he who is God by nature became flesh, or rather became man ensouled with a rational soul, then what reason could anyone have to be ashamed of these sayings of his, if they were made as befits a man? If he had refused to use words that are proper to a man, who was it that was compelling him to become a man like us in the first place? But since he abased himself for our sake into a willing self-emptying, what reason would he have for refusing these words that were proper to that very self-emptying? This is why all the sayings in the Gospels are to be attributed to one prosopon, and to the one enfleshed hypostasis of the Word, just as according to the scriptures there is One Lord Jesus Christ (1 Cor. 8:6).

9. If he is also called "apostle" and "high priest of our confession" (cf. Heb. 3:1), insofar as he ministers to God the Father, on our behalf, that confession of faith which is rendered for him and through him to God the Father, and indeed to the Holy Spirit as well, again we insist that he is by nature the Only Begotten Son of God; and we do not attribute the title or reality of the priesthood to any man different to him, since it was he who

became the mediator between God and men (1 Tim. 2:5) and a reconciler for peace (cf. Acts 7:26) by offering himself up as a fragrant sacrifice to God the Father (cf. Eph. 5:2). This is why he said: "You did not want sacrifice or offering, but prepared a body for me. You took no pleasure in holocausts and sin offerings. Then I said: look I come. In the scroll of the book it stands written of me, O God, to do your will" (Heb. 10:5-7; Ps. 39:7-9). For he offered his own body as a fragrant sacrifice on our behalf, not indeed for himself, for what offerings or sacrifices did he need for himself since as God he is greater than all sin? Even if "all sinned and fell short of the glory of God" (Rom. 3:23) insofar as we became prone to stray, and the nature of man was infected with sin, nonetheless he is not like this. This is why it is his glory that we fall short of; and so how could any doubt remain that the true lamb has been slain for us and on our behalf? To say that: "He offered himself for his own sake as well as ours" cannot fail to incur the charge of blasphemy, for he was guilty of no transgression whatsoever and committed no sin (cf. 1 Pet. 2:22), so what offerings did he need when there was no sin for which they had to be made?

10. When he says of the Spirit: "And he shall glorify me" (John 16:14), if we want to think correctly we will not say that the One Christ and Son received glory from the Holy Spirit as if he stood in need of glory from another; for his own Spirit is neither greater than him nor above him. But since he used his own Spirit in great miracles for the manifestation of his own Godhead, this is why he says that he is glorified by him, just as any one of us might say about our internal strength, perhaps, or a special skill we have, as being "our glory." Although the Spirit exists in his own hypostasis and is indeed recognized in himself, that is as Spirit and not Son, nonetheless he is not alien to the Son; for he is called the Spirit of Truth (John 16:13) and Christ is the truth (John 14:6), and he is poured forth from him just as he himself is from God the Father. This was how the Spirit worked wonders through the hands of the holy apostles after the ascension of our Lord Jesus Christ into heaven, and so glorified him. He himself was believed to be God by nature because he worked personally through his own Spirit. This is why he said: "He shall take from what is mine and shall announce it to you" (John 16:14). Not for a second do we admit that the Spirit is wise and powerful by participation, for he is all-perfect and wanting in no good thing whatsoever, and since he is the Spirit of the Father's wisdom and power (1 Cor. 1:24), that is the Spirit of the Son, he himself is wisdom and power itself.

11. Since the holy virgin gave birth in the flesh to God hypostatically united to flesh, for this reason we say that she is the "Mother of God." This does not mean that the Word's nature took the beginning of its existence from the flesh, for he "was in the beginning" and "the Word was God, and the Word was with God" (John 1:1) and he is the maker of the ages, coeternal with the Father and maker of all things. As we have said before, it means rather that he hypostatically united the human condition to himself and underwent a fleshly birth from her womb. He had no natural need, or external necessity, of a temporal birth in these last times of this age, but he did this so that he might bless the very beginning of our own coming into being, and that since a woman had given birth to him as united to the flesh, from that point onwards the curse upon our whole race should cease that drives our earthly bodies to death. He did it to annul that sentence: "In sorrow shall you bring forth children" (Gen. 3:16), and also to demonstrate the truth of the prophet's words: "Death swallowed us up in its power, but God wiped every tear from every face" (Isa. 25:8 LXX). This is why we say that in the economy he himself blessed marriage, and being invited went to Cana of Galilee with the holy apostles (John 2:1f.).

12. We have been taught to think these things by the holy apostles and evangelists, and by all the God-inspired scriptures, and from the true confessions of the holy Fathers. It is necessary that your Reverence gives assent to all of these things and accepts them without any evasion. All that your Reverence must anathematize is appended to this letter of ours:

1. If anyone does not confess the Emmanuel to be truly God, and hence the holy virgin to be

Mother of God (for she gave birth in the flesh to the Word of God made flesh), let him be anathema.

2. If anyone does not confess that the Word of God the Father was hypostatically united to the flesh so as to be One Christ with his own flesh, that is the same one at once God and man, let him be anathema.

3. If anyone divides the hypostases of the One Christ after the union, connecting them only by a conjunction in terms of honor or dignity or sovereignty, and not rather by a combination in terms of natural union, let him be anathema.

4. If anyone interprets the sayings in the Gospels and apostolic writings, or the things said about Christ by the saints, or the things he says about himself, as referring to two prosopa or hypostases, attributing some of them to a man conceived of as separate from the Word of God, and attributing others (as divine) exclusively to the Word of God the Father, let him be anathema.

5. If anyone should dare to say that Christ was a God-bearing man and not rather that he is truly God as the one natural Son, since the Word became flesh and "shared in flesh and blood just like us" (Heb. 2:14), let him be anathema.

6. If anyone says that the Word of God the Father is the God or Lord of Christ, and does not rather confess the same one is at once God and man, since according to the scriptures the Word has become flesh, let him be anathema.

7. If anyone says that Jesus as a man was activated by the Word of God and invested with the glory of the Only Begotten, as being someone different to him, let him be anathema.

8. If anyone should dare to say that the assumed man ought to be worshipped along with God the Word and co-glorified and called "God" as if he were one alongside another (for the con-

tinual addition of the phrase "along with" demands this interpretation) and does not rather worship the Emmanuel with a single veneration and render him a single doxology since the Word became flesh, let him be anathema.

9. If anyone says that the One Lord Jesus Christ was glorified by the Spirit, using the power that came through him as if it were foreign to himself, and receiving from him the power to work against unclean spirits and to accomplish divine signs for men, and does not rather say that the Spirit is his very own, through whom he also worked the divine signs, let him be anathema.

10. The divine scripture says that Christ became "the high priest and apostle of our confession" (Heb. 3:1) and "offered himself for our sake as a fragrant sacrifice to God the Father" (Eph. 5:2). So if anyone says that it was not the very Word of God who became our high priest and apostle when he became flesh and man as we are, but it was someone different to him, a separate man born of a woman; or if anyone says that he made the offering also for himself and not rather for us alone (for he who knew no sin had no need of offerings), let him be anathema.

11. If anyone does not confess that the Lord's flesh is life-giving and the very-own flesh of the Word of God the Father, but says that it is the flesh of someone else, different to him, and joined to him in terms of dignity, or indeed only having a divine indwelling, rather than being life-giving, as we have said, because it has become the personal flesh of the Word who has the power to bring all things to life, let him be anathema.

12. If anyone does not confess that the Word of God suffered in the flesh, was crucified in the flesh, and tasted death in the flesh, becoming the first-born from the dead, although as God he is life and life-giving, let him be anathema.

35. Definition of Faith
of the Council of Chalcedon

The decades following the Council of Ephesus witnessed increased hostility between different parties in the christological controversies. Hoping that religious unity would bring political unity to the Roman Empire, Emperor Marcian called the Council of Chalcedon in 451. Though participants were hesitant to draw up another creed, imperial commissioners insisted that the council produce a statement that would resolve the bitter disputes over the nature of Christ. Affirming the full humanity and full divinity of Christ, the Chalcedonian formula attempted to take a middle road between more extreme christological positions.

But, forasmuch as persons undertaking to make void the preaching of the truth have through their individual heresies given rise to empty babblings; some of them daring to corrupt the mystery of the Lord's incarnation for us and refusing [to use] the name Mother of God (θεοτοκος) in reference to the Virgin, while others, bringing in a confusion and mixture, and idly conceiving that the nature of the flesh and of the Godhead is all one, maintaining that the divine Nature of the Only Begotten is, by mixture, capable of suffering; therefore this present holy, great, and ecumenical synod, desiring to exclude every device against the Truth, and teaching that which is unchanged from the beginning, has at the very outset decreed that the faith of the Three Hundred and Eighteen Fathers shall be preserved inviolate. And on account of them that contend against the Holy Ghost, it confirms the doctrine afterwards delivered concerning the substance of the Spirit by the One Hundred and Fifty holy Fathers who assembled in the imperial City; which doctrine they declared unto all men, not as though they were introducing anything that had been lacking in their predecessors, but in order to explain through written documents their faith concerning the Holy Ghost against those who were seeking to destroy his sovereignty. And, on account of those who have taken in hand to corrupt the mystery of the dispensation [i.e., the Incarnation] and who shamelessly pretend that he who was born of the holy Virgin Mary was a mere man, it receives the synodical letters of the Blessed Cyril, Pastor of the Church of Alexandria, addressed to Nestorius and the Easterns, judging them suitable, for the refutation of the frenzied folly of Nestorius, and for the instruction of those who long with holy ardor for a knowledge of the saving symbol. And, for the confirmation of the orthodox doctrines, it has rightly added to these the letter of the President of the great and old Rome, the most blessed and holy Archbishop Leo, which was addressed to Archbishop Flavian of blessed memory, for the removal of the false doctrines of Eutyches, judging them to be agreeable to the confession of the great Peter, and as it were a common pillar against misbelievers. For it opposes those who would rend the mystery of the dispensation into a Duad of Sons; it repels from the sacred assembly those who dare to say that the Godhead of the Only Begotten is capable of suffering; it resists those who imagine a mixture or confusion of the two natures of Christ; it drives away those who fancy his form of a servant is of an heavenly or some substance other than that which was taken of us, and it anathematizes those who foolishly talk of two natures of our Lord before the union, conceiving that after the union there was only one.

SOURCE: *A Select Library of Nicene and Post-Nicene Fathers of the Christian Church*, second series, vol. 14, ed. Philip Schaff and Henry Wace (New York: Charles Scribner's Sons; Oxford and London: Parker & Company, 1900), 263-64.

Following the holy Fathers we teach with one voice that the Son [of God] and our Lord Jesus Christ is to be confessed as one and the same [person], that he is perfect in Godhead and perfect in manhood, very God and very man, of a reasonable soul and [human] body consisting, consubstantial with the Father as touching his Godhead, and consubstantial with us as touching his manhood; made in all things like unto us, sin only excepted; begotten of his Father before the worlds according to his Godhead; but in these last days for us men and for our salvation born [into the world] of the Virgin Mary, the Mother of God according to his manhood. This one and the same Jesus Christ, the only-begotten Son [of God] must be confessed to be in two natures, unconfusedly, immutably, indivisibly, inseparably [united], and that without the distinction of natures being taken away by such union, but rather the peculiar property of each nature being preserved and being united in one Person and subsistence, not separated or divided into two persons, but one and the same Son and only-begotten, God the Word, our Lord Jesus Christ, as the Prophets of old time have spoken concerning him, and as the Lord Jesus Christ hath taught us, and as the Creed of the Fathers hath delivered to us.

These things, therefore, having been expressed by us with the greatest accuracy and attention, the holy Ecumenical Synod defines that no one shall be suffered to bring forward a different faith (ἑτέραν πίστιν), nor to write, nor to put together, nor to excogitate, nor to teach it to others. But such as dare either to put together another faith, or to bring forward or to teach or to deliver a different Creed (ἕτερον σύμβολον) to such as wish to be converted to the knowledge of the truth from the Gentiles, or Jews or any heresy whatever, if they be Bishops or clerics let them be deposed, the Bishops from the Episcopate, and the clerics from the clergy; but if they be monks or laics: let them be anathematized.

36. Zacharias the Scholastic, *Life of Severus of Antioch*

Perhaps the most famous of the non-Chalcedonian theologians (known in older scholarship as "monophysites," a term now generally avoided) was Severus of Antioch (ca. 465-538). Severus studied rhetoric in Alexandria, then law in Beirut, where he was involved in an avid group of Christian students who met together to study the Church Fathers and to pray. He became a monk in Palestine, was ordained bishop of Antioch in 512, but was deposed upon the accession of the Chalcedonian emperor, Justin I, in 518. The following excerpts from his Life *(itself a Syriac translation of a Greek original, now lost) include an episode from his student days and a description of ongoing dissension among Eastern Christians in the wake of Chalcedon.*

Let no one suppose that this history has gone outside its purpose.[1] My intention is to show that the great Severus, so far from the accusation made against him, was always among these who showed such zeal against the pagans, and was praising what had been done by them. Far from ever being subject to the blame and fault of pagan error, he was a Christian in his faith, although then only a cate-

SOURCE: Tr. James F. Coakley. Syriac text: *Patrologia Orientalis* 2:44-46, 58-63, 100-115.
1. The previous section related how Christian zealots destroyed ancient "idols" from a village outside Alexandria.

chumen; but being engaged in secular study he did not have the opportunity to show himself as one in the way that in Phoenicia he appeared to everyone.

Even in Alexandria he rose above any suspicion of paganism, as the following indicates. Some time after the destruction of the idols the Christ-loving Menas—he who had prophesied that Severus would become patriarch[2]—departed this human life and went on straightaway to Him whom he had loved, taking with him many virtues: virginity of soul and body, love for others, exalted love, and great calmness and humility. At that time I myself was seized with a bodily illness, and the pagans supposed that we were being requited for what we did to their gods out of zeal for religion, and the flames by which we had burned them. They were proclaiming that I too would certainly die at the same time. Subsequently by the grace of our Lord Jesus Christ I was wonderfully delivered from the illness, and in the eulogy that I subsequently gave at the grave of the illustrious Menas I mentioned the overthrow of the idols of the pagans, and I told the story of their burning in front of all the people of the city. It was fitting that I recounted everything that had happened, there next to the grave of him who had been, before the act of zeal that was shown against them, so much admired by the pagans on account of his sweetness and love of others. And the great Severus took delight and rejoiced in relations like these, and he gloried in the things I said against the gods of the pagans, as if they had come from him himself, so that he applauded more than anyone. The pagans, however, who had been invited and came, not knowing what would be said, were weeping on their own account. One of them said in anger, "If you wanted to speak against the gods, why did you bring us to the tomb of your friend?"

. . .

It happened that certain people who were studying law in Beirut[3] had acquired notoriety for sorcery. They were George from Thessalonica, which is the first city of Illyricum, and Chrysaorius, from Tralles, a city of Asia, and Asklepi-odotus from Heliopolis, along with an Armenian and others like themselves; and they were abetted by John, known as the Fuller, who was from Thebes in Egypt.

They did not refrain from being involved in such atheistic practices as these.[4] They collected books of sorcery from everywhere, and showed them to people who took delight in disturbances. They were all supposed to be planning something murderous and full of wickedness. According to a report that got about concerning them, they were going to the Hippodrome at night to sacrifice to the demons an Ethiopian slave who belonged to the man from Thebes. By this God-offending act they would acquire a demon to be theirs, as they said, and, as they supposed, it would carry out the things that they wanted. What they wanted was, in general, everything illicit; but in particular, that they should bring by force to the master of that slave a woman with whom he had fallen in love, a woman who was then living in chastity, by the passion of love and the compulsion of the demons.

So they brought this slave on some pretext at an untimely hour of the night to the Hippodrome. But just when the murder was about to be committed, God, who concerns Himself in the affairs of men, took pity on the unhappy slave, and provided that some people should be passing that way. The men, being afraid on account of their assault and this happening that they had not expected, fled, and in this way the Ethiopian was given the opportunity to escape from their murderous hands that had been so ready for his killing.

This man told one of his master's fellow countrymen, a fervent Christian who feared the judgment of God, what had been devised against him. He, being both solicitous for the master of the slave and pitiful toward the slave himself, told us about the assault of these men and their intention of murder. He asked for some kind of Christian help for the soul of his fellow countryman that had been attacked by demons, for he was solicitous for him, he said, as a compatriot. When we

---

2. Another incident related earlier.

3. Lit. "that city." At this point in the text Severus has gone from Alexandria to Beirut to study law.

4. The exact sense of the following paragraph is not clear.

heard these things, we asked him if the other man had books of sorcery—for everyone who studied law in the city knew more or less that he was a sorcerer. He said, "The Ethiopian said so." I and Evagrius with Isidore and Athanasius who were from Alexandria and brothers and fervent in religion, and with our informant, decided to take Constantine and Polycarp who were from Beirut into our counsel to consider what to do. The former had for a long time had the profession of lawyer in that city, and the latter was a soldier in the cohort of the prefect. They were both experienced men of affairs, and were attenders with us of holy churches. Also, the accused man was thought to be a friend of Constantine.

So having told those men the relevant facts, and having considered at length how with God's help we could free the man from the error of demons and from the danger in which he stood, we all of us decided that we should go to his house and speak words of friendship to him. We would tell him that we had come to him as to a brother and that we were anxious about his reputation, and we would ask to examine his books on account of the report that had taken hold concerning him, so that we would be able with God's help to put a stop to the report that was diffused in the whole city concerning him, if indeed we found that in fact he was free of blame.

Since this seemed good to us, we went to his house. He received us for the sake of his fellow countryman and his friend Constantine, and also because all of us appeared pleasant and unassuming. The things that we together had agreed to say, we said to him in all courtesy, so that he would receive them in a brotherly way and not consider the mention of them as an offense. Now because he had hidden his books of sorcery under the seat of his chair, which he had made into a sort of box for them that would be concealed from those who were with him, he said confidently, "Since this is what you want, friends, examine my books just as you like." Having said this, he brought all the books that were in view in his house. But when we had examined these and found nothing of what we sought, the man's slave—the one against whom, as he said, they had plotted the slaying and foul murder—secretly indicated to us his chair,

and motioned as if to say, "If you just remove one board, you will see at once the books that you are seeking." When we did this, he knew that his practice had become clear to all, and he fell on his face and entreated us with tears that we, being Christians and religious in our ways, should not take him to law. We told him that, as God witnessed, we had not come to do him ill but were desirous of the salvation and health of his soul; but it was right that he should burn those books of sorcery with his own hands. The books had various pictures of evil demons in them and barbarous names, vain and wicked oracles, full of arrogance and becoming only to the evil demons. Some of them were ascribed to Zoroaster the Magian, others to Ostanes the sorcerer, others to Manetho.

The man promised to do this, and ordered fire to be brought. He recounted to us how he had fallen in love with a woman and supposed that, when she would have nothing to do with him, he would gain power over her by these books; and so he came to this wicked practice. He added that the practice of sorcerers was so impotent and its promises so vain that the woman for whom he had taken up magic and sorcery now hated him even more. Not only had he done so, but others too, and he counted off their names, saying that they too possessed similar books. When the fire was brought to him, he put the sorcery books into it with his own hands, thanking God that he had made him worthy of his visitation and freed him from the slavery and error of demons. He said he was a Christian, the son of Christian parents, but that he had gone astray at the aforementioned time, and had worshipped idols for the favor of evil demons, and that he would rightly offer the penitence and tears that befitted his sin.

After the burning of these books abhorrent to God, we all of us ate together, first praying and glorifying God and giving thanks for what had happened. For it was already the time of the midday meal. We ate what each of us brought from his own house which had been prepared for his dinner. Among this food was meat, and we took care that the man should partake with us because it is said that those who are under the influence of sorcery and consort with evil demons abstain from meat and consider this food as impure.

. . .

[*Later, Severus has become a monk and priest, and is living in a monastery near Gaza in Palestine.*]

So, while the way of life of these men [i.e., Severus and his associates in the monastery] was such that all the bishops in Egypt and in Palestine were boasting of their virtue, suddenly envy was awakened against all those in Palestine who were in communion with the bishops of Egypt and Alexandria. Nephalius, an Alexandrian monk, having quite forgotten practical virtue, sharpened his tongue to speak and, assuming a kind of sophistry, set himself up against all those who had grown old in the labors of asceticism. He stirred up the people of his land on account of the union that Peter, the metropolitan of Alexandria, had reached with Acacius the archbishop of Constantinople,[5] acting, he said, out of zeal against the synod that had been convened in Chalcedon. And he became the cause of a myriad of uprisings and killings in his land, all because of his enmity toward Peter, who was much loved by the people of the city and especially by those who made up the circus-factions in the city. He went so far as to arouse Zeno, of pious memory, against Peter, saying that Peter had evicted from their monasteries those people who had separated themselves from his communion on account of his union with Acacius; and to stir up thirty thousand monks from Egypt and to prepare to enter Alexandria by force to secure the overthrow of that union. At length Cosmas the Emperor's eunuch was sent to give aid to those who were said to have been evicted.

When Peter departed this life, Nephalius made a pretense of having repented and being sorry for the things he had so many times stirred up against him on account of the union with Acacius. He was careful to appear orthodox in the synodical letter that he sent to Fravitus the heir of Acacius. Later he wished to receive ordination to the priesthood and be entrusted with the management of a church. He got many people at court to press for this in a letter to Athanasius, who had succeeded

to the metropolitanate after Peter. But people of good will who held Peter in remembrance rightly hated him as one who was responsible for a myriad of troubles. And in their grief they said that he was a demoniac who needed to be tied up, and they affirmed that it was an impossibility that he should get what he was trying to lay hands on.

Finally, he had the audacity to turn around and accept the synod that he had previously denounced. He joined the clergy of Jerusalem, returning again to the zeal by which he had been the cause of so many upheavals, going many times to the Emperor and back. Stirring up opposition in every way to the union of the churches, he destroyed the peace and order of his land. Later, by way of a proof of his conversion, he planned an attack against the heirs of the great Peter and those of their persuasion, and against all those whom he had formerly admired. When he came to the region along the coast around the city of Gaza where their monasteries were, even though he knew that the God-loving Severus was invincible in his teaching of religion, and resolute against all heresies, in particular those of the enemies of God Apollinaris and Nestorius and Eutyches, he planned to engage him in battle. But because he could not withstand his invincible tongue or the depth of his arguments or the purity of his doctrines, he made a speech in front of the church against him and against the other monks whom he had defended before the Emperor. In it he divided our one Lord Jesus Christ into two natures. Finally with the aid of those from the churches he evicted them from their monasteries—the aid, that is, of those who had always been quietly disposed to them and had considered the difference between them to be a family quarrel. They had previously called them "orthodox" until the agitation against them took place in the way I have described.

This was the reason why Severus, that lover of divine contemplation [lit., "philosophy"] and of silence, should have come to Constantinople. When our Christ-loving Emperor learned what had happened—the governor of the place had

---

5. Lit. "this imperial city," here and always in this text.

informed him, and he himself already knew the troublesomeness of Nephalius and the virtues of those who had been evicted by him—he stood up against him with righteous anger so that all would know the religious will of the Emperor. As a result, those who had been evicted sent the great Severus as an emissary to address the injustice that had been done to them.

When he arrived, he sought me out and also John the soldier of our Lord Jesus Christ. And when he had learned from us concerning those who were diligent in orthodoxy, he went before the Emperor. Clementinus, who had then the title of consul and patrician, and the Christ-loving Eupraxius of victorious memory who was one of the eunuchs of the imperial chambers, supported him. And he recounted everything exactly that had befallen them, how they, being blameless of any heresies but conforming to the doctrines of the church in everything and being in communion with the bishops of Egypt, had been evicted from their monasteries where they had been living in peace. It aroused the pity of the Emperor and those who were in positions of power, when he informed them, he and the monks who were with him, of what had happened, and he won their admiration for his wise and spiritual conduct. The Emperor at once commanded that on the initiative of the magistrate then in office, those who had been wrongfully deprived of their monasteries should immediately have them given back. He also wrote a doctrinal letter to those who were in charge of these monasteries, in which he confessed our Lord Jesus Christ as "from two natures" and exhorted them to consider the unity of the holy catholic church of God.

The opponents, having thus taken a beating, then claimed that the admirable Severus and those of his party had formerly been in the grip of the heresy of the impious Eutyches. Severus, in order to refute such a slander, wrote a treatise to Apion and Paul, of illustrious memory, who were patricians, which he dedicated to them, against the heresy of Eutyches; and he wrote similar letters to other people against Eutyches and Apollinaris and Nestorius.

He learned that those who favored Nestorius had taken the God-inspired writings of Cyril the patriarch of Alexandria, and had attempted, by means of words construed in a forced sense and severed from their context and reference, to show that he favored the impious Nestorius. When a book like this came into his hands, he refuted the error that was fabricated against the simple folk: by citing the words that preceded and followed the quotations, he exposed the slander that had been insolently made against that godly man. From this he took his cue to name the work *Philalethes* ["Lover of Truth"].

I will here pass tacitly over the writings that he composed for many people who were in the imperial palace, especially Eupraxius, the lover of doctrine and lover of Christ whom I have mentioned, one of the imperial eunuchs, who asked him about some ecclesiastical matters and points of doctrine and contention which seemed utterly perplexing. He likewise refuted the testament of Lampetius that gave birth to the heresy of the Adelphians. And when he came to Nicomedia, he exposed Isidore, that is, John, who had left the monastic life, by which action and by the opinions of Origen he went astray and led many others astray. Likewise, he spoke[6] to those with Rabban Theodore, one of the heirs of the famous Peter the Iberian [the late bishop of Maiuma near Gaza], when they later came to Constantinople on account of the very same cause, that is, the cause of unity for which they were eagerly working. Having begun with this, he spoke then to the holy Sergius, bishop of Philadelphia in the province of Seleucia, and he spoke in the same way with Asterius of Kelendres—for it happened that they too had come there; and to Mama the abbot of the monastery of St. Romanos, and to the venerable Eunomius, abbot of the monastery of the blessed Acacius.

By means of these men he obtained unity with all the Isaurian bishops, while putting to shame by means of the same actions those who were saying of them that they were fleeing from communion with every bishop in the catholic church of God. (For this reason they wrongfully gave them the

---

6. Supplying a verb in this obscure passage.

name of *Akephaloi* [lit., "Headless Ones"]. Likewise, when the monks of the great city of Antioch came on account of the same affair, happily pronouncing [lit., "taking delight in"] fearful anathemas and becoming a hindrance to the unity of the church, he and those from Palestine, considering what was possible, did not extenuate the correctness of their own doctrines, and gave no pretext to the bishops who did not want to gather to themselves the disjoined members of the holy catholic church of God.

He brought the debasement of the *Plerophoria*[7] of Flavian, who was bishop of Antioch, up to the high level of doctrine, and as far as possible he tempered the obstinacy of those who had been divided by it. He persuaded the Emperor to order that there should be unity, on the basis of the *Type*.[8] Flavian of Antioch and Elia of Jerusalem, who would not be persuaded, and some from those who opposed these things, brought confusion on themselves and on the people generally.

What should we say? How he attracted to himself some of the more reasonable bishops, some by what he wrote and some by what he spoke, so that they became his supporters in the contest with the doctrines of Nestorius? Let me pass over that, and say just this: in three years of his living here on account of the cause of unity, he did not relax in any way his monastic way of life or the rule and rigor of ascetics, or live a life without witness (for this was the command of the great Peter the Iberian). He lived all this time, first with the monks who had come with him on account of the cause, and later with holy men who had come up from Palestine in the same way as himself—with Theodore, that is, whom I mentioned, who was called "the Righteous" in Beirut, and those with him. Everyone who knew the man testified that he was the complete image of virtue and virginity. Even councilors and people of seniority studied with him. As I said before, he was one of those who along with the holy John were heirs of Peter, that chosen vessel, and they had bestowed the habit of monasticism on the admirable Severus and anointed him for virtue and elevated him to the high position of divine contemplation.

After these things Severus's disciple Peter, whom I mentioned above,[9] came and reminded him about returning to his monastery. To all of us who saw him and tested him at that time he was seen to be adorned with all the different virtues, and perfect in the ascetic life of monasticism and in the practice of suffering. And he was admired too by those in the company of the great Theodore on account of his chastity and these other virtues.

People were moved by all these things and by the incident with Macedonius [Patriarch of Constantinople]—after a contest and debate with him concerning doctrine that Severus arranged before judges appointed by the emperor—to confer on him election to the patriarchate.[10] Many more agreed with them, and it lacked only a little for the Emperor to be of this mind, if only the envy and jealously of certain people had not put an end to any such idea. Even so, the Emperor urged him repeatedly to live with Timotheus, Macedonius's successor and a man admirable in virtue and rich in his charity to the needy, and to take care of matters pertaining to the unity of the church and with him to lead the affairs of the church. He declined such urgings, recalling his love of quietness and the life of monasticism and contemplation. Now, having urged others to such a life, and having now completed as far as possible the mission on account of which he had come to Constantinople, he returned with them to his own monastery. For himself and for all the inhabitants of Palestine he had obtained quietness, but more than all these other things he honored the life of monasticism.

But after these things, God wished to show this man as patriarch of the great city of Antioch, and He made ready that the mandate should come to him by the choice of all the monks of the East. Many of them had proved his faith and the orthodoxy of his doctine and had seen the other contemplative qualities of his life, when they had gone

---

7. Lit., "assurance," but here the name of a christological declaration. The sense of this paragraph is not completely clear.

8. Another christological formula, probably composed by Severus himself.

9. Not in the present extract.

10. Lit., "chief priesthood," here and always in this text.

up to Constantinople for the same reason as him. Even before these events he was known to the monks of the monastery of Turgis. They were evicted from one of the villages near Apamea by the order of Flavian on account of the zeal that they showed against the doctrines of Nestorius, and reached Palestine—nearly a hundred men, all having taken their cross on their shoulders and come. They were received by Severus and by the heirs of the illustrious Peter: Isaiah, Romanos, Solomon and Acacius. Severus was chosen too by the whole people, who were already marvelling at the excellent reports of him, that he was contending for orthodoxy here and that in the synod that took place later in Phoenicia he appeared to the orthodox bishops, bringing his own pains to bear along with those of the great Theodore, so that they would be victorious in the wider conflict.[11]

Our Christ-loving Emperor approved the choice of patriarch. Flavian having already fallen, by the common decision of the bishops of the East on account of his innovation in matters of faith, the Emperor ordered that for the sake of concord and unity among the bishops and the monks, Severus should leave his monastery and go to Antioch and take up the patriarchate, and obtain the unity for all that Flavian had destroyed by giving offices to Macedonius and others who had Nestorian views and wanted to introduce the teachings of Diodore and Theodore into the church.

Similar to those were certain others in Persia, who were once again stirring up controversies, on which account, those who were holding onto orthodoxy in that place sent repeated missions to our Emperor asking our bishops to state what they wanted to do about them. Most of all they asked about Barsauma [Bishop of Nisibis], who was said to be not only trying to make them embrace heretical doctrines but also perverting the canons of the church. To please the Emperor of the Persians, who had been angered by the large number of Christians abstaining from marriage, he had enacted laws to the contrary: that by compulsion each bishop, clergyman, monk, and in general all Christian men should be joined to a wife in marriage, and live with her. Then Acacius who was patriarch of Constantinople, rebuked him—the snake having shed the doctrines of Nestorius and Theodore, was still hissing[12]—and rejected the canons of Barsauma as entirely out of agreement with the apostolic tradition.

Our Christ-loving Emperor wished to remove all such innovations as these that the Nestorians were making up contrary to the *Henotikon* of Zeno of pious memory. Sometime later Macedonius too began to be thus tempted. At his consecration he promised to accept the *Henotikon* and to be in communion with all the bishops, but later he betrayed the sense of his statement and renounced union with the Egyptians. After a certain time Flavian adhered to this mind in what he did. He filled all the monks of the East with confusion when he persecuted many there who were devoted to divine contemplation, who were radiant with the labor and sweat of asceticism, and who anathematized equally the heresies of Nestorius, Eutyches, and of the enemy of God Apollinaris and all false teaching that stood against the holy catholic church of God. The Emperor did not want to turn aside from the sense of the *Henotikon*, but he wanted to restrain innovations and persecutions like these. He accepted the nomination of the great Severus, as I said, and he reckoned him the right person to receive the patriarchate.

As soon as I knew this, I recalled to Severus, in a letter, the prophecy that had been made about him by the blessed Menas, and I said that the call was a divine one and it would not be right to refuse it. Thus God himself, having brought to pass the promise concerning him, made him accept the patriarchate, while the whole city saw him as a second Peter. So he accepted the patriarchate, and the union of the bishops of the east and clergy and monks and the different peoples, and he at once restored the union with the Egyptians that his predecessor had broken to the destruction of ecclesiastical concord. Only Epiphanius bishop

---

11. An obscure sentence. This synod seems to have been a defeat for Severus's party.

12. An incoherent sentence. It might mean "deprived him of office on account of the doctrines of Nestorius and Theodore, the snake still hissing."

of Tyre, because of his affection for Flavian, who was his brother, would not come near the union at all; and likewise Julian bishop of Bostra. These men subsequently left the cities where they were bishops, though no one compelled them to do so.

But the man of God effected union with all the others, and he would have sent synodical letters to them if he had not been prevented by the envy of demons and the jealousy of men who did not at all rejoice in the peace of the churches. There was also a disturbance that took place in Constantinople by reason of the *Trisagion* hymn used in the East in which the phrase "who was crucified for us, have mercy on us" was added. It seemed good to some that here also it should be said thus. But great dangers resulted, in the disturbances that were then brought about among the simple folk by those who sympathized with Nestorius and reported this hymn to Rome.[13] By these things was the union frustrated.

Severus, at the time when he accepted the patriarchate, spoke his first discourse in the church of God. In it he mocked all heresies, so that everyone marveled at the soundness of his doctrines, and the scriptural proof-texts, and the clarity of the speech—reckoning him a second John.

My friend, I have recounted the life of the great Severus up until the time of his patriarchate. An account of the other part I leave to the city that received him and to all those who were governed by him and enjoyed his apostolic teaching, for they have already made a proof of his way of life and his ascetic labors. I will bring to an end the treatise that I have written, at your urging, for the glory of our great God and savior Jesus Christ, who is the substance, the beginning and the end of all religion and of every true account.

End of the account of the life of the holy Severus before his episcopate, by Zechariah the Scholasticus.

---

13. Emending a word. The text has "prepared this hymn for Rome."

---

37. John of Ephesus,
Life of Susan

Christians who opposed the creedal definition of Chalcedon—primarily in Syria, Egypt, Ethiopia, and Armenia—gradually formed separate non-Chalcedonian churches. Though deemed heretical and even persecuted by the officially Chalcedonian regime in the sixth century, non-Chalcedonian Christians persevered in their faith. In the 560s, John of Ephesus (ca. 507-586), a non-Chalcedonian monk, bishop, and missionary, wrote the Lives of the Eastern Saints, *a collection of inspiring accounts of the careers of fifty-eight of these holy ascetic men and women. The* Life of Susan *was one of them.*

And now the twenty-seventh story, about the blessed virgin of Christ whose name was Susan.

The mighty strength of Christ God is wont to be celebrated and manifested in human weakness so that no flesh may glorify itself before him, the strengthener of the weak. However, it is apt to show its activity not only in men who are powerful in appearance and mighty and forceful, but also in weak, feeble, frail women. Thus it fortifies and gives them courage until they too bear the struggle

---

SOURCE: *Holy Women of the Syrian Orient,* ed. and tr. Sebastian P. Brock and Susan Ashbrook Harvey (Berkeley: University of California Press, 1987), 133-41. Copyright © 1987 by The Regents of the University of California. Used by permission.

with undaunted strength—not simply with flesh and blood, enticing passions, the yearnings of fleshly lusts, and so on; but even against principalities, powers, and those ruling the world of this darkness, and against evil spirits under heaven. Against these are they mightily given courage, and they mock them as a powerful man mocks a band of children or infants preparing to come and fight against him. This was also revealed to us through Paul, wise in all things, when he said, "In Christ Jesus there is neither male nor female, nor slave nor free" (Gal. 3:28). This woman, then, holy and manly in Christ, so astonished me by her appearance, words, and strength in God that she seemed to me not at all out of place in this series of stories of holy men, with whom she strains to enter the same narrow gate as indeed she already has done.

Now this blessed woman (as we discovered when we managed to learn the details from her) belonged to a family from Persian Arzanene. It was a noble family; but from the beginning, since the age of eight, the light of her life shone out in her mind until people marveled at her sensibility, modesty, and devotion. For as if through prophecy her parents had named her "Blessing," she who truly received a heavenly blessing.

This virtuous girl decided that she should go and worship in the holy places, where the salvation of our lives took place, and she implored her parents. But they laughed at her, a mere child, and said, "You haven't even learned to understand the Scriptures, and yet you want to go to Jerusalem!" So she was silent, keeping watch in her heart; and during that time she prayed and said, "Lord if you wish for the salvation of my miserable soul, 'Make straight your way for me,' and present me with an escort. Save my soul from the defilement of this world's filthy mire!" Then the child (as she related to us when I pressed her greatly) placed her soul in the hands of God and ran away.

After crossing three or four miles, she chanced upon a large caravan of women and men traveling toward Jerusalem. And when she had mixed with them, inquiring and learning their purpose, she jumped and danced for joy, praising God, saying, "Blessed am I that the Lord wishes for my salvation, and as I asked He answered me! God forbid that I should return to the world and family and

parents, and so die; I go to Him who leads me and is my father, brother, and kinsman in both worlds." Thus she reached Jerusalem joyously. But when she had worshipped there, her companions wished to return and begged her to go back with them to her own country, saying, "We can't leave you here." So she parted from them, and they did not see her again.

Now she searched around to find a convent where she could live, and learning that there was a large community of women between Ascalon and Gaza, she set her course there. She revealed her desire to the woman at the gate, but because of that convent's strictness, the old woman said to her, "My daughter, you can't live here because you are a child. You couldn't bear the hardship and labor. Besides, your genteel upbringing doesn't make you suited for a convent."

The devout girl, because she was a stranger and in a foreign country, was very upset, and sat at the gate weeping for seven days. The women tried to drive her away, but she would not leave. Then, learning that she was a foreigner, they took her in; and she entered, though they looked down on her because she was so young. But when they learned where she had come from and where she had gone, they said to her as if concerned, "What good is it, child, for you to go out and ruin your soul this way in the mire of sin? For seeing you so young, and what's more alone, who—even if he were unwilling—would Satan not bring against you in order to destroy you prematurely?" Then (as the blessed women with her used to relate to me, and as they themselves had learned at the outset from her), she said, "For our Lord's sake pray for me, since I trust in Him to whom I have committed my soul, that He did not desert me to be destroyed, and He does not desert me now." And so they praised God.

From that time forward she took up great ascetic practices and virtuous feats of labor, abstinence, and devotion, while they hindered her and would slap her because she was a child, so that she would not apply herself to these things more than the other sisters. But she would strive even more and would keep vigil all night, standing in a corner. Not a single word would leave her mouth for anyone all day unless begged for; nor, from her arrival at the convent, did any of her companions ever see her face uncovered or all of her eye exposed; and no laughter came from her mouth.

Now when they saw the blessed girl's way of life—that however much they might strive to hinder her because she was a child, she would simply spend an extra year or two in this burdensome practice—those who had treated her disdainfully because of her youth saw her as one who was excellent. Then she changed the name that was hers before entering the convent, lest someone from her family come making inquiries, and find her; and she called herself Susan.

After she had been laboring ten years in these practices, persecution fell upon their convent, forcing them either to submit to Chalcedonian faith or to leave. Since theirs was a great and well-known community of women, the majority of them were seized and these then submitted to their persecutors; but some scattered here and there. Thus two choices were facing the blessed woman: either to leave the convent, or to risk falling into evil faith; so she decided to go out, and entering the desert beyond Alexandria, live there. Immediately she left. But there was great division even among those sisters who had surrendered themselves, and some women were saying, "Since Susan has gone we won't stay." Then five of the more prominent women from those who had not surrendered joined themselves to her, although she had intended to go alone, saying, "There is no way that we will be parted from you."

So Susan revealed her intentions to them, since they compelled her, and said, "Do not come with me. For to be brief, if the Lord profits me as is His wont, I am going to the desert." They also declared their decision: "We, too, will come with you to the desert." Then, as they would not be dissuaded, they boarded a ship together and crossed over to Alexandria.

There the blessed woman heard rumor of a place in the desert outside the monastery of Mar Menas, and she directed her course there—about two miles from a village called Mendis. This place eventually belonged to the blessed Syrians, but its beginning lay with Susan's arrival. Now there was a tower there that had been built as a watchtower against barbarians; and entering it enthusiasti-

cally, she and the five others dwelt there. Then one of them went and brought them work from the village. Thus they labored with their hands for their needs, and they sustained themselves. And God took care of them, seeing their zeal and trust in him.

Away from the tower was a cave underground, where once a holy man had lived. Susan used to leave human habitation to go out wandering and praying in the desert; on one occasion as she was going along she came across that cave and immediately jumped in. None of her companions or anyone else was aware of it, nor had she taken food or anything with her. Then, just as it is written about Ishmael the son of Abraham, "he sat in the desert of Paran and was instructed in the bow" (Gen. 21:20, 21), so also is it fitting to say about her that she was sitting in a desert cave, being instructed in struggle and manliness against hideous demons that especially show the fervor of their wickedness in the desert.

But when a day or two had passed without her coming, her companions sat day and night in bitter distress and tears, saying, "She in whose trust we came here has left us and gone." After about ten days, some people from the village learned of it and went to the blessed women to find out what had happened. When they saw their grief and weeping, they wondered whether she might have gone to that cave in the desert. Since they knew the place, they went out, and reaching the cave, they peered down and saw the blessed woman thrown on her face, groaning. They spoke to her, but she mistook them for the demons who were showing her fearful and hideous shapes there, and so did not stop the crying out of her prayer. Seeing that she would not answer them, they left and went to report to her companions.

Then all of them hastened to the cave and found the blessed woman in the same state, weeping and praying. With difficulty, and only after they had spoken many things to her, at last she believed who they were; for on the previous day demons had come to her in their guise, so as to drive her out from there. Tearfully the women begged her, "Don't you know that we came out to the desert trusting in you after our Lord? And now why do you seek to destroy all our souls, and that you alone should be delivered? Don't you know that without you we can't exist?" But that mighty woman, weeping with her head bent down, said to them, "My sisters, leave me alone. I am with you for all time; but because the Lord prepared this place for me, so that I might easily live in quietude here, go and stay in peace. And on Sundays let one of you come and see if I am alive or dead." Then the women stood over her to lift her up, trying to get her to go with them; but they could not do it.

Finally they exacted a promise from her, lest she also depart from there without letting them know; and she promised them. They begged her to let them make a small dish of lentils and bring it to her, since she had tasted nothing in ten days; but she did not even want to hear it, saying, "You want to take care of my food when I am lying flat on my face, and make me eat the sweat of your faces; God forbid! For the sustenance of my body it is enough if you bring me a pitcher of water on Sundays, and a small hunk of dried bread for each day."

This they did for three years. But after the report of the blessed women and where they lived was heard abroad, many people came to them from Alexandria and the villages of Libya. Now there was a certain great old man who had about ten disciples with him, and they had been neighbors of the women's convent in Palestine. He and his disciples had also been persecuted greatly and driven from place to place, but then had learned of the blessed women and where they were, and about the quietude and sweetness of that desert. So he made straight for that place, arriving there with his disciples—one of whom was the brother of the woman who had been made superior of the blessed women. He, too, was admirable in his way of life, and was named Samuel. The old man was named Maro and by birth was from Amida, while his disciple Samuel, with his sister, was from the environs of Edessa.

When these men came, the blessed women were comforted by them; and the men, too, were glad and gave thanks to the Lord that they had been refreshed with the quiet of the desert. Then they began to found a cell in that desert, and others, as well, were brought together there—some of whom we wrote about in an earlier chapter. So that place was settled, with the blessed women among them. But they determined to prepare a separate place for the women, so as not to give room for abuse by outsiders, and also because it was hard for them to speak without offending Susan. Indeed she was concerned over that very thought, "For God has provided his servants with this place, but it is not possible for our female sex to live among men—since the attack of the evil one against holy men is mostly made through women, even when they are far away, how much more so when they are near?—even if we should happen to continue warily pursuing spiritual things. Now then, let us depart for the desert beyond this."

Because those blessed men were ashamed by the sobriety of the holy woman, she herself said these things to them. But when they heard, they praised God and took upon themselves to build and make ready for the women a place at the boundary of that village, while she prepared again to penetrate further into the desert. Then they rose up, resisting her, and said, "For you, mother, a city would be a desert if you dwelt in it. But look at these souls that depend on you." Thus she was convinced by them. And they built for the women an enclosed convent with a tower inside it, and they dwelt in it.

Now the blessed woman gained valiance against demons through the strength that comes from grace, as night and day they arrayed themselves in successive ranks for battle against her in the form of men, and attacked her with every kind of weapon. But she mocked them, as a mighty man would despise sickly men who were threatening him. Report of her strength was heard everywhere; and after she had been in that desert for fifteen years, the news of her perfection incited us, as well, to desire the sight of her and of the holy men who were also there. Still, when we were deemed worthy of seeing her whom I can hardly call a woman, I was astonished at the words of suffering and wisdom of God that issued from her mouth—and I was with those holy men twenty days or more, going and coming in order to hear her gentle conversation.

Nor could I see her head held erect or any sign of her face except the tip of her nose, so sorrowful and weepy was she. She undertook to speak to us about this world, held fast by erring: how men see their companions rotting and corrupted and putrefying in their graves, while creepy things crawl and mingle in their putrefaction—yet those who see these things go astray through the empty vanities of this deceptive world. She spoke, too, of how it does not occur to the hearts of men that the dreadful hour of this world's destruction hastily approaches, when they will stand before the dreadful judgment seat of God. For, she said, "It is ridiculous that we hear about the chasm of fire, the flaming depths, the darkness, the rest of the tortures, but we do not take it to heart and beg for mercy while we have the opportunity, so that we might be delivered from these things." Again, the divine woman related to us many things more frightening than these; and we were left in great wonder at her words.

She also received the gift of healing, so that she could cure every sickness or disease she stretched her hand against. Now while we were there, a certain blessed man, great and God-loving, dwelt in a place in the desert not far away. Against him the demons would openly prepare for combat, and he would see their battle with the blessed woman, and she his. But because she was stronger than he, she both conquered the demons and had no fear at all of them. She became firm like adamant and unmoveable—so much so that the demons would cry out at her, "This is a woman, but she is stone, and instead of flesh she is iron!" Such were the things the demons said to her.

To such an extent was she thus steadfast that when visions prevailed against the blessed man, he would go to her as if to a mighty woman. While I was there, he came, pale, smitten in his mind, and disturbed. When she saw him, she understood, and asked, "Why are you worn out, father?" He told her, "The demons have waxed strong and taken away my senses. All week we have been engaged in an ever increasing battle, then last night and today they showed me fearful, terrible forms. My heart was shaken, my wits were seized, and I was confounded. I fled from fright. I am terrified to enter my cell because of the apparitions I saw. I'm not going back to that place anymore."

But when she heard, she shook her head, saying, "Come and have a look at some people who are called men—and not only men but servants of Christ. Do you deserve to be called servants of Christ? Do you thus think Christ your Lord to be feeble? Are you showing your own weakness that the mighty and invincible power of Him who has cast down and overthrown and annihilated all the power of Satan is actually weaker than that of demons? Does Christ thus now appear as one who flees and is conquered by devils? Do they turn out to be powerful and victorious over the power of God? How can you be a disciple of Him who said, 'You will trample all the power of the enemy'? (Luke 10:19). Forgive me, father, you have grieved me because you have gladdened the hearts of demons. Last night I only heard the shapes and voices resembling the battles of demons, and I wondered. But I am aware that the strength of the Lord surrounds my weakness like a wall of bronze, and there is no other power that can rise against it."

While the weak woman courageously said these things in front of us, we looked at each other, although she did not look at either of us. Then she spoke confidently to the blessed man, "In the name of the Lord Jesus Christ, stand up; go back to your cell. As He is accustomed, He will make humble all the power of the evil one." The blessed man was abashed at what the woman said, and quaking in his shame he agreed to go.

Then we rose from beside her and spoke amongst ourselves, marveling at her spiritual strength and courage, and I said to him, "Why can one not see the face of this woman?" He told me, "One day while we were speaking, I said to her, 'Why do you conceal your face from us?' And she swore an oath to me, saying, 'He who placed His yoke upon me by His grace knows, our brother, that ever since I accepted His yoke twenty-five years ago I have not seen a man's face. And do you want me to look at yours now?' So I said to her, 'For our Lord's sake, tell me the truth. Are you afraid that you will suffer harm at the sight of a man, or that he would at the sight of you?' She answered, 'Because of both these things.'"

So marveling at the practice of the holy woman and the constancy of Susan, Christ's virgin, we departed from there praising God.

The story of the blessed virgin of Christ whose name was Susan is ended.

38. The Evangelization of Nubia: John of Ephesus, *Ecclesiastical History*

Archaeologists have traced Africa's ancient black culture of Nubia back to 3100 B.C.E. Located in modern southern Egypt and northern Sudan, Nubia comprised three kingdoms (Nobatia, Makouria, and Alwa) that converted to Christianity in the sixth century. The following account of the non-Chalcedonian bishop, John of Ephesus (ca. 507-586; see also Text 37), describes the rivalry between the Chalcedonian emperor, Justinian, and his non-Chalcedonian wife, Theodora, who both sent missionaries to evangelize the Nobatai. Though neighboring Egypt fell to the Arabs in the seventh century, strong Christian kingdoms in Nubia resisted conquest and conversion to Islam until the fourteenth century.

Among the clergy in attendance upon pope Theodosius was a presbyter named Julian, an old man of great worth, who conceived an earnest spiritual desire to christianize the wandering people who dwell on the eastern borders of the Thebais [a region of upper Egypt], beyond Egypt, and who are not only not subject to the authority of the Roman empire, but even receive a subsidy on condition that they do not enter nor pillage Egypt. The blessed Julian, therefore, being full of anxiety for this people, went and spoke about them to the late queen Theodora, in the hope of awakening in her a similar desire for their conversion; and as the queen was fervent in zeal for God, she received the proposal with joy, and promised to do everything in her power for the conversion of these tribes from the errors of idolatry. In her joy, therefore, she informed the victorious king Justinian of the purposed undertaking, and promised and anxiously desired to send the blessed Julian thither. But when the king heard that the person she intended to send was opposed to the council of Chalcedon, he was not pleased, and determined to write to the bishops of his own side in the Thebais, with orders for them to proceed thither and instruct them, and plant among them the name of the synod. And as he entered upon the matter with great zeal, he sent thither, without a moment's delay, ambassadors with gold and baptismal robes, and gifts of honor for the king of that people, and letters for the duke of the Thebais, enjoining him to take every care of the embassy, and escort them to the territories of the Nobadæ [i.e., the people of Nobatia, one of the Nubian kingdoms]. When, however, the queen learnt these things, she quickly, with much cunning, wrote letters to the duke of the Thebais, and sent a mandatory of her court to carry them to him; and which were as follows: "Inasmuch as both his majesty and myself have purposed to send an embassy to the people of the Nobadæ, and I am now despatching a blessed man named Julian; and further my will is, that my ambassador should arrive at the aforesaid people before his majesty's; be warned, that if you permit his ambassador to arrive there before mine, and do not hinder him by various pretexts until mine shall have reached you, and have passed through your province, and arrived at his destination, your life shall answer for it; for I will immediately send and take off your head." Soon after the receipt of this letter the king's ambassador also came, and the duke said to him, "You must wait a little, while we look out and procure beasts of burden, and men who know the deserts; and then you will be able to proceed." And thus he delayed him until the arrival of the merciful queen's embassy, who found horses and guides in waiting, and the same day, without loss

SOURCE: *The Third Part of the Ecclesiastical History of John of Ephesus*, tr. R. Payne Smith (Oxford: Oxford University Press, 1860), 251-57, 315-16, 319-24.

of time, under a show of doing it by violence, they laid hands upon them, and were the first to proceed. As for the duke, he made his excuses to the king's ambassador, saying, "Lo! when I had made my preparations, and was desirous of sending you onward, ambassadors from the queen arrived, and fell upon me with violence, and took away the beasts of burden I had got ready, and have passed onward. And I am too well acquainted with the fear in which the queen is held, to venture to oppose them. But abide still with me, until I can make fresh preparations for you, and then you also shall go in peace." And when he heard these things, he rent his garments, and threatened him terribly, and reviled him; and after some time he also was able to proceed, and followed the other's track, without being aware of the fraud which had been practiced upon him.

The blessed Julian, meanwhile, and the ambassadors who accompanied him, had arrived at the confines of the Nobadæ, whence they sent to the king and his princes, informing him of their coming: upon which an armed escort set out, who received them joyfully, and brought them into their land unto the king. And he too received them with pleasure, and her majesty's letter was presented, and read to him, and the purport of it explained. They accepted also the magnificent honors sent them, and the numerous baptismal robes, and everything else richly provided for their use. And immediately with joy they yielded themselves up, and utterly abjured the error of their forefathers and confessed the God of the Christians, saying "that He is the one true God, and there is no other beside Him." And after Julian had given them much instruction, and taught them, he further told them about the council of Chalcedon, saying, that "inasmuch as certain disputes have sprung up among Christians touching the faith; and the blessed Theodosius being required to receive the council, and having refused, was ejected by the king from his throne, whereas the queen received him and rejoiced in him, because he stood firm in the right faith, and left his throne for its sake: on this account her majesty has sent us to you, that you also may walk in the ways of pope Theodosius, and stand in his faith, and imitate his constancy. And moreover the

king has sent unto you ambassadors, who already are on their way in our footsteps." They then instructed them how they should receive them, and what answer they should give: and when everything was fully settled, the king's ambassador also arrived. And when he had obtained an audience, he also gave the king the letters and presents, and began to inform and tell him, according to his instructions, as follows: "The king of the Romans has sent us to you, that in case of your becoming Christians, you may cleave to the church and those who govern it, and not be led astray after those who have been expelled from it." And when the king of the Nobadæ and his princes heard these things, they answered them, saying, "The honorable present which the king of the Romans has sent us we accept, and will also ourselves send him a present. But his faith we will not accept: for if we consent to become Christians, we shall walk after the example of pope Theodosius, who, because he was not willing to accept the wicked faith of the king, was driven away by him and expelled from his church. If, therefore, we abandon our heathenism and errors, we cannot consent to fall into the wicked faith professed by the king." In this manner then they sent the king's messengers away, with a written answer to the same effect. As for the blessed Julian, he remained with them for two years, though suffering greatly from the extreme heat. For he used to say that from nine o'clock until four in the afternoon he was obliged to take refuge in caverns, full of water, where he sat undressed and girt with a linen garment, such as the people of the country wear. And if he left the water his skin, he said, was blistered by the heat. Nevertheless, he endured it patiently, and taught them, and baptized both the king and his nobles, and many of the people also. He had with him also a bishop from the Thebais, an old man, named Theodore, and after giving them instruction and setting things in order, he delivered them over to his charge, and himself departed, and arrived in safety at Constantinople, where he was most honorably received by the queen. And to her he related many wonderful particulars concerning that numerous people, but they are too long for us to write, nor can we spare space for more than we have already inserted.

The chief charge of the new converts was vested in Theodosius, as being patriarch of Alexandria; nor were they forgotten by him: for on the very day of his departure from this world he had them in his memory, and especially because the blessed Julian their teacher had died but a very short time before, and also because her late majesty, the queen Theodora, had given orders that the excellent Longinus should be made bishop there, as being an earnest man admirably adapted to convert and establish them in the doctrines of Christianity. Immediately therefore after the pope's decease, Longinus was consecrated bishop of those parts, and made ready to proceed thither. But scarcely had he embarked his goods on board ship, when men were found, such as those of whom it is written, that "their teeth are spears and arrows, and their tongue a sharp sword" (Ps. 57:4), who went and told the king that "Longinus, the enemy of our palace, has been made bishop, and has embarked his goods on board ship, ready to start. And should he go, for he is a passionate man, and arrive among that people in safety, he will immediately stir them up to make war upon and pillage the territory of the Romans. Give orders therefore for his immediate arrest." When the king heard these things, he was stirred up to anger, and gave orders for his arrest, and had his baggage removed from the vessel. Thus then he was not permitted to depart, and three years passed by, during which he was waiting for an opportunity; and finally, as he was aware that he was watched, and would not be permitted to leave, he disguised himself, and put a wig on his head—for he was very bald—and taking with him two servants, he fled, and God delivered him, and caused him to arrive in safety at that land. And there he was magnificently received, and great joy testified at his coming: and immediately he began to instruct them afresh, and enlighten them, and teach them. And next he built them a church, and ordained clergy, and taught them the order of divine service, and all the ordinances of Christianity.

. . .

For far more pleasing is the subject to which we alluded above, namely, the conversion of the peo-ple whom the Greeks call Alodæi [i.e., the people of Alodia (or Alwa), another of the Nubian kingdoms] . . . to the Christian faith. For to repeat some part of our previous narrative, it was by the zeal of the late queen Theodora that the blessed Julian was originally sent to the powerful people called Nobadæ, and taught both the king and his princes, and most of the tribes in his dominions, for a period of two years. And on his departure thence, he intrusted all that people to a certain Theodore, a very old man, and bishop of the city called Philæ, situated in the further part of the Thebais, on their borders, who went to them, and visited them, and gave them counsel, and returned to his own city; and so they continued for a period of eighteen years, more or less. And then it was that Longinus escaped in disguise, and went to them, and taught and instructed them afresh, and baptized such of them as had never partaken of this rite, and continued with them six years and ambassadors moreover were sent by them to the king, and arrived at the capital, and we were repeatedly in their company, and heard them praising and extolling Longinus in the highest terms. And when the people of the Alodæi heard of the conversion of the Nobadæ, their king sent to the king of the Nobadæ, requesting him to permit the bishop who had taught and baptized them, to come and instruct them in like manner.

. . .

Meanwhile the king of the Alodæi had, as we have mentioned, sent a second embassy to the king of the Nobadæ, requesting that the bishop Longinus might be sent to teach and baptize both him and his people: and it was plainly visible that the conversion of that kingdom was the good purpose of the grace of God. The Lord therefore stirred up the spirit of Longinus to go to them; and though the Nubians were grieved at being separated from him, they nevertheless sent with him nobles and princes and men well acquainted with the desert. Upon the journey, however, he became ill, as also did his companions: and so great were their privations, and the intensity of the heat, that, as he mentions in a letter, he lost in the desert no less than seventeen camels out of the baggage animals which accompanied him. Nor was this their only or chief danger; for between the Nobadæ and the Alodæi is a country inhabited by another people, called the Makoritæ; and when their king heard that Longinus had started on his journey, Satan in his envy stirred him up to set watchers in all the passes of his kingdom on all the roads, both in the mountains and in the plains, as far as the sea of weeds, in hopes of arresting Longinus, and so hindering the salvation of the powerful people of the Alodæi. But God preserved him, and blinded the eyes of those who wanted to seize him; and he passed through them, and went on his way, and they saw him not. And on his arrival at the borders of the kingdom to which he was travelling, the king, as he tells us in his letters, on hearing of it, sent one of his nobles to meet him, named Aitekia, who received him honorably, and made him pass over into their land with great pomp: and on approaching nearer, the king went out in person to meet him, and received him with great joy. And immediately upon his arrival, he spake unto the king and to all his nobles the word of God, and they opened their understandings, and listened with joy to what he said; and after a few days' instruction, both the king himself was baptized and all his nobles; and subsequently, in process of time, his people also. And so the king, being glad and joyful, wrote a letter of thanks to the king of the Nobadæ, as follows:

Letter of the King of Alodia to the King of the Nubians.

"Your love is remembered by us, my lord, our brother Orfiulo, because you have now shown yourself my true kinsman, and that not only in the body, but also in the spirit, in having sent me hither our common spiritual father, who has shown me the way of truth, and of the true light of Christ our God, and has baptized me, and my nobles, and all my family. And in everything the work of Christ is multiplied, and I have hope in the holy God, and am desirous moreover of doing your pleasure, and driving your enemies from your land. For he is not your enemy alone, but also mine: for your land is my land, and your people my people. Let not your courage therefore fail, but be manful and take courage: for it is impossible for me to be careless of you and your land,

especially now that I have become a Christian, by the help of my father, the holy father Longinus. As we have need, however, of church furniture, get some ready for us: for I feel certain that you will send me these things with carefulness, and I will make you an answer: but on the day on which I was keeping festival, I did not wish to write, lest my letters should fail. Be not anxious then, but encourage yourself, and play the man: for Christ is with us." Such then was the letter which this new confessor, the king of the Alodæi, wrote to the king of the Nobadæ. And next we will also give a short extract from a letter of the blessed Longinus, which he wrote from that land, and sent to the king of the Nobadæ, with a request that he would forward it to Alexandria: which also he did; and it is as follows:

" . . . Not then to trouble you with our annoyances, and make the letter tedious, I have omitted all such matters, and will tell you, secondly, that which will rejoice all who are real Christians, and strict members of the orthodox communion: and I do rejoice with you all, and will rejoice, and you in like manner must rejoice with me. And, moreover, rejoice with me in this, that He Who wills that everyone should be saved, and does not desire the death of a sinner, such as I am, but forgets all my sins, has remembered His mercy and grace towards me, and opened for me the door of His mercy, and delivered me from those who were hunting after my life, and led me safely through them, and blinded their eyes so that they did not see me. Nor were we unvisited by His loving kindness in chastening us, in that all of us, with my unworthy self, fell ill, from the greatest even to the least; and I was the first to suffer: for it was but right that I should be chastened first, because I am guilty of many sins, and many are the offenses into which I have fallen. And not only did we become ill ourselves, and despaired of our safety, but also the animals that were with us died, not being able to bear the heat, and the thirst in the mountains, and the unwholesomeness of the water, so that we lost no less than seventeen camels. And when the king of the Alodæi heard that I had determined to come to him, he sent one of his princes, named Itika, who led me with great pomp into their land. And on our arrival at the river's bank, we went on board a vessel; and the king hearing of our coming rejoiced, and came out in person to meet us, and received us with great joy. And by the grace of God we taught him, and have baptized him and his nobles and all his family; and the work of God grows daily. But inasmuch as there are certain Abyssinians, who have fallen into the malady of the fancy of [the theologian] Julian [of Halicarnassus] and say, that Christ suffered in a body not capable of pain, or of death, we have told them what is the correct belief, and have required them to anathematize this heresy in writing, and have received these persons upon their presenting their recantation." . . . And again, after some things which we have omitted, he thus proceeds; ". . . And let all your rulers and people, on learning these things, offer up with spiritual joy their praises and thanksgivings to our merciful God, for all these His innumerable gifts; and let the fathers take care that there be sent down hither bishops, who will be able to labor and minister in this divine work, which is pleasing both to God and humans, and in the reality of which they may feel confident, and that it is going on prosperously. For there are a thousand thousand here who are hastening to salvation, to the glory of Him Who is the Savior of us all, even Christ. And believe what I say, that a short time ago a sort of purpose suggested by the weakness of human nature came to me, not to write to any one: but when I considered the danger which those incur who are negligent in their use of spiritual gifts, I have addressed this short letter to your spiritual love. For I desire neither silver, nor gold, nor dresses, as God is my witness, Who tries the hearts of people, and Who knows all I do, and that I have not bread for my daily use, and am even glad to see with my eyes food of vegetables only. And thus far then let it suffice me to have told you." This then was written by the holy Longinus himself, being extracts from the letter he sent from the land of the Alodæi to the king of the Nobadæ, with a request that he would forward it to Alexandria, which he accordingly did, to Theodore, whom Longinus had himself appointed as patriarch: and at the same time the king himself sent him a letter to inform him of Longinus' arrival among them, and his subsequent departure, and the trials and difficulties which stood in his way, and the gracious aid which God in His goodness gave him.

39. Christians in India:
Cosmas Indicopleustes, *Christian Topography*

Cosmas Indicopleustes, "The Indian Navigator," was a sixth-century native of Alexandria who traveled extensively in his early life as a seafaring merchant. After retiring from commercial enterprises, Cosmas became a monk and devoted himself to writing treatises on geography, cosmography, and scriptural exegesis. The only text to survive is his Christian Topography, *in which, in his description of the island of Sielediba—the present-day Sri Lanka—he provides the earliest surviving testimony to the presence of Christians in the area of the Indian subcontinent.*

SOURCE: *The Christian Topography of Cosmas, an Egyptian Monk*, tr. J. W. McCrindle (London: Hakluyt Society, 1897), 363-68.

Concerning the Island of Taprobanê

This is a large oceanic island lying in the Indian sea. By the Indians it is called Sielediba, but by the Greeks Taprobanê, and therein is found the hyacinth stone. It lies on the other side of the pepper country. Around it are numerous small islands all having fresh water and cocoanut trees. They nearly all have deep water close up to their shores. The great island, as the natives report, has a length of three hundred *gaudia*, that is, of nine hundred miles, and it is of the like extent in breadth. There are two kings in the island, and they are at feud the one with the other. The one has the hyacinth country, and the other the rest of the country where the harbor is, and the centre of trade. It is a great mart for the people in those parts. The island has also a church of Persian Christians who have settled there, and a Presbyter who is appointed from Persia, and a Deacon and a complete ecclesiastical ritual. But the natives and their kings are heathens. In this island they have many temples, and on one, which stands on an eminence, there is a hyacinth as large as a great pine-cone, fiery red, and when seen flashing from a distance, especially if the sun's rays are playing round it, a matchless sight. The island being, as it is, in a central position, is much frequented by ships from all parts of India and from Persia and Ethiopia, and it likewise sends out many of its own. And from the remotest countries, I mean Tzinista and other trading places, it receives silk, aloes, cloves, sandalwood and other products and these again are passed on to marts on this side, such as Male, where pepper grows, and to Calliana which exports copper and sesame-logs, and cloth for making dresses, for it also is a great place of business. And to Sindu also where musk and castor is procured and androstachys, and to Persia and the Homerite country, and to Adulê. And the island receives imports from all these marts which we have mentioned and passes them on to the remoter ports, while, at the same time, exporting its own produce in both directions. Sindu is on the frontier of India, for the river Indus, that is, the Phison, which discharges into the Persian Gulf, forms the boundary between Persia and India. The most notable places of trade in India are these: Sindu, Orrhotha, Calliana, Sibor, and then the five marts of Male which export pepper: Parti, Mangarouth, Salopatana, Nalopatana, Poudopatana. Then out in the ocean, at the distance of about five days and nights from the continent lies Sielediba, that is Taprobanê. And then again on the continent is Marallo, a mart exporting chank shells, then Caber which exports alabandenum, and then farther away is the clove country, then Tzinista which produces the silk. Beyond this there is no other country, for the ocean surrounds it on the east. This same Sielediba then, placed as one may say, in the centre of the Indies and possessing the hyacinth receives imports from all the seats of commerce and in turn exports to them, and is thus itself a great seat of commerce.

The Coming of Age of Latin Christianity

40. Augustine of Hippo,
City of God

Bishop of the North African town of Hippo Regius from 395 until his death, Augustine (354-430) remains the most influential theologian of the West- ern (Latin) tradition. In the City of God, *written between 412 and 426, he refutes the charge that Christianity caused the evils that had befallen the Roman Empire, but also opposes any triumphalist notion that Christianity necessarily makes the world a better place; the "city of God" or "heavenly city" is for him a transcendent reality, not to be identified with the "earthly city" in which its human members temporarily reside.*

Chapter 4

If I am asked what stand the City of God would take on the issues raised and, first, what this City thinks of the supreme good and ultimate evil, the answer would be: She holds that eternal life is the supreme good and eternal death the supreme evil, and that we should live rightly in order to obtain the one and avoid the other. Hence the Scriptural expression, "the just man lives by faith" (Gal. 3:11)—by faith, for the fact is that we do not now behold our good and, therefore, must seek it by faith; nor can we of ourselves even live rightly, unless He who gives us faith helps us to believe and pray, for it takes faith to believe that we need His help.

Those who think that the supreme good and evil are to be found in this life are mistaken. It makes no difference whether it is in the body or in the soul or in both—or, specifically, in pleasure or virtue or in both—that they seek the supreme good. They seek in vain whether they look to serenity, to virtue, or to both; whether to pleasure plus serenity, or to virtue, or to all three; or to the satisfaction of our innate exigencies, or to virtue, or to both. It is in vain that men look for beatitude on earth or in human nature. Divine Truth, as expressed in the Prophet's words, makes them look foolish: "The Lord knows the thoughts of men" (Ps. 93:11) or, as the text is quoted by St. Paul: "The Lord knows the thoughts of the wise that they are vain" (1 Cor. 3:20).

For, what flow of eloquence is sufficient to set forth the miseries of human life? Cicero did the best he could in his *Consolatio de morte filiae*, but how little was his very best? As for the primary sat- isfactions of our nature, when or where or how can they be so securely possessed in this life that they are not subject to the ups and downs of for- tune? There is no pain of body, driving out plea- sure, that may not befall the wise man; no anxiety that may not banish calm. A man's physical integrity is ended by the amputation or crippling of any of his limbs; his beauty is spoiled by defor- mity, his health by sickness, his vigor by weariness,

SOURCE: Augustine, *The City of God Books XVII-XXII*, tr. Gerald G. Walsh, S.J., and Daniel J. Honan (New York: Fathers of the Church, 1954), 194-202, 210-24, 232, 243-48. Used by permission of The Catholic University of America Press.

his agility by torpor and sluggishness. There is not one of these that may not afflict the flesh even of a philosopher. Among our elementary require-ments we reckon a graceful and becoming erect-ness and movement; but what happens to these as soon as some sickness brings on palsy or, still worse, a spinal deformity so severe that a man's hands touch the ground as though he were a four-footed beast? What is then left of any beauty or dignity in a man's posture or gait? Turn, now, to the primary endowments of the soul: senses to perceive and intelligence to understand the truth. How much sensation does a man have left if, for example, he goes deaf and blind? And where does the reason or intelligence go, into what strange sleep, when sickness unsettles the mind? We can hardly hold back our tears when mad men say or do extravagant things—things wholly unlike their customary behavior and normal goodness. To witness such things, even to recall them, makes a decent man weep. Still worse is the case of those possessed by demons. Their intelligence seems driven away, not to say destroyed, when an evil spirit according to its will makes use of their body and soul. And who can be sure that even a philosopher will not be such a victim at some time in his life?

Further, what is to be said of our perception of the truth, at the very best? What kind of truth and how much of it can we reach through our bodily senses? Do we not read in the truth-speaking Book of Wisdom: "For the corruptible body is a load upon the soul, and the earthly habitation presseth down the mind that museth upon many things"? (Wis. 9:15).

And what of the urge and appetite for action—*hormé*, as the Greeks call it—which is reckoned among the primary goods of our nature? Is not this the root, too, of those restless energies of the madmen who fill us with tears and fears when their senses deceive them and their reason refuses to function?

So much for the elementary endowments of nature. Look, now, at virtue herself, which comes later with education and claims for herself the topmost place among human goods. Yet, what is the life of virtue save one unending war with evil inclinations, and not with solicitations of other people alone, but with evil inclinations that arise within ourselves and are our very own.

I speak especially of temperance—*sōphrosynē*, as the Greeks call it—which must bridle our fleshly lusts if they are not to drag our will to con-sent to abominations of every sort. The mere fact that, as St. Paul says, "the flesh is at war with the spirit," is no small flaw in our nature; and virtue is at war with this evil inclination when, in the same Apostle's words, "the spirit lusts against the flesh." These are opposed to each other to such a degree that "we do not the things that we would" (Gal. 5:17). And when we seek final rest in the supreme good, what do we seek save an end to this conflict between flesh and spirit, freedom from this propensity to evil against which the spirit is at war? Yet, will as we may, such liberty cannot be had in mortal life.

This much, however, we can do with the help of God—not yield by surrender of the spirit and be dragged into sin willingly. Meanwhile, we must not fondly imagine that, so long as we wage this inward war, we may achieve that longed-for beati-tude which can be solely the prize of the victor. For there lives no man so perfected in wisdom as not to have some conflict with excessive desires.

Take, next, the virtue called prudence. Is not this virtue constantly on the lookout to distin-guish what is good from what is evil, so that there may be no mistake made in seeking the one and avoiding the other? So it bears witness to the fact that we are surrounded by evil and have evil within us. This virtue teaches that it is evil to con-sent to desires leading to sin and good to resist them. And what prudence preaches temperance puts into practice. Yet, neither prudence nor tem-perance can rid this life of the evils that are their constant concern.

Finally, there is justice. Its task is to see that to each is given what belongs to each. And this holds for the right order within man himself, so that it is just for the soul to be subordinate to God, and the body to the soul, and thus for body and soul taken together to be subject to God. Is there not abun-dant evidence that this virtue is unremittingly struggling to effect this internal order—and is far from finished? For, the less a man has God in his thoughts, the less is his soul subject to God; the more the flesh lusts counter to the spirit, the less the flesh is subject to the soul. So long, then, as such weakness, such moral sickliness remains within us, how can we dare to say that we are out of danger; and, if not yet out of danger, how can we say that our happiness is complete?

Look, now, at the great virtue called fortitude. Is not its very function—to bear patiently with misfortune—overwhelming evidence that human life is beset with unhappiness, however wise a man may be? It is beyond my comprehension how the Stoics can boldly argue that such ills are not really ills, meanwhile allowing that, if a philosopher should be tried by them beyond his obligation or duty to bear, he may have no choice but to take the easy way out by committing suicide. So stultifying is Stoic pride that, all evidences to the contrary, these men still pretend to find the ultimate good in this life and to hold that they are themselves the source of their own happiness. Their kind of sage—an astonishingly silly sage, indeed—may go deaf, dumb and blind, may be crippled, wracked with pain, visited with every imaginable affliction, driven at last to take his own life, yet have the colossal impertinence to call such an existence the happy life! Happy life, indeed, which employs death's aid to end it! If such a life is happy, then I say, live it! Why pretend that evils are not evils, when they not only overcome the virtue of fortitude and force it to yield to evil, but make a man so irrational as to call one and the same life both happy and unlivable? How can anyone be so blind as not to see that if life is happy it should not be shunned? Yet, the moment sickness opens her mouth they say one must choose a way out. If so, why do they not bow their stiff necks and admit life's unhappiness? Now, let me ask: Was it courage or cowardice that made their hero Cato kill himself? Certainly, he would not have done what he did had he not been too cowardly to endure the victory of Caesar. Where, then, was his fortitude? It was a fortitude that yielded, that surrendered, that was so beaten that Cato ran away, deserted, abandoned the happy life. Or, maybe it was no longer the happy life? In that case, it was unhappy. If so, how can anyone deny that the ills that made Cato's life unhappy and unlivable were real evils?

From this it follows that those who admit that such things are evils, so do the Aristotelians and those of the Old Academy whom Varro defends, are nearer the truth than the Stoics, even though Varro also makes the egregious mistake of maintaining that this life is still the happy life in spite of evils so grievous that, for one who suffers them, suicide becomes imperative. "The pains and afflictions of the body," Varro admits, "are evils; and the worse the pains, the greater the evil. To escape them you should end your life." I ask: Which life? He answers: "This life which is made grievous by so many evils." Life, then, is the happy life in the midst of evils which drive a man to escape from life? Is it, perhaps, the happy life precisely because you are allowed to escape its unhappiness by death? Suppose you should be bound by a divine law to remain in its evils and be permitted neither to die nor ever to be free from such misfortunes? Then, at least, you would have to say that such a life would be unhappy. And, surely, if you admit it would be unhappy if unending, you cannot say that it is not unhappy just because there is a quick way out. You cannot maintain that just because unhappiness is short-lived it is really not unhappiness at all; or, what is more preposterous, that because unhappiness is short-lived it deserves to be called happiness.

No, these ills of life must be very real indeed if they can drive even a sage of their type to take his life. For, these philosophers say—and rightly say—that the first and most fundamental command of nature is that a man should cherish his own human life and, by his very nature, shun death; that a man should be his own best friend, wanting and working with all his might and main to keep himself alive and to preserve the union of his body and soul. These ills must be very real indeed if they can subdue the very instinct of nature that struggles in every possible way to put death off; overwhelm it so utterly that death, once shunned, is now desired, sought, and, when all else fails, is self-inflicted. Yes, very real, when they can turn courage into a killer, if, indeed, there be any question of genuine courage, when this virtue, devised to support and steel a man, is so battered down by misfortune that—having failed to sustain him—it is driven, against its very function, to finish him off. It is true, of course, that a philosopher should face death as well as all other trials, with fortitude, but that means death coming upon him from without.

If then, as these philosophers held, even a wise man must yield to suicide, they ought logically to admit that there are evils—even insufferable evils—that account for this tragic compulsion; and that a life so burdensome, so exposed to fortune's ebb and flow, should not be called happy! Nor would those who talk of "the happy life" ever have called life happy if they had yielded to the truth and the cogency of reason in their search for the happy life as readily as they yield to unhappiness and the weight of evils when they lose their life by suicide; and if, further, they had given up the idea that they could enjoy the supreme good in this mortal life. They would have realized that man's very virtues, his best and most useful possessions, are the most solid evidences of the miseries of life, precisely because their function is to stand by him in perils and problems and pains.

For, when virtues are genuine virtues—and that is possible only when men believe in God—they make no pretense of protecting their possessors from unhappiness, for that would be a false promise; but they do claim that human life, now compelled to feel the misery of so many grievous ills on earth, can, by the hope of heaven, be made both happy and secure. If we are asked how a life can be happy before we are saved, we have the answer of St. Paul: "For in hope were we saved. But hope that is seen is not hope. For how can a man hope for what he sees? But if we hope for what we do not see, we wait for it with patience" (Rom. 8:24, 25).

Of course, the Apostle was not speaking of men lacking prudence, fortitude, temperance, and justice, but of men whose virtues were true virtues because the men were living by faith. Thus, as "we are saved by hope," so we are made happy by hope. Neither our salvation nor our beatitude is here present, but "we wait for it" in the future, and we wait "with patience," precisely because we are surrounded by evils which patience must endure until we come to where all good things are sources of inexpressible happiness and where there will be no longer anything

to endure. Such is to be our salvation in the hereafter, such our final blessedness. It is because the philosophers will not believe in this beatitude which they cannot see that they go on trying to fabricate here below an utterly fraudulent felicity built on virtue filled with pride and bound to fail them in the end.

Chapter 10

Not even the holy and faithful followers of the one true and supreme God are beyond the reach of demonic trickery and temptation in its many forms. Yet our anxiety in this matter is good for us, so long as we inhabit this frail body in this evil world, for it sends us seeking more ardently after that heavenly peace which is to be unshakeable and unending. There, all of our natural endowments—all that the Creator of all natures has given to our nature—will be both good and everlasting, where every wound in the soul is to be healed by wisdom and every weakness of body to be removed by resurrection; where our virtues will be no longer at war with passion or opposition of any kind, but are to have, as the prize of victory, an eternally imperturbable peace. This is what is meant by that consummate beatitude, that limitless perfection, that end that never ends.

On earth we are happy, after a fashion, when we enjoy the peace, little as it is, which a good life brings; but such happiness compared with the beatitude which is our end in eternity is, in point of fact, misery. When we mortal men, living amid the realities of earth, enjoy the utmost peace which life can give us, then it is the part of virtue, if we are living rightly, to make a right use of the goods we are enjoying. When, on the other hand, we do not enjoy this temporal peace, then it is the function of virtue to make a right use of the misfortunes which we are suffering. By genuine Christian virtue we mean here that we refer not only all good things which are being rightly used, and all the right use we are making of blessings and misfortunes, but our very virtue itself to that End in which there will be a peace so good that no peace could be better, a peace so great that a greater would be impossible.

Chapter 11

Thus, we may say of peace what we have said of eternal life—that it is our highest good; more particularly because the holy Psalmist was addressing the City of God (the nature of which I am trying, with so much difficulty, to make clear) when he said: "Praise the Lord, O Jerusalem; praise thy God, O Sion. Because he hath strengthened the bolts of thy gates, he hath blessed thy children within you. He hath placed peace in thy borders." For, when the bolts of that city's gates will have been strengthened, none will enter in and none will issue forth. Hence, its borders [fines] must be taken to mean that peace which I am trying to show is our final good. Note, too, that Jerusalem, the mystical name which symbolizes this City, means, as I have already mentioned, "the vision of peace."

However, the word "peace" is so often applied to conditions here on earth, where life is not eternal, that it is better, I think, to speak of "eternal life" rather than of "peace" as the end or supreme good of the City of God. It is in this sense that St. Paul says: "But now being made free from sin, and become servants of God, you have your fruit unto sanctification, and the end life everlasting" (Rom. 6:22).

It would be simplest for all concerned if we spoke of "peace in eternal life," or of "eternal" or of "eternal life in peace," as the end or supreme good of this City. The trouble with the expression "eternal life" is that those unfamiliar with the Scriptures might take this phrase to apply also to the eternal loss of the wicked, either because, as philosophers, they accept the immortality of the soul, or even because, as Christians, they know by faith that the punishment of the wicked has no end and, therefore, that they could not be punished forever unless their life were eternal.

The trouble with "peace" is that, even on the level of earthly and temporal values, nothing that we can talk about, long for, or finally get, is so desirable, so welcome, so good as peace. At any rate, I feel sure that if I linger a little longer on this topic of peace I shall tire very few of my readers. After all, peace is the end of this City which is the theme of this work; besides, peace is so universally loved that its very name falls sweetly on the ear.

Chapter 12

Any man who has examined history and human nature will agree with me that there is no such thing as a human heart that does not crave for joy and peace. One has only to think of men who are bent on war. What they want is to win, that is to say, their battles are but bridges to glory and to peace. The whole point of victory is to bring opponents to their knees—this done, peace ensues. Peace, then, is the purpose of waging war; and this is true even of men who have a passion for the exercise of military prowess as rulers and commanders.

What, then, men want in war is that it should end in peace. Even while waging a war every man wants peace, whereas no one wants war while he is making peace. And even when men are plotting to disturb the peace, it is merely to fashion a new peace nearer to the heart's desire; it is not because they dislike peace as such. It is not that they love peace less, but that they love their kind of peace more. And even when a secession is successful, its purpose is not achieved unless some sort of peace remains among those who plotted and planned the rebellion. Take even a band of highwaymen. The more violence and impunity they want in disturbing the peace of other men, the more they demand peace among themselves. Take even the case of a robber so powerful that he dispenses with partnership, plans alone, and single-handed robs and kills his victims. Even he maintains some kind of peace, however shadowy, with those he cannot kill and whom he wants to keep in the dark with respect to his crimes. Certainly in his own home he wants to be at peace with his wife and children and any other members of his household. Of course, he is delighted when his every nod is obeyed; if it is not obeyed, he rages, and scolds, and demands peace in his own home and, if need be, gets it by sheer brutality. He knows that the price of peace in domestic society is to have everyone subject in the home to some head—in this instance, to himself.

Suppose, now, a man of this type were offered the allegiance of a larger society, say of a city or of a nation, with the pledge that he would be obeyed as he looks to be obeyed under his own roof. In this case, he would no longer hide himself away in a darksome robber's den; he would show himself off as a high and mighty king—the same man, however, with all of his old greed and criminality. Thus it is that all men want peace in their own society, and all want it in their own way. When they go to war what they want is to make, if they can, their enemies their own, and then to impose on them the victor's will and call it peace.

...

It is even more so with man. By the very laws of his nature, he seems, so to speak, forced into fellowship and, as far as in him lies, into peace with every man. At any rate, even when wicked men go to war they want peace for their own society and would like, if possible, to make all men members of that society, so that everyone and everything might be at the service of one head. Of course, the only means such a conqueror knows is to have all men so fear or love him that they will accept the peace which he imposes. For, so does pride perversely copy God. Sinful man hates the equality of all men under God and, as though he were God, loves to impose his sovereignty on his fellow men. He hates the peace of God which is just and prefers his own peace which is unjust. However, he is powerless not to love peace of some sort. For, no man's sin is so unnatural as to wipe out all traces whatsoever of human nature. Anyone, then, who is rational enough to prefer right to wrong and order to disorder can see that the kind of peace that is based on injustice, as compared with that which is based on justice, does not deserve the name of peace.

Of course, even disorder, in whole or in part, must come to some kind of terms either with the situation in which it finds itself or with the elements out of which it takes its being—otherwise it would have no being at all.

Take a man hanging upside down. Certainly his members are in disorder and the posture of the body as a whole is unnatural. The parts which nature demands should be above and below have become topsy-turvy. Such a position disturbs the peace of the body and is therefore painful. Nevertheless, the soul remains at peace with the body and continues to work for its welfare. Otherwise, the man would not live to feel the agony. And even

if the soul is driven from the body by excess of pain, nevertheless, so long as the limbs hold together, some kind of peace among these parts remains. Otherwise, there would be no corpse to go on dangling there. Further, the fact that by gravity the corpse, made out of earth, tends to fall to the ground and pulls at the noose that holds it up proves that there is some order in which it seeks peace, and that its weight is, as it were, crying out for a place where it can rest. Lifeless and insensible though the body now is, it does not renounce that appropriate peace in the order of nature which it either has or seeks to have.

So, too, when a corpse is treated to embalming, to prevent dissolution and decay, there is a kind of peace which holds the parts together while the whole is committed to the earth, its proper resting place, and, therefore, a place with which the body is at peace. If, on the other hand, embalming is omitted and nature is allowed to take its course, the corpse remains a battleground of warring exhalations (that attack our senses with the stench we smell) only until such time as they finally fall in with the elements of this world and, slowly, bit by bit, become indistinguishable in a common peace.

Even afterward, however, the law and ordering of the Creator who is supreme in the whole cosmos and the regulator of its peace are still in control. Even when tiny bacteria spring from the corpse of a larger animal, it is by the same law of the Creator that all these minute bodies serve in peace the organic wholes of which they are parts. Even when the flesh of dead animals is eaten by other animals, there is no change in the universal laws which are meant for the common good of every kind of life, the common good that is effected by bringing like into peace with like. It makes no difference what disintegrating forces are at work, or what new combinations are made, or even what changes or transformations are effected.

Chapter 13

The peace, then, of the body lies in the ordered equilibrium of all its parts; the peace of the irrational soul, in the balanced adjustment of its appetites; the peace of the reasoning soul, in the harmonious correspondence of conduct and conviction; the peace of body and soul taken together, in the well-ordered life and health of the living whole. Peace between a mortal man and his Maker consists in ordered obedience, guided by faith, under God's eternal law; peace between man and man consists in regulated fellowship. The peace of a home lies in the ordered harmony of authority and obedience between the members of a family living together. The peace of the political community is an ordered harmony of authority and obedience between citizens. The peace of the heavenly City lies in a perfectly ordered and harmonious communion of those who find their joy in God and in one another in God. Peace, in its final sense, is the calm that comes of order. Order is an arrangement of like and unlike things whereby each of them is disposed in its proper place.

This being so, those who are unhappy, insofar as they are unhappy, are not in peace, since they lack the calm of that Order which is beyond every storm; nevertheless, even in their misery they cannot escape from order, since their very misery is related to responsibility and to justice. They do not share with the blessed in their tranquility, but this very separation is the result of the law of order. Moreover, even the miserable can be momentarily free from anxiety and can reach some measure of adjustment to their surroundings and, hence, some tranquility of order and, therefore, some slender peace. However, the reason why they remain unhappy is that, although they *may* be momentarily free from worry and from pain, they are not in a condition where they *must* be free both from worry and pain. Their condition of misery is worse when such peace as they have is not in harmony with that law which governs the order of nature. Their peace can also be disturbed by pain and in proportion to their pain; yet, some peace will remain, so long as the pain is not too acute and their organism as a whole does not distintegrate.

Notice that there can be life without pain, but no pain without some kind of life. In the same way, there can be peace without any kind of war, but no war that does not suppose some kind of peace. This does not mean that war as war involves peace; but war, insofar as those who wage

it or have it waged upon them are beings with organic natures, involves peace—for the simple reason that to be organic means to be ordered and, therefore, to be, in some sense, at peace.

Similarly, there can be a nature without any defect and, even, a nature in which there can be no kind of evil whatever, but there can be no nature completely devoid of good. Even the nature of the Devil, insofar as it is a nature, is not evil; it was perversity—not being true to itself—that made it bad. The Devil did not "stand in the truth" (John 8:44) and, therefore, did not escape the judgment of truth. He did not stand fast in the tranquility of order—nor did he, for all that, elude the power of the Ordainer. The goodness which God gave to his nature does not withdraw him from the justice of God by which that nature is subject to punishment. Yet, even in that punishment, God does not hound the good which He created, but only the evil which the Devil committed. So it is that God does not take back the whole of His original gift. He takes a part and leaves a part; He leaves a nature that can regret what God has taken back. Indeed, the very pain inflicted is evidence of both the good that is lost and the good that is left. For, if there were no good left, there would be no one to lament the good that has been lost.

A man who sins is just that much worse if he rejoices in the loss of holiness; but one who suffers pain, and does not benefit by it, laments, at least, the loss of his health. Holiness and health are both good things and, because the loss of any good is more a cause for grief than for gladness (unless there be some higher compensation—the soul's holiness, to be sure, is preferable to the body's health), it is more in accordance with nature that a sinner grieve over his punishment than that he rejoice over his offense. Consequently, just as a man's happiness in abandoning the good of wrongdoing betrays his bad will, so his sorrowing for the good he has lost when in pain bears witness to the good of his nature. For, anyone who grieves over the loss of peace to his nature does so out of some remnant of that peace wherewith his nature loves itself. This is what happens—deservedly, too—in eternal punishment. In the midst of their agonies the evil and the godless weep for the loss of their nature's goods, knowing, meanwhile, that

God whose great generosity they condemned was perfectly just when He took these goods away.

God, the wise Creator and just Ordainer of all natures, has made the mortal race of man the loveliest of all lovely things on earth. He has given to men good gifts suited to their existence here below. Among these is temporal peace, according to the poor limits of mortal life, in health, security, and human fellowship; and other gifts, too, needed to preserve this peace or regain it, once lost—for instance, the blessings that lie all around us, so perfectly adapted to our senses: daylight, speech, air to breathe, water to drink, everything that goes to feed, clothe, cure, and beautify the body. These good gifts are granted, however, with the perfectly just understanding that whoever uses the goods which are meant for the mortal peace of mortal men, as these goods should be used, will receive more abundant and better goods—nothing less than immortal peace and all that goes with it, namely, the glory and honor of enjoying God and one's neighbor in God everlastingly; but that whoever misuses his gifts on earth will both lose what he has and never receive the better gifts of heaven.

Chapter 14

In the earthly city, then, temporal goods are to be used with a view to the enjoyment of earthly peace, whereas, in the heavenly City, they are used with a view to the enjoyment of eternal peace. Hence, if we were merely unthinking brutes, we would pursue nothing beyond the orderly interrelationship of our bodily part and the appeasing of our appetites, nothing, that is, beyond the comfort of the flesh and plenty of pleasures, so that the peace of body might contribute to peace of the soul. For, if order in the body be lacking, the peace of an irrational soul is checked, since it cannot attain the satisfaction of its appetites. Both of these forms of peace meanwhile subserve that other form of peace which the body and soul enjoy between them, the peace of life and health in good order.

For, just as brutes show that they love the peace or comfort of their bodies by shunning pain, and the peace of their souls by pursuing pleasure to satisfy their appetites, so, too, by running from death, they make clear enough how much they love the peace which keeps body and soul together.

Because, however, man has a rational soul, he makes everything he shares with brutes subserve the peace of his rational soul, so that he first measures things with his mind before he acts, in order to achieve that harmonious correspondence of conduct and conviction which I called the peace of the rational soul. His purpose in desiring not to be vexed with pain, nor disturbed with desire, nor disintegrated by death is that he may learn something profitable and so order his habits and way of life. However, if the infirmity of his human mind is not to bring him in his pursuit of knowledge to some deadly error, he needs divine authority to give secure guidance, and divine help so that he may be unhampered in following the guidance given.

And because, so long as man lives in his mortal body and is a pilgrim far from the Lord, he walks, not by vision, but by faith. Consequently, he refers all peace of body or soul, or their combination, to that higher peace which unites a mortal man with the immortal God and which I defined as "ordered obedience guided by faith, under God's eternal law."

Meanwhile, God teaches him two chief commandments, the love of God and the love of neighbor. In these precepts man finds three beings to love, namely, God, himself, and his fellow man, and knows that he is not wrong in loving himself so long as he loves God. As a result, he must help his neighbor (whom he is obliged to love as himself) to love God. Thus, he must help his wife, children, servants, and all others whom he can influence. He must wish, moreover, to be similarly helped by his fellow man, in case he himself needs such assistance. Out of all this love he will arrive at peace, as much as in him lies, with every man—at that human peace which is regulated fellowship. Right order here means, first, that he harm no one, and, second, that he help whomever he can. His fundamental duty is to look out for his own home, for both by natural and human law he has easier and readier access to their requirements.

St. Paul says: "But if any does not take care of his own, and especially of his household, he has denied the faith and is worse than an unbeliever"

(1 Tim. 5:8). From this care arises that peace of the home which lies in the harmonious interplay of authority and obedience among those who live there. For, those who have the care of the others give the orders—a man to his wife, parents to their children, masters to their servants. And those who are cared for must obey—wives their husband, children their parents, servants their masters. In the home of a religious man, however, of a man living by faith and as yet a wayfarer from the heavenly City, those who command serve those whom they appear to rule—because, of course, they do not command out of lust to domineer, but out of a sense of duty—not out of pride like princes but out of solicitude like parents.

Chapter 17

While the homes of unbelieving men are intent upon acquiring temporal peace out of the possessions and comforts of this temporal life, the families which live according to faith look ahead to the good things of heaven promised as imperishable, and use material and temporal goods in the spirit of pilgrims, not as snares or obstructions to block their way to God, but simply as helps to ease and never to increase the burdens of this corruptible body which weighs down the soul. Both types of homes and their masters have this in common, that they must use things essential to this mortal life. But the respective purposes to which they put them are characteristic and very different.

So, too, the earthly city which does not live by faith seeks only an earthly peace, and limits the goal of its peace, of its harmony of authority and obedience among its citizens, to the voluntary and collective attainment of objectives necessary to mortal existence. The heavenly City, meanwhile – or, rather, that part that is on pilgrimage in mortal life and lives by faith—must use this earthly peace until such time as our mortality which needs such peace has passed away. As a consequence, so long as her life in the earthly city is that of a captive and an alien (although she has the promise of ultimate delivery and the gift of the Spirit as a pledge), she has no hesitation about keeping in step with the civil law which governs matters pertaining to our existence here below. For, as mortal life is the same for all, there ought to be common cause between the two cities in what concerns our purely human living.

Now comes the difficulty. The city of this world, to begin with, has had certain "wise men" of its own mold, whom true religion must reject, because either out of their own day-dreaming or out of demonic deception these wise men came to believe that a multiplicity of divinities was allied with human life, with different duties, in some strange arrangement, and different assignments ...

The heavenly City, on the contrary, knows and, by religious faith, believes that it must adore one God alone and serve Him with that complete dedication which the Greeks call *latreia* and which belongs to Him alone. As a result, she has been unable to share with the earthly city a common religious legislation, and has had no choice but to dissent on this score and so to become a nuisance to those who think otherwise. Hence, she has had to feel the weight of their anger, hatred, and violence, save in those instances when, by sheer numbers and God's help, which never fails, she has been able to scare off her opponents.

So long, then, as the heavenly City is wayfaring on earth, she invites citizens from all nations and all tongues, and unites them into a single pilgrim band. She takes no issue with that diversity of customs, laws, and traditions whereby human peace is sought and maintained. Instead of nullifying or tearing down, she preserves and appropriates whatever in the diversities of divers races is aimed at one and the same objective of human peace, provided only that they do not stand in the way of the faith and worship of the one supreme and true God.

Thus, the heavenly City, so long as it is wayfaring on earth, not only makes use of earthly peace but fosters and actively pursues along with other human beings a common platform in regard to all that concerns our purely human life and does not interfere with faith and worship. Of course, though, the City of God subordinates this earthly peace to that of heaven. For this is not merely true peace, but, strictly speaking, for any rational creature, the only real peace, since it is, as I said, "the perfectly ordered and harmonious communion of those who find their joy in God and in one another in God."

When this peace is reached, man will be no longer haunted by death, but plainly and perpetually endowed with life, nor will his body, which now wastes away and weighs down his soul, be any longer animal, but spiritual, in need of nothing, and completely under the control of our will.

This peace the pilgrim City already possesses by faith and it lives holily and according to this faith so long as, to attain its heavenly completion, it refers every good act done for God or for his fellow man. I say "fellow man" because, of course, any community must emphasize social relationships.

Chapter 21

I have arrived at the point where I must keep my promise to prove, as briefly and clearly as I can that, if we accept the definitions of Scipio, cited by Cicero in his book *On the Republic*, there never existed any such thing as a Roman Republic.

Scipio gives a short definition of a commonwealth as the weal of the people. Now, if this is a true definition, there never was any Roman Republic, because there never was in Rome any true "weal of the people." Scipio defines the people as "a multitude bound together by a mutual recognition of rights and a mutual co-operation for the common good." As the discussion progresses, he explains what he means by "mutual recognition of rights," going on to show that a republic cannot be managed without justice, for, where there is not true justice, there is no recognition of rights.

Chapter 24

It is possible to define a "people" not as Cicero does but as "a multitude of reasonable beings voluntarily associated in the pursuit of common interests." In that case, one need only consider what these interests are in order to determine of what kind any particular people may be. Still, whatever these interests are, so long as we have a multitude of rational beings—and not of irresponsible cattle—who are voluntarily associated in the pursuit of common interests, we can reasonably call them a "people," and they will be a better or worse people according as the interests which have brought them together are better or worse interests.

This definition certainly makes the Roman people a "people" and their weal a "commonwealth" or "republic." However, we know from history what kind of interests this people had, both in primitive times and more recently, and also what kind of morals brought on the rupture and corruption of their voluntary association (which is the health, so to speak, of any community), first, by sanguinary seditions, and, later, by social and civil war. On this subject, I had a good deal to say earlier in this work. However, I would still call the Romans a "people" and their affairs a "commonwealth," so long as they remain a multitude of reasonable beings voluntarily associated in the pursuit of common interests.

Of course, what I have said of the Romans and their Republic applies not less to the Athenians and other Greek communities, to the Egyptians, to the early Assyrians of Babylonia, and, in general, to any other pagan people whose government exercised real political control, however much or little. The fact is that any civil community made up of pagans who are disobedient to God's command that He alone receive sacrifices and who, therefore, are devoid of the rational and religious control of soul over body and of reason over sinful appetite must be lacking in true justice.

Chapter 25

There may seem to be some control of soul over body and of reason over passion, even when soul and reason do not serve God as He demands. Actually, however, there is no such thing. For, what species of control can there be of the body and its bad tendencies if the mistress mind is ignorant of the true God, insubmissive to His authority, and, as a result, a plaything to the corrupting influences of thoroughly evil demons? No, the virtues on which the mind preens itself as giving control over the body and its urges, and which aim at any other purpose or possession than God, are in point of fact vices rather than virtues.

Although some people claim that virtues are authentic and worthy of the name so long as their end is in themselves and they are not means to something else, even they are spoiled by the puff of pride and must, consequently, be reckoned as vices rather than virtues.

Just as our flesh does not live by its own power but by a power above it, so what gives to a man the life of blessedness derives not from himself, but from a power above him. And this applies not just to man but to every heavenly Power and Domination.

Chapter 26

As the life of the body is the soul, so the "blessed life" of a man is God. As the sacred writings of the Hebrews have it: "Happy is that people whose God is the Lord." Wretched, then, must be any people that is divorced from this God.

Yet, even such a people cherishes a peace of its own which is not to be scorned although in the end it is not to be had because this peace, before the end, was abused. Meanwhile, it is to our advantage that there be such peace in this life. For, as long as the two cities are mingled together, we can make use of the peace of Babylon. Faith can assure our exodus from Babylon, but our pilgrim status, for the time being, makes us neighbors.

All of this was in St. Paul's mind when he advised the Church to pray for this world's kings and high authorities—in order that "we may lead a quiet and peaceful life in all piety and worthy behavior" (1 Tim. 2:2). Jeremias, too, predicting the Babylonian captivity to the Old Testament Jews, gave them orders from God to go submissively and serve their God by such sufferings, and meanwhile to pray for Babylon. "For in the peace thereof," he said, "shall be your peace" (Jer. 29:7)—referring, of course, to the peace of this world which the good and bad share in common.

Chapter 27

The City of God, however, has a peace of its own, namely, peace with God in this world by faith and in the world to come by vision. Still, any peace we have on earth, whether the peace we share with Babylon or our own peace through faith, is more like a solace for unhappiness than the joy of beatitude. Even our virtue in this life, genuine as it is because it is referred to the true goal of every good, lies more in the pardoning of sins than in any perfection of virtues. Witness the prayer of God's whole City, wandering on earth and calling out to Him through all her members: "Forgive us our debts as we also forgive our debtors" (Matt. 6:12).

This prayer is effective, not on the lips of those whose faith without works is dead (cf. Jas. 2:17), but only on the lips of men whose faith works through charity (Gal. 5:6). This prayer is necessary for the just because their reason, though submissive to God, has only imperfect mastery over their evil inclinations so long as they live in this world and in a corruptible body that "is a load upon the soul" (Wis. 9:15). Reason may give commands, but can exercise no control without a struggle. And, in this time of weakness, something will inevitably creep in to make the best of soldiers—whether in victory or still in battle with such foes—offend by some small slip of the tongue, some passing thought, if not by habitual actions. This explains why we can know no perfect peace so long as there are evil inclinations to master. Those which put up a fight are put down only in perilous conflict; those that are already overcome cannot be kept so if one relaxes, but only at the cost of vigilant control. These are the battles which Scripture sums up in the single phrase: "The life of man upon earth is a warfare" (Job 7:1).

Who, then, save a proud man, will presume that he can live without needing to ask God: "Forgive us our debts"? Not a great man, you may be sure, but one blown up with the wind of self-reliance—one whom God in His justice resists while He grants His grace to the humble. Hence, it is written: "God resists the proud, but gives grace to the humble" (Jas. 4:6; 1 Pet. 5:5).

This, then, in this world, is the life of virtue. When God commands, man obeys; when the soul commands, the body obeys; when reason rules, our passions, even when they fight back, must be conquered or resisted; man must beg God's grace to win merit and the remission of his sins and must thank God for the blessings he receives.

But, in that final peace which is the end and purpose of all virtue here on earth, our nature, made whole by immortality and incorruption, will have no vices and experience no rebellion from within or without. There will be no need for reason to govern non-existent evil inclinations. God will hold sway over man, the soul over the body;

and the happiness in eternal life and law will make obedience sweet and easy. And in each and all of us this condition will be everlasting, and we shall know it to be so. That is why the peace of such blessedness or the blessedness of such peace is to be our supreme good.

Chapter 28

On the other hand, the doom in store for those who are not of the City of God is an unending wretchedness that is called "the second death" (Rev. 21:8), because neither the soul, cut off from the life of God, nor the body, pounded by perpetual pain, can there be said to live at all. And what will make that second death so hard to bear is that there will be no death to end it.

Now, since unhappiness is the reverse of happiness, death of life, and war of peace, one may reasonably ask: If peace is praised and proclaimed as the highest good, what kind of warfare are we to think of as the highest evil? If this inquirer will reflect, he will realize that what is hurtful and destructive in warfare is mutual clash and conflict, and, hence, that no one can imagine a war more unbearably bitter than one in which the will and passions are at such odds that neither can ever win the victory, and in which violent pain and the body's very nature will so clash that neither will ever yield. When this conflict occurs on earth, either pain wins and death puts an end to all feeling, or nature wins and health removes the pain. But, in hell, pain permanently afflicts and nature continues to feel it, for neither ever comes to term, since the punishment must never end.

However, it is through the last judgment that good men achieve that highest good (which all should seek) and evil men that highest evil (which all should shun), and so, as God helps me, I shall discuss that judgment in the Book that comes next.

41. Pelagius, *To Demetrias*

Pelagius, an ascetic teacher in Rome in the last years of the fourth century and early years of the fifth, probably came from Britain. His central teaching—for which he came into conflict with Augustine (see text 42)—was that human beings have the innate ability to choose good and reject evil. He wrote this letter in 413 at the request of the mother of Demetrias, a young woman of a prominent Christian Roman family who had taken a vow of virginity.

2, 1. Whenever I have to speak on the subject of moral instruction and the conduct of a holy life, it is my practice first to demonstrate the power and quality of human nature and to show what it is capable of achieving, and then to go on to encourage the mind of my listener to consider the idea of different kinds of virtues, in case it may be of little or no profit to him to be summoned to pursue ends which he has perhaps assumed hitherto to be beyond his reach; for we can never enter upon the path of virtue unless we have hope as our guide and companion and if every effort expended in seeking something is nullified in effect by despair of ever finding it. I also think that on this occasion, when the good in our nature calls for a fuller exposition commensurate with the greater perfec-

SOURCE: *Letters of Pelagius and His Followers*, ed. and tr. Brinley Roderick Rees (Woodbridge, U.K., and Rochester, N.Y.: Boydell Press, 1991), 36-40, 43-45. Used by permission of Boydell & Brewer Ltd.

tion of life which has to be inculcated in the listener's mind, I have special grounds for adhering to the same sequence of exhortation as I have followed in my other minor works, in order that the mind may not become more negligent and sluggish in its pursuit of virtue as it comes to believe less in its ability to achieve it, supposing itself not to possess something simply because it is unaware that it is present within. When it is desirable for a man to put a certain capacity to use, it always has to be brought to his attention, and any good of which human nature is capable has to be revealed, since what is shown to be practicable must be put into practice. Let us then lay this down as the first basis for a holy and spiritual life: the virgin must recognize her own strengths, which she will be able to employ to the full only when she has learned that she possesses them. The best incentive for the mind consists in teaching it that it is possible to do anything which one really wants to do: in war, for example, the kind of exhortation which is most effective and carries most authority is the one which reminds the combatant of his own strengths.

2. First, then, you ought to measure the good of human nature by reference to its creator, I mean God, of course: if it is he who, as report goes, has made all the works of and within the world good, exceeding good, how much more excellent do you suppose that he has made man himself, on whose account he has clearly made everything else? And before actually making man, he determines to fashion him in his own image and likeness and shows what kind of creature he intends to make him. Next, since he has made all animals subject to man and set him as lord over creatures which have been made more powerful than men either by their bodily size and greater strength or by the weapons which they have in their teeth, he makes it abundantly clear how much more gloriously man himself has been fashioned and wants him to appreciate the dignity of his own nature by marveling that strong animals have been made subject to him. For he did not leave man naked and defenseless nor did he expose him in his weakness to a variety of dangers; but, having made him seem unarmed outwardly, he provided him with a better armament inside, that is, with reason

and wisdom, so that by means of his intelligence and mental vigor, in which he surpassed the other animals, man alone was able to recognize the maker of all things and to serve God by using those same faculties which enabled him to hold sway over the rest. Moreover, the Lord of Justice wished man to be free to act and not under compulsion; it was for this reason that 'he left him free to make his own decisions' (Sir. 15:14) and set before him life and death, good and evil, and he shall be given whatever pleases him (ibid. 17). Hence we read in the Book Deuteronomy also: I have set before you life and death, blessing and curse; therefore choose life, that you may live (Deut. 30:19).

3, 1. That is why we must now take precautions to prevent you from being embarrassed by something in which the ignorant majority is at fault for lack of proper consideration, and so from supposing, with them, that man has not been created truly good simply because he is able to do evil and is not obliged by the overpowering inclination of his own nature to do good on compulsion and without any possibility of variation. If you reconsider this matter carefully and force your mind to apply a more acute understanding to it, it will be revealed to you that man's status is better and higher for the very reason for which it is thought to be inferior: it is on this choice between two ways, on this freedom to choose either alternative, that the glory of the rational mind is based, it is in this that the whole honor of our nature consists, it is from this that its dignity is derived and all good men win others' praise and their own reward. Nor would there be any virtue at all in the good done by the man who perseveres, if he could not at any time cross over to the path of evil.

2. It was because God wished to bestow on the rational creature the gift of doing good of his own free will and the capacity to exercise free choice, by implanting in man the possibility of choosing either alternative, that he made it his peculiar right to be what he wanted to be, so that with his capacity for good and evil he could do either quite naturally and then bend his will in the other direction too. He could not claim to possess the good of his own volition, unless he were the kind of crea-

ture that could also have possessed evil. Our most excellent creator wished us to be able to do either but actually to do only one, that is, good, which he also commanded, giving us the capacity to do evil only so that we might do his will by exercising our own. That being so, this very capacity to do evil is also good—good, I say, because it makes the good part better by making it voluntary and independent, not bound by necessity but free to decide for itself. We are certainly permitted to choose, oppose, approve, reject, and there is no ground for preferring the rational creature to the others except that, while all the others possess only the good derived from their own circumstances and necessity, it alone possesses the good of free will also.

3. But most of those who, from lack of faith as much as of knowledge, deplore the status of man, are—I am ashamed to admit it—criticizing the Lord's work and asserting that man ought to have been so made that he could do no evil at all, and we are then in a position where what is molded says to its molder: Why have you made me thus? (Rom. 9:20). And these most shameless of men, while hiding the fact that they are managing quite well with what they have been made, would prefer to have been made otherwise; and so those who are unwilling to correct their own way of life appear to want to correct nature itself instead, the good of which has been so universally established in all that it sometimes reveals itself and brings itself to notice even in pagans who do not worship God. For how many of the pagan philosophers have we heard and read and even seen for ourselves to be chaste, tolerant, temperate, generous, abstinent and kindly, rejecters of the world's honors as well as its delights, lovers of justice no less than knowledge? Whence, I ask you, do these good qualities pleasing to God come to men who are strangers to him? Whence *can* these good qualities come to them, unless it be from the good of nature? And since we see the qualities of which I have spoken contained either all in one person or severally in several persons and since the nature of all is one and the same, by their example they show each other that all qualities which are found either all together in all or severally in each one are able to exist in all alike. But if even men without

God can show what kind of creatures they were made by God, consider what Christians are able to do whose nature and life have been instructed for the better by Christ and who are assisted by the aid of divine grace as well.

4, 1. Come now, let us approach the secret places of our soul, let everyone examine himself more attentively, let us ask what opinion our own personal thoughts have of this matter, let our conscience itself deliver its judgment on the good of nature, let us be instructed by the inner teaching of the mind, and let us learn about each of the good qualities of the mind from no other source but the mind itself. Why is it, I ask you, that we either blush or fear at every sin we commit, displaying our guilt for what we have done at one moment by the blush on our countenance, at another by its pallor, anxiously trying to avoid any witness even of our smallest offenses and suffering pangs of conscience all the while? And why, on the other hand, are we happy, resolute, bold after every good deed we have done and, if this fact is hidden from sight, desire and wish it to be seen in broad daylight? Why else unless it is because nature itself is its own witness and discloses its own good by the very fact of its disapproval of evil and, by putting its trust only in a good deed, shows what alone benefits it? Hence it comes about that frequently, though a murderer's identity remains concealed, torments of conscience make furious attacks on the author of the crime, and the secret punishment of the mind takes vengeance on the guilty man in hiding; nor is there any room for escape from punishment after the crime has been committed, since guilt is itself the penalty. That is why the innocent man, contrariwise, enjoys the peace of mind that comes from a good conscience even while undergoing torture and, though he fears punishment, still glories in his innocence.

2. There is, I maintain, a sort of natural sanctity in our minds which, presiding as it were in the mind's citadel, administers judgment equally on the evil and the good and, just as it favors honorable and upright actions, so too condemns wrong deeds and, on the evidence of conscience, distinguishes the one side from the other by a kind of

inner law; nor, in fine, does it seek to deceive by any display of cleverness or of counterfeit brilliance in argument but either denounces or defends us by our thoughts themselves, surely the most reliable and incorruptible of witnesses. This is the law which the apostle recalls when he writes to the Romans, testifying that it is implanted in all men and written as it were on the tablets of the heart: For when gentiles who have not the law do by nature what the law requires, they are a law to themselves, even though they do not have the law. They show that what the law requires is written in their hearts, while their conscience also bears them witness and their conflicting thoughts accuse or perhaps excuse them (Rom. 2:15, 16). It is this law that all have used whom scripture records as having lived in sanctity and having pleased God between the time of Adam and that of Moses: some of these must be set before you as examples, so that you may not find it difficult to understand how great is the good of nature, when once you have satisfied yourself that it has replaced the law in the task of teaching righteousness.

8, 1. Yet we do not defend the good of nature to such an extent that we claim that it cannot do evil, since we undoubtedly declare also that it is capable of good and evil; we merely try to protect it from an unjust charge, so that we may not seem to be forced to do evil through a fault in our nature, when, in fact, we do neither good nor evil without the exercise of our will and always have the freedom to do one of the two, being always able to do either. For on what grounds are some to be judges, others to be judged, unless it is because the will works in different ways in one and the same nature and because, though all of us are able to do the same, we actually do different things? And so, in order that this essential fact may stand out more clearly, we must cite some examples. Adam is cast out of paradise, Enoch is snatched away from the world; in both the Lord shows freedom of choice at work, for, just as the one who sinned could have pleased the Lord, so the other, who did please him, could have sinned instead. Neither would the former have deserved to be punished nor the latter to be chosen by a just God, unless both had been able to choose either course of action. This is how we are to understand the matter of Cain and Abel and also of Jacob and Esau, the twin brothers, and we have to realize that, when merits differ in the same nature, it is will that is the sole cause of an action.

2. Noah in his righteousness rejected the world when it was destroyed by flood because of its sins, Lot in his holiness passed judgment on the crimes of the Sodomites; and the fact that those first men were without the rebukes of the law for the space of so many years gives us no small grounds for acknowledging the good of nature, not, assuredly, because God at any time did not care for his creatures but because he knew that he had made human nature such that it would suffice them in place of the law for the practice of righteousness. In a word, as long as a nature which was still comparatively fresh was in vigorous use and long habituation to sinning did not draw a dark veil, as it were, over human reason, nature was set free and left without law; but when it had now become buried beneath an excess of vices and as if tainted with the rust of ignorance, the Lord applied the file of the law to it, and so, thoroughly polished by its frequent admonishments, it was enabled to recover its former brilliance.

3. Nor is there any reason why it is made difficult for us to do good other than that long habit of doing wrong which has infected us from childhood and corrupted us little by little over many years and ever after holds us in bondage and slavery to itself, so that it seems somehow to have acquired the force of nature. We now find ourselves being resisted and opposed by all that long period in which we were carelessly instructed, that is, educated in evil, in which we even strove to be evil, since, to add to the other incentives to evil, innocence itself was held to be folly. That old habit now attacks our new-found freedom of will, and, as we languish in ignorance through our sloth and idleness, unaccustomed to doing good after having for so long learned to do only evil, we wonder why sanctity is also conferred on us as if from an outside source.

4. So much then by way of a cursory explanation of the good of nature, as it is also stated in another of my works: it was something which we

had to provide in order to pave your way to perfect righteousness and make it more level and easier for you to run along in the knowledge that there is nothing uneven or unapproachable confronting you. Even before the law was given to us, as we have said, and long before the arrival of our Lord and Savior some are reported to have lived holy and righteous lives; how much more possible must we believe that to be after the light of his coming, now that we have been instructed by the grace of Christ and reborn as better men: purified and cleansed by his blood, encouraged by his example to pursue perfect righteousness, we ought surely to be better than those who lived before the time of the law, better even than those who lived under the law, since the apostle says: For sin will have no dominion over you, since you are not under law but under grace (Rom. 6:14).

42. Augustine of Hippo, *On Nature and Grace*

Pelagius (see text 41) had objected publicly to what he saw as Augustine's denial of free will as early as 405, and Augustine (see text 40) wrote his first work opposing what we recognize as "Pelagian" ideas in 412. But his first direct response to Pelagius was in On Nature and Grace, *in 415. In the opening chapters, presented here, Augustine summarizes the issues in the controversy as he saw them and explains his theology of grace. He is responding directly to Pelagius's treatise* On Nature *(now lost), from which the passages italicized here are probably quotations.*

Introduction

The book which you have sent to me, dearly beloved sons Timasius and James, I have read through somewhat rapidly—having set aside for a little while the books which I was reading—but with considerable attention. I saw [in this book] a man inflamed with a very ardent zeal against those who, although they ought, when they sin, to censure the human will, try instead to accuse the nature of human beings and thus to excuse themselves. He has flared up excessively against this plague, which even writers of secular literature have strongly reproved, exclaiming: "The human race wrongly brings a complaint against its own nature." With all the strength of his intellectual talents, your author also has piled up support for precisely this judgment. I fear, nevertheless, that he will instead give support to those "who have a zeal for God, but not according to knowledge; for they, not knowing the justice of God, and seeking to establish their own, have not submitted themselves to the justice of God" (Rom. 10:2-3). The Apostle makes clear the meaning of "the justice of God" in this passage by adding immediately, "For the end of the law is Christ, to justice for everyone who believes" (Rom. 10:4). Therefore, whoever understands that the justice of God lies not in the precept of the law, which incites fear, but in the help given by the grace of Christ—and it is to this grace alone that the fear of the law, as of a pedagogue (cf. Gal. 3:24), leads—he understands why he is a Christian. "For if justice is through the law,

SOURCE: Augustine, *Four Anti-Pelagian Writings*, tr. John A. Mourant and William J. Collinge (Washington: Catholic University of America Press, 1992), 22-26, 35-37. Used by permission of The Catholic University of America Press.

then Christ died in vain" (Gal. 2:21). However, if he did not die in vain, then only in him is the ungodly man justified, and to him who "believes in him who justifies the ungodly, his faith is attributed for his justification" (Rom. 4:5). "For all have sinned and are deprived of the glory of God and are justified freely through his blood" (Rom. 3:23, 24). But those who do not believe that they belong to the "all" who "have sinned and are deprived of the glory of God," do not, of course, have any necessity to become Christians, for those who are healthy do not need a physician, but rather those who are ill. For this reason Christ came to call, not the just, but sinners (Matt. 9:12, 13).

2.(2) And thus the nature of the human race, born from the flesh of the one transgressor, ought, if it could be sufficient to itself to fulfill the law and to achieve justice, to be sure of its reward, that is, of eternal life, *even if in some nation or in some past time faith in the blood of Christ was not known to it. For God is not unjust and would not deprive the just of their reward for justice, if the mystery of Christ's nature as both human and divine, which was manifest in the flesh, had not been proclaimed to them. For how could they believe what they had not heard? Or how could they hear without a preacher?* (cf. Rom. 10:14). For *"Faith is from hearing,"* as Scripture says, *"and hearing by the word of Christ. But I say,"* says St. Paul, *"Have they not heard? 'Their sound has gone forth into all the earth, and their words unto the ends of the whole world'"* (Rom. 10:17, 18; cf. Ps. 18:5). *However, before all this has begun to be accomplished, before that preaching itself finally reaches the ends of the whole earth—for there still exist some people in remote places, although it is said that they are few in number, to whom the gospel has not yet been preached— what should human nature do or what has it done, either before when it had not yet heard that salvation was to come to pass, or now if it has not learned that it was accomplished? What should it do except fulfill God's will by believing in him who made heaven and earth, and who created human nature itself (as it naturally perceives) and by living rightly, even though it has not been tinged with any faith in the passion and resurrection of Christ?* If this could have been done or can be done, I also say what the Apostle said about the law: [235] "Christ died in

vain" (Gal. 2:21). For if he declared this regarding the law accepted by the one Jewish people, how much more truly may it be said concerning the law of nature which all mankind has received, "If justice is derived from [human] nature, then Christ died in vain." But if he did not die in vain, then human nature can in no way be justified and redeemed from the most righteous wrath of God, that is from punishment, unless through faith and the sacrament of the blood of Christ.

3.(3) In the beginning man's nature was created without any fault and without any sin; however, this human nature in which we are all born from Adam now requires a physician, because it is not healthy. Indeed, all the good qualities which it has in its organization, life, senses, and understanding, it possesses from the most high God, its creator and shaper. On the other hand, the defect which darkens and weakens all those natural goods, so that there is a need for illumination and healing, is not derived from its blameless maker but from that original sin that was committed through free will. Consequently, that criminal nature draws upon itself the most righteous punishment. For, if we are now a new creation in Christ (cf. 1 Cor. 5:17), "we were," nevertheless, "children of wrath, even as the rest. But God, who is rich in mercy, because of the great love with which he loved us, even when we were dead through our offenses, has given us life together with Christ, by whose grace you have been saved" (Eph. 2:3-5).

4.(4) This grace of Christ, then, without which neither children nor adults can be saved, is given gratuitously and not for our merits, and for this reason it is called "grace." "[They are] justified," says the Apostle, "freely by his blood" (Rom. 3:24). Consequently, those who are not liberated through grace, either because they have not yet been able to hear, or because [236] they have not wished to obey, or also because, when on account of their age they were not capable of hearing, they did not receive the bath of regeneration, which they could have received and by means of which they would have been saved, are justly condemned. For they are not without sin, either that which they contracted originally or that which they added through their own misconduct. "For all have sinned," either in Adam or in themselves, "and are deprived of the glory of God" (Rom. 3:23).

5.(5) Consequently, the whole human mass ought to be punished, and if the deserved punishment of damnation were rendered to all, beyond all doubt it would be justly rendered. This is why those who are liberated from it by grace are not called vessels of their own merits but "vessels of mercy" (Rom. 9:23). But whose mercy was it but his who sent Jesus Christ into this world to save sinners (cf. 1 Tim. 1:15), whom he foreknew, predestined, called, justified, and glorified? (cf. Rom. 8:29-30). Hence, who could be so advanced in foolish insanity as not to render ineffable thanks to the mercy of this God who liberates those whom he has wished, considering that one could not in any way reproach the justice of God in condemning all entirely?

6.(6) If we understand this according to Scripture, we are not obliged to dispute against the grace of Christ nor to try to show that human nature, in infancy, needs no physician because it is sound and, in adults, can be sufficient, if it wishes, to obtain justice for itself. These opinions indeed seem here to be expressed incisively, but in a "wisdom of speech" (1 Cor. 1:17), which makes void the cross of Christ. "For this is not wisdom descending from above" (Jas. 3:15). I do not wish to quote the words that follow, that we may not be thought to do injustice to our friends, whose most strong and quick minds we wish to see run in a straight, rather than a perverse, course.

7.(7) Therefore, however great is the zeal with which the author of this book which you have sent is inflamed against those who base a defense plea for their sins on the infirmity of human nature, with equal and more ardent zeal must we be inflamed, so that the cross of Christ may not be made void (cf. 1 Cor. 1:17). But it is made void if it is said that one can arrive at justice and eternal life in any way besides its sacrament. And that is what is done in this book—I do not wish to say by someone who knows what he is doing, so that I may not judge that he who wrote it should not even be considered a Christian, but, as I tend to believe, by someone who writes in ignorance, though admittedly with great power. I only wish

his powers were sound, and not the sort which madmen are accustomed to display.

The Nature and Effects of Sin

19.(21) Now consider—which is most central to our subject—how Pelagius tries to present human nature as if it were entirely without fault and how, against the clearest evidence of God's Scriptures, he prefers that "wisdom of speech" by which the cross of Christ is made void (cf. 1 Cor. 1:17). But certainly it will not be made void, rather this "wisdom" will be overturned. When we have shown this, perhaps the mercy of God will intervene, so that Pelagius may regret that he ever said these things. *First*, he says, *we must dispute the view which maintains that our nature has been weakened and changed through sin. I think, therefore, that before all else we must inquire what sin is. Is it some substance, or is it a name wholly lacking substance, by which is expressed neither a thing, nor an existence, nor some kind of body, but the action of doing something evil?* Then he adds, *I believe it is the latter, and if it is,* he says, *how could that which lacks substance have weakened or changed human nature?* Observe, I beseech you, how he endeavors in his ignorance to distort the most salutary words of our health-giving Scriptures: "I said, O Lord, be merciful to me; heal my soul, for I have sinned against you" (Ps. 40:5). But what is healed if nothing is wounded, nothing injured, nothing weakened and corrupted? But if there is something to be healed, whence came the injury? You hear the Psalmist confessing—what need is there for discussion? "Heal my soul," he says. Ask him how the soul, which he prays to be healed, became injured, and listen to what follows: "For I have sinned against you." Let our author question him, let him ask of him what he thinks ought to be asked and say, "Oh you who cry, 'Heal my soul, for I have sinned against you,' tell me, what is sin? Is it some substance, or is it a name lacking all substance, by which is expressed neither a thing nor an existence nor some kind of body, but merely the action of doing something evil?" The Psalmist replies, "It is just as you say: sin is not some substance, but only the act of doing something evil is expressed by this name." Then Pelagius objects, "Then why do you cry out, 'Heal my soul, for I have sinned against you'? How could that which lacks substance have injured your soul?" Then would not his respondent, exhausted by the anguish of his wound, briefly, so that he may not be diverted from prayer by the discussion, answer, "Leave me, I beg of you!

Instead discuss the issue, if you can, with him who said, 'They that are in health need not a physician, but they that are ill. . . . I am not come to call the just, but sinners' (Matt. 9:12-13), where clearly he calls the just 'healthy,' while he calls sinners 'ill.'"

43. Ambrose of Milan,
Letters 2 and 3

Ambrose (ca. 339-397) became bishop of Milan, where the Roman emperors had their western residence, in 373 or 374. He became famous as a preacher, wrote hymns that set lasting patterns for Latin hymnody, and asserted the authority of his office in several encounters with emperors. In the first of the letters below he rebukes the emperor Theodosius I for commanding the rebuilding of a synagogue at Callinicum that had been destroyed by a bishop's order. In the second he excommunicates the same emperor for a massacre of citizens at Thessalonica.

2. To the most clement prince and blessed Emperor Theodosius Augustus, Ambrose, bishop (December, 388)

I am continually beset with almost unending cares, O most blessed Emperor, but never have I felt such anxiety as now, for I see that I must be careful not to have ascribed to me anything resembling an act of sacrilege. I beg you, therefore, give ear with patience to what I say. For, if I am not worthy of a hearing from you, I am not worthy of offering sacrifice for you, I to whom you have entrusted the offering of your vows and prayers. Will you yourself not hear one whom you wish heard when he prays in your behalf? Will you not hear one who pleads in his own defense, one whom you have heard plead for others? And do you not fear for your own decision that, if you think him unworthy to be heard by you, you will make him unworthy of being heard for you?

It is not fitting for an emperor to refuse freedom of speech, or for a bishop not to say what he thinks. There is no quality in you emperors so popular and so lovable as the cherishing of liberty even in those whom you have subdued on the battlefield. In fact, it spells the difference between good and bad emperors that the good love liberty; the bad, slavery. And there is nothing in a bishop so fraught with danger before God, so base before men, as not to declare freely what he thinks. Indeed, it is written: "And I spoke of thy precepts in the presence of kings and I was not ashamed" (Ps. 118:46), and elsewhere: "Son of man, I have made you a watchman to the house of Israel," in order, it is said, "that if the just man shall turn away from his justice and shall commit iniquity, because thou hast not given him warning," that is, not told him what to guard against, "his righteousness shall not be remembered, and I will

SOURCE: Ambrose, *Letters*, tr. Sr. Mary Melchior Beyenka (New York: Fathers of the Church, 1954), 6-26. Used by permission of The Catholic University of America Press.

require his blood at thy hand. But if thou warn the righteous that he sin not, and he doth not sin, the righteous shall surely live because thou hast warned him, and thou wilt deliver thy soul" (Ezek. 3:17-21).

I would rather, O Emperor, have partnership with you in good deeds than in evil. Therefore, the bishop's silence should be disagreeable to your Clemency; his freedom, agreeable. You are involved in the peril of my silence, but you are helped by the boon of my freedom. I am not, then, intruding in bothersome fashion where I have no obligation; I am not interfering in the affairs of others; I am complying with my duty; I am obeying the commands of our God. This I do, first of all, out of love for you, in gratitude to you, from a desire to preserve your well-being. If I am not believed or am forbidden a hearing, I speak, nonetheless, for fear of offending God. If my personal peril would set you free, I should offer myself patiently, though not willingly, for you, for I would rather you were acceptable to God and glorious without peril to me. But, if the guilt of silence and untruthfulness should weigh heavily upon me and set you free, I had rather that you think me too bothersome than useless and dishonest. Indeed, it is written in the words of the holy Apostle Paul, whose teaching you cannot disprove: "Be urgent in season, out of season; reprove, entreat, rebuke with all patience and teaching" (2 Tim. 4:2).

We have one whom it is more perilous to displease, especially since even emperors are not displeased when each man performs his task, and you patiently listen to each as he makes suggestions in his own sphere; in fact, you chide him if he does not act in accordance with his rank in service. Can this seem offensive in bishops, the very thing you are willing to accept from those who are in your service, since we are saying, not what we wish, but what we are bidden to say? You know the passage: "When you will stand before kings and governors, take no thought of what you are to speak; for what you are to speak will be given you in that hour. For it is not you who are speaking, but the Spirit of your Father who speaks through you" (Matt. 10:19, 20). If I were speaking in a case involving the commonwealth (even though justice must be maintained there), I would not feel such dread if I were not given a hearing. But in a case involving God, whom will you listen to if not the bishop, who sins at a greater peril? Who will dare tell you the truth if the bishop does not?

I know that you are God-fearing, merciful, gentle, and calm, that you have the faith and fear of God in your heart, but often some things escape our notice. Some persons have zeal for God, but not according to knowledge (cf. Rom. 10:2). Care must be taken, I think, lest this condition steal upon pious souls. I know your devotion to God, your leniency toward men. I myself am indebted to you for many kind favors. Therefore, I fear the more, I am the more anxious lest you condemn me later in your judgment for the fault you did not avoid, because of my want of openness and my flattery of you. If I saw you sinning against me, I would not have to be silent, for it is written: "If thy brother sin against you, first take hold of him, then rebuke him before two or three witnesses. If he refuse to hear you, tell the Church" (Matt. 18:15-17). Shall I, then, keep silence in the cause of God? Let us then consider wherein lies my fear.

It was reported by a count of military affairs in the East that a synagogue was burned, and this at the instigation of a bishop. You gave the order for those who were involved to be punished and the synagogue rebuilt at the bishop's expense. My charge is not that you should have waited for the bishop's testimony, for bishops quell disturbances and are eager for peace unless they deeply feel some wrong against God or insult to the Church. But suppose that this particular bishop was over-impetuous in burning the synagogue, and too timid at the judgment seat; are you not afraid, Emperor, that he may comply with your pronouncement and do you not fear he may become an apostate?

Are you not afraid of what will perhaps ensue, his resisting the count in so many words? Then he [the count] will have to make him either an apostate or a martyr, either alternative very different from this era of your reign, either one equivalent to persecution if he is forced to apostatize or undergo martyrdom. You see what the outcome of this case will be. If you know that the bishop is firm, beware of making him a martyr if he becomes more firm; if you consider him inconstant, have no part in the downfall of one who is frail. He incurs a heavier obligation who compels the weak to fall.

I am supposing that in the present state of affairs the bishop will admit that he spread the fires, gathered the crowd, and brought the people together in order not to lose the chance of martyrdom and to present a strong individual instead of many weak ones. O happy falsehood, which wins acquittal for others and for himself grace! This, I ask, O Emperor, that you rather take your vengeance on me, and, if you consider this a crime, attribute it to me. Why pronounce judgment on those who are far away? You have someone at hand, you have someone who admits his guilt. I declare that I set fire to the synagogue, at least that I gave the orders, so that there would be no building in which Christ is denied. If the objection is raised that I did not burn the synagogue here, I answer that its burning was begun by God's judgment, and my work was at an end. If you want the truth, I was really remiss, for I did not think such a deed was to be punished. Why should I have done what was to be without one to punish, and without reward? These words cause me shame but they bring me grace, lest I offend the most high God.

Let no one call the bishop to task for performing his duty: that is the request I make of your Clemency. And although I have not read that the edict was revoked, let us consider it revoked. What if other more timid persons should, through fear of death, offer to repair the synagogue at their expense, or the count, finding this previously determined, should order it to be rebuilt from the funds of Christians? Will you, O Emperor, have the count an apostate, and entrust to him the insignia of victory, or give the labarum, which is sanctified by Christ's name, to one who will rebuild a synagogue which knows not Christ? Order the labarum carried into the synagogue and let us see if they [the Jews] do not resist.

Shall a place be provided out of the spoils of the Church for the disbelief of the Jews, and shall this patrimony, given to Christians by the favor of Christ, be transferred to the treasuries of unbelievers? We read that, of old, temples were reared for idols from the plunder taken from the Cimbrians and from the spoils of the enemy. The Jews will write on the front of their synagogue the inscription: "The Temple of Impiety, erected from the spoils of the Christians."

Is your motive a point of discipline, O Emperor? Which is of more importance: a demonstration of discipline or the cause of religion? The maintenance of civil law should be secondary to religion.

Have you not heard how, when Julian had ordered the Temple of Jerusalem rebuilt, those who were clearing the rubbish were burned by fire from heaven? Are you not afraid that this will also happen now? In fact, you should never have given an order such as Julian would have given.

What is your motive? Is it because a public building of some sort has been burned, or because it chanced to be the synagogue there? If you are disturbed by the burning of a very unimportant building (for what could there be in so mean a town?), do you remember, O Emperor, how many homes of prefects at Rome have been burned and no one has exacted punishment? In fact, if any of the emperors wanted to punish such a deed more severely, he only aggravated the cause of all who had suffered such a great loss. If there is going to be any justice at all, which is more fitting, that a fire on some part of the building of Callinicum be avenged, or one at Rome? Some time ago the bishop's residence at Constantinople was burned, and your Clemency's son pleaded with his father, begging you not to punish the insult done to him, the emperor's son, in the burning of the episcopal residence. Do you not think, O Emperor, that if you were to order this burning to be punished, he would again plead that it be not so? It was very suitable for your son to gain that favor from his father, for it was fitting that he first forgive what was done to him. Besides, there was a good division of grace there, since the son made the entreaty regarding his injury, and so did the father for the son's. Here is nothing for you to waive in your son's behalf; be careful, then, to derogate nothing from God.

There is really no adequate cause for all this commotion, people being punished so severely for the burning of a building, and much less so, since a synagogue has been burned, an abode of unbelief, a house of impiety, a shelter of madness under the damnation of God Himself. For we read by the mouth of Jeremias, the Lord our God speaking: "And I will do to this house in which my name is called upon, and which you trust, and to the place which I have given you and your father, as I did to Silo. And I will cast you away from before my face, as I have cast away all your brethren, the whole seed of Ephraim. Therefore do not thou pray for this people, nor show mercy for them and do not approach me for them; for I will not hear you. Seest thou not what they do in the cities of Juda?" (Jer. 7:14-17). God forbids us to make intercession for those that you think should be vindicated.

If I were pleading according to the law of the nations, I would mention how many of the Church's basilicas the Jews burned in the time of Julian, two at Damascus—one of which is scarcely yet repaired, and that at the expense of the Church, not of the synagogue—while the other basilica is still a rough heap of unsightly ruins. Basilicas were burned at Gaza, Ascalon, Beirut, in fact, almost all over that region, and no one demanded punishment. A basilica of surpassing beauty at Alexandria was burned by heathens and Jews, but the Church was not avenged, and shall the synagogue be avenged?

Shall the burning of the temple of the Valentinians also be avenged? What is it but a temple where the heathens gather? Although the heathens worship twelve gods, the Valentinians worship thirty-two Aeons, whom they call gods. I have found out that a law was passed and orders given for the punishment of some monks to whom the Valentinians denied the right of way as they sang the psalms by an ancient custom and practice, going on their way to the feast of the martyrs, the Maccabees. In anger at their effrontery they [the monks] burned their hurriedly built shrine in some country village.

How many can entertain such hope when they remember that in the time of Julian a man who had thrown down an altar and disturbed the sacrifice was sentenced by the judge and suffered martyrdom? The judge who heard the case was never considered other than a persecutor. No one ever thought him worth meeting or saluting with a kiss. And if he were not dead, I would be afraid, O Emperor, that you would punish him, although he did not escape heaven's vengeance, for he outlived his heir.

But it is said that a trial of the judge was demanded and the decision handed down that he should not have reported the deed, but punished it; and money chests which had been taken had to be restored. I shall omit any other details. The churches' basilicas were burned by the Jews and nothing was restored, nothing was demanded in return, nothing was required. Moreover, what could a synagogue in a distant town contain, when everything there is not much, is of no value, is of no account? In fine, what could those scheming Jews have lost in this act of plunder? These are but the devices of Jews wishing to bring false charges, so that by reason of their complaints an extraordinary military inquiry may be demanded and soldiers sent who will perhaps say what was said here some time before your accession, O Emperor: "How will Christ be able to help us who are sent to avenge Jews? They lost their own army, they wish to destroy ours."

Furthermore, into what false charges will they not break forth, when they even falsely accused Christ with their false witnesses? Into what false charges will men not break forth when they were liars even in matters divine? Whom will they not name as the instigators of the sedition? Whom will they not attack, even though they know them not, just so that they may see countless Christians in chains, see the necks of faithful people bowed in captivity, that the servants of God may go into dark hiding places, be struck with axes, given to the flames, and delivered to the mines, so that their sufferings may not pass hurriedly?

Will you grant the Jews this triumph over God's Church? this trophy over Christ's people? these joys, O Emperor, to unbelievers? this festival to the synagogue? this grief to the Church? The Jewish people will put this solemnity among their feast days, and doubtless they will rank it with their triumphs over the Amorites and the Canaanites, or their deliverance from Pharaoh, the king of Egypt, or from the hand of Nabuchodonosor, the king of Babylon. They will have this solemnity marking the triumphs they have wrought over the people of Christ.

And although they refuse to be bound by the laws of Rome, thinking them outrageous, they now wish to be avenged, so to speak, by Roman laws. Where were those laws when they set fire to the domes of the sacred basilicas? If Julian did not avenge the Church, because he was an apostate, will you, O Emperor, avenge the harm done the synagogue, because you are a Christian?

And what will Christ say later to you? Do you not recall that He sent word to blessed David through Nathan the Prophet? (cf. 2 Kgs. 7:8-17). "I have chosen you, the youngest of your brethren, and have made you an emperor from a private individual. The fruits of your seed I have put upon the imperial throne. I have made barbarian nations subject to you; I have given you peace; I have brought your captive enemy into power. You had no grain to feed your army; I threw open the gates to you; I opened the granaries to you by the hand of the enemies themselves. Your enemy prepared provisions for themselves and gave them to you. I troubled the counsels of your enemy so that he laid himself bare. I so fettered the usurper of the Empire and bound his mind that while he still had a chance to flee, as though afraid that one of his men should elude you, he shut himself in with them all. His officer and forces on the other element, whom I had routed earlier, so that they would not join battle against you, I brought together again to complete your victory. Your army gathered from many unruly nations I bade keep faith and peace and concord, as if of one nation. And when there was great danger that the perfidious plans of the barbarians would penetrate the Alps, in order that you might conquer and suffer no loss, I brought you victory within the very ramparts of the Alps. I, then, caused you to triumph over your enemy, and are you giving my enemies a triumph over my people?"

Was not Maximus undone because, when he heard that the synagogue at Rome had been burned, before the set time for his expedition, he sent an edict to Rome, as if he were the champion of public order? On this account the Christian people said: "No good is in store for him! The king has turned Jew, we have heard he is a defender of those whom Christ soon made trial of, He who died for sinners" (Rom. 5:6). If this was said of his mere words, what will be said of your actual punishment? He was soon conquered by the Franks, by the Saxon nation, in Sicily, at Siscia, at Pettau; in fact, everywhere. What has the believer in common with this unbeliever? Marks of his baseness should die with the base one. The victor should not imitate, but condemn his injury of the vanquished for his offenses.

I have recounted these details for you, not through ingratitude, but I have enumerated them as rightly due to you, so that by heeding these warnings you, who have been given more, will love the more. When Simon answered in these words, the Lord Jesus said: "Thou hast judged rightly," and turning at once to the woman anointing His feet, setting forth an example for the Church, He said to Simon: "Wherefore I say to you, her sins, many as they are, shall be forgiven her, because she has loved much. But he to whom little is forgiven, loves little" (Luke 7:43, 47). This is the woman who entered the house of the Pharisee and cast off the Jew, but gained Christ, for the Church shut out the synagogue. Why is trial again being made within the household of Christ? Is it that the synagogue may shut out the Church from the bosom of faith, from the house of Christ?

These matters, O Emperor, I have gathered together in this address out of love and attachment to you. I am under obligation for your kindnesses at my requests when you released many from exile, from prisons, and from the extreme penalty of death. I am bound to prefer hurting your feelings for the sake of your welfare (for no one has greater confidence than one who loves from the heart, and certainly no one should harm one whose interests he has at heart); and I should not fear to lose in one moment the favor which other bishops and I have enjoyed for so many years. Yet it is not the loss of that favor that I would avert, but the peril to salvation.

How important it is for you, O Emperor, not to feel bound to investigate or punish a matter which no one up to now has investigated or punished! It is a serious matter to jeopardize your faith in behalf of the Jews. When Gideon had slain the sacred calf, the heathens said: "Let the gods themselves avenge the injury done to them" (Judg. 5:32). Whose task is it to avenge the synagogue? Christ whom they slew, whom they denied? Or will God the Father avenge those who did not accept the Father, since they did not accept the Son? Whose task is it to avenge the heresy of the Valentinians? How can your Piety avenge them when it has given orders for them to be denied entrance and has denied them the right of assembly? If I give you the example of Josias as a king approved by God, will you condemn in them what was approved in him? (cf. 2 Chron. 22:1, 2).

Yet, if you have little faith in me, bid those bishops assemble whom you do esteem. Discuss with them, O Emperor, what ought to be done without injury to the faith. If you consult your officers on money matters, how much fairer is it to consult the Lord's priests on a religious matter!

Let your Clemency consider how many persons plot and spy on the Church. If they find a slight crack, they drive in an arrow. I speak in the manner of men, but God is more feared than men, for He is rightly preferred even to emperors. If someone considers it proper to show deference to a friend, or parents or relatives, I think it rightly should be shown to God and that He should be preferred to all. Consult your best interests, O Emperor, or allow me to consult mine.

What shall be my excuse later if it is found out that by authority emanating from here some Christians were slain by the sword or clubs or leaden balls? How will I justify such a deed? How will I make excuse to those bishops who sorely lament the fact that priests or other ministers of the Church who have performed their office for thirty years and more are dragged away from their sacred tasks and assigned to curial offices? If men who war for you are kept for a set time of service, how much more ought you to be considerate of those who war for God? How, I say, shall I justify this before bishops who complain about the clergy and write that the churches are being ruined by the serious attacks being made on them?

For this reason, I wanted this to come to the notice of your Clemency. You will, when it pleases you, condescend to consult and temper your wishes; but exclude and put an end to that which troubles me, and rightly so. Do yourself what you ordered to be done, even if he [the count] is not going to do it. I would rather that you be merciful than that he fail to do what he was ordered.

In return for those whom you now have, you ought to cultivate and win the Lord's mercy for the Roman Empire, for you have more for them than you hoped for yourself. Let their favor, their well-being, appeal to you in these words of mine. I fear that you will entrust your cause to another's will. You still have everything in its original state. In this I pledge myself to our God for you: Have no scruple over your oath. Can that displease God which is corrected for His honor? Alter nothing in that letter, whether it was sent or not. Order another to be written, which will be filled with faith, with piety. You can still correct yourself; I cannot hide the truth.

You forgave the people of Antioch the injury they offered you; you recalled your enemy's daughters and gave them to a relative to rear, and from your own treasury you sent your enemy's mother a pension. This great faith and piety toward God will be blackened by the present deed. I beg you, after sparing enemies in arms and saving personal enemies, do not presume to punish Christians with such intensity.

Now, O Emperor, I beg you not to hear me with contempt, for I fear for you and for myself, as says the holy man: "Wherefore was I born to see the ruin of my people" (1 Macc. 2:7), that I should commit an offense against God? Indeed, I have done what I could do honorably, that you might hear me in the palace rather than make it necessary to hear me in the Church.

3. *To the most august Emperor Theodosius, Ambrose, bishop*

Sweet to me is the recollection of your friendship in the past, and I recall the favor of benefits which you have bestowed with supreme favor upon others at my frequent requests. Hence, you may infer that I could not have avoided meeting you through any feeling of ingratitude, for I had always heretofore ardently desired your coming. I shall briefly set forth the reason for acting as I did.

I saw that I alone of your court had been deprived of the natural right of a hearing, so that I was also shorn of the privilege of speaking. You were disturbed several times because certain decisions in your consistory came to my knowledge. I, therefore, am without a share in the common privilege, although the Lord Jesus says: "Nothing is hidden that will not be made manifest" (Luke 8:17). As far as I could, then, I reverently complied with the will of the emperor, and took heed that you yourself should have no cause for displeasure for I managed to have none of the imperial decrees brought to my knowledge. And if I am ever present, either I shall not hear out of fear of all giving me a reputation for conniving, or I shall hear in such a way that, though my ears are open, my voice is stifled so that I cannot utter what I have heard, lest I do injury to those who have incurred the suspicion of treachery.

What, therefore, could I do? Not hear? I could not stop my ears with the wax of which old fables [tell]. Should I disclose what I heard? But I had to be on my guard in what I said for fear of your orders, lest a bloody deed be committed. Should I keep silence? Then would my conscience be bound, my voice snatched from me—most wretched of all conditions. And where would be the significance of the saying that if a bishop declare not to the wicked, the wicked shall die in his iniquity, and the bishop shall be guilty of punishment because he has not warned the wicked? (Ezek. 3:19, 20).

Understand this, august Emperor! I cannot deny that you are zealous for the faith; I do not disavow that you have a fear of God—but you have a natural vehemence which you quickly change to pity when one endeavors to soothe it. When one stirs it up, you so excite it that you can hardly check it. If only no one would enkindle it, if no one would arouse it! This I gladly commend to you: Restrain yourself, and conquer by love of duty your natural impetuosity.

This vehemence I have preferred to commend privately to your own considerations rather than to rouse it publicly perchance by any action of mine. I preferred to fail somewhat in my duty rather than in submission, that others should look for priestly authority in me instead of your failing to find reverence in me, who am most devoted. The result would be that, though you restrained your vehemence, your ability to get counsel might be unimpaired. I proffered the excuse of bodily illness, truly severe, and only to be eased by men

being milder. Yet I would have preferred to die rather than not await your arrival in two or three days. But that was not what I did.

The affair which took place in the city of Thessalonica and with no precedent within memory, that which I could not prevent from taking place, which I had declared would be most atrocious when I entered pleas against it so many times, and which you yourself, by revoking it too late, manifestly considered to have been very serious, this when done I could not extenuate. It was first heard of when the synod had met on the arrival of Gallican bishops. No one failed to lament, no one took it lightly. Your being in fellowship with Ambrose was not an excuse for your deed; blame for what had been done would have been heaped upon me even more had no one said there must needs be a reconciliation with our God.

Are you ashamed, O Emperor, to do what King David the Prophet did, the forefather of the family of Christ according to the flesh? He was told that a rich man who had many flocks had seized and killed a poor man's one ram on the arrival of a guest, and recognizing that he himself was being condemned in this tale, for he had himself done so, he said: "I have sinned against the Lord" (2 Kgs. 12:13). Do not be impatient, O Emperor, if it is said to you: "You have done what was declared to King David by the prophet." For if you listen carefully to this and say: "I have sinned against the Lord," if you repeat the words of the royal Prophet: "Come, let us adore and fall down before him, and weep before our Lord who made us" (Ps. 94:6), it will be said also to you: "Since you repent, the Lord forgives you your sin and you shall not die" (2 Kgs. 12:13).

Again, when David had ordered the people to be numbered, he was smitten in heart and said to the Lord: "I have sinned very much in the command I have made, and now, O Lord, take away the iniquity of thy servant, because I have sinned exceedingly." And the Prophet Nathan was sent again to him to offer him the choice of three things, that he might select what he chose: a famine in the land for three years, flight from the face of his enemies for three months, or pestilence in the land for three days. And David answered: "These three things are a great strait to me, yet I shall fall into the hand of the Lord since his mercies are exceedingly great, and I shall not fall into the hands of men" (2 Kgs. 24:10, 14). His fault was that he desired to know the number of all the people who were with him, and the knowledge of this he should have left to God alone.

And it is said that when the pestilence came upon the people on the first day at dinner time, when David saw the angel striking the people, he said: "I have sinned, I, the shepherd, have done evil and this flock, what has it done? Let your hand be upon me, and upon my father's house" (2 Kgs. 24:17). So the Lord repented and He bade the angel to spare the people, but David to offer sacrifice, for sacrifices were then offered for sin, but now they are sacrifices of penance. Thus, by his humility he became more acceptable to God, for it is not strange that man sins, but it is reprehensible if he does not acknowledge that he has erred and humble himself before God.

Holy Job, also powerful in this world, says: "I have not hid my sin, but declared it before all the people" (Job 31:34 LXX). To fierce King Saul his own son Jonathan said: "Sin not against thy servant David," and "Why wilt thou sin against innocent blood by killing David, who is without fault?" (1 Kgs. 19:4, 5). Although he was a king, he sinned if he killed the innocent. Finally, even David, when he was in possession of his kingdom and had heard that an innocent man named Abner was slain by Joab, the leader of his army, said: "I and my kingdom are innocent now and forever of the blood of Abner the son of Ner" (2 Kgs. 3:28), and he fasted in sorrow.

These things I have written not to disconcert you but that the examples of kings may stir you to remove this sin from your kingdom, for you will remove it by humbling your soul before God. You are a man, you have met temptation—conquer it. Sin is not removed except by tears and penance. No angel or archangel can remove it; it is God Himself who alone can say: "I am with you" (Matt. 28:20); if we have sinned, He does not forgive us unless we do penance.

I urge, I ask, I beg, I warn, for my grief is that you, who were a model of unheard-of piety, who had reached the apex of clemency, who would not allow the guilty to be in peril, are not now mourning that so many guiltless have perished. Although

you waged battles most successfully, and were praiseworthy also in other respects, the apex of your deeds was always your piety. The Devil envied you this, your most outstanding possession. Conquer him while you still have the means of doing so. Do not add another sin to your sin nor follow a course of action which has injured many followers.

I among all other men, a debtor to your Piety, to whom I cannot be ungrateful, this piety which I discover in many emperors and match in only one, I, I say, have no charge of arrogance against you, but I do have one of fear. I dare not offer the Holy Sacrifice if you intend to be present. Can that which is not allowable, after the blood of one man is shed, be allowable when many persons' blood was shed? I think not.

Lastly, I am writing with my own hand what you alone may read. Thus, may the Lord free me from all anxieties, for I have learned very definitely what I may not do, not from man nor through man. In my anxiety, on the very night that I was preparing to set forth you appeared [in my dreams] to have come to the church and I was not allowed to offer the Holy Sacrifice. I say nothing of the other things I could have avoided, but bore for love of you, as I believe. May the Lord make all things pass tranquilly. Our God admonishes us in many ways, by heavenly signs, by the warnings of the Prophets, and He wills that we understand even by the visions of sinners. So we will ask Him to remove these disturbances, to preserve peace for you who are rulers, that the faith and peace of the Church continue, for it avails much if her emperors be pious Christians.

You certainly wish to be approved by God. "There is a time for everything" (Eccles. 3:1), as it is written: "It is time to act, O Lord" (Ps. 118:126), and "The time of mercy, O God" (Ps. 68:14). You will make your offering then when you receive permission to sacrifice, when your offering has been acceptable to God. Would it not delight me to have the emperor's favor, so that I could act in accord with your will if the case allowed? Prayer by itself is sacrifice, it brings pardon when the other [sacrifice] causes offense, for the one bespeaks humility, the other contempt. We have God's word that He prefers the doing of His command to the offering of sacrifice. God proclaims this,

Moses declares it to the people, Paul preaches it to the Gentiles. Do at the right moment what you know is of greater value. "I desire mercy," it says, "and not sacrifice" (Matt. 9:13). Are they not more Christian who condemn their sin than they who hope to defend it, for "The just is first accuser of himself" (Prov. 18:17 LXX). One who accuses himself when he has sinned is just, not one who praises himself.

I wish, O Emperor, that before this you had relied upon me rather than on your own habits. Since I realize that you are quick to pardon, quick to retract, as you have so often done, you have now been prevented and I have not shirked what I had no need to fear. But, thanks be to the Lord who wills to chastise His servants lest He lose them. This I have in common with the Prophets and you will have it in common with the saints.

Shall I not value the father of Gratian more than my eyes? Your other blessed offspring deserves pardon. I conferred a sweet name formerly on those to whom I bore a mutual love. I love, I cherish, I attend you with prayers. If you trust me, follow me; if, I say, you trust me, acknowledge what I say; if you do not trust me, pardon what I do in esteeming God more than you. May you, the most blessed and eminent Emperor Augustus, together with your holy offspring, enjoy perpetual peace.

44. Patrick, *Confession*

Patrick, who was probably a bishop, devoted himself to evangelistic and pastoral work in Ireland in the fifth century. He wrote this Confession *late in his career, apparently in response to an attack on his character. Though the text is obscure at points, we learn that Patrick was abducted at age sixteen from his home in Britain to slavery in Ireland where he experienced conversion (though already nominally Christian) and, after returning home, received a revelation to go again to Ireland "for the salvation of others." The italicized passages below show the extent of Patrick's scriptural allusions; for readability, we identify sources only when he quotes explicitly.*

I am Patrick, a sinner, most unlearned, the least of all the faithful, and utterly despised by many. My father was Calpornius, a deacon, son of Potitus, a priest, of the village Bannavem Taburniae; he had a country seat nearby, and there I was taken captive.

I was then about sixteen years of age. I did not know the true God. I was taken into captivity to Ireland with many thousands of people—and deservedly so, because we turned away from God, and did not keep His commandments, and did not obey our priests, who used to remind us of our salvation. And the Lord *brought over us the wrath of His anger and scattered us among many nations*, even *unto the utmost part of the earth*, where now my littleness is placed among strangers.

2. And there *the Lord opened the sense of my unbelief* that I might at last remember my sins and *be converted with all my heart to the Lord my God*, who *had regard for my abjection*, and mercy on my youth and ignorance, and watched over me before I knew Him, and before I was able to distinguish between good and evil, and guarded me, and comforted me as would a father his son.

SOURCE: *The Works of St. Patrick*, ed. and tr. Ludwig Bieler (Westminster, Md.: Newman Press, 1953; London: Longmans, Green and Co., 1953), 21-40. Copyright © by Rev. Johannes Quasten and Rev. Joseph C. Plumpe. Used by permission of Paulist Press, Inc., New York/Mahwah, N.J.

3. Hence I cannot be silent—*nor, indeed, is it expedient*—about the great benefits and the great grace which the Lord has deigned to bestow upon me *in the land of my captivity*; for this we can give to God in return after having been chastened by Him, *to exalt and praise His wonders* before *every nation that is* anywhere *under the heaven*.

4. Because there is no other God, nor ever was, nor will be, than God the Father unbegotten, without beginning, from whom is all beginning, the Lord of the universe, as we have been taught; and His son Jesus Christ, whom we declare to have always been with the Father, spiritually and ineffably begotten by the Father before the beginning of the world, before all beginning; and by Him are made all things visible and invisible. He was made man, and, having defeated death, was received into heaven by the Father; *and He hath given Him all power over all names in heaven, on earth, and under the earth, and every tongue shall confess to Him that Jesus Christ is Lord and God*, in whom we believe, and whose advent we expect soon to be, *judge of the living and of the dead*, who will render to every man according to his deeds; and *He has poured forth upon us abundantly the Holy Spirit, the gift* and *pledge* of immortality, who makes those who believe and obey *sons of God* and *joint heirs with Christ*; and Him do we confess and adore, one God in the Trinity of the Holy Name.

5. For He Himself has said through the Prophet: *Call upon me in the day of thy trouble, and I will deliver you, and thou shall glorify me* (Ps. 49:15). And again He says: *It is honorable to reveal and confess the works of God* (Tob. 12:7).

6. Although I am imperfect in many things, I nevertheless wish that my brethren and kinsmen should know what sort of person I am, so that they may understand my heart's desire.

7. I know well *the testimony of my Lord*, who in the Psalm declares: *Thou wilt destroy them that speak a lie* (Ps. 5:7). And again He says: *The mouth that belieth killeth the soul* (Wis. 1:11). And the same Lord says in the Gospel: *Every idle word that men shall speak, they shall render an account for it on the day of judgment* (Matt. 12:36).

8. And so I should dread exceedingly, *with fear and trembling*, this sentence on that day when no one will be able to escape or hide, but we all, with-out exception, shall have *to give an account* even of our smallest sins *before the judgment seat of* the Lord *Christ*.

9. For this reason I long had in mind to write, but hesitated until now; I was afraid of exposing myself to the talk of men, because I have not studied like the others, who thoroughly imbibed law and Sacred Scripture, and never had to change from the language of their childhood days, but were able to make it still more perfect. In our case, what I had to say had to be translated into a tongue foreign to me, as can be easily proved from the savor of my writing, which betrays how little instruction and training I have had in the art of words; for, so says Scripture, *by the tongue will be discovered the wise man, and understanding, and knowledge, and the teaching of truth* (Ecclus. 4:29).

10. But of what help is an excuse, however true, especially if combined with presumption, since now, in my old age, I strive for something that I did not acquire in youth? It was my sins that prevented me from fixing in my mind what before I had barely read through. But who believes me, though I should repeat what I started out with?

As a youth, nay, almost as a boy not able to speak, I was taken captive, before I knew what to pursue and what to avoid. Hence today I blush and fear exceedingly to reveal my lack of education; for I am unable to tell my story to those versed in the art of concise writing—in such a way, I mean, as my spirit and mind long to do, and so that the sense of my words expresses what I feel.

11. But if indeed it had been given to me as it was given to others, then I would not be silent *because of my desire of thanksgiving*; and if perhaps some people think me arrogant for doing so in spite of my lack of knowledge and my slow tongue, it is, after all, written: *The stammering tongues shall quickly learn to speak peace* (Isa. 32:4 LXX).

How much more should we earnestly strive to do this, we, who are, so Scripture says, *a letter of Christ for salvation unto the utmost part of the earth*, and, though not an eloquent one, yet . . . *written in your hearts, not with ink, but with the spirit of the living God!* (cf. 2 Cor. 3:2, 3). And again the Spirit witnesses that *even rusticity was created by the Highest* (Ecclus. 7:16).

12. Whence I, once rustic, exiled, unlearned, who does not know how to provide for the future, this at least I know most certainly that before I was humiliated I was like a stone lying in the deep mire; and He that is mighty came and in His mercy lifted me up, and raised me aloft, and placed me on the top of the wall. And therefore I ought to cry out aloud and so also render something to the Lord for His great benefits here and in eternity—benefits which the mind of men is unable to appraise.

13. Wherefore, then, be astonished, *ye great and little that fear God*, and you men of letters on your estates, listen and pore over this. Who was it that roused up me, the fool that I am, from the midst of those who in the eyes of men are wise, and expert in law, and powerful in word and in everything? And He inspired me—me, the outcast of this world—before others, to be the man (if only I could!) who, *with fear and reverence and without blame*, should faithfully serve the people to whom the love of Christ conveyed and gave me for the duration of my life, if I should be worthy; yes indeed, to serve them humbly and sincerely.

14. In the light, therefore, of our faith in the Trinity I must make this choice, regardless of danger I must make known the gift of God and everlasting consolation, without fear and frankly I must spread everywhere the name of God so that after my decease I may leave a bequest to my brethren and sons whom I have baptized in the Lord—so many thousands of people.

15. And I was not worthy, nor was I such that the Lord should grant this to His servant; that after my misfortunes and so great difficulties, after my captivity, after the lapse of so many years, He should give me so great a grace in behalf of that nation—a thing which once, in my youth, I never expected nor thought of.

16. But after I came to Ireland—every day I had to tend sheep, and many times a day I prayed—the love of God and His fear came to me more and more, and my faith was strengthened. And my spirit was moved so that in a single day I would say as many as a hundred prayers, and almost as many in the night, and this even when I was staying in the woods and on the mountain; and I used to get up for prayer before daylight, through snow, through frost, through rain, and I felt no harm, and there was no sloth in me—as I now see, because the spirit within me was then fervent.

17. And there one night I heard in my sleep a voice saying to me: "It is well that you fast, soon you will go to your own country." And again, after a short while, I heard a voice saying to me: "See, your ship is ready." And it was not near, but at a distance of perhaps two hundred miles, and I had never been there, nor did I know a living soul there; and then I took to flight, and I left the man with whom I had stayed for six years. And I went in the strength of God who directed my way to my good, and I feared nothing until I came to that ship.

18. And the day that I arrived the ship was set afloat, and I said that I was able to pay for my passage with them. But the captain was not pleased, and with indignation he answered harshly: "It is of no use for you to ask us to go along with us." And when I heard this, I left them in order to return to the hut where I was staying. And as I went, I began to pray; and before I had ended my prayer, I heard one of them shouting behind me, "Come, hurry, we shall take you on in good faith; make friends with us in whatever way you like." And so on that day I refused to suck their breasts for fear of God, but rather hoped they would come to the faith of Jesus Christ, because they were pagans. And thus I had my way with them, and we set sail at once.

19. And after three days we reached land, and for twenty-eight days we traveled through deserted country. And they lacked food, and hunger overcame them; and the next day the captain said to me: "Tell me, Christian: you say that your God is great and all-powerful; why, then, do you not pray for us? As you can see, we are suffering from hunger; it is unlikely indeed that we shall ever see a human being again."

I said to them, full of confidence: "*Be truly converted with all your heart to the Lord my God*, because nothing is impossible for Him, that this day He may send you food on your way until you be satisfied; for He has abundance everywhere." And, with the help of God, so it came to pass: suddenly a herd of pigs appeared on the road before our eyes, and they killed many of them; and there they stopped for two nights and fully recovered their strength, and their hounds received their fill, for many of them had grown weak and were half-dead along the way.

And from that day they had plenty of food. They also found wild honey, and offered some of it to me, and one of them said: "This we offer in sacrifice." Thanks be to God, I tasted none of it.

20. That same night, when I was asleep, Satan assailed me violently, a thing I shall remember *as long as I shall be in this body*. And he fell upon me like a huge rock, and I could not stir a limb. But whence came it into my mind, ignorant as I am, to call upon Helias? And meanwhile I saw the sun rise in the sky, and while I was shouting "Helias! Helias!" with all my might, suddenly the splendor of that sun fell on me and immediately freed me of all misery. And I believe that I was sustained by Christ my Lord, and that His Spirit was even then crying out in my behalf, and I hope it will be so *on the day of my tribulation*, as is written in the Gospel: *On that day*, the Lord declares, *it is not you that speak, but the Spirit of your Father that speaketh in you* (Matt. 10:19, 20).

21. And once again, after many years, I fell into captivity. On that first night I stayed with them. I heard a divine message saying to me: "Two months will you be with them." And so it came to pass: on the sixtieth night thereafter *the Lord delivered me out of their hands*.

22. Also on our way God gave us food and fire and dry weather every day, until, on the tenth day, we met people. As I said above, we traveled twenty-eight days through deserted country, and the night that we met people we had no food left.

23. And again after a few years I was in Britain with my people, who received me as their son, and sincerely besought me that now at last, having suffered so many hardships, I should not leave them and go elsewhere.

And there I saw in the night the vision of a man, whose name was Victoricus, coming as it were from Ireland, with countless letters. And he gave me one of them, and I read the opening words of the letter, which were, "The voice of the Irish"; and as I read the beginning of the letter I thought that at the same moment I heard their voice—they were those beside the Wood of Voclut, which is near the Western Sea—and thus did they cry out *as with one mouth*: "We ask you, boy, come and walk among us once more."

And I was quite broken in heart, and could read no further, and so I woke up. Thanks be to God, after many years the Lord gave to them according to their cry.

24. And another night—whether within me, or beside me, *I know not, God knoweth*—they called me most unmistakably with words which I heard but could not understand, except that at the end of the prayer He spoke thus: "*He that has laid down His life for you*, it is He that speaketh in you"; and so I awoke full of joy.

25. And again I saw Him praying in me, and I was as it were within my body, and I heard Him above me, that is, over *the inward man*, and there He prayed mightily with groanings. And all the time I was astonished, and wondered, and thought with myself who it could be that prayed in me. But at the end of the prayer He spoke, saying that He was the Spirit; and so I woke up, and remembered the Apostle saying: *The Spirit helpeth the infirmities of our prayer. For we know not what we should pray for as we ought; but the Spirit Himself asketh for us with unspeakable groanings, which cannot be expressed in words*; and again: *The Lord our advocate asketh for us* (cf. 1 John 2:1; Rom. 8:26).

26. And when I was attacked by a number of my seniors who came forth and brought up my sins against my laborious episcopate, on that day indeed was I struck so that I might have fallen now and for eternity; but the Lord graciously spared the stranger and sojourner for His name and came mightily to my help in this affliction. Verily, not slight was the shame and blame that fell upon me! I ask God that *it may not be reckoned to them as sin*.

27. As cause for proceeding against me they found—after thirty years!—a confession I had made before I was a deacon. In the anxiety of my troubled mind I confided to my dearest friend what I had done in my boyhood one day, nay, in one hour, because I was not yet strong. *I know not, God knoweth*—whether I was then fifteen years old; and I did not believe in the living God, nor did I so from my childhood, but lived in death and unbelief until I was severely chastised and really humiliated, by hunger and nakedness, and that daily.

28. On the other hand, I did not go to Ireland of my own accord, not until I had nearly perished; but this was rather for my good, for thus was I

purged by the Lord; and He made me fit so that I might be now what was once far from me—that I should care and labor for the salvation of others, whereas then I did not even care about myself.

29. On that day, then, when I was rejected by those referred to and mentioned above, in that night I saw a vision of the night. There was a writing without honor against my face, and at the same time I heard God's voice saying to me: "We have seen with displeasure the face of Deisignatus" (thus revealing his name). He did not say, "Thou hast seen," but, "We have seen," as if He included Himself, as He sayeth: *He who toucheth you toucheth as it were the apple of my eye* (Zech. 2:8).

30. Therefore *I give Him thanks who hath strengthened me* in everything, as He did not frustrate the journey upon which I had decided, and the work which I had learned from Christ my Lord; but I rather felt after this no little strength, and my trust was proved right before God and men.

31. And so I say boldly, my conscience does not blame me now or in the future: God is my witness that I have not lied in the account which I have given you.

32. But the more am I sorry for my dearest friend that we had to hear what he said. To him I had confided my very soul! And I was told by some of the brethren before that defense—at which I was not present, nor was I in Britain, nor was it suggested by me—that he would stand up for me in my absence. He had even said to me in person: "Look, you should be raised to the rank of bishop!"—of which I was not worthy. But whence did it come to him afterwards that he let me down before all, good and evil, and publicly, in a matter in which he had favored me before spontaneously and gladly—and not he alone, but the Lord, who *is greater than all*?

33 . Enough of this. I must not, however, hide God's gift which He bestowed upon me *in the land of my captivity*; because then I earnestly sought Him, and there I found Him, and He saved me from all evil *because*—so I believe—*of His Spirit that dwelleth* in me. Again, boldly said. But God knows it, had this been said to me by a man, I had perhaps remained silent for the love of Christ.

34. Hence, then, I give unwearied thanks to God, who kept me faithful *in the day of my tempta-* *tion*, so that today I can confidently offer Him my soul as a living sacrifice—to Christ my Lord, who *saved me out of all my troubles*. Thus I can say: "*Who am I, O Lord*, and to what hast Thou called me, Thou who didst assist me with such divine power that to-day I constantly *exalt* and magnify Thy name *among the heathens* wherever I may be, and not only in good days but also in tribulations? So indeed I must accept with equanimity whatever befalls me, be it good or evil, and always give thanks to God, who taught me to trust in Him always without hesitation, and who must have heard my prayer so that I, however ignorant I was, *in the last days* dared to undertake such a holy and wonderful work—thus imitating somehow those who, as the Lord once foretold, would preach His Gospel *for a testimony to all nations* before *the end of the world*. So we have seen it, and so it has been fulfilled: indeed, we are witnesses that the Gospel has been preached unto those parts beyond which there lives nobody.

35. Now, it would be tedious to give a detailed account of all my labors or even a part of them. Let me tell you briefly how the merciful God often freed me from slavery and from twelve dangers in which my life was at stake—not to mention numerous plots, which I cannot express in words; for I do not want to bore my readers. But God is my witness, who knows all things even before they come to pass, as He used to forewarn even me, poor wretch that I am, of many things by a divine message.

36. *How came I by this wisdom*, which was not in me, who neither *knew the number of my days* nor knew what God was? Whence was given to me afterwards the gift so great, so salutary—to know God and to love Him, although at the price of leaving my country and my parents?

37. And many gifts were offered to me in sorrow and tears, and I offended the donors, much against the wishes of some of my seniors; but, guided by God, in no way did I agree with them or acquiesce. It was not grace of my own, but God, who is strong in me and resists them all—as He had done when I came to the people of Ireland to preach the Gospel, and to suffer insult from the unbelievers, *hearing the reproach of my going abroad*; and many persecutions even unto bonds, and to give my free birth for the benefit of others;

and, should I be worthy, I am prepared to give even my life without hesitation and most gladly for His name, and it is there that I wish to spend it until I die, if the Lord would grant it to me.

38. For I am very much God's debtor, who gave me such great grace that many people were reborn in God through me and afterwards confirmed, and that clerics were ordained for them everywhere, for a people just coming to the faith, whom the Lord took from the utmost parts of the earth, as He once had promised through His prophets: *To You the gentiles shall come from the ends of the earth and shall say: "How false are the idols that our fathers got for themselves, and there is no profit in them"*; and again: *I have set You as a light among the gentiles, that Thou mayest be for salvation unto the utmost part of the earth* (Jer. 16:19 LXX; Acts 13:47).

39. And there I wish to wait for His promise who surely never deceives, as He promises in the Gospel: *They shall come from the east and the west, and shall sit down with Abraham and Isaac and Jacob*—as we believe the faithful will come from all the world.

40. For that reason, therefore, we ought to fish well and diligently, as the Lord exhorts in advance and teaches, saying: *Come ye after me, and I will make you to be fishers of men* (Matt. 4:19; Mark 1:17). And again He says through the prophets: *Behold, I send many fishers and hunters, saith God*, and so on (cf. Jer. 16:16). Hence it was most necessary to spread our nets so that a great multitude and throng might be caught for God, and that there be clerics everywhere to baptize and exhort a people in need and want, as the Lord in the Gospel states, exhorts, and teaches, saying: *Going therefore now, teach ye all nations, baptizing them in the name of the Father, and the Son, and the Holy Spirit, teaching them to observe all things whatsoever I have commanded you: and behold I am with you all days even to the consummation of the world* (Matt. 28:19-20). And again He says: *Go ye therefore into the whole world, and preach the Gospel to every creature. He that believeth and is baptized shall be saved; but he that believeth not shall be condemned* (Mark 16:15). And again: *This Gospel of the kingdom shall be preached in the whole world for a testimony to all nations, and then shall come the end* (Matt. 24:14). And so too the Lord announces

through the prophet, and says: *And it shall come to pass, in the last days, saith the Lord, I will pour out of my Spirit upon all flesh; and your sons and your daughters shall prophesy, and your young men shall see visions, and your old men shall dream dreams. And upon my servants indeed, and upon my handmaids will I pour out in those days of my Spirit, and they shall prophesy* (Joel 2:28, 29; Acts 2:17-18). And *in Osee He saith: "I will call that which was not my people, my people; . . . and her that had not obtained mercy, one that hath obtained mercy. And it shall be in the place where it was said: 'You are not my people,' there they shall be called the sons of the living God"* (Hos. 1:10; Rom. 9:25, 26).

41. Hence, how did it come to pass in Ireland that those who never had a knowledge of God, but until now always worshipped idols and things impure, have now been made a people of the Lord, and are called sons of God, that the sons and daughters of the kings of the Irish are seen to be monks and virgins of Christ?

42. Among others, a blessed Irishwoman of noble birth, beautiful, full-grown, whom I had baptized, came to us after some days for a particular reason: she told us that she had received a message from a messenger of God, and he admonished her to be a virgin of Christ and draw near to God. Thanks be to God, on the sixth day after this she most laudably and eagerly chose what all virgins of Christ do. Not that their fathers agree with them; no—they often even suffer persecution and undeserved reproaches from their parents; and yet their number is ever increasing. How many have been reborn there so as to be of our kind, I do not know—not to mention widows and those who practice continence.

But greatest is the suffering of those women who live in slavery. All the time they have to endure terror and threats. But the Lord gave His grace to many of His maidens; for, though they are forbidden to do so, they follow Him bravely.

43. Wherefore, then, even if I wished to leave them and go to Britain—and how I would have loved to go to my country and my parents, and also to Gaul in order to visit the brethren and to see the face of the saints of my Lord! God knows it that I much desired it; but I am bound by the Spirit, who gives evidence against me if I do this,

telling me that I shall be guilty; and I am afraid of losing the labor which I have begun—nay, not I, but Christ the Lord who bade me come here and stay with them for the rest of my life, if the Lord will, and will guard me from every evil way that I may not sin before Him.

44. This, I presume, I ought to do, but I do not trust myself *as long as I am in this body of death*, for strong is he who daily strives to turn me away from the faith and the purity of true religion to which I have devoted myself to the end of my life to Christ my Lord. But the hostile flesh is ever dragging us unto death, that is, towards the forbidden satisfaction of one's desires; and I know that in part I did not lead a perfect life as did the other faithful; but I acknowledge it to my Lord, and do not blush before Him, because I lie not: from the time I came to know Him in my youth, the love of God and the fear of Him have grown in me, and up to now, thanks to the grace of God, I have kept the faith.

45. And let those who will, laugh and scorn—I shall not be silent; nor shall I hide the signs and wonders which the Lord has shown me many years before they came to pass, as He knows everything even *before the times of the world.*

46. Hence I ought unceasingly to give thanks to God who often pardoned my folly and my carelessness, and on more than one occasion spared His great wrath on me, who was chosen to be His helper and who was slow to do as was shown me and as the Spirit suggested. And the Lord had mercy on me thousands and thousands of times because He saw that I was ready, but that I did not know what to do in the circumstances. For many tried to prevent this my mission; they would even talk to each other behind my back and say: "Why does this fellow throw himself into danger among enemies who have no knowledge of God?" It was not malice, but it did not appeal to them because—and to this I own myself—of my rusticity. And I did not realize at once the grace that was then in me; now I understand that I should have done so before.

47. Now I have given a simple account to my brethren and fellow servants who have believed me because of what I said and still say in order to strengthen and confirm your faith. Would that

you, too, would strive for greater things and do better! This will be my glory, for *a wise son is the glory of his father.*

48. You know, and so does God, how I have lived among you from my youth in the true faith and in sincerity of heart. Likewise, as regards the heathen among whom I live, I have been faithful to them, and so I shall be. God knows it, I have overreached none of them, nor would I think of doing so, for the sake of God and His Church, for fear of raising persecution against them and all of us, and for fear that through me the name of the Lord be blasphemed; for it is written: *Woe to the man through whom the name of the Lord is blasphemed* (Matt. 18:7; Rom. 2:24).

49. *For although I be rude in all things*, nevertheless I have tried somehow to keep myself safe, and that, too, for my Christian brethren, and the virgins of Christ, and the pious women who of their own accord made me gifts and laid on the altar some of their ornaments; and I gave them back to them, and they were offended that I did so. But I did it for the hope of lasting success—in order to preserve myself cautiously in everything so that they might not seize upon me or the ministry of my service, under the pretext of dishonesty, and that I would not even in the smallest matter give the infidels an opportunity to defame or defile.

50. When I baptized so many thousands of people, did I perhaps expect from any of them as much as half a screpall [a small coin]? *Tell me, and I will restore it to you.* Or when the Lord ordained clerics everywhere through my unworthy person and I conferred the ministry upon them free, if I asked any of them as much as the price of my shoes, *speak against me and I will return it to you.*

51. On the contrary, I spent money for you that they might receive me; and I went to you and everywhere for your sake in many dangers, even to the farthest districts, beyond which there lived nobody and where nobody had ever come to baptize, or to ordain clergy, or to confirm the people. With the grace of the Lord, I did everything lovingly and gladly for your salvation.

52. All the while I used to give presents to the kings, besides the fees I paid to their sons who travel with me. Even so they laid hands on me and

my companions, and on that day they eagerly wished to kill me; but my time had not yet come. And everything they found with us they took away, and me they put in irons; and on the fourteenth day the Lord delivered me from their power, and our belongings were returned to us because of God and our dear friends whom we had seen before.

53. You know how much I paid to those who administered justice in all those districts to which I came frequently. I think I distributed among them not less than the price of fifteen men, so that you might enjoy me, and I might always enjoy you in God. I am not sorry for it—indeed it is not enough for me; I still spend and shall spend more. God has power to grant me afterwards *that I myself may be spent for your souls.*

54. Indeed, *I call God to witness upon my soul that I lie not*; neither, I hope, am I writing to you in order to make this an occasion of flattery or covetousness, nor because I look for honor from any of you. Sufficient is the honor that is not yet seen but is anticipated in the heart. *Faithful is He that promised; He never lieth.*

55. But I see myself exalted even in the present world beyond measure by the Lord, and I was not worthy nor such that He should grant me this. I know perfectly well, though not by my own judgment, that poverty and misfortune becomes me better than riches and pleasures. For Christ the Lord, too, was poor for our sakes; and I, unhappy wretch that I am, have no wealth even if I wished for it. Daily I expect murder, fraud, or captivity, or whatever it may be; *but I fear none of these things* because of the promises of heaven. I have cast myself into the hands of God Almighty, who rules everywhere, as the prophet says: *Cast thy thought upon God, and He shall sustain you* (Ps. 54:23).

56. So, now *I commend my soul to my faithful* God, *for whom I am an ambassador* in all my wretchedness; but God *accepteth no person*, and chose me for this office—to be, although among His least, one of His ministers.

57. Hence let me *render unto Him for all He has done to me.* But what can I say or what can I promise to my Lord, as I can do nothing that He has not given me? May He *search the hearts and reins*; for greatly and exceedingly do I wish, and

ready I was, that He should give me His chalice to drink, as He gave it also to the others who loved Him.

58. Wherefore may God never permit it to happen to me that I should lose His people which He purchased in the utmost parts of the world. I pray to God to give me perseverance and to deign that I be a faithful witness to Him to the end of my life for my God.

59. And if ever I have done any good for my God whom I love, I beg Him to grant me that I may shed my blood with those exiles and captives for His name, even though I should be denied a grave, or my body be woefully torn to pieces limb by limb by hounds or wild beasts, or the fowls of the air devour it. I am firmly convinced that if this should happen to me, I would have gained my soul together with my body, because on that day without doubt we shall rise in the brightness of the sun, that is, in the glory of Christ Jesus our Redeemer, as sons of the living God and *joint heirs with Christ, to be made conformable to His image*; for *of Him, and by Him, and in Him* we shall reign.

60. For this sun which we see rises daily for us because He commands so, but it will never reign, nor will its splendor last; what is more, those wretches who adore it will be miserably punished. Not so we, who believe in, and worship, the true sun—Christ—who will never perish, nor will he *who doeth His will*; but he *will abide forever as Christ abideth forever*; who reigns with God the Father Almighty and the Holy Spirit before time, and now, and in all eternity. Amen.

61. Behold, again and again would I set forth the words of my confession. *I testify* in truth and in joy of heart *before God* and *His holy angels* that I never had any reason except the Gospel and its promises why I should ever return to the people from whom once before I barely escaped.

62. I pray those who believe and fear God, whosoever deigns to look at or receive this writing which Patrick, a sinner, unlearned, has composed in Ireland, that no one should ever say that it was my ignorance if I did or showed forth anything however small according to God's good pleasure; but let this be your conclusion and let it so be thought, that—as is the perfect truth—it was the gift of God. This is my confession before I die.

PART THREE

600–1000 C.E.

Early Medieval Christianity in Asia

45. Apology of Patriarch Timothy of Baghdad before the Caliph Mahdi

When the Abbasid caliphate established its new Islamic capital in Baghdad (750), the patriarch of the Persian or East Syrian church (that is, the Church of the East) moved to Baghdad as well. In 780 the reforming, missionary-minded bishop Timothy became patriarch. In 781 he participated in a two-day interreligious dialogue with the Abbasid caliph, Mahdi, and later wrote an account of their interchange that circulated as an apology. In matters of Christology, some of the dyophysite (i.e., two-nature) emphases of the East Syrian church are evident in this fascinating conversation between a Muslim caliph and a Christian bishop.

The Questions and Answers of the Second Day

The next day I had an audience of his Majesty. Such audiences had constantly taken place previously, sometimes for the affairs of the State, and some other times for the love of wisdom and learning which was burning in the soul of his Majesty. He is a lovable man, and loves also learning when he finds it in other people, and on this account he directed against me the weight of his objections, whenever necessary.

After I had paid to him my usual respects as King of Kings, he began to address me and converse with me not in a harsh and haughty tone, since harshness and haughtiness are remote from his soul, but in a sweet and benevolent way.

And our King of Kings said to me: "O Catholicos, did you bring a Gospel with you, as I had asked you?"—And I replied to his exalted Majesty: "I have brought one, O our victorious and God-loving King."—And our victorious Sovereign said to me: "Who gave you this Book?"—And I replied

to him: "It is the Word of God that gave us the Gospel, O our God-loving King."—And our King said: "Was it not written by four Apostles?" And I replied to him: "It was written by four Apostles, as our King has said, but not out of their own heads, but out of what they heard and learned from the Word-God. If then the Gospel was written by the Apostles, and if the Apostles simply wrote what they heard and learned from the Word-God, the Gospel has, therefore, been given in reality by the Word-God. Similarly, the Torah was written by Moses, but since Moses heard and learned it from an angel, and the angel heard and learned it from God, we assert that the Torah was given by God and not by Moses.

"In the same way also the Muslims say that they have received the Qur'an from Muḥammad, but since Muḥammad received knowledge and writing from an angel, they, therefore, affirm that the Book that was divulged through him was not Muḥammad's or the angel's but God's. So also we Christians believe that although the Gospel was

SOURCE: A. Mingana, ed. and tr., *Woodbrooke Studies*, vol. 2 (Cambridge: Heffer, 1928), 60-73, 77-84, 87-90.

given to us by the Apostles, it was not given as from them but as from God, His Word and His Spirit. Further, the letters and official documents of your Majesty are written by the hands of scribes and clerks, but they are not said to be those of scribes, but those of your Majesty, and of the Commander of the Faithful."

And our gracious and wise King said to me: "What do you say about Muḥammad?"—And I replied to his Majesty: "Muḥammad is worthy of all praise, by all reasonable people, O my Sovereign. He walked in the path of the prophets, and trod in the track of the lovers of God. All the prophets taught the doctrine of one God and since Muḥammad taught the doctrine of the unity of God, he walked, therefore, in the path of the prophets. Further, all the prophets drove men away from bad works, and brought them nearer to good works, and since Muḥammad drove his people away from bad works and brought them nearer to the good ones, he walked, therefore, in the path of the prophets. Again, all the prophets separated men from idolatry and polytheism, and attached them to God and to His cult, and since Muḥammad separated his people from idolatry and polytheism, and attached them to the cult and the knowledge of one God, beside whom there is no other God, it is obvious that he walked in the path of the prophets. Finally Muḥammad taught about God, His Word and His Spirit, and since all the prophets had prophesied about God, His Word and His Spirit, Muḥammad walked, therefore, in the path of all the prophets.

"Who will not praise, honor and exalt the one who not only fought for God in words, but showed also his zeal for Him in the sword? As Moses did with the Children of Israel when he saw that they had fashioned a golden calf which they worshipped, and killed all of those who were worshipping it, so also Muḥammad evinced an ardent zeal towards God, and loved and honored Him more than his own soul, his people and his relatives. He praised, honored and exalted those who worshipped God with him, and promised them kingdom, praise and honor from God, both in this world and in the world to come in the Garden. But those who worshipped idols and not God he fought and opposed, and showed to them the tor-ments of hell and of the fire which is never quenched and in which all evildoers burn eter-nally.

"And what Abraham, that friend and beloved of God, did in turning his face from idols and from his kinsmen, and looking only towards one God and becoming the preacher of one God to other peoples, this also Muḥammad did. He turned his face from idols and their worshippers, whether those idols were those of his own kins-men or of strangers, and he honored and wor-shipped only one God. Because of this God honored him exceedingly and brought low before his feet two powerful kingdoms which roared in the world like a lion and made the voice of their authority heard in all the earth that is below heaven like thunder, viz.: the Kingdom of the Per-sians and that of the Romans. The former king-dom, that is to say the Kingdom of the Persians, worshipped the creatures instead of the Creator, and the latter, that is to say the Kingdom of the Romans, attributed suffering and death in the flesh to the one who cannot suffer and die in any way and through any process. He further extended the power of his authority through the Commander of the Faithful and his children from east to west, and from north to south. Who will not praise, O our victorious King, the one whom God has praised, and will not weave a crown of glory and majesty to the one whom God has glori-fied and exalted? These and similar things I and all God-lovers utter about Muḥammad, O my sover-eign."

And our King said to me: "You should, there-fore, accept the words of the Prophet."—And I replied to his gracious Majesty: "Which words of his our victorious King believes that I must accept?"—And our King said to me: "That God is one and that there is no other one besides Him."—And I replied: "This belief in one God, O my Sovereign, I have learned from the Torah, from the Prophets and from the Gospel. I stand by it and shall die in it."—And our victorious King said to me: "You believe in one God, as you said, but one in three."—And I answered his sentence: "I do not deny that I believe in one God in three, and three in one, but not in three different God-heads, however, but in the persons of God's Word and His Spirit. I believe that these three constitute one God, not in their person but in their nature. I have shown how in my previous words."

And our King asked: "How is it that these three persons whom you mention do not constitute three Gods?"—And I answered his Majesty: "Because the three of them constitute one God, O our victorious King, and the fact that He is only one God precludes the hypothesis that there are three Gods."—And our King retorted: "The fact that there are three precludes the statement that there is only one God. If there are three, how can they be one?"—And I replied: "We believe that they are three, O our Sovereign, not in Godhead, but in persons, and that they are one not in persons but in Godhead."—And our King retorted: "The fact that they are three precludes the statement that they are one, and the fact that they are one precludes the statement that they are three. This everybody will admit."—And I said to him: "The three in Him are the cause of one, and the one that of three, O our King. Those three have always been the cause of one, and that one of three."—And our King said to me: "How can one be the cause of three and three of one? What is this?"—And I answered his question: "One is the cause of three, O our King, because this number one is the cause of the number two, and the number two that of the number three. This is how one is the cause of three, as I said, O King. On the other hand the number three is also the cause of the number one because since the number three is caused by the number two and this number two by the number one, the number three is therefore the cause of number one."

And our King said to me: "In this process the number four would also be the cause of number five and so on, and the question of one Godhead would resolve itself into many Godheads, which, as you say, is the doctrine not of the Christians but of the Magians."—And I replied to our King: "In every comparison there is a time at which one must stop, because it does not resemble reality in everything. We should remember that all numbers are included in number three. Indeed the number three is both complete and perfect and all numbers are included in a complete and perfect number. In this number three all other numbers

are included, O our victorious King. Above three all other numbers are simply numbers added to themselves, by means of that complete and perfect number, as it is said. It follows from all this that one is the cause of three and three of one, as we suggested."—And our King said to me: "Neither three nor two can possibly be said of God."—And I replied to his Majesty: "Neither, therefore, one."—And our King asked: "How?"—And I answered: "If the cause of three is two, the cause of two would be one, and in this case the cause of three would also be one. If then God cannot be said to be three, and the cause of three is two and that of two one, God cannot, therefore be called one either. Indeed this number one being the cause and the beginning, of all numbers, and there being no number in God, we should not have applied it to Him. As, however, we do apply this number to God without any reference to the beginning of an arithmetical number, we apply to Him also the number three without any implication of multiplication or division of Gods, but with a particular reference to the Word and the Spirit of God, through which heaven and earth have been created, as we have demonstrated in our previous colloquy. If the number three cannot be applied to God, since it is caused by the number one, the latter could not by inference be applied to God either, but if the number one can be applied to God, since this number one is the cause of the number three, the last number can therefore be applied also to God."

And our victorious King said: "The number three denotes plurality, and since there cannot be plurality in Godhead, this number three has no room at all in Godhead."—And I replied to his Majesty: "The number one is also the cause and the beginning of all numbers, O our King, and number is the cause of plurality. Since there cannot be any kind of plurality in God, even the number one would have no room in Him."—And our King said: "The number one as applied to God is attested in the Book."—And I said: "So also is the case, O our King, with a number implying plurality. We find often such a number in the Torah, in the Prophets and in the Gospel, and as I hear, in your Book also, not, however, in connection with Godhead but in relation to humanity."

"So far as the Torah is concerned it is written in it, 'Let us make humankind in our image, after our likeness' (Gen. 1:26); and 'The man is become as one of us' (Gen. 3:22); and, 'Let us go down, and there confound their language' (Gen. 11:7). As to the Prophets, it is written in them, 'Holy, holy, holy, is the Lord of Hosts' (Isa. 7:3); and 'The Lord God and his Spirit hath sent me' (Isa. 48:16); and 'By the Word of the Lord were the heavens made, and all His hosts by the Spirit of His mouth' (Ps. 30:6 Peshitta). As to the Gospel, it is written in it, 'Go and teach all nations, baptizing them in the name of the Father, and of the Son and of the Holy Ghost' (Matt. 28:9). As to your Book, it is written in it, 'And we sent to her our Spirit' (Qur'an 19:17), and 'We breathed into her from our Spirit' (Qur'an 21:91), and 'We fashioned,' 'We said,' 'We did,' and all such expressions which are said of God in a plural form. If the Holy Books refer these words to God in a plural form, what the Books say concerning God we have to say and admit. Since we had to preserve without change the number one as applied to God, we had also by inference to preserve without modification the number three, that is to say plurality, as applied to Him. The number one refers to nature and Godhead, and the number three to God, His Word and His Spirit, because God has never been, is not, and will never be, without Word and Spirit."

And our wise Sovereign said: "The plural form in connection with God, in the expressions 'We sent,' 'We breathed,' 'We said,' etc., has been used in the Books not as a sign of persons or of Trinity, but as a mark of Divine majesty and power. It is even the habit of the kings and governors of the earth to use such a mode of speech."—And I replied to the wealth of his intelligence: "What your glorious Majesty has said is true. To you God gave knowledge and understanding along with power and greatness, more than to all other countries and kings. The community of all humankind, whether composed of freemen or of subjected races is personified in the kings, and the community of mankind being composed of innumerable persons, the kings rightly make use of the plural form in expressions such as, 'We ordered,' 'We said,' 'We did,' etc. Indeed the kings represent collectively all the community of humankind individually. If all people are one with the king, and

the king orders, says and does, all people order, say and do in the king, and he says and does in the name of all.

"Further, the kings are human beings, and human beings are composed of body and soul, and the body is in its turn composed of the power of the four elements. Because a human being is composed of many elements, the kings make use not unjustly of the plural form of speech, such as 'We did,' 'We ordered,' etc. As to God who is simple in His nature and one in His essence and remote from all division and bodily composition, what greatness and honor can possibly come to Him when He, who is one and undivided against Himself, says in the plural form, 'We ordered,' and, 'We did'? The greatest honor that can be offered to God is that He should be believed in by all as He is. In His essence He is one, but He is three because of His Word and His Spirit. This Word and this Spirit are living beings and are of His nature, as the word and the spirit of our victorious King are of his nature, and he is one King with his word and spirit, which are constantly with him without cessation, without division and without displacement.

"When, therefore, expressions such as, 'We spoke,' 'We said,' 'We did,' and 'Our image and likeness,' are said to refer to God, His Word and His Spirit, they are referred in the way just described, O King of Kings. Who is more closely united to God than His Word through which He created all, governs all and directs all? Or who is nearer to Him than His Spirit through which He vivifies, sanctifies and renews all? David spoke thus: 'By the Word of the Lord were the heavens made, and all His hosts by the Spirit of His mouth' (Ps. 33:6 Peshitta); and, 'He sent His Word and healed them, and delivered them from destruction' (Ps. 107:20); and 'You send forth Your Spirit and they are created, and You renew the face of the earth' (Ps. 104:30).

"If one asserts that the expressions, 'Our image' and 'Our likeness' used by Moses and the expressions, 'We made,' and 'We breathed,' used by Muḥammad, do not refer to God but to the angels, how disgraceful it would be to believe that the image and the likeness of God and those of the angels, that is of the creator and the created, are one! How dishonorable it would be to affirm that

God says, orders and does with the angels and His creatures! God orders and does like the Lord and the creator, and orders and does in a way that transcends that of all others; but the angels being creatures and servants, do not order with God, but are under the order of God; they do not create with God, but are very much created by God. The angels are what David said about them, 'Who makes His angels spirits and His ministers a flaming fire' (Ps. 104:4). In this he shows that they are made and created.

"As to the Word and Spirit of God the prophet David says that they are not created and made, but creators and makers: '*By* the Word of the Lord were the heavens made,' and not His Word alone; and 'the heavenly hosts were created *by* His Spirit' and not His Spirit alone; and, 'Because He said and they were made, and He commanded and they were created' (Ps. 148:5). It is obvious that one who 'says,' 'says' and 'commands' by word, and that the word precedes the action, and the thought precedes the deed. Since God is one without any other before Him, with Him and after Him, and since all the above expressions which denote plurality cannot be ascribed to angels, and since the nature of God is absolutely free from all compositions—to whom could we ascribe then all such expressions? I believe, O our victorious King, that they refer to the Word and the Spirit of God. If it is right that the expression 'One God' is true, it is also right that the expression 'We ordered,' 'We said' and 'We breathed from our Spirit' are without doubt true and not false. It is also possible that the three letters placed before some Sūrahs in the Qurʾan, as I have learned, such as A.L.R and Ṭ.S.M. and Y.S.M. and others, which are three in number, refer also in your Book to God, His Word and His Spirit."

And our victorious King said: "And what did impede the Prophet from saying that this was so, that is that these letters clearly referred to God, His Word and His Spirit?"—And I replied to his Majesty: "The obstacle might have come from the weakness of those people who would be listening to such a thing. People whose ears were accustomed to the multiplicity of idols and false gods could not have listened to the doctrine of Father, Son, and Holy Spirit, or to that of one God, His Word, and His Spirit. They would have believed

that this also was polytheism. This is the reason why your Prophet proclaimed openly the doctrine of one God, but that of the Trinity he only showed it in a somewhat veiled and mysterious way, that is to say through his mention of God, and of His Spirit and through the expressions 'We sent our Spirit' and 'We fashioned a complete man.' He did not teach it openly in order that his hearers may not be scandalized by it and think of polytheism, and he did not hide it completely in order that he may not deviate from the path followed by Moses, Isaiah, and other prophets, but he showed it symbolically by means of the three letters that precede the Sūrahs.

"The ancient prophets had also spoken of the unity of the nature of God and used words referring to this unity in an open and clear way, but the words which referred to His three persons they used them in a somewhat veiled and symbolical way. They did so not for any other reason than that of the weakness of men whose mind was bound up in idolatry and polytheism. When, however, Christ appeared to us in the flesh, He proclaimed openly and clearly what the prophets had said in a veiled and symbolical way. 'Go ye,' said He to His Disciples, 'and baptize all nations in the name of the Father, and of the Son and of the Holy Ghost' (Matt. 28:19). Moses also uttered the same thing in a way that means both one and three, 'Hear, O Israel,' said he, 'The Lord your God is one Lord' (Deut. 6:4). In saying He 'is one,' he refers to the one nature of Godhead, and in saying the three words, 'Lord, God, and Lord' he refers to the three persons of that Godhead, as if one was saying that God, His Word and His Spirit were one eternal God. Job also said, 'The Lord gave, and the Lord hath taken; blessed be the name of the Lord' (Job 1:21). In blessing the single name of the Lord, Job used it three times, in reference to one in three."

And our King said to me: "If He is one, He is not three; and if He is three, He is not one; what is this contradiction?"—And I answered: "The sun is also one, O our victorious King, in its spheric globe, its light and its heat, and the very same sun is also three, one sun in three powers. In the same way the soul has the powers of reason and intelligence, and the very same soul is one in one thing and three in another thing. In the same way also a piece of three gold denarii, is called one and three, one in its gold that is to say in its nature, and three in its persons that is to say in the number of denarii. The fact that the above objects are one does not contradict and annul the other fact—that they are also three, and the fact that they are three does not contradict and annul the fact that they are also one.

"In the very same way the fact that God is one does not annul the other fact that He is in three persons, and the fact that He is in three persons does not annul the other fact that He is one God. The human is a living, rational and mortal being, and the human is one and three, one in being one person and three in being living, rational and mortal, and this idea gives rise to three notions not contradictory but rather confirmatory to one another. By the fact that the human being is one, it is by necessity living, rational and mortal, and by the fact that it is a living, rational and mortal being, the human is by necessity one person. This applies also to God in whom the fact of His being three does not annul the other fact that He is one and *vice versa*, but these two facts confirm and corroborate each other. If He is one God, He is the Father, the Son, and the Holy Spirit; and if He is the Father, the Son, and the Holy Spirit, He is one God, because the eternal nature of God consists in Fatherhood, Filiation, and Procession, and in the three of them He is one God, and in being one God He is the three of them."

And our King said to me: "Do you say that the nature of God is composed of the above three, as the human nature is composed of its being living, rational, and mortal, and as the sun is composed of light, heat, and sphericity, and as the soul is composed of reason and intelligence, and as gold is composed of height, depth, and width?"—And I denied this and said: "No, this is not so."—And our King said to me: "Why then do you wish to demonstrate with bodily demonstrations One who has no body and is not composed?"—And I answered his Majesty: "Because there is no other God like Him, from whom I might draw a demonstration as to what is a being that has no beginning and no end."—And our King said to me: "It is never allowed to draw a demonstration from the creatures concerning the Creator."—And I said to

Him: "We will then be in complete ignorance of God, O King of Kings."

And our King said: "Why?"—And I answered: "Because all that we say about God is deducted from natural things that we have with us; as such are the adjectives: King of all Kings, Lord of all Lords, Mighty, Powerful, Omnipotent, Light, Wisdom, and Judge. We call God by these and similar adjectives from things that are with us, and it is from them that we take our demonstration concerning God. If we remove Him from such demonstrations and do not speak of Him through them, with what and through what could we figure in our mind Him who is higher than all image and likeness?"

And our victorious King said to me: "We call God by these names, not because we understand Him to resemble things that we have with us, but in order to show that He is far above them, without comparison. In this way, we do not attribute to God things that are with us, we rather ascribe to ourselves things that are His, with great mercy from Him and great imperfection from us. Words such as: kingdom, life, power, greatness, honor, wisdom, sight, knowledge, and justice, etc., belong truly, naturally and eternally to God, and they only belong to us in an unnatural, imperfect, and temporal way. With God they have not begun and they will not end, but with us children of humanity they began and they will end."

And I replied to his Majesty: "All that your Majesty said on this subject, O our victorious King, has been said with perfect wisdom and great knowledge; this is especially true of what you have just now said. It was not indeed with the intention of lowering God to a comparison with His creatures, that from the latter I drew a comparison concerning Him who in reality has no comparison with the created beings at all. I made use of such similes solely for the purpose of uplifting my mind from the created things to God. All the things that we have with us compare very imperfectly with the things of God. Even in saying of God that He is one, we introduce in our mind division concerning Him, because when we say for instance one person, one angel, one denarius, one pearl, we immediately think of a division that singles out and separates one denarius from many denarii, one pearl from many pearls, one angel from many angels, and one person from many persons.

"One would not be counting rightly but promiscuously if one were to say: one person and two angels, one horse and two asses, one denarius and two pence, one pearl and two emeralds. Every entity is counted with the entities of its own species, and we say: one, two, or three persons; one, two, or three angels; one, two, or three denarii; one, two, or three pearls, as the case may be. With all these calculations in saying one we introduce, as I said, the element of division, but in speaking of God we cannot do the same thing, because there are no other entities of the same species as Himself which would introduce division in Him in the same sense as in our saying: one angel or one person. He is one, single and unique in His nature. Likewise when we say three we do not think of bodies or numbers, and when we say: Father, Son, and Holy Spirit, we do not say it in a way that implies division, separation, or promiscuity, but we think of it as something high above us in a divine, incomprehensible, and indescribable way.

"Our fathers and our children were born from marital union and intercourse, and their fatherhood and filiation have a beginning and an end. Further, a father was a son before becoming a father, and all relationships are liable to natural dissolution and cessation. As to Fatherhood, Filiation, and Procession in God they are not in a way similar to those of our humanity, but in a divine way that mind cannot comprehend. They do not arise from any intercourse between them, nor are they from time or in the time but eternally without beginning and without end. Since the above three attributes are of the nature of God, and the nature of God has no beginning and no end, they also are without a beginning and without an end. And since He who is without a beginning and without an end is also unchangeable, that Fatherhood, therefore, that Filiation and that Procession are immutable and will remain without any modification. The things that are with us give but an imperfect comparison with the things that are above, because things that are God's are above comparison and likeness, as we have already demonstrated."

And our victorious King said: "The mind of rational beings will not agree to speak of God who is eternally one in Himself in terms of Trinity."— And I answered: "Since the mind of the rational beings is created, and no created being can comprehend God, you have rightly affirmed, O King of Kings, that the mind of the rational beings will not agree to speak of one God in terms of Trinity. The mind, however, of the rational beings can only extend to the acts of God, and even then in an imperfect and partial manner; as to the nature of God we learn things that belong to it not so much from our rational mind as from the Books of Revelation, i.e., from what God Himself has revealed and taught about Himself through His Word and Spirit:

"The Word of God said, 'No one knows the Father but the Son, and no one knows the Son but the Father' (John, *passim*), and, 'The Spirit searches all things even the deep things of God' (1 Cor. 2:10). No one knows what there is in man except man's own spirit that is in him, so also no one knows what is in God except the Spirit of God. The Word and the Spirit of God, being eternally from His own nature—as heat and light from the sun, and as reason and mind from the soul—alone see and know the Divine nature, and it is they who have revealed and taught us in the sacred Books that God is one and three, as I have already shown in my above words from the Torah, the Prophets, the Gospel, and the Qur'an according to what I have learned from those who are versed in the knowledge of your Book.

"Were it not for the fact that His Word and His Spirit were eternally from His own nature God would not have spoken of Himself in the Torah, as, '*Our* image and *Our* likeness' (Gen. 1:26); and 'Behold the man is become as one of *us*' (Gen. 3:22); and 'Let us go down and there confound their language' (Gen. 11:7); and the Qur'an would not have said, 'And we sent to her *our* Spirit' (Qur'an 19:17); and 'We breathed into her from *our* Spirit' (Qur'an 21:91); and '*We* did,' '*We* said,' and so on. By such expressions (The Qur'an) refers to God and His Word and His Spirit as we have said above. Has not the mind of the rational beings, O our victorious Sovereign, to follow the words of God rather than its own fanciful conceptions? The inspired Books are surely right, and since we find in them that one and the same prophet speaks of God as one and as three, we are compelled by the nature of the subject to believe it."

. . .

And our King said to me: "O Catholicos, if this is your religion and that of the Christians, I will say this, that the Word and the Spirit are also creatures of God, and there is no one who is uncreated except one God."—And I replied: "If the Word and the Spirit are also creatures of God like the rest, by means of whom did God create the heaven and the earth and all that they contain? The Books teach us that He created the world by means of His Word and His Spirit—by means of whom did He then create this Word and this Spirit? If He created them by means of another word and another spirit, the same conclusion would also be applied to them: will they be created or uncreated? If uncreated, the religion of the Catholicos and of the Christians is vindicated; and if created, by means of whom did God create them? And this process of gibberish argumentation will go on indefinitely until we stop at that Word and that Spirit hidden eternally in God, by means of whom we assert that the worlds were created."

And the King said: "You appear to believe in three heads, O Catholicos."—And I said "This is certainly not so, O our victorious King. I believe in one head, the eternal God the Father, from whom the Word shone and the Spirit radiated eternally, together, and before all times, the former by way of filiation and the latter by way of procession, not in a bodily but in a divine way that befits God. This is the reason why they are not three separate Gods. The Word and the Spirit are eternally from the single nature of God, who is not one person divested of word and spirit as the weakness of the Jewish belief has it. He shines and emits rays eternally with the light of His Word and the radiation of His Spirit, and He is one head with His Word and His Spirit. I do not believe in God as stripped of His Word and Spirit, in the case of the former without mind and reason, and in the case of the latter without spirit and life. It is only the idolaters

who believe in false gods or idols who have neither reason nor life."

And our victorious King said: "It seems to me that you believe in a vacuous God since you believe that He has a child."—And I answered: "O King, I do not believe that God is either vacuous or solid, because both these adjectives denote bodies. If vacuity and solidity belong to bodies, and God is a Spirit without a body, neither of the two qualifications can be ascribed to Him."—And the King said: "What then do you believe that God is if He is neither vacuous nor solid?"—And I replied to His Majesty: "God is a Spirit and an incorporeal light, from whom shine and radiate eternally and divinely His Word and His Spirit. The soul begets the mind and causes reason to proceed from it, and the fire begets the light and causes heat to proceed from its nature, and we do not say that either the soul or fire are hollow or solid. So also is the case with regard to God, about Whom we never say that He is vacuous or solid when He makes His Word shine and His Spirit radiate from His essence eternally."

And our victorious King said: "What is the difference in God between shining and radiating?"—And I replied: "There is the same difference between shining and radiating in God as that found in the illustration furnished by the fire and the apple: the fire begets the light and causes heat to proceed from it, and the apple begets the scent and causes the taste and savor to proceed from it. Although both the fire and the apple give rise, the former to light and heat, and the latter to scent and savor, yet they do not do it in the same manner and with an identical effect on the one and the same sense of our body. We receive the heat of the fire with the sense of feeling, the light with the eyes, the scent of the apple with the sense of smell, and the sweetness of its savor with the palate. From this it becomes clear that the mode of filiation is different from that of procession. This is as far as one can go from bodily comparisons and similes to the realities and to God."

And the King said: "You will not go very far with God in your bodily comparisons and similes."—And I said: "O King, because I am a bodily man I made use of bodily metaphors, and not of those that are without any body and any composition. Because I am a bodily man, and not a spiritual being, I make use of bodily comparisons in speaking of God. How could I or any other human being speak of God as He is with a tongue of flesh, with lips fashioned of mud, and with a soul and mind closely united to a body? This is far beyond the power of people and angels to do. God Himself speaks with the prophets about Himself not as He is, because they cannot know and hear about Him as He is, but simply in the way that fits in with their own nature, a way they are able to understand. In His revelations to the ancient prophets sometimes He revealed Himself as human, sometimes as fire, sometimes as wind, and some other times in some other ways and similitudes.

"The divine David said, 'He then spoke in visions to His holy ones' (Ps. 89:19 Peshitta); and the Prophet Hosea said on behalf of God, 'I have multiplied my visions and used similitudes by the ministry of the prophets' (Hos. 12:10); and one of the Apostles of Christ said, 'God at sundry times and in divers manners spoke in time past unto our fathers by the prophets' (Heb. 1:1). If God appeared and spoke to the ancient in bodily similitudes and symbols, we with stronger reason find ourselves completely unable to speak of God and to understand anything concerning Him except through bodily similitudes and metaphors. I shall here make bold and assert that I hope I shall not deserve any blame from your Majesty if I say that you are in the earth the representative of God for the earthly people; now God makes His sun to rise on the evil and on the good, and sends His rain on the just and the unjust (Matt. 5:45). Your Majesty also in the similitude of God will make us worthy of forgiveness, if in the fact of being earthly beings we speak of God in an earthly way and not in a spiritual way like spiritual beings."

And our victorious King said: "You are right in what you said before and say now on the subject that God is above all the thoughts and minds of created beings, and that all the thoughts and minds of created beings are lower not only than God Himself but also His work. The fact, however, that you put the servant and the Lord on the same footing you make the creator equal with the created, and in this you fall into error and falsehood."

And I replied: "O my Sovereign, that the Word and the Spirit of God should be called servants and created I considered and consider not far from unbelief. If the Word and the Spirit are believed to be from God, and God is conceived to be a Lord and not a servant, His Word and Spirit are also, by inference, lords and not servants. It is one and the same freedom that belongs to God and to His Word and Spirit, and they are called Word and Spirit of God not in an unreal, but in a true, sense. The kingdom which my victorious Sovereign possesses is the same as that held by his word and his spirit, so that no one separates his word and his spirit from his kingdom, and he shines in the diadem of kingdom together with his word and his spirit in a way that they are not three Kings, and in a way that he does not shine in the diadem of kingdom apart from his word and his spirit.

"If it please your Majesty, O my powerful Sovereign, I will also say this: the splendor and the glory of the kingdom shine in one and the same way in the Commander of the Faithful and in his sons Mūsa and Hārūn, and in spite of the fact that kingdom and lordship in them are one, their personalities are different. For this reason no one would venture to consider, without the splendor of kingdom, not only the Commander of the Faithful but also the beautiful flowers and majestic blossoms that budded and blossomed out of him; indeed the three of them blossom in an identical kingdom, and this one and the same kingdom shines and radiates in each one of them, so that no one dares to ascribe servitude to any of them. In a small and partial way the same light of kingdom, lordship, and divinity shines and radiates eternally in the Father, the Son and the Holy Spirit, or if one prefers to put it, in God, His Word, and His Spirit, and no one is allowed to give to any of them the name of servant. If the Word and the Spirit are servants of God, while they are from God Himself, the logical conclusion to be drawn I leave to a tongue other than mine to utter."

And the King said: "It is very easy for your tongue, O Catholicos, to prove the existence of that Lord and God, and the existence also of that consubstantial servant, and to draw conclusions sometimes or to abstain from them some other times, but the minds and the will of rational beings are induced to follow not your mind which is visible in your conclusions, but the law of nature and the inspired Books."

And I replied: "O our victorious King, I have proved my words that I have uttered in the first day and today both from nature and from Book. So far as arguments from nature are concerned, I argued, confirmed, and corroborated my words sometimes from the soul with its mind and its reason; sometimes from the fire with its light and its heat; sometimes from the apple with its scent and its savor; and some other times from your Majesty and from the rational and royal flowers that grew from it: Mūsa and Hārūn, the sons of your Majesty. As to the inspired Books, I proved the object under discussion sometimes from Moses, sometimes from David, and some other times I appealed to the Qurʾan, as a witness to prove my statement.

"God said to the prophet David and caused him further to prophesy in the following manner concerning His Word and His Spirit, 'I have set up my King on my holy hill of Zion' (Ps. 2:6). Before this He had called Him His Christ, 'Against the Lord and against His Christ' (Ps. 2:2). If the Christ of God is a King, it follows that the Christ is not a servant but a King. Afterwards David called Him twice Son, 'Thou art my Son and this day I have begotten Thee' (Ps. 2:7), and, 'Kiss the Son lest the Lord be angry and ye perish from His way' (Ps. 2:12). If the Christ, therefore, is a Son, as God called Him through the prophet David, and if no son is a servant, it follows, O King, that the Christ is not a servant. In another passage the same prophet David called the Christ 'Lord,' 'Son,' and 'A priest forever,' because he said, 'The Lord said unto my Lord, Sit Thou at my right hand' (Ps. 90:1, 4). And in order to show that Christ is of the same nature and power as God, he said on behalf of the Father as follows, 'In the beauties of holiness from the womb I have begotten Thee from the beginning' (Ps. 110:3 Peshitta). God, therefore, called Christ 'a Lord' through the prophet David, and since no true Lord is a servant, it follows that Christ is not a servant.

"Further, Christ has been called through David one 'begotten of God' both 'from eternity' and 'In the beauties of holiness from the womb.' Since no one begotten of God is a servant, the Christ, therefore, O King of Kings, is not a servant and created,

but He is uncreated and a Lord. God said also through the prophet Isaiah to Ahaz, King of Israel, 'Behold a virgin shall conceive and bear a Son, and His name shall he called—not a servant—but Emmanuel, which being interpreted is, God with us' (Isa. 7:14; Matt. 1:23). The same Isaiah said, 'For unto us a Child—and not a servant—is born, and unto us a Son—not a servant and a created being—is given, and His name has been called Wonderful, Counselor, the Mighty God of the Worlds' (Isa. 9:6). If the Christ, therefore, is the Son of God, this Son of God, as God Himself spoke through the prophet Isaiah, is the 'mighty God of the worlds,' and not a servant in subjection, but a Lord and a Prince. It follows, O our victorious King, that the Christ is surely a Lord and a Prince, and not a servant in subjection.

"As your Majesty would wax angry if your children were called servants, so also God will be wrathful if anybody called His Word and His Spirit servants. As the honor and dishonor of the children of your Majesty redound on you, so also and in a higher degree the honor and dishonor of God's Word and Spirit redound on Him. It is for this reason that Christ said in the Gospel, 'He that honors not the Son, honors not the Father who has sent Him' (John 5:23), and, 'He who honors not the Son shall not see life, but the wrath of God shall abide on him' (John 3:36).

"The above is written in the Gospel. I heard also that it is written in the Qurʾan that Christ is the Word and the Spirit of God (Qurʾan 4:169; cf. 3:40), and not a servant. If Christ is the Word and the Spirit of God, as the Qurʾan testifies, He is not a servant but a Lord, because the Word and the Spirit of God are Lords. It is by this method, O our God-loving King, based on the law of nature and on divinely inspired words, and not on purely human argumentation, word, and thought, that I both in the present and in the first conversation have demonstrated the lordship and the sonship of Christ, and the Divine Trinity."

Our victorious King said: "Has not the Christ been called also several times a servant by the prophets?"—And I said: "I am aware, O my Sovereign, of the fact that the Christ has also been called a servant, but that this appellation does not imply a real servitude is borne out by the illustration that may be taken from the status of Hārūn, the blossom and the flower of your Majesty. He is now called by everybody 'Heir Presumptive,' but after your long reign, he will he proclaimed King and Sovereign by all. He served his military service through the mission entrusted to him by your Majesty to repair to Constantinople against the rebellious and tyrannical Byzantines. Through this service and mission he will not lose his royal sonship and his freedom, nor his princely honor and glory, and acquire the simple name of servitude and subjection, like any other individual. So also is the case with the Christ, the Son of the heavenly King. He fulfilled the will of His Father in His coming on His military mission to mankind, and in His victory over sin, death, and Satan. He did not by this act lose His royal Sonship, and did not become a stranger to Divinity, Lordship, and Kingdom, nor did He put on the dishonor of servitude and subjection like any other individual.

. . .

"If Christ has been called by the prophets God and Lord, and if it has been said by some people that God suffered and died in the flesh, it is evident that it is the human nature which the Word-God took from us that suffered and died, because in no Book, neither in the prophets nor in the Gospel, do we find that God Himself died in the flesh, but we do find in all of them that the Son and Jesus Christ died in the flesh. The expression that God suffered and died in the flesh is not right."

And our victorious King asked: "And who are those who say that God suffered and died in the flesh."—And I answered: "The Jacobites and Melchites say that God suffered and died in the flesh, as to us we not only do not assert that God suffered and died in our nature, but that He even removed the passibility of our human nature that He put on from Mary by His impassibility, and its mortality by His immortality, and He made it to resemble divinity, to the extent that a created being is capable of resembling his Creator. A created being cannot make himself resemble his Creator, but the Creator is able to bring His creature to His own resemblance. It is not the picture that makes the painter paint a picture in its own

resemblance, but it is the painter that paints the picture to his own resemblance; it is not the wood that works and fashions a carpenter in its resemblance, but it is the carpenter that fashions the wood in his resemblance. In this same way it is not the mortal and passible nature that renders God passible and mortal like itself, but it is by necessity God that renders the passible and mortal human nature impassible and immortal like Himself. On the one hand, this is what the Jacobites and Melchites say, and, on the other, this is what we say. It behooves your Majesty to decide who are those who believe rightly and those who believe wrongly."

And our victorious King said: "In this matter you believe more rightly than the others. Who dares to assert that God dies? I think that even demons do not say such a thing. In what, however, you say concerning one Word and Son of God, all of you are wrong."—And I replied to his Majesty: "O our victorious King, in this world we are all of us as in a dark house in the middle of the night. If at night and in a dark house a precious pearl happens to fall in the midst of people, and all become aware of its existence, everyone would strive to pick up the pearl, which will not fall to the lot of all but to the lot of one only, while one will get hold of the pearl itself, another one of a piece of glass, a third one of a stone or of a bit of earth, but everyone will be happy and proud that he is the real possessor of the pearl. When, however, night and darkness disappear, and light and day arise, then everyone of those people who had believed that they had the pearl, would extend and stretch their hand towards the light, which alone can show what everyone has in hand. The one who possesses the pearl will rejoice and be happy and pleased with it, while those who had in hand pieces of glass and bits of stone only will weep and be sad, and will sigh and shed tears.

"In this same way we children of humanity are in this perishable world as in darkness. The pearl of the true faith fell in the midst of all of us, and it is undoubtedly in the hand of one of us, while all of us believe that we possess the precious object. In the world to come, however, the darkness of mortality passes, and the fog of ignorance dissolves, since it is the true and the real light to which the fog of ignorance is absolutely foreign. In it the possessors of the pearl will rejoice, be happy and pleased, and the possessors of mere pieces of stone will weep, sigh, and shed tears, as we said above."

And our victorious King said: "The possessors of the pearl are not known in this world, O Catholicos."—And I answered: "They are partially known, O our victorious King."—And our victorious and very wise King said: "What do you mean by partially known, and by what are they known as such?"—And I answered: "By good works, O our victorious King, and pious deeds, and by the wonders and miracles that God performs through those who possess the true faith. As the luster of a pearl is somewhat visible even in the darkness of the night, so also the rays of the true faith shine to some extent even in the darkness and the fog of the present world. God indeed has not left the pure pearl of the faith completely without testimony and evidence, first in the prophets and then in the Gospel. He first confirmed the true faith in Him through Moses, once by means of the prodigies and miracles that He wrought in Egypt, and another time when He divided the waters of the Red Sea into two and allowed the Israelites to cross it safely, but drowned the Egyptians in its depths. He also split and divided the Jordan into two through Joshua, son of Nun, and allowed the Israelites to cross it without any harm to themselves, and tied the sun and the moon to their own places until the Jewish people were well avenged upon their enemies. He acted in the same way through the prophets who rose in different generations, viz.: through David, Elijah, and Elisha.

"Afterwards He confirmed the faith through Christ our Lord by the miracles and prodigies which He wrought for the help of the children of humanity. In this way the Disciples performed miracles greater even than those wrought by Christ. These signs, miracles, and prodigies wrought in the name of Jesus Christ are the bright rays and the shining luster of the precious pearl of the faith, and it is by the brightness of such rays that the possessors of this pearl which is so full of luster and so precious that it outweighs all the world in the balance, are known."

And our victorious King said: "We have hope in God that we are the possessors of this pearl, and

that we hold it in our hands."—And I replied: "Amen, O King. But may God grant us that we too may share it with you, and rejoice in the shining and beaming luster of the pearl! God has placed the pearl of His faith before all of us like the shining rays of the sun, and everyone who wishes can enjoy the light of the sun.

"We pray God, who is King of Kings, and Lord of Lords, to preserve the crown of the kingdom and the throne of the Commander of the Faithful for multitudinous days and numerous years! May He also raise after him Mūsa and Hārūn and ʿAli to the throne of his kingdom forever and ever! May He subjugate before them and before their descendants after them all the barbarous nations, and may all the kings and governors of the world serve our Sovereign and his sons after him till the day in which the Kingdom of Heaven is revealed from heaven to earth!"

And our victorious King said: "Miracles have been and are sometimes performed even by unbelievers."—And I replied to his Majesty: "These, O our victorious King, are not miracles but deceptive similitudes of the demons, and are performed not by the prophets of God and by holy men, but by idolaters and wicked men. This is the reason why I said that good works and miracles are the luster of the pearl of the faith. Indeed, Moses performed miracles in Egypt, and the sorcerers Jannes and Jambres performed them also there, but Moses performed them by the power of God, and the sorcerers through the deceptions of the demons. The power of God, however, prevailed, and that of the demons was defeated.

"In Rome also Simon Cephas and Simon Magus performed miracles, but the former performed them by the power of God, and the latter by the power of the demons, and for this reason Simon Cephas was honored and Simon Magus was laughed at and despised by everyone, and his deception was exposed before the eyes of all celestial and terrestrial beings."

At this our victorious King rose up and entered his audience chamber, and I left him and returned in peace to my patriarchal residence.

Here ends the controversy of the Patriarch Mar Timothy I. with Mahdi, the Caliph of the Muslims. May eternal praise be to God!

46. Inscription of the Monument of the Church of the East at Xian

By 635 East Syrian Christian monks, often erroneously referred to as "Nestorians," had reached Ch'ang-an, China, the capital of the T'ang dynasty. An account of the mission of the Syrian monk Alopen (or Alouben), the favorable reception of the emperor, and the varied responses to Christianity by a succession of T'ang emperors is recorded on a remarkable stone monument erected in 781 and inscribed primarily in Chinese characters. Detailing the spread of Christianity as well as the struggles Christians faced over a 150-year period in early medieval China, the full inscription is reproduced here.

Part One

[Across the top of the monument:]
[1]The Record of the Transmission
of the Religion of Light
of the West in China

[2]The Minister of the Administration of
Monasteries bestows the Purple Robe to
Yeli,
the Chief Priest of the Monastery.

[At the bottom of the monument:]
[3]The erection of this monument is supervised
by the monk Gongdong
[with] monk Lingbao.

[At top upper right:]
[4]Monument commemorating the
transmission of the Religion of Light in
China

[At middle right:]
[5]Related by the monk Jingjing of the
Da Qin Monastery

Part Two

[1]In the beginning was the natural constant, the true stillness of the Origin, and the primordial void of the Most High. [2]Then, the spirit of the void emerged as the Most High Lord, moving in mysterious ways to enlighten the holy ones. [3]He is Joshua, my True Lord of the Void, who embodies the three subtle and wondrous bodies, and who was condemned to the cross so that the people of the four directions can be saved.

[4]He beat up the primordial winds and the two vapors were created. [5]He differentiated the gray emptiness and opened up the sky and the earth. [6]He set the sun and moon on their course and day and night came into being. [7]He crafted the myriad things and created the first people. [8]He gave to them the original nature of goodness and appointed them as the guardians of all creation. [9]Their minds were empty; they were content; and their hearts were simple and innocent. [10]Originally they had no desire, but under the influence of Satan, they abandoned their pure and simple goodness for the glitter and the gold. [11]Falling into the trap of death and lies, they became embroiled in the three hundred and sixty-five forms of sin. [12]In doing so, they have woven the web of retribution and have bound themselves inside it. [13]Some believe in the material origin of things; some have sunk into chaotic ways; some think that they can receive blessings simply by reciting prayers; and some have abandoned kindness for treachery.

Source: "The Stone Sutra," tr. Martin Palmer et al., in Martin Palmer, *The Jesus Sutras: Rediscovering the Lost Scrolls of Taoist Christianity* (New York: Ballantine, 2001), 224-32. Copyright © 2001 by Martin Palmer. Used by permission of Ballantine Books, a division of Random House, Inc.

[14]Despite their intelligence and their passionate pleas, they have got nowhere. [15]Forced into the everturning wheel of fire, they are burned and obliterated. [16]Having lost their way for eons, they can no longer return.

[17]Therefore, my Lord Ye Su, the One emanating in three subtle bodies, hid his true power, became a human, and came on behalf of the Lord of Heaven to preach the good teachings. [18]A virgin gave birth to the sacred in a dwelling in the Da Qin Empire. [19]The message was given to the Persians who saw and followed the bright light to offer Him gifts. [20]The twenty-four holy ones have given us the teachings, and heaven has decreed that the new religion of the "Three-In-One Purity that cannot be spoken of" should be proclaimed. [21]These teachings can restore goodness to sincere believers, deliver those living within the boundaries of the eight territories, refine the dust and transform it into truth, reveal the gate of the three constants, lead us to life, and destroy death. [22]The Religion of Light teachings are like the resplendent sun: they have the power to dissolve the dark realm and destroy evil forever.

[23]He set afloat the raft of salvation and compassion so that we can use it to ascend to the palace of light and be united with the spirit. [24]He carried out the work of deliverance, and when the task was completed, He ascended to immortality in broad daylight. [25]He left twenty-seven books of scriptures to inspire our spirit; He revealed the workings of the Origin; and He gave to us the method of purification by water.

[26]Borne on gentle winds and brilliant clouds of purity, the white seal carves the words, gathering the four radiances to be united with the void. [27]The sound of wood striking propagates the voice of virtue and benevolence:

[28]"The Eastern-facing Rites can give you the path of life. [29]Those who choose to grow beards, shave their heads, travel on the open roads, renounce desire, have neither male nor female slaves, see all people as equal, and do not hoard material goods, are followers of My rites of purification."

[30]We use abstinence to subdue thoughts of desire; and we use stillness to build our foundation. [31]At seven we gather for service to pray for the salvation of all. [32]Every seven days we have an audience with heaven. [33]We purify our hearts and return to the simple and natural way of the truth. [34]This truth cannot be named but its function surpasses all expectations. [35]When forced to give it a name we call it the Religion of Light. [36]As it is with the Way, that which is sacred is not sacred unless it is highly sacred, and that which is the Way is not the Way unless it is the Great Way.

Part Three

[1]The sacred doctrine that has brought light to the world came here during the reign of the Emperor Taizong. [2]The glorious teachings were carried by Aluoben, a man of high virtue from the Da Qin Empire. [3]He came on azure clouds bearing the true scriptures, and after a long and arduous journey, arrived in Chang-an during the ninth year of Zhenguan. [4]The emperor sent his minister Fang Xuanling to greet him at the western suburb. [5]The visitor was welcomed into the palace where he was asked to translate his scriptures. [6]When the emperor heard the teachings, he realized deeply that they spoke the truth. [7]He therefore asked that these teachings be taught, and in the seventh month in the autumn of the twelfth year of Zhenguan, he issued a decree:

[8]"The Way does not have a common name and the sacred does not have a common form. [9]Proclaim the teachings everywhere for the salvation of the people. [10]Aluoben, the man of great virtue from the Da Qin Empire, came from a far land and arrived at the capital to present the teachings and images of his religion. [11]His message is mysterious and wonderful beyond our understanding. [12]The teachings tell us about the origin of things and how they were created and nourished. [13]The message is lucid and clear; the teachings will benefit all; and they should be practiced throughout the land."

[14]On the street named Yining in the capital, the Da Qin Monastery was erected for twenty-one Religion of Light monks. [15]Through His great virtue and His ascension to the blue skies in the west, the fight of the Way and the Religion of Light spirit has reached the Great Tang. [16]On the eastern gate of the monastery is an imperial decla-

ration penned by the Emperor: "Reveal the splendor and brightness of heaven; glorify the Religion of Light saints; and let the benevolent teachings illuminate this realm of existence."

[17]According to the maps of the western territories and the records of the Han and Wei histories, the southern part of the Da Qin Empire touches the coral seas. [18]Northward it stretches toward the Mountains of the Many Treasures. [19]Westward it overlooks the flowering woods of paradise. [20]Eastward it extends to lands where the wind never stops and the rivers are few. [21]From there came cotton-filling to make warm clothing, frankincense, shining pearls, and bright gemstones. [22]In that land there are no thieves. [23]People are happy and healthy. [24]Only the Religion of Light teachings are practiced, and nothing other than virtue is promoted. [25]The buildings are large and spacious, and the country is rich in culture and learning.

[26]The Emperor Gaozong praised his ancestor for recognizing the value of the true teachings and decreed the building of Religion of Light Monasteries in many provinces. [27]He conferred on Alouben the title "Lord Protector of the Great Teachings." [28]The teaching spread to the ten directions and the country prospered. [29]Monasteries were built in hundreds of cities and many people received blessings from the Religion of Light Church.

[30]In the following years, the Buddhist teachers from the eastern district spread vicious rumors and gathered a group of dishonorable people in the western suburb to slander [the Religion of Light Church]. [31]The chief priest, the Honorable Lo-hsieh, brought out the golden religious objects, and the high monks defended the wondrous doctrine. [32]Thus, a disaster was averted.

[33]The pious Emperor Xuanzong ordered five princes from the dukedom of Ning to supervise the building of a church where the doctrine could be taught to more people in simple and straightforward ways. [34]Within a short time, many people were converted.

[35]In the early years of Tianbao, the emperor ordered General Gao Lishi to attend the consecration of the Acts of the Five Saints Church. [36]He also sent gifts of one hundred bolts of satin and a commemorative tapestry. [37]On the tapestry was embroidered: "The Dragon may be far away, but the bow and sword can reach the corners of the sun to bring light and celestial music to the three realms." [38]From the Da Qin Empire came the monk Jiehe, who observed changes in the stars and gazed at the sun in an audience with the Lord. [39]The emperor also asked the Honorable Jiehe, Lexie, Bulun, and seventeen other monks to perform a high ceremony of prayer and offering at the Celebration Hall. [40]At the Tiandi Monastery there is a plaque written by the emperor. [41]Decorated with sparkling jade and suspended from a high rafter, it floats like a many-colored cloud from heaven. [42]On it is written:

[43]"As great as the Southern Mountains, as grand as the largest lakes, and as deep as the Eastern Seas, the Way can accomplish anything, and what it accomplishes must be described. [44]There is nothing that the holy ones cannot achieve, and what they have achieved will always be recorded."

[45]The enlightened Emperor Suzong established Religion of Light Monasteries in Ling-wu and four other provinces. [46]He supported charitable works and celebrated the great festivals. [47]Thus he was blessed, and his reign was prosperous.

[48]The scholar and military Emperor Daizong continued to promote the Sacred Way and follow the principles of wu-wei. [49]On the morning of the Holy Birthday, he offered incense and honored the Religion of Light Christians with an imperial declaration. [50]It read: "Due to your wonderful and meritorious works, many people have found salvation. [51]Because the sacred took on human form, the poisons of the world can be stopped."

[52]During the years of Jianzhong [of the Emperor Dezong], my pious emperor issued eight edicts and drove away the darkness. [53]He opened the nine realms and renewed the life of the Religion of Light Church.

[54]To penetrate the mysteries, to bless with a good conscience, to be great and yet empty, to return to stillness and be forgiving, to be compassionate and to deliver all people, to do good deeds and help people reach the other shore—these are the great benefits of our path of cultivation. [55]To calm people in stormy times, to help them understand the nature of things, to maintain purity, to nourish all things, to respect all life, and to answer

the needs of those whose beliefs come from the heart—these are the services the Religion of Light Church can offer.

[56]The Minister of Religious Affairs and the Assistant Provincial Governor of the tribute kingdoms bestowed the purple robe on the monk Yishi in the Examination Room on behalf of the emperor. [57]In a harmonious and benevolent way, this monk dedicated his life to spreading the teachings from the capital to the heart of the country. [58]His skill was impeccable and his learning was without peer. [59]In the beginning he befriended the Governor. [60]Later, he made himself known in the community of scribes. [61]Finally, he got Duke Guo of Hanyang to introduce the rites of abstinence in the tribute kingdoms.

[62]When the Emperor Suzong saw that his father was bedridden and unable to walk, he vowed that he would continue the policy of his ancestor. [63]He sent messages to his ministers and ordered them to distribute his wealth generously, and to send gifts of cloth and gold [to the Religion of Light]. [64]He offered to renovate the older monasteries, rebuild the churches, and redecorate the halls and chambers. [65]He also asked the Luminous Religion Church to follow the principles of virtue and benevolence. [66]Every year, he invited the monks of the four monasteries to plan their charitable activities together with him. [67]He bid them to feed the crippled, give clothing to those suffering from cold, heal the sick, and bury the dead. [68]His devotion was so great that he asked a white-robed Religion of Light priest to write a plaque to glorify the luminous doctrine. [69]The text reads:

[70]"The True Lord of the Primordial Void, in absolute stillness and constant naturalness, crafted and nourished all things. [71]He raised the earth and established the sky. [72]He took on human form and His compassion was limitless. [73]The sun rises; darkness is banished; and we are witnesses to the true wonder."

[74]Throughout the reigns of the emperors there were records documenting the history of the Religion of Light Church [in China]. [75]They tell us that the Religion of Light teachings were brought into the Tang Empire, that the scriptures were translated, and that monasteries were built.

[76]These teachings are like a raft, carrying salvation, blessings, and goodwill to the people of my country.

[77]Following the footsteps of his ancestors, the Emperor Gaozong built beautiful monasteries and churches throughout the land. [78]The True Way was proclaimed and the title "Lord Protector of the Great Teachings" was conferred. [79]The people were happy and there was prosperity everywhere.

[80]The Emperor Xuanzong promoted the sacred doctrine even further. [81]He followed the true teachings, penned declarations to endorse them, and issued imperial decrees to support them. [82]In simple and glorious words, he praised the deeds [of the Religion of Light] and deemed them worthy of celebration.

[83]The Emperor Suzong revived the Way of Heaven and observed the holy days. [84]Within one night, the fair winds swept away the impurities that have corrupted the palace. [85]The dust was cleared and the country was made whole again.

[86]The Emperor Daizong was filial and virtuous. [87]His piety was as great as heaven and earth. [88]He opened the imperial treasury and gave gifts of precious materials and jasmine incense. [89]To those who were virtuous, he rewarded them with gemstones that were as bright as the full moon.

[90]The reigning Emperor of Jianzhang [the Emperor Dezong] believed in the enlightened teachings. [91]During his time, the military and the generals kept peace in the four corners of land and the scholar officials were honest and upright. [92]He encouraged everyone to examine the nature of things with the hidden mirror. [93]People in the six directions were enlightened, and the hundred unruly tribes were brought under jurisdiction.

Part Four

[1]This doctrine is great and its workings are powerful and mysterious. [2]If forced to describe it, I would call them the work of the Three-in-one Lord. [3]All this humble servant has done is to record on the monument what has happened and to glorify the Primordial Lord.

[4]Erected in the second year of Jianzhang of the Great Tang, accompanied by the proper ceremonial music and rites, in the seventh month, on a day when the bright sun illuminated the forest.

[5]Attended by Chief Priest Ningshu and the followers of the Religion of Light teachings from the East.

[6]The calligrapher is the former military adviser of the Dai Province, the Honorable Imperial Appointee Lu Xiuyan.

47. Chinese Christian Sutras

Resembling Buddhist sutras in style, several Chinese Christian treatises have been found that attest to early medieval missionary activity in China. The Sutra of Jesus Christ *has been dated as early as 638 and may originate with Alopen's original mission. Using terms like "Lord of the Universe" for Christ and "Cool Wind" for the Holy Spirit, it retells the message of the gospel in language that would have been more accessible to a Buddhist and Taoist audience. Composed ca. 720, the* First Liturgical Sutra, *with its prayer to the "Jade-faced One," illustrates the adaptation of Christian liturgy to the Chinese context.*

The Fourth Sutra:
The Sutra of Jesus Christ
Chapter One

[1]At this time the messiah taught the laws of God, of Yahweh. [2]He said: There are many different views as to the real meaning of the Sutras, and on where God is, and what God is, and how God was revealed.

[3]The Messiah was orbited by the Buddhas and arhats [disciples of the Buddha who have attained semidivine status]. [4]Looking down he saw the suffering of all that is born, and so he began to teach.

[5]Nobody has seen God. [6]Nobody has the ability to see God. [7]Truly, God is like the wind. [8]Who can see the wind? [9]God is not still but moves on the earth at all times. [10]He is in everything and everywhere. [11]Humanity lives only because it is filled with God's life-giving breath. [12]Peace comes only when you can rest secure in your own place, when your heart and mind rest in God. [13]Day in, day out there you exist in contentment, open to where you may be led. [14]God leads the believer to that place of contentment and great bliss.

[15]All great teachers such as the Buddhas are moved by this Wind and there is nowhere in the world where this Wind does not reach and move. [16]God's Palace is in this place of peace and happiness yet he knows the suffering and actions of the whole world.

[17]Everyone in the world knows how the Wind blows. [18]We can hear it but not see its shadow. [19]Nobody knows what it really looks like, whether it is pleasing to look upon or not, nor whether it is yellow, white, or even blue. [20]Nobody knows where the Wind dwells.

[21]God's sacred spirit force allows him to be in one place, but where it is nobody knows, or how to get there. [22]God is beyond the cycle of death and birth, beyond being called male or female. [23]God made both Heaven and Earth. [24]God's sacred spirit force has never been fully manifested. [25]This power can grant longevity and lead to immortality.

SOURCE: "The Fourth Sutra: The Sutra of Jesus Christ" and "The First Liturgical Sutra: Taking Refuge in the Trinity," tr. Martin Palmer et al., in Martin Palmer, *The Jesus Sutras: Rediscovering the Lost Scrolls of Taoist Christianity* (New York: Ballantine, 2001), 159-68, 180-81. Copyright © 2001 by Martin Palmer. Used by permission of Ballantine Books, a division of Random House, Inc.

[26]When people are afraid they call upon Buddha's name. [27]Many folk are sadly ignorant. [28]God is a sacred spirit force. [29]God is always beside the believer. [30]There are the Sutras. [31]People say they know who God is but they do not. [32]It is in Buddha's nature to bestow grace, and with this grace comes also a deep, clear understanding that lifts us above folly. [33]This way anybody can attain Heaven, even if he is not a scholar. [34]The sacred spirit power of God works in everybody, bringing all to fullness. [35]All existence is an act of grace, every physical form is created, God has brought everything into being. [36]Everything is born, dies, and decays, returning into the earth and continued suffering.

Chapter Two

[1]All that has life, know in your hearts that this is so and by grace understand how to do that which is good. [2]Everything that is born must die. [3]Everything that lives exists only because the Winds give it life. [4]When it is time for life to end, the Winds depart from the body. [5]A person's heart and mind are not their own, but are created by the Winds. [6]The Winds' departure is a time of great distress, but nobody can see the Winds at that time. [7]Nobody can see them because they have no form, no color, not red or green or any other. [8]The Winds of Life are invisible. [9]The path is unknown. [10]Similarly, people want to know where God is. [11]The path is unknown, and so it is impossible to see God.

[12]Only the virtuous can enter into the presence of God, can see God. [13]It is not possible for everyone to see God. [14]Those who are blessed and fortunate can feel God close by, but those who do evil will remain sunk in evil. [15]People must first understand that God cannot be seen, and never has been seen. [16]So the question arises: How can anyone practice the correct way to be blessed? [17]If they avoid the Way of Earth, of Hell, they can attain the Way of Heaven. [18]However, even if they do attain the Way of Heaven, it is still easy for them to sink into the Way of Evil again.

[19]If what they do does not show wisdom, then they are not following the Way of Heaven. All that lives, regard this grace well. [20]There is a great, a very great, distance between Heaven and Earth.

[21]Some lives are shaped by evil. [22]Those who put their souls into serving the nation receive much wealth as a reward, but those who live wicked lives, not doing what is ordered by the Power of Heaven, will never achieve success or a good post. [23]Instead they will be exiled, to die in ignominy. Is this not the Power of Heaven? [24]All such evil stems from the first beings, and the disobedience in the fruitful garden. [25]All that lives is affected by the karma of previous lives. [26]God suffered terrible woes so that all should be freed from karma, for nobody is beyond the reach of this Buddha principle. [27]Those who do good will be blessed and fortunate, but those who do evil will suffer.

Chapter Three

[1]Foolish people make wooden statues of camels, cows, horses, and so on. [2]They may make them seem very lifelike and worship them, but this does not really bring them to life. [3]If you can understand all this, then understand the process of karma's cause and effect. [4]This is a gift unique to human beings. [5]In today's world there are so many who create images of people, of scholars and gurus. [6]They think this makes them like God, but they cannot give life to their creations. [7]They really are confused! [8]They make gold, silver, or bronze statues of spirits, then venerate them. [9]They even make wooden statues of the spirits, people, and animals. [10]But no matter how much the human statue looks like a human, or the horse statue like a horse, or the cow statue like a cow, or the donkey statue like a donkey, they cannot walk, they cannot speak, they cannot eat or drink. [11]They have no real flesh, or skin, or organs, or bones. [12]Even though these statues cannot talk, everybody today wants to talk to them. [13]If you eat something, you should know by its taste and smell whether it is good or bad.

[14]Only somebody who truly worships God can teach the Sutras and expound the texts. [15]Someone who fears punishment does what is right, and tells others to do likewise. [16]God loves such a one, and they are known as one who follows God's Law. [17]However, somebody who knows in their heart the right way to follow, but does not do good and encourages others not to do good, is unacceptable to God. [18]Such people are trapped by lux-

uries and illusions, too preoccupied with appearances, too attracted to life's pleasures, and they are following the wrong path. ¹⁹Such people will end up in the hands of King Yama, God of Judgment and Rebirth. ²⁰But even those who accept the teachings of God, who often say "I obey God," who teach others to obey God, should fear God. ²¹Be watchful every day of slipping. ²²Remember all life depends on God. ²³Everybody should seek the right relationship by resolving their bad actions. ²⁴Life and death are controlled by the sacred spirit, and everyone should fear God.

²⁵This fear is like the fear of the Emperor. ²⁶The Emperor is who he is because of his previous lives which have led to his being placed in this fortunate position. ²⁷He is chosen by God, so cannot call himself God, because he has been appointed by God to do what is expected. ²⁸This is why the people obey the Emperor, and this is right and proper. ²⁹Everyone should obey the Commands. ³⁰If anybody disobeys then they are punished. ³¹Wise people understand this and teach others to act likewise. ³²Those are the people who live by the Precepts. ³³If you do not fear God, even if you live by the Law of the Buddha, you will not be saved. ³⁴Indeed, you will be counted among the traitors.

³⁵The third aspect is to fear your parents. ³⁶You should honor your parents just as you honor God and the Emperor. ³⁷If you honor the Emperor and not your parents then God will not bless you with good fortune.

Chapter Four

¹Of these three aspects, the first and most important is to honor God. ²The second is to honor the Emperor. ³The third is to honor your parents. ⁴The whole of Heaven and Earth follows this way. ⁵Everything follows this way of respecting parents; throughout the world everything owes its existence to parents. ⁶The sacred spirits have ordained that the Emperor is born as the Emperor. ⁷We should fear God, the Sacred One, and the Emperor. ⁸Also, fear your parents and do good. ⁹If you understand the Law and Precepts, do not disobey, but instead teach all people true religion. ¹⁰Buddha creates Buddha's own bitterness and suffering. ¹¹Heaven and Earth have been made to show clearly the causes of creation. ¹²The Emperor should be the embodiment of enlightenment. ¹³He does what is naturally right to do. ¹⁴The first covenant of God is that anything that exists and does evil will be punished, especially if they do not respect the elderly.

¹⁵The second covenant is to honor and care for elderly parents. ¹⁶Those who do this will be true followers of Heaven's Way.

¹⁷The third covenant is to acknowledge we have been brought into existence through our parents. ¹⁸Nothing exists without parents.

¹⁹The fourth covenant is that anybody who understands the precepts should know to be kind and considerate to everything, and to do no evil to anything that lives.

²⁰The fifth covenant is that any living being should not only not take the life of another living being, but should also teach others to do likewise.

²¹The sixth covenant is that nobody should commit adultery, or persuade anyone else to do so.

²²The seventh covenant is not to steal.

²³The eighth covenant is that nobody should covet a living man's wife, or his lands, or his palace, or his servants.

²⁴The ninth covenant is not to let your envy of somebody's good wife, or son, or house or gold, lead you to bear false witness against them.

²⁵The tenth covenant is to offer to God only that which is yours to give.

²⁶But there is much more than this.

²⁷Do not bully those weaker than you. ²⁸Do not despise those more powerful than you. ²⁹If someone is hungry, even if he is your enemy, care for him, forgive and forget. ³⁰If someone is hardworking, help and support him. ³¹Clothe the naked. ³²Do not abuse or try to deceive your workers, especially if you have no real work for them. ³³To do so, and thus fail to pay them, brings suffering to their families. ³⁴If you see someone abusing their workers like this, know that the sacred spirit will severely punish them.

³⁵If a poor person begs for money, give generously. ³⁶If you have no money, have the courtesy to explain why you can give only a little help. ³⁷If someone is seriously ill or handicapped do not mock, because this is the result of karma and not to be ridiculed. ³⁸Do not laugh at poor people in rags and tatters. ³⁹Do not obtain anything by

deception or force. If someone is arrested tell only the truth. [40]Never try to use false means to achieve anything. [41]If someone who is alone, or a widow, or orphan, brings a complaint against anyone, their quest for justice should not be hindered. [42]Do not boast or brag. [43]Do not cause dissent and strife by picking quarrels, arguments, or fights, and do not side with one party against another.

[44]Someone who has power and authority should not abuse it to make things go his way, so do not use your influence with authority to win a case. [45]Keep quiet. [46]Those who follow the precepts should be charitable and humble. [47]Turn away from evil to good. [48]Doing good will save you from tribulation, so do good to all. [49]Those that do so, and follow the covenants, are those who know the precepts. [50]If while studying the Sutras you come to believe, then you have received the precepts.

[51]If you study, but do not believe, then you have not received the precepts. [52]All rests ultimately with God. [53]Our saintly ancestors, both great and small, will stand before us and judge us in the end. [54]The first thing is to obey God. [55]God protects all that lives; everything that lives does so as a result of this. [56]It is forbidden to take a life even for a sacrifice, for these teachings forbid taking any life. [57]All sacrifice and slaying of the lamb is to be offered for the sacred spirits' blessing and forgiveness. [58]If any living being does not follow this, does not do good or sets out to do evil in secret, God will track them down. [59]God will not look with compassion on such behavior, but God does look with compassion on those who turn away from rejecting God and doing evil. [60]God responded by coming to promote good deeds and replace the former law.

Chapter Five

[1]So God caused the Cool Breeze to come upon a chosen young woman called Mo Yan, who had no husband, and she became pregnant. [2]The whole world saw this, and understood what God had wrought. [3]The power of God is such that it can create a bodily spirit and lead to the clear, pure path of compassion. [4]Mo Yan gave birth to a boy and called him Ye Su, who is the Messiah and whose father is the Cool Breeze. [5]Some people claimed they could not understand how this was possible, and said that if the Cool Breeze had made Mo Yan conceive, then such a child must have been created at the bottom of the world.

[6]If the Emperor sends a command, all loyal citizens must obey it. [7]God looks down in compassion from Heaven, and controls everything in Heaven and Earth. [8]When Ye Su the Messiah was born, the whole world saw a bright mystery in the Heavens. [9]Everybody saw from their homes a star as big as a wagon wheel. [10]This mysterious light shone over the place where God was to be found, for at this time the One was born in the city of Wen-li-shih-ken [Jerusalem] in the orchard of But Lam [Bethlehem]. [11]After five years had passed the Messiah began to talk. [12]He did many miraculous and good things while teaching the Law. [13]When he was twelve he assumed the Holy Word and began teaching.

[14]He came to a place of running water called Shu-Nan [Jordan] so that he might be given a name. [15]Thus he came to one called the Brother who dwelt in the wilderness and who, from his birth, had never eaten meat or drunk wine, but instead lived on vegetables and honey gathered from the wilderness.

[16]At that time many people came to the Messiah, bringing gifts, and worshiped him. [17]These people were deeply troubled. [18]The Messiah went to them, bringing the precepts. [19]When he emerged from the waters the Cool Breeze visited him from Heaven and a voice proclaimed "This is my son, obey him."

[20]The Messiah showed everyone that the way of God is the way of Heaven. [21]He spoke the words of the sacred spirit, telling people to renounce evil and talking about doing good. [22]This began when he was twelve and he preached until he was thirty-two. [23]He found people who were living evil lives and brought them back to the way of goodness, the True Way. [24]He instructed his followers, especially his twelve disciples, and traveled the land teaching and healing. [25]Those departed from this world were restored to life. [26]The blind were able to see. [27]The crippled and sick were restored and able to walk. [28]Those troubled by ghosts had them cast out. [29]Some of the sick were healed simply by asking, others by holding on to his gown—but all were healed.

[30]Those who do evil, and do not recognize the True Way or the words teaching of God's religion, as well as the unclean ones, can never be truly saved, not today or even in this generation. [31]The scholars, fearing the Messiah, attacked and denounced him, but the people believed his holy teachings, so he could not be taken.

[32]The evil ones schemed together, pretending to be speakers of truth and purity. [33]They tried to slander him, but could not trap him, so they went to the great king Pilate, wanting him to kill the Messiah. [34]The Messiah ignored all this and continued teaching the people about true religion and how to do good. [35]He became famous.

[36]When he was thirty-two the evil men came before the great king Pilate and were able to state their case, saying that the Messiah must die. [37]The great king said that he would not kill him, as there seemed to be no clear case against him. [38]The seekers of evil in this affair argued that he must die, because otherwise what would become of us?

[39]The great king Pilate ordered water brought and washed his hands showing the evil ones he washed his hands clean of the case. [40]The evil ones continued to press their case until he had no option but to kill the Messiah.

[41]The Messiah gave up his body to the wicked ones for the sake of all living beings. [42]Through this the whole world knows that all life is as precarious as a candle flame. [43]In his compassion he gave up his life.

[44]The evil ones brought the Messiah to a place set apart, and after washing his hair led him to the place of execution called Chi-Chu [Golgotha]. [45]They hung him high upon a wooden scaffold, with two criminals, one on either side of him. [46]He hung there for five hours. [47]That was on the sixth cleansing, vegetarian day. [48]Early that morning there was bright sunlight, but as the sun went West, darkness came over the world, the earth quaked, the mountains trembled, the tombs opened and the dead walked. [49]Those who saw this believed that he was who he said he was. [50]How can anyone not believe? [51]Those who take these words to heart are true disciples of the Messiah. [52]As a result . . . [here the text breaks off].

. . .

The First Liturgical Sutra: Taking Refuge in the Trinity

[1]Da Qin/Syrian Christian liturgy of taking Refuge in the Three

[2]All reverence to the Great Holy Compassionate Father of All Things—Allaha!

[3]Priest: Oh radiant Jade-faced One
Exalted as the sun and moon
Your virtues are greater than those
Of all the Holy Ones and Dharma Lords—

[4]Congregation: The laws of Compassion save us all!

[5]Echoing through the world like a tolling golden bell. . . .

[6]Priest: Great Holy Law Giver
You bring us back to our original nature.

[7]And the souls that are saved are countless:
Divine compassion lifts them up from the dust
Redeeming them from the saddened realm of ghosts

[8]Congregation: The hundred Ways bring us clarity and kindhearted mercy. . . .

[9]Priest: Now I draw close to our Holy Compassionate Father
The One who creates salvation—
See the angelic spirits crossing the Ocean of Dharma!

[10]We know to practice peace in our hearts through You.

[11]This whole gathering unites in singing to You, Honored One:

[12]All: The Great Law is now the Heavenly Wheel
Of returning—to You.

[13]Worship the Dharma Kings. Begin with the Sutra of Dharma King John. Then continue with the Sutra of the Psalms and the Path of Grace Sutra.

[14]On the 2nd day in the 5th month of Hai Yun [720], Su Yun of the Da Qin Religion of Light in the Great Holy Oneness of the Dharma, a monk of the Da Qin monastery at Shachou [Qansu], wrote this faithfully for the faithful.

251

Early Medieval Christianity in the West

48. Acts of the Third Council of Toledo

Reccared, the Arian Visigothic king of Spain, converted to Catholic Christianity in 587. Two years later he convened the so-called Third Council of Toledo, the first of sixteen church councils that met in Toledo under royal supervision between 589 and 702. Aimed at the public conversion of the Goths and strengthening the Catholic faith throughout the land, it ruled that the creed be recited before the Lord's Prayer whenever the Eucharist was celebrated. We find in the acts of this council the first occurrence of the filioque *clause, the addition of the phrase "and the Son" to the Nicene Creed. Here is the king's opening address to the council.*

In the name of our Lord Jesus Christ, in the fourth year of the reign of the most glorious and pious and God-believing lord Reccared, on the eighth day of the Ides of May in the year 627 [589 C.E.], this holy synod was held in the royal city of Toledo by bishops of the whole of Spain and Gaul . . .

When, out of the sincerity of his faith, that most glorious prince had charged all the bishops of his kingdom to come together as one to rejoice at his own conversion and at the return of the Gothic people to the Lord, and to give thanks to the divine dignity for such a gift, the most holy prince spoke to the venerable council saying: "I believe that you know that I called you to our serene presence in order to formulate the discipline of the church. For although in times past the heresy that threatened the whole catholic church kept synods from meeting, now that God has been pleased to use us to remove the obstacle of heresy, he has directed that the church's ordinances be restored. Therefore let it be a matter of delight and

joy for you that, because of our glory, the canonical customs will be brought back to the land of our fathers in the sight of God. But first I admonish and exhort you to give yourselves over to fasting, vigils and prayer, so that the canonical order, which priests have long forgotten and which our age frankly knows nothing about, might be disclosed again as a gift of God."

At that the whole council cried out its approval, with thanks to God and to the most religious prince. Three days of fasting followed. Then on the eighth day of the Ides of May the priests of God came together in one assembly and, after prayer was offered, each of the priests sat in his proper seat; and into their midst came the most serene prince. Having united with the priests of God in prayer and being thereafter filled with divine spirit, he spoke: "We believe it is not unknown to your holinesses how long Spain has labored under the error of the Arians, and we believe that not long after our father's decease, when your holinesses came to know that we had

SOURCE: Tr. John W. Coakley. Latin text: *Concilios Visigóticos e Hispano-Romanos*, ed. José Vives, et al. (Madrid: Instituto Enrique Flórez, 1963), 107-13.

associated ourselves with the holy catholic faith, there was great eternal joy. And so, venerable fathers, we have directed you to gather at this synod to bring to the Lord the thanks of those who just now have come to Christ. The matters to be acted upon by your priestliness concerning the faith and the hope that we manifest, we have written and bound in this volume. Let it be read aloud in your midst. And let our glory shine for all time, tested by the judgment of the synod and adorned by the testimony of the faith."

The priests of God received the volume of the sacred faith from the king who offered it, and they gave it their consideration while the clerk read it out in a clear voice, as follows:

"Although almighty God has bestowed on us the highest place in the kingdom, and has committed to our royal care the government of no small number of people, still we are mindful that we are bound by the condition of mortals and so cannot acquire the happiness of future blessedness unless we give our attention to the defense of the true faith and please our creator by at least making the confession of which he is worthy. And the higher we have been raised over our subordinates by the glory of kingship, the more prudent we ought to be in those things that are of God, both for the increase of our hope and for the care of the people God has entrusted to us. What then shall we give to the divine omnipotence for such benefits, since all things are his own and he has no need of any of our goods—except to believe in him with total devotion, according to the manner in which, in the sacred scriptures, he has wanted us to understand him and has directed us to believe?

"Therefore we confess that there exists the Father, who generates from his very substance a Son co-equal and co-eternal with himself, but not in such a way as to be both child and parent; rather, the Father who generates is one person, and the Son who is generated is another, even though they both subsist in one divinity of substance. For the Father from whom the Son exists, himself exists from nothing else; and the Son has a Father, yet he subsists in divinity without beginning and without diminution, in such a way as to be coequal and coeternal with the Father. And in a similar way, we confess and preach that the Holy Spirit proceeds from the Father and the Son and is one in substance with the Father and Son; indeed that the Holy Spirit is a third person in the Trinity, albeit that it has in common with the Father and the Son the essence of divinity. For this Holy Trinity is one God, Father and Son and Holy Spirit, by whose goodness—by which all things were created good—we are transformed from our cursed inheritance back to our original beatitude, by means of the human form assumed by the Son. But just as it is a sign of true health to perceive the Trinity in Unity and the Unity in Trinity, so we shall come to the perfection of righteousness if we hold to that same faith within the universal church and preserve the teachings of the apostles, resting on the apostolic foundation. It is also important for you priests of God to bear in mind how many troubles the catholic church of God in Spain will have to suffer from the enemy, for as Catholics maintain their agreement in the faith and defend the truth, the heretics will maintain their own falsehood with all the more obstinate animosity. But so that you might see real results, the Lord has raised me up and kindled my zeal for the faith, so that once the obstinacy of infidelity has been expelled and the fury of discord has been removed, I shall recall the people, who have been enslaved to error in the name of religion, to the knowledge of the faith and the fellowship of the catholic church.

"For present here is the renowned nation of the Goths, whom all other nations consider to possess genuine vigor. Even though the depravity of their teachers has thus far separated them from the faith and the unity of the catholic church, now they join their assent to mine and participate together in the communion of the church, which receives the multitude of diverse nations in its maternal bosom and nourishes them with the breasts of charity, and of which the prophet sang: 'my house shall be called a house of prayer for all nations.' Nor is it only the conversion of the Goths that has added to the sum of our reward, but also that of the great multitude of the people of the Suevi, whom with the help of heaven we have subjected to our kingdom; although they had been led astray in the vice of heresy, our zeal has recalled them to the fount of truth. So it is, most holy fathers, that I offer these noble nations, whom we have brought near to the benefits of the Lord, as a holy and appeasing sacrifice to eternal God by your hands; when the righteous are rewarded, there will an unfading crown and joy for me, if these peoples who because of our adroitness have come running to the unity of the church, have been established in it and remain steadfast. For just as, by divine command, it was our concern to draw those nations to the unity of the church of Christ, so let them be educated by your teaching in the catholic dogmas, so that being instructed in all knowledge of the truth they may be able firmly to reject the error of pernicious heresy, stay on the pathway of the true faith in love, and embrace the communion of the catholic church with all the more avid desire.

"Furthermore, just as I believe that such an illustrious nation will find pardon easily for having erred unaware, so I do not doubt that it will be a weightier matter, if they hold their understanding of the truth with a doubtful heart and avert their eyes from the clear light. For that reason I have considered it necessary to convene your beatitude, having faith in the saying of the Lord that 'where two or three are gathered in my name, there will I be in the midst of them' (Matt. 18:20). For I believe that the blessed divinity of the holy Trinity is present in this holy council; and I have brought my faith into your midst as though into the sight of God, being aware of the divine saying, 'I have not hidden your mercy and your truth from the great congregation' (Ps. 40:10); and I have heard the apostle Paul directing his disciple Timothy: 'Fight the good fight of faith, lay hold on eternal life, to which you have been called, and of which you made a good confession before many witnesses' (1 Tim. 6:12).

"For the saying of our redeemer in the Gospel is true, that the one who confesses him before others confesses him before the Father, and that whoever denies him will be denied (Luke 12:8-9). For it is profitable for us to confess by the mouth what we believe in the heart, according to the heavenly directive: 'in the heart one believes for righteousness, and with the mouth one makes confession for salvation'" (Rom. 10:10).

[*Reccared then endorses the Councils of Nicaea, Constantinople, Ephesus, and Chalcedon.*]

"Therefore let your reverences hasten to put this faith of ours into the canonical records, and to hear from bishops and religious and nobles of our people the faith that they wisely confess within the catholic church, noted in writing, affirmed by their signatures and reserved for a human and divine testimony in future times, so that these peoples over whom in the name of God we preside in royal power, and which, ancient error being wiped away through the unction of the holy chrisms or the imposition of hands will perceive the Paraclete Spirit in the church of God, which Spirit they confess as one and equal with the Father and the Son, its gifts being located in the bosom of the holy catholic church. If any persons wish to doubt this upright and holy confession of ours, let them receive the anger of God with eternal anathema, and let their ruin be a joy to believers and an example to unbelievers. To this confession of mine I have joined the holy constitutions of the aforementioned councils, and, God being my witness, in all simplicity of heart I have added my signature. . . . "

49. Columbanus, *Letter 2*

Part of the great age of Irish monasticism and missions, Columbanus (d. 615) was educated at the monastery of Bangor in Ireland. Among the Irish peregrini, wandering monks and nuns who began to spread across the

SOURCE: *Sancti Columbani Opera*, ed. and tr. G. S. M. Walker (Dublin: Institute for Historical Studies, 1957), 15-23. Used by permission of The Dublin Institute for Advanced Studies (School of Celtic Studies).

European continent by the late sixth century, Columbanus traveled to Gaul in the 580s. He established several important monasteries in southern France and northern Italy and composed a monastic rule based on rigorous Irish ascetic practices. He wrote the following letter in 603 to a synod of bishops in Gaul in defense of his adherence to customs of the Irish church (especially regarding Easter) that were at odds with Roman and Gallic practice.

5. Therefore let us all together, whether clergy or monks, first frankly execute these true and unique rules of our Lord Jesus Christ, and thus thereafter, laying aside the swelling growth of pride, seek to record a unanimous verdict on the rest. If we all choose to be humble and poor for Christ's sake, Who for our sakes became poor though He was rich, then, with our various lusts laid aside and our mortal cares cast out from the sinful clay, by humility and by the willing poverty which the gospel teaches, as it were with the causes of disagreement and difference cut off, all the sons of God shall mutually enjoy between themselves a true peace and entire charity, by the likeness of their characters and the agreement of their single will. For great harm has been done and is done to the church's peace by difference of character and diversity of practice; but yet if, as I have said, we first hasten by the exercise of true humility to heal the poisons of pride and envy and vain glory, through the teaching of our Savior Who says for our example, Learn of Me for I am meek and lowly of heart, and so on, then let us all, made perfect with no further blemish, with hatred rooted out, as the disciples of our Lord Jesus Christ, love one another with our whole heart. And if there be some variety of traditional practice, as there is over Easter, while the humble cannot strive, nor does the church have such a custom, while those will soon know more truly, who with the same purpose and the same desire of knowing truth seek jointly what they may more rightly follow, when none is vanquished except error, and when none boasts in himself but in the Lord; let us then seek together, I beseech you, my most loving fathers and brethren, and let us see which be the more true tradition—yours, or that of your brethren in the West. For, as I have noted in the book of my reply, which I have now sent you, though it was written three years ago, all the churches of the entire West do not consider that the resurrection should take place before the passion, that is, Easter before the equinox, and they do not wait beyond the twentieth moon, lest they should hold a sacrament of the New Testament without authority of the Old. But this I leave to another time; for the rest, I have informed the holy father in three books of their opinions upon Easter, and in a short pamphlet I have further ventured to write the same to your holy brother Arigius.

6. One thing therefore I request of your holiness, that with peace and charity you bear my ignorance and, as some say, my proud impudence in writing, which has been extorted by necessity, not pride, as my very baseness proves; and since I am not the author of this difference, and it is for the sake of Christ the Savior, our common Lord and God, that I have entered these lands a pilgrim, I beseech you by our common Lord, and entreat you by Him Who is to judge the quick and the dead, if you deserve His recognition Who shall say to many, Amen I say to you that I never knew you, that I may be allowed with your peace and charity to enjoy the silence of these woods and to live beside the bones of our seventeen dead brethren, even as up till now we have been allowed to live twelve years among you, so that, as up till now we have done, we may pray for you as we ought. Let Gaul, I beg, contain us side by side, whom the kingdom of heaven shall contain, if our deserts are good; for we have one kingdom promised and one hope of our calling in Christ, with Whom we shall together reign, if indeed we first suffer here with Him, that also together with Him we may be glorified. I know that to many this verbosity of mine will seem excessive; but I judged it better that you too should know what we here discuss and ponder

amongst ourselves. For these are our rules, the commands of the Lord and the apostles, in these our confidence is placed; these are our weapons, shield and sword, these are our defense; these brought us from our native land; these here too we seek to maintain, though laxly; in these we pray and hope to continue up till death, as we have seen our predecessors do. But do you, holy fathers, look what you do to your poor veterans and aged pilgrims; as I judge, it will be better for you to comfort them than to confound.

7. I however did not venture to appear before you, lest perhaps when present I might strive contrary to the apostle's precept when he says, Do not strive with words, and again, If any man is quarrelsome, we have no such custom nor has the church of God; but I admit the inmost convictions of my conscience, that I have more confidence in the tradition of my native land in accordance with the teaching and reckoning of eighty-four years and with Anatolius, who was commended by Bishop Eusebius the author of the ecclesiastical history and by Jerome the holy writer of the catalogue, for the celebration of Easter, rather than to do so in accordance with Victorius who writes recently and in a doubtful manner, and without defining anything where it was needed, as he himself bears witness in his prologue, and who, after the age of great Martin and great Jerome and Pope Damasus, under Hilary covered a hundred and three years with his compilation. But do you yourselves choose whom you prefer to follow, and whom you rather trust, in accordance with that saying of the apostle, Prove all things, hold what is good. Far be it then that I should maintain the need to quarrel with you, so that a conflict among us Christians should rejoice our enemies, I mean the Jews or heretics or Gentile heathen—far be it indeed, far be it; for the rest, we may agree in some other way, so that either each should remain before God in the condition in which he was called, if both traditions are good, or else both books should be read over in peace and humility without any argument, and what agrees better with the Old and New Testament should be maintained without ill-will at any. For if it is of God that you should drive me hence from the place of seclusion, which I have sought from overseas for

the sake of my Lord Jesus Christ, it will be my part to use—that prophetic speech. If on my account this storm is upon you, take me and cast me into the sea, that this tempest may recede from you in calm; yet let it first be your part like those mariners to seek to save the shipwrecked by the bowels of godliness, and to draw the ship to land, as they, though Gentiles, did, according to the scripture, which says, And the men sought to return to land and could not, for the sea ran and the swell increased the more. Finally as my last word I advise, admittedly with presumption, that, since many walking on the roomy and broad roadway of this age hasten towards the narrow crossing, if some few are found, who pass through the strait and narrow gate, that leads to life according to the Lord's command, you should rather help them on to life than hinder them, lest perhaps you also with the Pharisees be smitten by the word of the Lord, saying, Woe unto you, scribes and Pharisees, since you shut the kingdom of heaven before men, and Neither do you enter yourselves, nor do you allow them that are entering to enter.

8. But someone will say: Are we really not entering the kingdom of heaven? Why can you not by the Lord's grace, if you become as little children, that is, humble and chaste, simple-hearted and guileless in evil, yet wise in goodness, easy to be entreated and not retaining anger in your heart? But all these things can very hardly be fulfilled by those who often look at women and who more often quarrel and grow angry over the riches of the world. Thus our party, once renouncing the world, and cutting off sins' causes and strifes' incentives at the start, consider that they may more easily fulfill the Lord's word in nakedness than wealth. For before the acquisition of these four qualities there is no entrance to the kingdom of heaven, as St. Jerome witnesses to three and Basil to the fourth, who expound the character of children in accordance with the tenor of the gospel saying. For a child is humble, does not harbor the remembrance of injury, does not lust after a woman when he looks on her, does not keep one thing on his lips and another in his heart. And these, as I have said, will be better maintained by one who is still and sees that God Himself is Lord,

than by one who sees and hears all manner of things. Let none disparage the benefits of silence; for unless they grow lax, the secluded live better than the social, except for that still stricter life which has the greater reward; for where the battle is more stubborn, there is found a crown of higher glory. But yet, as says St. Gregory, they are not credited with private virtues who do not avoid notorious ills. Therefore knowing this, St. Jerome bade bishops imitate the apostles, but taught monks to follow the fathers who were perfect. For the patterns of clergy and of monks are different, and widely distinct from one another. Let each maintain what he has grasped; but let all maintain the gospel, and both parties, like single harmonious members of one body, follow Christ the head of all by His own commands, which were revealed by Him to be accomplished in charity and peace. And these two cannot be perfectly accomplished, save by truly humble and unitedly spiritual men, who fulfill Christ's commands, as the Lord Himself bears witness, If ye love Me, keep My commandments, this is My commandment, that ye love one another, as I also have loved you, for in this shall all know that ye are My disciples, if ye love one another. Thus unity of minds and peace and charity then can be assured, spread abroad in the bowels of believers by the Holy Ghost, when all alike long to fulfill the divine commands; for the fiction of peace and charity between the imperfect will be such as is the measure of disagreement in their practical pursuits. Therefore, that we may love one another in charity unfeigned, let us carefully ponder the commands of our Lord Jesus Christ, and hasten to fulfill them when understood, that by His teaching the whole church may hasten to the heavenly places with one impulse of unbounded zeal. May His free grace afford us this, that we all may shun the world and love Him only and long for Him with the Father and the Holy Ghost, to Whom is the glory unto ages of ages. Amen.

9. For the rest, fathers, pray for us as we also do for you, wretched though we be, and refuse to consider us estranged from you; for we are all joint members of one body, whether Franks or Britons or Irish or whatever our race be. Thus let all our races rejoice in the comprehension of faith and the apprehension of the Son of God, and let us all hasten to approach to perfect manhood, to the measure of the completed growth of the fullness of Jesus Christ, in Whom let us love one another, praise one another, correct one another, encourage one another, pray for one another, that with Him in one another we may reign and triumph. Pray pardon my verbosity and presumption as I toil beyond my strength, most long-suffering and holy fathers and brethren all.

50. Bede, *Ecclesiastical History*

A monk and the greatest of Anglo-Saxon scholars, the "Venerable" Bede (ca. 673-735) composed what is our principal source for the study of the early English church. The conversion of England to Christianity in the seventh century was partly the work of Irish monks and partly the work of Benedictine missionaries sent out by Rome under Pope Gregory I. The following selections from Bede's History *focus on the ideals and strategy of the Roman mission and the eventual resolution of tensions in the English church caused by the different traditions of Irish and Roman Christianity.*

SOURCE: Bede, *A History of the English Church and People*, tr. Leo Sherley-Price (New York: Penguin, 1955), 66-67, 68-71, 86-87, 185-92. Copyright © Leo Sherley-Price, 1955, 1968. Reproduced by permission of Penguin Books Ltd.

Book One

CHAPTER 23: *The holy Pope Gregory sends Augustine and other monks to preach to the English nation, and encourages them in a letter to persevere in their mission* [596 C.E.].

In the year of our Lord 582, Maurice, fifty-fourth in succession from Augustus, became Emperor, and ruled for twenty-one years. In the tenth year of his reign, Gregory, an eminent scholar and administrator, was elected Pontiff of the apostolic Roman see, and ruled it for thirteen years, six months, and ten days. In the fourteenth year of this Emperor, and about the one hundred and fiftieth year after the coming of the English to Britain, Gregory was inspired by God to send his servant Augustine with several other God-fearing monks to preach the word of God to the English nation. Having undertaken this task in obedience to the Pope's command and progressed a short distance on their journey, they became afraid, and began to consider returning home. For they were appalled at the idea of going to a barbarous, fierce, and pagan nation, of whose very language they were ignorant. They unanimously agreed that this was the safest course, and sent back Augustine—who was to be consecrated bishop in the event of their being received by the English—so that he might humbly request the holy Gregory to recall them from so dangerous, arduous, and uncertain a journey. In reply, the Pope wrote them a letter of encouragement, urging them to proceed on their mission to preach God's word, and to trust themselves to his aid. This letter ran as follows:

"GREGORY, Servant of the servants of God, to the servants of our Lord. My very dear sons, it is better never to undertake any high enterprise than to abandon it when once begun. So with the help of God you must carry out this holy task which you have begun. Do not be deterred by the troubles of the journey or by what men say. Be constant and zealous in carrying out this enterprise which, under God's guidance, you have undertaken: and be assured that the greater the labor, the greater will be the glory of your eternal reward. When Augustine your leader returns, whom We have appointed your abbot, obey him humbly in all things, remembering that whatever he directs

you to do will always be to the good of your souls. May Almighty God protect you with His grace, and grant me to see the result of your labors in our heavenly home. And although my office prevents me from working at your side, yet because I long to do so, I hope to share in your joyful reward. God keep you safe, my dearest sons.

"Dated the twenty-third of July, in the fourteenth year of the reign of the most pious Emperor Maurice Tiberius Augustus, and the thirteenth year after his Consulship: the fourteenth indiction."

CHAPTER 25: *Augustine reaches Britain, and first preaches in the Isle of Thanet before King Ethelbert, who grants permission to preach in Kent* [597 C.E.].

Reassured by the encouragement of the blessed father Gregory, Augustine and his fellow servants of Christ resumed their work in the word of God, and arrived in Britain. At this time the most powerful king there was Ethelbert, who reigned in Kent and whose domains extended northwards to the river Humber, which forms the boundary between the north and south Angles. To the east of Kent lies the large island of Thanet, which by English reckoning is six hundred hides in extent; it is separated from the mainland by a waterway about three furlongs broad called the Wantsum, which joins the sea at either end and is fordable only in two places. It was here that God's servant Augustine landed with companions, who are said to have been forty in number. At the direction of blessed Pope Gregory, they had brought interpreters from among the Franks, and they sent these to Ethelbert, saying that they came from Rome bearing very glad news, which infallibly assured all who would receive it of eternal joy in heaven and an everlasting kingdom with the living and true God. On receiving this message, the king ordered them to remain in the island where they had landed, and gave directions that they were to be provided with all necessaries until he should decide what action to take. For he had already heard of the Christian religion, having a Christian wife of the Frankish royal house named Bertha, whom he had received from her parents on condition that she should have freedom to hold and practice her faith unhindered with Bishop Liudhard, whom they had sent as her helper in the faith.

After some days, the king came to the island and, sitting down in the open air, summoned Augustine and his companions to an audience. But he took precautions that they should not approach him in a house; for he held an ancient superstition that, if they were practicers of magical arts, they might have opportunity to deceive and master him. But the monks were endowed with power from God, not from the Devil, and approached the king carrying a silver cross as their standard and the likeness of our Lord and Savior painted on a board. First of all they offered prayer to God, singing a litany for the eternal salvation both of themselves and of those to whom and for whose sake they had come. And when, at the king's command, they had sat down and preached the word of life to the king and his court, the king said: "Your words and promises are fair indeed; but they are new and uncertain, and I cannot accept them and abandon the age-old beliefs that I have held together with the whole English nation. But since you have traveled far, and I can see that you are sincere in your desire to impart to us what you believe to be true and excellent we will not harm you. We will receive you hospitably and take care to supply you with all that you need; nor will we forbid you to preach and win any people you can to your religion." The king then granted them a dwelling in the city of Canterbury, which was the chief city of all his realm, and in accordance with his promise he allowed them provisions and did not withdraw their freedom to preach. Tradition says that as they approached the city, bearing the holy cross and the likeness of our great King and Lord Jesus Christ as was their custom, they sang in unison this litany: "We pray Thee, O Lord, in all Thy mercy, that Thy wrath and anger may be turned away from this city and from Thy holy house, for we are sinners. Alleluia."

CHAPTER 26: *The life and doctrine of the primitive Church are followed in Kent: Augustine establishes his episcopal see in the king's city.*

As soon as they had occupied the house given to them they began to emulate the life of the apostles and the primitive Church. They were constantly at prayer; they fasted and kept vigils; they preached the word of life to whomsoever they could. They regarded worldly things as of little importance, and accepted only the necessities of life from those they taught. They practiced what they preached, and were willing to endure any hardship, and even to die for the truth which they proclaimed. Before long a number of heathen, admiring the simplicity of their holy lives and the comfort of their heavenly message, believed and were baptized. On the east side of the city stood an old church, built in honor of Saint Martin during the Roman occupation of Britain, where the Christian queen of whom I have spoken went to pray. Here they first assembled to sing the psalms, to pray, to say Mass, to preach, and to baptize, until the king's own conversion to the Faith gave them greater freedom to preach and to build and restore churches everywhere.

At length the king himself, among others, edified by the pure lives of these holy men and their gladdening promises, the truth of which they confirmed by many miracles, believed and was baptized. Thenceforward great numbers gathered each day to hear the word of God, forsaking their heathen rites and entering the unity of Christ's holy Church as believers. While the king was pleased at their faith and conversion, it is said that he would not compel anyone to accept Christianity; for he had learned from his instructors and guides to salvation that the service of Christ must be accepted freely and not under compulsion. Nevertheless, he showed greater favor to believers, because they were fellow citizens of the kingdom of heaven. And it was not long before he granted his teachers in his capital of Canterbury a place of residence appropriate to their station, and gave them possessions of various kinds to supply their wants.

CHAPTER 30: *A copy of the letter sent by Pope Gregory to Abbot Mellitus on his departure for Britain* [601 C.E.].

When these messengers had left, the holy father Gregory sent after them letters worthy of our notice, which show most clearly his unwearying interest in the salvation of our nation. The letter runs as follows:

"To our well loved son Abbot Mellitus: Gregory, servant of the servants of God.

"Since the departure of those of our fellowship who are bearing you company, we have been seriously anxious, because we have received no news of the success of your journey. Therefore, when by God's help you reach our most reverend brother, Bishop Augustine, we wish you to inform him that we have been giving careful thought to the affairs of the English, and have come to the conclusion that the temples of the idols among that people should on no account be destroyed. The idols are to be destroyed, but the temples themselves are to be aspersed with holy water, altars set up in them, and relics deposited there. For if these temples are well-built, they must be purified from the worship of demons and dedicated to the service of the true God. In this way, we hope that the people, seeing that their temples are not destroyed, may abandon their error and, flocking more readily to their accustomed resorts, may come to know and adore the true God. And since they have a custom of sacrificing many oxen to demons, let some other solemnity be substituted in its place, such as a day of Dedication or the Festivals of the holy martyrs whose relics are enshrined there. On such occasions they might well construct shelters of boughs for themselves around the churches that were once temples, and celebrate the solemnity with devout feasting. They are no longer to sacrifice beasts to the Devil, but they may kill them for food to the praise of God, and give thanks to the Giver of all gifts for the plenty they enjoy. If the people are allowed some worldly pleasures in this way, they will more readily come to desire the joys of the spirit. For it is certainly impossible to eradicate all errors from obstinate minds at one stroke, and whoever wishes to climb to a mountain top climbs gradually step by step, and not in one leap. It was in this way that the Lord revealed Himself to the Israelite people in Egypt, permitting the sacrifices formerly offered to the Devil to be offered thenceforward to Himself instead. So He bade them sacrifice beasts to Him, so that, once they became enlightened, they might abandon one element of sacrifice and retain another. For, while they were to offer the same beasts as before, they were to offer them to God instead of to idols, so that they

would no longer be offering the same sacrifices. Of your kindness, you are to inform our brother Augustine of this policy, so that he may consider how he may best implement it on the spot. God keep you safe, my very dear son."

Book Three

CHAPTER 25: *Controversy arises with the Scots over the date of Easter* [664 C.E.].

When Bishop Aidan departed this life, he was succeeded in the Bishopric by Finan, who had been consecrated and sent by the Scots. He built a church in the Isle of Lindisfarne suitable for an episcopal see, constructing it, however, not of stone, but of hewn oak thatched with reeds after the Scots manner. It was later dedicated by the most reverend Archbishop Theodore in honor of the blessed Apostle Peter. But Eadbert, a later Bishop of Lindisfarne, removed the thatch, and covered both roof and walls with sheets of lead.

About this time there arose a great and recurrent controversy on the observance of Easter, those trained in Kent and Gaul maintaining that the Scottish observance was contrary to that of the universal Church. The most zealous champion of the true Easter was a Scot named Ronan, who had been instructed in Gaul and Italy in the authentic practice of the Church. He disputed against Finan and convinced many, or at least persuaded them to make more careful enquiry into the truth. But he entirely failed to move Finan, a hot-tempered man whom reproof made more obstinate and openly hostile to the truth. James, formerly the deacon of the venerable Archbishop Paulinus, of whom I have spoken, kept the true and Catholic Easter with all whom he could persuade to adopt the right observance. Also Queen Eanfled and her court, having a Kentish priest named Romanus who followed the Catholic practice, observed the customs she had seen in Kent. It is said that the confusion in those days was such that Easter was sometimes kept twice in one year, so that when the King had ended Lent and was keeping Easter, the Queen and her attendants were still fasting and keeping Palm Sunday. During Aidan's lifetime these differences of Easter observance were patiently tolerated by everyone; for it was realized that, although he was in loyalty bound to retain the customs of those who sent him, he nevertheless labored diligently to cultivate the faith, piety, and love that marks out God's saints. He was therefore rightly loved by all, even by those who differed from his opinion on Easter, and was held in high respect not only by ordinary folk, but by Honorius of Canterbury and Felix of the East Angles.

When Finan, who followed Aidan as bishop, died, he was succeeded by another Irishman, Colman, under whom an even more serious controversy arose about Easter and also about other rules of Church discipline. This dispute rightly began to trouble the minds and consciences of many people, who feared that they might have received the name of Christian in vain. Eventually the matter came to the notice of King Oswy and his son Alchfrid. Oswy thought nothing could be better than the Scots teaching, having been instructed and baptized by the Scots and having a complete grasp of their language. But Alchfrid, who had been instructed in the Faith by Wilfrid—a very learned man who had gone to Rome to study the doctrine of the Church, and spent a long time at Lyons under Dalfin, Archbishop of Gaul, from whom he had received the tonsure—knew that Wilfrid's doctrine was in fact preferable to all the traditions of the Scots. He had therefore given him a monastery with forty hides of land at In-Hrypum. Actually, he had given this not long previously to the adherents of the Scottish customs; but since, when offered the alternative, these preferred to give up the place rather than alter their customs, he then offered it to Wilfrid, whose life and teaching made him a worthy recipient. About this time, Agilbert, Bishop of the West Saxons, whom I have mentioned, had come to visit the province of the Northumbrians. He was a friend both of King Alchfrid and of Abbot Wilfrid and stayed with them for some time, and at the king's request he made Wilfrid a priest in his monastery. He also had with him a priest named Agatho. So when discussion arose there on the questions of Easter, the tonsure, and various other church matters, it was decided to hold a synod to put an end to this dispute at the monastery of Streanaeshalch, which means The Bay of the Beacon, then ruled by the Abbess Hilda, a woman devoted to God. Both kings, father and son, came to this synod, and so did Bishop Colman with his Scots clergy, and Bishop Agilbert with the priests Agatho and Wilfrid. James and Romanus supported the latter, while Abbess Hilda and her community, together with the venerable bishop Cedd, supported the Scots. Cedd, who as already mentioned had long ago been ordained by the Scots, acted as a most careful interpreter for both parties at the council.

King Oswy opened by observing that all who served the One God should observe one rule of life, and since they all hoped for one kingdom in heaven, they should not differ in celebrating the sacraments of heaven. The synod now had the task of determining which was the truer tradition, and this should be loyally accepted by all. He then directed his own bishop Colman to speak first, and to explain his own rite and its origin. Then Colman said: "The Easter customs which I observe were taught me by my superiors, who sent me here as a bishop; and all our forefathers, men beloved of God, are known to have observed these customs. And lest anyone condemn or reject them as wrong, it is recorded that they owe their origin to the blessed evangelist Saint John, the disciple especially loved by our Lord, and all the churches over which he presided." When he had concluded these and similar arguments, the king directed Agilbert to explain the origin and authority of his own customs. Agilbert replied: "May I request that my disciple the priest Wilfrid be allowed to speak in my place? For we are both in full agreement with all those here present who support the traditions of our Church, and he can explain our view in the English language more competently and clearly than I can do through an interpreter." When Wilfrid had received the king's command to speak, he said: "Our Easter customs are those that we have seen universally observed in Rome, where the blessed Apostles Peter and Paul lived, taught, suffered, and are buried. We have also seen the same customs generally observed throughout Italy and Gaul when we traveled through these countries for study and prayer. Furthermore, we have learnt that Easter is observed by men of different nations and languages at one and the same time, in Africa, Asia, Egypt, Greece, and throughout the world wherever the Church of Christ has spread. The only people who stupidly contend against the whole world are these Scots and their partners in obstinacy the Picts and Britons, who inhabit only a portion of these the two uttermost islands of the ocean." In reply to this statement, Colman answered: "It is strange that you call us stupid when we uphold customs that rest on the authority of so great an Apostle, who was considered worthy to lean on our Lord's breast, and whose great wisdom is acknowledged throughout the world." Wilfrid replied: "Far be it from us to charge John with stupidity, because he literally observed the Law of Moses at a time when the Church followed many Jewish practices, and the Apostles were not able immediately to abrogate the observances of the Law once given by God, lest they gave offense to believers who were Jews (whereas idols, on the other hand, being inventions of the Devil, must be renounced by all converts). For this reason Paul circumcised Timothy, offered sacrifice in the Temple, and shaved his head at Corinth with Aquila and Priscilla, for no other reason than that of avoiding offense to the Jews. For James said to Paul: '*Thou seest, brother, how many thousands of Jews there are which believe; and they are all zealous of the law*' [Acts 21:20]. But today, as the Gospel spreads throughout the world, it is unnecessary and indeed unlawful for the faithful to be circumcised or to offer animals to God in sacrifice. John, following the custom of the Law, used to begin the Feast of Easter on the evening of the fourteenth day of the first month, not caring whether it fell on the Sabbath or on any other day. But Peter, when he preached in Rome, remembering that it was on the day after the Sabbath that our Lord rose from the dead and gave the world the hope of resurrection, realized that Easter should be kept as follows: like John, in accordance with the Law, he waited for moonrise on the evening of the fourteenth day of the first month. And if the Lord's Day, then called the morrow of the Sabbath, fell on the following day, he began to observe Easter the same evening, as we all do today. But, if the Lord's Day did not fall on the day following the fourteenth day of the moon, but on the sixteenth, seventeenth, or any other day up to the twenty-first, he waited until that day, and on the Sabbath evening preceding it he began the observance of the Easter Festival. This evangelical and apostolical tradition does not abrogate but fulfill the Law, which ordained that the Passover be kept between the eve of the fourteenth and twenty-first days of the moon of that month. And this is the custom of all the successors of blessed John in Asia since his death, and is also that of the worldwide Church. This is the true and only Easter to be observed by the faithful. It was not newly decreed by the Council of Nicaea, but reaffirmed by it, as Church history records. It is quite apparent, Colman, that you follow neither the example of John, as you imagine, nor that of Peter, whose tradition you deliberately contradict. Your keeping of Easter agrees neither with the Law nor with the Gospel. For John, who kept Easter in accordance with the decrees of Moses, did not keep to the first day after the Sabbath; but this is not your practice, for you keep Easter only on the first day after the Sabbath. Peter kept Easter between the fifteenth and twenty-first days of the moon; you do not, for you keep it between the fourteenth and twentieth days of the moon. As a result, you often begin Easter on the evening of the thirteenth day, which is not mentioned in the Law. Nor did our Lord, the Author and Giver of the Gospel, eat the old Passover or institute the Sacrament of the New Testament to be celebrated by the Church in memory of His Passion on that day, but on the fourteenth. Furthermore, when you keep Easter, you totally exclude the twenty-first day, which the Law of Moses particularly ordered to be observed. Therefore, I repeat, you follow neither John nor Peter, the Law nor the Gospel, in your keeping of our greatest Festival."

Colman in reply said: "Do you maintain that Anatolius, a holy man highly spoken of in Church history, taught contrary to the Law and the Gospel, when he wrote that Easter should be kept between the fourteenth and twentieth days of the moon? Are we to believe that our most revered Father Columba and his successors, men so dear to God, thought or acted contrary to Holy Scripture when they followed this custom? The holiness of many of them is confirmed by heavenly signs, and their virtues by miracles; and having no doubt that they are Saints, I shall never cease to emulate their lives, customs, and discipline."

"It is well established that Anatolius was a most holy, learned, and praiseworthy man," answered Wilfrid; "but how can you claim his authority when you do not follow his directions? For he followed the correct rule about Easter, and observed a cycle of nineteen years; but either you do not know of this general custom of the Christian Church, or else you ignore it. He calculated the fourteenth day of the moon at Easter according to the Egyptian method, counting it in the evening as the fifteenth; similarly, he assigned the twentieth to Easter Sunday, regarding it after sunset as the twenty-first day. But it appears that you do not realize this distinction, since you sometimes keep Easter before full moon, that is, on the thirteenth day. And with regard to your Father Columba and his followers, whose holiness you claim to imitate and whose rules and customs you claim to have been supported by heavenly signs, I can only say that when many shall say to our Lord at the day of judgment: *'Have we not prophesied in Thy name, and cast out devils, and done many wonderful works?'* the Lord will reply, *'I never knew you'* [Matt: 7:22-23]. Far be it from me to apply these words to your fathers; for it is more just to believe good rather than evil of those whom one does not know. So I do not deny that they were true servants of God and dear to Him, and that they loved Him in primitive simplicity but in devout sincerity. Nor do I think that their ways of keeping Easter were seriously harmful, so long as no one came to show them a more perfect way to follow. Indeed, I feel certain that, if any Catholic reckoner had come to them, they would readily have accepted his guidance, as we know that they readily observed such of God's ordinances as they already knew. But you and your colleagues are most certainly guilty of sin if you reject the decrees of the Apostolic See, indeed of the universal Church, which are confirmed by Holy Writ. For, although your Fathers were holy men, do you imagine that they, a few men in a corner of a remote island, are to be preferred before the universal Church of Christ throughout the world? And even if your Columba—or, may I say, ours also if he was the servant of Christ—was a Saint potent in miracles, can he take precedence before the most blessed Prince of the Apostles, to whom our Lord said; *'Thou art Peter, and upon this rock I will build my Church, and the gates of hell shall not prevail against it, and I will give unto thee the keys of the kingdom of heaven'*?" [Matt. 16:18-19].

When Wilfrid had ended, the king asked: "Is it true, Colman, that these words were spoken to that Peter by our Lord?" He answered: "It is true, Your Majesty." Then the king said: "Can you show that a similar authority was given to your Columba?" "No," replied Colman. "Do you both agree," the king continued, "that these words were indisputably addressed to Peter in the first place, and that our Lord gave him the keys of the kingdom of heaven?" Both answered: "We do." At this, the king concluded: "Then, I tell you, Peter is guardian of the gates of heaven, and I shall not contradict him. I shall obey his commands in everything to the best of my knowledge and ability; otherwise, when I come to the gates of heaven, there may be no one to open them, because he who holds the keys has turned away."

When the king said this, all present, both high and low, signified their agreement and, abandoning their imperfect customs, hastened to adopt those which they had learned to be better.

51. Rudolf of Fulda,
Life of Leoba

Despite limitations they faced as females, women had a very important place in English religious life. Some even ruled "double monasteries" com-

SOURCE: *The Anglo-Saxon Missionaries in Germany*, tr. C. H. Talbot (New York: Sheed & Ward, 1954), 207-8, 210-18, 222-23, 224. Used by permission of The Continuum International Publishing Group Ltd.

prising communities of men and women under a single abbess. Others formed part of a great Anglo-Saxon missions effort that spread the Christian faith to still largely pagan areas of Europe. Known for her avid reading, piety, and leadership, the nun Leoba (ca. 700-780) was summoned by Boniface to aid in his missionary work in Germany. There she founded Bischofsheim monastery, a model for convents throughout the land. Leoba's biography was written some fifty years after her death.

In the island of Britain, which is inhabited by the English nation, there is a place called Wimbourne, an ancient name which may be translated "Winestream." It received this name from the clearness and sweetness of the water there, which was better than any other in that land. In olden times the kings of that nation had built two monasteries in the place, one for men, the other for women, both surrounded by strong and lofty walls and provided with all the necessities that prudence could devise. From the beginning of the foundation the rule firmly laid down for both was that no entrance should be allowed to a person of the other sex. No woman was permitted to go into the men's community, nor was any man allowed into the women's, except in the case of priests who had to celebrate Mass in their churches; even so, immediately after the function was ended the priest had to withdraw. Any woman who wished to renounce the world and enter the cloister did so on the understanding that she would never leave it. She could only come out if there was a reasonable cause and some great advantage accrued to the monastery. Furthermore, when it was necessary to conduct the business of the monastery and to send for something outside, the superior of the community spoke through a window and only from there did she make decisions and arrange what was needed.

It was over this monastery, in succession to several other abbesses and spiritual mistresses, that a holy virgin named Tetta was placed in authority, a woman of noble family (for she was a sister of the king), but more noble in her conduct and good qualities. Over both the monasteries she ruled with consummate prudence and discretion. She gave instruction by deed rather than by words, and whenever she said that a certain course of action was harmful to the salvation of souls she

showed by her own conduct that it was to be shunned. She maintained discipline with such circumspection (and the discipline there was much stricter than anywhere else) that she would never allow her nuns to approach clerics. She was so anxious that the nuns, in whose company she always remained, should be cut off from the company of men that she denied entrance into the community not merely to laymen and clerics but even to bishops. There are many instances of the virtues of this woman which the virgin Leoba, her disciple, used to recall with pleasure when she told her reminiscences.

. . .

We will now pursue our purpose of describing the life of her spiritual daughter, Leoba the virgin.

As we have already said, her parents were English, of noble family and full of zeal for religion and the observance of God's commandments. Her father was called Dynno, her mother Aebba. But as they were barren, they remained together for a long time without children. After many years had passed and the onset of old age had deprived them of all hope of offspring, her mother had a dream in which she saw herself bearing in her bosom a church bell, which on being drawn out with her hand rang merrily. When she woke up she called her old nurse to her and told her what she had dreamt. The nurse said to her: "We shall yet see a daughter from your womb and it is your duty to consecrate her straightaway to God. And as Anna offered Samuel to serve God all the days of his life in the temple, so you must offer her, when she has been taught the Scripture from her infancy, to serve Him in holy virginity as long as she shall live." Shortly after the woman had made this vow she conceived and bore a daughter, whom she called Thrutgeba, surnamed Leoba because she was beloved, for this is what Leoba means. And when the child had grown up her mother consecrated her and handed her over to Mother Tetta to be taught the sacred sciences. And because the nurse had foretold that she should have such happiness, she gave her her freedom.

The girl, therefore, grew up and was taught with such care by the abbess and all the nuns that she had no interests other than the monastery and the pursuit of sacred knowledge. She took no pleasure in aimless jests and wasted no time on girlish romances, but, fired by the love of Christ, fixed her mind always on reading or hearing the Word of God. Whatever she heard or read she committed to memory, and put all that she learned into practice. She exercised such moderation in her use of food and drink that she eschewed dainty dishes and the allurements of sumptuous fare, and was satisfied with whatever was placed before her. She prayed continually, knowing that in the Epistles the faithful are counseled to pray without ceasing. When she was not praying she worked with her hands at whatever was commanded her, for she had learned that he who will not work should not eat. However, she spent more time in reading and listening to Sacred Scripture than she gave to manual labor. She took great care not to forget what she had heard or read, observing the commandments of the Lord and putting into practice what she remembered of them. In this way she so arranged her conduct that she was loved by all the sisters. She learned from all and obeyed them all, and by imitating the good qualities of each one she modeled herself on the continence of one, the cheerfulness of another, copying here a sister's mildness, there a sister's patience. One she tried to equal in attention to prayer, another in devotion to reading. Above all, she was intent on practicing charity, without which, as she knew, all other virtues are void.

When she had succeeded in fixing her attention on heavenly things by these and other practices in the pursuit of virtue she had a dream in which one night she saw a purple thread issuing from her mouth. It seemed to her that when she took hold of it with her hand and tried to draw it out there was no end to it; and as if it were coming from her very bowels, it extended little by little until it was of enormous length. When her hand was full of thread and it still issued from her mouth she rolled it round and round and made a ball of it. The labor of doing this was so tiresome that eventually, through sheer fatigue, she woke from her sleep and began to wonder what the meaning of the dream might be. She understood quite clearly that there was some reason for the dream, and it seemed that there was some mystery hidden in it. Now there was in the same monastery an aged nun who was known to possess the spirit of prophecy, because other things that she had foretold had always been fulfilled. As Leoba was diffident about revealing the dream to her, she told it to one of her disciples just as it had occurred and asked her to go to the old nun and describe it to her as a personal experience and learn from her the meaning of it. When the sister had repeated the details of the dream as if it had happened to her, the nun, who could foresee the future, angrily replied: "This is indeed a true vision and presages that good will come. But why do you lie to me in saying that such things happened to you? These matters are no concern of yours: they apply to the beloved chosen by God." In giving this name, she referred to the virgin Leoba. "These things," she went on, "were revealed to the person whose holiness and wisdom make her a worthy recipient, because by her teaching and good example she will confer benefits on many people. The thread which came from her bowels and issued from her mouth signifies the wise counsels that she will speak from the heart. The fact that it filled her hand means that she will carry out in her actions whatever she expresses in her words. Furthermore, the ball which she made by rolling it round and round signifies the mystery of the divine teaching, which is set in motion by the words and deeds of those who give instruction and which turns earthwards through active works and heavenwards through contemplation, at one time swinging downwards through compassion for one's neighbor, again swinging upwards through the love of God. By these signs God shows that your mistress will profit many by her words and example, and the effect of them will be felt in other lands afar off whither she will go." That this interpretation of the dream was true later events were to prove.

At the time when the blessed virgin Leoba was pursuing her quest for perfection in the monastery the holy martyr Boniface was being ordained by Gregory, Bishop of Rome and successor to Constantine, in the Apostolic See. His mission was to preach the Word of God to the people in Germany. When Boniface found that the people were ready to receive the faith and that, though the harvest was great, the laborers who worked with him were few, he sent messengers and letters to England, his native land, summoning from different ranks of the clergy many who were learned in the divine law and fitted both by their character and good works to preach the Word of God. With their assistance he zealously carried out the mission with which he was charged, and by sound doctrine and miracles converted a large part of Germany to the faith. As the days went by, multitudes of people were instructed in the mysteries of the faith and the Gospel was preached not only in the churches but also in the towns and villages. Thus the Catholics were strengthened in their belief by constant exhortation, the wicked submitted to correction, and the heathen, enlightened by the Gospel, flocked to receive the grace of Baptism. When the blessed man saw that the Church of God was increasing and that the desire of perfection was firmly rooted he established two means by which religious progress should be ensured. He began to build monasteries, so that the people would be attracted to the church not only by the beauty of its religion but also by the communities of monks and nuns. And as he wished the observance in both cases to be kept according to the Holy Rule, he endeavored to obtain suitable superiors for both houses. For this purpose he sent his disciple Sturm, a man of noble family and sterling character, to Monte Cassino, so that he could study the regular discipline, the observance and the monastic customs which had been established there by St. Benedict. As the future superior, he wished him to become a novice and in this way learn in humble submission how to rule over others. Likewise, he sent messengers with letters to the abbess Tetta, of

whom we have already spoken, asking her to send Leoba to accompany him on this journey and to take part in this embassy: for Leoba's reputation for learning and holiness had spread far and wide and her praise was on everyone's lips. The abbess Tetta was exceedingly displeased at her departure, but because she could not gainsay the dispositions of divine providence she agreed to his request and sent Leoba to the blessed man. Thus it was that the interpretation of the dream which she had previously received was fulfilled. When she came, the man of God received her with the deepest reverence, holding her in great affection, not so much because she was related to him on his mother's side as because he knew that by her holiness and wisdom she would confer many benefits by her word and example.

In furtherance of his aims he appointed persons in authority over the monasteries and established the observance of the Rule: he placed Sturm as abbot over the monks and Leoba as abbess over the nuns. He gave her the monastery at a place called Bischofsheim, where there was a large community of nuns. These were trained according to her principles in the discipline of monastic life and made such progress in her teaching that many of them afterwards became superiors of others, so that there was hardly a convent of nuns in that part which had not one of her disciples as abbess. She was a woman of great virtue and was so strongly attached to the way of life she had vowed that she never gave thought to her native country or her relatives. She expended all her energies on the work she had undertaken in order to appear blameless before God and to become a pattern of perfection to those who obeyed her in word and action. She was ever on her guard not to teach others what she did not carry out herself. In her conduct there was no arrogance or pride; she was no distinguisher of persons, but showed herself affable and kindly to all. In appearance she was angelic, in word pleasant, clear in mind, great in prudence, Catholic in faith, most patient in hope, universal in her charity. But though she was always cheerful, she never broke out into laughter through excessive hilarity. No one ever heard a bad word from her lips; the sun never went down upon her anger. In the matter of food and drink she always showed the utmost understanding for others but was most sparing in her own use of them. She had a small cup from which she used to drink and which, because of the meager quantity it would hold, was called by the sisters "the Beloved's little one." So great was her zeal for reading that she discontinued it only for prayer or for the refreshment of her body with food or sleep: the Scriptures were never out of her hands. For, since she had been trained from infancy in the rudiments of grammar and the study of the other liberal arts, she tried by constant reflection to attain a perfect knowledge of divine things so that through the combination of her reading with her quick intelligence, by natural gifts and hard work, she became extremely learned. She read with attention all the books of the Old and New Testaments and learned by heart all the commandments of God. To these she added by way of completion the writings of the church Fathers, the decrees of the Councils and the whole of ecclesiastical law. She observed great moderation in all her acts and arrangements and always kept the practical end in view, so that she would never have to repent of her actions through having been guided by impulse. She was deeply aware of the necessity for concentration of mind in prayer and study, and for this reason took care not to go to excess either in watching or in other spiritual exercises. Throughout the summer both she and all the sisters under her rule went to rest after the midday meal, and she would never give permission to any of them to stay up late, for she said that lack of sleep dulled the mind, especially for study. When she lay down to rest, whether at night or in the afternoon, she used to have the Sacred Scriptures read out at her bedside, a duty which the younger nuns carried out in turn without grumbling. It seems difficult to believe, but even when she seemed to be asleep they could not skip over any word or syllable whilst they were reading without her immediately correcting them. Those on whom this duty fell used afterwards to confess that often when they saw her becoming drowsy they made a mistake on purpose to see if she noticed it, but they were never able to escape undetected. Yet it is not surprising that she could not be deceived even in her sleep, since He who keeps watch over Israel and neither slumbers nor sleeps possessed her heart, and she was able to say with the spouse in the Song of Songs: "I sleep, but my heart watcheth."

She preserved the virtue of humility with such care that, though she had been appointed to govern others because of her holiness and wisdom, she believed in her heart that she was the least of all. This she showed both in her speech and behavior. She was extremely hospitable. She kept open house for all without exception, and even when she was fasting gave banquets and washed the feet of the guests with her own hands, at once the guardian and the minister of the practice instituted by our Lord.

Whilst the virgin of Christ was acting in this way and attracting to herself everyone's affection, the devil, who is the foe of all Christians, viewed with impatience her own great virtue and the progress made by her disciples. He therefore attacked them constantly with evil thoughts and temptations of the flesh, trying to turn some of them aside from the path they had chosen. But when he saw that all his efforts were brought to nought by their prayers, fasting and chaste lives, the wily tempter turned his attention to other means, hoping at least to destroy their good reputation, even if he could not break down their integrity by his foul suggestions.

There was a certain poor little crippled girl, who sat near the gate of the monastery begging alms. Every day she received her food from the abbess's table, her clothing from the nuns and all other necessities from them; these were given to her from divine charity. It happened that after some time, deceived by the suggestions of the devil, she committed fornication, and when her appearance made it impossible for her to conceal that she had conceived a child she covered up her guilt by pretending to be ill. When her time came, she wrapped the child in swaddling clothes and cast it at night into a pool by the river which flowed through that place. In this way she added crime to crime, for she not only followed fleshly sin by murder, but also combined murder with the poisoning of the water. When day dawned, another woman came to draw water and, seeing the corpse of the child, was struck with horror. Burning with womanly rage, she filled the whole village with her uncontrollable cries and reproached the holy nuns with these indignant words: "Oh, what a chaste community! How admirable is the life of nuns, who beneath their veils give birth to children and exercise at one and the same time the function of mothers and priests, baptizing those to whom they have given birth. For, fellow citizens, you have drawn off this water to make a pool, not merely for the purpose of grinding corn, but unwittingly for a new and unheard-of kind of Baptism. Now go and ask those women, whom you compliment by calling them virgins, to remove this corpse from the river and make it fit for us to use again. Look for the one who is missing from the monastery and then you will find out who is responsible for this crime." At these words all the crowd was set in uproar and everybody, of whatever age or sex, ran in one great mass to see what had happened. As soon as they saw the corpse they denounced the crime and reviled the nuns. When the abbess heard the uproar and learned what was afoot she called the nuns together, told them the reason, and discovered that no one was absent except Agatha, who a few days before had been summoned to her parents' house on urgent business: but she had gone with full permission. A messenger was sent to her without delay to recall her to the monastery, as Leoba could not endure the accusation of so great a crime to hang over them. When Agatha returned and heard of the deed that was charged against her she fell on her knees and gazed up to heaven, crying: "Almighty God, who knowest all things before they come to pass, from whom nothing is hid and who hast delivered Susanna from false accusations when she trusted in Thee, show Thy mercy to this community gathered together in Thy name and let it not be besmirched by filthy rumors on account of my sins; but do Thou deign to unmask and make known for the praise and glory of Thy name the person who has committed this misdeed."

On hearing this, the venerable superior, being assured of her innocence, ordered them all to go to the chapel and to stand with their arms extended in the form of a cross until each one of them had sung through the whole psalter, then three times each day, at Tierce, Sext and None, to go round the monastic buildings in procession with the crucifix at their head, calling upon God to free them, in His mercy, from this accusation. When they had done this and they were going into the church at None, having completed two rounds, the blessed Leoba went straight to the altar and, standing before the cross, which was being prepared for the third procession, stretched out her hands towards heaven, and with tears and groans prayed, saying: "O Lord Jesus Christ, King of virgins, Lover of chastity, unconquerable God, manifest Thy power and deliver us from this charge, because the reproaches of those who reproached Thee have fallen upon us." Immediately after she had said this, that wretched little woman, the dupe and the tool of the devil, seemed to be surrounded by flames, and, calling out the name of the abbess, confessed to the crime she had committed. Then a great shout rose to heaven: the vast crowd was astounded at the miracle, the nuns began to weep with joy, and all of them with one voice gave expression to the merits of Leoba and of Christ our Savior.

So it came about that the reputation of the nuns, which the devil had tried to ruin by his sinister rumor, was greatly enhanced, and praise was showered on them in every place. But the wretched woman did not deserve to escape scot-free and for the rest of her life she remained in the power of the devil. Even before this God had performed many miracles through Leoba, but they had been kept secret. This one was her first in Germany and, because it was done in public, it came to the ears of everyone.

. . .

The blessed virgin, however, persevered unwaveringly in the work of God. She had no desire to gain earthly possessions but only those of heaven, and she spent all her energies on fulfilling her vows. Her wonderful reputation spread abroad and the fragrance of her holiness and wisdom drew to her the affections of all. She was held in veneration by all who knew her, even by kings. Pippin, King of the Franks, and his sons Charles and Carloman treated her with profound respect, particularly Charles, who, after the death of his father and brother, with whom he had shared the throne for some years, took over the reins of government. He was a man of truly Christian life, worthy of the power he wielded and by far the bravest and wisest king that the Franks had produced. His love for the Catholic faith was so sincere that, though he governed all, he treated the servants and handmaids of God with touching humility. Many times he summoned the holy virgin to his court, received her with every mark of respect and loaded her with gifts suitable to her station. Queen Hiltigard also revered her with a chaste affection and loved her as her own soul. She would have liked her to remain continually at her side so that she might progress in the spiritual life and profit by her words and example. But Leoba detested the life at court like poison. The princes loved her, the nobles received her, the bishops welcomed her with joy. And because of her wide knowledge of the Scriptures and her prudence in counsel they often discussed spiritual matters and ecclesiastical discipline with her. But her deepest concern was the work she had set on foot. She visited the various convents of nuns and, like a mistress of novices, stimulated them to vie with one another in reaching perfection.

Sometimes she came to the Monastery of Fulda to say her prayers, a privilege never granted to any woman either before or since, because from the day that monks began to dwell there entrance was always forbidden to women. Permission was only granted to her, for the simple reason that the holy martyr St. Boniface had commended her to the seniors of the monastery and because he had ordered her remains to be buried there. The following regulations, however, were observed when she came there. Her disciples and companions were left behind in a nearby cell and she entered the monastery always in daylight, with one nun older than the rest; and after she had finished her prayers and held a conversation with the brethren, she returned towards nightfall to her disciples whom she had left behind in the cell. When she was an old woman and became decrepit through age she put all the convents under her care on a sound footing and then, on Bishop Lull's advice, went to a place called Scoranesheim, four miles south of Mainz. There she took up residence with some of her nuns and served God night and day in fasting and prayer.

. . .

She died in the month of September, the fourth of the kalends of October. Her body, followed by a long cortège of noble persons, was carried by the monks of Fulda to their monastery with every mark of respect. Thus the seniors there remembered what St. Boniface had said, namely, that it was his last wish that her remains should be placed next to his bones. But because they were afraid to open the tomb of the blessed martyr, they discussed the matter and decided to bury her on the north side of the altar which the martyr St. Boniface had himself erected and consecrated in honor of our Savior and the twelve Apostles.

After some years, when the church had grown too small and was being prepared by its rectors for a future consecration, Abbot Eigil, with permission of Archbishop Heistulf, transferred her bones and placed them in the west porch near the shrine of St. Ignatius the martyr, where, encased in a tomb, they rest glorious with miracles. For many who have approached her tomb full of faith have many times received divine favors.

52. *The Heliand*

After a brutal conquest and forced baptism at the hands of Charlemagne's armies in the late eighth century, the Saxons were evangelized primarily by English and Frankish missionary monks who worked among these conquered people. The Heliand *or* The Saxon Gospel, *an anonymous ninth-century narrative poem, shows the effort to translate the story of the gospel into the Germanic cultural idiom. A harmonization of the four gospels composed in Old Saxon, it presented Jesus' life and ministry in terms that would particularly resonate with the chieftain society for which it was written.*

Song 1
*The Creator's spell, by which
the whole world is held together
is taught to four heroes.*

There were many whose hearts told them that they should begin to tell the secret runes, the word of God, the famous feats that the powerful Christ accomplished in words and in deeds among human beings. There were many of the wise who wanted to praise the teaching of Christ, the holy Word of God, and wanted to write a bright-shining book with their own hands, telling how the sons of men should carry out His commands. Among all these, however, there were only four who had the power of God, help from heaven, the Holy Spirit, the strength from Christ to do it. They were chosen. They alone were to write down the evangelium in a book, and to write down the commands of God, the holy heavenly word. No one else among the heroic sons of men was to attempt it, since these four had been picked by the power of God: Matthew and Mark, Luke and John were their names. They were dear to God, worthy of the work. The ruling God had placed the Holy Spirit firmly in those heroes' hearts, together with many a wise word, as well as a devout attitude and a powerful mind, so that they could lift up their holy voices to chant God's spell. There is nothing like it in words anywhere in this world! Nothing can ever glorify the Ruler, our dear Chieftain, more! Nor is there anything that can better fell every evil creature or work of wickedness, nor better withstand the hatred and aggression of enemies. This is so, because the one who taught them God's Spell, though generous and good, had a powerful mind: the noble, the almighty Creator Himself.

These four were to write it down with their own fingers; they were to compose, sing, and proclaim what they had seen and heard of Christ's powerful strength—all the many wonderful things, in word and deed, that the mighty Chieftain Himself said, taught, and accomplished among human beings—and also all the things which the Ruler spoke from the beginning, when He, by His own power, first made the world and formed the whole universe with one word. The heavens and the earth and all that is contained within them, both inorganic and organic, everything, was firmly held in place by the Divine words. He then determined which of the peoples was to rule the greatest territory, and at what times the ages of the world were to come to an end. One age still stood before the sons of men; five were past. The blessed sixth age was to come by the power of God the Holy Spirit and the birth of Christ. He is the Best of Healers, come here to the middle world to be a help to many, to give human beings an advantage against the hatred of the enemy and the hidden snare.

At that time the Christian God granted to the Roman people the greatest kingdom. He strength-

Source: *The Heliand: The Saxon Gospel*, tr. G. Ronald Murphy, S.J. (New York: Oxford University Press, 1992), 24, 38, 58-59, 68-69. Copyright © 1992 by Oxford University Press, Inc. Used by permission of Oxford University Press, Inc.

ened the heart of their army so that they had conquered every nation. Those helmet-lovers from hill-fort Rome had won an empire. Their military governors were in every land and they had authority over the people of every noble race.

In Jerusalem, Herod was chosen to be king over the Jewish people. Caesar, ruling the empire from the hill-fort Rome, placed him there—among the warrior-companions—even though Herod did not belong by clan to the noble and well-born descendants of Israel. He did not come from their kinsmen. It was only thanks to Caesar in hill-fort Rome, who ruled the empire, that the descendants of Israel, those fighting men renowned for their toughness, had to obey him. They were Herod's very unwavering friends—as long as he held power, for as long as he had authority over the Jewish people.

At that time there was in that place an old man, a man of experience and wisdom. He was from the people, from Levi's clan, Jacob's son, of good family. His name was Zachary. He was a blessedly happy man, since he loved to serve God and acted according to God's will. His wife did the same. She was an elderly woman. An heir had not been granted to them when they were young. They lived far from any vice and were highly respected. Their obedience was to the King of Heaven, they honored our Chieftain; they never desired to be the cause of anything bad or treacherous, illegal or sinful, among mankind. But they did live in a worried state of mind because they did not have an heir of their own; they had no children.

There, in Jerusalem, Zachary fulfilled the divine command whenever his turn came. Whenever the times informed him in their bright and clear way that he was to perform the holy worship of the Ruler at the shrine, the divine service of God, the King of Heaven, he was very happy and carried it out with a devout mind.

Song 5
The Chieftain of mankind
is born in David's hill-fort.

Then there came a decree from Fort Rome, from the great Octavian who had power over the whole world, an order from Caesar to his wide realm, sent to every king enthroned in his home-land and to all Caesar's army commanders governing the people of any territory. It said that everyone living outside their own country should return to their homeland upon receipt of the message. It stated that all the warrior heroes were to return to their assembly place, each one was to go back to the clan of which he was a family member by birth in a hill-fort.

That command was sent out over the whole world. People came together at all the hill-forts. The messengers who had come from Caesar were men who could read and write, and they wrote everyone's name down very carefully in a report—both name and nationality—so that no human being could escape from paying the tax which each warrior had on his head.

The good Joseph went also with his household, just as God, ruling mightily, willed it. He made his way to his shining home, the hill-fort at Bethlehem. This was the assembly place for both of them, for Joseph the hero and for Mary the good, the holy girl. This was the place where in olden days the throne of the great and noble good King David stood for as long as he reigned, enthroned on high, an earl of the Hebrews. Joseph and Mary both belonged by birth to his household, they were of good family lineage, of David's own clan.

I have heard it told that the shining workings [of fate] and the power of God told Mary that on this journey a son would be granted her, born in Bethlehem, the strongest child, the most powerful of all kings, the Great One come powerfully to the light of mankind—just as foretold by many visions and signs in this world many days before.

At that time it all came to pass, just as wise men had said long ago: that the Protector of People would come in a humble way, by His own power, to visit this kingdom of earth. His mother, that most beautiful woman, took Him, wrapped Him in clothes and precious jewels, and then with her two hands laid Him gently, the little man, that child, in a fodder-crib, even though He had the power of God, and was the Chieftain of mankind. There the mother sat in front of Him and remained awake, watching over the holy Child and holding it. And there was no doubt in the mind or in the heart of the holy maid.

What had happened became known to many

over this wide world. The guards heard it. As horse-servants they were outside, they were men on sentry duty, watching over the horses, the beasts of the field: they saw the darkness split in two in the sky, and the light of God came shining through the clouds and surrounded the guards out in the fields. Those men began to feel fear in their hearts. They saw the mighty angel of God coming toward them. He spoke to the guards face to face and told them that they should not fear any harm from the light. "I am going to tell you," he said, "something very wonderful, something very deeply desired. I want to let you know something very powerful: Christ is now born, on this very night, God's holy Child, the good Chieftain, at David's hill-fort. What happiness for the human race, a boon for all men! You can find Him, the most powerful Child, at Fort Bethlehem. Take what I now tell you in truthful words as a sign: He is there, wrapped up, lying in a fodder-crib—even though He is king over all the earth and the heavens and over the sons of all the peoples, the Ruler of the world." Just as he said that word, an enormous number of the holy army, the shining people of God, came down to the one angel from the meadows of heaven, saying many words of praise for the Lord of Peoples. They then began to sing a holy song as they wended their way through the clouds towards the meadows of heaven.

The guards heard how the angels in their power praised the all-mighty God most worshipfully in words: "Glory now be," they said, "to the Lord-Chieftain Himself, in the highest reaches of heaven, and peace on earth to the sons of men, men of good will, those who because of their clear minds recognize God!"

The herdsmen understood that something great had been told to them—a merry message! They decided to go to Bethlehem that night, they wanted very much to be able to see Christ Himself.

Song 16
*The Chieftain's instructions
on the mountain;
the eight Good Fortunes.*

Then the warrior-companions whom He chose from among the people gathered closer around Christ, the Ruler and Rescuer. Wise men were very eager and willing to stand around God's Son, intent on His words. They thought and kept silent and wondered what the Chieftain of Peoples, the Ruler Himself, would want to say out of love for these people.

Then the Land's Herdsman, God's own Son, sat down in front of the men. He wanted with His talk to teach the people many wise sayings, how they could perform the praise of God in this world-kingdom. The holy Chieftain sat there in silence and looked at them for a long time with tender feelings for them in His mind and generosity toward them in His heart. Then He unlocked His mouth, and the Ruler's Son instructed them in words about many amazing things. Moreover, Christ spoke in wise words to the men whom He had picked to come to His talk, to those men who were of all the inhabitants of earth, of all mankind, the most precious to God—to them He spoke in soothsaying.

He said that those were fortunate here in this middle world who were poor in their hearts through humility, "to them is granted the eternal kingdom in all holiness, eternal life on the meadows of heaven."

He said that those too were fortunate who were gentle people, "they will be allowed to possess the great earth, the same kingdom."

He said that those also were fortunate who cried here over their evil deeds, "in return, they can expect the very consolation they desire in their Master's kingdom."

"Those too are fortunate who desired to do good things here, those fighting men who wanted to judge fairly. With good things they themselves will be filled to satisfaction in the Chieftain's kingdom for their wise actions; they will attain good things, those fighting men who judged fairly here. Nor will any people want to deceive them with secrets when they are seated there at the banquet!"

"Fortunate as well are those who have kind and generous feelings within a hero's chest, the powerful, holy Chieftain will Himself be kind and generous to them."

"Fortunate also are the many people who have cleaned their hearts, they will see Heaven's Ruler in His kingdom."

He said that those too were fortunate "who live

peacefully among the people and do not want to start any fights or court cases by their own actions, they will be called the Chieftain's sons for He will be gracious to them, they will long enjoy His kingdom."

He said that fortunate too are the fighting men who wanted justice, "and, because of that, suffer more powerful men's hatred and verbal abuse. To them is granted afterwards God's meadow and spiritual life for eternal days—thus the end will never come of their beatific happiness!"

So the ruling Christ had told the earls in front of Him the eight Good Fortunes. With them, anyone will always reach God's kingdom, if he wants to. If not, he will afterwards do without possessions and happiness for endless days, from the moment he gives up this world, the fate of life on earth, and goes to the other light—for better or for worse—depending on how he treated people here in this world, just as Christ the All-Ruler said it there with His words, the most powerful of kings, God's own Son, to His followers.

"You too will also be fortunate," He said to them, "the people of this country will sue you in court cases and say repulsive things about you, they will make fun of you, and arrange to hurt you greatly in this world. They will punish you and cover you with verbal abuse and hostility, deny your teaching, and do great wickedness and harm to you because of your Lord. But let your minds always enjoy life, since in God's kingdom your reward is standing ready for you: every good thing, in full strength and diversity! That is given to you as payment, since beforehand you suffered hardship and punishment here in this world.

"Something worse will be given to those others, a more horrible thing, to those who had possessions here and were very well-to-do in the world. They used up their happiness here. They enjoyed it to the full here; in return those heroes will suffer with something more skimpy after their departure. They will weep over their misery, those who here before were joyful, who lived according to their every desire, the ones who did not want to omit a single thing, no immoral idea or dirty deed, which their emotions spurred them on to. When their reward comes to them, evil hardship, they will look toward its end with grave concern. Those

who so much followed the will of this world will become deeply worried in mind and in heart.

"Now, you are to reprove them for such evil deeds, and stop them with words, as I will now teach you, My companions, in true words, in soothsaying. From now on you are to become this world's salt, sinful men's salt, to heal their deadly deeds, so that they, the people, can turn to better things, and cease from doing the enemy's work, the devil's deeds, and head toward the kingdom of their Chieftain.

"Thus you are to turn many of the people with your teaching toward following My will. If, however, any of you turns away from this and abandons the teaching which he is supposed to be doing, then he is like the salt which people scatter all over the beach, the sons of men kick it with their feet when they are on the sand. It is worthless. So it will also be with the man who is to tell God's word to human beings. If he lets his feelings doubt, so that he does not, with a clear mind, want to urge people toward the kingdom of heaven with his speech, nor to recite God's spell, but rather vacillates in his words, the Ruler will become extremely exasperated, enraged at him—and so also will the sons of men! He will be despised by all the peoples of the world, by everyone, if his teaching is worthless."

Song 17
The instructions on the mountain.

Thus He spoke wisely and told God's spell. The Guardian of the land taught His people with a clear mind. Heroes were very eager and willing to stand around God's Son, intent on His words. They thought and kept silent. They listened to the Chieftain of the People giving law to the nobly-born. He promised them the heaven-kingdom and said to the heroes, "I can also tell you, My companions, in truthful words, that from now on you will be, for the human race, this world's light, shining peacefully among men, over many peoples, bright and beautiful. Your great works cannot be hidden, nor the intent with which you proclaim them, any more than a hill-fort on a mountain, a high steep-sided hill, can be hidden with its gigantic works. So also your words and deeds cannot be concealed from human beings in this middle world. Do as I teach you: let your powerful light shine for people, for the sons of men, so that they understand your feelings, your works, and your will, and therefore they will praise the ruling God, the heavenly Father, with a clear mind in this light, because He gave you such teaching.

"Nor should anyone who has light hide it from people, keeping it well concealed, but rather he should set it up high in the house so that all who are inside, the heroes in the hall, can see it together.

"So you should not hide your holy word from the people of this country, concealing it from mankind's heroes, but instead you should spread God's command high and wide throughout all this countryside, so that everyone born will understand it and carry it out. Just as in the olden days when earls held the old law, very wise men spoke in words, so now I tell you all the more: just as it was commanded in the old law—each and every man is to serve God.

"Do not think for a moment that I have come to this world to destroy the old law, to chop it down among the people and to throw down the word of the prophets—they were truthful men, clear in their commands. Heaven and earth standing now united will both fall apart before even a minute bit of their words, in which they gave true commands to the people here, goes unaccomplished in this world. I did not come to this world to fell the word of the prophets, but to fulfill them; to increase them and to make them new again for the children of men, for the good of this people.

"It was written before in the old law—you have often heard word-wise men say it—whosoever in this world so acts that he steals another's old age from him, robs him of his life, the sons of men shall put such a person to death. I now want to add more depth to this concept, to push it further: whosoever is hostile to another in his feelings, angry in his heart—they are all brothers after all, the blessed people of God, they belong to the clan, they are family relatives!—if someone, however, becomes so hostile to another in his feelings that he would rob the man of his life if he could do so, then he is already guilty, condemned to lose his life-spirit, receiving the very same sentence as the other man who by the strength of his hand robbed another earl of his head.

"It is also written in the law in true words, as you all know, that one should love his neighbor zealously in his heart, be kind to his relatives, be good to his fellow clansmen, be generous in his giving, be loving to each of his friends, and shall hate his enemies, resisting them in battle, and with a strong mind shall defend himself against their wrath.

"Now I say to you truthfully, with greater fullness for the people, that you are to love your enemies in your feelings, just as you love your family relatives, in God's name. Do a great deal of good for them, extend friendly loyalty to them with a clear mind—love versus their hatred. This is longlasting advice for every man, this is how a person's feelings against his enemy should be directed. Then, you will have as your own, the gift that you can be called the Heaven-King's sons, His happy children—and you cannot obtain anything better than that in this world.

"I would also like to say to you in all truth, to everyone born, that you cannot donate anything of your goods to God's house that would be worthy of His acceptance with an angry mind—or for as long as you are thinking anything hostile or vicious against another human being. You are to reconcile yourself with your opponent beforehand, talk out an agreement, then afterwards you may donate your treasures at God's altar; then they are worthy of the King of Heaven. You should serve God more according to His graciousness, following His will, more than other Jews do, if you want to own the eternal kingdom and see everlasting life.

"I shall also tell you that it is commanded in the old law that one earl must not seduce another man's woman, the other's wife, into immorality. But then I say to you in all truth that a man's eyes can quickly lead him off into murky evil behavior, if he lets his emotions goad him on so that he begins to yearn for someone who can never go with him. At that point he has already committed a sin himself, on his own, and chained the penalty of Hel to his heart. If, then, a man's eye or his right hand, or any other member of his body, wants to lead him off onto the path of evil, then it is better for any earl, any of the sons of men, that he remove it from his body and throw it away. It is better to come up to heaven without it than, with all his members intact, a man wend his way hale and hearty to the inferno, to the bottom of Hel.

"Human weakness dictates that no one should follow a close friend if the friend is going to urge him on to crimes, to court trials; it does not matter how closely he is related to him by clan, nor how powerful their family relationship is—if the friend is urging him to murder, pushing him to commit crime. It is better for him that he cast the friend far away from himself, avoid this relative, and not have any love for him, so that he will be able to go up to the high kingdom of heaven by himself, rather than that they both go together to the extensive tortures and hideous hardship of Hel's confinement."

Song 18

The instructions on the mountain.

"It is also written in the law in true words, as you all know, that all of mankind should avoid false oaths, that no one should perjure himself, since that is a great sin and leads people off onto the loathsome path. But I want to tell you that no one should swear any oaths at all, neither by high heaven—since that is the Lord's throne, nor by earth beneath it—since that is the Lord's bright footstool. Nor should any human being swear any oath by his own head—since he cannot turn a hair of it black or white unless God in His power decided to make it so. Earls should very much avoid taking oaths. Anyone who swears often, always gets worse, since he cannot control himself.

"I will now tell you in true words, that you are never to swear any oaths more serious and heavy to human beings than the ones that I most truly command you here with My words. If a man is on trial, let him tell the truth; say 'yes,' if it is so, admit what is true; say 'no,' if it is not so. Let that be enough for him. Whatever a man does beyond that, all comes to no good for the human race, since one earl will not believe the word of another because of [earls'] unfaithfulness [to their word].

"Then I say to you also in truth, that it was commanded in the old law: whoever takes the eye of another man, separating it, or any other limb, from his body, he shall immediately pay for it with the same limb of his own. But now what I teach

you is that you should not avenge wrongful deeds in that way, but that you humbly tolerate all the evil and wrongs whatsoever that people do to you in this world. Let every earl do good and profitable things for the other man, just as he wishes that the sons of man do good for him in return. God will then be generous with him and with every person who desires to behave in this way.

"Honor poor people! Share your possessions with needy folk! Do not be concerned whether you will receive any thanks or repayment in this passing world; instead, think of your beloved Lord for compensation for your gifts; be aware that God, the powerful Protector, pays you for them, for whatever you do out of His love. If, despite that, you want to give your gleaming coins to good men through such people, because you think to make more profit in return, then why would you expect any reward from God as repayment in this world for what is only transitory wealth?

"So it is with everything which you do out of love of other people. If you intend to get similar things back in return in both word and action, then why would our Ruler owe you anything for giving in such a way as to get back what you want in return? Give your possessions to the poor people who never pay you back in this world, and strive toward your Ruler's kingdom. When you are giving your alms to the poor man with your own hands, do not do it loudly! Do it for the man gladly and humbly and for God's appreciation. Then you will be able to receive wealth in return, the very lovely payment in the place where you will long enjoy its more beautiful profits!

"Whatever you give away in secret and with good intentions is valued by Our Chieftain. Do not brag too much about your giving, no one should do that, for then it will not be worth any return—miserably lost for the sake of the vanity of fame. It is before the eyes of God that you should receive the reward for good works.

"I shall also command you that when you want to bow in prayer, and you want to ask the Lord for help, to free you from loathsomeness—from the crimes and sins that you yourselves have wrongfully done here—do not do it in front of other people! Do not tell it to everybody so that people will praise you for it and hold your action in high esteem, because then your prayer to your Chieftain goes lost for the sake of the vanity of fame. If you want to pray to the Lord and modestly ask His help—something you really need—so that your Victory-Chieftain will take away your sins, then do it very secretly. Your holy Chieftain in heaven already knows it Himself, since there is nothing in words or deeds that is hidden from Him. He then lets it all happen just the way you ask Him when you bow down to pray with a clear mind."

Heroes were very eager and willing to stand around God's Son, intent on His words. They thought and kept silent. They needed very much to think about the many brilliant things that the holy Child had told them this first time in words. Then one of the twelve, one of the more intelligent men, spoke in reply to God's Son.

Song 19
The instructions on the mountain;
the secret runes of the Lord's Prayer.

"Our good Lord," he said, "we need Your gracious help in order to carry out Your will and we also need Your own words, Best of all born, to teach us, Your followers, how to pray—just as John, the good baptist, teaches his people with words every day how they are to speak to the ruling God. Do this for Your own followers—teach us the secret runes." The powerful One, the Son of the Chieftain, had a good word ready right after that in reply. "When you men want to speak to the ruling God," He said, "to address the most powerful of all kings, then say what I now teach you:

Father of us, the sons of men,
You are in the high heavenly kingdom,
Blessed be Your name in every word.
May Your mighty kingdom come.
May Your will be done over all this world—
just the same on earth as it is up there
in the high heavenly kingdom.
Give us support each day, good Chieftain,
Your holy help, and pardon us, Protector of
  Heaven,
our many crimes, just as we do to other
  human beings.
Do not let evil little creatures lead us off
to do their will, as we deserve,
but help us against all evil deeds.

That is how you men should pray in your words when you bow in prayer to ask the ruling God to pardon the evil of mankind. If you are willing to pardon the violent crimes and sins that they do against you yourselves here, then the ruling God, the all-mighty Father, will forgive your enormous deeds of evil and many culpable acts. But if your emotions get too strong for you so that you are not willing to forgive other earls, other men, their wrongdoing, then God the Ruler will also not forgive you your grim actions—and you will receive His payment, the extremely loathsome reward that lasts a long, long time, for all the injustice that you did to others here in this light, since you did not reconcile yourselves with your fellow human beings over a problem before you departed on the journey from this world.

. . .

Song 24
The marriage feast in
the guest-hall at Fort Cana.

Three nights afterwards the Chieftain of these people decided to go to Galileeland. He, God's Son, had been invited to a wedding. There a bride was to be given away, a beautiful maiden. Mary, the happy virgin, the mighty One's mother, was there with her Son. The Protector of People, God's own Child, went with His followers to the high house where the crowd of Jewish people were drinking in the guest-hall. He was there at the wedding too, and it was there that He made known that He had God's strength, Holy Spirit, help from the Father in heaven, the wisdom of the Ruler.

The warriors were merry, the people were enjoying themselves together, the men were feeling good. The servants went around pouring from pitchers, they had clear wine in steins and barrels. The conviviality of the earls in the drinking hall was a beautiful sight, and the men on the benches had reached a very high level of bliss, they were really happy! Then the wine ran out on them; the people had no more apple wine. There was not the smallest drop left in the house that the servants could still bring to the crowd. The vats were empty; the liquor was gone.

Now it was not very long before the loveliest lady, Christ's mother, found out about it. She went and spoke with her Child, with her Son Himself, and told Him in words that the hosts did not have any more wine for the guests at the wedding. Then she asked the holy Christ earnestly to arrange some help for the people, for the sake of their happiness. The mighty Son of God had His answer ready and said to His mother, "What is it to Me and you," He said, "what happens to these people's liquor, to these warriors' wine? Why are you talking so much like this, woman, admonishing me in front of all these people? My times have not yet come."

The holy virgin, however, trusted well in her mind that, even after these words, the Ruler's Son, the Best of healers, would help. Then the most beautiful of women told the servants, those pouring and those in charge of the wine barrels, all the ones who were serving the crowd, that they were not to let out a whit of the words or actions that the holy Christ would tell them to do for the people.

Six stone vats were standing there empty. God's mighty Child gave His orders very quietly so that a lot of people would not know for sure how He said it with His words. He told those who were pouring to fill the vats there with clear water, and then He made the sign of the cross over it with His fingers, with His own hands—He worked it into wine! Then He ordered it poured into a drinking vessel, drawn off with a pitcher, and then speaking to a servant, He told him to give it to the most important person at the wedding, to put it right into the hands of the one who had the most authority over these people after the host.

As soon as he drank the wine the man could not contain himself from speaking, in front of the crowd, to the bridegroom. He said that it was always the best apple wine that every earl serves first at his wedding, "men's minds wake up with the wine, so that they start feeling ever more merry—drunk, they rejoice! Then, after that happens, one can serve the cheaper apple wine: that is the custom of these people.

"Now you, as host, have made your arrangements for the crowd in a most amazing way! You ordered your servants to bring the worst of all your wine to these folks and to serve it first at your wedding. Now your guests are full, the whole wedding party is very drunk; they are all intoxicated. Now you have ordered the loveliest of all apple wines brought out that I have ever seen lifted anywhere in this world. This is what you should have given to the guests earlier today; at that time, every one of us would have received it with gratitude!"

After those words, and after they had drunk this wine, many a thane became aware that the holy Christ had performed a sign there inside the house. They had more trust in His protection after that, more confidence that He had the power and authority of God in this world. It became widely known to the Jewish people throughout Galilee-land how the Chieftain's Son, right there in their country, had changed water to wine. That was the first of the wonders which He performed there in Galilee for the Jewish people as signs.

There is no one who can tell, no one who can say for certain, what the wonders were that were done afterwards among the people, as Christ the Ruler taught the Jewish people in God's name all day long. He promised them the kingdom of heaven and He protected them against Hel's oppression with words. He told them to look for God's attention and eternal life—that is where there is the light of souls, God's comings and goings, daylight, the glory of God! There many a guest lives most happily—they are the ones who kept obedience to the Heaven-King's command well in mind here.

Song 68
The body is removed
from the gallows tree and
buried in the earth; Christ's spirit
returns at night to the corpse;
Christ rises.

When the bright sun, together with the heavenly stars, had sunk nearer to its rest on that gloomy day, our Chieftain's thane set off on his way. An intelligent man, he had been a follower of Christ for a long time, although not many people really knew of it, since he concealed it with his words from the Jewish people. Joseph was his name, secretly our Chieftain's follower. He did not want to follow wicked people of the clan into doing anything sacrilegious, and so he waited among the Jewish people in holiness for the kingdom of the heavens.

At that moment he was on his way to speak with the military governor, to deal with emperor Caesar's thane. Joseph urged the man earnestly to release Christ's body from the cross on which it now was, dead, freeing the good man from the gallows, and to lay it in a grave, commit it to the earth. The military governor had no desire to refuse what Joseph wanted, and so he granted him the authority to carry it out. From there, Joseph set off for the gallows, walking to the place where he knew that God's Son, the corpse of his Lord, was hanging. He removed it from the new gallows pole and pulled the nails out of it. He took the beloved body in his arms, just as one should with one's lord, wrapped it in linen, and carried it devoutly—as the Chieftain deserved—to the place where they had hewn out the inside of a rock with their hands, a place where no hero's son, no one, had ever been buried. There they committed God's Son, the holiest of corpses into the folds of the earth in the way customary in their country, and closed the most godlike of all graves with a stone. The poor women who had seen all of this man's terrible death sat there crying and distraught. Then the weeping women decided to go away from there—they noted carefully the way back to the grave—they had seen enough of sorrow and overpowering sadness. The poor distraught women were all called Mary. Evening came then, and the night fog.

The next morning many of the hateful Jewish people were assembled . . . they were holding a secret meeting. "You are well aware how this whole kingdom was divided and the people were confused because of this one man. Now He lies buried, overcome with wounds, in a deep grave. He always said that He was to get up from death on the third day. This clan's people believe much too much in His words. Order the grave now to be put under guard and watched, so that His followers do not steal Him from the rock and then say that the powerful One has arisen from His rest. The clan's fighting men will be even more provoked if they start to spread that story around here."

Warriors were picked from the Jewish battle-group for the guard. They set off with their weapons and went to the grave where they were to guard the corpse of God's Son. The holy day of the Jews had now passed. The warriors sat on top of the grave on their watch during the dark starlit night. They waited under their shields until bright day came to mankind all over the middle world, bringing light to people.

It was not long then until: there was the spirit coming, by God's power, the holy breath, going under the hard stone to the corpse!

Light was at that moment opened up, for the good of the sons of men; the many bolts on the doors of Hel were unlocked; the road from this world up to heaven was built! Brilliantly radiating, God's Peace-Child rose up! He went about, wherever He pleased, in such a way that the guards, tough soldiers, were not at all aware of when He got up from death and arose from His rest.

The Jewish warriors, the fighting men with their shields, were sitting outside, around the grave. The brilliant sunlight continued to glide upward. The women were on their way, walking to the grave, women of good family, the Marys most lovely. They had traded many jewels, silver and gold to buy salves, and given much wealth to get roots, the best they could obtain, so that they could pour salve on the corpse of their beloved Lord, the Chieftain's Son, and into the wounds carved into Him. The women were very concerned in their minds and some were speaking about who could roll the huge stone off to one side of the grave. They had seen the men lay it over the corpse when they had buried the body in the rock.

When the noble ladies had come into the garden so that they could look at the grave itself, an angel of the All-Ruler came down out of the skies above, moving along on its coat of feathers like a roaring wind so that all the ground was set to shaking; the earth reverberated; and the resolve of the earls, the Jewish guards, weakened; and they fell down out of fear. They did not think that they would have their life-spirits—simply be alive—much longer!

Song 69
The angel of the All-Ruler
tells the women that the Chieftain
is on His way to Galileeland.

The guards were lying there, the warrior-companions were as if half dead. Suddenly the great stone lifted up, uncovering the grave, as God's angel pushed it aside. The Chieftain's great messenger then sat down on the grave. In his movements and in his face, for anyone who attempted to look directly at him, he was as radiant and blissfully beaming as a brilliant light! His clothes were like a cold winter's snow. The women saw him sitting there on top of the stone which had been removed, and terror came over them because of the nearness of such radiance. All of the noble ladies were shocked and became very frightened. They did not dare to take a step farther toward the grave, until God's angel, the Ruler's messenger, spoke to them in words and said that he was very aware of their errand, their works, their good will and intentions, and told the women not to be afraid of him. "I know that you are looking for your Chieftain, Christ the Rescuer, from hill-fort Nazareth, whom the Jewish people tortured, crucified and, though innocent, laid here in the grave. He is not here now, He has gotten up for you. This place, this grave in the sand, is empty. You may come up much closer to it now. I know that you long to look inside this rock. The places are still clearly visible where His body was lying."

The pale women felt strong feelings of relief taking hold in their hearts—radiantly beautiful women. What the angel of the All-Ruler said to them about their Lord was a most welcome message for them to hear. He told them to go back again from the grave, and journey to Christ's followers and to tell His warrior-companions in soothsaying words that their Chieftain had gotten up from death. He told them especially to tell Simon Peter the wonderful and welcome message in words, and to let him know: the Chieftain is coming! He is already in Galileeland Himself, "where His followers, His warrior-companions, will see Him again, just as He promised them in His own true words." Just as the women were intending to leave, two other angels in completely white, brilliantly shining clothing stood there in front of them. The angels spoke to them in holy words. The women's minds were stupefied, they were in sheer terror! They could not look at God's angels because of the radiance, the brilliance was far too strong for them to gaze at.

The Ruler's messengers spoke to them immediately and asked the women why they came looking where the dead are for Christ, the Chieftain's Son, who was a living person and full of life-spirit. "You will never find Him here in this rock-grave now; He has already risen up in His body. You should believe this, and remember the words which He often said to you so truthfully when He was one of your companions in Galileeland—how He, the holy Chieftain, was to be given over and sold into the hands of sinful, hate-filled men, that they would torture, crucify, and kill Him, and that for the good of the people He would get up, alive, on the third day, by the Chieftain's power. Now He has done all this, it has been accomplished among human beings. Hurry now, go forth quickly and let His followers know!"

53. Hrotsvit of Gandersheim,
Dulcitius

The tenth-century religious Hrotsvit of Gandersheim stands in a tradition of Saxon nuns distinguished for their intellectual achievements. She not only wrote legends and contemporary history in verse, but her six short plays written in imitation of Terence represent the first medieval drama. As she explains in the prefaces to these plays, she aimed to transform the pagan Roman playwright's treatment of licentious women into a glorification of

SOURCE: *The Plays of Roswitha*, tr. Christopher St. John (London: Chatto & Windus, 1923), 35-47.

DULCITIUS

the chastity of Christian virgins. The play Dulcitius *is set during the reign of the pagan Roman emperor Diocletian.*

Scene I

DIOCLETIAN. The pure and famous race to which you belong and your own rare beauty make it fitting that you should be wedded to the highest in our court. Thus we decree, making the condition that you first promise to deny your Christ and sacrifice to the gods.

AGAPE. We beg you not to concern yourself about us, and it is useless to make preparations for our marriage. Nothing can make us deny that Name which all should confess, or let our purity be stained.

DIOCLETIAN. What does this madness mean?

AGAPE. What sign of madness do you see in us?

DIOCLETIAN. It is clear enough.

AGAPE. In what way are we mad?

DIOCLETIAN. Is it not madness to give up practicing an ancient religion and run after this silly new Christian superstition?

AGAPE. You are bold to slander the majesty of Almighty God. It is dangerous.

DIOCLETIAN. Dangerous? To whom?

AGAPE. To you, and to the state you rule.

DIOCLETIAN. The girl raves. Take her away.

CHIONIA. My sister does not rave. She is right.

DIOCLETIAN. This mænad seems even more violent than the other! Remove her also from our presence, and we will question the third.

IRENA. You will find her as rebellious and as determined to resist.

DIOCLETIAN. Irena, you are the youngest in years. Show yourself the oldest in dignity.

IRENA. Pray tell me how.

DIOCLETIAN. Bow your head to the gods, and set an example to your sisters. It may rebuke and save them.

IRENA. Let those who wish to provoke the wrath of the Most High prostrate themselves before idols! I will not dishonor this head which has been anointed with heavenly oil by abasing it at the feet of images.

DIOCLETIAN. The worship of the gods does not bring dishonor to those who practice it, but, on the contrary, the greatest honor.

IRENA. What could be more shameful baseness, what baser shame, than to venerate slaves as if they were lords?

DIOCLETIAN. I do not ask you to worship slaves, but the gods of princes and the rulers of the earth.

IRENA. A god who can be bought cheap in the marketplace, what is he but a slave?

DIOCLETIAN. Enough of this presumptuous chatter. The rack shall put an end to it!

IRENA. That is what we desire. We ask nothing better than to suffer the most cruel tortures for the love of Christ.

DIOCLETIAN. Let these obstinate women who dare to defy our authority be laden with chains and thrown into a dungeon. Let them be examined by Governor Dulcitius.

Scene II

DULCITIUS. Soldiers, produce your prisoners.

SOLDIERS. The ones you wanted to see are in there.

DULCITIUS. Ye gods, but these girls are beautiful! What grace, what charm!

SOLDIERS. Perfect!

DULCITIUS. I am enraptured!

SOLDIERS. No wonder!

DULCITIUS. I'm in love! Do you think they will fall in love with me?

SOLDIERS. From what we know, you will have little success.

DULCITIUS. Why?

SOLDIERS. Their faith is too strong.

DULCITIUS. A few sweet words will work wonders!

SOLDIERS. They despise flattery.

DULCITIUS. Then I shall woo in another fashion—with torture!

SOLDIERS. They would not care.

DULCITIUS. What's to be done, then?

SOLDIERS. That is for you to find out.

DULCITIUS. Lock them in the inner room—the one leading out of the passage where the pots and pans are kept.

SOLDIERS. Why there?

DULCITIUS. I can visit them oftener.

SOLDIERS. It shall be done.

Scene III

DULCITIUS. What can the prisoners be doing at this hour of night?

SOLDIERS. They pass the time singing hymns.

DULCITIUS. Let us approach.

SOLDIERS. Now you can hear their silver-sweet voices in the distance.

DULCITIUS. Take your torches, and guard the doors. I will go in and enjoy myself in those lovely arms!

SOLDIERS. Enter. We will wait for you here.

Scene IV

AGAPE. What noise is that outside the door?

IRENA. It is that wretch Dulcitius.

CHIONIA. Now may God protect us!

AGAPE. Amen.

CHIONIA. There is more noise! It sounds like the clashing of pots and pans and fire-irons.

IRENA. I will go and look. Come quick and peep through the crack of the door!

AGAPE. What is it?

IRENA. Oh, look! He must be out of his senses! I believe he thinks that he is kissing us.

AGAPE. What is he doing?

IRENA. Now he presses the saucepans tenderly to his breast, now the kettles and frying-pans! He is kissing them hard!

CHIONIA. How absurd!

IRENA. His face, his hands, his clothes! They are all as black as soot. He looks like an Ethiopian.

AGAPE. I am glad. His body should turn black—to match his soul, which is possessed of a devil.

IRENA. Look! He is going now. Let us watch the soldiers and see what they do when he goes out.

Scene V

SOLDIERS. What's this? Either one possessed by the devil, or the devil himself. Let's be off!

DULCITIUS. Soldiers, soldiers! Why do you hurry away? Stay, wait! Light me to my house with your torches.

SOLDIERS. The voice is our master's voice, but the face is a devil's. Come, let's take to our heels! This devil means us no good.

DULCITIUS. I will hasten to the palace. I will tell the whole court how I have been insulted.

Scene VI

DULCITIUS. Ushers, admit me at once. I have important business with the Emperor.

USHERS. Who is this fearsome, horrid monster? Coming here in these filthy rags! Come, let us beat him and throw him down the steps. Stop him from coming further.

DULCITIUS. Ye gods, what has happened to me? Am I not dressed in my best? Am I not clean and fine in my person? And yet everyone who meets me expresses disgust at the sight of me and treats me as if I were some foul monster! I will go to my wife. She will tell me the truth. But here she comes. Her looks are wild, her hair unbound, and all her household follow her weeping.

Scene VII

WIFE OF DULCITIUS. My lord, my lord, what evil has come on you? Have you lost your reason, Dulcitius? Have the Christ-worshippers put a spell on you?

DULCITIUS. Now at last I know! Those artful women have made an ass of me!

WIFE OF DULCITIUS. What troubled me most, and made my heart ache, was that you should not know there was anything amiss with you.

DULCITIUS. Those impudent wenches shall be stripped and exposed naked in public. They shall have a taste of the outrage to which I have been subjected!

Scene VIII

SOLDIERS. Here we are sweating like pigs and what's the use? Their clothes cling to their bodies like their own skin. What's more, our chief, who ordered us to strip them, sits there snoring, and there's no way of waking him. We will go to the Emperor and tell him all that has passed.

Scene IX

DIOCLETIAN. I grieve to hear of the outrageous way in which the Governor Dulcitius has been insulted and hoaxed! But these girls shall not boast of having blasphemed our gods with impunity, or of having made a mock of those who worship them. I will entrust the execution of my vengeance to Count Sisinnius.

Scene X

SISINNIUS. Soldiers, where are these impudent hussies who are to be put to the torture?

SOLDIERS. In there.

SISINNIUS. Keep Irena back, and bring the others here.

SOLDIERS. Why is one to be treated differently?

SISINNIUS. She is young, and besides she may be more easily influenced when not intimidated by her sisters.

SOLDIERS. That may be so.

Scene XI

SOLDIERS. We have brought the girls you asked for.

SISINNIUS. Agape, and you, Chionia, take my advice.

AGAPE. And if we do, what then?

SISINNIUS. You will sacrifice to the gods.

AGAPE. We offer a perpetual sacrifice of praise to the true God, the eternal Father, to His Son, co-eternal, and to the Holy Ghost.

SISINNIUS. I do not speak of that sacrifice. That is prohibited on pain of the most severe penalties.

AGAPE. You have no power over us, and can never compel us to sacrifice to demons.

SISINNIUS. Do not be obstinate. Sacrifice to the gods, or by order of the Emperor Diocletian I must put you to death.

CHIONIA. Your Emperor has ordered you to put us to death, and you must obey, as we scorn his decree. If you were to spare us out of pity, you also would die.

SISINNIUS. Come, soldiers! Seize these blasphemers and fling them alive into the flames.

SOLDIERS. We will build a pyre at once. The fierceness of the fire will soon put an end to their insolence,

AGAPE. O Lord, we know Thy power! It would not be anything strange or new if the fire forgot its nature and obeyed Thee. But we are weary of this world, and we implore Thee to break the bonds that chain our souls, and to let our bodies be consumed that we may rejoice with Thee in heaven.

SOLDIERS. O wonderful, most wonderful! Their spirits have left their bodies, but there is no sign of any hurt. Neither their hair, nor their garments, much less their bodies, have been touched by the flames!

SISINNIUS. Bring Irena here.

SOLDIERS. There she is.

Scene XII

SISINNIUS. Irena, take warning from the fate of your sisters, and tremble, for if you follow their example you will perish.

IRENA. I long to follow their example, and to die, that I may share their eternal joy.

SISINNIUS. Yield, yield!

IRENA. I will yield to no man who persuades me to sin.

SISINNIUS. If you persist in your refusal, I shall not grant you a swift death. I shall eke it out, and every day I shall increase and renew your torments.

IRENA. The greater my pain, the greater my glory!

SISINNIUS. You are not afraid of being tortured, I know, but I can use another means that will be abhorrent to you.

IRENA. By Christ's help I shall escape from all you can devise against me.

SISINNIUS. I can send you to a house of ill-fame, where your body will be abominably defiled.

IRENA. Better far that my body should suffer outrage than my soul.

SISINNIUS. When you are dishonored and forced to live among harlots, you can no longer be numbered among the virgins.

IRENA. The wage of sin is death; the wage of suffering a crown. If the soul does not consent, there is no guilt.

SISINNIUS. In vain I try to spare her, and show pity to her youth!

SOLDIERS. We could have told you as much. She is not to be frightened, and nothing can make her worship the gods.

SISINNIUS. I will show her no more mercy.

SOLDIERS. That is the only way to deal with her.

SISINNIUS. Have no pity. Be rough with her, and drag her to the lowest brothel you can find.

IRENA. They will never take me there.

SISINNIUS. Indeed! What can prevent them?

IRENA. The power that rules the world.

SISINNIUS. We shall see.

IRENA. Yes! Sooner than you will like!

SISINNIUS. Soldiers, do not let the absurd prophecies of this woman interfere with your duty.

SOLDIERS. We are not likely to be frightened by a slip of a girl! We will carry out your orders at once.

Scene XIII

SISINNIUS. Who are these men hurrying towards us? They cannot be the soldiers who took away Irena. Yet they resemble them. Yes, these are the men! Why have you returned so suddenly? Why are you panting for breath?

SOLDIERS. We ran back to find you.

SISINNIUS. Where is the girl?

SOLDIERS. On the crest of the mountain.

SISINNIUS. What mountain?

SOLDIERS. The mountain yonder, nearest this place.

SISINNIUS. O fools, madmen! Have you lost your senses ?

SOLDIERS. What's the matter? Why do you look at us so threateningly, and speak with such anger?

SISINNIUS. May the gods crush you with their thunder!

SOLDIERS. What have we done? How have we offended? We have only obeyed your orders.

SISINNIUS. Fools! Did I not tell you to take this rebellious girl to a brothel?

SOLDIERS. That is so, but while we were on the way up came two young strangers and told us you had sent them to take Irena to the summit of the mountain.

SISINNIUS. I learn this for the first time from you.

SOLDIERS. So we see.

SISINNIUS. What were these strangers like?

SOLDIERS. They were gorgeously dressed and looked like people of rank.

SISINNIUS. Did you not follow them?

SOLDIERS. Yes, we followed them.

SISINNIUS. What did they do?

SOLDIERS. They placed themselves one on each side of Irena, and told us to hasten and tell you what we had seen.

SISINNIUS. Then there is nothing to do but for me to mount my horse and ride to the mountain to discover who has dared to play us this trick.

SOLDIERS. We will come too.

Scene XIV

SISINNIUS. What has happened to me? These Christians have bewitched me. I wander blindly round this hill, and when I stumble on a path I can neither follow it nor return upon my steps.

SOLDIERS. We are all the sport of some strange enchantment. We are exhausted. If you let this madwoman live an hour longer it will be the death of us all.

SISINNIUS. Take a bow one of you, bend it as far as you can, and loose a shaft that shall pierce this devilish witch.

SOLDIERS. That's the way!

IRENA. You wretched Sisinnius! Do you not blush for your shameful defeat? Are you not ashamed that you could not overcome the resolution of a little child without resorting to force of arms ?

SISINNIUS. I accept the shame gladly, since now I am sure of your death.

IRENA. To me my death means joy, but to you calamity. For your cruelty you will be damned in Tartarus. But I shall receive the martyr's palm, and, adorned with the crown of virginity, I shall enter the azure palace of the Eternal King, to Whom be glory and honor forever and ever!

54. Adso of Montier-en-Der, *Letter on the Origin and Time of the Antichrist*

For the Frankish lands, the tenth century was a time of extreme violence and constant threat of invasion by Vikings, Muslims, and Magyars. The collapse of the Carolingian Empire provoked social disorder while political and religious renovatio (renewal) became a focus of new hope. In the tradition of apocalyptic literature, Abbot Adso of Montier-en-Der's biography of the Antichrist attempted to make sense of the crises of his day in terms of the end, which gives ultimate meaning to history. Written ca. 950, it became a "best-seller" that influenced the presentation of similar themes in later medieval apocalyptic literature.

Prologue to Gerberga

Brother Adso, the last of all her servants, sends best wishes and eternal peace to her highness Gerberga, most excellent Queen, mighty in royal dignity, beloved of God and cherished by all the saints, mother of monks and leader of holy virgins.

Because I have won the favor of your kindness, Royal Mother, I have been always faithful to you in everything like a dutiful servant. Even though my prayers do not deserve anything from God, I beseech the mercy of our God for you and for your husband, the Lord King, as well as for the safety of your sons. May he deign to preserve the imperial dignity for you in this life and after it cause you to reign happy with him in heaven. If the Lord gives you good fortune and bestows longer life on your sons, we know without doubt and do believe that God's Church must be exalted and the monastic order must be multiplied more and more. As your faithful one, I wish for this and strongly desire it. If I were able to gain the whole kingdom for you, I would do it most gladly; but since I cannot do that, I will beseech the Lord for the salvation of you and your sons that his grace may always precede you in your works and his glory may follow you in loving kindness. Because grace is directed to the divine commandments, you can fulfill the good that you desire so that the crown of the heavenly kingdom will be given to you.

You have a pious desire to listen to the scriptures and often to speak about our Redeemer. You even want to learn about the wickedness and persecution of the Antichrist, as well as of his power and origin. Since you have deigned to ask your servant, I wish to write to you to tell you something about the Antichrist, although you do not need to hear it from me because you have Don Rorico at your side, that most prudent pastor and brilliant mirror of all wisdom and eloquence, a man indispensable to our age.

The Treatise

When you wish to be informed about the Antichrist the first thing you want to know is why he is so called. This is because he will be contrary to Christ in all things and will do things that are against Christ. Christ came as a humble man; he will come as a proud one. Christ came to raise the lowly, to justify sinners; he, on the other hand, will cast out the lowly, magnify sinners, exalt the wicked. He will always exalt vices opposed to virtues, will drive out the evangelical law, will revive the worship of demons in the world, will seek his own glory (John 7:18), and will call himself Almighty God. The Antichrist has many min-

Source: *Apocalyptic Spirituality*, ed. and tr. Bernard McGinn (New York: Paulist Press, 1979), 89-96. Copyright © 1979 by The Missionary Society of St. Paul the Apostle in the State of New York. Used by permission of Paulist Press, Inc., New York/Mahwah, N.J.

isters of his malice. Many of them have already existed, like Antiochus, Nero, and Domitian. Even now in our own time we know there are many Antichrists, for anyone, layman, cleric, or monk, who lives contrary to justice and attacks the rule of his way of life and blasphemes what is good (Rom. 14:16) is an Antichrist, the minister of Satan.

Now let us see about the Antichrist's origin. What I say is not thought out or made up on my own, but in my attentive reading I find it all written down in books. As our authors say, the Antichrist will be born from the Jewish people, that is, from the tribe of Dan, as the Prophet says: "Let Dan be a snake in the wayside, an adder on the path." He will sit in the wayside like a serpent and will be on the path in order to wound those who walk in the paths of justice (Ps. 22:3) and kill them with the poison of his wickedness. He will be born from the union of a mother and father, like other men, not, as some say, from a virgin alone. Still, he will be conceived wholly in sin (Ps. 50:7), will be generated in sin, and will be born in sin (John 9:34). At the very beginning of his conception the devil will enter his mother's womb at the same moment. The devil's power will foster and protect him in his mother's womb and it will always be with him. Just as the Holy Spirit came into the mother of Our Lord Jesus Christ and overshadowed her with his power and filled her with divinity so that she conceived of the Holy Spirit and what was born of her was divine and holy (Luke 1:35), so too the devil will descend into the Antichrist's mother, will completely fill her, completely encompass her, completely master her, completely possess her within and without, so that with the devil's cooperation she will conceive through a man and what will be born from her will be totally wicked, totally evil, totally lost. For this reason that man is called the "Son of Perdition" (2 Thess. 2:3), because he will destroy the human race as far as he can and will himself be destroyed at the last day.

You have heard how he is to be born; now hear the place where he will be born. Just as Our Lord and Redeemer foresaw Bethlehem for himself as the place to assume humanity and to be born for us, so too the devil knew a place fit for that lost man who is called Antichrist, a place from which

the root of all evil (1 Tim. 6:10) ought to come, namely, the city of Babylon. Antichrist will be born in that city, which once was a celebrated and glorious pagan center and the capital of the Persian Empire. It says that he will be brought up and protected in the cities of Bethsaida and Corozain, the cities that the Lord reproaches in the Gospel when he says, "Woe to you, Bethsaida, woe to you Corozain!" (Matt. 11:21). The Antichrist will have magicians, enchanters, diviners, and wizards who at the devil's bidding will rear him and instruct him in every evil, error, and wicked art. Evil spirits will be his leaders, his constant associates, and inseparable companions. Then he will come to Jerusalem and with various tortures will slay all the Christians he cannot convert to his cause. He will erect his throne in the Holy Temple, for the Temple that Solomon built to God that had been destroyed he will raise up to its former state. He will circumcise himself and will pretend that he is the son of Almighty God.

He will first convert kings and princes to his cause, and then through them the rest of the peoples. He will attack the places where the Lord Christ walked and will destroy what the Lord made famous. Then he will send messengers and his preachers through the whole world. His preaching and power will extend "from sea to sea, from East to West" (Ps. 71:8), from North to South. He will also work many signs, great and unheard-of prodigies (Apoc. 13:13). He will make fire come down from heaven in a terrifying way, trees suddenly blossom and wither, the sea become stormy and unexpectedly calm. He will make the elements change into differing forms, divert the order and flow of bodies of water, disturb the air with winds and all sorts of commotions, and perform countless other wondrous acts. He will raise the dead "in the sight of men in order to lead into error, if possible, even the elect" (Matt. 24:24). For when they shall have seen great signs of such a nature even those who are perfect and God's chosen ones will doubt whether or not he is the Christ who according to the scriptures will come at the end of the world.

He will arouse universal persecution against the Christians and all the elect. He will lift himself up against the faithful in three ways, that is, by terror, by gifts, and by prodigies. To those who believe in him he will give much gold and silver. Those he is not able to corrupt with gifts, he will overcome with terror; those he cannot overcome with terror, he will try to seduce with signs and prodigies. Those he cannot seduce with prodigies, he will cruelly torture and miserably put to death in the sight of all. "Then there will be tribulation such as has not been on earth from when the nations began to exist up to that time. Then those who are in the field will flee to the mountains, and he who is on the roof will not go down into his house to take anything from it" (Matt. 24:21, 16; Dan. 12:1). Then every faithful Christian who will be discovered will either deny God, or, if he will remain faithful, will perish, whether through sword, or fiery furnace, or serpents, or beasts, or through some other kind of torture. This terrible and fearful tribulation will last for three and a half years in the whole world. "Then the days will be shortened for the sake of the elect, for unless the Lord had shortened those days, mankind would not have been saved" (Matt. 24:22).

The Apostle Paul reveals the time when the Antichrist will come and when Judgment Day will begin in the Epistle to the Thessalonians, chapter two ("We beseech you through the coming of Our Lord Jesus Christ"), in the place where he says: "Unless the defection shall have come first and the man of sin and the Son of Perdition shall have been revealed" (2 Thess. 2:3). For we know that after the Greek Empire, or even after the Persian Empire, each of which in its time had great glory and flourished with the highest power, at last after all the other empires there came into existence the Roman Empire, which was the strongest of all and had all the kingdoms of the earth under its control. All nations were subject to the Romans and paid tribute to them. This is why the Apostle Paul says that the Antichrist will not come into the world "unless the defection shall have come first," that is, unless first all the kingdoms that were formerly subject shall have defected from the Roman Empire. This time has not yet come, because even though we may see the Roman Empire for the most part in ruins, nonetheless, as long as the Kings of the Franks who now possess the Roman Empire by right shall last, the dignity of the Roman Empire will not completely perish because it will endure in its kings. Some of our learned men say that one of the Kings of the Franks will possess anew the Roman Empire. He will be in the last time and will be the greatest and the last of all kings. After he has successfully governed his empire, he will finally come to Jerusalem and will lay aside his scepter and crown on the Mount of Olives. This will be the end and the consummation of the Roman and Christian Empire.

Immediately, according to the saying of Paul the Apostle cited above, they say that the Antichrist will be at hand. And then will be revealed the man of sin, namely, the Antichrist. Even though he is a man, he will still be the source of all sins and the Son of Perdition, that is, the son of the devil, not through nature but through imitation because he will fulfill the devil's will in everything. The fullness of diabolical power and of the whole character of evil will dwell in him in bodily fashion; for in him will be hidden all the treasures of malice and iniquity.

"He is the Enemy," that is, he is contrary to Christ and all his members, "and he is lifted up, that is, raised up in pride above everything that is called God" (2 Thess. 2:4), that is, above all the heathen gods, Hercules, Apollo, Jupiter and Mercury, whom the pagans think are gods. Antichrist will be lifted up above these gods because he will make himself greater and stronger than all of them. He will be lifted up not only above these gods, but also "above everything that is worshiped," that is, above the Holy Trinity, which alone is to be worshiped and adored by every creature. "He will exalt himself in such a way that he will be enthroned in God's Temple displaying himself as if he were God."

As we said above, he will be born in the city of Babylon, will come to Jerusalem, and will circumcise himself and say to the Jews: "I am the Christ promised to you who has come to save you, so that I can gather together and defend you who are the Diaspora." At that time all the Jews will flock to him, in the belief that they are receiving God, but rather they will receive the devil. Antichrist also "will be enthroned in God's Temple, that is, in Holy Church, and he will make all Christians martyrs. He will be lifted up and made great,

287

because in him will be the devil, the fountainhead of all evil "who is the king above all the sons of pride" (Job 41:25).

Lest the Antichrist come suddenly and without warning and deceive and destroy the whole human race by his error, before his arrival the two great prophets Enoch and Elijah will be sent into the world. They will defend God's faithful against the attack of the Antichrist with divine arms and will instruct, comfort, and prepare the elect for battle with three and a half years of teaching and preaching. These two very great prophets and teachers will convert the sons of Israel who will live in that time to the faith, and they will make their belief unconquerable among the elect in the face of the affliction of so great a storm. At that time what scripture says will be fulfilled: "If the number of sons of Israel be like the sand of the sea, their remnant will be saved" (Rom. 9:27). When, after three and a half years, they shall have finished their preaching, the Antichrist's persecution will soon begin to blaze out. He will first take up his arms against them and will slay them, as it says in the Apocalypse: "And when they have finished their witness the beast which will ascend from the abyss will make war against them and will conquer and kill them" (Apoc. 11:7). After these two have been slain, he will then persecute the rest of the faithful, either by making them glorious martyrs or by rendering them apostates. And whoever shall have believed in him will receive his brand on the forehead (Apoc. 20:4).

Since we have spoken about his beginning, let us say what end he will have. This Antichrist, the devil's son and the worst master of evil, as has been said, will plague the whole world with great persecution and torture the whole people of God with various torments for three and a half years. After he has killed Elijah and Enoch and crowned with martyrdom the others who persevere in the faith, at last God's judgment will come upon him, as Saint Paul writes when he says, "The Lord Jesus will kill him with the breath of his mouth" (2 Thess. 2:8). Whether the Lord Jesus will slay him by the power of his own might, or whether the Archangel Michael will slay him, he will be killed through the power of Our Lord Jesus Christ and not through the power of any angel or archangel. The teachers say that Antichrist will be killed on the Mount of Olives in his tent and upon his throne, in the place opposite to where the Lord ascended to heaven. You ought to know that after Antichrist has been killed the Judgment Day will not come immediately, nor will the Lord come to judge at once (Isa. 3:14); but as we understand from the Book of Daniel, the Lord will grant the elect forty days to do penance because they were led astray by the Antichrist. No one knows how much time there may be after they shall have completed this penance until the Lord comes to judgment; but it remains in the providence of God who will judge the world in that hour in which for all eternity he predetermined it was to be judged.

Epilogue

So, Your Highness, I your loyal servant have faithfully fulfilled what you commanded. I am prepared to obey in other matters what you shall deem worthy to command.

The Byzantine Commonwealth

55. John of Damascus,
On the Divine Images

Born into a prosperous Chalcedonian Christian family in Damascus, John of Damascus (ca. 650-ca. 749) resigned a ministerial post in the caliph's court to enter the monastery of Mar Saba near Jerusalem. Ordained a priest, John devoted himself to scholarly writing on theology, philosophy, and liturgy. Known for his resistance to the iconoclast policies of Emperor Leo III, yet living beyond Byzantine borders in Muslim territory, John could write in relative freedom. His treatise On the Divine Images *is one of the most important reflections on the theological issues at stake in the iconoclastic controversies.*

First Apology of Saint John of Damascus against Those Who Attack the Divine Images

1. Although it is best for us to be ever aware of our unworthiness and to confess our sins before God, nevertheless it is good and necessary to speak when the times demand it, for I see the Church which God founded on the apostles and prophets, her cornerstone being Christ His Son, tossed on an angry sea, beaten by rushing waves, shaken and troubled by the assaults of evil spirits. Impious men seek to rend asunder the seamless robe of Christ and to cut His Body in pieces: His Body, which is the Word of God and the ancient tradition of the Church. Therefore I deem it unreasonable to keep silence and hold my tongue, remembering the warning of Scripture: "If he shrinks back, my soul has no pleasure in him" (Heb. 10:38), and, "If you see the sword coming and do not warn your brother, I shall require his blood at your hand" (cf. Ezek. 33:8). Fear compels me to speak; the truth is stronger than the might of kings. I heard David, the ancestor of God, singing: "I will speak of Thy testimony before kings, and shall not be put to shame" (Ps. 119:46). Therefore I am stirred to speak even more vehemently, for the commanding words of a king must be fearful to his subjects. Yet few men can be found who know enough to despise the evil laws of kings, even though the authority of earthly monarchs does come from above.

2. First of all, I grasp the teaching of the Church, through which salvation is planted in us, as both foundation and pillar. I will make the meaning of this teaching evident because it is both the starting line and the finish line for the race; it is the bridle of a tightly-reined horse. I see it to be a great calamity that the Church, progressing in dazzling superiority and adorned with the highest examples of the saints of old, should regress to the weak and beggarly elemental spirits, and be greatly afraid when there is nothing to fear. It is disastrous to suppose that the Church does not know God as He really is; that she has degenerated into idolatry, for if she declines one iota from perfection, it will be a blot on her unblemished face, destroying by its ugliness the beauty of the whole. A small thing is not small when it leads to something great; and it is no small

SOURCE: John of Damascus, *On the Divine Images: Three Apologies against Those Who Attack the Divine Images,* tr. David Anderson (Crestwood, N.Y.: St. Vladimir's Seminary Press, 1997), 13-33. Used by permission of St. Vladimir's Seminary Press, 575 Scarsdale Rd., Crestwood, NY 10707.

matter to forsake the ancient tradition of the Church which was upheld by all those who were called before us, whose conduct we should observe, and whose faith we should imitate.

3. In the first place before I speak to you, I beg Almighty God before whom all things lie open to bless the words of my mouth, for He knows my humble purpose and my sincere intention. May He enable me to bridle my mouth and direct it to Him and to walk in His straight path, not turning aside to the right, however convincing it may seem, or knowing anything about the left. Secondly I ask all God's people, the holy nation, the royal priesthood, together with him who has been called to shepherd the flock of Christ's priesthood in his own person, to receive my treatise with kindness. They must not dwell on my unworthiness, or expect eloquence, for I am only too conscious of my shortcomings. Rather, they must consider the power of the thoughts themselves. The kingdom of heaven does not consist of words, but of deeds. My aim is not to conquer, but to raise a hand which fights for the truth—a hand which is helped by guidance from Him who is all-powerful. Relying on the invincible truth as my help, I will begin my treatise.

4. I heed the words of Him who cannot deceive: "The Lord our God, the Lord, is one" (Deut. 6:4), and, "You shall adore the Lord your God, and worship Him alone," and, "You shall not have strange gods" (cf. Deut. 6:13). "You shall not make for yourself a graven image or any likeness of anything that is in heaven above, or that is in the earth beneath" (Exod. 20:4), and, "All worshipers of images are put to shame, who make their boast in worthless idols" (Ps. 97:7). And again, "The gods who did not make the heavens and the earth shall perish from the earth and from under the heavens" (Jer. 10:11). In this way and in a similar manner God spoke in times past to the fathers by the prophets, but last of all in these days He has spoken to us by His only-begotten Son, by whom He made the ages. He says: "This is eternal life, that they know Thee, the only true God, and Jesus Christ, whom Thou hast sent" (John 17:3). I believe in one God, the source of all things, without beginning, uncreated, immortal and unassail-

able, eternal, everlasting, incomprehensible, bodiless, invisible, uncircumscribed, without form. I believe in one superessential Being, one Godhead greater than our conception of divinity, in three persons: Father, Son, and Holy Spirit, and I adore Him alone. I worship one God, one Godhead, but I adore three persons: God the Father, God the Son made flesh, and God the Holy Spirit, one God. I do not adore the creation rather than the Creator, but I adore the one who became a creature, who was formed as I was, who clothed Himself in creation without weakening or departing from His divinity, that He might raise our nature in glory and make us partakers of His divine nature. Together with my King, my God and Father, I worship Him who clothed Himself in the royal purple of my flesh, not as a garment that passes away, or as if the Lord incarnate constituted a fourth person of the Trinity—God forbid! The flesh assumed by Him is made divine and endures after its assumption. Fleshly nature was not lost when it became part of the Godhead, but just as the Word made flesh remained the Word, so also flesh became the Word, yet remained flesh, being united to the person of the Word. Therefore I boldly draw an image of the invisible God, not as invisible, but as having become visible for our sakes by partaking of flesh and blood. I do not draw an image of the immortal Godhead, but I paint the image of God who became visible in the flesh, for if it is impossible to make a representation of a spirit, how much more impossible is it to depict the God who gives life to the spirit?

5. Now some say that God commanded Moses the lawgiver: "You shall worship the Lord your God, and adore Him alone," and, "You shall not make yourself a graven image, or any likeness of anything that is in heaven above, or that is in the earth beneath."

They truly are in error, brothers, for they do not know the Scriptures, that the letter kills, but the Spirit gives life. They do not find in the written word its hidden, spiritual meaning. I can justly say to those people: He who teaches you this will also teach you the following. Listen to the lawgiver's interpretation, which you read in Deuteronomy: "The Lord spoke to you out of the midst of the fire; you heard the sound of words but saw no form; there was only a voice" (Deut. 4:12). And shortly thereafter: "Take good heed to yourselves. Since you saw no form on the day that the Lord spoke to you at Horeb out of the midst of the fire, beware lest you act corruptly by making a graven image for yourself, in the form of any figure, the likeness of male or female, the likeness of any beast that is on the earth, or the likeness of any bird that flies in the air" (Deut. 4:15-17). And again, "Beware lest you lift up your eyes to heaven, and when you see the sun and the moon and the stars, all the host of heaven, you be drawn away and worship them and serve them" (Deut. 4:19).

6. You see that the one thing aimed for is that no created thing can be adored in place of the Creator, nor can adoration be given to any save Him alone. Therefore to worship Him always means to offer Him adoration. For again He says: "You shall have no other gods before Me. You shall not make for yourself a graven image, or any likeness of anything that is in heaven above, or that is on the earth beneath. You shall not worship them or adore them, for I am the Lord your God" (Deut. 5:7-9). And again, "You shall tear down their altars, and dash in pieces their pillars, and burn their Asherim with fire; you shall hew down the graven images of their gods, for you shall not worship other gods" (Deut. 12:3). And again, "You shall make for yourself no molten gods" (Exod. 34:17).

7. You see that He forbids the making of images because of idolatry, and that it is impossible to make an image of the immeasurable, uncircumscribed, invisible God. For "You heard the sound of words, but saw no form; there was only a voice" (Deut. 4:12). This was Paul's testimony as he stood in the midst of the Areopagus: "Being then God's offspring, we ought not to think that the Deity is like gold, or silver, or stone, a representation by the art and imagination of man" (Acts 17:29).

8. These commandments were given to the Jews because of their proneness to idolatry. But to us it is given, on the other hand, as Gregory the Theologian says, to avoid superstitious error and to come to God in the knowledge of the truth; to adore God alone, to enjoy the fullness of divine knowledge, to attain to mature manhood, that we may no longer be children, tossed to and fro and carried about

with every wind of doctrine. We are no longer under custodians, but we have received from God the ability to discern what may be represented and what is uncircumscript. "You cannot see My form" (cf. Exod. 33:20), the Scripture says. What wisdom the Lawgiver has! How can the invisible be depicted? How does one picture the inconceivable? How can one draw what is limitless, immeasurable, infinite? How can a form be given to the formless? How does one paint the bodiless? How can you describe what is a mystery? It is obvious that when you contemplate God becoming man, then you may depict Him clothed in human form. When the invisible One becomes visible to flesh, you may then draw His likeness. When He who is bodiless and without form, immeasurable in the boundlessness of His own nature, existing in the form of God, empties Himself and takes the form of a servant in substance and in stature and is found in a body of flesh, then you may draw His image and show it to anyone willing to gaze upon it. Depict His wonderful condescension, His birth from the Virgin, His baptism in the Jordan, His transfiguration on Tabor, His sufferings which have freed us from passion, His death, His miracles which are signs of His divine nature, since through divine power He worked them in the flesh. Show His saving cross, the tomb, the resurrection, the ascension into the heavens. Use every kind of drawing, word, or color. Fear not; have no anxiety; discern between the different kinds of worship. Abraham bowed down to the sons of Hamor, men who had neither faith nor knowledge of God, when he bought the double cave intended to become a tomb. Jacob bowed to the ground before Esau, his brother, and also before the tip of his son Joseph's staff. He bowed down, but he did not adore. Joshua, the son of Nun, and Daniel bowed in veneration before an angel of God, but they did not adore him. For adoration is one thing, and that which is offered in order to honor something of great excellence is another.

9. Since we are speaking of images and worship, let us analyze the exact meaning of each. An image is of like character with its prototype, but with a certain difference. It is not like its archetype in every way. The Son is the living, essential, and precisely similar Image of the invisible God, bear-

ing the entire Father within Himself, equal to Him in all things, except that He is begotten by Him, the Begetter. It is the nature of the Father to cause; the Son is the effect. The Father does not proceed from the Son, but the Son from the Father. The Father who begets is what He is because of His Son, though not in a second place after Him.

10. There are also in God images and models of His acts yet to come: those things which are His will for all eternity, which is always changeless. That which is divine is immutable; there is no variation in Him or shadow due to change. Blessed Dionysius, who has great knowledge of divine things, says that these images and models were marked out beforehand, for in His will, God has prepared all things that are yet to happen, making them unalterable before they come to pass, just as a man who wishes to build a house would first write out a plan and work according to its prescriptions.

11. Again, visible things are corporeal models which provide a vague understanding of intangible things. Holy Scripture describes God and the angels as having descriptive form, and the same blessed Dionysius teaches us why. Anyone would say that our inability immediately to direct our thoughts to contemplation of higher things makes it necessary that familiar everyday media be utilized to give suitable form to what is formless, and make visible what cannot be depicted, so that we are able to construct understandable analogies. If, therefore, the Word of God, in providing for our every need, always presents to us what is intangible by clothing it with form, does it not accomplish this by making an image using what is common to nature and so brings within our reach that for which we long but are unable to see? A certain perception takes place in the brain, prompted by the bodily senses, which is then transmitted to the faculties of discernment, and adds to the treasury of knowledge something that was not there before. The eloquent Gregory says that the mind which is determined to ignore corporeal things will find itself weakened and frustrated. Since the creation of the world the invisible things of God are clearly seen by means of images. We see images in the creation which, although they are only dim lights, still remind us of God. For instance, when we speak of the holy and eternal Trinity, we use the images of

the sun, light, and burning rays; or a running fountain; or an overflowing river; or the mind, speech, and spirit within us; or a rose tree, a flower, and a sweet fragrance.

12. Again, an image foreshadows something that is yet to happen, something hidden in riddles and shadows. For instance, the ark of the covenant is an image of the Holy Virgin and Theotokos, as are the rod of Aaron and the jar of manna. The brazen serpent typifies the cross and Him who healed the evil bite of the serpent by hanging on it. Baptismal grace is signified by the cloud and the waters of the sea.

13. Again, things which have already taken place are remembered by means of images, whether for the purpose of inspiring wonder, or honor, or shame, or to encourage those who look upon them to practice good and avoid evil. These images are of two kinds: either they are words written in books, as when God had the law engraved on tablets and desired the lives of holy men to be recorded, or else they are material images, such as the jar of manna, or Aaron's staff, which were to be kept in the ark as a memorial. So when we record events and good deeds of the past, we use images. Either remove these images altogether, and reject the authority of Him who commanded them to be made, or else accept them in the manner and with the esteem which they deserve. In speaking of the proper manner, let us consider the question of worship.

14. Worship is the means by which we show reverence and honor. Let us understand that there are different degrees of worship. First of all there is adoration, which we offer to God, who alone by nature is worthy to be worshipped. Then, for the sake of Him who is by nature to be worshipped, we honor His friends and companions, as Joshua, the son of Nun, and Daniel bowed in worship before an angel, or as David venerated God's holy places, when he says, "Let us go to His dwelling place; let us worship at His footstool" (Ps. 132:7), or as when the people of Israel once offered sacrifices and worshipped in His tent, or encircled the temple in Jerusalem, fixing their gaze upon it from all sides and worshipping as their kings had commanded, or as Jacob bowed to the ground before

Esau, his elder brother, and before Pharaoh, the ruler whose authority was established by God. Joseph's brothers prostrated themselves in homage on the ground before him. Other worship is given to show respect, as was the case with Abraham and the sons of Nahor. Either do away with worship completely, or else accept it in the manner and with the esteem it deserves.

15. Answer me this question: "Is there one God?" You will answer, Yes, I assume there is only one Lawgiver. What? Does He then command contrary things? The cherubim are not outside creation. How can He allow cherubim, carved by the hands of men, to overshadow the mercy-seat? Is it not obvious that since it is impossible to make an image of God, who is uncircumscribed and unable to be represented, or of anything like God, creation is not to be worshipped and adored as God? But He allows the image of cherubim who are circumscribed, to be made and shown as prostrate in adoration before the divine throne, overshadowing the mercy-seat, for it was fitting that the image of the heavenly servants should overshadow the image of the divine mysteries. Would you say that the ark, or the staff, or the mercy-seat, were not made by hands? Are they not the handiwork of men? Do they not owe their existence to what you call contemptible matter? What is the meeting-tent itself, if not an image? Was it not a type, a figure? Well then, listen to the holy apostle's words concerning those things that are of the law! "They serve as a copy and shadow of the heavenly sanctuary, for when Moses was about to erect the tent, he was instructed by God saying, 'See that you make everything according to the pattern which was shown you on the mountain'" (Heb. 8:5; Exod. 25:40). But the law was not an image, but the shadow of an image, for as the same apostle says: "For since the law has but a shadow of the good things to come instead of the true form of the realities . . ." (Heb. 10:1). If the law forbids images, and yet is itself the forerunner of images, what shall we say? If the meeting tent was a shadow and the image of an image, how can it be true that the law does not forbid the making of images? But this is not at all the case, for there is a season for everything; a time for every matter under heaven (cf. Eccles. 3:1).

16. In former times God, who is without form or body, could never be depicted. But now when God is seen in the flesh conversing with men, I make an image of the God whom I see: I do not worship matter; I worship the Creator of matter who became matter for my sake, who willed to take His abode in matter; who worked out my salvation through matter. Never will I cease honoring the matter which wrought my salvation! I honor it, but not as God. How could God be born out of things which have no existence in themselves? God's body is God because it is joined to His person by a union which shall never pass away. The divine nature remains the same; the flesh created in time is quickened by a reason-endowed soul. Because of this I salute all remaining matter with reverence, because God has filled it with His grace and power. Through it my salvation has come to me. Was not the thrice-happy and thrice-blessed wood of the cross matter? Was not the holy and exalted mountain of Calvary matter? What of the life-bearing rock, the holy and life-giving tomb, the fountain of our resurrection, was it not matter? Is not the ink in the most holy Gospel-book matter? Is not the life-giving altar made of matter? From it we receive the bread of life! Are not gold and silver matter? From them we make crosses, patens, chalices! And over and above all these things, is not the Body and Blood of our Lord matter? Either do away with the honor and veneration these things deserve, or accept the tradition of the Church and the veneration of images. Reverence God and His friends; follow the inspiration of the Holy Spirit. Do not despise matter, for it is not despicable. God has made nothing despicable. To think such things is Manichaeism. Only that which does not have its source in God is despicable—that which is our own invention, our willful choice to disregard the law of God—namely, sin. If you despise and abhor the command to make images because they are material things, consider the words of Scripture: "And the Lord said to Moses: See, I have called by name Bezalel the son of Uri, son of Aur, of the tribe of Judah, and I have filled him with the spirit of God, with ability and intelligence, with knowledge and all craftsmanship to devise artistic designs, to work in gold, silver and bronze, in cutting stones for setting and in carving wood, for work in every

craft. And behold, I have appointed with him Oholiab, the son of Ahisamach, of the tribe of Dan, and I have given ability to all able men, that they may make all that I have commanded you" (Exod. 31:1-6). And again, "Moses said to all the congregation of the people of Israel: This is the thing which the Lord has commanded. Take from among you an offering to the Lord; whoever is of a generous heart, let him bring the Lord's offering: gold, silver, and bronze; blue and purple and scarlet stuff and fine twined linen; goats' hair, tanned rams' skins and goatskins; acacia wood, oil for the light, spices for the anointing oil and for the fragrant incense, and onyx stones and stones for setting, for the ephod and for the breastplate. And let every able man among you come and make all that the Lord has commanded, the tabernacle, etc." (Exod. 35:4-10). Behold the glorification of matter, which you despise! What is more insignificant than colored goatskins? Are not blue and purple and scarlet merely colors? Behold the handiwork of men becoming the likeness of the cherubim! How can you make the law a reason for refusing to do what the law itself commands? If you invoke the law in your despising of images, you might just as well insist on keeping the sabbath and practicing circumcision. But it is certain that "if you receive circumcision, Christ will be of no advantage to you. I testify again to every man that if he receive circumcision, he is bound to keep the whole law. You are severed from Christ, you who would be justified by the law; you have fallen away from grace" (Gal. 5:2-4). Israel of old did not see God, but "we all, with unveiled face, behold the glory of the Lord" (2 Cor. 3:18).

17. We use all our senses to produce worthy images of Him, and we sanctify the noblest of the senses, which is that of sight. For just as words edify the ear, so also the image stimulates the eye. What the book is to the literate, the image is to the illiterate. Just as words speak to the ear, so the image speaks to the sight; it brings us understanding. For this reason God ordered the ark to be constructed of wood which would not decay, and to be gilded outside and in, and for the tablets to be placed inside, with Aaron's staff and the golden urn containing the manna, in order to provide a remembrance of the past, and an image of the future. Who can say that these were not images, heralds sounding from far off? They were not placed aside in the meeting-tent, but were brought forth in the sight of all the people, who gazed upon them and used them to offer praise and worship to God. Obviously they were not adored for their own sake, but through them the people were led to remember the wonders of old and to worship God, the worker of wonders. They were images serving as memorials; they were not divine, but led to the remembrance of divine power.

18. God ordered twelve stones to be taken from the Jordan, and specified why, for He says: "When your children ask their fathers in time to come, what do these stones mean? Then you shall let your children know, Israel passed over this Jordan on dry ground, for the Lord your God dried up the waters of the Jordan for you until you passed over" (Josh. 4:21-22), and thus the ark was saved and all the people. Shall we not then record with images the saving passion and miracles of Christ our God, so that when my son asks me, "What is this?" I may say that God the Word became man, and that through him not only Israel passed through the Jordan, but the whole human race regained its original happiness? Through Him, human nature rose from the lowest depths to the most exalted heights, and in Him sat on the Father's throne.

19. Some would say: Make an image of Christ and of His Mother, the Theotokos, and let that be enough. What foolishness! Your own impious words prove that you utterly despise the saints. If you make an image of Christ, and not of the saints, it is evident that you do not forbid images, but refuse to honor the saints. You make images of Christ as one who is glorified, yet you deprive the saints of their rightful glory, and call truth falsehood. The Lord says, "I will glorify those who glorify me" (1 Sam. 2:30). The divinely-inspired apostle writes, "So through God you are no longer a slave but a son, and if a son, then an heir" (Gal. 4:17). And "if children, then heirs, heirs of God and fellow heirs with Christ, provided we suffer with Him in order that we may also be glorified with Him" (Rom. 8:17). You are not waging war against images, but against the saints themselves. St. John the Theologian, who leaned on the breast

of Christ, says "We shall become like Him" (1 John 3:2). Just as something in contact with fire becomes fire not by its own nature, but by being united, burned, and mingled with fire, so it is also, I say, with the assumed flesh of the Son of God. By union with His person, that flesh participates in the divine nature and by this communion becomes unchangeably God; not only by the operation of divine grace, as was the case with the prophets, but by the coming of grace Himself. The Scripture calls the saints gods, when it says, "God has taken His place in the divine council; in the midst of the gods He holds judgment" (Ps. 82:1). St. Gregory interprets these words to mean that God takes His place in the assembly of the saints, determining the glory due each. The saints during their earthly lives were filled with the Holy Spirit, and when they fulfill their course, the grace of the Holy Spirit does not depart from their souls or their bodies in the tombs, or from their likenesses and holy images, not by the nature of these things, but by grace and power.

20. God told David that through his son a temple would be built, and that His resting-place would be prepared. As the Books of Kings tell us, Solomon, while he was building the temple, also made the cherubim. "And he overlaid the cherubim with gold and carved all the walls of the house round about with carved figures of cherubim and palm trees and open flowers, in the inner and outer rooms." Is it not even better to adorn the Lord's house with holy forms and images, instead of beasts and plants? What has become of this law which declares "You shall make for yourself no graven image?" Solomon was given the gift of wisdom, and built the temple, the image of heaven. He made the likenesses of bulls and lions, which the law forbade. Now if we make images of Christ, and images of the saints, which are filled with the Holy Spirit, will they not increase our reverence? Just as the people and the temple were once purified by the blood of goats and bulls and the sprinkling of a heifer's ashes, so we are cleansed by Christ, who in His testimony before Pontius Pilate made the good confession, and who is Himself the example of martyrs. He builds His Church on the foundation of the blood of the saints. There the

forms of lifeless beasts adorned the temple; here we use living and reasonable images.

21. We depict Christ as our King and Lord, then, and do not strip Him of His army. For the saints are the Lord's army. If the earthly emperor wishes to deprive the Lord of His army, let him also dismiss his own troops. If he wishes in his tyranny to refuse due honor to these valiant conquerors of evil, let him also cast aside his own purple. For if the saints are heirs of God and co-heirs with Christ, they will also share in the divine glory and dominion. If they have partaken of Christ's sufferings, and are His friends, shall they not receive a share of glory from the Church on earth? "No longer do I call you servants," God says, "but I have called you friends" (John 15:15). Shall we strip them of the glory given them by the Church? What audacity! What effrontery of mind, to fight with God, refusing to follow His commands! You who refuse to bow before images also refuse to bow before the Son of God who is the living image of the invisible God, and His unchanging likeness. I bow before the images of Christ, the incarnate God; of our Lady, the Theotokos and Mother of the Son of God; and of the saints, who are God's friends. In struggling against evil they have shed their blood; they have imitated Christ who shed His Blood for them by shedding their blood for Him. I make a written record of the prowess and sufferings of those who have walked in His footsteps, that I may be sanctified, and be set on fire to imitate them zealously. St. Basil says, "the honor given to the image is transferred to its prototype." If you build churches to honor the saints of God, then make images of them as well. The temple of old was not built in the name of any man, nor was the death of the righteous an occasion for feasting, but rather for tears. He who touched a corpse was considered unclean, even if the corpse was Moses himself. But now the memory of the saints is kept with rejoicing. There was weeping at the death of Jacob, but there was joy at the death of Stephen. Therefore either give up the joyful feasts of the saints, since they are not part of the old law, or accept the images which you say are contrary to the law. But it is impossible not to keep the memory of the saints with rejoicing, for the choir of holy apostles and God-bearing fathers insist that we do so.

From the time that God the Word became flesh, He is like us in everything except sin, and partakes of our nature without mingling or confusion. He has deified our flesh forever, and has sanctified us by surrendering His Godhead to our flesh without confusion. And from the time that God, the Son of God, who is unchangeable by reason of His Godhead, chose to suffer voluntarily, He wiped out our debt, by paying for us a most admirable and precious ransom. We are all made free through the blood of the Son, which pleads for us to the Father, and by His descent into the grave, when He went and preached to the souls imprisoned there for many ages, and gave freedom to the captives, sight to the blind, and bound the strong one. He rose by the excellence of His power, keeping the immortal flesh by which He had saved us from corruption. And from the time when we were born again of water and the Spirit, we have become sons of God and members of His household. For this reason St. Paul calls the faithful saints. Therefore we do not grieve but rejoice over the death of the saints. We are not under the law but under grace, having been justified by faith, and having seen the one true God. For the law is not laid down for the just, nor do we serve as children, held under the law, but we have reached the estate of mature manhood, and are fed on solid food, not on that which leads to idolatry. The law was good, as a lamp shining in a dark place until the day dawns, and the morning star rose in our hearts. The living water of divine knowledge has driven away pagan seas, and now all may know God. The old creation has passed away, and all things are made new. The holy apostle Paul said to Peter the prince of the apostles: "If you, though a Jew, live like a Gentile and not like a Jew, how can you compel the Gentiles to live like Jews?" (Gal. 2:14). And he writes to the Galatians: "I testify again to every man who receives circumcision that he is bound to keep the whole law" (Gal. 5:3).

22. Of old, those who did not know God were in bondage to beings that by nature are no gods. But now that we have come to know God, or rather to be known by Him, how can anyone turn back again to the weak and beggarly elemental spirits, and be their slaves once more? For I have seen God in human form, and my soul has been saved. I gaze upon the image of God, as Jacob did, but in a different way. For he only saw with spiritual sight what was promised to come in the future, while the memory of Him who became visible in the flesh is burned into my soul. Peter's shadow, or handkerchiefs and aprons carried from Paul's body, healed the sick and put demons to flight. Shall the paintings and images of the saints not be glorified? Either refuse to worship any matter, or stop your innovations. Do not remove age-old boundaries, erected by your fathers.

23. The tradition of the Church is not only passed on in written documents, but has also been given in unwritten form. In chapter twenty-seven of St. Basil's book of thirty chapters written to Amphilochius concerning the Holy Spirit, he says "Among the carefully guarded teachings and doctrines of the Church, there are some teachings we received from written documents, while others we receive secretly, for they have been handed on to us from the apostolic tradition. Both sources have equal power to lead us to righteousness. No one who values the seasoned discipline of the Church will dispute with this, for if we neglect unwritten customs as not having much force, we then bury much of the Gospel which is vitally important." Those are the words of Basil the Great. How then can we know anything about the holy place of Calvary or the life-giving tomb? Is not such unwritten information handed down from father to sons? For it is written that the Lord was crucified at the place of the skull, and buried in a tomb which was hewn out of a rock by Joseph; but it is from unwritten tradition that we know the locations of these places, and worship there now. There are other examples. What is the origin of the three immersions at baptism, or praying toward the east, or the manner in which we celebrate the eucharist? Therefore the holy apostle Paul says: "So then, brethren, stand firm and hold to the traditions which you were taught by us, either by word of mouth or by letter" (2 Thess. 2:15). Therefore, since so much that is unwritten has been handed down in the Church and is still observed now, why do you despise images?

24. If you speak of pagan abuses, these abuses do not make our veneration of images loathsome. Blame the pagans, who made images into gods! Just because the pagans used them in a foul way, that is no reason to object to our pious practice. Sorcerers and magicians use incantations and the Church prays over catechumens; the former conjure up demons while the Church calls upon God to exorcise the demons. Pagans make images of demons which they address as gods, but we make images of God incarnate, and of his servants and friends, and with them we drive away the demonic hosts.

25. If you object that the great St. Epiphanius utterly forbade images, in the first place the writing in question is fictitious and inauthentic. It is the work of someone who used Epiphanius' name, which is a common enough practice. Secondly, we know that the blessed Athanasius objected to the relics of the saints being put into chests, and that he preferred them to be buried in the earth, wishing to abolish the disgusting custom of the Egyptians, who did not bury their dead under the earth, but displayed them on beds and couches. Let us suppose that the great Epiphanius really wrote this work, wishing to correct a similar abuse by forbidding the making of images. Even so, the proof that he did not object to them is found in his own church, which we see adorned with images to this very day. Thirdly, one exception cannot be a law for the Church, nor does a single swallow's song mean that spring has come to stay, as Gregory, the theologian and teacher of truth, says. Nor can a

single opinion overturn the unanimous tradition of the whole Church, which has spread to the ends of the earth.

26. Accept, therefore, the teaching of the Scriptures and the fathers. If the Scripture says, "The idols of the nations are silver and gold, the work of men's hands" (Ps. 135:15), it is not forbidden to bow before inanimate things, or the handiwork of men, but only before those images which are the devil's work.

27. We have seen that prophets bowed before angels, and men, and kings, and those who knew not God, and even a staff. David says, ". . . and worship at His footstool" (Ps. 99:5). Isaiah, speaking in God's name, says, "Heaven is my throne and the earth is my footstool" (Isa. 66:1). It is obvious to all that the heavens and the earth are created things. Moses, Aaron, and all the people worshipped before things made with hands. Paul, the golden voice of the Church, says in the Epistle to the Hebrews, "But when Christ appeared as a high priest of the good things to come, then He entered once for all through the greater and more perfect tent, not made with hands, a type of the true one, but into heaven itself" (Heb. 9:11, 24). Thus the former holy things, the tent, and everything therein were made by hands, and no one can deny that they were venerated.

56. Letters of Patriarch Photius of Constantinople and Pope Nicholas I on Disputed Issues

The correspondence of Patriarch Photius of Constantinople and Pope Nicholas I exposes several issues that increased alienation between the Greek and Latin churches in the second half of the ninth century. The Bulgar khan Boris had recently received baptism according to the Greek tradition, yet he had also written to the pope with a series of religious questions. Along with the tension over Bulgaria, the following letters reveal strong personalities, liturgical differences, and especially the conflict over the filioque *addition to the creed, all of which contributed to the schism of the churches.*

Source: "The Photian Schism, 866-867," tr. Monks of St. John's Abbey, in *Readings in Church History*, vol. 1, ed. Colman J. Barry (Westminster, Md.: Christian Classics, 1960), 316-21.

A. Patriarch Photius of Constantinople: Encyclical Letter to the Archiepiscopal Sees of the East, 866

Encyclical letter to the archiepiscopal sees of the East, that is, Alexandria and the rest, in which the solutions of certain doubtful conclusions are considered, and that it is not permissible to say that the Holy Spirit proceeds from the Father and the Son, but from the Father alone.

These [heresies of Arius, Macedonius, Nestorius, Eutyches, and Dioscorus] although at one time very prominent, have been consigned to silence and oblivion. Bright and solid hope that there would be a time in the near future when no fresh contriver of impieties would spring up seemed encouraging, because in all things that the devil has attempted the opposite effect has turned out. . . .

Moreover, now the barbarian tribe of the Bulgarians, who were hostile and inimical to Christ, has been converted to a surprising degree of meekness and knowledge of God. Beyond all expectation they have in a body embraced the faith of Christ, departing from the worship of devils and of their ancestral gods, and rejecting the error of pagan superstition.

But what a wicked and malignant design, what an ungodly state of affairs! Here is the story: The previous assumption of good news has been turned into dejection, delight and joy are changed into sadness and tears. That people had not embraced the true religion of Christians for even two years when certain impious and ominous men (or by whatever name a Christian refers to them) emerged from the darkness (for they have risen up out of the West)—Oh, how will I go on to tell the rest?—These, as I have said, in a tribe so recently established in piety, which joined the Church just a short time ago, as lightning or an earthquake or a heavy hail—actually I should say, like a wild boar greedily leaping into the much loved and newly planted vineyard of the Lord with feet and bared teeth—on paths of dishonorable administration and corrupted doctrine, thus boldly dividing up the country for themselves, have brought ruin on the people. They have villainously devised to lead them away from the true

and pure doctrine and from an unblemished Christian faith and in this way destroy them.

The first unlawful practice they have set up is fasting on Saturday. Such slight disregard for the traditional teaching usually leads to the complete abandonment of the entire doctrine.

They separated the first week of Lent from the rest and allowed them milk, cheese and other gluttonous practices during this time. From here they made the road of transgressions wider and wider and removed the people more and more from the straight and royal road.

They taught them to despise the priest living in lawful matrimony and by rejecting matrimony spread the seed of Manichaeism, while they themselves practiced adultery.

They did not shrink from reconfirming those who had been anointed by priests with the chrism, and presenting themselves as bishops, they declared the confirmation administered by priests to be useless and invalid. Whoever heard of such a preposterous idea as these insane men have produced, of confirming those who are already confirmed and thereby making fun of the supernatural and divine mysteries of Christians. . . . They claim that bishops only have the right to confirm. But who made this law? Which apostle, which father of the Church, which synod made it? Where and when was this synod held? Who confirmed the resolution? If the priest is not allowed to confirm, then neither is he allowed to baptize or to offer sacrifice. He may as well return to the lay state. Whoever sacrifices the Body of the Lord and the Blood of Christ and by it sanctifies the already blessed members of the Church must certainly be able to sanctify with oil those already blessed. The priest baptizes . . . how then do you deprive him of bringing to perfection with its guard and seal the purification which he has really only begun? Then he would be only a priest in name. . . .

They have not only introduced the committing of such outrages, but now the crown of all evils is sprung up. Besides these offenses that have already been mentioned, they have attempted to adulterate the sacred and holy creed, which has been approved by the vote of all the ecumenical synods and has unconquerable strength, with spurious arguments, interpolated words, and rash exaggerations. They are preaching a novel doctrine: that the Holy Spirit proceeds not from the Father alone, but from the Son as well.

This is the impiety which those bishops of darkness (at least they call themselves bishops) have spread among the Bulgarians. There are also other unlawful practices which they have introduced. When the report of these things reached my ears it struck a mortal blow right to my heart. I felt just like a father who sees his own children torn to pieces and dragged about by ferocious animals and snakes. For our sufferings and labors and sweat laid the foundation for their regeneration and initiation. In proportion to these it is permissible to sympathize with the unbearable pain and misfortune of these perishing children. The greater the joy was over the rebirth of this people, the greater must be the affliction over their misfortune. I have deeply mourned and I am mourning yet. I will give my eyes no rest until I have lifted up the deceived and returned them to the house of the Lord.

These new forerunners of apostasy, these servants of the anti-Christ, who have deserved death a thousand times, ... these deceivers and enemies of God, we have by the resolution of a holy synod sentenced, or rather declared, that by previous resolutions of synods and by apostolic laws, they are already condemned and are made manifest to all. People are so constituted by nature that they are more restrained by present and visible punishments than by previously inflicted ones. Thus because these men remain in their manifold errors, we consider them banished by public proclamation from the company of Christians. The sixty-fourth canon of the holy apostles, rejecting those who make it their practice to fast on Saturdays, says:

"If any cleric is found fasting on the Lord's Day or on Saturday, except for one [Saturday], he is to be deposed; if a lay person is found doing this he is to be excommunicated...."

The fourth canon of the Synod of Gangra, against those who have a horror for marriage, says, "If any priest who is married thinks that this forbids him from partaking in the offering when he officiates at the sacred liturgy, let him be anathema...."

As for doing away with the first week [of Lent] and the re-anointing of those who were anointed at the time they were baptized, there is no need to speak, since these abuses have their condemnation in the canons already mentioned....

But the blasphemy against the Holy Spirit, or rather against the whole Trinity, has nothing to compare with it, and if all the other false teachings were not present, this alone would be enough to bring ten thousand anathemas upon them....

It is necessary that those whom you send as your representatives will uphold you and that they be dispatched with your full and free power, that, namely, which is bestowed upon you by the Holy Spirit. The reason for this is that they may be able to give an opinion and vote on the matter proposed and on any other matter which might be treated, with that liberty which befits the apostolic sees. This is especially the case since from Italy a synodal letter has reached us full of accusations against their Roman bishop. With it was a request not to allow the Italian Christians to perish in such a lamentable way on account of a cruel tyranny which overrides all ecclesiastical laws. But this is not the first complaint to reach us, for previously we have been informed of the situation by a priest who escaped from there and by some monks. Basilius, Zosimus, and Metrophanes have complained of this heavy yoke, and have called upon us with tears to avenge the tyrannized Church. Just now several letters from different persons have arrived full of bitter complaints and tragic stories. According to the wishes of the senders, we have sent special copies of these to the apostolic sees together with this letter for your appraisal. We have done this so that the holy and ecumenical synod which is about to be convened in the Lord, will be seen to conform with the canons and will be confirmed by their unanimous vote, and thus a deep peace may take hold of the Church of Christ.

B. Pope St. Nicholas I: Letter to Archbishop Hincmar of Rheims and the Bishops of the Western Empire, 23 October 867

Nicholas, bishop and servant of the servants of God, to the worthy and Most Reverend Hincmar and to our other brothers, archbishops and bishops, ruling the churches established in the kingdom of glorious King Charles:

You evidently know that the most blessed Peter, who protects and defends us, the heirs of his ministry, bears the burdens which weigh down all of us. In fact he bears them in us. Assuredly among the difficulties which cause us great concern are those, especially disturbing to us, which the Greek emperors, Michael and Basil, and their subjects inflict on us, and truly on the whole West.

Inflamed with hate and envy against us, as we will specify later, they attempt to accuse us of heresy. With hatred indeed, for we not only disapproved but even condemned by deposition and anathematization the advancement attained by Photius, a neophyte, usurper, and adulterer of the Church of Constantinople. The ejection from this church of Ignatius, our brother and co-minister, perpetrated by his own subjects and the imperial power, did not receive our approval. And with envy, because they learned that Michael, king of the Bulgarians, and his people received the faith of Christ and now desired St. Peter's See to provide teachers and instruction for them.

Instead they wish, rather, eagerly try to lead the Bulgarians from obedience to blessed Peter and to subject them shrewdly to their own authority under the pretext of the Christian religion. They preach such things about the Roman Church, which is without spot or wrinkle or anything of the kind, that those ignorant of the faith who hear these things avoid us, shy away, and almost desert us as criminals spotted with the filth of various heresies. . . .

While we were beset by these anxieties and overcome by great trials, the promised legates of the Bulgarian king suddenly presented themselves. Who can guess how great our joy and delight was! For we realized that their health-giving conversion came through the rich kindness of God. We also found out that they had diligently sought the teaching of the blessed apostle Peter and of his See, and so even though they lived far away, were nevertheless made close to us by their faith. And finally we saw that an easy land passage to the East lay open for our messengers through their kingdom.

Just as we had arranged for what was suited to the fundamentals of the faith of the Bulgarian people, so also we took care of what to send to Constantinople. We directed our messengers with the legates now ready to pass through the region of the above-mentioned king. The Greeks not only refused to receive them, but were even furious at the Bulgarians for permitting them to travel across their country. They intimated, undoubtedly, that if our messengers had crossed over territory subject to them, they would have delivered them over to the danger to which the above-mentioned heads of the heretical city are often read to have delivered the legates of the Holy See sent to them for the sake of the faith or ecclesiastical reform.

Further, while they remained with the king of the Bulgarians, and while our messengers tried to reach Constantinople, these officials sent a letter to the Bulgarian king. When he received it he loyally decided to pass it on to us through our legates. Thus we received it and after examining it along with other writings there could not be any doubt that the often mentioned leaders had not written this except with a pen moistened in a pool of blasphemy and with the mud of error for ink.

They strive particularly to find fault with our church and generally with every church which speaks Latin, because we fast on Saturdays and profess that the Holy Spirit proceeds from the Father and the Son, whereas they confess that He proceeds merely from the Father. Besides this, they claim that we detest marriage, since we do not allow priests to marry. They try to blame us because we prohibit priests from anointing the foreheads of the baptized with chrism (which chrism, however, they falsely hold we make from fresh water).

They try to blame us nevertheless because we do not fast, according to our custom, from meat during the eight weeks before Easter, and from cheese and eggs during the seven weeks before the Pasch. They also lie, as their other writings show, when they say that we bless and offer a lamb on the altar, after Jewish custom, together with the Lord's Body on the feast of the Passover. They are certainly content with fault finding!

They complain that our priests do not refuse to shave their beards, and that we ordain a deacon not yet raised to the order of the priesthood to the episcopacy. They complain even though they appointed as their patriarch a layman, hastily become a monk and tonsured, and then, as they realized, to advance him without any fear by a leap to the episcopacy through imperial power and favor.

Yet what is more insulting and foolish, they tried to demand a testimony of faith from our messengers, if they wished to be received by them, something which is against every rule and custom. In it these doctrines and those holding them are anathematized. They even impudently demanded a canonical letter from them, to give to the one they call their "ecumenical patriarch."

It is certainly right, brothers, that you exert yourselves to the utmost in this affair, and put your other cares aside. Since these taunts are common, for they are hurled against the universal Church as we have shown, at least that part of it which is singled out by its use of Latin, all together who are raised to the divine priesthood ought to fight to keep the ancient traditions from being exposed to such derogation. But these traditions, which such depraved men, lying and erring, try to defile by their contentiousness, must be entirely cleared of every blemish of blasphemy by the hand of common defense.

It is ridiculous and certainly detestably shameful to allow the holy Church of God either to be falsely charged today, or its ancient customs handed down from our fathers to be disparaged at the pleasure of those always erring. Therefore, it is necessary to resist their efforts and to oppose to their deceitful barbs the shield of truth. . . .

Each and every one of you who enjoy metropolitan rank, joined with your brothers and their auxiliaries, are to take diligent care of these things. Take pains to search for whatever may be needed to rebut their hostile detractions. Eagerly search out, and by no means think it a light matter to send quickly what is found. Thus we will be able to send your answer along with our other declarations against their ragings. . . .

We should stimulate each other's zeal and be found not as stragglers, but as an orderly line of defense arrayed against the common enemy. Then, while we gain your adherence in the common conflict as you also enter into our struggles, we will be seen to esteem you with an affectionate heart and to honor you as a brother. And you will be known as not being separated in any way from the See of Peter, the head of the Church.

With what great malice and foolishness these aforementioned Greek leaders and their henchmen are armed against us, because we did not consent to their evil ragings, is clearly revealed. Their charges, with which they try to stain us, are either false, or against what has been guarded in the Roman Church, indeed in the entire West, from the earliest times without any contradiction. When great doctors of the Church began to rise among them, none of them was critical of these things. Only those among them who burned not with a just zeal but driven by an evil zeal seek to tear to pieces the traditions of the Church.

This is especially true since the Saturday fast was fully discussed and disputed during the time of St. Sylvester, a confessor of Christ, and defined to be observed everywhere. No one after that time has rashly presumed to attack it, nor even to murmur against it. Rather, on the contrary, what the Holy See instituted and subsequently observed was hitherto found to be one and the same fountain of the saving law.

As regards the procession of the Holy Spirit— who does not know that distinguished men, especially among the Latins, have written much about this matter? Supported by their authority we can reply fully and reasonably to their senselessness. Does any custom demand that they should go unrefuted, or that we should not answer their yelps and disputatious tongues with reasonable argument?

Is it even strange that they should allege such things since they even glory in the assertion that when the emperors moved from Rome to Constantinople the primacy of the Roman See also went to Constantinople, and with the royal dignities even the privileges of the Roman Church were transferred? So that this same Photius, a usurper in the Church, even entitles himself in his writings, "archbishop and universal patriarch."

Therefore, consider, brethren, if these things do not prejudice the Church of Christ. See if they can be judged to be tolerable. Consider whether these men have the right to inflict derogations and detractions of this kind on the Roman Church. From the time the Christian religion began to be spread she has held immutable and taught uncorrupted throughout the world the doctrines which she once received from her patron and founder, St. Peter. Nor has anyone appeared, at least through all these past years, who detracted from her traditions, or presumed to oppose her. . . .

57. *Life of Constantine [Cyril]*

After diplomatic missions to the caliph in Baghdad and the rulers of Khazaria, the scholar Constantine the Philosopher set out with his brother Methodius on a mission to the Slavs of Moravia. At the request of the Moravian prince for Christian teachers, the Byzantine emperor and patriarch sent the brothers on the famous mission that would eventually earn them the title Apostles to the Slavs. The tenth-century Slavonic Vita *of Constantine, who eventually became a monk and took the name Cyril, describes different phases and struggles of his career.*

The *Vita* and Life of Our Blessed Teacher

Constantine the Philosopher, the First Preceptor of the Slavic People

Bless us, Father

1. Merciful and compassionate is God, who awaits the repentance of Man and will have all to be saved, and to come unto the knowledge of the truth; for He wishes the sinner not death but repentance and life even if he be given to malice. Neither does He allow mankind to fall away through weakness or be led into temptation by the Adversary and perish. Rather, in each age and epoch He has not ceased to grant us His abundant grace, even now just as it was in the beginning. . . . He did so also in our generation, having raised up for us this teacher who enlightened our nation, which did not wish to walk in the light of God's commandments, and whose understanding was obscured by weakness and even more by the Devil's wiles.

Stated briefly, his *Vita* reveals what sort of man he was, so that hearing it, he who wishes—taking courage and rejecting idleness—can follow him. For as the Apostle has said: "Be ye followers of me, even as I also am of Christ" (1 Cor. 11:1).

2. There was a certain noble and rich man named Leo in the city of Thessalonica who held the rank of *drungarios* under the *strategos*. He was, as Job once was, a pious man, and kept faithfully all God's commandments. He begot seven children of which the youngest, the seventh, was Constantine the Philosopher, our preceptor and teacher. And when his mother bore him, he was given over to a wet-nurse for nursing. However, until the child was weaned he would not take any other breast but his mother's. This was by God's design so that there be a good offshoot from a good root. And after this the good parents agreed not to lie with each other. They never once transgressed their vow, but lived that way in the Lord for 14 years, parting in death. And when that devout man was wanted on Judgment Day, the mother of this child cried, saying: "I am worried about nought save this one child and how he will be nurtured." Then he said: "Believe me, wife, I place my hope in God. He will give him for a

SOURCE: *Medieval Slavic Lives of Saints and Princes,* ed. and tr. Marvin Kantor (Ann Arbor: Michigan Slavic Publications, 1983), 25–31, 35–39, 41–49, 61–81. Used by permission of Michigan Slavic Publications.

father and steward one such as guides all Christians." And so it came to pass.

3. When he was seven the boy had a dream which he recounted to his father and mother, saying: "After the *strategos* had assembled all the girls of our city, he said to me: 'Choose her whom you wish as your wife and helpmate from among them.' Gazing upon them and taking note of each one, I discerned the most beautiful of all, with a radiant face, richly adorned in gold necklaces and pearls, and all manner of finery. Her name was Sophia, that is, Wisdom. I chose her."

When his parents heard these words, they said to him: "Son, keep thy father's commandment, and forsake not the law of thy mother. For the commandment is a lamp; and the law is light. Say unto Wisdom, Thou art my sister; and call Understanding thy kinswoman. For Wisdom shines even more than the sun. And if you then take her to yourself as your wife, you will be delivered from much evil through her" (cf. Wis. 9:1-5). When they sent him for instruction he surpassed all his fellow students in learning, as his memory was very keen. He was then a marvel. . . .

Upon hearing of the keenness, wisdom, and zeal for learning with which he was imbued, the Emperor's administrator, called the *Logothete*, sent for Constantine to study together with the Emperor. Learning of this, the boy joyfully set out . . .

4. When he arrived in the Imperial City he was entrusted to teachers to be taught. In three months he mastered grammar and began other studies. He studied Homer and geometry with Leo, and dialectics and all philosophical studies with Photius; and in addition to that, rhetoric and arithmetic, astronomy and music, and all the other Hellenic arts. He mastered them all just as though he were mastering only one of them. For keenness joined with zeal, the one vying with the other, by which ability studies are perfected. But more than studiousness, a newly serene countenance became him. He conferred with those who were more beneficial and turned from those who turned to malice, for he thought and acted only to acquire heavenly things in place of earthly ones and to quit his body and live with God . . .

[Having gained a reputation for great learning, Constantine is persuaded to accept an academic chair in Constantinople and to teach philosophy to his countrymen and foreigners. Soon after he debates the iconoclast patriarch John the Grammarian (837-843).]

6. Afterward the Hagarites, who were called Saracens, blasphemed the single Deity of the Holy Trinity, saying: "How is it, O Christians, that you, while holding that God is one, further divide Him into three, saying He is Father, Son, and Spirit? If you can explain clearly, send us men who can speak of this and convince us."

At that time the Philosopher was 24 years of age. Having convened a council, the Emperor summoned Constantine and said to him: "Do you hear, Philosopher, what the nasty Hagarites are saying against our faith? Since you are a servant and disciple of the Holy Trinity, go and oppose them. And may God, the Accomplisher of all, Who is glorified in the Trinity, the Father and Son and Holy Spirit, grant you grace and strength in words. And may He reveal you a second David against Goliath whom he defeated with three stones, and return you to us made worthy of the heavenly kingdom."

Upon hearing this, Constantine answered: "I shall gladly go for the Christian faith. For what in this world could be sweeter for me than to live and die for the Holy Trinity!"

And they assigned the court secretary, George, to him and sent them.

When they came there they saw strange and vile things which the God-fighting Hagarites did to deride and mock Christians. In these places all those living in piety in Christ were caused much grief. Thus on the outside doors of all Christians they painted images of demons playing games and grimacing. And they asked the Philosopher, saying: "Philosopher, can you understand what this sign means?"

Then he said: "I see demonic images and assume that Christians dwell within. However, the demons are unable to live with them and flee from them. But wherever this sign is not present on the outside, the demons dwell with those inside."

At dinner the Hagarites, a wise people, well versed in scholarship, geometry, astronomy and other sciences, tested Constantine and questioned him, saying: "Philosopher, perceive you the wondrous miracle, how the Prophet Mohammed brought us joyful tidings from God and converted many people; and how we all keep his law without transgressing in any way? But in keeping Christ's law, you act and do whatever pleases each of you, one this, another that."

To this the Philosopher answered: "Our God is like the breadth of the sea. Thus did the Prophet speak of Him: 'And who shall declare His generation? for He was cut off out of the land of the living' (Isa. 53:8). For the sake of this search many set out on this sea. And with His help, the strong in mind sail across and return, receiving a wealth of understanding. But the weak in mind, some sink like those attempting to cross in rotten ships, while others flounder in impotent idleness, barely breathing from exhaustion. However, your sea is deceptive and self-serving, so that anyone, great and small can leap across. For it is not beyond the wonts of man but something one can easily do. Now Mohammed forbade you nothing else. Since he did not restrain your anger and lust but allowed them, do you know into which abyss he will cast you? Let the sensible understand: Christ is not that way. Rather, He raises up what is difficult from beneath through faith and divine action. As the Creator of everything, He created man between the angels and beasts. For man is distinguished from beasts by his speech and intelligence, and from angels by his anger and lust. And he shall participate either in higher or lower realms in accordance with the realm he approaches."

And again they questioned him: "Since God is one, why do you glorify Him as three? If you know, explain this! For you call Him Father, Son, and Spirit. If this be so, give Him a wife as well, so that many gods might be sired by Him."

To this the Philosopher answered: "Do not speak such despicable blasphemies. For well have we learned from the prophets and fathers and teachers to glorify the Trinity, the Father, the Word and the Spirit, three hypostases in one being. And the Word became flesh in the Virgin and was born for the sake of our salvation, as your prophet Mohammed bore witness when he wrote the following: 'We sent our spirit, to the Virgin, having consented that She gave birth' (Qur'an 19:17). From this I apprise you of the Trinity."

Defeated by these words, they turned to another matter . . .

[*Constantine continues to debate with the Muslims. He returns to his native land and joins his brother, Methodius, a monk of the monastery of Mount Olympus in Bithynia.*]

8. And then to the Greek Emperor came emissaries from the Khazars, saying: "From the beginning we have known one God who is above all, and worshipped Him facing east. However, we keep other shameful customs. The Jews exhort us to accept their faith and ways, while on the other hand the Saracens, offering us peace and many gifts, press us, saying: 'Our faith is better than that of all other peoples.' Maintaining our former love and friendship, we therefore have come to you. For you are a great people and your empire is from God. And in requesting your counsel, we ask of you a learned man. Should he prevail over the Jews and Saracens, we shall accept your faith."

Then the Emperor sought the Philosopher and, after finding him, told him of the Khazars' words, saying: "Philosopher, go to these people, preach and answer for the Holy Trinity with Its help. For no one else is capable of doing this properly."

He said: "If you command, lord, on such a mission I shall gladly go on foot and unshod, lacking all the Lord forbade His disciples to bring."

The Emperor answered, saying: "Well spoken; were you to do this! But bear in mind the imperial power and honor, and go honorably and with imperial help."

He immediately set out on his way. After coming to Kherson, he learned the Hebrew language and scriptures and translated eight parts of the grammar, from which he acquired understanding. A certain Samaritan living there would come to Constantine and debate with him. And he brought Samaritan scriptures and showed them to him. The Philosopher asked him for them, locked himself in his room and gave himself up to prayer. And having obtained understanding from God, he began to read the scriptures without error. When the Samaritan saw this, he cried out in a loud voice and said: "Verily, those who believe in Christ quickly receive Grace and the Holy Spirit." His son was baptized immediately and he himself was baptized after him.

And Constantine found there the Gospels and the Psalter written in Russian letters. And he also found a man who spoke that language. And having conversed with him and acquiring the power of his speech by comparing it to his own language, he distinguished letters, vowels and consonants, and offering a prayer to God, he soon began to read and speak. And they were amazed at him and praised God.

And when he heard that St. Clement was still lying in the sea, he prayed and said: "I believe in God and place my hope in St. Clement, that I shall find him and take him from the sea."

After persuading the Archbishop, they boarded a ship with all the clergy and pious men and set out for that spot. A great calm came over the sea and they arrived and began to dig, chanting. And immediately a strong fragrance arose as if there were many censers, and then the holy relics appeared. To the glory of all the townsmen, they raised them with great reverence and carried them into the city, as Constantine writes in his *Discovery*.

A Khazar commander came with his troops, surrounded a certain Christian city, and laid siege to it. Upon learning of this, the Philosopher went to him without hesitation. Conversing with him, he imparted his edifying words and calmed him. He promised Constantine to be baptized.

The Philosopher continued on his way. And while he was reciting the prayer of the first hour, Hungarians fell upon him howling like wolves and wishing to kill him. But he was not frightened and did not forsake his prayers, crying out only, "Lord, have mercy!" for he had already completed the office. Seeing him, they were calmed by God's design and began to bow to him. And upon hearing edifying words from his lips, they released him and his entire retinue in peace.

9. Having boarded a ship, Constantine set out for the land of the Khazars by way of the Meotis Sea and Caspian Gates of the Caucasus Mountains. The Khazars sent a cunning and resourceful man to meet him, who entered into conversation with him and said to him: "Why do you follow the evil custom of replacing one emperor with another of a different lineage? We do this only according to lineage."

The Philosopher said to him: "Yet in place of Saul, who did nothing to please Him, God chose David, who was pleasing to Him, and David's lineage."

And furthermore the Khazar said: "Why is it you hold the Scriptures in hand, and recite all parables from it? However, we do not do so, but take all wisdom from the heart as though it were absorbed. We do not pride ourselves in writing as you do."

And the Philosopher said to him: "I shall answer you in regard to this. If you meet a naked man and he says: 'I have many garments and gold,' would you believe him, seeing him naked?"

He said: "No."

Then Constantine said to him: "So I say unto you. If you have absorbed all wisdom as you boast, tell me how many generations are there from Adam to Moses, and how many years did each generation endure?"

Unable to answer this, the Khazar fell silent.

When Constantine came for the feast at the Kagan's and they wished to seat him, they questioned him, saying: "What is your station so that we may seat you according to your rank?"

And he said: "I had a great and very renowned forefather who stood close to the Emperor. But he voluntarily rejected the great honor granted him and was banished. He became impoverished after going to a foreign land, and there he begot me. Though I have sought my forefather's former station, I have not succeeded in obtaining it, for I am Adam's scion."

They then said: "O guest, you speak worthily and rightly." And from that moment they began to confer honor upon him.

Taking up his cup, the Kagan said: "Let us drink in the name of the One God who made all creation."

Taking up his cup, the Philosopher said: "I drink in the name of the One God and His Word, who by His Word made all creation and through Whom the heavens were established; and in the name of the life-giving Spirit through Whom all their power exists."

The Kagan answered him: "We say the same but maintain the following difference: you glorify the Trinity, while we, having obtained Scriptures, the One God."

Then the Philosopher said: "The Scriptures proclaim the Word and the Spirit. If someone renders honor unto you but will not honor your word and spirit, whereas yet another will honor all three, which of the two renders greater honor?"

He said: "The one who honors all three."

And the Philosopher answered: "Thus, we do more by revealing it in deeds and obeying the prophets. For Isaiah said: 'Hearken unto me, O Jacob and Israel, my called; I am the first, I am forever. And now the Lord, and His Spirit, hath sent me'" (Isa. 48:12, 16).

Then the Jews standing around Constantine said to him: "Tell us now, how is it possible for a woman to bear God in her womb upon whom she may not even look, let alone give birth to."

And pointing his finger at the Kagan and his first counselor, the Philosopher said: "If someone says: 'The first counselor cannot entertain the Kagan' but furthermore says: 'The latter's lowest slave can entertain the Kagan and render honor unto him,' what are we to call him, tell me, insane or sensible?"

And they said: "Very much insane."

Then the Philosopher said to them: "Which of the visible creatures is the most honored of all?"

They answered him: "Man, for he was created in the image of God."

And again the Philosopher said to them: "Indeed, are they not raving who say it is not possible for God to be contained in man, since He was contained in the bush and in the cloud, in the whirlwind and smoke, having appeared so to Moses and Job. Otherwise how can the sick be healed? For when mankind comes to perdition, from whom can it further await renewal if not from the very Creator Himself? Answer me! If a doctor wishes to apply a plaster to the sick, would he or would he not apply it to a tree or to a stone? And will he be able to heal a man by this?"

"And how could Moses in his prayer through the Holy Spirit say with outstretched arms, 'In the thunder of stones and in the voice of trumpets reveal yourself unto us no more, merciful Lord, but having removed our sins, abide inside us.'" For thus speaks Aquila. And thus they departed from the feast after setting a day when they would speak about all this. . . .

[*Constantine continues to dialogue with the Khazars, both Muslims and Jews.*]

11. . . . At that time about two hundred of these people were baptized, having cast off heathen abominations and lawless marriages. And the Kagan wrote the following epistle to the Emperor: "Lord, you have sent us a man who in word and deed has shown us that the Christian faith is holy. We are convinced it is the true faith and, in the hope that we too shall attain it, we have commanded all to be baptized voluntarily. We all are friends of your Empire and are at your service wherever you require it."

Seeing the Philosopher off, the Kagan offered him many gifts, but he did not accept them, saying: "Give me as many Greek captives as you have here. That means more to me than all your gifts."

Having gathered about two hundred captives, they gave them to him. And he went on his way, rejoicing.

[*Constantine and his delegation return to Constantinople.*]

14. While the Philosopher was rejoicing in God, yet another matter arose, and a task no less than the former. For Rastislav, the Prince of Moravia, through God's admonition, took counsel with his Moravian princes and appealed to Emperor Michael, saying: "Though our people have rejected paganism and observe Christian law, we do not have a teacher who can explain to us in our language the true Christian faith, so that other countries which look to us might emulate us. Therefore, O lord, send us such a bishop and teacher; for from you good law issues to all countries." And having gathered his council, the Emperor summoned Constantine the Philosopher and had him listen to this matter. And he said: "Philosopher, I know that you are weary, but it is necessary that you go there. For no one can attend to this matter like you."

And the Philosopher answered: "Though I am weary and sick in body, I shall go there gladly if they have a script for their language."

Then the Emperor said to him: "My grandfather and my father, and many others have sought this but did not find it. How then can I find it?"

And the Philosopher answered: "Who can write a language on water and acquire for himself a heretic's name?"

And together with his uncle, Bardas, the Emperor answered him again: "If you wish, God may give you this as He gives to everyone that asks without doubt, and opens to them that knock."

The Philosopher went and, following his old habit, gave himself up to prayer together with his other associates. Hearing the prayer of His servants, God soon appeared to him. And immediately Constantine composed letters and began to write the language of the Gospel, that is: "In the beginning was the Word, and the Word was with God, and the Word was God" (John 1:1), and so forth.

The Emperor rejoiced, and together with his counselors glorified God. And he sent Constantine with many gifts, after writing the following epistle to Rastislav: "God, who will have all men come unto the knowledge of the truth and raise themselves to a greater station, having noted your faith and struggles, arranged now, in our time, to fulfill your request and reveal a script for your language, which did not exist in the beginning but only in later times, so that you may be counted among the great nations that praise God in their own language. Therefore, we have sent you the one to whom God revealed this, a venerable and pious and very learned man, a philosopher. Thus, accept this gift which is greater and more valuable than all gold and silver, precious stones and transient riches. And strive zealously with him to strengthen his work, and with all your heart to seek God. And do not reject universal salvation. Convince all not to be idle, but to take the true path. So that, having led them to divine understanding through your struggles, you too shall receive your reward—both in this age and the next—for the souls of all who wish to believe in Christ our God now and evermore. Thus shall you leave your memory to future generations like the great Emperor Constantine."

15. When Constantine arrived in Moravia, Rastislav received him with great honor. And he gathered students and gave them over to Constantine for instruction. As soon as all the church offices were accepted, he taught them Matins and the Hours, Vespers and the Compline, and the Liturgy. And according to the word of the prophet, the ears of the deaf were unstopped, the Words of the Scriptures were heard, and the tongues of stammerers spoke clearly. And God rejoiced over this, while the Devil was shamed.

Because God's Word was spreading, the evil envier from the days of creation, the thrice-accursed Devil, was unable to bear this good and entered his vessels. And he began to rouse many, saying to them: "God is not glorified by this. For if this were pleasing unto Him, could He not have ordained from the beginning that they should glorify Him, writing their language in their own script? But only three languages, Hebrew, Greek, and Latin, were chosen as appropriate for rendering glory unto God."

These were the cohorts of the Latins speaking, archpriests, priests, and their disciples. And having fought with them like David with the Philistines, Constantine defeated them with words from the Scriptures, and called them trilinguists, since Pilate had thus written the Lord's title.

And this was not all they were saying, but they also were teaching other impieties, saying: "Underground live people with huge heads; and all reptiles are the creation of the Devil, and if one kills a snake, he will be absolved of nine sins because of this. If one kills a man, let him drink from a wooden cup for three months and not touch one of glass." And they forbade neither the offering of sacrifices according to the ancient custom, nor shameful marriages.

Cutting all this down like thorns, Constantine burned them with the fire of Scripture, saying: "Offer unto God a sacrifice of thanksgiving; and pay thy vows unto the Most High. Send not away the wife of thy youth. For if having begun to hate her, thou send her away, wickedness covers not thy lust, saith the Lord Almighty. And take heed to your spirit, and let none leave the wife of thy youth; and that which I hated ye have done, because the Lord hath been witness between thee and the wife of thy youth, whom thou hast forsaken: Yet is she thy companion and the wife of thy covenant. And in the Gospel the Lord says: 'Ye have heard that it was said to them of old time, Thou shalt not commit adultery: But I say unto you, That whosoever looketh on a woman to lust after her, hath committed adultery with her already in his heart' (Matt. 5:27, 28). And furthermore: 'But I say unto you: That whosoever shall put away his wife, saving for the cause of fornication, causeth her to commit adultery: and whosoever shall marry her that is divorced, committeth adultery' (Matt. 5:32). And the Apostle said: 'What God hath joined together, let no man put asunder'" (Mark 10:9).

Constantine spent forty months in Moravia, and then left to ordain his disciples. On the way Kocel, Prince of Pannonia, received him and took a great liking to the Slavic letters. He learned them himself, and gave him about fifty students to be taught them. He rendered him great honor, and accompanied him. But Constantine took neither gold nor silver nor other things from either Rastislav or Kocel. He set down the word of the Gospel without sustenance, asked only for nine hundred captives, and released them.

16. When he was in Venice, bishops, priests and monks gathered against him like ravens against a falcon. And they advanced the trilingual heresy, saying: "Tell us, O man, how is it that you now teach, having created letters for the Slavs, which none else have found before, neither the Apostle, nor the pope of Rome, nor Gregory the Theologian, nor Jerome, nor Augustine? We know of only three languages worthy of praising God in the Scriptures, Hebrew, Greek, and Latin."

And the Philosopher answered them: "Does not God's rain fall upon all equally? And does not the sun shine also upon all? And do we not all breathe air in the same way? Are you not ashamed to mention only three tongues, and to command all other nations and tribes to be blind and deaf? Tell me, do you render God powerless, that He is incapable of granting this? Or envious, that He does not desire this? We know of numerous peoples who possess writing and render glory unto God, each in its own language. Surely these are obvious: Armenians, Persians, Abkhazians, Iberi-

ans, Sogdians, Goths, Avars, Turks, Khazars, Arabs, Egyptians, and many others. If you do not wish to understand this, at least recognize the judgment of the Scriptures. For David cries out, saying: 'O sing unto the Lord, all the earth: sing unto the Lord a new song' (Ps. 96:1). And again: 'Make a joyful noise unto the Lord, all the earth: make a loud noise, and rejoice, and sing praise' (Ps. 98:4). And likewise: 'Let all the earth worship Thee, and sing unto Thee; let it sing to Thy name, God on High' (Ps. 66:4). And furthermore: 'O praise the Lord, all ye nations: praise Him, all ye people. Let every thing that hath breath praise the Lord' (Ps. 117:1; 150:6). And in the Gospel according to John it says: 'But as many as received Him, to them gave He power to become the children of God' (John 1:12). And again in the same Gospel: 'Neither pray I for these alone, but for them also which shall believe in Me through their word, that they all may be one; as Thou, Father, art in Me, and I in Thee' (John 17:20, 21).

"And Matthew said: 'All power is given unto Me in heaven, and on earth. Go ye, therefore, and teach all nations, baptizing them in the name of the Father, and of the Son, and of the Holy Ghost; Teaching them to observe all things whatsoever I have commanded you: and, lo, I am with you always, even unto the end of time. Amen' (Matt. 28:18-20).

"And Mark says again: 'Go into all the world, and preach the Gospel to every creature. He that believeth and is baptized, shall be saved; but he that believeth not, shall be damned. And these signs shall follow them that believe; In my name shall they cast out devils; they shall speak with new tongues' (Mark 16:15-17).

"And unto you also is said, teachers of the law: 'Woe unto you, scribes and Pharisees, hypocrites! for ye shut up the kingdom of heaven against men: for ye neither go in yourselves, neither suffer ye them that are entering to go in' (Matt. 23:13).

"And furthermore: 'Woe unto you, lawyers! for ye have taken away the key of knowledge: ye entered not in yourselves, and them that were entering in, ye hindered' (Luke 11:52).

"And Paul said to the Corinthians: 'I would that ye all spake with tongues, but rather that ye prophesied: for greater is he that prophesieth, than he that speaketh with tongues, except he interpret, that the church may receive edifying . . .'" (1 Cor. 14:5-40).

[*Constantine continues the long citation from 1 Corinthians 14.*]

. . . And with these words and many more, he shamed them and went away, leaving them.

17. Upon learning of Constantine, the Pope of Rome sent for him. And when he came to Rome, the Apostolic Father himself, Hadrian and all the townspeople came out to meet him, carrying candles. For he was carrying the relics of St. Clement the Martyr and Pope of Rome. And at once God wrought glorious miracles for his sake: a paralytic was healed, and many others were cured of various maladies. And even captives were at once liberated from the hands of their captors when they invoked Christ and St. Clement.

Accepting the Slavic Scriptures, the Pope placed them in the Church of St. Mary called Phatne. And the holy liturgy was celebrated over them. Then the Pope commanded two bishops, Formosus and Gauderich, to consecrate the Slavic disciples. And when they were consecrated they at once celebrated the liturgy in the Slavic language in the Church of the Apostle Peter. And the next day they celebrated in the Church of St. Petronilla, and on the following day in the Church of St. Andrew. And then they celebrated the entire night, glorifying God in Slavic once again in the Church of the Apostle Paul, the great universal teacher. And in the morning they again celebrated the liturgy over his blessed grave with the help of Bishop Arsenius, one of the seven bishops, and of Anastasius the librarian . . .

18. And his many labors overtook him, and he fell ill. Enduring his illness for many days, he once had a divine revelation and began to chant the following: "When they said unto me, Let us go into the house of the Lord, my spirit rejoiced, and my heart was gladdened" (Ps. 122:1).

Having put on his venerable garments, he thus spent that entire day rejoicing and saying: "Henceforth I am neither a servant of the Emperor nor of anyone else on earth, but only of God Almighty. I was not, and I came to be, and am forever. Amen."

On the following day he put on holy monastic dress and, receiving light to light, called himself Cyril. He spent fifty days in that dress. And when the hour to repose and remove to the eternal dwellings approached, he raised his arms to God and, in tears, prayed, saying thus: "O Lord, my God, who hast created all the ranks of angels and incorporeal powers, stretched out the heavens and founded the earth, and brought all things into being from non-being, who hast always heeded those that work Thy will, fear Thee and keep Thy commandments, heed my prayer and preserve Thy faithful flock which Thou appointed to me, Thy useless and unworthy servant. Deliver them from the godless and heathen malice of those speaking blasphemy against Thee, and destroy the trilingual heresy belief. Increase Thy church to a multitude, gather all together in unanimity, and make a chosen people of those who are of one mind in Thy true faith and just confession. And inspire in their hearts the Word of Thy Son, for it is Thy gift. If Thou hast accepted us, unworthy ones, to preach the Gospel of Thy Christ, then those who are striving for good deeds and doing what pleases Thee, whom Thou hast given to me, I return to Thee as Thine. Guide them with Thy firm right hand and shelter them with the cover of Thy wings, so that all might praise and glorify Thy name, the Father, Son and Holy Spirit. Amen."

He kissed everyone with a holy kiss and said: "Blessed be God, who hath not given us as prey into the teeth of our invisible enemies, but hath smashed their snare and saved us from their corruption." And thus he reposed in the Lord at 42 years of age, on the 14th day of the month of February, of the second indiction, the 6370th year from the creation of this world.

And the Apostolic Father commanded all Greeks residing in Rome, as well as Romans, to gather with candles, chant over him and join his funeral procession, as they would for the Pope himself. And this they did. Then Methodius, his brother, entreated the Apostolic Father saying: "Our mother adjured us that the one of us first to pass away be brought to his brother's monastery to be buried there."

And the Pope commanded that he be put into a coffin and that it be nailed shut with iron nails. He kept him this way for seven days, preparing for the journey. But the Roman bishops said to the Apostolic Father: "Though he traveled through many lands, God led him here, and here He received his soul. Thus, it is proper that he be buried here as a venerable man."

Then the Apostolic Father said: "For the sake of his saintliness and charity I shall transgress Roman custom and bury him in my tomb, in the Church of the Holy Apostle Peter."

And his brother said: "Since you do not heed me and do not give him up, let him, if it pleases you, rest in the Church of St. Clement, for he came here with him."

And the Apostolic Father commanded that this be done. Gathering again with all the people who wished to join the procession of honor, the bishops said: "Let us unnail the coffin and see whether anything has been taken from him."

After much effort, they were unable to unnail the coffin, by God's command. And thus they put him with the coffin into a tomb to the right of the altar in the Church of St. Clement, where many miracles began to occur. When the Romans saw these miracles, they became even more attached to his saintliness and honor. Painting his icon over the tomb, they began to light candles over it day and night and praise God, who thus glorifies those who glorify Him. Unto Him glory, honor, and reverence forever. Amen.

58. The Christianization of Russia:
Russian Primary Chronicle

Although the Russian princess Olga had become a Christian in 957 while on a diplomatic mission in Constantinople, the final conversion of Russia awaited the reign of her grandson, Prince Vladimir of Kiev, in 987-988. Compiled in the eleventh and early twelfth centuries, the Russian Primary Chronicle *recounts the traditional story with its charming blend of fact and fiction. The account not only suggests the reasons for Vladimir's acceptance of the Christian faith from Byzantium but also reveals a distinct anti-Latin bias in the catechetical instruction that ensued.*

6495 (987). Vladimir summoned together his boyars and the city-elders, and said to them, "Behold, the Bulgars came before me urging me to accept their religion. Then came the Germans and praised their own faith; and after them came the Jews. Finally the Greeks appeared, criticizing all other faiths but commending their own, and they spoke at length, telling the history of the whole world from its beginning. Their words were artful, and it was wondrous to listen and pleasant to hear them. They preach the existence of another world. 'Whoever adopts our religion and then dies shall arise and live forever. But whosoever embraces another faith, shall be consumed with fire in the next world.' What is your opinion on this subject, and what do you answer?" The boyars and the elders replied, "You know, oh Prince, that no man condemns his own possessions, but praises them instead. If you desire to make certain, you have servants at your disposal. Send them to inquire about the ritual of each and how he worships God."

Their counsel pleased the prince and all the people, so that they chose good and wise men to

SOURCE: *The Russian Primary Chronicle: Laurentian Text,* tr. Samuel Hazzard Cross and Olgerd P. Sherbowitz-Wetzor (Cambridge, Mass.: Medieval Academy of America, 1953), 110-17.

the number of ten, and directed them to go first among the Bulgars and inspect their faith. The emissaries went their way, and when they arrived at their destination they beheld the disgraceful actions of the Bulgars and their worship in the mosque; then they returned to their country. Vladimir then instructed them to go likewise among the Germans, and examine their faith, and finally to visit the Greeks. They thus went into Germany, and after viewing the German ceremonial, they proceeded to Tsar'grad, where they appeared before the Emperor. He inquired on what mission they had come, and they reported to him all that had occurred. When the Emperor heard their words, he rejoiced, and did them great honor on that very day.

On the morrow, the Emperor sent a message to the Patriarch to inform him that a Russian delegation had arrived to examine the Greek faith, and directed him to prepare the church and the clergy, and to array himself in his sacerdotal robes, so that the Russes might behold the glory of the God of the Greeks. When the Patriarch received these commands, he bade the clergy assemble, and they performed the customary rites. They burned incense, and the choirs sang hymns. The Emperor accompanied the Russes to the church, and placed them in a wide space, calling their attention to the beauty of the edifice, the chanting, and the pontifical services and the ministry of the deacons, while he explained to them the worship of his God. The Russes were astonished, and in their wonder praised the Greek ceremonial. Then the Emperors Basil and Constantine invited the envoys to their presence, and said, "Go hence to your native country," and dismissed them with valuable presents and great honor.

Thus they returned to their own country, and the Prince called together his boyars and the elders. Vladimir then announced the return of the envoys who had been sent out, and suggested that their report be heard. He thus commanded them to speak out before his retinue. The envoys reported, "When we journeyed among the Bulgars, we beheld how they worship in their temple, called a mosque, while they stand ungirt. The Bulgar bows, sits down, looks hither and thither like one possessed, and there is no happiness among

them, but instead only sorrow and a dreadful stench. Their religion is not good. Then we went among the Germans, and saw them performing many ceremonies in their temples; but we beheld no glory there. Then we went to Greece and the Greeks led us to the edifices where they worship their God, and we knew not whether we were in heaven or on earth. For on earth there is no such splendor or such beauty, and we are at a loss how to describe it. We only know that God dwells there among men, and their service is fairer than the ceremonies of other nations. For we cannot forget that beauty. Every man, after tasting something sweet, is afterward unwilling to accept that which is bitter, and therefore, we cannot dwell longer here." Then the boyars spoke and said, "If the Greek faith were evil, it would not have been adopted by your grandmother Olga who was wiser than all other men." Vladimir then inquired where they should all accept baptism, and they replied that the decision rested with him.

After a year had passed, in 6496, Vladimir proceeded with an armed force against Kherson, a Greek city, and the people of Kherson barricaded themselves therein. Vladimir halted at the farther side of the city beside the harbor, a bowshot from the town, and the inhabitants resisted energetically while Vladimir besieged the town. Eventually, however, they became exhausted, and Vladimir warned them that if they did not surrender, he would remain on the spot for three years. When they failed to heed this threat, Vladimir marshaled his troops and ordered the construction of an earthwork in the direction of the city. While this work was under construction, the inhabitants dug a tunnel under the city-wall, stole the heaped-up earth, and carried it into the city, where they piled it up in the center of the town. But the soldiers kept on building, and Vladimir persisted. Then a man of Kherson, Anastasius by name, shot into the Russ camp an arrow on which he had written, "There are springs behind you to the east, from which water flows in pipes. Dig down and cut them off." When Vladimir received this information, he raised his eyes to heaven and vowed that if this hope was realized, he would be baptized. He gave orders straightaway to dig down above the pipes, and the water supply was thus cut off. The inhabitants were accordingly overcome by thirst, and surrendered.

Vladimir and his retinue entered the city, and he sent messages to the Emperors Basil and Constantine, saying, "Behold, I have captured your glorious city. I have also heard that you have an unwedded sister. Unless you give her to me to wife, I shall deal with your own city as I have with Kherson." When the Emperors heard this message they were troubled, and replied, "It is not meet for Christians to give in marriage to pagans. If you are baptized, you shall have her to wife, inherit the kingdom of God, and be our companion in the faith. Unless you do so, however, we cannot give you our sister in marriage." When Vladimir learned their response, he directed the envoys of the Emperors to report to the latter that he was willing to accept baptism, having already given some study to their religion, and that the Greek faith and ritual, as described by the emissaries sent to examine it, had pleased him well. When the Emperors heard this report, they rejoiced, and persuaded their sister Anna to consent to the match. They then requested Vladimir to submit to baptism before they should send their sister to him, but Vladimir desired that the Princess should herself bring priests to baptize him. The Emperors complied with his request, and sent forth their sister, accompanied by some dignitaries and priests. Anna, however, departed with reluctance. "It is as if I were setting out into captivity," she lamented; "better were it for me to die at home." But her brothers protested, "Through your agency God turns the land of Rus' to repentance, and you will relieve Greece from the danger of grievous war. Do you not see how much harm the Russes have already brought upon the Greeks? If you do not set out, they may bring on us the same misfortunes." It was thus that they overcame her hesitation only with great difficulty. The Princess embarked upon a ship, and after tearfully embracing her kinfolk, she set forth across the sea and arrived at Kherson. The natives came forth to greet her, and conducted her into the city, where they settled her in the palace.

By divine agency, Vladimir was suffering at that moment from a disease of the eyes, and could see nothing, being in great distress. The Princess declared to him that if he desired to be relieved of this disease, he should be baptized with all speed, otherwise it could not be cured. When Vladimir heard her message, he said, "If this proves true, then of a surety is the God of the Christians great," and gave order that he should be baptized. The Bishop of Kherson, together with the Princess's priests, after announcing the tidings, baptized Vladimir, and as the Bishop laid his hand upon him, he straightway received his sight. Upon experiencing this miraculous cure, Vladimir glorified God, saying, "I have now perceived the one true God." When his followers beheld this miracle, many of them were also baptized.

Vladimir was baptized in the Church of St. Basil, which stands at Kherson upon a square in the center of the city, where the Khersonians trade. The palace of Vladimir stands beside this church to this day, and the palace of the Princess is behind the altar. After his baptism, Vladimir took the Princess in marriage. Those who do not know the truth say he was baptized in Kiev, while others assert this event took place in Vasil'ev, while still others mention other places.

After Vladimir was baptized, the priests explained to him the tenets of the Christian faith, urging him to avoid the deceit of heretics by adhering to the following creeds:

I believe in God, the Father Almighty, Maker of Heaven and Earth; and also: I believe in one God the Father, who is unborn, and in the only Son, who is born, and in one Holy Ghost emanating therefrom: three complete and thinking Persons, divisible in number and personality, but not in divinity; for they are separated without distinction and united without confusion. God the Father Everlasting abides in Fatherhood, unbegotten, without beginning, himself the beginning and the cause of all things. Because he is unbegotten, he is older than the Son and the Spirit. From him the Son was born before all worlds, and from him the Holy Ghost emanates intemporally and incorporeally. He is simultaneously Father, Son and Holy Ghost.

The Son, being like the Father, is distinguished from the Father and the Spirit in that he was born. The Spirit is Holy, like to the Father and the Son, and is everlasting. The Father possesses Fatherhood, and Son Sonship, and the Holy Ghost Emanation. For the Father is not transformed into the Son or the Spirit, nor the Son to the Father and the Spirit, nor the Spirit to the Son and the Father, since their attributes are invariable. Not three Gods, but one God, since there is one divinity in three Persons.

In consequence of the desire of the Father and the Spirit to save his creation, he went out of the bosom of the Father, yet without leaving it, to the pure womb of a Virgin, as the seed of God. Entering into her, he took on animated, vocal, and thinking flesh which had not previously existed, came forth God incarnate, and was ineffably born, while his Mother preserved her virginity immaculate. Suffering neither combination, nor confusion, nor alteration, he remained as he was, became what he was not, and assumed the aspect of a slave in truth, not in semblance, being similar to us in every respect except in sin.

Voluntarily he was born, voluntarily he suffered want, voluntarily he thirsted, voluntarily he endured, voluntarily he feared, voluntarily he died in truth and not in semblance. All these were genuine and unimpeachable human sufferings. He gave himself up to be crucified. Though immortal, he tasted death. He arose in the flesh without knowing corruption; he ascended into Heaven, and sat upon the right hand of the Father. And as he ascended in glory and in the flesh so shall he descend once more.

Moreover, I acknowledge one Baptism of water and the Spirit, I approach the Holy Mysteries, I believe in the True Body and Blood, I accept the traditions of the Church, and I venerate the sacred images. I revere the Holy Tree and every Cross, the sacred relics, and the sacred vessels.

Believe, also, they said, in the seven councils of the Church: the first at Nicaea, comprising three hundred and eighteen Fathers, who cursed Arius and proclaimed the immaculate and orthodox faith; the second at Constantinople, attended by one hundred and fifty Fathers, who anathematized Macedonius (who denied the Holy Spirit), and proclaimed the oneness of the Trinity; the third at Ephesus, comprising two hundred Fathers, against Nestorius, whom they cursed, while they also proclaimed the dignity of the Mother of God; the fourth council of six hundred and thirty Fathers held at Chalcedon, to condemn Eutyches and Dioscorus, whom the Holy Fathers cursed after they had proclaimed the Perfect God and the Perfect Man, our Lord Jesus Christ; the fifth council of one hundred and sixty-five Fathers, held at Constantinople, which was directed against the teachings of Origen and Evagrius, whom the Fathers anathematized; the sixth council of one hundred and seventy Holy Fathers, likewise held at Constantinople, which condemned Sergius and Cyrus, whom the Holy Fathers cursed; and the seventh council, comprising three hundred and fifty Holy Fathers, which was held at Nicaea, and cursed those who do not venerate images.

Do not accept the teachings of the Latins, whose instruction is vicious. For when they enter the church, they do not kneel before the images, but they stand upright before kneeling, and when they have knelt, they trace a cross upon the ground and then kiss it, but they stand upon it when they arise. Thus while prostrate they kiss it, and yet upon arising they trample it underfoot. Such is not the tradition of the Apostles. For the Apostles prescribed the kissing of an upright cross, and also prescribed the use of images. For the Evangelist Luke painted the first image and sent it to Rome. As Basil has said, the honor rendered to the image redounds to its original. Furthermore, they call the earth their mother. If the earth is their mother, then heaven is their father, for in the beginning God made heaven and earth. Yet they say, "Our Father which art in Heaven." If, according to their understanding, the earth is their mother, why do they spit upon their mother, and pollute her whom they caress?

In earlier times, the Romans did not so act, but took part in all the councils, gathering together from Rome and all other Sees. At the first Council in Nicaea, directed against Arius, Silvester sent bishops and priests from Rome, as did Athanasius from Alexandria; and Metrophanes also dispatched his bishops from Constantinople. Thus they corrected the faith. At the second council took part Damasus of Rome, Timotheus of Alexandria, Meletius of Antioch, Cyril of Jerusalem, and Gregory the Theologian. In the third council participated Coelestinus of Rome, Cyril of Alexandria, Juvenal of Jerusalem. At the fourth council participated Leo of Rome, Anatolius of Constantinople, and Juvenal of Jerusalem; and at the fifth, Vigilius of Rome, Eutychius of Constantinople, Apollinaris of Alexandria, and Domnus of Antioch. At the sixth council took part Agathon of Rome, Georgius of Constantinople, Theophanes of Antioch, and Peter the Monk of Alexandria; at the seventh, Adrian of Rome, Tarasius of Constantinople, Politian of Alexandria, Theodoret of Antioch, and Elias of Jerusalem. These Fathers, with the assistance of the bishops, corrected the faith.

After the seventh council, Peter the Stammerer came with the others to Rome and corrupted the faith, seizing the Holy See. He seceded from the Sees of Jerusalem, Alexandria, Constantinople, and Antioch. His partisans disturbed all Italy, disseminating their teaching in various terms. For some of these priests who conduct services are married to one wife, and others are married to seven. Avoid their doctrine; for they absolve sins against money payments, which is the worst abuse of all. God guard you from this evil, oh Prince!

Hereupon Vladimir took the Princess and Anastasius and the priests of Kherson, together with the relics of St. Clement and of Phoebus his disciple, and selected also sacred vessels and images for the service. In Kherson he thus founded a church on the mound which had been heaped up in the midst of the city with the earth removed from his embankment; this church is standing at the present day. Vladimir also found and appropriated two bronze statues and four bronze horses, which now stand behind the Church of the Holy Virgin, and which the ignorant think are made of marble. As a wedding present for the Princess, he gave Kherson over to the Greeks again, and then departed for Kiev.

When the Prince arrived at his capital, he directed that the idols should be overthrown, and that some should be cut to pieces and others burned with fire. He thus ordered that Perun should be bound to a horse's tail and dragged down Borichev to the stream. He appointed twelve men to beat the idol with sticks, not because he thought the wood was sensitive, but to

affront the demon who had deceived man in this guise, that he might receive chastisement at the hands of men. Great art thou, oh Lord, and marvelous are thy works! Yesterday he was honored of men, but today held in derision. While the idol was being dragged along the stream to the Dnieper, the unbelievers wept over it, for they had not yet received holy baptism. After they had thus dragged the idol along, they cast it into the Dnieper. But Vladimir had given this injunction "If it halts anywhere, then push it out from the bank, until it goes over the falls. Then let it loose." His command was duly obeyed. When the men let the idol go, and it passed through the rapids, the wind cast it out on the bank, which since that time has been called Perun's sandbank, a name that it bears to this very day.

Thereafter Vladimir sent heralds throughout the whole city to proclaim that if any inhabitants, rich or poor, did not betake himself to the river, he would risk the Prince's displeasure. When the people heard these words, they wept for joy, and exclaimed in their enthusiasm, "If this were not good, the Prince and his boyars would not have accepted it." On the morrow, the Prince went forth to the Dnieper with the priests of the Princess and those from Kherson, and a countless multitude assembled. They all went into the water: some stood up to their necks, others to their breasts, and the younger near the bank, some of them holding children in their arms, while the adults waded farther out. The priests stood by and offered prayers. There was joy in heaven and upon earth to behold so many souls saved. But the devil groaned, lamenting, "Woe is me! how am I driven out hence! For I thought to have my dwelling place here, since the apostolic teachings do not abide in this land. Nor did this people know God, but I rejoiced in the service they rendered unto me. But now I am vanquished by the ignorant, not by apostles and martyrs, and my reign in these regions is at an end."

When the people were baptized, they returned each to his own abode. Vladimir, rejoicing that he and his subjects now knew God himself, looked up to heaven and said, "Oh God, who has created heaven and earth, look down, I beseech thee, on this thy new people, and grant them, oh Lord, to know thee as the true God, even as the other Christian nations have known thee. Confirm in them the true and inalterable faith, and aid me, oh Lord, against the hostile adversary, so that, hoping in thee and in thy might, I may overcome his malice." Having spoken thus, he ordained that wooden churches should be built and established where pagan idols had previously stood. He thus founded the Church of St. Basil on the hill where the idol of Perun and the other images had been set, and where the Prince and the people had offered their sacrifices. He began to found churches and to assign priests throughout the cities, and to invite the people to accept baptism in all the cities and towns.

He took the children of the best families, and sent them for instruction in book learning. The mothers of these children wept bitterly over them, for they were not yet strong in faith, but mourned as for the dead. When these children were assigned for study, there was fulfilled in the land of Rus' the prophecy which says, "In those days, the deaf shall hear words of Scripture, and the voice of the stammerers shall be made plain" (Isa. 29:18). For these persons had not ere this heard words of Scripture, and now heard them only by the act of God, for in his mercy the Lord took pity upon them, even as the Prophet said, "I will be gracious to whom I will be gracious" (Exod. 33:19).

PART FOUR
1000–1453 C.E.

Reform, Crusade, Reconquest

59. Pope Gregory VII,
Letter to Hermann of Metz

After becoming pope in 1073, Gregory VII (d. 1085) extended the reform program of his predecessors by issuing decrees against clerical marriage and simony and soon went so far as to prohibit any intervention by lay persons in the election of bishops. This move met resistance, most famously from the German king Henry IV. In this letter to the bishop of Metz, Gregory defends his second excommunication of Henry in 1080 by arguing the superiority of spiritual to temporal authority—a point that his twelfth- and thirteenth-century successors would continue to press.

To HERMANN OF METZ, IN DEFENSE OF THE PAPAL POLICY TOWARD HENRY IV
Book VIII, 21, p. 547. March 15, 1081.

Gregory . . . to his beloved brother in Christ, Hermann, bishop of Metz, greeting . . .

We know you to be ever ready to bear labor and peril in defense of the truth, and doubt not that this is a gift from God. It is a part of his unspeakable grace and his marvelous mercy that he never permits his chosen ones to wander far or to be completely cast down; but rather, after a time of persecution and wholesome probation, makes them stronger than they were before. On the other hand, just as among cowards one who is worse than the rest is broken down by fear, so among the brave one who acts more bravely than the rest is stirred thereby to new activity. We remind you of this by way of exhortation that you may stand more joyfully in the front ranks of the Christian host, the more confident you are that they are the nearest to God the conqueror.

You ask us to fortify you against the madness of those who babble with accursed tongues about the authority of the Holy Apostolic See not being able to excommunicate King Henry as one who despises the law of Christ, a destroyer of churches and of the empire, a promoter and partner of heresies, nor to release anyone from his oath of fidelity to him; but it has not seemed necessary to reply to this request, seeing that so many and such convincing proofs are to be found in Holy Scripture. Nor do we believe that those who abuse and contradict the truth to their utter damnation do this as much from ignorance as from wretched and desperate folly. And no wonder! It is ever the way of the wicked to protect their own iniquities by calling upon others like themselves; for they think it of no account to incur the penalty of falsehood.

To cite but a few out of the multitude of proofs: Who does not remember the words of our Lord and Savior Jesus Christ: "Thou art Peter and on this rock I will build my Church, and the gates of hell shall not prevail against it. And I will give thee the keys of the kingdom of heaven and whatsoever thou shalt bind on earth shall be bound in heaven and whatsoever thou shalt loose on earth

SOURCE: *Correspondence of Pope Gregory VII*, ed. and tr. Ephraim Emerton (New York: Columbia University Press, 1932), 166-75. Reprinted by permission of the publisher.

shall be loosed in heaven" (Matt. 16:18-19). Are kings excepted here? Or are they not of the sheep which the Son of God committed to St. Peter? Who, I ask, thinks himself excluded from this universal grant of the power of binding and loosing to St. Peter unless, perchance, that unhappy man who, being unwilling to bear the yoke of the Lord, subjects himself to the burden of the Devil and refuses to be numbered in the flock of Christ? His wretched liberty shall profit him nothing; for if he shakes off from his proud neck the power divinely granted to Peter, so much the heavier shall it be for him in the day of judgment.

This institution of the divine will, this foundation of the rule of the Church, this privilege granted and sealed especially by a heavenly decree to St. Peter, chief of the Apostles, has been accepted and maintained with great reverence by the holy fathers, and they have given to the Holy Roman Church, as well in general councils as in their other acts and writings, the name of "universal mother." They have not only accepted her expositions of doctrine and her instructions in [our] holy religion, but they have also recognized her judicial decisions. They have agreed as with one spirit and one voice that all major cases, all especially important affairs, and the judgments of all churches ought to be referred to her as to their head and mother, that from her there shall be no appeal, that her judgments may not and cannot be reviewed or reversed by anyone.

Thus Pope Gelasius, writing to the emperor Anastasius, gave him these instructions as to the right theory of the principate of the Holy and Apostolic See, based upon divine authority:

Although it is fitting that all the faithful should submit themselves to all priests who perform their sacred functions properly, how much the more should they accept the judgment of that prelate who has been appointed by the supreme divine ruler to be superior to all priests and whom the loyalty of the whole later Church has recognized as such. Your Wisdom sees plainly that no human capacity [concilium] whatsoever can equal that of him whom the word of Christ raised above all others and whom the reverend Church has always confessed and still devotedly holds as its Head.

So also Pope Julius, writing to the eastern bishops in regard to the powers of the same Holy and Apostolic See, says:

You ought, my brethren, to have spoken carefully and not ironically of the Holy Roman and Apostolic Church, seeing that our Lord Jesus Christ addressed her respectfully [decenter], saying, "Thou art Peter and upon this rock I will build my church, and the gates of hell shall not prevail against it; and I will give thee the keys of the kingdom of heaven" (Matt. 16:18-19). For it has the power, granted by a unique privilege, of opening and shutting the gates of the celestial kingdom to whom it will.

To whom, then, the power of opening and closing Heaven is given, shall he not be able to judge the earth? God forbid! Do you remember what the most blessed Apostle Paul says: "Know ye not that we shall judge angels? How much more things that pertain to this life?" (1 Cor. 6:3).

So Pope Gregory declared that kings who dared to disobey the orders of the Apostolic See should forfeit their office. He wrote to a certain senator and abbot in these words:

If any king, priest, judge or secular person shall disregard this decree of ours and act contrary to it, he shall be deprived of his power and his office and shall learn that he stands condemned at the bar of God for the wrong that he has done. And unless he shall restore what he has wrongfully taken and shall have done fitting penance for his unlawful acts he shall be excluded from the sacred body and blood of our Lord and Savior Jesus Christ and at the last judgment shall receive condign punishment.

Now then, if the blessed Gregory, most gentle of doctors, decreed that kings who should disobey his orders about a hospital for strangers should be not only deposed but excommunicated and condemned in the last judgment, how can anyone blame us for deposing and excommunicating Henry, who not only disregards apostolic judgments but, so far as in him lies, tramples upon his mother the Church, basely plunders the whole kingdom and destroys its churches—unless indeed it were one who is a man of his own kind?

As we know also through the teaching of St. Peter in his letter touching the ordination of Clement, where he says: "If any one were friend to those with whom he [Clement] is not on speaking terms, that man is among those who would like to destroy the Church of God and, while he seems to be with us in the body, he is against us in mind and heart, and he is a far worse enemy than those who are without and are openly hostile. For he, under the forms of friendship, acts as an enemy and scatters and lays waste the Church." Consider then, my best beloved, if he passes so severe a judgment upon him who associates himself with those whom the pope opposes on account of their actions, with what severity he condemns the man himself to whom the pope is thus opposed.

But now, to return to our point: Is not a sovereignty invented by men of this world who were ignorant of God subject to that which the providence of Almighty God established for his own glory and graciously bestowed upon the world? The Son of God we believe to be God and man, sitting at the right hand of the Father as High Priest, head of all priests and ever making intercession for us. He despised the kingdom of this world wherein the sons of this world puff themselves up and offered himself as a sacrifice upon the cross.

Who does not know that kings and princes derive their origin from men ignorant of God who raised themselves above their fellows by pride, plunder, treachery, murder—in short, by every kind of crime—at the instigation of the Devil, the prince of this world, men blind with greed and intolerable in their audacity? If, then, they strive to bend the priests of God to their will, to whom may they more properly be compared than to him who is chief over all the sons of pride? For he, tempting our High Priest, head of all priests, son of the Most High, offering him all the kingdoms of this world, said: "All these will I give thee if thou wilt fall down and worship me" (Matt. 4:9).

Does anyone doubt that the priests of Christ are to be considered as fathers and masters of kings and princes and of all believers? Would it not be regarded as pitiable madness if a son should try to rule his father or a pupil his master and to bind with unjust obligations the one through whom he expects to be bound or loosed, not only on earth but also in heaven? Evidently recognizing this the emperor Constantine the Great, lord over all kings and princes throughout almost the entire earth, as St. Gregory relates in his letter to the emperor Mauritius, at the holy synod of Nicaea took his place below all the bishops and did not venture to pass any judgment upon them but, even addressing them as gods, felt that they ought not to be subject to his judgment but that he ought to be bound by their decisions.

Pope Gelasius, urging upon the emperor Anastasius not to feel himself wronged by the truth that was called to his attention said: "There are two powers, O august Emperor, by which the world is governed, the sacred authority of the priesthood and the power of kings. Of these the priestly is by so much the greater as they will have to answer for kings themselves in the day of divine judgment;" and a little further: "Know that you are subject to their judgment, not that they are to be subjected to your will."

In reliance upon such declarations and such authorities, many prelates have excommunicated kings or emperors. If you ask for illustrations: Pope Innocent excommunicated the emperor Arcadius because he consented to the expulsion of St. John Chrysostom from his office. Another Roman pontiff deposed a king of the Franks, not so much on account of his evil deeds as because he was not equal to so great an office, and set in his place Pippin, father of the emperor Charles the Great, releasing all the Franks from the oath of fealty which they had sworn to him. And this is often done by Holy Church when it absolves fighting men from their oaths to bishops who have been deposed by apostolic authority. So St. Ambrose, a holy man but not bishop of the whole Church, excommunicated the emperor Theodosius the Great for a fault which did not seem to other prelates so very grave and excluded him from the Church. He also shows in his writings that the priestly office is as much superior to royal power as gold is more precious than lead. He says: "The honor and dignity of bishops admit of no comparison. If you liken them to the splendor of kings and the diadem of princes, these are as lead compared to the glitter of gold. You see the necks of kings and princes bowed to the knees of priests, and by the kissing of hands they believe that they share the benefit of their prayers." And again:

"Know that we have said all this in order to show that there is nothing in this world more excellent than a priest or more lofty than a bishop."

Your Fraternity should remember also that greater power is granted to an exorcist when he is made a spiritual emperor for the casting out of devils than can be conferred upon any layman for the purpose of earthly dominion. All kings and princes of this earth who live not piously and in their deeds show not a becoming fear of God are ruled by demons and are sunk in miserable slavery. Such men desire to rule, not guided by the love of God, as priests are, for the glory of God and the profit of human souls, but to display their intolerable pride and to satisfy the lusts of their mind. Of these St. Augustine says in the first book of his Christian doctrine: "He who tries to rule over men—who are by nature equal to him—acts with intolerable pride." Now if exorcists have power over demons, as we have said, how much more over those who are subject to demons and are limbs of demons! And if exorcists are superior to these, how much more are priests superior to them!

Furthermore, every Christian king when he approaches his end asks the aid of a priest as a miserable suppliant that he may escape the prison of hell, may pass from darkness into light and may appear at the judgment seat of God freed from the bonds of sin. But who, layman or priest, in his last moments has ever asked the help of any earthly king for the safety of his soul? And what king or emperor has power through his office to snatch any Christian from the might of the Devil by the sacred rite of baptism, to confirm him among the sons of God and to fortify him by the holy chrism? Or—and this is the greatest thing in the Christian religion—who among them is able by his own word to create the body and blood of the Lord? or to whom among them is given the power to bind and loose in Heaven and upon earth? From this it is apparent how greatly superior in power is the priestly dignity.

Or who of them is able to ordain any clergyman in the Holy Church—much less to depose him for any fault? For bishops, while they may ordain other bishops, may in no wise depose them except by authority of the Apostolic See. How, then, can even the most slightly informed person doubt that priests are higher than kings? But if kings are to be judged by priests for their sins, by whom can they more properly be judged than by the Roman pontiff?

In short, all good Christians, whosoever they may be, are more properly to be called kings than are evil princes; for the former, seeking the glory of God, rule themselves rigorously; but the latter, seeking their own rather than the things that are of God, being enemies to themselves, oppress others tyrannically. The former are the body of the true Christ; the latter, the body of the Devil. The former rule themselves that they may reign forever with the supreme ruler. The power of the latter brings it to pass that they perish in eternal damnation with the prince of darkness who is king over all the sons of pride.

It is no great wonder that evil priests take the part of a king whom they love and fear on account of honors received from him. By ordaining any person whomsoever, they are selling their God at a bargain price. For as the elect are inseparably united to their Head, so the wicked are firmly bound to him who is head of all evil—especially against the good. But against these it is of no use to argue, but rather to pray God with tears and groans that he may deliver them from the snares of Satan, in which they are caught, and after trial may lead them at last into knowledge of the truth.

So much for kings and emperors who, swollen with the pride of this world, rule not for God but for themselves. But since it is our duty to exhort everyone according to his station, it is our care with God's help to furnish emperors, kings and other princes with the weapons of humility that thus they may be strong to keep down the floods and waves of pride. We know that earthly glory and the cares of this world are wont especially to cause rulers to be exalted, to forget humility and, seeking their own glory, strive to excel their fellows. It seems therefore especially useful for emperors and kings, while their hearts are lifted up in the strife for glory, to learn how to humble themselves and to know fear rather than joy. Let them therefore consider carefully how dangerous, even awesome is the office of emperor or king, how very few find salvation therein, and how those who are saved through God's mercy have become far less famous in the Church by divine judgment than many humble persons. From the beginning of the world to the present day we do not find in all authentic records [seven] emperors or kings whose lives were as distinguished for virtue and piety as were those of a countless multitude of men who despised the world—although we believe that many of them were saved by the mercy of God. Not to speak of Apostles and Martyrs, who among emperors and kings was famed for his miracles as were St. Martin, St. Antony and St. Benedict? What emperor or king ever raised the dead, cleansed lepers or opened the eyes of the blind? True, Holy Church praises and honors the emperor Constantine, of pious memory, Theodosius and Honorius, Charles and Louis, as lovers of justice, champions of the Christian faith and protectors of churches, but she does not claim that they were illustrious for the splendor of their wonderful works. Or to how many names of kings or emperors has Holy Church ordered churches or altars to be dedicated or masses to be celebrated?

Let kings and princes fear lest the higher they are raised above their fellows in this life, the deeper they may be plunged in everlasting fire. Wherefore it is written: "The mighty shall suffer mighty torments." They shall render unto God an account for all men subject to their rule. But if it is no small labor for the pious individual to guard his own soul, what a task is laid upon princes in the care of so many thousands of souls! And if Holy Church imposes a heavy penalty upon him who takes a single human life, what shall be done to those who send many thousands to death for the glory of this world? These, although they say with their lips, *mea culpa*, for the slaughter of many, yet in their hearts they rejoice at the increase of their glory and neither repent of what they have done nor regret that they have sent their brothers into the world below. So that, since they do not repent with all their hearts and will not restore what they have gained by human bloodshed, their penitence before God remains without the fruits of a true repentance.

Wherefore they ought greatly to fear, and they should frequently be reminded that, as we have said, since the beginning of the world and throughout the kingdoms of the earth very few kings of saintly life can be found out of an innumerable multitude, whereas in one single chair of successive bishops—the Roman—from the time of the blessed Apostle Peter nearly a hundred are counted among the holiest of men. How can this be, except because the kings and princes of the earth, seduced by empty glory, prefer their own interests to the things of the Spirit, whereas pious pontiffs, despising vainglory, set the things of God above the things of the flesh. The former readily punish offenses against themselves but are not troubled by offenses against God; the latter quickly forgive those who sin against them but do not easily pardon offenders against God. The former, far too much given to worldly affairs, think little of spiritual things; the latter, dwelling eagerly upon heavenly subjects, despise the things of this world.

All Christians, therefore, who desire to reign with Christ are to be warned not to reign through ambition for worldly power. They are to keep in mind the admonition of that most holy pope Gregory in his book on the pastoral office: "Of all these things what is to be followed, what held fast, except that the man strong in virtue shall come to his office under compulsion? Let him who is without virtue not come to it even though he be urged thereto." If, then, men who fear God come under compulsion with fear and trembling to the Apostolic See where those who are properly ordained become stronger through the merits of the blessed Apostle Peter, with what awe and hesitation should men ascend the throne of a king where even good and humble men like Saul and David become worse! What we have said above is thus stated in the decrees of the blessed pope Symmachus—though we have learned it by experience: "He, that is St. Peter, transmitted to his successors an unfailing endowment of merit together with an inheritance of innocence"; and again: "For who can doubt that he is holy who is raised to the height of such an office, in which if he is lacking in virtue acquired by his own merits, that which is handed down from his predecessor is sufficient. For either he [Peter] raises men of distinction to bear this burden or he glorifies them after they are raised up."

Wherefore let those whom Holy Church, of its own will and with deliberate judgment, not for fleeting glory but for the welfare of multitudes, has called to royal or imperial rule—let them be obedient and ever mindful of the blessed Gregory's declaration in that same pastoral treatise: "When a man disdains to be the equal of his fellow men, he becomes like an apostate angel. Thus Saul, after his period of humility, swollen with pride, ran into excess of power. He was raised in humility, but rejected in his pride, as God bore witness, saying: 'Though thou wast little in thine own sight, wast thou not made the head of the tribes of Israel?'" (1 Sam. 15:17), and again: "I marvel how, when he was little to himself he was great before God, but when he seemed great to himself he was little before God." Let them watch and remember what God says in the Gospel: "I seek not my own glory" (John 8:50), and, "He who would be first among you, let him be the servant of all" (Mark 10:44). Let them ever place the honor of God above their own; let them embrace justice and maintain it by preserving to everyone his right; let them not enter into the counsels of the ungodly, but cling to those of religion with all their hearts. Let them not seek to make Holy Church their maidservant or their subject, but recognizing priests, the eyes of God, as their masters and fathers, strive to do them becoming honor.

If we are commanded to honor our fathers and mothers in the flesh, how much more our spiritual parents! If he that curseth his father or his mother shall be put to death, what does he deserve who curses his spiritual father or mother? Let not princes, led astray by carnal affection, set their own sons over that flock for whom Christ shed his blood if a better and more suitable man can be found. By thus loving their own son more than God they bring the greatest evils upon the Church. For it is evident that he who fails to provide to the best of his ability so great and necessary an advantage for our holy mother, the Church, does not love God and his neighbor as befits a Christian man. If this one virtue of charity be wanting, then whatever of good the man may do will lack all saving grace.

But if they do these things in humility, keeping their love for God and their neighbor as they ought, they may count upon the mercy of him who said: "Learn of me, for I am meek and lowly of heart" (Matt. 11:29). If they humbly imitate him, they shall pass from their servile and transient reign into the kingdom of eternal liberty.

60. Guibert of Nogent,
The Deeds of God through the Franks

The French abbot Guibert of Nogent (d. ca. 1125) produced his history of the First Crusade, The Deeds of God through the Franks, *between 1106 and 1109. We include two excerpts here: Guibert's account of Urban II's proclamation of the Crusade at the Council of Clermont in 1095, and his account of the fall of Jerusalem in 1099 to the crusading armies. Guibert, who was not an eyewitness to these events, relied heavily on an earlier work by an anonymous crusader,* The Deeds of the Franks, *to which he added an interpretive framework emphasizing the role of divine Providence.*

Source: *The Deeds of God through the Franks: A Translation of Guibert de Nogent's* Gesta Dei per Francos, tr. Robert Levine (Woodbridge, U.K.: Boydell Press, 1997), 40-45, 126-33. Used by permission of Boydell Brewer Ltd.

Book Two

Pope Urban, whose name was Odo before becoming pope, was descended from a noble French family from the area and parish of Rheims, and they say, unless the report is in error, that he was the first French pope. A cleric, he was made a monk of Cluny, after the abbot of glorious memory who aided Hugo; not long afterwards he was made prior, and then, because of his abilities, he was appointed bishop of the city of Ostia, by order of Pope Gregory VII; finally, he was elected supreme pontiff of the Apostolic See. His greatness of spirit was made manifest when he urged that the journey be undertaken, because when he first showed how it was to be done the whole world was astonished. His death, resplendent in miracles, attests to the state of his mind. According to what the bishop who succeeded him at Ostia wrote, many signs were seen after he was dead and buried; a certain young man stood at his tomb, and swore by his own limbs that no sign had ever been given or might be given by the merit of Urban, who was called Odo. Before he could move a step, he was struck dumb, and paralyzed on one side; he died the next day, offering testimony to the power of Urban. This great man, although honored with great gifts, and even with prayers, by Alexius, prince of the Greeks, but driven much more by the danger to all of Christendom, which was diminished daily by pagan incursions (for he heard that Spain was steadily being torn apart by Saracen invasions), decided to make a journey to France, to recruit the people of his country. It was, to be sure, the ancient custom for pontiffs of the Apostolic See, if they had been harmed by a neighboring people, always to seek help from the French: the Pontiffs Stephen and Zacharias, in the time of Pepin and Charles, took refuge with them; Pepin made an expedition to Ticinum to restore to the church its patrimony, and to place Stephen back on his throne. Charles compelled King Desiderius, by the mere threat of combat, to return what he had seized by force. More respectful and humble than other nations toward blessed Peter and pontifical decrees, the French, unlike other peoples, have been unwilling to behave insolently against God. For many years we have seen the Germans, particularly the entire kingdom of Lotharingia, struggling with barbaric obstinacy against the commands of Saint Peter and of his pontiffs. In their striving, they prefer to remain under a daily, or even eternal excommunication rather than submit. Last year while I was arguing with a certain archdeacon of Mainz about a rebellion of his people, I heard him vilify our king and our people, merely because the king had given a gracious welcome everywhere in his kingdom to his Highness Pope Paschal and his princes; he called them not merely Franks, but, derisively, "Francones." I said to him, "If you think them so weak and languid that you can denigrate a name known and admired as far away as the Indian Ocean, then tell me upon whom did Pope Urban call for aid against the Turks? Wasn't it the French? Had they not been present, attacking the barbarians everywhere, pouring their sturdy energy and fearless strength into the battle, there would have been no help for your Germans, whose reputation there amounted to nothing." That is what I said to him. I say truly, and everyone should believe it, that God reserved this nation for such a great task. For we know certainly that, from the time that they received the sign of faith that blessed Remigius brought to them until the present time, they succumbed to none of the diseases of false faith from which other nations have remained uncontaminated either with great difficulty or not at all. They are the ones who, while still laboring under the pagan error, when they triumphed on the battlefield over the Gauls, who were Christians, did not punish or kill any of them, because they believed in Christ. Instead, those whom Roman severity had punished with sword and fire, native French generosity encased in gold and silver, covered with gems and amber. They strove to welcome with honor not only those who lived within their own borders, but they also affectionately cared for people who came from Spain, Italy, or anywhere else, so that love for the martyrs and confessors, whom they constantly served and honored, made them famous, finally driving them to the glorious victory at Jerusalem. Because it has carried the yoke since the days of its youth, it will sit in isolation, a nation noble, wise, war-like, generous, brilliant above all kinds of nations. Every nation borrows the name as an honorific title; do we not see the Bretons, the English, the Ligurians call men "Frank" if they behave well? But now let us return to the subject.

When the pope crossed our borders, he was greeted with such great joy by crowds in the cities, towns, and villages, because no one alive could remember when the bishop of the apostolic see had come to these lands. The year of the incarnate Word 1097 was hastening to its end, when the bishop hastily convoked a council, choosing a city in Auvergne, famous for the most learned of all bishops, Sidonius, although its name has now been changed to Clermont. The council was even more crowded because of the great desire to see the face and to hear the words of such an excellent, rarely seen person. In addition to the multitudes of bishops and abbots, whom some, by counting their staves, estimated at approximately four hundred, learned men from all of France and the dependent territories flowed to that place. One could see there how he presided over them with serene gravity, with a dignified presence, and, if I may use the words of Sidonius, with what peppery eloquence the most learned pope answered whatever objections were raised. It was noted with what gentleness the most brilliant man listened gently to the most vehemently argued speeches, and how little he valued the social position of people, judging them only by God's laws.

Then Philip, King of the French, who was in the thirty-seventh year of his reign, having put aside his own wife, whose name was Berta, and having carried off Bertrada, the wife of the Count of Anjou, was excommunicated by the pope, who spurned both the attempts by important people to intercede for the king, and the offers of innumerable gifts. Nor was he afraid because he was now within the borders of the kingdom of France. In this council, just as he had planned before leaving Rome and seeking out the French for this reason, he gave a fine speech to those who were in attendance. Among other things which were said to exceed the memories of the listeners, he spoke about this project. His eloquence was reinforced by his literary knowledge; the richness of his speech in Latin seemed no less than that of any lawyer nimble in his native language. Nor did the crowd of disputants blunt the skill of the speaker.

Surrounded by praiseworthy teachers, apparently buried by clouds of cases being pressed upon him, he was judged to have overcome, by his own literary brilliance, the flood of oratory and to have overwhelmed the cleverness of every speech. Therefore his meaning, and not his exact words, follow: "If, among the churches scattered through the whole world, some deserve more reverence than others because they are associated with certain people and places, then, because of certain persons, I say, greater privileges are granted to apostolic sees; in the case of places, some privilege is granted to royal cities, as is the case with the city of Constantinople. We are grateful for having received from this most powerful church the grace of redemption and the origin of all Christianity. If what was said by the Lord remains true, namely that 'salvation is from the Jews,' and it remains true that the Lord of the Sabbath has left his seed for us, lest we become like those of Sodom and Gomorrah, and that Christ is our seed, in whom lies salvation and blessing for all people, then the earth and the city in which he lived and suffered is called holy by the testimony of Scripture. If this land is the inheritance of God, and his holy temple, even before the Lord walked and suffered there, as the sacred and prophetic pages tell us, then what additional sanctity and reverence did it gain then, when the God of majesty took flesh upon Himself there, was fed, grew up, and moving in his bodily strength walked here and there in the land? To abbreviate a matter that could be spun out at much greater length, this is the place where the blood of the Son of God, holier than heaven and earth, was spilled, where the body, at whose death the elements trembled, rested in its tomb. What sort of veneration might we think it deserves? If, soon after our Lord's death, while the city was still in the possession of the Jews, the Evangelist called it sacred, when he said, 'Many bodies of the saints that have been asleep here have awoken, and come to the holy city, and they have been seen by many' (Matt. 27:53), and it was said by the prophet Isaiah, 'His tomb will be glorious' (Isa. 11:10), since this very sanctity, once granted by God the sanctifier himself, cannot be overcome by any evil whatsoever, and the glory of his tomb in the same way remains undiminished, then, O my dearly beloved brothers, you must exert yourselves, with all your strength, and with God leading you and fighting for you, to cleanse the holiness of the city and the glory of the tomb, which has been polluted by the thick crowd of pagans, if you truly aspire to the author of that holiness and glory, and if you love the traces that he has left on earth. If the Maccabees once deserved the highest praise for piety because they fought for their rituals and their temple, then you too, O soldiers of Christ, deserve such praise, for taking up arms to defend the freedom of your country. If you think you must seek with such effort the thresholds of the apostles and of others, then why do you hesitate to go to see and to snatch up the cross, the blood, and to devote your precious souls to rescuing them? Until now you have waged wrongful wars, often hurling insane spears at each other, driven only by greed and pride, for which you have deserved only eternal death and damnation. Now we propose for you battles which offer the gift of glorious martyrdom, for which you will earn present and future praise. If Christ had not died and been buried in Jerusalem, had not lived there at all, if all these things had not taken place, surely this fact alone should be enough to drive you to come to the aid of the land and the city: that the law came from Zion and the word of God from Jerusalem. If all Christian preaching flows from the fountain of Jerusalem, then let the rivulets, wherever they flow over the face of the earth, flow into the hearts of the Catholic multitude, so that they may take heed of what they owe to this overflowing fountain. If 'rivers return to the place whence they flow, so that they may continue to flow' (Eccles. 1:7), according to the saying of Solomon, it should seem glorious to you if you are able to purify the place whence you received the cleansing of baptism and the proof of faith. And you should also consider with the utmost care whether God is working through your efforts to restore the church that is the mother of churches; he might wish to restore the faith in some of the eastern lands, in spite of the nearness of the time of the Antichrist. For it is clear that the Antichrist makes war neither against Jews, nor against pagans, but, according to the etymology of his name, he will

move against Christians. And if the Antichrist comes upon no Christian there, as today there is scarcely any, there will be no one to resist him, or any whom he might justly move among. According to Daniel and Jerome his interpreter, his tent will be fixed on the Mount of Olives, and he will certainly take his seat, as the Apostle teaches, in Jerusalem, 'in the temple of God, as though he were God' (2 Thess. 2:4), and, according to the prophet, he will undoubtedly kill three kings preeminent for their faith in Christ, that is, the kings of Egypt, of Africa, and of Ethiopia. This cannot happen at all, unless Christianity is established where paganism now rules. Therefore if you are eager to carry out pious battles, and since you have accepted the seedbed of the knowledge of God from Jerusalem, then you may restore the grace that was borrowed there. Thus through you the name of Catholicism will be propagated, and it will defeat the perfidy of the Antichrist and of the Antichristians. Who can doubt that God, who surpasses every hope by means of his overflowing strength, may so destroy the reeds of paganism with your spark that he may gather Egypt, Africa and Ethiopia, which no longer share our belief, into the rules of his law, and 'sinful man, the son of perdition' (1 Thess. 2:3), will find others resisting him? See how the Gospel cries out that 'Jerusalem will be trodden down by the Gentiles, until the time of the nations will be fulfilled' (Luke 21:24). 'The time of nations' may be understood in two ways: either that they ruled at will over the Christians, and for their own pleasures have wallowed in the troughs of every kind of filth, and in all of these things have found no obstruction (for 'to have one's time' means that everything goes according to one's wishes, as in 'My time has not yet come, but your time is always ready' (John 7:6), and one customarily says to voluptuaries, 'You have your time'); or else the 'time of nations' means the multitudes of nations who, before Israel is saved, will join the faith. These times, dearest brothers, perhaps will now be fulfilled, when, with the aid of God, the power of the pagans will be pushed back by you, and, with the end of the world already near, even if the nations do not turn to the Lord, because, as the Apostle says, 'there must be a falling away from faith'

(2 Thess. 2:3). Nevertheless, first, according to the prophecies, it is necessary, before the coming of the Antichrist in those parts, either through you or through whomever God wills that the empire of Christianity be renewed, so that the leader of all evil, who will have his throne there, may find some nourishment of faith against which he may fight. Consider, then, that Almighty providence may have destined you for the task of rescuing Jerusalem from such abasement. I ask you to think how your hearts can conceive of the joy of seeing the holy city revived by your efforts, and the oracles, the divine prophecies fulfilled in our own times. Remember that the voice of the Lord himself said to the church, 'I shall lead your seed from the East, and I shall gather you from the West' (Isa. 43:5). The Lord has led our seed from the East, in that he brought forth for us in a double manner out of the Eastern land the early progeny of the Church. But out of the West he assembled us, for through those who last began the proof of faith, that is the Westerners (we think that, God willing, this will come about through your deeds), Jerusalem's losses will be restored. If the words of Scripture and our own admonitions do not move your souls, then at least let the great suffering of those who wish to visit the holy places touch you. Think of the pilgrims who travel the Mediterranean; if they are wealthy, to what tributes, to what violence are they subjected; at almost every mile they are compelled to pay taxes and tributes; at the gates of the city, at the entrances of churches and temples, they must pay ransoms. Each time they move from one place to another they are faced with another charge, compelled to pay ransom, and the governors of the Gentiles commonly coerce with blows those who are slow to give gifts. What shall we say about those who have taken up the journey, trusting in their naked poverty, who seem to have nothing more than their bodies to lose? The money that they did not have was forced from them by intolerable tortures; the skin of their bones was probed, cut, and stripped, in search of anything that they might have sewed within. The brutality of these evildoers was so great that, suspecting that the wretches had swallowed gold and silver, they gave them purgatives to drink, so that they would either vomit or burst their insides.

Even more unspeakable, they cut their bellies open with swords, opening their inner organs, revealing with a hideous slashing whatever nature holds secret. Remember, I beg you, the thousands who died deplorably, and, for the sake of the holy places, whence the beginnings of piety came to you, take action. Have unshakable faith that Christ will be the standard bearer and inseparable advance guard before you who are sent to His wars."

The superb man delivered this speech, and by the power of the blessed Peter absolved everyone who vowed to go, confirming this with an apostolic benediction, and establishing a sign of this honorable promise. He ordered that something like a soldier's belt, or rather that for those about to fight for the Lord, something bearing the sign of the Lord's passion, the figure of a Cross, be sewn onto the tunics and cloaks of those who were going. If anyone, after accepting this symbol, and after having made the public promise, then went back on his good intentions, either out of weak regretfulness, or out of domestic affection, such a person, according to the pope's decree, would be considered everywhere an outlaw, unless he came to his senses and fulfilled the obligation which he had foully laid aside. He also cursed with a horrible anathema all those who might dare to harm the wives, sons, and possessions of those who took up God's journey for all of the next three years.

Finally, he entrusted the leadership of the expedition to the most praiseworthy of men, the bishop of the city of Puy (whose name, I regret, I have never discovered or heard). He granted him the power to teach the Christian people as his representative, wherever they went, and therefore, in the manner of the apostles, he laid hands upon him and gave him his blessing as well. How wisely he carried out his commission the results of this wonderful effort demonstrate.

. . .

Book Seven

Finally they reached the place which had provoked so many hardships for them, which had brought upon them so much thirst and hunger for such a long time, which had stripped them, kept them sleepless, cold, and ceaselessly frightened, the most intensely pleasurable place, which had been the goal of the wretchedness they had undergone, and which had lured them to seek death and wounds. To this place, I say, desired by so many thousands of thousands, which they had greeted with such sadness and jubilation, they finally came, to Jerusalem. As one reads that the sojourners ate and worshiped the Body of the Lord, so it may be said of these men that they adored Jerusalem and took it by storm. On Tuesday, the sixth of June, the siege was begun with remarkable energy, by a remarkable combination of forces. From the north, Count Robert of Normandy laid siege to it, near the church of the blessed Saint Stephen, who, because he said that he had seen the Son of man standing at the right hand of God, was covered with a rain of stones by the Jews. From the west, Duke Godfrey, the Count of Flanders, and Tancred attacked. From the south, the Count of Saint-Gilles laid siege, on the mount of Zion, near the church of the blessed Mary, mother of God, where the Lord is said to have sat at dinner with his disciples, the day before his Passion. On the third day after they had arrived at the city, Raymond, whose deeds on the Lord's expedition were well known, this man, I say, whom they called Pelet, together with another man who had the same name, and several others, marched some distance from the place of siege, to see if he could find any of the enemy wandering into our ambushes, as they often did. Suddenly a band of near two hundred Arabs fell upon them; as soon as Raymond saw them, he attacked as fiercely as a lion, and, in spite of their boldness, with the aid of God, they were subdued. After killing many of them, and capturing thirty horses, they brought the victory back to the army, which took pleasure in their glorious deed. At dawn, on the second day of the next week, the outer, smaller wall of the city was attacked with such force and with such teamwork that both the city and its outskirts would have immediately fallen to the Franks, if they had not lacked ladders. After the outer wall was broken, and a broad passage opened through its rubble, the ladder they did have was extended towards the battlements of the main wall. Some of our knights climbed it quickly and began to fight at long range. And when the arrows ran out, they fought with

lances and swords; both the defenders of the city and the besiegers battled hand-to-hand with steel. Many of our men fell, but more of their men.

One should know that while Antioch was under siege, Jerusalem was held by the Turks, under the authority of the King of Persia. Moreover, the Emperor of Babylon, as I mentioned previously, had sent ambassadors to our army, for the sole purpose of determining the condition of our enterprise. When they saw the terrible need that afflicted the Christian army, and when they discovered that the nobles had become foot soldiers because of a lack of horses, they considered us valueless in a struggle against the Turks, whom they hated intensely. The King of Persia had taken a great part of the Babylonian empire, which was very large, for his people were wiser and more energetic in military matters. When the Babylonian prince heard, however, that the Franks—that is, God working through the Franks—had taken Antioch, and had defeated Kherboga himself, together with the pride of Persia, before the walls of Antioch, he quickly gathered his courage, bore arms against the Turks, and laid siege to them in Jerusalem, which they occupied. Then, I don't know whether by force or by some agreement, they entered the town, and placed many Turks, whether to guard it or to take charge of it I don't know, in the tower bearing the name of David, which we think more correctly should be called the tower of Zion. In any case, during the siege they harmed none of us, merely watching peacefully over their assigned tower. As a result, our men fought only with the Saracens.

They were unable to buy bread during the siege, and for nearly ten days food was difficult to find anywhere, until God brought help, and our fleet reached the port of Jaffa. In addition, the army also suffered from thirst, and they not only were worn out by this great discomfort, but they had to drive their horses and pack animals a great distance, six miles, to find water, all the while fearful that the enemy might attack them. The fountain of Siloah, famous for having cured the blind man in the Gospel, which rises from springs on mount Zion, supplied them with water, which was sold to them at the highest prices. After messengers had announced that the fleet had arrived at

Jaffa, the leaders held a meeting and decided to send a group of knights to the harbor to guard the ships and the men in them. Early in the morning, at the crack of dawn, Raymond, of whom we have spoken often, together with two other nobles, took one hundred knights from the army of his lord, the Count of Saint-Gilles, and set out for the port, with his customary decisiveness. Thirty of the knights separated from the main group and came upon approximately seven hundred Turks, Arabs, and Saracens, whom the King of Babylon had sent to watch our comings and goings. Although greatly outnumbered, our men forcefully attacked their troops, but the strength and ferocity of the enemy was so great that we were threatened on all sides with imminent death. They killed one of the two leaders, whose name was Achard, as well as some of the most respected among the poor and the foot soldiers. As they were surrounding our men, pressing them with arms on all sides, so that they were about to despair utterly, one man came to the above-mentioned Raymond and told him of the plight of his peers. "Why do you and your men remain here? See how your men, who recently separated from you, are now fiercely surrounded by a swarm of Saracens and Arabs. Unless you bring them help very quickly, you will undoubtedly soon find them dead, if they have not already perished. Therefore fly, hurry, I say, so that you may not be too late." Together with all of his nobles, Raymond quickly set off to look at the place where the fighting was going on. In preparing for combat he placed his faith not in arms, not in strength, but in faith in the Savior. When the Gentile troops saw the Christian army, they swiftly broke up into two groups. Calling upon the Most High for support, our men attacked with such force that each man knocked the opponent charging at him to the ground. Judging themselves unable to withstand the onslaught of the Christians, the pagans stopped, and, driven by fear, fled swiftly. Our men followed them quickly, pursuing them for four miles. After having killed many of them, they brought back 103 horses as trophies of victory. They refrained from killing only one man, whom they brought back with them, and from whom they learned everything that was going on among their enemies, including what the prince of Babylon was planning against us.

Meanwhile the army was suffering from a terrible thirst, which compelled them to sew together the hides of cattle and oxen, in which they carried water from six miles away. They used the water carried in such bags, which were putrid with recent sweat, and multiplied the great suffering caused by hunger, to make barley bread for the army. How many jaws and throats of noble men were eaten away by the roughness of this bread. How terribly were their fine stomachs revolted by the bitterness of the putrid liquid. Good God, we think that they must have suffered so, these men who remembered their high social position in their native land, where they had been accustomed to great ease and pleasure, and now could find no hope or solace in any external comfort, as they burned in the terrible heat. Here is what I and I alone think: never had so many noble men exposed their own bodies to so much suffering for a purely spiritual benefit. Although the hearts of the pilgrims burned for the dear, distant pledges of their affections, for their sweet wives and for the dignity of their possessions, nevertheless they remained steadfastly in place there, and did not cease to pursue the battle for Christ.

The Saracens were always waiting in ambush around the springs and rivers, eager to kill our men wherever they found them, strip their bodies, and, if they happened to gain booty and horses, to hide them in caves and caverns. Terrible hunger and thirst raged through the army surrounding the city, and the very great rage of the enemy prowling here and there thundered against them as well. But the leaders of the sacred army, seeing that so many men of such different capacities could scarcely endure such pain any longer, urged the use of machines by means of which the city might be made more vulnerable, so that, after all they had gone through, they might finally stand before the monuments of the passion and burial of the Savior. In addition to the many other instruments, like battering rams with which they might tear down the walls, or catapults to topple the towers and walls, they ordered two wooden castles to be built, which we usually call "falas." Duke Godfrey was the first to build his castle, together with other machines; and Raymond, Count of Saint-Gilles, who permitted himself to be second to no one, also built his own. When they saw the machines being built, the castles being constructed, the missile launchers and equipment being moved up to the towers, the Saracens began, with unusual speed, to extend and to repair their walls and towers. Working all night long, they surprised our men by the speed with which they accomplished things. Moreover, the wood from which our men had built the castles and other machines was brought from a distant region. When the leaders of the army of the Lord perceived which side of the city was most vulnerable, on a certain Sunday night they brought the castle, together with some other machines, to that place. At dawn they set up the machines on the eastern side, and on Monday, Tuesday, and Wednesday they established them firmly in place. The Count of Saint-Gilles, however, set up his machine on the southern side. As they burned with eagerness for the siege, their hearts were burning with intolerable thirst, and a silver coin could not purchase enough water to quench a man's thirst. Finally, on the fourth and fifth day, gathering all their forces, they started to attack the walled city. But before the attack took place, the bishops and priests directed the people who were their subjects to sing litanies, and to undertake fasts, to pray, and to give alms. The bishops remembered what had once happened at Jericho, that the walls of the perfidious city had fallen when the Israelites' trumpets sounded, and they marched seven times around the city, carrying the sacred ark, and the walls of the faithless city fell down. They too circled Jerusalem in their bare feet, their spirits and bodies contrite, as they tearfully cried out the names of the saints. Both the leaders and the people came together in this time of necessity, to implore divine assistance. When this was accomplished with great humility, on the sixth day of the week, after they had attacked the city with great forcefulness, and their common effort had proved to be of no avail, such a great torpor fell upon the whole army that their strength vanished, and the steady misfortunes undermined the determination of the most courageous men. As God is my witness, I have heard, from men renowned for their truthfulness, who were present in the divine army, that after

their unsuccessful assault upon the walls of the city, you would have seen the best of the knights who had returned from the walls striking their hands, shouting angrily, lamenting that God had deserted them. And I also learned, from sources no less reliable, that Robert, Count of Normandy, and the other Robert, Prince of Flanders, met and shared their mutual grief, weeping copiously, and declaring themselves the most wretched of men, since the Lord Jesus had judged them unworthy of worshipping His Cross, and of seeing, or rather of adoring, His tomb. But as the hour drew near at which Jesus, who for the second time delivered the people from the prison of Egypt, is believed to have ascended the Cross, Duke Godfrey and his brother, Count Eustace, who had not stopped battling from their castle, steadily struck the lower walls with battering rams, while at the same time attacking the Saracens, who were fighting to protect their lives and country, with stones, with various other kinds of missiles, and even with the points of their swords.

Meanwhile, Lietaud, one of the knights, who will be known for generations to come for his daring and for his deeds, was the first to leap onto the walls of the city, startling the Gentiles who surrounded him, and robbing them of their confidence. When he had mounted the wall, several of the young Franks whose pious boldness had made them preeminent rushed forward, unwilling to seem inferior to him who had preceded them, and they climbed to the top of the wall. I would insert their names on this page, were I not aware of the fact that, after they returned, they became infamous for criminal acts; therefore, according to the judgment of men who love the name of God, my silence is not unjust. Very soon, when the Saracens saw the Franks breaching the walls, they quickly fled over the walls and through the city. While they were retreating, our entire army rushed in, some through the breaches made by the battering rams, others by jumping from the tops of their machines. Their struggle to enter resulted in harmful speed; with each man wanting to be perceived as the first, they got in each other's way. Moreover, near the entrance to the gates to the city, the Saracens had built secret covered pits, which injured many of our men, not to speak of the difficulties caused by the narrowness of the entrance as our men rushed in. The Franks chased the fleeing pagans fiercely, killing everyone they came upon, more in slaughter than in battle, through the streets, squares, and crossroads, until they reached what was called the Temple of Solomon. So much human blood flowed that a wave of damp gore almost covered the ankles of the advancing men. That was the nature of their success that day.

Raymond, the Count of Saint-Gilles, moved his army from the southern flank and had a very large machine on wheels brought to the wall, but between the machine, which was called the Castle, and the wall, was a very deep pit. The princes soon conferred about how to accomplish the breaching of the wall quickly, and ordered a messenger to announce throughout the army that anyone who carried three stones into the ditch would certainly receive a penny. In the space of scarcely three days the moat was filled in, since night did not prevent them from carrying out their project. When the moat had been filled in by this means, they pushed the machine against the walls. However, those who had taken on the defense of the inner city resisted us, not out of bravery I say, but out of obstinate madness, hurling what they call Greek fire at our men, and damaging the wheels of the machine with stones. The Franks, however, with remarkable skill, often managed to evade their blows and efforts. Meanwhile, at the eastern side of the city, the tumult of battle alone made the aforementioned count think that the Franks had broken into the city, and were racing through it, spreading death. "Why," he said to his men, "do we delay? Don't you see that the Franks have taken the city, and are now triumphantly seizing great booty?" The count, together with his men, then swiftly invaded the city. When he learned that some of the Franks had spread through the city's palaces, some into the Temple of the Lord, and that many were fighting at the altars of the Temple of Solomon, as it was formerly called, in order to retain power in the captured city he spoke with the emir (as they called him) in charge of the tower of David, which was called Zion, demanding that he hand over the tower with which he had been entrusted. Thus the satrap, after a pact had been agreed upon between

them, opened for him the gate through which the pilgrims used to pass when they entered Jerusalem, and where they were cruelly and unfairly compelled to pay tribute, which was called *musellae*. When the Provencals, that is, the army of the Count of Saint-Gilles, and all the others had entered the city, a general slaughter of the pagans took place. No one was spared because of tender years, beauty, dignity, or strength: one inescapable death awaited them all. Those who had retreated to the Temple of Solomon continued to battle against us throughout the day, but our men, enraged at the feeble arrogance of these desperate men, attacked them with united force, and by means of their combined efforts penetrated to the depths of the temple, where they inflicted such slaughter on the wretches within the temple that the blood of the innumerable crowd of those who were killed nearly submerged their boots. An innumerable crowd, of mingled sexes and ages, had poured into this Temple; the Franks granted some of them a few moments of life, so that they might remove from the Temple the bodies of the fallen, of whom a foul pile lay scattered here and there. After they had removed the bodies, they were themselves put to the sword. Those who had climbed to the top of the Temple, a large crowd of the common people, received the standards of Tancred and Gaston as a sign that peace had been granted to them in the meantime. However, whether Gaston, a famous and very wealthy man, was a Gascon or a Basque, I don't exactly remember, but I am certain that he was one or the other. The army then ran amok, and the entire city was looted. Palaces and other buildings lay open, and silver, gold, and silken garments were seized as booty. They found many horses and mules, and in the houses they found great abundance of every kind of food. This was right and proper for the army of God, that the finest things that offered themselves to each man, no matter how poor, became his by right, without doubt or challenge, no matter the social class of the man who first came upon them. And then, putting these things aside, they ran, equally joyful and sad, towards that which they had thirsted for so fervently.

They approached the sepulcher of the Lord and thanked Him for what they had sought, the liberation of the Blessed Places; He had performed such great deeds with them as his instruments, that neither those who had performed them nor any other men could properly evaluate these great deeds. They kept in mind how much anguish they had endured to achieve this, and how they had accomplished what they could not have hoped for, and when they considered that they themselves had done deeds which had been unknown for centuries, no man could understand how blessed were the tears which they poured forth. Omnipotent God, what deep emotion, what joy, what grief they felt, after unheard-of sufferings, never experienced by any army, like the tortures of childbirth, when, like newborn children, they saw that they had attained the fresh joys of the long-desired vision. Therefore they were sad, and after they had joyfully wept tears sweeter than any bread, they rejoiced, and with overflowing emotions they embraced the most pious Jesus, the cause of their excruciating daily labors, as though he had been hanging on the cross, or had been held until that moment in the shelter of the tomb from time immemorial. Magnificent gifts of gold and silver were offered there, but sincere devotion was more valuable than any gift.

At last the next day shone forth, and the Franks, sorry that they had permitted those who had climbed to the top of the Temple (to whom Tancred and Gaston had given their own standards, as we said earlier) to remain alive, invaded the heights of the temple and cut the Saracens to pieces, killing the women together with the men. Some of them, preferring suicide, threw themselves from the top of the Temple. Tancred, however, because he and Gaston had given their pledges of security, was much disturbed by this killing. Then our men ordered some of the Saracens to carry off the dead, because the foul stench of the bodies was oppressive, and the city was filled with so many corpses that the Franks were unable to move without stepping on dead bodies. Therefore the pagans, when they had carried the bodies from the city, in front of the main gates piled up mountains of corpses, and burned them in a huge pile. We merely read about, and have never seen, such a killing of Gentiles anywhere; God repaid them who had inflicted such pain and death upon the pilgrims—who had suffered for such a long time in that land—by exacting a retribution equal to their hideous crimes. For no one except God himself can calculate how much suffering, how many labors, how much destruction all of those who sought the Holy Places endured at the hands of the arrogant Gentiles. God certainly must have grieved more over their suffering than over the delivery of his Cross and Tomb into profane hands. But before we turn our stylus to other matters, it should be made clear that the Temple of Solomon, to which we referred earlier, is not the structure which Solomon himself built, which the Lord had predicted would not continue to stand, "one stone upon another" (Matt. 24:2), and which was destroyed, but an imitation of it, built by I don't know whom, as tribute to the noble ancient House. It certainly was a place of very great beauty, built out of gold and silver, of immeasurable price, and of incredible variety, with walls and gates plated with layers of precious metals. Count Raymond then had the prefect who had been in charge of the citadel, to whom he had sent his banners, brought out of the citadel that night, together with his entire retinue, and given safe conduct to Ascalon.

Then, when the holy places had been liberated, the entire Christian army was ordered to give alms and offerings, so that their souls might be properly receptive to the divine grace that they needed to choose the man who would rule the holy city as its king. On the eighth day after the taking of the city, they made an offer to the Count of Saint-Gilles, because of his excellence, but he, although mindful of his high position, refused to take on such an onerous task, for good reason (he was an old man, who had only one eye, but was famous for his remarkable feats of arms and for his energy). Finally, they approached Duke Godfrey, and, at the urgent insistence of everyone, the labor rather than the honor of this task was imposed upon him, for he would have to battle unremittingly against the great strength of the Gentiles, and to show good will towards the neighboring Christians. Slender, relatively tall, eloquent, and even-tempered, he had made himself known for his strength in battle on the Lord's expedition. According to reliable, accurate testimony, the following story is told about a remarkable deed he did, when he met at Antioch, on the bridge over the Pharphar, a Turk, wearing no cuirass, but riding a horse. Godfrey struck his guts so forcefully with his sword that the trunk of his body fell to the earth, while the legs remained seated as the horse moved on. The men of Lotharingia customarily had remarkably long as well as sharp swords.

61. Ibn al-Athīr
on the Fall of Jerusalem, 1099

The Arab historian Ibn al-Athīr (1160-1233), himself an eyewitness to later phases of the Crusades, included this account of the 1099 fall of Jerusalem to the crusaders in his comprehensive history of the Muslim world.

Taj ad-Daula Tutūsh was the Lord of Jerusalem but had given it as a feoff to the amīr Suqmān ibn Artūq the Turcoman. When the Franks defeated the Turks at Antioch the massacre demoralized them, and the Egyptians, who saw that the Turkish armies were being weakened by desertion, besieged Jerusalem under the command of al-Afdal ibn Badr al-Jamali. Inside the city were Artūq's sons, Suqmān and Ilghazi, their cousin Sunij and their nephew Yaquti. The Egyptians brought more than forty siege engines to attack Jerusalem and broke down the walls at several points. The inhabitants put up a defense, and the siege and fighting went on for more than six weeks. In the end the Egyptians forced the city to capitulate, in Sha'bān 489/August 1096. Suqmān, Ilghazi and their friends were well treated by al-Afdal, who gave them large gifts of money and let them go free. They made for Damascus and then crossed the Euphrates. Suqmān settled in Edessa and Ilghazi went on into Iraq. The Egyptian governor of Jerusalem was a certain Iftikhār ad-Daula, who was still there at the time of which we are speaking.

After their vain attempt to take Acre by siege, the Franks moved on to Jerusalem and besieged it for more than six weeks. They built two towers, one of which, near Sion, the Muslims burnt down, killing everyone inside it. It had scarcely ceased to burn before a messenger arrived to ask for help and to bring the news that the other side of the city had fallen. In fact Jerusalem was taken from the north on the morning of Friday 22 Sha'bān 492/15 July 1099. The population was put to the sword by the Franks, who pillaged the area for a week. A band of Muslims barricaded themselves into the Oratory of David and fought on for several days. They were granted their lives in return for surrendering. The Franks honored their word, and the group left by night for Ascalon. In the Masjid al-Aqsa the Franks slaughtered more than 70,000 people, among them a large number of Imams and Muslim scholars, devout and ascetic men who had left their homelands to live lives of pious seclusion in the Holy Place. The Franks stripped the Dome of the Rock of more than forty silver candelabra, each of them weighing 3,600 drams, and a great silver lamp weighing forty-four Syrian pounds, as well as a hundred and fifty smaller silver candelabra and more than twenty gold ones, and a great deal more booty. Refugees from Syria reached Baghdād in Ramadan, among them the qadi Abu Sa'd al-Hárawi. They told the Caliph's ministers a story that wrung their hearts and

SOURCE: F. Gabrieli, *Arab Historians of the Crusades* (London: Routledge and Kegan Paul, 1969), 10-12. Used by permission of Taylor & Francis Books.

brought tears to their eyes. On Friday they went to the Cathedral Mosque and begged for help, weeping so that their hearers wept with them as they described the sufferings of the Muslims in that Holy City: the men killed, the women and children taken prisoner, the homes pillaged. Because of the terrible hardships they had suffered, they were allowed to break the fast.

It was the discord between the Muslim princes, as we shall describe, that enabled the Franks to overrun the country. Abu 1-Muzaffar al-Abiwardi composed several poems on this subject, in one of which he says:

We have mingled blood with flowing tears, and there is no room left in us for pity(?)

To shed tears is a man's worst weapon when the swords stir up the embers of war.

Sons of Islām, behind you are battles in which heads rolled at your feet.

Dare you slumber in the blessed shade of safety, where life is as soft as an orchard flower?

How can the eye sleep between the lids at a time of disasters that would waken any sleeper?

While your Syrian brothers can only sleep on the backs of their chargers, or in vultures' bellies!

Must the foreigners feed on our ignominy, while you trail behind you the train of a pleasant life, like men whose world is at peace?

When blood has been spilt, when sweet girls must for shame hide their lovely faces in their hands!

When the white swords' points are red with blood, and the iron of the brown lances is stained with gore!

At the sound of sword hammering on lance young children's hair turns white.

This is war, and the man who shuns the whirlpool to save his life shall grind his teeth in penitence.

This is war, and the infidel's sword is naked in his hand, ready to be sheathed again in men's necks and skulls.

This is war, and he who lies in the tomb at Medina seems to raise his voice and cry: 'O sons of Hashim!

I see my people slow to raise the lance against the enemy: I see the Faith resting on feeble pillars.

For fear of death the Muslims are evading the fire of battle, refusing to believe that death will surely strike them.'

Must the Arab champions then suffer with resignation, while the gallant Persians shut their eyes to their dishonor?

62. Nicetas Choniates on the Sack of Constantinople, 1204

The Fourth Crusade was launched in 1202 to attack Egypt, but the crusading army was diverted to Constantinople instead. The ostensible goal was to restore a deposed emperor, but in 1204 the crusaders themselves took over the city—as described here by the Byzantine scholar Nicetas Choniates (1155/7-1217)—and installed one of their own, Baldwin of Flanders, on the imperial throne, doing long-term damage both to the Greek empire itself and to the tenuous relationship between the Greek and Latin churches.

SOURCE: D. C. Munro, *Translations and Reprints from the Original Sources of European History,* series 1, vol. 3:1, rev. ed. (Philadelphia: University of Pennsylvania Press, 1912), 15-16.

. . . How shall I begin to tell of the deeds wrought by these nefarious men! Alas, the images, which ought to have been adored, were trodden under foot! Alas, the relics of the holy martyrs were thrown into unclean places! Then was seen what one shudders to hear, namely, the divine body and blood of Christ was spilled upon the ground or thrown about. They snatched the precious reliquaries, thrust into their bosoms the ornaments which these contained, and used the broken remnants for pans and drinking cups—precursors of Antichrist, authors and heralds of his nefarious deeds, which we momentarily expect. Manifestly, indeed, by that race then, just as formerly, Christ was robbed and insulted and His garments were divided by lot; only one thing was lacking, that His side, pierced by a spear, should pour rivers of divine blood on the ground.

Nor can the violation of the Great Church [note: Hagia Sophia] be listened to with equanimity. For the sacred altar, formed of all kinds of precious materials and admired by the whole world, was broken into bits and distributed among the soldiers, as was all the other sacred wealth of so great and infinite splendor.

When the sacred vases and utensils of unsurpassable art and grace and rare material, and the fine silver, wrought with gold, which encircled the screen of the tribunal and the ambo, of admirable workmanship, and the door and many other ornaments, were to be borne away as booty, mules and saddled horses were led to the very sanctuary of the temple. Some of these which were unable to keep their footing on the splendid and slippery pavement, were stabbed when they fell, so that the sacred pavement was polluted with blood and filth.

4. Nay more, a certain harlot, a sharer in their guilt, a minister of the furies, a servant of the demons, a worker of incantations and poisonings, insulting Christ, sat in the patriarch's seat, singing an obscene song and dancing frequently. Nor, indeed, were these crimes committed and others left undone, on the ground that these were of lesser guilt, the others of greater. But with one consent all the most heinous sins and crimes were committed by all with equal zeal. Could those, who showed so great madness against God Himself, have spared the honorable matrons and maidens or the virgins consecrated to God?

Nothing was more difficult and laborious than to soften by prayers, to render benevolent, these wrathful barbarians, vomiting forth bile at every unpleasing word, so that nothing failed to inflame their fury. Whoever attempted it was derided as insane and a man of intemperate language. Often they drew their daggers against anyone who opposed them at all, or hindered their demands.

No one was without a share in the grief. In the alleys, in the streets, in the temples, complaints, weeping, lamentations, grief, the groaning of men, the shrieks of women, wounds, rape, captivity, the separation of those most closely united. Nobles wandered about ignominiously, those of venerable age in tears, the rich in poverty. Thus it was in the streets, on the corners, in the temple, in the dens, for no place remained unassailed or defended the suppliants. All places everywhere were filled full of all kinds of crime. Oh, immortal God, how great the afflictions of the people, how great the distress!

63. James I of Aragon on the Fall of Valencia, 1238

From the mid-eleventh century through the mid-thirteenth, the Christian kingdoms of northern Spain gradually effected the so-called "reconquest" of

SOURCE: *Chronicle of James I, King of Aragon*, vol. 1, tr. John Forster (London: Chapman and Hall, 1883), 392-99.

most of the large portion of the Iberian peninsula that had come under Muslim control in the eighth century. (The major holdout, Granada, would remain Muslim until 1492.) In his colorful autobiography, King James I of Aragon (1208-1276)—or someone writing on his behalf—recounts his own conquest of the Muslim kingdom of Valencia in 1238 in the late phase of this process.

CCLXXVIII

On the third day the Rais sent me word that if I would give him an escort he would come out to me. I sent one of my barons to him, and he came immediately. He told me that the King of Valencia, Zaen, had considered the thing, and that he knew that the town could not hold out in the end; wherefore, that he might not cause the Valencians to bear more ill than they had already borne, he would surrender the city on this condition: that the Saracens, men and women, might take away all their effects; that they should not be searched, nor should any outrage be done to them, and they all, himself and they, should go under escort to Cullera. Since it was the will of God that I should have the city, he had to will it so. On that I said that I would consult the Queen, who alone was in the secret. He said that he thought that was good, and he went out of the house, where I and the Queen remained. I then asked her what she thought of Zaen's proposal. She said, that if it seemed right to me to take those terms, she thought it right also; for Valencia was not a thing that one who could have it would risk from one day to another. I felt that she gave me good advice, and I told her that I agreed with what she said, but I would add what I thought a very good reason for accepting Zaen's terms, namely, that should the town be taken by force, it would go hard for me if a wrangling (*baralla*) over it arose in the army. Not for base lucre nor for apparel of any sort ought I to put off what my ancestors and myself had so long desired to take and have; and even yet, if I were wounded or fell ill before the town could be taken by force, the whole thing might still be lost. Wherefore, so good a work as that should not be put to risk, and one should follow it up well, and end it.

CCLXXIX

After saying that, I sent for Rais Abnalmalet, and answered him in this wise:—"Rais, you know well that I have made a great outlay in this business of mine; yet notwithstanding the outlay that I and my people have made and the ills we have suffered, for all that it shall not be but that I will agree to your terms, and have you escorted to Cullera, with all the goods that the Saracens, men and women, may be able to carry. For love of the King and of you, who have come here, will I do your people that grace, that they may go safely and securely with their apparel and with what they can carry, and wish to carry."

CCLXXX

When the Rais heard that, he was content; and he said he gave me great thanks, though their loss was to be great; withal he thanked me much for the grace I did them. After a time, I asked him on what day it should be. He said they needed ten days for clearing out. I told him that he asked too much, that the army was growing weary of the delay, for nothing was being done, and it was not for their good nor for mine. And so after long discourse we agreed that on the fifth day they would surrender the town, and would begin to depart.

When that was settled between me and him, I told the Rais to keep the thing secret till I had spoken with the Archbishop of Narbonne, with the other bishops, and with my barons. He said he would do so, and I told him I would speak with them that very evening, and would give orders that from that time no harm should be done to them.

CCLXXXI

When that was done, and I had eaten, drunk, and taken sleep in a pavilion beside my quarters, I sent for the Archbishop [of Tarragona], for the bishops and the barons, as well as for the Archbishop of Narbonne, who was there in the camp. When all were present, I told them how Our Lord had done me many favors, and among others had now done me one for which I and they ought to give Him great thanks. As they had a good share in that great gain of mine, I would make them know, that they all might rejoice in it, that Valencia was ours at last. When I had said that, Don Nuño, Don Exemen de Urrea, Don Pedro, Fernandez de Açagra, and Don Pedro Cornell, lost color, as if someone had stabbed them to the heart; all murmured except the Archbishop and some of the bishops, who said that they thanked Our Lord for giving me that gain, and that grace; not one of the others thanked God for it, or took it well. Then Don Nuño and Don Pedro Fernandez de Açagra asked how it was done, and in what wise? I said that I had engaged for the safety of the King of Valencia and of the Saracens, all those living in the town, men and women, and for escorting them to Cullera and Denia; and that they were to surrender the town on the fifth day from that. All said that since I had done it, they approved of it. And the Archbishop of Narbonne added: "This is the work of God, and I do not believe but that of three things one must be; either you have done service to God, or you are now serving Him in this, or you will serve Him hereafter." And En Ramon Berenguer said: "We ought to give God great thanks for the love He has shown you, and since that which you and your ancestors had desired is now fulfilled through you, we ought to be very thankful to Our Lord."

CCLXXXII

Next day, at vespers, I sent to tell the King and the Rais Abnalmalet that, in order that the Christians might know that Valencia was ours, and might do nothing against it, they should hoist my standard on the tower, which now is that called of the Temple; they said they were content, and I went on the Rambla, between the camp and the tower. When I saw my standard upon the tower I dismounted, turned myself towards the east, and wept with my eyes, kissing the ground, for the great mercy that had been done to me.

CCLXXXIII

Meantime the Saracens busied themselves about departing within the five days I had agreed on with them, so that on the third day they were all ready to quit; and I myself, with knights and armed men about me, brought them all out into the fields between Ruçafa and the town. I had, however, to put some of my own men to death because of their attempting to take goods from the Saracens, and carry off some women and children. So it was, that though the people who came out of Valencia were so numerous—there being between men and women well fifty thousand—by the grace of God they did not lose between them one thousand souls, so well did I escort, and have them escorted, as far as Cullera.

CCLXXXIV

When that was done I made my entrance into the city, and on the third day began the division of the houses among the Archbishop of Narbonne, the bishops, and the barons who were with me, as well as the knights who were entitled to heritages in the district. I also gave shares to the corporations of the cities [of Aragon and Catalonia], according to the number of men-at-arms each had there.

CCLXXXV

At the end of three weeks I appointed partitioners to divide the lands of the district of Valencia. I made the yoke, "jouvada," to be of six "caficades." I had the whole land of the district measured, and the grants I had made carefully examined. When this was done, I found that, in consequence of the grants made to some of the men, the charters came to more "jouvadas" than the land itself. Many men there were who had asked for a small portion of land, and I found afterwards that, through their cheating, it was twice or three times as much as they ought to have had. As there was not enough land for the grants, I took away from those who had too much, and redistributed it, so that all had some, as was fitting.

Spirituality and Theology in the Latin West in the Twelfth and Thirteenth Centuries

64. Anselm of Canterbury, *Cur Deus Homo*

Anselm (ca. 1033-1099) spent more than thirty years in the monastic life at Bec in Normandy before becoming archbishop of Canterbury in 1093. In addition to meditations and prayers that, in their strong affectivity, set a new direction for medieval devotional literature, Anselm wrote theological works of enduring importance. In Cur Deus Homo (Why God Became Human) he explains Christ's atonement in a way that ascribes to humanity an active role in the drama of salvation, in contrast to earlier theories that had cast humans as ransomed captives. Anselm's application of reason to matters of faith ("faith seeking understanding") anticipates the spirit of the later scholastic theologians.

Book I

Chapter I

The question on which the whole work rests.

I have been often and most earnestly requested by many, both personally and by letter, that I would hand down in writing the proofs of a certain doctrine of our faith, which I am accustomed to give to inquirers; for they say that these proofs gratify them, and are considered sufficient. This they ask, not for the sake of attaining to faith by means of reason, but that they may be gladdened by understanding and meditating on those things which they believe; and that, as far as possible, they may be always ready to convince anyone who demands of them a reason of that hope which is in us. And here is a question that infidels are accustomed to bring up against us, ridiculing Christian simplicity as absurd, but also that many believers ponder in their hearts: for what cause or necessity did God become human, and by his own death, as we believe and affirm, restore life to the world, when he might have done this by means of some other being, angelic or human, or merely by his will? Not only the learned, but also many unlearned persons interest themselves in this inquiry and seek for its solution. Many, therefore, desire to consider this subject, and even though the investigation of it may seem very difficult; still the solution is plain to all, and attractive for the value and beauty of the reasoning. And although what ought to be sufficient has been said by the holy fathers and their successors, yet I will take pains to disclose to inquirers what God has seen fit to lay open to me. And since investigations that are carried on by question and answer, are more plain to many people, and especially to those with less quick minds and on that account are more gratifying, I will take to argue with me one of those

Source: Anselm, *Proslogium, Monologium . . . and Cur Deus Homo*, tr. Sidney Norton Deane (Chicago: Open Court Publishing Company, 1903), 203-10, 225-28, 237-45.

persons who agitate this subject, indeed the person who more than anyone else has earnestly impelled me to it: so Boso will question, and Anselm will reply.

Chapter XII

Whether it were proper for God to put away sins by compassion alone, without any payment of debt.

Anselm. Let us return and consider whether it were proper for God to put away sins by compassion alone, without any payment of the honor taken from him.

Boso. I do not see why it is not proper.

Anselm. To remit sin in this manner is nothing else than not to punish; and since it is not right to cancel sin without compensation or punishment; if it be not punished, then is it passed by undischarged.

Boso. What you say is reasonable.

Anselm. It is not fitting for God to pass over anything in his kingdom undischarged.

Boso. If I wish to oppose this, I fear to sin.

Anselm. It is, therefore, not proper for God thus to pass over sin unpunished.

Boso. Thus it follows.

Anselm. There is also another thing which follows if sin be passed by unpunished, viz., that with God there will be no difference between the guilty and the not guilty; and this is unbecoming to God.

Boso. I cannot deny it.

Anselm. Observe this also. Everyone knows that justice to humans is regulated by law, so that, according to the requirements of law, the measure of award is bestowed by God.

Boso. This is our belief.

Anselm. But if sin is neither paid for nor punished, it is subject to no law.

Boso. I cannot conceive it to be otherwise.

Anselm. Injustice, therefore, if it is cancelled by compassion alone, is more free than justice, which seems very inconsistent. And to these is also added a further incongruity, viz., that it makes injustice like God. For as God is subject to no law, so neither is injustice.

Boso. I cannot withstand your reasoning. But when God commands us in every case to forgive those who trespass against us, it seems inconsistent to enjoin a thing upon us which it is not proper for him to do himself.

Anselm. There is no inconsistency in God's commanding us not to take upon ourselves what belongs to Him alone. For to execute vengeance belongs to none but Him who is Lord of all; for when the powers of the world rightly accomplish this end, God himself does it who appointed them for the purpose.

Boso. You have obviated the difficulty which I thought to exist; but there is another to which I would like to have your answer. For since God is so free as to be subject to no law, and to the judgment of no one, and is so merciful as that nothing more merciful can be conceived; and nothing is right or fit save as he wills; it seems a strange thing for us to say that he is wholly unwilling or unable to put away an injury done to himself, when we are wont to apply to him for indulgence with regard to those offenses which we commit against others.

Anselm. What you say of God's liberty and choice and compassion is true; but we ought so to interpret these things as that they may not seem to interfere with His dignity. For there is no liberty except as regards what is best or fitting; nor should that be called mercy which does anything improper for the Divine character. Moreover, when it is said that what God wishes is just, and that what He does not wish is unjust, we must not understand that if God wished anything improper it would be just, simply because he wished it. For if God wishes to lie, we must not conclude that it is right to lie, but rather that he is not God. For no will can ever wish to lie, unless truth in it is impaired, nay, unless the will itself be impaired by forsaking truth. When, then, it is said: "If God wishes to lie," the meaning is simply this: "If the nature of God is such as that he wishes to lie"; and, therefore, it does not follow that falsehood is right, except it be understood in the same manner as when we speak of two impossible things: "If this be true, then that follows; because neither *this* nor *that* is true"; as if someone should say: "Supposing water to be dry, and fire to be moist"; for neither is the case. Therefore, with regard to these things, to speak the whole truth: If God desires a thing, it is right that he should desire that which involves no unfitness. For if God chooses that it should rain, it is right that it should rain; and if he desires that anyone should die, then is it right that he should die. Wherefore, if it be not fitting for God to do anything unjustly, or out of course, it does not belong to his liberty or compassion or will to let the sinner go unpunished who makes no return to God of what the sinner has defrauded him.

Boso. You remove from me every possible objection which I had thought of bringing against you.

Anselm. Yet observe why it is not fitting for God to do this.

Boso. I listen readily to whatever you say.

Chapter XIII

*How nothing less was to be endured,
in the order of things, than that the creature
should take away the honor due the Creator
and not restore what he takes away.*

Anselm. In the order of things, there is nothing less to be endured than that the creature should take away the honor due the Creator, and not restore what he has taken away.

Boso. Nothing is more plain than this.

Anselm. But there is no greater injustice suffered than that by which so great an evil must be endured.

Boso. This, also, is plain.

Anselm. I think, therefore, that you will not say that God ought to endure a thing than which no greater injustice is suffered, viz., that the creature should not restore to God what he has taken away.

Boso. No; I think it should be wholly denied.

Anselm. Again, if there is nothing greater or better than God, there is nothing more just than supreme justice, which maintains God's honor in the arrangement of things, and which is nothing else but God himself.

Boso. There is nothing clearer than this.

Anselm. Therefore God maintains nothing with more justice than the honor of his own dignity.

Boso. I must agree with you.

Anselm. Does it seem to you that he wholly

preserves it, if he allows himself to be so defrauded of it as that he should neither receive satisfaction nor punish the one defrauding him.

Boso. I dare not say so.

Anselm. Therefore the honor taken away must be repaid, or punishment must follow; otherwise, either God will not be just to himself, or he will be weak in respect to both parties; and this it is impious even to think of.

Boso. I think that nothing more reasonable can be said.

Chapter XIV

*How the honor of God exists
in the punishment of the wicked.*

Boso. But I wish to hear from you whether the punishment of the sinner is an honor to God, or how it is an honor. For if the punishment of the sinner is not for God's honor when the sinner does not pay what he took away, but is punished, God loses his honor so that he cannot recover it. And this seems in contradiction to the things which have been said.

Anselm. It is impossible for God to lose his honor; for either the sinner pays his debt of his own accord, or, if he refuse, God takes it from him. For either humanity renders due submission to God of his own will, by avoiding sin or making payment, or else God subjects him to himself by torments, even against humanity's will, and thus shows that he is the Lord of humanity, though humanity refuses to acknowledge this of its own accord. And here we must observe that as humanity in sinning takes away what belongs to God, so God in punishing gets in return what pertains to humanity. For not only does that belong to a person which that person has in present possession, but also that which it is in the person's power to have. Therefore, since humanity was so made as to be able to attain happiness by avoiding sin; if, on account of his sin, it is deprived of happiness and every good, it repays from its own inheritance what it has stolen, even if unwillingly. For although God does not apply what he takes away to any object of his own, as one transfers the money taken from another to one's own use; yet what he takes away serves the purpose of his own honor, for this very reason, that it is taken away. For by this act he shows that the sinner and all that pertains to that sinner are under his subjection.

Chapter XV

Whether God suffers his honor to be violated even in the least degree.

Boso. What you say satisfies me. But there is still another point which I should like to have you answer. For if, as you make out, God ought to sustain his own honor, why does he allow it to be violated even in the least degree? For what is in any way made liable to injury is not entirely and perfectly preserved.

Anselm. Nothing can be added to or taken from the honor of God. For this honor which belongs to him is in no way subject to injury or change. But as the individual creature preserves, naturally or by reason, the condition belonging, and, as it were, allotted to him, he is said to obey and honor God; and to this, rational nature, which possesses intelligence, is especially bound. And when the being chooses what he ought, he honors God; not by bestowing anything upon him, but because he brings himself freely under God's will and disposal, and maintains his own condition in the universe, and the beauty of the universe itself, as far as in him lies. But when he does not choose what he ought, he dishonors God, as far as the being himself is concerned, because he does not submit himself freely to God's disposal. And he disturbs the order and beauty of the universe, as relates to himself, although he cannot injure nor tarnish the power and majesty of God. For if those things which are held together in the circuit of the heavens desire to be elsewhere than under the heavens, or to be further removed from the heavens, there is no place where they can be but under the heavens, nor can they fly from the heavens without also approaching them. For both whence and whither and in what way they go, they are still under the heavens; and if they are at a greater distance from one part of them, they are only so much nearer to the opposite part. And so, though human being or evil angel refuse to submit

to the Divine will and appointment, yet they cannot escape it; for if they wish to fly from a will that commands, they fall into the power of a will that punishes. And if you ask whither they go, it is only under the permission of that will; and even this wayward choice or action of theirs becomes subservient, under infinite wisdom, to the order and beauty of the universe before spoken of. For when it is understood that God brings good out of many forms of evil, then the satisfaction for sin freely given, or if this be not given, the exaction of punishment, hold their own place and orderly beauty in the same universe. For if Divine wisdom were not to insist upon these things, when wickedness tries to disturb the right appointment, there would be, in the very universe which God ought to control, an unseemliness springing from the violation of the beauty of arrangement, and God would appear to be deficient in his management. And these two things are not only unfitting, but consequently impossible; so that satisfaction or punishment must needs follow every sin.

Boso. You have relieved my objection.

Anselm. It is then plain that no one can honor or dishonor God, as he is in himself; but the creature, as far as he himself is concerned, appears to do this when he submits or opposes his will to the will of God.

Boso. I know of nothing which can be said against this.

Anselm. Let me add something to it.

Boso. Go on, until I am weary of listening.

Chapter XX

That satisfaction ought to be proportionate to guilt; and that humanity is of itself unable to accomplish this.

Anselm. Neither, I think, will you doubt this, that satisfaction should be proportionate to guilt.

Boso. Otherwise sin would remain in a manner exempt from control (*inordinatum*), which cannot be, for God leaves nothing uncontrolled in his kingdom. But this is determined, that even the smallest unfitness is impossible with God.

Anselm. Tell me, then, what payment you make God for your sin?

Boso. Repentance, a broken and contrite heart, self-denial, various bodily sufferings, pity in giving and forgiving, and obedience.

Anselm. What do you give to God in all these?

Boso. Do I not honor God, when, for his love and fear, in heartfelt contrition I give up worldly joy, and despise, amid abstinence and toils, the delights and ease of this life, and submit obediently to him, freely bestowing my possessions in giving to and releasing others?

Anselm. When you render anything to God which you owe him, irrespective of your past sin, you should not reckon this as the debt which you owe for sin. But you owe God every one of those things which you have mentioned. For, in this mortal state, there should be such love and such desire of attaining the true end of your being, which is the meaning of prayer, and such grief that you have not yet reached this object, and such fear lest you fail of it, that you should find joy in nothing which does not help you or give encouragement of your success. For you do not deserve to have a thing which you do not love and desire for its own sake, and the want of which at present, together with the great danger of never getting it, causes you no grief. This also requires one to avoid ease and worldly pleasures such as seduce the mind from real rest and pleasure, except so far as you think suffices for the accomplishment of that object. But you ought to view the gifts which you bestow as a part of your debt, since you know that what you give comes not from yourself, but from him whose servant both you are and he also to whom you give. And nature herself teaches you to do to your fellow servant, person to person, as you would be done by; and that those who will not bestow what they have ought not to receive what they do not have. Of forgiveness, indeed, I speak briefly, for, as we said above, vengeance in no sense belongs to you, since you are not your own, nor is he who injures you yours or his, but you are both the servants of one Lord, made by him out of nothing. And if you avenge yourself upon your fellow servant, you proudly assume judgment over him when it is the peculiar right of God, the judge of all. But what do you give to God by your obedience, which is not owed him already, since he demands from you all that you are and have and can become?

Boso. Truly I dare not say that in all these things I pay any portion of my debt to God.

Anselm. How then do you pay God for your transgression?

Boso. If in justice I owe God myself and all my powers, even when I do not sin, I have nothing left to render to him for my sin.

Anselm. What will become of you then? How will you be saved?

Boso. Merely looking at your arguments, I see no way of escape. But, turning to my belief, I hope through Christian faith, "which works by love," that I may be saved, and the more, since we read that if the sinner turns from his iniquity and does what is right, all his transgressions shall be forgotten.

Anselm. This is only said of those who either looked for Christ before his coming, or who believe in him since he has appeared. But we set aside Christ and his religion as if they did not exist, when we proposed to inquire whether his coming were necessary to humanity's salvation.

Boso. We did so.

Anselm. Let us then proceed by reason simply.

Boso. Though you bring me into straits, yet I very much wish you to proceed as you have begun.

Chapter XXV

How humanity's salvation by Christ is necessarily possible.

Anselm. Is it not sufficiently proved that humanity can be saved by Christ, when even infidels do not deny that humanity can be happy somehow, and it has been sufficiently shown that, leaving Christ out of view, no salvation can be found for humanity? For, either by Christ or by someone else can humanity be saved, or else not at all. If, then, it is false that humanity cannot be saved at all, or that it can be saved in any other way, its salvation must necessarily be by Christ.

Boso. But what reply will you make to a person who perceives that humanity cannot be saved in any other way, and yet, not understanding how it can be saved by Christ, sees fit to declare that there cannot be any salvation either by Christ or in any other way?

Anselm. What reply ought to be made to one

who ascribes impossibility to a necessary truth, because he does not understand how it can be?

Boso. That he is a fool.

Anselm. Then what he says must be despised.

Boso. Very true; but we ought to show him in what way the thing is true which he holds to be impossible.

Anselm. Do you not perceive, from what we have said above, that it is necessary for some people to attain to felicity? For, if it is unfitting for God to elevate humanity with any stain upon it, to that for which he made it free from all stain, lest it should seem that God had repented of his good intent, or was unable to accomplish his designs; far more is it impossible, on account of the same unfitness, that no one should be exalted to that state for which he was made. Therefore, a satisfaction such as we have above proved necessary for sin, must be found apart from the Christian faith, which no reason can show; or else we must accept the Christian doctrine. For what is clearly made out by absolute reasoning ought by no means to be questioned, even though the method of it be not understood.

Boso. What you say is true.

Anselm. Why, then, do you question further?

Boso. I come not for this purpose, to have you remove doubts from my faith, but to have you show me the reason for my confidence. Therefore, as you have brought me thus far by your reasoning, so that I perceive that human beings as sinners owe God for their sin what they are unable to pay, and cannot be saved without paying; I wish you would go further with me, and enable me to understand, by force of reasoning, the fitness of all those things which the Catholic faith enjoins upon us with regard to Christ, if we hope to be saved; and how they avail for the salvation of humanity, and how God saves humanity by compassion; when he never remits human sin, unless humanity shall have rendered what was due on account of that sin. And, to make your reasoning the clearer, begin at the beginning, so as to rest it upon a strong foundation.

Anselm. Now God help me, for you do not spare me in the least, nor consider the weakness of my skill, when you enjoin so great a work upon me. Yet I will attempt it, as I have begun, not trust-ing in myself but in God, and will do what I can with his help. But let us separate the things which remain to be said from those which have been said, by a new introduction, lest by their unbroken length, these things become tedious to one who wishes to read them.

Book II

Chapter I

How humanity was made holy by God, so as to be happy in the enjoyment of God.

Anselm. It ought not to be disputed that rational nature was made holy by God, in order to be happy in enjoying Him. For to this end is it rational, in order to discern justice and injustice, good and evil, and between the greater and the lesser good. Otherwise it was made rational in vain. But God made it not rational in vain. Wherefore, doubtless, it was made rational for this end. In like manner is it proved that the intelligent creature received the power of discernment for this purpose, that he might hate and shun evil, and love and choose good, and especially the greater good. For else in vain would God have given him that power of discernment, since human beings' discretion would be useless unless they loved and avoided according to it. But it does not befit God to give such power in vain. It is, therefore, established that rational nature was created for this end, viz., to love and choose the highest good supremely, for its own sake and nothing else; for if the highest good were chosen for any other reason, then something else and not itself would be the thing loved. But intelligent nature cannot fulfill this purpose without being holy. Therefore that it might not in vain be made rational, it was made, in order to fulfill this purpose, both rational and holy. Now, if it was made holy in order to choose and love the highest good, then it was made such in order to follow sometimes what it loved and chose, or else it was not. But if it were not made holy for this end, that it might follow what it loves and chooses, then in vain was it made to love and choose holiness; and there can be no reason why it should be ever bound to follow holiness. Therefore, as long as it will be holy in loving and choosing the supreme good, for which it was made, it will be miserable; because it will be impotent despite of its will, inasmuch as it does not have what it desires. But this is utterly absurd. Wherefore rational nature was made holy, in order to be happy in enjoying the supreme good, which is God. Therefore humanity, whose nature is rational, was made holy for this end, that it might be happy in enjoying God.

Chapter II

How human beings would never have died, unless they had sinned.

Anselm. Moreover, it is easily proved that humanity was so made as not to be necessarily subject to death; for, as we have already said, it is inconsistent with God's wisdom and justice to compel humanity to suffer death without fault, when he made it holy to enjoy eternal blessedness. It therefore follows that had human beings never sinned they never would have died.

Chapter III

How humans will rise with the same bodies which they have in this world.

Anselm. From this the future resurrection of the dead is clearly proved. For if humanity is to be perfectly restored, the restoration should make it such as it would have been had human beings never sinned.

Boso. It must be so.

Anselm. Therefore, as human beings, had they not sinned, were to have been transferred with the same body to an immortal state, so when they shall be restored, it must properly be with their own bodies as they lived in this world.

Boso. But what shall we say to one who tells us that this is right enough with regard to those in whom humanity shall be perfectly restored, but is not necessary as respects the reprobate?

Anselm. We know of nothing more just or proper than this, that as humanity, had it continued in holiness, would have been perfectly happy

for eternity, both in body and in soul; so, if it persevere in wickedness, it shall be likewise completely miserable forever.

Boso. You have promptly satisfied me in these matters.

Chapter IV

How God will complete, in respect to human nature, what he has begun.

Anselm. From these things, we can easily see that God will either complete what he has begun with regard to human nature, or else he has made to no end so lofty a nature, capable of so great good. Now if it be understood that God has made nothing more valuable than rational existence capable of enjoying him; it is altogether foreign from his character to suppose that he will suffer that rational existence utterly to perish.

Boso. No reasonable being can think otherwise.

Anselm. Therefore is it necessary for him to perfect in human nature what he has begun. But this, as we have already said, cannot be accomplished save by a complete expiation of sin, which no sinner can effect for himself.

Boso. I now understand it to be necessary for God to complete what he has begun, lest there be an unseemly falling off from his design.

Chapter V

How, although the thing may be necessary, God may not do it by a compulsory necessity; and what is the nature of that necessity which removes or lessens gratitude, and what necessity increases it.

Boso. But if it be so, then God seems as it were compelled, for the sake of avoiding what is unbecoming, to secure the salvation of humanity. How, then, can it be denied that he does it more on his own account than on ours? But if it be so, what thanks do we owe him for what he does for himself? How shall we attribute our salvation to his grace, if he saves us from necessity?

Anselm. There is a necessity which takes away or lessens our gratitude to a benefactor, and there is also a necessity by which the favor deserves still greater thanks. For when one does a benefit from a necessity to which he is unwillingly subjected, less thanks are due him, or none at all. But when he freely places himself under the necessity of benefiting another, and sustains that necessity without reluctance, then he certainly deserves greater thanks for the favor. For this should not be called necessity but grace, inasmuch as he undertook or maintains it, not with any constraint, but freely. For if that which today you promise of your own accord you will give tomorrow, you do give tomorrow with the same willingness; though it be necessary for you, if possible, to redeem your promise, or make yourself a liar; notwithstanding, the recipient of your favor is as much indebted for your precious gift as if you had not promised it, for you were not obliged to make yourself his debtor before the time of giving it: just so is it when one undertakes, by a vow, a design of holy living. For though after his vow he ought necessarily to perform, lest he suffer the judgment of an apostate, and, although he may be compelled to keep it even unwillingly, yet, if he keep his vow cheerfully, he is not less but more pleasing to God than if he had not vowed. For he has not only given up the life of the world, but also his personal liberty, for the sake of God; and he cannot be said to live a holy life of necessity, but with the same freedom with which he took the vow. Much more, therefore, do we owe all thanks to God for completing his intended favor to humanity though, indeed, it would not be proper for him to fail in his good design, because wanting nothing in himself he began it for our sake and not his own. For what humans were about to do was not hidden from God at their creation; and yet by freely creating them, God as it were bound himself to complete the good which he had begun. In fine, God does nothing by necessity, since he is not compelled or restrained in anything. And when we say that God does anything to avoid dishonor, which he certainly does not fear, we must mean that God does this from the necessity of maintaining his honor; which necessity is after all no more than this, viz., the immutability of his honor, which belongs to him in himself, and is not derived from another; and therefore it is not properly called necessity. Yet we may say, although the whole work which God does for humanity is of grace, that it is necessary for God, on account of his unchangeable goodness, to complete the work which he has begun.

Boso. I grant it.

Chapter VI

How no being, except the God-man, can make the atonement by which humanity is saved.

Anselm. But this cannot be effected, except the price paid to God for the sin of humanity be something greater than all the universe besides God.

Boso. So it appears.

Anselm. Moreover, it is necessary that he who can give God anything of his own which is more valuable than all things in the possession of God, must be greater than all else but God himself.

Boso. I cannot deny it.

Anselm. Therefore none but God can make this satisfaction.

Boso. So it appears.

Anselm. But none but a human being ought to do this, otherwise humanity does not make the satisfaction.

Boso. Nothing seems more just.

Anselm. If it be necessary, therefore, as it appears, that the heavenly kingdom be made up of human beings, and this cannot be effected unless the aforesaid satisfaction be made, which no one but God can make and no one but human beings ought to make, it is necessary for the God-man to make it.

Boso. Now blessed be God! We have made a great discovery with regard to our question....

65. Bernard of Clairvaux,
On Loving God

Bernard of Clairvaux (1090-1153) was abbot of the Cistercian monastery of Clairvaux from 1115 until his death. An influential public figure, he supported Innocent II after the disputed papal election of 1130, worked to condemn Peter Abelard at the Council of Sens in 1140, and afterward took the lead in promoting the Second Crusade. Bernard also wrote brilliantly about the internal dynamic of the soul in its relation to God—a theme that typified twelfth-century spirituality—in such works as his masterpiece, Sermons on the Song of Songs, *and this little treatise,* On Loving God.

VI. 16. Briefly repeating what has been said so far, consider first how God merits to be loved, that there is to be no limit to that love, for he loved us first. Such a one loved us so much and so freely, insignificant as we are and such as we are, that, as you recall I said in the beginning, we must love God without any limit. Finally, as love offered to God has for object the one who is immeasurable and infinite—for God is both infinite and immeasurable—what, I ask, should be the aim or degree of our love? What about the fact that our love is not given gratuitously but in payment of a debt? Thus the Immeasurable loves, the Eternal loves, that Charity which surpasses knowledge loves; God, whose greatness knows no end, to whose wisdom there is no limit, whose peace exceeds all understanding, loves—and we think we can requite him with some measure of love? "I shall love you, O Lord, my fortress, my strength, my refuge, my deliverer" (Ps. 17:2-3), and whatever can be held desirable and lovable for me. My God, my help, I shall love you as much as I am able for your gift. My love is less than is your due, yet not less than I am able, for even if I cannot love you as much as I should, still I cannot love you more than I can. I shall only be able to love you more when you give me more, although you can never find my love worthy of you. For, "Your eyes have seen my imperfections, and all shall be written down in your book" (Ps. 138:16), all who do what they can, even if they cannot do all they should. As far as I can see, it is clear enough to what extent God ought to be loved and that by his own merit. By his own merit, I say, but to whom is the degree of this merit really clear? Who can say? Who can understand it?

VII. 17. Let us see now how he is to be loved for our advantage. How far from the reality is our knowledge of it? Nevertheless, it is not right to keep silent about what has been seen, even if it falls short of the truth. When asking above why and how God is to be loved, I said the question may be understood in two ways: it may mean by what merit of his God deserves our love or what benefit do we acquire in loving him. Both questions it seems may be asked. After speaking of God's merit in a way no doubt unworthy of him, but according to the gift I have received, it remains for me to speak of the reward insofar as it also will be given to me.

God Is Not Loved without a Reward

God is not loved without a reward, although he should be loved without regard for one. True charity cannot be worthless, still, as "it does not seek its own advantage" (1 Cor. 13:5), it cannot be termed mercenary. Love pertains to the will, it is

Source: *On Loving God by Bernard of Clairvaux* [anonymous translation] *with an Analytical Commentary by Emero Stiegman* (Kalamazoo, Mich.: Cistercian Publications, 1995), 19-35. Translation copyright © Cistercian Publications, Inc., 1973. Used by permission.

not a transaction; it cannot acquire or be acquired by a pact. Moving us freely, it makes us spontaneous. True love is content with itself; it has its reward, the object of its love. Whatever you seem to love because of something else, you do not really love; you really love the end pursued and not that by which it is pursued. Paul does not evangelize in order to eat; he eats in order to evangelize; he loves the Gospel and not the food. True love merits its reward, it does not seek it. A reward is offered him who does not yet love; it is due him who loves; it is given to him who perseveres. When we have to persuade people in lesser affairs we cajole the unwilling with promises and rewards, not those who are willing. Who would dream of offering a man a reward for doing something he wants to do? No one, for example, pays a hungry man to eat, a thirsty man to drink, or a mother to feed the child of her womb. Who would think of using prayers or prizes to remind a man to fence in his vine, to dig around his tree, or to build his own home? How much more the soul that loves God seeks no other reward than that God whom it loves. Were the soul to demand anything else, then it would certainly love that other thing and not God.

18. Every rational being naturally desires always what satisfies more its mind and will: It is never satisfied with something which lacks the qualities it thinks it should have. A man with a beautiful wife, for example, looks at a more attractive woman with a wanton eye or heart; a well-dressed man wants more costly clothes; and a man of great wealth envies anyone richer than he. You can see men who already own many farms and possessions, still busy, day after day, adding one field to another, driven by an excessive passion to extend their holdings. You can see men living in homes worthy of a king and in sumptuous dwellings, nonetheless daily adding house to house, through restless curiosity building up, then tearing down, changing squares into circles. What about men promoted to high honors? Do we not see them striving more and more in an insatiable ambition to go higher still? There is no end to all this, because no single one of these riches can be held to be the highest or the best. Why wonder if man cannot be content with what is lower or worse, since he cannot find peace this side of what is highest or

best? It is stupidity and madness to want always that which can neither satisfy nor even diminish your desire. While enjoying those riches, you strive for what is missing and are dissatisfied, longing for what you lack. Thus the restless mind, running to and fro among the pleasures of this life, is tired out but never satisfied; like the starving man who thinks whatever he stuffs down his throat is not enough, for his eyes see what remains to be eaten. Thus man craves continually for what is missing with no less fear than he possesses with joy what is in front of him. Who can have everything? A man clings to the fruits of his work (however small they may be), never knowing when he will have the sorrow of losing them, yet he is certain to lose them some day. In like manner a perverted will contends for what is best, and hastens in a straight line toward what will afford it the most satisfaction. Rather vanity makes sport of it in those tortuous ways, and evil deceives itself. If you wish to accomplish in this way what you desire, to gain hold of that which leaves nothing further to be desired, why bother about the rest? You are running on crooked roads and will die long before you reach the end you are seeking.

19. The wicked, therefore, walk round in circles, naturally wanting whatever will satisfy their desires, yet foolishly rejecting that which would lead them to their true end, which is not in consumption but in consummation. Hence they exhaust themselves in vain instead of perfecting their lives by a blessed end. They take more pleasure in the appearance of things than in their Creator, examining all and wanting to test them one by one before trying to reach the Lord of the universe. They might even succeed in doing so if they could ever gain hold of what they wish for; that is, if any one man could take possession of all things without him who is their Principle. By the very law of man's desire which makes him want what he lacks in place of what he has and grow weary of what he has in preference to what he lacks, once he has obtained and despised all in heaven and on earth, he will hasten toward the only one who is missing, the God of all. There he will rest, for just as there is no rest this side of eternity, so there will be no restlessness to bother him on the other side. Then he will say for sure: "It is good for me to adhere to God" (Ps. 72:28). He will even add to

that: "What is there for me in heaven and what have I desired on earth, if you?" (Ps. 72:25). And, also: "God of my heart, God, my lot forever" (Ps. 72:26). Therefore, as I said, whoever desires the greatest good can succeed in reaching it, if he can first gain possession of all he desires short of that good itself.

20. This is altogether impossible because life is too short, strength too weak, competition too keen, men too fatigued by the long road and vain efforts; wishing to attain all they desire, yet unable to reach the end of all their wants. If they could only be content with reaching all in thought and not in deed. They could easily do so and it would not be in vain, for man's mind is more comprehensive and subtle than his senses. It even anticipates the senses in all things and they dare not contact an object unless the mind approves its utility beforehand. I think this is what is alluded to in the text: "Test all and hold on to what is good" (1 Thess. 5:21). The mind looks ahead for the senses and these must not pursue their desires unless the mind gives its consent. Otherwise, you do not ascend the Lord's mountain or stand in his holy place, because you have received your soul in vain, that is, your rational soul; while you follow your senses like a dumb beast, your sleepy reason offers no resistance. Those who do not think ahead run alongside the road, they do not follow the Apostle's counsel: " . . . run, then to win . . ." (1 Cor. 9:24). When will they reach him whom they do not want to reach until they have tested all the rest? The desire to experience all things first is like a vicious circle, it goes on forever.

21. The just man is not like that. Hearing about the evil conduct of those who remain inside the circle (for many follow the wide road which leads to death), he prefers the royal road which turns neither to the right nor to the left. Finally the Prophet confirms: "The path of the just is straight, and straightforward for walking" (Isa. 26:7). These are the ones who take a salutary short-cut and avoid the dangerous, fruitless round-about way, choosing the shortened and shortening word, not desiring everything they see, but rather selling all they have and giving it to the poor. It is clear that "Blessed are the poor, for theirs is the kingdom of heaven" (Matt. 5:3). All run, indeed, but one must distinguish between

runners. At length, "The Lord knows the way of the just, the way of the wicked will perish" (Ps. 1:6). As a result, "Better is a little to the just than all the wealth of the wicked" (Ps. 36:16). As Wisdom says and folly learns, money never satisfies those who love it. Rather, ". . . they that hunger and thirst for justice will have their fill" (Matt. 5:6). Justice is the vital, natural food of the rational soul; money can no more lessen the mind's hunger than air can that of the body. If you see a hungry man open wide his mouth to the wind and puff up his cheeks with air to satisfy his hunger, will you not think he is out of his mind? It is no less folly to think a rational soul will be satisfied rather than merely puffed up by any kind of material goods. What do material things mean to the mind? The body cannot live on ideas or the mind subsist on meat. "Bless the Lord, my soul, he satisfies your desires with good things" (Ps. 102:1, 5). He satisfies with good things, he incites to good, maintains in goodness, anticipates, sustains, fulfills. He makes you desire, he is what you desire.

22. I said above that God is the reason for loving God. That is right, for he is the efficient and final cause of our love. He offers the opportunity, creates the affection, and consummates the desire. He makes, or rather is made himself lovable. He hopes to be so happily loved that he will not be loved in vain. His love prepares and rewards ours. Obligingly he leads the way; reasonably he requites us; he is our sweet hope. Rich for all who call on him, although he can give us nothing better than himself. He gave himself to merit for us; he keeps himself to be our reward; he serves himself as food for holy souls; he sold himself in ransom for captive souls. O Lord, you are so good to the soul who seeks you, what must you be to the one who finds you? More wonderful still, no one can seek you unless he has already found you. You wish to be found that you may be sought for, and sought for to be found. You may be sought and found, but nobody can forestall you. Even when we say: "In the morning my prayer will come before you" (Ps. 87:14), we must remember that, without our first receiving divine inspiration, all prayer becomes lukewarm. Let us now see where our love begins, for it has been shown where it ends.

VIII. 23. Love is one of the four natural passions. There is no need to name them, for they are well known. It would be right, however, for that which is natural to be first of all at the author of nature's service. That is why the first and greatest commandment is: "You shall love the Lord, your God . . ." (Matt. 22:37).

The First Degree of Love:
Man Loves Himself for His Own Sake

Since nature has become more fragile and weak, necessity obliges man to serve it first. This is carnal love by which a man loves himself above all for his own sake. He is only aware of himself; as St. Paul says: "What was animal came first, then what was spiritual" (1 Cor. 15:46). Love is not imposed by a precept; it is planted in nature. Who is there who hates his own flesh? Yet should love, as it happens, grow immoderate, and, like a savage current, burst the banks of necessity, flooding the fields of delight, the overflow is immediately stopped by the commandment which says: "You shall love your neighbor as yourself" (Matt. 22:39). It is just indeed that he who shares the same nature should not be deprived of the same benefits, especially that benefit which is grafted in that nature. Should a man feel overburdened at satisfying not only his brethren's just needs but also their pleasures, let him restrain his own if he does not want to be a transgressor. He can be as indulgent as he likes for himself providing he remembers his neighbor has the same rights. O man, the law of life and order imposes on you the restraint of temperance, lest you follow after your wanton desires and perish, lest you use nature's gifts to serve through wantonness the enemy of the soul. Would it not be more just and honorable to share them with your neighbor, your fellow man, than with your enemy? If, faithful to the Wiseman's counsel, you turn away from sensual delights and content yourself with the Apostle's teaching on food and clothing, you will soon be able to guard your love against "carnal desires which war against the soul" (1 Pet. 2:11) and I think you will not find it a burden to share with those of your nature that which you have withheld from the enemy of your soul. Then your love will be sober and just if you do not refuse your brother that which he needs of what you have denied yourself in pleasure. Thus carnal love becomes social when it is extended to others.

24. What would you do if, while helping out your neighbor, you find yourself lacking what is necessary for your life? What else can you do than to pray with all confidence to him "who gives abundantly and bears no grudges (Jas. 1:5), who opens his hand and fills with blessings every living being" (Ps. 144:16)? There is no doubt that he will assist us willingly in time of need, since he helps us so often in time of plenty. It is written: "Seek first the kingdom of God and his justice, and the rest will be added thereto" (Matt. 6:33; Luke 12:31). Without being asked he promises to give what is necessary to him who withholds from himself what he does not need and loves his neighbor. This is to seek the kingdom of God and implore his aid against the tyranny of sin, to prefer the yoke of chastity and sobriety rather than let sin reign in your mortal flesh. And again, it is only right to share nature's gifts with him who shares that nature with you.

25. Nevertheless, in order to love one's neighbor with perfect justice, one must have regard to God. In other words, how can one love one's neighbor with purity, if one does not love him in God? But it is impossible to love in God unless one loves God. It is necessary, therefore, to love God first; then one can love one's neighbor in God. Thus God makes himself lovable and creates whatever else is good. He does it this way. He who made nature protects it, for nature was created in a way that it must have its creator for protector. The world could not subsist without him to whom it owes its very existence. That no rational creature may ignore this fact concerning itself or dare lay claim through pride to benefits due the creator, by a deep and salutary counsel, the same creator wills that man be disciplined by tribulations so that when man fails and God comes to his help, man, saved by God, will render God the honor due him. It is written: "Call to me in the day of sorrow; I will deliver you, and you shall honor me" (Ps. 49:15). In this way, man who is animal and carnal, and knows how to love only himself, yet starts loving God for his own benefit, because he learns from frequent experience that he can do everything that is good for him in God and that without God he can do nothing good.

The Second Degree of Love:
Man Loves God for His Own Benefit

IX. 26. Man, therefore, loves God, but for his own advantage and not yet for God's sake. Nevertheless, it is a matter of prudence to know what you can do by yourself and what you can do with God's help to keep from offending him who keeps you free from sin. If man's tribulations, however, grow in frequency and as a result he frequently turns to God and is frequently freed by God, must he not end, even though he had a heart of stone in a breast of iron, by realizing that it is God's grace which frees him and come to love God not for his own advantage but for the sake of God?

The Third Degree of Love:
Man Loves God for God's Sake

Man's frequent needs oblige him to invoke God more often and approach him more frequently. This intimacy moves man to taste and discover how sweet the Lord is. Tasting God's sweetness entices us more to pure love than does the urgency of our own needs. Hence the example of the Samaritans who said to the woman who had told them the Lord was present: "We believe now not on account of what you said; for we have heard him and we know he is truly the Savior of the world" (John 4:42). We walk in their footsteps when we say to our flesh, "Now we love God, not because of your needs; for we have tasted and know how sweet the Lord is" (Ps. 33:9). The needs of the flesh are a kind of speech, proclaiming in transports of joy the good things experienced. A man who feels this way will not have trouble in fulfilling the commandment to love his neighbor. He loves God truthfully and so loves what is God's. He loves purely and he does not find it hard to obey a pure commandment, purifying his heart, as it is written, in the obedience of love. He loves with justice and freely embraces the just commandment. This love is pleasing because it is free. It is chaste because it does not consist of spoken words but of deed and truth. It is just because it renders what is received. Whoever loves this way, loves the way he is loved, seeking in turn not what is his but what belongs to Christ, the same way Christ sought not what was his, but what was

ours, or rather, ourselves. He so loves who says: "Confess to the Lord for he is good" (Ps. 117:1). Who confesses to the Lord, not because he is good to him but because the Lord is good, truly loves God for God's sake and not for his own benefit. He does not love this way of whom it is said: "He will praise you when you do him favors" (Ps. 48:19). This is the third degree of love: in it God is already loved for his own sake.

The Fourth Degree of Love:
Man Loves Himself for the Sake of God

X. 27. Happy the man who has attained the fourth degree of love, he no longer even loves himself except for God. "O God, your justice is like the mountains of God" (Ps. 35:7). This love is a mountain, God's towering peak. Truly indeed, it is the fat, fertile mountain. "Who will climb the mountain of the Lord?" (Ps. 23:3). "Who will give me the wings of a dove, that I may fly away to find rest?" (Ps. 54:7). "This place is made peaceful, a dwelling-place in Sion" (Ps. 75:3). "Alas for me, my exile has been lengthened" (Ps. 119:5). When will flesh and blood, this vessel of clay, this earthly dwelling, understand the fact? When will this sort of affection be felt that, inebriated with divine love, the mind may forget itself and become in its own eyes like a broken dish, hastening towards God and clinging to him, becoming one with him in spirit, saying: "My flesh and my heart have wasted away; O God of my heart, O God, my share for eternity" (Ps. 72:26). I would say that man is blessed and holy to whom it is given to experience something of this sort, so rare in life, even if it be but once and for the space of a moment. To lose yourself, as if you no longer existed, to cease completely to experience yourself, to reduce yourself to nothing is not a human sentiment but a divine experience. If any mortal, suddenly rapt, as has been said, and for a moment is admitted to this, immediately the world of sin envies him, the evil of the day disturbs him, the mortal body weighs him down, the needs of the flesh bother him, the weakness of corruption offers no support, and sometimes with greater violence than these, brotherly love calls him back. Alas, he has to come back to himself, to descend again into his being, and wretchedly cry out: "Lord, I suffer violence"

(Isa. 38:14), adding: "Unhappy man that I am, who will free me from this body doomed to death?" (Rom. 7:24).

28. All the same, since Scripture says God made everything for his own purpose, the day must come when the work will conform to and agree with its Maker. It is therefore necessary for our souls to reach a similar state in which, just as God willed everything to exist for himself, so we wish that neither ourselves nor other beings to have been nor to be except for his will alone; not for our pleasure. The satisfaction of our wants, chance happiness, delights us less than to see his will done in us and for us, which we implore every day in prayer saying: ". . . your will be done on earth as it is in heaven . . ." (Matt. 6:10). O pure and sacred love! O sweet and pleasant affection! O pure and sinless intention of the will, all the more sinless and pure since it frees us from the taint of selfish vanity, all the more sweet and pleasant, for all that is found in it is divine. It is deifying to go through such an experience. As a drop of water seems to disappear completely in a big quantity of wine, even assuming the wine's taste and color; just as red, molten iron becomes so much like fire it seems to lose its primary state; just as the air on a sunny day seems transformed into sunshine instead of being lit up; so it is necessary for the saints that all human feelings melt in a mysterious way and flow into the will of God. Otherwise, how will God be all in all if something human survives in man? No doubt, the substance remains though under another form, another glory, another power. When will this happen? Who will see it? Who will possess it? "When shall I come and when shall I appear in God's presence?" (Ps. 41:3). O my Lord, my God, "My heart said to you: my face has sought you; Lord, I will seek your face" (Ps. 26:8). Do you think I shall see your holy temple?

29. I do not think that can take place for sure until the word is fulfilled: "You will love the Lord your God with all your heart, all your soul, and all your strength" (Mark 12:30), until the heart does not have to think of the body and the soul no longer has to give it life and feeling as in this life. Freed from this bother, its strength is established in the power of God. For it is impossible to assemble all these and turn them toward God's face as long as the care of this weak and wretched body keeps one busy to the point of distraction. Hence it is in a spiritual and immortal body, calm and pleasant, subject to the spirit in everything, that the soul hopes to attain the fourth degree of love, or rather to be possessed by it; for it is in God's hands to give it to whom he wishes, it is not obtained by human efforts. I mean he will easily reach the highest degree of love when he will no longer be held back by any desire of the flesh or upset by troubles as he hastens with the greatest speed and desire toward the joy of the Lord. All the same, do we not think the holy martyrs received this grace, at least partially, while they were still in their victorious bodies? The strength of this love seized their souls so entirely that, despising the pain, they were able to expose their bodies to exterior torments. No doubt, the feeling of intense pain could only upset their calm; it could not overcome them.

XI. 30. But what about those souls which are already separated from their bodies? We believe they are completely engulfed in that immense ocean of eternal light and everlasting brightness.

The Condition of Souls after Death before the Resurrection

But if, which is not denied, they wish that they had received their bodies back or certainly if they desire and hope to receive them, there is no doubt that they have not altogether turned from themselves, for it is clear they still cling to something of their own to which their desires return though ever so slightly. Consequently, until death is swallowed up in victory and eternal light invades from all sides the limits of night and takes possession to the extent that heavenly glory shines in their bodies, souls cannot set themselves aside and pass into God. They are still attached to their bodies, if not by life and feeling, certainly by a natural affection, so that they do not wish nor are they able to realize their consummation without them. This rapture of the soul which is its most perfect and highest state, cannot, therefore, take place before the resurrection of the bodies, lest the spirit, if it could reach perfection without the body, would no longer desire to be united to the flesh. For indeed, the body is not deposed or resumed without profit for the soul. To be brief. "The death of his saints is precious in the sight of the Lord" (Ps. 115:15). If death is precious, what must life be, especially that life? Do not be surprised if the glorified body seems to give the spirit something, for it was a real help when man was sick and mortal. How true that text is which says that all things turn to the good of those who love God. The sick, dead and resurrected body is a help to the soul who loves God; the first for the fruits of penance, the second for repose, and the third for consummation. Truly the soul does not want to be perfected, without that from whose good services it feels it has benefited by in every way.

31. The flesh is clearly a good and faithful partner for a good spirit, it helps if it is burdened; it relieves if it does not help; it surely benefits and is by no means a burden. The first state is that of fruitful labor; the second is restful but by no means tiresome; the third is above all glorious. Listen to the bridegroom in the Canticle inviting us to this triple progress: "Eat, friends, and drink; be inebriated, dearest ones" (Song 5:1). He calls to those working in the body to eat; he invites those who have set aside their bodies to drink; and he impels those who have resumed their bodies to inebriate themselves, calling them his dearest ones, as if they were filled with charity. There is a difference between those who are simply called friends, who sigh under the weight of the flesh, who are held to be dear for their charity, and those who are free from the bonds of the flesh, who are all the more dear because they are more ready and free to love. More than the other two, these last ones are called dearest and are so. Receiving a second garment, they are in their resumed and glorified bodies. They are that much more freely and willingly borne toward God's love because nothing at all remains to solicit them or hold them back. This neither of the first two states can claim because, in the first state the body is endured with distress, in the second state it is hoped for as for something missing.

32. In the first state, therefore, the faithful soul eats its bread, but, alas, in the sweat of its brow. While in the flesh it moves by faith which necessarily acts through charity, for if it does not act, it dies. Moreover, according to our Savior, this work is food: "My food is to do the will of my Father" (John 4:34). Afterwards, having cast off its flesh, the soul no longer feeds on the bread of sorrow, but, having eaten, it is allowed to drink more deeply of the wine of love, not pure wine, for it is written of the bride in the Song of Songs: "I drank my wine mixed with milk" (Song 5:1). The soul mixes the divine love with the tenderness of that natural affection by which it desires to have its body back, a glorified body. The soul, therefore, glows already with the warmth of charity's wine, but not to the stage of intoxication, for the milk moderates its strength. Intoxication disturbs the mind and makes it wholly forgetful of itself, but the soul which still thinks of the resurrection of its own body has not forgotten itself completely. For the rest, after finding the only thing needed, what is there to prevent the soul from taking leave of itself and passing into God entirely, ceasing all the more to be like itself as it becomes more and more like God? Then only, the soul is allowed to drink wisdom's pure wine, of which it is said: "How good is my cup, it inebriates me!" (Ps. 22:5). Why wonder if the soul is inebriated by the riches of the Lord's dwelling, when free from worldly cares it can drink pure, fresh wine with Christ in his Father's house?

33. Wisdom presides over this triple banquet, composed of charity which feeds those who labor, gives drink to those who are resting, and inebriates those who reign. As at an earthly banquet, edibles are served before liquid refreshments. Nature has set this order which Wisdom also observes. First, indeed, up to our death, while we are in mortal flesh we eat the work of our hands, laboriously masticating what is to be swallowed. In the spiritual life after death, we drink with ease whatever is offered. Once our bodies come back to life we shall be filled with everlasting life, abounding in a wonderful fullness. This is what is meant by the Bridegroom in the Canticle saying: "Eat, my friends, and drink; dearest ones, be inebriated" (Song 5:1). Eat before death, drink after death, be inebriated after the resurrection. It is right to call them dearest who are drunk with love; they are rightly inebriated who deserve to be admitted to the nuptials of the Lamb, eating and drinking at his table in his kingdom when he takes his Church to him in her glory without a blemish, wrinkle, or any defect of the sort. By all means he will then intoxicate his dearest ones with the torrent of his

delight, for in the Bridegroom and bride's most passionate yet most chaste embrace, the force of the river's current gives joy to the city of God. I think this is nothing other than the Son of God who in passing waits on us as he in a way promised: "The just are feasting and rejoicing in the sight of God, delighting in their gladness" (Ps. 67:4). Here is fullness without disgust; here is insatiable curiosity without restlessness; here is that eternal, inexplicable desire knowing no want. At last, here is that sober intoxication of truth, not from overdrinking, not reeking with wine, but burning for God. From this then that fourth degree of love is possessed forever, when God alone is loved in the highest way, for now we do not love ourselves except for his sake, that he may be the reward of those who love him, the eternal recompense of those who love him forever.

66. Thomas of Celano,
First Life of Francis of Assisi

The son of a wealthy merchant, Francis of Assisi (1181/2-1226) undertook a literal obedience to the gospel such as some of the urban heretics of his time had done; but he cast himself instead as an obedient son of the church, and obtained Pope Innocent III's approval of his new religious order, the Friars Minor, in 1209. At the time of Francis's canonization in 1228, Pope Gregory IX (who as Cardinal Hugolino had been the order's first protector) commissioned the friar Thomas of Celano to write this vita, which carefully charts the emergence of Francis's sense of calling and the origins of the order.

[*After years of vanity and frivolous behavior, in his mid-twenties Francis has become more serious. Having begun to devote himself to prayer to discover the will of God for his life, one day he sets out for Foligno.*]

8. . . . [Francis] prepared his horse, mounted, and taking with him scarlet cloths [from his father's inventory] to sell, arrived in a hurry at the city called Foligno. There, as a successful merchant, he sold as usual all the goods he had brought, then got a price for the horse he had been riding, and left it behind. So having laid aside his burdens, he turned back, pondering with a devout mind what to do with the money. Soon, in a marvelous way, he was turned completely to the work of God, and feeling that to carry that money even for an hour would sorely oppress him, he hurried to get rid of it, considering all its benefits to be as so much sand. And as he was returning toward Assisi, he found by the wayside a church that had been built long ago in honor of St. Damian, but was in danger of collapsing soon from excessive age. 9. When Christ's new knight came to it he was moved with compassion for such need, and went in with awe and reverence. Finding a poor priest there, he kissed his hands with great faith, offered him the money he was carrying and explained, in order, his plans. The priest was amazed and, wondering at such a sudden change of circumstances, refused to believe what he heard. And because he thought he was being made sport of, he would not keep the offered money—for almost the day before, so to speak, he had seen Francis living riotously among his kinsfolk and acquaintance and surpassing the others in folly. But with obstinate persistence

SOURCE: *The Lives of S. Francis of Assisi by Brother Thomas of Celano*, tr. A. G. Ferrers Howell (London: Methuen, 1908), 10-12, 14-20, 22-24, 31-38, 42-45, as revised with reference to *Vita prima s. Francisci Assisiensis*, ed. a pp. Collegii S. Bonaventurae (Quaracchi: Ex typographia Collegii S. Bonaventurae, 1926).

Francis kept trying to gain credit for his words, praying and earnestly entreating the priest to let him stay with him for the Lord's sake. At last the priest agreed to this, but would not take the money for fear of Francis' parents; and the true despiser of money cast it on a windowsill, heeding it as little as dust. For he longed to possess wisdom, which is better than gold, and to get prudence, which is more precious than silver.

10. So while the servant of God Most High was dwelling in the aforesaid place his father went all round about like a diligent spy, wanting to know what was become of his son. And when he understood that his son was leading such a life in that place, he was inwardly grieved at heart, and very greatly disturbed at the sudden turn of events. Calling his friends and neighbors together, he hurried to the place where the servant of God was dwelling. But he, as a new athlete of Christ, upon hearing of the threats of his persecutors and getting wind of their coming, wanted to give place to wrath, and so concealed himself in a hidden pit that he had made ready for the purpose. That pit—known perhaps only to one person—was in the house, and there he lay constantly hidden for a month, so that he hardly dared come out for the human necessities. When food was given him he ate it in the secrecy of the pit, and every service was rendered to him secretly. He prayed constantly amid showers of tears that the Lord would deliver him from the hands of those who were persecuting his soul. In fasting and weeping he prevailed upon the mercy of the Savior to fulfill his devout wishes with kindly favor, and, distrusting his own efforts, cast all his care on the Lord; and though he was in darkness and in the pit yet he was filled with an ineffable gladness of which till then he had had no experience. Wholly fired by this gladness, he left the pit and exposed himself openly to the curses of his persecutors.

. . .

[Francis's father finds him then and imprisons him at home.]

13. When his father had departed for awhile from his home on business, the man of God remained bound and in confinement in the house; but his mother, who had been left alone at home with him, disapproved of what her husband had done, and spoke to her son kindly. And though she saw that she could not recall him from his purpose, she yearned over him with maternal compassion, and she loosed his chains and let him go free. But he, giving thanks to Almighty God, was moved to return to the place where he had been [i.e., the church of St. Damian]. But now he gave himself greater freedom, having been tested in the lessons of temptation; and his many struggles had given him a more cheerful countenance. The wrongs that had been done him had given him a more confident temper, and, with higher spirit than before, he went about freely everywhere. In the meantime his father came back, and, not finding his son, heaped sin on sin and turned upon his wife in violent reproach. Then, raging and blustering, he ran to the place where his son was, so that, if he could not call him back, he might at least drive him out of the province. But because the fear of the Lord is the confidence of strength, when the son of grace heard his carnal father coming to him, he went out to meet him, fearless and joyful. Of his own accord he called out that he cared nothing for his father's chains and beatings, and declared that he would gladly undergo any evils for the name of Christ.

14. But when his father saw that he would not be able to recall Francis from the journey he had begun, he was fully roused to get the money back. The man of God had wanted to offer it all to be spent on feeding the poor and on the repair of that church. But he who had no love for money as not to be misled by any show of good that it might bring, and, not being held back by any affection for it, he was not disturbed at the loss of it. Therefore when the money was found where it been thrown aside into the dust of the window by that greatest despiser of earthly things, that most eager searcher after heavenly riches, the raging father's fury was somewhat appeased, and the dew of the discovery somewhat slaked the thirst of his avarice. Then he brought his son before the bishop of the city, so that by a formal renunciation of all his property in the bishop's presence he might give back what he had. Francis not only did

not refuse to do this, but, with great rejoicing and a ready mind he hastened to do what was demanded of him.

15. When brought before the bishop, Francis would allow no delay nor did he hesitate in anything: but rather, without waiting to be spoken to and without speaking he immediately put off and cast aside all his clothes and gave them back to his father. Moreover he did not even keep his drawers but stripped himself stark naked before all the bystanders. But the bishop, observing his disposition, greatly admiring his fervor and steadfastness, got up immediately, gathered him into his arms and covered him with the mantle that he himself was wearing. He understood clearly that the counsel was of God, and perceived that the actions of the man of God that he was seeing at that moment enfolded a mystery. Immediately therefore the bishop became his helper, and, cherishing and encouraging him, he embraced him in the bowels of charity. . . .

16. He who formerly wore scarlet array was now going clad in scanty garments, and as he was singing praises to the Lord in French in a certain wood, some robbers suddenly rushed upon him. On their asking him in no friendly tone who he was, the man of God answered confidently with a loud voice, "I am a herald of the great King. What is that to you?" But they beat him and cast him into a pit filled with deep snow, saying, "Lie there, you clownish herald of God!" But he turned himself this way and that to shake off the snow, and when they went away he jumped out of the pit, and exhilarated by great joy, with a loud voice he began to fill the grove with praises to the Creator of all things. At length he reached a cloister of monks where he spent several days as a servant, wearing nothing but a wretched shirt, and desiring at least to get his fill of broth. But when, meeting with no pity there, he could not even get any old clothing, he left the place (not moved by anger but urged by need) and came to the city of Gubbio where he got a small tunic from a former friend of his. (But some time afterwards when the fame of the man of God was spreading everywhere and his name was noised abroad among the people, the prior of the aforesaid monastery remembered and realized how the man of God had been treated,

and came to him and for reverence of the Savior humbly begged forgiveness for himself and his monks.)

17. And then the holy lover of all humility took himself to the lepers, and was with them, serving them all most zealously for God's sake, washing all foulness from them and even wiping away the matter from the ulcers, "for," as he himself says in his Testament, "when I was in sin it seemed to me exceeding bitter to look on lepers, but the Lord brought me among them, and I showed mercy to them." For indeed at one time the sight of lepers was, as he used to say, so bitter to him that when in the days of his vanity he looked at their houses about two miles off, he stopped his nostrils with his hands. But when now by the grace and power of the Highest he was beginning to think of holy and profitable things, one day, while still in the habit of the world, he met a leper, and, having become stronger than himself, went near and kissed him.

Thereafter also he began to despise himself more and more, until by the Redeemer's mercy he attained to perfect conquest of himself. While remaining in the world and still following the world he was a helper of other poor also, stretching forth the hand of mercy to the destitute and pitying the afflicted. For one day when (contrary to his custom, for he was very courteous), he had upbraided a poor man who asked alms of him, immediately he was brought to penitence and began to say to himself that it was a great reproach and shame to deny the request of one asking in the name of so great a King. And then he settled it in his heart that in the future, according to his power, he would never deny anything to any one asking him for the sake of God. Which thing he most diligently performed and fulfilled, to the point that he gave himself fully and in every way [to others], becoming first a follower of that counsel of the Gospel which he himself would later teach: "Give to the one who asks of you (it says) and do not turn away from the one who would borrow from you" (Matt. 5:42).

18. Now the first work that blessed Francis undertook after having been delivered from the hand of his carnal father was to build a house for God: but he did not try to build it anew, but rather

repaired the old and restored the ancient; he did not pull up the foundation, but built upon it, always, though unwittingly, respecting the prerogative of Christ, for "no one can lay another foundation than that which has been laid, which is Christ Jesus" (1 Cor. 3:11). And when he had returned to the place where, as has been said, a church of St. Damian had been built in ancient times, he zealously repaired it in a short time, the grace of the Most High being with him. This is that blessed and holy place where, some six years after blessed Francis's conversion and by means of this same blessed man, the glorious religion and most excellent order of Poor Ladies and holy virgins had its happy beginning. Its foundation was Lady Clare, a native of the city of Assisi, a stone precious and strong above all the others of the pile. For when, after the beginning of the Order of the Brothers, that lady had been turned to God by the admonitions of the holy man, she lived for the advantage of many, and was an example for a countless multitude. . . .

[*Francis then repairs another church, that of St. Mary in Portiuncula.*]

22. One day in that church the Gospel lesson was read in which Christ sent his disciples out to preach. The saint of God, who was present, got some inkling of the Gospel words, and after the solemnities of Mass had been celebrated, he humbly begged the priest to explain the Gospel to him. When the priest had explained everything in order, and Francis had heard that Christ's disciples were not to possess gold, silver, or purse, nor to carry on their way a bag, wallet, bread or staff, nor to have shoes or two tunics, but to preach the Kingdom of God, and repentance, immediately he cried, rejoicing in the spirit of God: "This is what I wish, this is what I am seeking, this I desire in my inmost heart to do." Then the holy Father, overflowing with joy, hastens to fulfill that saving word, nor does he allow any delay before he begins devoutly to perform what he has heard. Straightaway he puts his shoes off from his feet, and the staff out of his hands, and, content with one tunic, exchanges his leather girdle for a small cord. Then he prepares a tunic for himself that

displays the image of the Cross, so that in it he may beat off all promptings of the devil; he makes it of the roughest material so that in it he may crucify the flesh with [its] vices and sins; lastly he makes it most poor and mean, so that it will in no way excite the world's covetousness . . .

23. Then with great fervor of spirit and joy of mind he began to preach repentance to all, edifying his hearers with simple words but largeness of heart. For his word was like a blazing fire piercing through the inmost heart, and it filled the minds of all with wonder. He seemed quite another man than he had been, and, gazing on heaven, he disdained to look on earth. . . . In all of his preaching, before he set forth God's word to the congregation he called for peace, saying, "The Lord give you peace"; and peace he always most devoutly proclaimed, to men and women, and to people who opposed each other. For that reason, many who had been haters of peace as well as of salvation embraced peace with their whole heart, with the Lord's help, and themselves became children of peace and zealots of eternal salvation.

. . .

[*Several young men join Francis. Francis prophesies the growth of the order. They all go out on preaching missions in pairs, and return.*]

32. Blessed Francis, seeing that the Lord God was daily increasing the number [of the friars] . . . wrote down simply and in few words for himself and for his present and future brothers a pattern and rule of life, using chiefly the language of the holy Gospel, whose perfection was the one thing he longed for. However he inserted a few other things necessarily concerned with the practice of a holy life. Then he came to Rome with all the said brothers, with the deep desire that what he had written might be confirmed by the Lord Pope Innocent III. . . . [He] waited upon the reverend Lord Bishop of Sabina, named John of St. Paul, who among the princes and great ones of the Roman Court appeared to despise earthly things and love heavenly things. This man received him with kindness and charity and warmly commended his will and purpose. 33. But, being a farseeing and judicious man, he began to question

St. Francis on many points, and urged him to embrace the life of a monk or of a hermit. St. Francis, however, as humbly as he could, refused to yield to the Cardinal's persuasion; not that he despised what had been urged upon him; but in his pious longing for another course of life he was carried on by a still loftier desire. The Cardinal marveled at his fervor, and fearing that he might flinch from so stern a purpose, pointed out easier paths. At length, overcome by the steadfastness of St. Francis's entreaties, he gave in, and after that zealously promoted his business with the Pope. At that time the Lord Pope Innocent III ruled over the Church, a glorious man, one moreover of abundant learning, renowned in discourse, fervent in zeal for righteousness in those things required by the business of promoting the Christian faith. When he knew the wish of the men of God, after first examining the matter, he granted their request and carried it into complete effect: and then, encouraging and admonishing them concerning many things, he blessed St. Francis and his brothers, and said to them: "Go, and the Lord be with you, brothers, and as he shall deign to inspire you, preach repentance to all. And when the Lord Almighty shall multiply you in number and in grace, report it to me with joy, and I will grant you more than this and shall with more confidence entrust greater things to you." . . .

34. St. Francis with his brothers, greatly exulting in the gift and favor of so great a father and lord, gave thanks to almighty God who sets the humble on high and cheers the sorrowful with deliverance. And he went immediately to visit the threshold of St. Peter; and, having finished his prayer, he left the city and set out with his companions on the journey toward the valley of Spoleto. And as they thus went along they talked together of what great gifts the most merciful God had given them; of their gracious reception by the Vicar of Christ, the lord and father of all Christendom; of their power to fulfill his admonitions and commands; of how they might sincerely observe and unfailingly guard the Rule they had received; of how they should walk in all holiness and religion before the Most High; and finally of how their life and behavior might, by increase of the holy virtues, be an example to their neighbors. . . .

35. . . . They discussed together, those true followers of righteousness, whether they ought to live among people, or gather in solitary places. But St. Francis, who did not trust in his own efforts, but anticipated all matters with holy prayer, chose not to live for himself alone, but for Him who died for all, knowing himself to have been sent for this, that he might gain for God souls that the devil was trying to take away.

. . .

[*Francis preaches and many are converted; the friars followed his example of humility, poverty, and patience.*]

42. The blessed Francis and the other brothers gathered again at a place called Rivo Torto near the city of Assisi. In that place there was a forsaken hovel beneath whose shelter those most strenuous despisers of large and beautiful houses lived, protecting themselves from storms of rain. For, as a saint has said, one ascends to heaven more quickly from a hovel than from a palace. All his sons and brothers lived with the blessed father there in that one place, laboring greatly and lacking everything; very often, wholly deprived of the solace of bread, they were content with turnips only, which in their distress they begged for here and there over the plain of Assisi. Their dwelling was so extremely cramped that they could scarcely sit down or rest in it. There was no sound of murmur or complaint at these things; but their heart being at peace, their mind was filled with joy and kept them patient. St. Francis most carefully examined himself and his companions daily, indeed continually; he would not allow any lewdness to linger in them, and drove away all negligence from their hearts. Rigid in discipline, he guarded himself watchfully at every hour; for if ever (as is usual) any fleshly temptation assailed him he would plunge in winter into a pit full of ice and remain there until all fleshly taint withdrew from him. And the others most eagerly followed the example of such mortification. 43. He taught them not only to mortify vices and to keep down the promptings of the flesh but also to control even the outward organs of sense, through which death

enters the soul. For when at that time the Emperor Otto [IV] was passing through those parts with great stir and pomp, to receive the crown of the earthly Empire, the most holy father and his companions in the said hovel were close to the road by which the Emperor was passing; but he did not go out to look, nor did he allow any others to do so, except for one, who was to announce [to the Emperor] very firmly that this glory of his would endure but for a short time. . . .

44. . . . One day while they were living there, a man leading an ass chanced to come to the shelter where the man of God was dwelling with his companions, and in order not to be driven away, he urged his ass to go in, saying these words: "Go in, for we shall do good to this place." When St. Francis heard these words and perceived what the man meant, he was moved in spirit; for the man thought that the brothers intended to stay there [as owners] in order to enlarge the place, and "add house to house." And St. Francis immediately went out from there, and abandoned that hovel, because of what the peasant had said, and he removed to another place not far from it called Portiuncula, where . . . the Church of St. Mary was, which he had repaired long before. He would have nothing in the way of property so that he might the more fully possess all things in the Lord.

45. At that time the brothers entreated St. Francis to teach them to pray, because, walking in simplicity of spirit, they did not as yet know the offices of the Church. And he said to them: "When you pray, say, 'Our Father' and 'We worship you, O Christ, [here] and at all your churches which are in all the world, and we bless you; by your holy

Cross you have redeemed the world.'" And this the brothers, dutiful disciples of their master, were most careful to observe, for not only those things which blessed Francis told them by way of brotherly advice or fatherly command, but even those things which he was thinking of or meditating on, if they could get to know them by any token, they strove most effectually to fulfill. For their blessed father used to tell them that true obedience is not only uttered, but thought out; not only enjoined, but desired. That is, if a subject brother should not only hear the voice of a superior brother but should understand his will, he ought forthwith to concentrate himself wholly on obedience and do what he understands by any sign to be the superior's will.

Moreover, in whatever place a church might be built, even if they were not present there, yet if they could see it from afar they bowed down toward it flat on the ground, and inclining the inward and the outward man, worshipped the Almighty, saying, "We worship you, O Christ, [here] and at all your churches," as the holy father had taught them. And (a thing not less to be wondered at) wherever they saw a cross, or a mark of a cross, whether on the ground, on a wall, on trees, or in hedges by the way, they did that same thing. 46. For holy simplicity had so filled them, innocence of life was so teaching them, purity of heart so possessed them, that they were utterly ignorant of duplicity of mind. For as they were one in faith, so they were one in spirit, one in will, one in charity: agreement in disposition, harmonious behavior, the practice of the virtues, conformity of mind and piety in action always prevailed among them.

67. Thomas Aquinas on the Existence of God

The Dominican Thomas Aquinas (ca. 1225-1274), whose thought has had a preeminent place in subsequent Catholic tradition, attained great stature as a theologian already in his own lifetime. These excerpts from his synthesis

SOURCE: Thomas Aquinas, *Summa Theologica*, vol. 1, tr. English Dominicans (London: Burns, Oates and Washburne, 1920), 22-27.

of Christian theology, Summa Theologiae, *illustrate the dialectical form of argument typical of high-medieval scholasticism. Thomas momentously affirmed that human reason, understood in Aristotelian fashion as proceeding from sense perception, can attain to some of the truths known otherwise from divine revelation (as here in respect to God's existence), and moreover will not contradict those revealed truths to which it cannot attain.*

Second Article
Whether It Can Be Demonstrated That God Exists?

We proceed thus to the Second Article:—

Objection 1. It seems that the existence of God cannot be demonstrated. For it is an article of faith that God exists. But what is of faith cannot be demonstrated, because a demonstration produces scientific knowledge; whereas faith is of the unseen (Heb. 11:1). Therefore it cannot be demonstrated that God exists.

Obj. 2. Further, the essence is the middle term of demonstration. But we cannot know in what God's essence consists, but solely in what it does not consist; as Damascene (*De Fid. Orth.* 1.4). Therefore we cannot demonstrate that God exists.

Obj. 3. Further, if the existence of God were demonstrated, this could only be from His effects. But His effects are not proportionate to Him, since He is infinite and His effects are finite; and between the finite and infinite there is no proportion. Therefore, since a cause cannot be demonstrated by an effect not proportionate to it, it seems that the existence of God cannot be demonstrated.

On the contrary, The Apostle says: *The invisible things of Him are clearly seen, being understood by the things that are made* (Rom. 1:20). But this would not be unless the existence of God could be demonstrated through the things that are made; for the first thing we must know of anything is, whether it exists.

I answer that, Demonstration can be made in two ways: One is through the cause, and is called *a priori,* and this is to argue from what is prior absolutely. The other is through the effect, and is called a demonstration *a posteriori*; this is to argue from what is prior relatively only to us. When an effect is better known to us than its cause, from the effect we proceed to the knowledge of the cause. And from every effect the existence of its proper cause can be demonstrated, so long as its effects are better known to us; because since every effect depends upon its cause, if the effect exists, the cause must pre-exist. Hence the existence of God, insofar as it is not self-evident to us, can be demonstrated from those of His effects which are known to us.

Reply Obj. 1. The existence of God and other like truths about God, which can be known by natural reason, are not articles of faith, but are preambles to the articles; for faith presupposes natural knowledge, even as grace presupposes nature, and perfection supposes something that can be perfected. Nevertheless, there is nothing to prevent a man, who cannot grasp a proof, accepting, as a matter of faith, something which in itself is capable of being scientifically known and demonstrated.

Reply Obj. 2. When the existence of a cause is demonstrated from an effect, this effect takes the place of the definition of the cause in proof of the cause's existence. This is especially the case in regard to God, because, in order to prove the existence of anything, it is necessary to accept as a middle term the meaning of the word, and not its essence, for the question of its essence follows on the question of its existence. Now the names given to God are derived from His effects; consequently, in demonstrating the existence of God from His effects, we may take for the middle term the meaning of the word "God."

Reply Obj. 3. From effects not proportionate to the cause no perfect knowledge of that cause can be obtained. Yet from every effect the existence of the cause can be clearly demonstrated, and so we can demonstrate the existence of God from His effects; though from them we cannot perfectly know God as He is in His essence.

Third Article
Whether God Exists?

We proceed thus to the Third Article:—

Objection 1. It seems that God does not exist; because if one of two contraries be infinite, the other would be altogether destroyed. But the word "God" means that He is infinite goodness. If, therefore, God existed, there would be no evil discoverable; but there is evil in the world. Therefore God does not exist.

Obj. 2. Further, it is superfluous to suppose that what can be accounted for by a few principles has been produced by many. But it seems that everything we see in the world can be accounted for by other principles, supposing God did not exist. For all natural things can be reduced to one principle, which is nature; and all voluntary things can be reduced to one principle, which is human reason, or will. Therefore there is no need to suppose God's existence.

On the contrary, It is said in the person of God: *I am Who am* (Exod. 3:14).

I answer that, The existence of God can be proved in five ways.

The first and more manifest way is the argument from motion. It is certain, and evident to our senses, that in the world some things are in motion. Now whatever is in motion is put in motion by another, for nothing can be in motion except it is in potentiality to that towards which it is in motion; whereas a thing moves inasmuch as it is in act. For motion is nothing else than the reduction of something from potentiality to actuality. But nothing can be reduced from potentiality to actuality, except by something in a state of actuality. Thus that which is actually hot, as fire, makes wood, which is potentially hot, to be actually hot, and thereby moves and changes it. Now it is not possible that the same thing should be at once in actuality and potentiality in the same respect, but only in different respects. For what is actually hot cannot simultaneously be potentially hot; but it is simultaneously potentially cold. It is therefore impossible that in the same respect and in the same way a thing should be both mover and moved, i.e., that it should move itself. Therefore, whatever is in motion must be put in motion by another. If that

by which it is put in motion be itself put in motion, then this also must needs be put in motion by another, and that by another again. But this cannot go on to infinity, because then there would be no first mover, and, consequently, no other mover; seeing that subsequent movers move only inasmuch as they are put in motion by the first mover; as the staff moves only because it is put in motion by the hand. Therefore it is necessary to arrive at a first mover, put in motion by no other; and this everyone understands to be God.

The second way is from the nature of the efficient cause. In the world of sense we find there is an order of efficient causes. There is no case known (neither is it, indeed, possible) in which a thing is found to be the efficient cause of itself; for so it would be prior to itself, which is impossible. Now in efficient causes it is not possible to go on to infinity; because in all efficient causes following in order, the first is the cause of the intermediate cause, and the intermediate is the cause of the ultimate cause, whether the intermediate cause be several, or one only. Now to take away the cause is to take away the effect. Therefore, if there be no first cause among efficient causes, there will be no ultimate, nor any intermediate cause. But if in efficient causes it is possible to go on to infinity, there will be no first efficient cause, neither will there be an ultimate effect, nor any intermediate efficient causes; all of which is plainly false. Therefore it is necessary to admit a first efficient cause, to which everyone gives the name of God.

The third way is taken from possibility and necessity, and runs thus. We find in nature things that are possible to be and not to be, since they are found to be generated, and to corrupt, and consequently, they are possible to be and not to be. But it is impossible for these always to exist, for that which is possible not to be at some time is not. Therefore, if everything is possible not to be, then at one time there could have been nothing in existence. Now if this were true, even now there would be nothing in existence, because that which does not exist only begins to exist by something already existing. Therefore, if at one time nothing was in existence, it would have been impossible for anything to have begun to exist; and thus even now nothing would be in existence—which is absurd.

Therefore, not all beings are merely possible, but there must exist something the existence of which is necessary. But every necessary thing either has its necessity caused by another, or not. Now it is impossible to go on to infinity in necessary things which have their necessity caused by another, as has been already proved in regard to efficient causes. Therefore we cannot but postulate the existence of some being having of itself its own necessity, and not receiving it from another, but rather causing in others their necessity. This all men speak of as God.

The fourth way is taken from the gradation to be found in things. Among beings there are some more and some less good, true, noble, and the like. But "more" and "less" are predicated of different things, according as they resemble in their different ways something which is the maximum, as a thing is said to be hotter according as it more nearly resembles that which is hottest; so that there is something which is truest, something best, something noblest, and, consequently, something which is uttermost being; for those things that are greatest in truth are greatest in being, as it is written in *Metaph.* 2. Now the maximum in any genus is the cause of all in that genus; as fire, which is the maximum of heat, is the cause of all hot things. Therefore there must also be something which is to all beings the cause of their being, goodness, and every other perfection; and this we call God.

The fifth way is taken from the governance of the world. We see that things which lack intelligence, such as natural bodies, act for an end, and this is evident from their acting always, or nearly always, in the same way, so as to obtain the best result. Hence it is plain that not fortuitously, but designedly, do they achieve their end. Now whatever lacks intelligence cannot move towards an end, unless it be directed by some being endowed with knowledge and intelligence; as the arrow is shot to its mark by the archer. Therefore some intelligent being exists by whom all natural things are directed to their end; and this being we call God.

Reply Obj. 1. As Augustine says (*Enchir.* 11): *Since God is the highest good, He would not allow any evil to exist in His works, unless His omnipotence and goodness were such as to bring good even out of evil.* This is part of the infinite goodness of God, that He should allow evil to exist, and out of it produce good.

Reply Obj. 2. Since nature works for a determinate end under the direction of a higher agent, whatever is done by nature must needs be traced back to God, as to its first cause. So also whatever is done voluntarily must also be traced back to some higher cause other than human reason or will, since these can change and fail; for all things that are changeable and capable of defect must be traced back to an immovable and self-necessary first principle, as was shown in the body of the *Article.*

68. Letters and Visions of Hadewijch of Brabant

Nothing is known of the life of the thirteenth-century writer Hadewijch of Brabant apart from her surviving letters, poems, and visionary narratives. She was probably a beguine, perhaps the head of a community of beguines, from which she was obliged to depart (as Letter 29 *suggests) for reasons that remain unclear. She characteristically explored mystical experience using a*

SOURCE: Hadewijch, *The Complete Works*, tr. Columba Hart, O.S.B. (New York: Paulist Press, 1983), 56-63, 114-15, 280-82, 289-93. Copyright © The Missionary Society of St. Paul the Apostle in the State of New York. Used by permission of Paulist Press, Inc., New York/Mahwah, N.J.

language of love (Minne) borrowed in part from courtly literature, and she treated in a fresh and profound way such typical themes of late-medieval spirituality as the imitation of Christ and devotion to the Eucharist.

Letter 6

To Live Christ

1. I wish to put you on your guard this time against one thing from which much harm results. I tell you that this is now one of the most pernicious evils that are found among souls, of all the evils found there, which are still numerous everywhere: Everyone wishes to demand fidelity from others and to test his friend, and continually complains on the subject of fidelity. These are the occupations souls are now living in, when they ought to be tendering high love to the God of all greatness!

11. If someone desires the good and wishes to uplift his life in God's sublimity, why is he preoccupied about who treats him with fidelity or infidelity, and whether he should be thankful or reproachful toward one who does evil or good to him? The man who fails in fidelity or justice toward another is the one who suffers the greatest harm; and the worst of it is that he himself lacks the sweetness of fidelity.

19. If anyone, no matter who, behaves toward you with fidelity and helps you in the things you need, do not fail to thank him and to render him service in return; but serve and love God more heartily because someone is faithful, and as far as thanking or not thanking goes, leave that to God. For he is just in himself, and it lies in his power to take and give what is right: For he is in the height of his fruition, and we are in the abyss of our privation. I mean you and I, who have not yet become what we are, and have not grasped what we have, and still remain so far from what is ours. We must, without sparing, lose all for all; and learn uniquely and intrepidly the perfect life of Love, who has urged on both of us to her work.

36. O dear child! First and above all I entreat you that you keep yourself from instability, for nothing could or can separate you from our Lord so quickly as instability.

40. And, also, do not be so self-willed in your-self at any unpleasantness that you ever let yourself doubt, in future, that anything less than the great God totally shall be yours in the being of love, so that doubt or self-will makes you neglect any good action. For if you abandon yourself to Love, you will soon attain full growth. And if you remain in doubt, you will become slothful and unwilling, so that everything you ought to do will be unwelcome to you. Do not be anxious about anything; and amid the tasks that lead to your goal, do not think there is anything so high that you cannot surely surmount it, or so remote that you cannot surely reach it. So you must be ardent and persistent, with ever new strength.

54. If you see a man who meets the needs of love and wishes eagerly to come to it, and consequently suffers misery and many griefs, be generous to him so far as lies in you, and pour yourself out in helping him—your heart in merciful kindness, your reasoning power in consolation, and your members in energetic service. Toward sinners be compassionate, with fervent petitions to God; but do not take on yourself to keep reciting prayers for them or earnestly wish that God withdraw them from that state; for you would waste your time, and in other respects it would not be of much use.

67. Those who already love God, you can sustain with love, helping to strengthen them so that their God may be loved; this is profitable, but nothing else is. And for the lowest, who are sinners and estranged from God, neither efforts nor prayers to God are profitable, but rather the love we give to God. And the stronger that love is, the more it frees sinners from their sins and gives security to those who love.

76. To live sincerely according to the will of Love is to be so perfectly one in the will of veritable Love, in order to content her, that—even if one had another wish—one would choose or wish nothing except to desire above all what Love wills, no matter who is condemned or blessed by it. And a person should consent to be deprived of repose

and pleasure for no other reason than that he knows he has not grown sufficiently in love.

86. We must be continually aware that noble service and suffering in exile are proper to man's condition; such was the share of Jesus Christ when he lived on earth as Man. We do not find it written anywhere that Christ ever, in his entire life, had recourse to his Father or his omnipotent Nature to obtain joy and repose. He never gave himself any satisfaction, but continually undertook new labors from the beginning of his life to the end. He said this himself to a certain person who is still living, whom he also charged to live according to his example, and to whom he himself said that this was the true justice of Love: where Love is, there are always great labors and burdensome pains. Love, nevertheless, finds all pains sweet: *Qui amat non laborat*; that is, he who loves does not labor.

102. When Christ lived on earth as Man, all his works had their time (John 7:6). When the hour came (John 2:4), he acted; in words, in deeds, in preaching, in doctrine, in reprimands, in consolation, in miracles, and in penance; and in labors, in pains, in shame, in calumny, in anguish, and in distress, even to the passion, and even to death. In all these things he patiently awaited his time. And when the hour came in which it befitted him to act, he was intrepid and powerful in consummating his work; and he paid, by the service of perfect fidelity, the debt of human nature to the Father's divine truth. *Then mercy and truth met together, and justice and peace kissed each other* (Ps. 84:11).

117. With the Humanity of God you must live here on earth, in the labors and sorrow of exile, while within your soul you love and rejoice with the omnipotent and eternal Divinity in sweet abandonment.

120. For the truth of both is one single fruition. And just as Christ's Humanity surrendered itself on earth to the will of the Majesty, you must here with Love surrender yourself to both in unity. Serve humbly under their sole power, stand always before them prepared to follow their will in its entirety, and let them bring about in you whatever they wish.

128. Do not, then, undertake anything else. But serve the Humanity with prompt and faithful hands and with a will courageous in all virtues.

Love the Divinity not merely with devotion but with unspeakable desires, always standing with new ardor before the terrible and wonderful countenance in which Love reveals herself and engulfs all works. Read in that most holy countenance all your judgments and all you have done in your life. Set aside all the melancholy to which you have yielded, and renounce the cowardice that is in you; prefer wandering in continual exile far from the Beloved to coming out (after the enjoyment of much happiness) somewhere below him. All your perfection depends on this: shunning every alien enjoyment, which is something less than God himself; and shunning every alien suffering, which is not exclusively for his sake.

146. O be most compassionate in all things! For myself this is urgently necessary. And turn with an upright will toward the Supreme Truth. We have an upright will when we wish no object or enjoyment, in heaven or on earth, in our soul or in our body, except those alone for which God has loved and chosen us (cf. Col. 3:2).

153. And count this the most important thing for you, without needing to question anyone: to stand always ready for God's good pleasure, sparing no trouble, without fearing that anyone might remark it, whether in mockery or reproach, anger or zeal.

158. Whether you make a good impression or a bad impression, do not renounce truth in your good works. We can willingly put up with derision when it is aimed at good works in which we recognize God's will; we can also willingly put up with praise that follows on virtues in which the sublimity of our God is honored. The affliction of our sweet God which he suffered when he lived as Man, merits our gladly bearing for his sake all affliction and every sort of derision; and it even merits our desiring every sort of affliction. And the eternal Nature of his sweet love also merits that each of us should perform with perfect good will the virtues in which God our Beloved is honored.

172. Do not shirk, therefore, either disgrace or honor. For all that we can suffer or accomplish is welcome to Love's insatiableness. For Love is that burning fire which devours everything and shall never, never cease in all the endless ages to come.

178. And since you are still young and as yet have had nothing to suffer, you must make the strongest efforts to grow as if out of nothing, like one who has nothing and who can attain nothing unless he struggles from the depths of his being. And whatever works you are able to accomplish, always fall back into the abyss of humility. That is what God wishes of you: that you walk at all times in humility of behavior with all the people with whom you associate on the way. And rise above all the low things that are something less than God himself if you wish to become what he wills you to be: that is your peace in the totality of your nature.

191. If you wish to follow your being in which God created you, you must in noble-mindedness fear no difficulty; and so in all hardihood and pride you must neglect nothing, but you should valiantly lay hold on the best part—I mean, the great totality of God—as your own good. And so must you also give generously, according to your wealth, and make all the poor rich: for veritable Charity never fails to prevail over those who began with the pride of their whole will; so that she gives truly what she wishes to give, overcomes what she wishes to overcome, and maintains what she wishes to maintain.

204. O dear child! I entreat you now that you will always work without grumbling, purely with your will accompanied by all the perfect virtues, in every good work small or great. And do not wish or demand any favor from God, either for your needs or for your friends; do not ask him for spiritual joys in any sort of repose or consolation, unless this is as he himself wills. Let him come and go according to his holy will, and let him do, as his sublimity demands, all his will with you and with all those whom you long to instruct in his love.

215. Both for your interests and for theirs you must desire his will; if you pray for them, do not pray for what they choose in accordance with their own sense of values. Under cover of holy desires, the majority of souls today go astray and find their refreshment in an inferior consolation that they can grasp. This is a great pity.

222. Be careful therefore to choose and love God's will aright in all things, in what concerns you or concerns your friends, as well as in what concerns God, whereas you would most gladly receive from him something that gave you pleasure, by which you might live out your time in consolation and repose.

227. Nowadays this is the way everyone loves himself; people wish to live with God in consolations and repose, in wealth and power, and to share the fruition of his glory. We all indeed wish to be God with God, but God knows there are few of us who want to live as men with his Humanity, or want to carry his cross with him, or want to hang on the cross with him and pay humanity's debt to the full. Indeed we can rightly discern this as regards ourselves, in that we are so little able to hold out against suffering in all respects. An unexpected sorrow, though slight, goes to our heart; or a slander, or a lie that people tell about us; or someone's robbing us of our honor, or our rest, or our own will: How quickly and deeply any of this wounds us all! And we know so well what we want or do not want, there are so many things and kinds of things for which we have an attraction or an aversion: now alike, now different; now sweetness, now bitterness; now here, now there; now off, now on; and as regards everything, we are so ready to provide for ourselves where any repose for us is in sight!

249. This is why we remain unenlightened in our views, inconstant in our whole manner of acting, and unreliable in our reason and our understanding. So we wander, poor and unhappy, exiled and robbed of everything, on the rough roads of a foreign land (Luke 15:11-20). And we all had little need of doing so, were it not that illusions assail us on every side. By this we show plainly that we do not live with Christ as he lived; neither do we forsake all as Christ did, nor are we forsaken by all as Christ was. We can discern this in many ways: for we strain every nerve in our own interests where anything can fall to our share, and we strive after honor wherever possible; we gladly carry our own will into effect, we esteem and love ourselves in our pleasure, and we gladly seize our outward and inward advantages. For every advantage fills us with delight and convinces us that we are something; and precisely through this conviction we become nothing at all. And thus we ruin ourselves in all respects: We do not live with Christ, and we do not carry that cross with the Son of God, but

we carry it with Simon who received pay because he carried our Lord's cross (Matt. 27:32).

274. So it is with our struggles and our suffering: for we demand God as a reward for our good works, and we wish to feel him present in this life, on the supposition that we have truly merited this, and consequently that he, in his turn, should rightly do what we want him to. We hold in great esteem what we do or suffer for him, and we never resign ourselves to being left without recompense, or without knowing and feeling that it pleases God; we very quickly accept from him pay in the hand, namely satisfaction and repose; we also accept pay a second time in our self-complacency; and a third time, when we are satisfied that we have pleased others, and we accept commendation, honor, and praise from them.

290. All this is to carry that cross with Simon, who carried the cross a short time; but he did not die on it. Thus it is with the people who live as I have just said—even if in their neighbor's eyes their behavior may be lofty and their works glorious and manifest, so that at times they appear to lead a life sincere and holy, nobly ordered and adorned with the moral virtues—God, all the same, has little pleasure in it; for they do not stand firm, and they do not go all the way to the end. Just when they shine forth, they quickly break down; the smallest obstacle they encounter shows what their soul's depths really are. In sweetness they are quickly elated, and in bitterness they are dejected, because they are not established in the truth; the depths of their soul continue untrustworthy and unstable. Whatever they erect on such a foundation, they remain inconstant and untrustworthy in their works and in their being. They neither stand firm nor go to the end, and they do not die with Christ. For although they practice virtues, their intentions are neither pure nor trustworthy; for there is an intermingling of many untruths, which so falsify the virtues that they no longer have the power to direct man aright, or enlighten him, or keep him in firm and constant truth, in which he must possess his eternity.

316. For it is man's obligation to practice virtues, not in order to obtain consideration, or joy, or wealth, or rank, or any enjoyment in heaven or on earth, but solely out of homage to the incomparable sublimity of God, who created our nature to this end and made it for his own honor and praise, and for our bliss in eternal glory.

324. This is the way on which the Son of God took the lead, and of which he himself gave us knowledge and understanding when he lived as Man. For from the beginning to the end of the time he spent on earth, he did and perfectly accomplished, amid multiplicity, the will of the Father in all things and at all times, with all that he was, and with all the service he could perform (Matt. 20:28), in words and works, in joy and pain, in grandeur and abasement, in miracles, and in the distress of bitter death. With his whole heart and his whole soul, and with all his strength (Deut. 6:5), in each and every circumstance, he was ready to perfect what was wanting on our part. And thus he uplifted us and drew us up by his divine power and his human justice to our first dignity, and to our liberty (Gal. 4:31), in which we were created and loved, and to which we are now called (Gal. 5:13) and chosen in his predestination (Eph. 1:4-5), in which he had foreseen us from all eternity.

344. The sign that anyone possesses grace is a holy life. The sign of predestination is the pure and genuine impulse by which the heart is borne, in living confidence and unspeakable desires, toward God's honor and toward what befits the incomprehensible divine sublimity.

350. That cross which we must bear with the Son of the living God (Matt. 12:38) is the sweet exile that we bear for the sake of veritable Love, during which we must await with longing confidence the festival when Love shall manifest herself and reveal her noble power and rich omnipotence on earth and in heaven. In this she shows herself so unreservedly to him who loves that she makes him beside himself; she robs him of heart and mind, and causes him to die to himself and live in devotion to veritable Love.

361. But before Love thus bursts her dikes, and before she ravishes man out of himself and so touches him with herself that he is one spirit and one being with her and in her, he must offer her noble service and the life of exile—noble service in

all works of virtue, and a life of exile in all obedi-ence. And thus we must always persevere with renewed ardor: with hands ever ready for all works in which virtue is practiced, our will ready for all virtues in which Love is honored, without other intention than to render Love her proper place in man, and in all creatures according to their due. This is to be crucified with Christ (Gal. 2:19), to die with him, and to rise again with him (Col. 3:1). To this end he must always help us; I pray him for this, calling upon his supreme good-ness.

Letter 29
Hadewijch Evicted

1. God be with you! and may he give you con-solation with the veritable consolation of himself, with which he suffices to himself and to all crea-tures according to their being and their deserts. O sweet child, your sadness, dejection, and grief give me pain! And this I entreat you urgently, and exhort you, and counsel you, and command you as a mother commands her dear child, whom she loves for the supreme honor and sweetest dignity of Love, to cast away from you all alien grief, and to grieve for my sake as little as you can. What happens to me, whether I am wandering in the country or put in prison—however it turns out, it is the work of Love.

14. I know well, also, that I am not the cause of such grief to you; and I am close to you in heart, and trusted; and for me, you—after Sara—are the dearest person alive. Therefore I well understand that you cannot easily leave off grieving over my disgrace. But be aware, dear child, that this is an alien grief. Think about it yourself; if you believe with all your heart that I am loved by God, and he is doing his work in me, secretly or openly, and that he renews his old wonders in me (cf. Ecclus. 36:6), you must also be aware that these are doings of Love, and that this must lead aliens to wonder at me and abhor me. For they cannot work in the domain of Love, because they know neither her coming nor her going. And with these persons I have little shared their customs in their eating, drinking, or sleeping; I have not dressed up in their clothes, or colors, or outward magnificence.

And from all the things that can gladden the human heart, from what it can obtain or receive, I never derived joy except for brief moments from the experience of the Love that conquers all.

38. But from its first awakening and upward turning, my enlightened reason (which, ever since God revealed himself in it, has enlightened me as to whatever in myself and in others was lacking in perfection) showed me and led me to the place where I am to have fruition of my Beloved in unity according to the worthiness of my ascent.

44. This place of Love which enlightened rea-son showed me, was so far above human thought that I was obliged to understand I might no longer have joy or grief in anything, great or small, except in this, that I was a human being, and that I expe-rienced Love with a loving heart; but that, since God is so great, I with my humanity may touch the Godhead without attaining fruition.

52. This desire of unattainable fruition, which Love has always given me for the sake of fruition of Love, has injured me and wounded me in the breast and in the heart: in *armariolo et in antisma*. *Amariolo*—that is, the innermost of the arteries of the heart, with which we love; and *antisma*—that is, the innermost of the spirits by which we live, and the one sensitive to the greatest preoccupa-tion.

61. I have lived with these persons nevertheless with all the works I could perform in their service. And they found me prepared with ready virtue for all their needs. This was no doubt unjustifiably. I have also been with them in all things; since God first touched me with the totality of love, I have felt everyone's need according to what he was. With God's charity I have felt and given favor to each one according to that person's needs. With his wisdom I have felt his mercy, and why one must forgive people so much, and how they fall and get up again; and how God gives and takes away (Job 1:21); and how he strikes and heals (Job 5:18); and how he gives himself gratuitously. With his sublimity I have felt the sins of all those whom in this life I have heard named and have seen. And this is why ever since, with God, I have passed just judgments according to the depths of his truth, on us all as we also were. With his unity in love I have felt constantly, since then, the experience of being

lost in the fruition of Love, or the suffering of being deprived of this fruition, and the ways of veritable Love in all things, and its mode of operation in God and in all men.

85. In love I have experienced all these attributes, and I have acted with justice toward these persons, however much they have failed me. But if I possess this in love with my eternal being, I do not possess it yet in fruition of Love in my own being. And I remain a human being, who must suffer to the death with Christ in Love; for whoever lives in veritable Love will suffer opprobrium from all aliens, until Love comes to herself, and until she is full-grown within us in virtues, whereby Love becomes one with men.

Vision 7

Oneness in the Eucharist

On a certain Pentecost Sunday I had a vision at dawn. Matins were being sung in the church, and I was present. My heart and my veins and all my limbs trembled and quivered with eager desire and, as often occurred with me, such madness and fear beset my mind that it seemed to me I did not content my Beloved, and that my Beloved did not fulfill my desire, so that dying I must go mad, and going mad I must die. On that day my mind was beset so fearfully and so painfully by desirous love that all my separate limbs threatened to break, and all my separate veins were in travail. 14. The longing in which I then was cannot be expressed by any language or any person I know; and everything I could say about it would be unheard-of to all those who never apprehended Love as something to work for with desire, and whom Love had never acknowledged as hers. I can say this about it: I desired to have full fruition of my Beloved, and to understand and taste him to the full. I desired that his Humanity should to the fullest extent be one in fruition with my humanity, and that mine then should hold its stand and be strong enough to enter into perfection until I content him, who is perfection itself, by purity and unity, and in all things to content him fully in every virtue. To that end I wished he might content me interiorly with his Godhead, in one spirit, and that for me he should be all that he is, without withholding anything from me. For above all the gifts that I ever longed for, I chose this gift: that I should give satisfaction in all great sufferings. For that is the most perfect satisfaction: to grow up in order to be God with God. For this demands suffering, pain, and misery, and living in great new grief of soul: but to let everything come and go without grief, and in this way to experience nothing else but sweet love, embraces, and kisses. In this sense I desired that God give himself to me, so that I might content him.

42. As my mind was thus beset with fear, I saw a great eagle flying toward me from the altar, and he said to me: "If you wish to attain oneness, make yourself ready!"

45. I fell on my knees and my heart beat fearfully, to worship the Beloved with oneness, according to his true dignity; that indeed was impossible for me, as I know well, and as God knows, always to my woe and to my grief.

50. But the eagle turned back and spoke: "Just and mighty Lord, now show your great power to unite your oneness in the manner of union with full possession!"

53. Then the eagle turned round again and said to me: "He who has come, comes again; and to whatever place he never came, he comes not."

57. Then he came from the altar, showing himself as a Child; and that Child was in the same form as he was in his first three years. He turned toward me, in his right hand took from the ciborium his Body, and in his left hand took a chalice, which seemed to come from the altar, but I do not know where it came from.

64. With that he came in the form and clothing of a Man, as he was on the day when he gave us his Body for the first time; looking like a Human Being and a Man, wonderful, and beautiful, and with glorious face, he came to me as humbly as anyone who wholly belongs to another. Then he gave himself to me in the shape of the Sacrament, in its outward form, as the custom is; and then he gave me to drink from the chalice, in form and taste, as the custom is. After that he came himself to me, took me entirely in his arms, and pressed me to him; and all my members felt his in full felicity, in accordance with the desire of my heart and my humanity. So I was outwardly satisfied

and fully transported. Also then, for a short while, I had the strength to bear this; but soon, after a short time, I lost that manly beauty outwardly in the sight of his form. I saw him completely come to nought and so fade and all at once dissolve that I could no longer recognize or perceive him outside me, and I could no longer distinguish him within me. Then it was to me as if we were one without difference. It was thus: outwardly, to see, taste, and feel, as one can outwardly taste, see, and feel in the reception of the outward Sacrament. So can the Beloved, with the loved one, each wholly receive the other in all full satisfaction of the sight, the hearing, and the passing away of the one in the other.

94. After that I remained in a passing away in my Beloved, so that I wholly melted away in him and nothing any longer remained to me of myself; and I was changed and taken up in the spirit, and there it was shown me concerning such hours.

Vision 11
The Abyss of Omnipotence

I was in a very depressed frame of mind one Christmas night, when I was taken up in the spirit. There I saw a very deep whirlpool, wide and exceedingly dark; in this abyss all beings were included, crowded together, and compressed. The darkness illuminated and penetrated everything. The unfathomable depth of the abyss was so high that no one could reach it. I will not attempt now to describe how it was formed, for there is no time now to speak of it; and I cannot put it in words, since it is unspeakable. Second, this is not a convenient time for it, because much pertains to what I saw. It was the entire omnipotence of our Beloved. In it I saw the Lamb (cf. Apoc. 5:6) take possession of our Beloved. In the vast space I saw festivities, such as David playing the harp, and he struck the harp strings. Then I perceived an Infant being born in the souls who love in secret, the souls hidden from their own eyes in the deep abyss of which I speak, and to whom nothing is lacking but that they should lose themselves in it. I saw the forms of many different souls, according to what each one's life had been. Of those whom I saw, the ones whom I already knew remained known to

me; and those I did not know became known to me; I received interior knowledge about some, and also exterior knowledge about many. And certain ones I knew interiorly, having never seen them exteriorly.

28. Then I saw coming as it were a bird, namely the one called phoenix. It devoured a grey eagle that was young, and a yellow eagle with new feathers that was old. These eagles kept flying about incessantly in the deep abyss.

33. Then I heard a voice like thunder (cf. Apoc. 6:1) that said: "Do you know who these different-colored eagles are?"

36. And I answered: "I should like to know this better."

37. And although I asked to know this, I nevertheless perceived the essence of all the things I saw. For all that is seen in the spirit when one is ravished by Love is understood, tasted, seen, and heard through and through. So was it also here. I wished, however, to hear the Voice that came to my hearing from the Beloved. And indeed the truth was told me concerning all this, in particular the natures and perfections comprised in my vision. All this would take too long; I pass over it. For a great book would be required if one were to write everything perfectly in full truth!

49. One of the eagles who were swallowed was Saint Augustine, and the other myself. The old feathers that were grey, and the eaglet that was young—this was I, for I was attaining to perfection, beginning, and growing in love. The feathers that were yellow and old—this was the full-grown-ness of Saint Augustine, who was old and perfect in the love of our Beloved. The old age I had was in the perfect nature of eternal being, even though I was youthful in created nature. The young feathers of the old eagle were the renewed splendor he received from me in the new heavenly glory of my love, with which I loved him and so greatly desired with him to pour forth one single love in the Trinity, where he himself was burning so totally with an unquenchable love. The youth that the old feathers that were yellow had signified also the renewal of Love, which continually grows in heaven and on earth (cf. Ps. 102:5). The phoenix that swallowed the eagles was the Unity in which the Trinity dwells, wherein both of us are lost.

72. When afterwards I returned to myself, where I found myself poor and miserable, I reflected on this union with Saint Augustine to which I had attained. I was not contented with what my dearly Beloved had just permitted, in spite of my consent and emotional attraction; it weighed on me now that this union with Saint Augustine had made me so perfectly happy, whereas previously I had possessed union far from saints and men, with God alone. From this I understood that neither in heaven nor in the spirit can one enjoy one's own will, except in accordance with the will of Love. And as I thought about this attitude, I asked my Beloved to deliver me from it. For I wished to remain in his deepest abyss, alone in fruition. And I understood that, since my childhood, God had drawn me to himself alone, far from all the other beings whom he welcomes to himself in other manners. But I well know that whatever was in him is, in highest measure, eternal glory and perfect enjoyment, but I likewise wished to remain in him alone. I understood this when I asked for it, and so greatly desired it, and suffered so much; then I remained free. No doubt I continued to belong to God alone while being united in Love to this creature. But my liberty I gained then was given me moreover for reasons of my own, which neither Augustine nor many others had.

98. I did not suggest this as a claim to be more privileged than Saint Augustine; but in the time when I knew the truth of Being, I did not want to receive any comfort from him insofar as he was a creature, or to accept any joy amid my pains, and so I would allow myself no satisfaction in the security that was given me in this union with Saint Augustine. For I am a free human creature, and also pure as to one part, and I can desire freely with my will, and I can will as highly as I wish, and seize and receive from God all that he is, without objection or anger on his part—what no saint can do. For the saints have their will perfectly according to their pleasure; and they can no longer will beyond what they have. I have hated many great wonderful deeds and experiences, because I wished to belong to Love alone, and because I could not believe that any human creature loved him so passionately as I—although I know it is a

fact and indubitable, still I cannot believe it or feel it, so powerfully am I touched by Love.

121. In this wonderful way I belong to God alone in pure love, and to my saint in love, and then to all the saints, each one according to his dignity, and to men according to what each one loved and also according to what he was and still is. But in striving for this I have never experienced Love in any sort of way as repose; on the contrary, I found Love a heavy burden and disgrace. For I was a human creature, and Love is terrible and implacable, devouring and burning without regard for anything. The soul is contained in one little rivulet; her depth is quickly filled up; her dikes quickly burst. Thus with rapidity the Godhead has engulfed human nature wholly in itself.

134. I used to love the blessedness of the saints, but I never ceased to desire the repose in which God within them had fruition of himself; their quietude was many a time my inquietude; yes, truly, it was always forty pains against one single pleasure. I could not but know that they were smiled at, while I wept; that they boasted themselves fortunate, while I pitied myself; and that they were honored by God, and that God was honored because of them in every land, while I was an object of derision. All this, nevertheless, was my greatest repose, for he willed it—but this was such repose as comes to those who desire love and fruition, and who have in this desire such woe as I do.

147. Now for persons, my repose lay in loving each of them in what was proper to him, and wishing for each of them that only what he held desirable and good might happen to him; whether this good was that of their will or of the divine will was a question with which I did not meddle. But what they had in love, I loved for God, in order that he might strengthen it for himself and cause it to grow to perfection; such was my desire. Because I loved God's being loved, I wished no pleasure from it but that.

156. As for persons who failed God and were strangers to him, they weighed heavy on me. For I was so laden with his love and captivated by it that I could scarcely endure that anyone should love him less than I. And charity for others wounded me cruelly, that he should let these souls be such

strangers to him and so deprived of all the good that he himself is in love. This was such an intolerable burden to me in many an hour that it happened to me as it did to Moses because of his love for his sister: I would have wished that he give his love to others or withdraw it from me. I would gladly have purchased love for them by accepting that he should love them and hate me. And sometimes, too, because he did not do this, I would willingly have turned away from him in love and would have loved them in spite of his wrath (cf. Rom. 9:3); seeing that these unfortunates could not know the sweet and ardent love that dwells in his holy Nature, I would most gladly have loved them, had I been able.

174. Also, charity has wounded me the most—except for actual Love. What is actual Love? It is the divine power that must have priority; and it does so in me. For the sovereign power that is actual Love spares no one, either in hate or in love; favor is never found in it. This power held me back once again when I had wished to free all men in the twinkling of an eye, otherwise than in accordance with how God had chosen them. When I could thus turn myself against him, it was a beautiful and free expression of life as a human being. Then I could desire what I wished. But when I did the opposite, I was more beautiful and taken up into a fuller participation in the Divine Nature.

188. Thus I have lived quietly as a human being, so that I have taken repose neither in saints nor in men on earth. And so I have lived in misery without love, in the love of God and of those who are his; and while I do not receive from him what is mine, and what God does not yet give me—I have it nevertheless, and it shall remain mine! Hence I never felt love, unless as an ever-new death—until the time of my consolation came, and God granted me to know the perfect pride of love; to know how we shall love the Humanity in order to come to the Divinity, and rightly know it in one single Nature. This is the noblest life that can be lived *in the kingdom of God* (Col. 4:11). This rich repose God gave me, and truly in a happy hour.

Asian and African Christianity
in the Late Middle Ages

69. The Lives of Mâr Yahbh-Allâhâ
and Rabban Ṣâwmâ

*The early Mongol rulers in Asia looked favorably on Christians of the
Church of the East, under the Patriarch of Baghdad, but by the end of the
thirteenth century the Christians' fortunes began to reverse as the Mongols
embraced Islam. The fourteenth-century Syriac* History of Yabh-Allâhâ III
and Rabban Ṣâwmâ *tells of two Christian monks from China who traveled
westward in about 1275, intending to visit Jerusalem, but found other des-
tinies instead. One of them, Rabban Ṣâwmâ, was sent by Arghon, the Mongol Ilkhan of Persia, as his ambassador to the Christian West to explore the
possibility of an anti-Muslim alliance. The other monk, Mark, was elected
Patriarch of Baghdad (i.e., Catholicus of the Church of the East) in 1281 as
Yabh-Allâhâ III, and he presided over the church amid the catastrophic
events that soon beset it.*

Chapter VII

*On the Departure of Rabban Ṣâwmâ
to the Country of the Romans
in the Name of King Arghôn
and of the Catholicus
Mâr Yahbh-Allâhâ*

Now Mâr Yahbh-Allâhâ, the Catholicus,
increased in power, and his honor before the King
and Queens grew greater daily. He pulled down
the church of Mâr Shalitâ, which was in Mârâghâh, and he rebuilt it at very great expense. And
instead of using [the old] beams [and making a
single roof] he made [the new church] with two
naves *(haikĕlê)*; and by the side of it he built a cell
in which to live. For his affection for the house of
King Arghôn was very warm, because Arghôn
loved the Christians with his whole heart. And

Arghôn intended to go into the countries of Palestine and Syria and to subjugate them and take possession of them, but he said to himself, "If the
Western Kings, who are Christians, will not help
me, I shall not be able to fulfill my desire." Thereupon he asked the Catholicus to give him a wise
man, "one who is suitable and is capable of undertaking an embassy, that we may send him to those
kings." And when the Catholicus saw that there
was no man who knew the language except Rabban Ṣâwmâ, and knowing that he was fully capable
of this, he commanded him to go [on the
embassy].

Rabban Ṣâwmâ in Byzantium

And Rabban Ṣâwmâ set out on his journey. . . .
And after [some] days he arrived at the great city
of Constantinople. . . . And after they had enjoyed

Source: *The Monks of Kûbla Khân, Emperor of China,* ed. and tr. E. A. Wallis Budge (London: Religious Tract Society,
1928), 165-69, 173-74, 177-79, 181-85, 189-91, 195-97, 210-30, 303-6.

food and drink Rabban Ṣâwmâ asked the king to be allowed to see the churches and the shrines [or tombs] of the Fathers [i.e., Patriarchs], and the relics of the saints that were therein. And the king handed Rabban Ṣâwmâ over to the nobles of his kingdom and they showed him everything that was there.

First of all he went unto the great church of ἡ Σοφία [i.e., the Church of Divine Wisdom], which has three hundred and sixty doors [i.e., pillars] all made of marble. As for the dome of the altar, it is impossible for a man to describe it [adequately] to one who has not seen it, and to say how high and how spacious it is. There is in this church a picture of the holy Mary which Luke, the Evangelist, painted. He saw there also the hand of Mâr John the Baptist, and portions [of the bodies of] Lazarus, and Mary Magdalene, and that stone which was laid on the grave of our Lord, when Joseph the βουλευτής brought Him down from the Cross. Now Mary wept on that stone, and the place whereon her tears fell is wet even at the present time; and however often this moisture is wiped away the place becomes wet again. And he saw also the stone bowl in which our Lord changed the water into wine at Kâtnê (Cana) of Galilee; and the funerary coffer of one of the holy women which is exposed to public view every year, and every sick person who is laid under it is made whole; and the coffer of Mâr John of the Mouth of Gold (Chrysostom). And he saw also the stone on which Simon Peter was sitting when the cock crew; and the tomb of King Constantine, the Conqueror, which was made of red stone (porphyry?); and also the tomb of Justinian, which was [built of] green stone; and also the Bêth Kâwmâ (resting place) of the Three Hundred and Eighteen [orthodox] Bishops who were all laid in one great church; and their bodies have not suffered corruption because they had confirmed the [True] Faith. . . .

Rabban Ṣâwmâ in Italy and in Great Rome

[Rabban Ṣâwmâ's embassy travels by sea from Constantinople to Naples, then inland to Rome on horses. En route they hear that Mâr Pâpâ (Honorius IV who died in 1287) has died. Cardinals assign Ṣâwmâ a mansion in which to rest.]

. . . Three days later the Cardinals sent and summoned Rabban Ṣâwmâ to their presence. And when he went to them they began to ask him questions, saying, "What is your quarter of the world, and why have you come?" And he replied in the selfsame words he had already spoken to them. And they said to him, "Where does the Catholicus live? And which of the Apostles taught the Gospel in your quarter of the world?" And he answered them, saying, "Mâr Thomas, and Mâr Addai, and Mâr Mârî taught the Gospel in our quarter of the world, and we hold at the present time the canons [or statutes] which they delivered unto us." The Cardinals said to him, "Where is the Throne of the Catholicus?" He said to them, "In Baghdâd." They answered, "What position have you there?" And he replied, "I am a deacon in the Cell of the Catholicus, and the director of the disciples, and the Visitor-General." The Cardinals said, "It is a marvelous thing that you who are a Christian and a deacon of the Throne of the Patriarch of the East have come on an embassy from the king of the Mongols." And Rabban Ṣâwmâ said to them, "Know, O our Fathers, that many of our Fathers have gone into the countries of the Mongols, and Turks, and Chinese and have taught them the Gospel, and at the present time there are many Mongols who are Christians. For many of the sons of the Mongol kings and queens have been baptized and confess Christ. And they have established churches in their military camps, and they pay honor to the Christians, and there are among them many who are believers. Now the king [of the Mongols], who is joined in the bond of friendship with the Catholicus, has the desire to take Palestine, and the countries of Syria, and he demands from you help in order to take Jerusalem. He has chosen me and has sent me to you because, being a Christian, my word will be believed by you." . . .

[A discussion of Ṣâwmâ's faith ensues, but the text here is complex and has several gaps.]

". . . If it be pleasing in your eyes, let us set aside discussion; and give attention and direct someone to show us the churches here and the shrines of the saints; [if you will do this] you will confer a very great favour on your servant and disciple."

Then the Cardinals summoned the Amîr of the city and certain monks and commanded them to show him the churches and the holy places that were there; and they went forth straightaway and saw the places which we will now mention. First of all they went into the church of Peter and Paul. Beneath the Throne is a naos, and in this is laid the body of Saint Peter, and above the throne is an altar. The altar which is in the middle of that great temple has four doorways, and in each of these two folding doors worked with designs in iron; Mâr Pâpâ celebrates the Mass at this altar, and no person besides himself may stand on the bench of that altar. Afterwards they saw the Throne of Mâr Peter whereon they make Mâr Pâpâ to sit when they appoint him. And they also saw the strip of fine [or thin] linen on which our Lord impressed His image and sent to King Abhgar of Ûrhâi (Edessa). Now the extent of that temple and its splendor cannot be described; it stands on one hundred and eight pillars. In it is another altar at which the King of their Kings receives the laying on of hands [i.e., is consecrated and crowned], and is proclaimed "Amprôr (Emperor) King of Kings," by the Pope. And they say that after the prayers Mâr Pâpâ takes up the Crown with his feet and clothes the Emperor with it, that is to say, places it upon his own head [to show], as they say, that priesthood reigns over sovereignty [or kingship].

And when they had seen all the churches and monasteries that were in Great Rome, they went outside the city to the church of Mâr Paul the Apostle, where under the altar is his tomb. And there, too, is the chain wherewith Paul was bound when he was dragged to that place. And in that altar there are also a reliquary of gold wherein is the head of Mâr Stephen the Martyr, and the hand of Mâr Khananyâ (Ananias) who baptized Paul. And the staff of Paul the Apostle is also there. And from that place they went to the spot where Paul the Apostle was crowned [with martyrdom]. They say that when his head was cut off it leaped up thrice into the air, and at each time cried out "Christ! Christ!" And that from each of the three

places on which his head fell there came forth waters which were useful for healing purposes, and for giving help to all those who were afflicted.

. . . And Rabban Ṣâwmâ asked from them permission to go to the king who dwells in Rome; and they permitted him to go, and said, "We cannot give you an answer until the [new] Pope is elected."

Rabban Ṣâwmâ in Fransâ or Frangestân

[*Rabban Ṣâwmâ's embassy travels to Paris, where he is received by King Philip IV of France.*]

. . . And when he had come the king stood up before him and paid him honor, and said to him, "Why have you come? And who sent you?" And Rabban Ṣâwmâ said unto him, "King Arghôn and the Catholicus of the East have sent me concerning the matter of Jerusalem." And he showed him all the matters which he knew, and he gave him the letters which he had with him, and the gifts, that is to say, presents which he had brought. And the king of France answered him, saying, "If it be indeed so that the Mongols, though they are not Christians, are going to fight against the Arabs for the capture of Jerusalem, it is fitting especially for us that we should fight [with them], and if our Lord wills, go forth in full strength."

. . . And Rabban Ṣâwmâ and his companions remained for a month of days in this great city of Paris, and they saw everything that was in it. There were in it thirty thousand scholars [i.e., pupils] who were engaged in the study of ecclesiastical books of instruction, that is to say, of commentaries and exegesis of all the Holy Scriptures, and also of profane learning; and they studied wisdom, that is to say, philosophy and [the art of] speaking (rhetoric?), and [the art of] healing, geometry, arithmetic, and the science of the planets and the stars; and they engaged constantly in writing [theses], and all these pupils received money for subsistence from the king. And they also saw one Great Church wherein were the funerary coffers of dead kings, and statues of them in gold and in silver were upon their tombs. And five hundred monks were engaged in performing commemoration services in the burial-place [i.e., mausoleum] of the kings, and they all ate and drank at the expense of the king. And they fasted and prayed continually in the burial-place of those kings. And the crowns of those kings, and their armor, and their apparel were laid upon their tombs. In short Rabban Ṣâwmâ and his companions saw everything which was splendid and renowned.

And after this the king sent and summoned them, and they went to him in the church, and they saw him standing by the side of the altar, and they saluted him. And he asked Rabban Ṣâwmâ, saying, "Have you seen what we have? And does there not remain anything else for you to see?" Then Rabban Ṣâwmâ thanked him [and said "There is not"]. Forthwith he went up with the king into an upper chamber of gold, which the king opened, and he brought forth from it a coffer of beryl wherein was laid the Crown of Thorns which the Jews placed upon the head of our Lord when they crucified Him. Now the Crown was visible in the coffer, which, thanks to the transparency of the beryl, remained unopened. And there was also in the coffer a piece of the wood of the Cross. And the king said to Rabban Ṣâwmâ and his companions, "When our fathers took Constantinople, and sacked Jerusalem, they brought these blessed objects from it." And we blessed the king and besought him to give us the order to return. And he said unto us, "I will send with you one of the great Amîrs whom I have here with me to give an answer to King Arghôn"; and the king gave Rabban Ṣâwmâ gifts and apparel of great price. . . .

Rabban Ṣâwmâ Returns to Rome

[*After being received by King Edward I of England, who also expresses support for Arghôn's plan, the embassy returns to Rome where they learn that a new pope, Nicholas IV, has been appointed.*]

. . . And straightaway Rabban Ṣâwmâ went into the presence of Mâr Pâpâ, who was seated on his throne. And he approached the Pope, bowing down to the ground as he did so, and he kissed his feet and his hands, and he withdrew walking backwards, with his hands clasped [on his breast]. And he said to Mâr Pâpâ, "May your throne stand forever, O our Father! And may it be blessed above all kings and nations! And may it make peace to reign in your days throughout the Church to the uttermost ends of the earth! Now that I have seen your face my eyes are illumined, and I shall not go away brokenhearted to the countries [of the East]. I give thanks to the goodness of God who has held me to be worthy to see your face." Then Rabban Ṣâwmâ presented unto him the gift of King Arghôn and his Letters, and the gift of Mâr Yahbh-Allâhâ the Catholicus, that is to say, a blessing [i.e., gift] and his Letter. And Mâr Pâpâ rejoiced and was glad, and he paid more honor to Rabban Ṣâwmâ than was customary, and he said to him, "It will be good if you will keep the festival with us, for you will see our use." Now that day [marked] the half of our Lord's Fast [i.e., Mid-Lent]. And Rabban Ṣâwmâ made answer, "Your command is high and exalted." And Mâr Pâpâ assigned to him a mansion in which to dwell, and he appointed servants to give him everything he might require.

Some days later Rabban Ṣâwmâ said to Mâr Pâpâ, "I wish to celebrate the Eucharist so that you might see our use"; and the Pope commanded him to do as he had asked. And on that day a very large number of people were gathered together in order to see how the ambassador of the Mongols celebrated the Eucharist. And when they had seen they rejoiced and said, "The language is different, but the use is the same." Now the day on which he celebrated was the Sunday [on which the prayer beginning] "ainâw âsyâ" [i.e., "Who is the physician"] is recited. And having performed the Mysteries, he went to Mâr Pâpâ and saluted him. And the Pope said unto Rabban Ṣâwmâ, "May God receive your offering, and bless you, and pardon your transgressions and sins." Then Rabban Ṣâwmâ said, "Besides the pardon of my transgressions and sins which I have received from you, O our Father, I beseech your Fatherhood, O our holy Father, to let me receive the Offering from your hands, so that the remission [of my sins] may be complete." And the Pope said, "So let it be!"

[*Rabban Ṣâwmâ stayed in Rome through Easter celebrating Holy Week with many bishops, metropolitans and cardinals.*]

. . . And when these things had taken place Rabban Ṣâwmâ asked Mâr Pâpâ for [his] command to return. And Mâr Pâpâ said unto him, "We wish you to remain with us, and to abide with us, and we will guard you like the pupil of our eye." But Rabban Sâwmâ replied, "O our Father, I came on an embassy for your service (?). If my coming had been the result of my personal wish, I would willingly bring to an end the days of this my useless life in your service at the outer door of your palace. [But I must return], and believe that when I go back and show the kings who are there the benefits which you have conferred upon my poor person, that the Christians will gain great content thereby. Now I beseech our Holiness to bestow upon me some of the relics [of the saints] which you have with you."

And Mâr Pâpâ said, "If we had been in the habit of giving away these relics to the people [who come] in myriads, even though the relics were as large as the mountains, they would have come to an end long ago. But since you have come from a far country, we will give you a few." And he gave to Rabban Sâwmâ a small piece of the apparel of our Lord Christ, and a piece of the cape (φακιόλιον), that is to say, kerchief of my Lady Mary, and some small fragments of the bodies of the saints that were there. And he sent to Mâr Yahbh-Allâhâ a crown for his head which was of fine gold, and was inlaid with precious stones; and sacred vestments made of red cloth through which ran threads of gold; and socks and sandals on which real pearls were sewn; and the ring from his finger; and a "Pethîkhâ," or Bull which authorized him to exercise Patriarchal dominion over all the Children of the East. And he gave to Rabban Sâwmâ a "Pethîkhâ" which authorized him to act as Visitor-General over all Christians. And Mâr Pâpâ blessed him, and he caused to be assigned to him for expenses on the road one thousand, five hundred *mathkâlê* of red gold. And to King Arghôn he sent certain gifts. And he embraced Rabban Sâwmâ and kissed him and dismissed him. And Rabban Sâwmâ thanked our Lord who had held him to be worthy of such blessings as these.

. . . And Rabban Sâwmâ returned. He crossed the seas which he crossed when he came, and he arrived in peace at the place where King Arghôn

was, sound in body, and with soul safely kept. And he gave to him the Letter of Blessings, and the gifts which he had brought from Mâr Pâpâ and from all the kings of the Franks. . . .

Chapter XI

The Persecution of Mâr Yahbh-Allâhâ and the Christians in Mârâghâh

[*King Arghôn died in 1291. Civil war broke out in 1295, and Muslim Arabs commenced raiding the country.*]

And a certain man, one of the Amîrs, who was called Nâwrûz, and who did not fear God, bestirred himself, and sent letters by the hands of envoys, and he made to fly to the four quarters of the dominions of this kingdom, an order to this effect:—"The churches shall be uprooted and the altars overturned, and the celebrations of the Eucharist shall cease, and the hymns of praise, and the sounds of calls to prayer shall be abolished; and the heads (or chiefs) of the Christians, and the heads of the congregations [i.e., synagogues] of the Jews, and the great men among them shall be killed."

And that same night [the Arabs] seized Mâr Catholicus in his Cell [i.e., palace] in Mârâghâh, and outside the building no one knew anything about the seizure of him until the day broke. And from the morning of that day, which was the second day of the week (Monday) they went into his Cell and plundered everything that was in it, both that which was old and that which was new, and they did not leave even a nail in the walls.

And the night of the third day of the week (Tuesday) following, which was the 27th day of 'Îlûl (September), the Catholicus was buffeted the whole night long by those who had seized him. And in respect of the venerable men who were with him, the Arabs tied some of them up naked with ropes; others cast aside their apparel and took to flight, and others cast themselves down from high places [and perished]. And they suspended the Catholicus by a rope head downwards, and they took a cloth used for cleaning, that is to say, a duster, and they put ashes in it, and tied it over his mouth, and one prodded him in the breast with a skewer (*bûksînâ*), saying, "Abandon this Faith of you so that you may not perish; become a Hagarâyâ (Muḥammadan) and you shall be saved." And the Catholicus, weeping, answered them never a word. And they smote him with a stick on the thighs and seat [i.e., posterior]. And they also took him up onto the roof of the Cell, saying, "Give us gold and we will let you go; point out to us your treasures, show us the things which you had hidden away, and reveal to us your hiding-things and we will let you go."

And Mâr Catholicus, because he was clothed with a body feeble and sensitive to pain, was afraid of death. And he began to cry out on the roof, "Where are the disciples? How is it that those whom I have brought up have betaken themselves to flight? Of what use are possessions (or riches) to us? Come and buy me back from those who would sell me wrongfully, redeem your master." Now the people, men, and women, and youths, and children, in the darkness of midnight were crying out with bitter tears, but no one was able to approach the Catholicus, because of fear. Nevertheless they received help from [their] weeping, and took refuge in [their] prayer, saying, "Yea, you mountains fall upon us! O you hills cover us" (Luke 23:30). And thus was fulfilled the prophecy of the prophet of the Syrians [Aphrêm Syrus], who said "Because we have despised the way, and have regarded it with great contempt, [God] has made us a reproach to those who are outside; that we may drink from them mockery. The filthy ones have ruined our churches, because we have not prayed in them in a right manner; they have defiled the altar which is before Him [because] we have not ministered thereto with pure service."

Finally, not to make our narrative too long, some of the disciples of the Patriarch's palace went and incurred a debt of fifteen thousand *zûzê* and gave the money, little by little [to the Arabs], with the hope of redeeming the Catholicus. And when those who had seized the Catholicus had received the sum of five thousand *dînârs*, and the chalices, and the eucharistic patens, and everything that was in the palace, and that debt [i.e., the money which the disciple had undertaken to pay], they went

forth from the palace at midday of the third day of the week.

And then a great tumult took place, and the peoples of the Arabs came with a great rush to destroy the great church of Mâr Shalîtâ, the holy martyr, and they destroyed it. And they took everything that was in it, the veils (or hangings), and the vessels and other objects used in the service. And the uproar made by their outcries, and the storm of their shoutings shook almost the earth itself and the inhabitants thereof. Perhaps the reader of this history, not having been caught up in the middle of that storm, may think that the writer is telling a fabulous story; but to speak the real truth, the one who states what is here written calls God to witness, that it is impossible for even one of the events which took place to be adequately described and written!

Then King Khêtâm (or Hâthôm), Takpûr (Tâkâwôr) of the Arîmnâyê (Armenians), came down into that church which Rabban Ṣâwmâ had built, and by means of the greatness of his gifts [i.e., bribes], and by his soldiers, saved it from destruction. And the Catholicus having made his escape from the hands of those who had seized him, fled to it and hid himself therein that night. In the morning of the following day, which was the fourth day of the week (Wednesday), a certain Amîr who was one of the envoys of the Nâwrûz mentioned above, came and brought certain letters [ordering] the murder of the Catholicus. And he seized many of the men, among whom were some belonging to the Takpûr, i.e., king, [and said unto them] "Show me the Catholicus, for I have certain business with him." When Mâr Catholicus heard this his heart quaked and he fled from the church and left Takpûr; and King Takpûr appeased the Amîr with certain gifts which he gave to him, and he departed from Mârâghâh.

After a few days, King Takpûr himself went to Tabhrîz, and Mâr Catholicus changed all his apparel, and went forth by himself in the guise of one of the servants, and he accompanied Takpûr as far as the city of Tabhrîz, where King Ḳâzân had arrived. And the Catholicus kept himself hidden for seven days, until Takpûr had been able to go unto the presence of King Ḳâzân, and make his story known to him, and then Takpûr asked him to go and see the king. Now, since the men who were in the regular service in the palace of the Catholicus were scattered, there remained with the Catholicus a certain number of poor young men who cleaved to him, and these went into the presence of King Kâzân with him. And the king did not know him. And when he had saluted him he asked him two questions: "Where do you come from?" and "What is your name?" and that was all. And the Catholicus answered him in a word, i.e., briefly, and blessed him, and then went forth, trembling having entered his bones. But this was not due to [his fear of] death, but to his seeing to what a pass the children of baptism [i.e., the Christians] had come! And because of the angel who consoled him, and his wakeful mind admonished him, saying, "No temptation has come to you except that which is of the children of men" (1 Cor. 10:13), he still kept up his courage with weeping and groaning, saying, "Who gave my head water, and my eyes fountains of tears, that I should weep by day and by night over the breaking of the daughter of my people?" (Jer. 9:1). Thus did these things happen.

Now it was cold in those days, and the Camp was removed to the winter station of Mûghân; and Nâwrûz, the accursed one, was at Tâbhrîz. And the Catholicus, without money for expenses, and without a beast to ride, and without any baggage-animal, returned to Mârâghâh. He remained a few days in [his] Cell, and then other men came seeking for him, but he escaped from their hands by flight, but, though with considerable risk, he went back there day after day. Now it was well known that all glory which is of this world brings upon itself in the end the humiliation which is from God, and that glory attaches in the end only to the abject humiliation which [is endured] for God's sake. That winter the Catholicus sent to the Camp [of the king] one of [his] disciples so that he might effect a change in the orders and make known [to the king] how matters were. And he returned as one fleeing [for his life], for there was no one who would espouse the cause of the Christians, or who would show compassion on those who were broken[hearted]. This disciple only escaped with the

greatest difficulty from the hands of a man who was an unbeliever, and who had abandoned his Faith and had become a Hagarâyâ [i.e., Muhammadan].

After the Feast of the Nativity of the year of the Greeks, one thousand six hundred and seven (A.D. 1295), on the Sunday [when the prayer beginning] "Mâre kûl kadh badhemûthâ" (i.e., "the Lord of all in the Image") [is said], messengers of Nâwrûz, the accursed one, again came down against the Catholicus. They bore in their hands orders which said, "Give us, O Catholicus, the ten thousand dînârs which you received in the time of King Kaihkâtô. Behold the 'Tamghâ,' that is to say, the document which is sealed with the seal of the Amîr and contains the order for giving them back. "Now the [treasury of the] palace of the Catholicus was empty, for it had been plundered long ago. When the servants of the palace heard this they straightaway dispersed and sought refuge in flight, and the Catholicus remained in the hands of the Mongols who had become Muhammadans and those who had brought them. And fear fell upon the sons of the Church (How [sad] would you say. How [sad]!), and even the reverend old men who were in the palace fled, Mâr Catholicus remained alone in the hands of those accursed and impudent men. That night he promised to give them a village, but they would accept nothing but gold. And when straightaway they threatened to beat him, he began to borrow [money] and to give it [to them], and throughout that day, which was the first of the week (Sunday), until towards the evening they took [from him] two thousand dînârs.

Then certain of [his] disciples took counsel with Mâr Catholicus in order to help him to flight, and to deliver him from the hands of those [impudent men]. He was afraid [at first] of this, but when they pressed him he hearkened [i.e., consented]. And at cock crow they brought him out through a small opening in the chamber in which he was imprisoned. Now the size of the opening was so small that a person would think that not even a child could come out through it, and they lowered him down, and he went to other places and kept himself hidden.

And when the day dawned the Muslim Mongols were sorely vexed and they did not know what they were to do. And they were also afraid lest someone should take vengeance on them, saying, "You have destroyed the Catholicus." Thereupon they straightway went forth from the city, and made their way to Baghdâd.

And whilst these men were in the act of departing, another messenger arrived, an evil man who was more wicked than Nâwrûz, the accursed. And there was with him a Christian who had become a Muḥammadan, and he brought with him another Order to the effect that thirty-six thousand dînârs should be given to him [by the Catholicus]. And because Mâr Catholicus was in hiding, those impudent messengers seized certain of the disciples in the palace, and by means of many blows and tortures they reduced the bodies of the disciples to a state of helplessness. And they hung them up head downwards [in the open air] during the days of frost and snow, when the cold was more intense than any which had ever before been experienced. And after all [the people] in the city had been gathered together to obtain their release, the disciples were only delivered from the hands of those wicked men with the greatest difficulty by paying them sixteen thousand dînârs. And the Catholicus and all those who cleaved to him, whether venerable old men, or monks, or members of the laity, were persecuted by every man, and were obliged to hide themselves in the houses of the laity. And when the persecutors knew that they were in a certain house [those who were hidden therein] straightway departed to other houses. [And this state of affairs lasted] until the great Feast of the Resurrection [A.D. 1296].

Chapter XII

King Kâzân Pays Honor
to Mâr Yahbhâ-Allâhâ

Now when the sun had descended into the sign of the Ram, and creation was warmed a little, the Catholicus sent one of the monks of the Cell to the victorious King Ḳâzân, to the place called Mûghân, the winter station of all the Mongol Kings, to bless him and to inform [him] concerning the events that had happened to him. And when that monk arrived at the Camp, and he had taken care to see all the Amîrs, they introduced him into the presence of the victorious king, and he declared unto him in their entirety all the words which Mâr Catholicus had spoken to him saying, "Blessed is your throne, O king, and it shall stand firm forever, and your seed shall be surely seated thereon forever." And the king asked, "Why did not the Catholicus come to us?" and the monk replied, "Because of the confused state [of his mind]. He was hung up and cruelly beaten, and his head touched the earth. Through the severe pain which hath been roused in him he was unable to come to do homage to the king, and it is for this reason that he hath sent me to pronounce his blessing upon you, O my lord, the king. But when the victorious king shall arrive in peace at Tabhrîz, whether the Catholicus is sick or whether he be well, he will come to salute you and do homage to you."

And God caused these words to find mercy in the eyes of the king, and he gave to the Catholicus a Pukdânâ, according to custom, in which it was laid down that poll-tax should not be exacted from the Christians; that none of them shall abandon his Faith; that the Catholicus shall live in the state to which he hath been accustomed; that he shall be treated with the respect due to his rank; that he shall rule over his Throne; and shall hold the staff of strength over his dominion [i.e., that he shall wield his scepter with vigor and determination]. And he promulgated an Edict throughout all countries, and addressed it to all the Amîrs by their names, and to the soldiers, ordering them to give back everything which they had taken from the Catholicus or from the holy old men by force, and to give back to him what those men of Baghdâd and their envoys, whom we have mentioned above, had taken. Moreover, he allotted and dispatched to the Catholicus five thousand dînârs for his expenses, saying, "These will serve him as a supply until he comes to us."

Because Christ does not forsake His Church, He binds up the brokenhearted, He redeems those who are humble in spirit, He is the refuge of the poor, and is their Helper in times of tribulation.

God chastises in mercy, and in order to possess [the sinner] He makes him suffer. His rebuke is for the man who hath understanding, and teaches him that he is not a stranger [to God]. And He doth not leave him that is tempted to be tempted more than his strength [will bear]. And again he envelops him with His mercies and sustains him; and He gathered him into the fold of life after He hath tried him. God—may His honor be adored!—turned the heart of the king towards His people, "for the heart of a king is set in His hands like a fountain of water; He turns it about in whatever direction He pleases" (Prov. 21:1).

And from that day the rays of salvation began to shine on the whole Church. In the districts of Arbîl the churches were laid waste long ago. In Tabhrîz and Hamâdân they were entirely destroyed, and their foundations had been uprooted from the earth. In Mâwsil (Môsul) and its provinces, and in Baghdâd, the churches had been ransomed at very large prices and tens of thousands of darics. But the Church which the Catholicus Makîkhâ (1257-63) built in Baghdâd by the command of Hûlâbhû (Hûlâgû), the victorious king, and Tûkôs Khâtûn, the believing queen, and the Cell of the Catholicus were taken, and the palace which had belonged to the Arab kings. When Hûlâbhû (Hûlâgû) the father of these kings [i.e., the Mongols] had taken and looted Baghdâd he gave that palace to Mâr Makîkhâ, the Catholicus, in order that he might establish in it services of prayer on behalf of himself and his seed forever. Now this was not sufficient—for those who took this church and the Cell of the Catholicus to set up [mosques upon it]—but they compelled the Christians to eject from it even the bones of the two Patriarchal Fathers [Mâr Makîkhâ and Mâr Denhâ], and those of the holy old men, and monks, and believers who had been buried therein. And these things were carried out by the command of that son of perdition, that accursed and damned man Nâwrûz, the hater of justice, the enemy of the truth, and the lover of falsehood.

And when that monk whom Mâr Catholicus [had sent to the king] returned, and brought with him the Pukdânâ [i.e., the royal Edict which

restored to him his authority], and showed him the affection of the Amîrs and the greatness of the victorious king's goodwill towards him, the door of the Cell was opened, and the Catholicus took his seat upon his Throne and gathered together his scattered adherents, and brought nigh to him the members of his household who had betaken themselves afar off. And the Pukdânê (Edicts) were read in the Dîwân (judical assembly) and every man brought back that which he had taken. From that sum of money the Catholicus took what was necessary for travelling to King Ḳâzân. And he went forth from Mârâghâh in the month of Tammuz (July) of that year, which fell in the month of Ramâdhân, and was the year of the Greeks one thousand six hundred and seven (A.D. 1296), to the place which is called Ûghân (or Ôghân).

Two days after his arrival he went into the presence of the king with appropriate state and ceremony. And the king burned incense according to custom, and made the Catholicus to sit on his right hand, and [the attendants] brought wine, and the king took the cup and presented it to the Catholicus, and also to all the holy men who were with him. And from that [time] he began [to treat him] with affection. And in proportion as the king, little [by little], was increasing the honor which he paid to the Catholicus, the hatred which was in the hearts of the enemies [of the Catholicus] increased and they forged evil plots, and they sent information about everything which took place to that son of perdition, that accursed man Nâwrûz.

Chapter XIII

Further Pillage and Murder in Mârâghâh

And in the year of the Greeks one thousand six hundred and eight (A.D. 1296-97), the victorious king came down to pass the winter in the city of Baghdâd, and Mâr Catholicus remained in Mârâghâh. And it fell out that a certain man who was called by the name of Shenâkh el-Tâmûr (or Shaing êl-Taimûr, or Shâkh êl-Taimûr) came into Mârâghâh, and he cast about a report that he had with him an Edict ordering that everyone who did not abandon Christianity and deny his Faith should be killed. And he added many threats and magnified the severity of the Edict, and inserted various [penalties] which had never before been heard of in the world. Now when the people of the Arabs heard this they became like savages, and they stirred themselves up to fight, and their hearts became bold and cruel, and in the fierceness of their strength the whole of their people rushed to the Cell, and plundered everything which they found [there]. This took place during the Fast of Lent, on the fourth day of the week (Wednesday) following the Sunday on which the prayer beginning "Tâu naudhê waneshabbakh" (i.e., "come ye, let us praise and glorify") [is said].

And when the story went forth that this impudent fellow had done this without any royal command, and had acted solely because of the evil of his disposition and the intensity of his wickedness, the Amîrs and the governors who were in Mârâghâh gathered together and took counsel, and decided to perform judgment on a following Sunday and to restore to the Cell the various valuable objects which those impudent men had carried off from it. Now these objects were of very great price, among them being the gold seal which the King of Kings Mangû Khân [the eldest son of Tûlûi Khân and grandson of Genghis Khân]—May our Lord give rest to his soul, and make his portion to be with the saints!—had given to the Patriarchal Cell, and that crown which Mâr Pâpâ (the Pope) had given to the Cell, and another seal, made of silver, which the deceased King Arghôn had given to the Catholicus.

And then [on the following Sunday] the people of the Arabs were assembled before the Amîrs and Judges, and the rods for the punishment of the evildoers had been brought [and they began] to beat [them], straightway with one voice they all uttered loud cries [of protest].

And they took stones in their hands, and, shut their ears, and chased the Amîrs and the governors, every man to his house. And every Christian who fell into their hands they smote and belabored pitilessly. In the impetuosity of their attack they came to the Cell, and they pulled down all the buildings as far as the beams of the roof. And they smashed in with stones the heads of the monks who were in the Cell, and of the young men who had gone up to the roof to hide themselves. When one of the disciples saw these things taking place, he hurled [the stones] back on the Arabs and wounded some of them. Thereupon the Arabs became more infuriated, and one of them went up behind that disciple, and smote him with [his] sword and cut off his head, and threw it down to the ground. Then the monks who were there cast themselves down [from the roof], and there were some of them whose bones were broken. And one of those impudent men who were thirsting for the blood of the Christians, seeing that the monks had cast themselves down in order to save their lives, stretched out his hand for [his] knife, and smote that monk and killed him. Certain believing men grasped the other monks and dragged them into [their] houses. And the treasury of the holy church of Mâr George, which Rabban Ṣâwmâ had built, was broken open, and everything that was in the Cell, the vessels of copper and iron, the carpets, and the chests of stores, which had escaped a previous looting, were all taken and carried off at the same time. But by the looting of those things the church itself was saved and delivered from pulling down and destruction. Those impudent men had fully intended to destroy the church, but God in His mercy on that church prevented them from doing this by means of the objects which they looted.

And to speak briefly, this last looting was so much worse than the first looting which took place at the beginning [of the persecution], that neither the tongue is capable of describing it, nor is the pen of the skilled scribe able to write [any account of it]. If God had not shown mercy, and the believing woman Queen Bûrgesîn Argî (?) had not hidden the Catholicus and the holy men in her house, and, with the help of God which supported [her], protected them, all that was left for the Church to do was to bow her head, and veil her face, for those turbulent men were determined to make a massacre.

After five days they departed to a place which is called Shâkâto, and thence they removed themselves to the mountain which is called Siyâ Kûh, until the king returned from Baghdâd to Hamâdân. And in the neighborhood of this city the Catholicus went to him, and when the king saw him he was sorry for him, and for his broken condition. And he issued a Pukdânâ (Edict) and sent a messenger and gave orders that all the people of the city of Mârâghâh should be seized, and bound with fetters, and beaten with stripes until they gave up what they had robbed from the Cell, and also that they should rebuild the churches and restore them to their former condition. And after great toil, and the beatings and tortures which they were made to suffer, the people had produced a very small part of what they had stolen and the rest remained [with them].

Chapter XIX

The Death of Mâr Yahbh-Allâhâ

Then the Catholicus, and the Mongols, and the clergy who were with him, who had come from the Amîr Gaidjâk to bring him, went to the village of Bêth Sayyâdhê, but with great fear, and terror, and great anguish and affliction. And they stayed in the village for a few days until they had collected some money, which they gave to the messenger of the Amîr Djôpân, and to the one hundred men who had come from the Amîr Gaidjâk, and to the Kurds, who were with them. Then they departed and went to the Camp, on the eighth day of the month Tammûz (July) of this year (A.D. 1310).

And the Catholicus visited the princess, the wife of the Amîr Gaidjâk, and she paid him great honor and also sent men with him to the Camp. When he arrived he went straightaway to visit the great Amîr Djôpân, who saw him, and paid him the honor which was his due, and thence he went to the city; and all the Amîrs were well acquainted with his history. And he went to the victorious king and blessed him according to custom and placed the cup in his hands, and the king likewise gave him the cup, but neither of them spake a word with the other. And sorely afflicted, the Catholicus went forth from the presence, for he had intended if the king had questioned him to make known to him all that had happened to himself and to his flock. At this treatment his heart

was broken grievously, and he sat down there for a month of days, hoping that, peradventure, some new thing might happen, or that someone would ask him about what had happened. And when certain necessary business connected with the Cell and the Christians had been accomplished, he went back and came to the monastery which he had built by the side of Mârâghâh. And he made up his mind that he would never again go to the Camp, saying, "I am wearied (or disgusted) with the service of the Mongols."

And in the year of the Greeks one thousand six hundred and twenty-two (A.D. 1310-11) he passed the winter in the monastery. In the summer he went to the city of Tâbhrîz because he heard that the Amîr Irnâdjîn—may our Lord preserve his life!—had arrived there; and the Catholicus having come thither met him straightaway. And Irnâdjîn paid him great honor, and he and his wife [Kekhshek], the daughter of King Ahmâd, the son of the deceased King Hûlâgû, gave him gifts and presents. And the princess [Kekhshek] was greatly honored in the kingdom, because the victorious King [Ûljâîtô] had taken her daughter [Kûtlûk-shâh Khâtûn] to wife, and she was then the greatest of his wives. The amount of money which the Amîr Irnâdjîn and his wife gave to the Catholicus was ten thousand [dînârs], which are [equal to] sixty thousand zûzê, and two riding horses. And the Amîr also gave a village to the church of Mâr Shalîtâ, the holy martyr, for his dead father was laid therein, and his mother and his wives were buried therein.

The Catholicus passed the winter of the year of the Greeks one thousand six hundred and twenty-three (A.D. 1311-12) in the monastery and the summer also. And when his case was represented to the king by the Council he bestowed upon him five thousand dînârs, which came to him for his maintenance every year. And the king also gave him villages [in the neighborhood] of the city of Baghdâd.

Now up to this year the number of the Fathers, Metropolitans, and Bishops which he has ordained for flocks by layings on of hands, is seventy-five. Thus are they. He lived in the monastery which he had built until the year of the Greeks, one thousand six hundred and twenty-nine [A.D. 1317]. He died on the night of the [Saturday preceding] the Sunday [of the prayer] "Mâ shêbhîh mashkĕnâkh ("How glorious is Your habitation"), the 15th day of the month the latter Teshrî (November), and was laid in the monastery which he had built. May his memory be for blessing! And may the prayers of Mâr Yahbh-Allâhâ, the Catholicus, and Rabban Ṣâwmâ be upon us, and upon the world, to the uttermost limit thereof, and upon the Holy Church and her children.

And to God be glory, and honor, and praise, and worship, forever and ever. Amen and Amen.

Here ends this "History of Mâr Yahbh-Allâhâ, the Catholicus and Patriarch of the East, and of Rabban Ṣâwmâ, the Visitor-General." And to God be constant glory, and to the sinner who wrote these lines, may there be forgiveness of debts, and remission of sins in the terrible Hall of Judgment! Amen.

70. *The War Chronicle of Amda Tseyon*

Amda Tseyon (d. 1344), grandson of the restorer of the Aksumite monarchy of Ethiopia (see Text 71), ruled that ancient Christian kingdom from 1314 to 1344, extending its borders by conquering neighboring Muslim states. His reign was also marked by a literary renaissance and the growth of an influential monastic reform movement in the country's central highlands, which, however, often opposed the king. This war chronicle was evidently composed by someone in the royal court, although, as M. Kropp has observed, it sounds less like a typical court chronicle than like a vita of a wonder-working saint. (Within this excerpt, the condensation is by the translator, whose comments are in italics.)

[*After defeating invading armies from the Muslim states of Ifat, Adal and Mora, Amda Tseyon goes on the attack, and meets an army of soldiers from seven Muslim provinces. In the midst of the battle, an opposing warrior attacks the king himself from the rear.*]

. . . But Amda Tseyon was preserved by the grace of God, and turning, hit his assailant with his spear and killed him.

As for his army, it threw itself in pursuit of the ungodly, but the latter went over to the offensive and gave battle to the Christians, who, unable to sustain the fight, cried out, "Where is the King?" because their King was strong, courageous, and

victorious in combat and there was no one who could equal him. While they were uttering these cries the King arrived behind them, riding on his horse; he entered the midst of the ungodly and hurled his spear at one of them who was struck down by it. Then, being unable to resist, they gave up the battle. The King pursued them with his army and there was much killing; the land was covered with their corpses.

Amda Tseyon returned to his camp glorifying God the Father, the Son, and the Holy Spirit, who had given him the victory; then he ordered the troops who had not taken part in the fighting to go off in pursuit of those enemies who survived and to wage war against them; obeying the orders of

Source: *Ethiopian Royal Chronicles*, ed. and tr. K. P. Pankhurst (Addis Ababa: Oxford University Press, 1967), 20-28.

the King these troops left during the night, reached the ungodly who were on the banks of a river in the morning and killed them. The soldiers then returned to the King, bringing with them their loot: swords, bows, spears and clothes in great quantity. At this sight the King was filled with joy and thanked God.

[*Amda Tseyon in this way defeated his enemies in battle after battle, and advanced into lands never previously occupied by any Ethiopian emperor. At first all went well, but later Jamal ad-Din (of Ifat) rebelled and joined forces with the ruler of Adal. The emperor was now greatly outnumbered by his enemies, for many of his best troops were on duty elsewhere. He was, moreover, a sick man.*]

King Amda Tseyon was in his tent lying on his bed and gravely ill. For seven days and seven nights he had neither eaten nor drunk and he had sent one of his officers, called Zana Yamanu, chief of the pages in charge of the dogs, to hunt wild animals. This officer on his journey met the army of the Muslims; he immediately abandoned the hunt and warned the King in these terms: "The enemy army, more numerous than all your troops, approaches, and we have returned to die with you." At this news the King sent scouts on horseback to reconnoiter the camp of the Muslims and to find out whether they were numerous or not. When these scouts saw the multitude of the unbelievers, resembling an immense cloud which obscured the sky or a vast number of locusts covering the earth, they became giddy and felt their hearts fail them. They returned to the King and said to him: "The entire earth cannot contain all these people, and if they were to attack, all the people of Ethiopia, great and small, could not resist them." On hearing these words the King rose, and attempted, though ill and weak, to leave his tent, but he could not put on his girdle nor stand on his feet, and he fell back on his bed, defeated by his illness. His servants lifted him up again, and put on his military girdle, then he left his tent and, stumbling now on one side and now on the other, was followed by the two Queens (i.e., his mother and his wife) who, crying bitterly, said

to him, "O, lord, how can you go to fight? Are your legs strong enough to allow you to run as before when you were in good health? Can your hand draw the bow or carry the shield and the spear? Have you the strength to ride the horse, enfeebled as you are by your illness?" In speaking to him thus they shed abundant tears. The King replied to them, "Must I die as a woman? No, I know how to die as a warrior!" Then he left them.

Then the younger Queen said to the elder, "Hold him back in the name of Christ and do not let him leave!" But the latter replied, "If he wishes to go I cannot prevent him. And why should I oppose his will when the unbelievers come to kill him? Shall I hold him so that they strike him in his tent? That idea is far from my thought; let him rather go and die like a man!" And at these words they both gave way to tears, because it seemed to them that they would never again see the King. At that moment he returned on foot, and said to them, "Go back to your tents and do not follow me!" Then he left, putting his confidence in God, who gives life and death, punishes and pardons, humbles and elevates, weakens the strong and fortifies the feeble. . . .

The King was thus fortified by the Lord; he forgot his illness and his weakness, girded the sword with two cutting edges, namely, prayer and supplication, and dressed himself in his victorious armor, that is to say, confidence and faith; then he cried out: "Come to my help, God of Moses and of Aaron!" and addressed himself to the priests: "Intercede for me with God," he said, "and do not forget me in your prayers!" He then went out of the camp and found himself alone.

[*The priests prayed as the Emperor had commanded. Amda Tseyon also prayed, according to his custom.*]

The King raised his eyes and his hands to heaven, and said, "Most powerful God, merciful God and friend of men, protect Your people, do not let it perish because of its sins, but have pity on it in Your mercy, because You are sweet, clement, and just; as for me, do with me what You please!" It was thus that the King prayed, imploring the help of God, not for himself, but for his people, thus conforming with the word of the Gospel which says, "The good shepherd gives his life for his sheep."

Then the army of the unbelievers advanced, bows extended, swords in hand, their swords shining like lightning. They were as numerous as locusts, as the stars of the sky, or the grains of sand on the edge of the sea, and resembled clouds full of rain which cover the sky. The noise which they made resembled the noise of waves driven by a hurricane, their voices resounded like the thunder which bursts in the middle of rain; their cries made the hills and mountains tremble and the earth shake under their feet.

[*The Muslim army was so terrifying that the emperor's forces fled, leaving Amda Tseyon almost alone with a mere handful of trusted followers.*]

His friends kissed his hands, feet, eyes, breast and shoulders, and, all taking flight, left him to die. He remained alone like a steadfast column, like a solid base, like a wall of granite, and he cried out to those who fled, "Stay a little to see how I fight, how I know how to die, and what God will do today by my hand!" But no one listened; everyone fled. And if I say that they all fled, do not believe that it was through cowardice and be not astonished, for I must add that the army of Shoa and of Damot, that of Gojam and of Tigre, that of Bugana and of Amhara and even all the armies of Ethiopia together could not have resisted, if not by the power of God.

When King Amda Tseyon saw his soldiers take flight, he cried to them in a loud voice, "Where are you going? Do you believe you can today reach your provinces? Have you forgotten, besides, that it is I who raised you, nourished you, and covered you with ornaments of gold and silver and precious clothes!" Then he threw himself forward like a tiger, jumped like a lion on his horse, which was called Harab Asfare, and told one of his followers, Zanasfare, the chief of the young cavaliers, to advance on the right in the midst of the unbelievers. Zanasfare, obeying the order of the King, penetrated their ranks and was followed by five other cavaliers, the first of whom was Takla, the second

Wanag Raad, the third Saf Sagad, the son of the King, the fourth Badl Wabaz, and the fifth Qedmaye. King Amda Tseyon attacked the enemy on their left flank, which was the weakest; he attacked without looking behind him and without turning back, despite the spears and arrows which fell like hail around him. The unbelievers surrounded him with their swords, but he, his face impassive as a rock, despising death, threw himself into their ranks, striking with such force that, by the power of God, he killed two of his enemies simultaneously with his spear. Then the unbelievers scattered and gave way to flight, feeling that they could not resist an old warrior like himself who had no equal in fighting. The six cavaliers of whom I have just spoken also struck at the enemies whom they found around them, and when the King put the unbelievers to flight the troops who had abandoned him rejoined him; they drove the enemy, though numerous and powerful, into a ditch which God seemed to have put there for that very purpose. Then the King descended from his horse, took his shield and struck at the Muslims. When his right hand was exhausted he used his left, and, when that had had its turn, he again used his right.

[*Amda Tseyon, if we can believe his admiring chronicler, had thus won the battle almost singlehandedly.*]

Permit me to return to the battle which took place that day, because there was nothing like it in the time of any of the kings of Ethiopia who preceded Amda Tseyon. This Prince fought against all the peoples placed under his rule. No one dared to make war against him, but the unbelievers had come resolutely to attack him when he was alone, without the help of his army, which, led by the hand of God, had gone into another country. God wished it thus in order to manifest His power and wisdom so that the troops of Amda Tseyon could not claim to have won by their own strength; it was for that reason that He helped with His own power the King who had with him no more than a handful of soldiers. . . . Amda Tseyon was himself worth ten thousand warriors: all by himself he dispersed and exterminated the infidels; he trampled on them like dust, he pounded them like grain, he split them like seeds, he scattered them like the leaves which the wind tears off and carries away, he destroyed them like grass burnt by a forest fire.

[At the end of the fighting the emperor once again gave thanks to God.]

At sunset the King left the battlefield and went back to his camp, covered with great glory; he entered the chapel, advanced to the altar and fell at the feet of the Crucifix, prostrating his face to the ground and crying abundantly: "Glory to you, O Christ, and to Your merciful Father and to the Holy Spirit," he said. "It is You who have given us the victory, who have saved us from the hands of the unbelievers and who have saved me from becoming the prey of the enemy."

The priests embraced one another crying, and large tears fell on their breasts because it had seemed to them that the light of the world, the King, our veritable sun, was going to pass away.

After having made his salutation, Amda Tseyon left the chapel and returned to his tent, where the Queen entered behind him. She kissed his hands, feet, and neck, and said to him in tears, "Is it possible that you are still alive, O master King? It seems to me that this is a dream like those which one has during sleep and which disappear in waking. I see you today as in a dream, but I have no certainty that this is reality. Are you really alive, O King, my master?" Uttering these words she threw herself at his feet and rolled in the dust, sobbing.

[Amda Tseyon at last felt that he had accomplished his mission. He therefore assembled his men to discuss their future course of action.]

The King then reassembled his troops and said to them, "Speak to me frankly, without fear, and tell me what you think. Must we send back to our country our women and children, our followers and our servants who give us their care; or must we leave them here and go further?" No one replying to him, he resumed, "Speak openly, and tell me what seems to you best, most useful and convenient. If your desire is to leave this very day and to return to Ethiopia, we will set forth this morn-

ing or this evening by day, or by night; we will set out at once if this pleases you. It is sometimes for the King to follow the council of his generals and sometimes for the generals to follow that of the King; he who acts without taking advice is a madman. Tell me then, I beg you, if you are of the opinion that we alone should go forward, without taking our wives, our children, our followers, our servants and our goods? Have no fear; if you get on to your horses and mules I will have even better ones than yours for myself, and if you have rivers to swim across I will swim also with the strength of God, because He who came to my help in this war and who saved me from the hand of the unbelievers when you were absent can again drag me from danger: it is in Him that I put my confidence and my hope. Tell me then what you wish!"

Then one of the great priests of the royal chapel, who was called Hezba Egziabher, rose and said, "It is certain that it is God who delivered you from the hands of the unbelievers and that without His help we would not have been saved. Listen O King, it was not His powerful angels, Mikael or Gabriel, whom God sent that day to bring us help and deliver us from danger, it was His own Son who descended from Heaven to save us by His power from the hands of the Muslims."

This priest did not speak thus through lack of faith in angels, but because of the multitude of the unbelievers. . . .

The King then once again resumed his discourse and said to the priest, "It seems to me that if the whole army of Ethiopia found itself in front of these people, even if the latter were without swords, bows, and spears, it could not in the space of six months have defeated them. But God, who can do all and whom no one can resist, annihilated them in an hour; He did not wish to remember my sins because He is merciful and loves mankind."

Then one of the chiefs of the army replied to the King, "You say that the unbelievers came armed with their swords to make war on us in these plains; but what would you say of us when we make war on them and pursue them on horseback?"

[The emperor and his followers thus discussed matters for some time. No one dared to tell Amda

Tseyon that they wished to return home. At length he himself again raised the matter.]

The King later returned to his soldiers and addressed them, saying, "Tell me what you think. Shall we return to our country by the road we took in coming, or shall we take another? Answer me I beg you because one cannot conclude an affair by silence. Once you had reason to fear when you saw bursting on us that black cloud full of rain which obscured the sky and the earth—I mean that innumerable multitude of unbelievers—but today you have no longer anything to dread since God has shown us His mercy and has saved us from the hands of our enemies." The army then replied, "You have fought for us night and day and you have delivered us from the unbelievers. Now allow us to return to our country."

"It is proper for the animal to return to its pasturage," replied the King. "As for me this is my intention: we will cross the country of Talag in the kingdom of Adal, we will kill the unbelievers who are still there, and we will return to our country by another road."

This proposition being well received, the King set forth.

71. *Kebra Nagast*

Kebra Nagast ("The Glory of Kings"), the national epic of Ethiopia, establishes the nation's connection to ancient Israel through the Aksumite kings' descent from King Solomon and their possession of the Tabernacle of the Covenant. Its main part tells of the encounter between Solomon and Queen Mâkĕdâ of Ethiopia, the birth of their son Bayna-Lehkem, the son's journey to meet his father, who anoints him and renames him David, and the removal of the Tabernacle from Jerusalem to Ethiopia when David returns home as king. It was composed in the Ethiopic language during the reign of Amda Tseyon (see text 70) in the early fourteenth century, though it includes translations of thirteenth-century Arabic texts, and the substance of the legends is probably much older.

[During her stay in Jerusalem, Queen Mâkĕdâ is persuaded by King Solomon to worship the God of Israel.]

28. . . .

And the Queen said [to Solomon], "From this moment I will not worship the sun, but will worship the Creator of the sun, the God of Israel. And that Tabernacle of the God of Israel shall be to me my Lady, and to my seed after me, and to all my kingdoms that are under my dominion. And because of this I have found favor before you, and before the God of Israel my Creator, who has brought me to you, and has made me to hear your voice, and has shown me your face, and has made me to understand your commandment." Then she returned to [her] house.

And the Queen used to go [to Solomon] and return continually, and hearken to his wisdom, and keep it in her heart. And Solomon used to go and visit her and answer all the questions which she put to him; and the Queen used to visit him and ask him questions, and he informed her concerning every matter that she wished to enquire about. And after she had dwelt [there] six months, the Queen wished to return to her own country,

SOURCE: *The Queen of Sheba and Her Only Son Menyelek*, ed. and tr. E. A. Wallis Budge (London, Liverpool, and Boston: Medici Society, 1922), 29, 33–36, 37–40, 42, 51–54, 64, 65, 66–68, 71–72, 80, 88.

and she sent a message to Solomon, saying, "I desire greatly to dwell with you, but now, for the sake of all my people, I wish to return to my own country. And as for that which I have heard, may God make it to bear fruit in my heart, and in the hearts of all those who have heard it with me. For the ear could never be filled with the hearing of your wisdom, and the eye could never be filled with the sight of the same."

. . .

30. Concerning How King Solomon Swore to the Queen

And Solomon answered and said to her, "I swear to you that I will not take you by force, but you must swear to me that you will not take by force anything that is in my house." And the Queen laughed and said to him, "Being a wise man why do you speak as a fool? Shall I steal anything, or shall I carry out of the house of the King that which the King has not given to me? Do not imagine that I have come here through love of riches. Moreover, my own kingdom is as wealthy as yours, and there is nothing which I wish for that I lack. Assuredly I have only come in quest of your wisdom." And he said to her, "If you would make me swear, swear to me, for a swearing is fitting for both [of us], so that neither of us may be unjustly treated. And if you will not make me swear I will not make you swear." And she said to him, "Swear to me that you will not take me by force, and I on my part will swear not to take by force your possessions"; and he swore to her and made her swear.

And the King went up on his bed on the one side [of the chamber], and the servants made ready for her a bed on the other side. And Solomon said to a young manservant, "Wash out the bowl and set in it a vessel of water whilst the Queen is looking on, and shut the doors and go and sleep." And Solomon spoke to the servant in another tongue which the Queen did not understand, and he did as the King commanded, and went and slept. And the King had not as yet fallen asleep, but he only pretended to be asleep, and he was watching the Queen intently. Now the house of Solomon the King was illumined as by day, for

in his wisdom he had made shining pearls which were like unto the sun, and moon, and stars [and had set them] in the roof of his house.

And the Queen slept a little. And when she woke up her mouth was dry with thirst, for the food which Solomon had given her in his wisdom had made her thirsty, and she was very thirsty indeed, and her mouth was dry; and she moved her lips and sucked with her mouth and found no moisture. And she determined to drink the water which she had seen, and she looked at King Solomon and watched him carefully, and she thought that he was sleeping a sound sleep. But he was not asleep, and he was waiting until she should rise up to steal the water to [quench] her thirst. And she rose up and, making no sound with her feet she went to the water in the bowl and lifted up the jar to drink the water. And Solomon seized her hand before she could drink the water, and said to her, "Why have you broken the oath that you have sworn, that you would not take by force anything that is in my house?" And she answered and said to him in fear, "Is the oath broken by my drinking water?" And the King said to her, "Is there anything that you have seen under the heavens that is better than water?" And the Queen said, "I have sinned against myself, and you are free from [your] oath. But let me drink water for my thirst." Then Solomon said to her, "Am I perchance free from the oath which you have made me swear?" And the Queen said, "Be free from your oath, only let me drink water." And he permitted her to drink water, and after she had drunk water he worked his will with her and they slept together.

And after he slept there appeared to King Solomon [in a dream] a brilliant sun, and it came down from heaven and shed exceedingly great splendor over Israel. And when it had tarried there for a time it suddenly withdrew itself, and it flew away to the country of Ethiopia, and it shone there with exceedingly great brightness forever, for it willed to dwell there. And [the King said], "I waited [to see] if it would come back to Israel, but it did not return. And again while I waited a light rose up in the heavens, and a Sun came down from them in the country of Judah, and it sent forth light which was very much stronger than before." And Israel, because of the flame of that Sun entreated that Sun evilly and would not walk in the light thereof. And that Sun paid no heed to Israel, and the Israelites hated Him, and it became impossible that peace should exist between them and the Sun. And they lifted up their hands against Him with staves and knives, and they wished to extinguish that Sun. And they cast darkness upon the whole world with earthquake and thick darkness, and they imagined that that Sun would never more rise upon them. And they destroyed His light and cast themselves upon Him and they set a guard over His tomb wherein they had cast Him. And He came forth where they did not look for Him, and illumined the whole world, more especially the First Sea and the Last Sea, Ethiopia and Rôm. And He paid no heed whatsoever to Israel, and He ascended His former throne.

And when Solomon the King saw this vision in his sleep, his soul became disturbed, and his understanding was snatched away as by [a flash of] lightning, and he woke up with an agitated mind. . . .

32. How the Queen Brought Forth and Came to Her Own Country

And the Queen departed and came into the country of Bâlâ Zadîsârĕyâ nine months and five days after she had separated from King Solomon. And the pains of childbirth laid hold upon her, and she brought forth a man child, and she gave it to the nurse with great pride and delight. And she tarried until the days of her purification were ended, and then she came to her own country with great pomp and ceremony. And her officers who had remained there brought gifts to their mistress, and made obeisance to her, and did homage to her, and all the borders of the country rejoiced at her coming. Those who were nobles among them she arrayed in splendid apparel, and to some she gave gold and silver, and hyacinthine and purple robes; and she gave them all manner of things that could be desired. And she ordered her kingdom aright, and none disobeyed her command; for she loved wisdom and God strengthened her kingdom.

And the child grew and she called his name Bayna-Lehkem. And the child reached the age of twelve years, and he asked his friends among the boys who were being educated with him, and said to them, "Who is my father?" And they said to him, "Solomon the King." And he went to the Queen his mother, and said to her, "O Queen, make me to know who is my father." And the Queen spoke to him angrily, wishing to frighten him so that he might not desire to go [to his father] saying, "Why do you ask me about your father? I am your father and your mother; seek not to know any more." And the boy went forth from her presence, and sat down. And a second time, and a third time he asked her, and he importuned her to tell him. One day, however, she told him, saying, "His country is far away, and the road thither is very difficult; would you not rather be here?" And the youth Bayna-Lehkem was handsome, and his whole body and his members, and the bearing of his shoulders resembled those of King Solomon his father, and his eyes, and his legs, and his whole gait resembled those of Solomon the King. And when he was twenty-two years old he was skilled in the whole art of war and of horsemanship, and in the hunting and trapping of wild beasts, and in everything that young men are wont to learn. And he said to the Queen, "I will go and look upon the face of my father, and I will come back here by the will of God, the Lord of Israel."

33. How the King of Ethiopia Traveled

And the Queen called Tâmrîn, the chief of her caravan men and merchants, and she said to him, "Get ready for your journey and take this young man with you, for he importunes me by night and by day. And you shall take him to the King and shall bring him back here in safety, if God, the Lord of Israel, pleases . . ."

Now there was a law in the country of Ethiopia that [only] a woman should reign, and that she must be a virgin who had never known man, but the Queen said [to her son], "henceforward a man who is of your seed shall reign, and a woman shall nevermore reign; only seed of yours shall reign and his seed after him from generation to generation. And this you shall inscribe in the letters of the rolls in the Book of their Prophets in brass, and you shall lay it in the House of God, which shall be built as a memorial and as a prophecy for the last days. And the people shall not worship the sun and the magnificence of the heavens, or the mountains and the forests, or the stones and the trees of the wilderness, or the abysses and that which is in the waters, or graven images and figures of gold, or the feathered fowl which fly; and they shall not make use of them in divining, and they shall not pay adoration to them. And this law shall abide forever. And if there be anyone who shall transgress this law, your seed shall judge him forever. Only give us the fringes of the covering of the holy heavenly Zion, the Tabernacle of the Law of God, which we would embrace (or, greet). Peace be to the strength of your kingdom and to your brilliant wisdom, which God, the Lord of Israel our Creator, has given to you."

And the Queen took the young man aside and when he was alone with her she gave him that symbol which Solomon had given her, that is to say, the ring on his finger, so that he might know his son, and might remember her word and her covenant which she had made [with him], that she would worship God all the days of her life, she and those who were under her dominion, with all [the power] which God had given her. And then the Queen sent him away in peace.

And the young man [and his retinue] made straight their way and they journeyed on and came into the country of the neighborhood of Gâzâ. Now this is the Gâzâ which Solomon the King gave to the Queen of Ethiopia. And in the Acts of the Apostles Luke the Evangelist wrote, saying, "He was the governor of the whole country of Gâzâ, a eunuch of Queen Hendakê, who had believed on the word of Luke the Apostle."

34. ...

[Report of the arrival of Bayna-Lehkem reaches Solomon.] ...

And when King Solomon heard this his heart was perturbed and he was glad in his soul, for in those days he had no children, except a boy who was seven years old and whose name was Îyôrbeʿâm (Rehoboam). It happened to Solomon even as Paul states, saying, "God has made foolishness the wisdom of this world," for Solomon had made a plan in his wisdom and said, "By one thousand women I shall beget one thousand men children, and I shall inherit the countries of the enemy, and I will overthrow [their] idols." But [God] only gave him three children. His eldest son was the King of Ethiopia, the son of the Queen of Ethiopia, and was the firstborn of whom [God] spoke prophetically, "God swore to David in righteousness, and repented not, 'Of the fruit of your body will I make to sit upon your throne.'" And God gave to David His servant grace before Him, and granted to him that there should sit upon the throne of Godhead One of his seed in the flesh, from the Virgin, and should judge the living and the dead, and reward all according to their works, One to whom praise is fitting, our Lord Jesus Christ, forever and ever, Amen. And He gave him one on the earth who should become king over the Tabernacle of the Law of the holy, heavenly Zion, that is to say, the King of Ethiopia. And as for those who reigned, who were not [of] Israel, that was due to the transgression of the law and the commandment, whereat God was not pleased.

. . .

[Solomon welcomes his son Bayna-Lehkem, and wants him to succeed him on the throne of Israel, but the son declines, resolute on returning to Ethiopia.]

38. How the King Planned to Send Away His Son with the Children of the Nobles

And then Solomon the King went back into his house, and he caused to be gathered together his councillors, and his officers, and the elders of his kingdom, and he said to them, "I am not able to make this young man consent [to dwell here]. And now, listen to me, and to what I shall say to you. Come, let us make him king of the country of Ethiopia, together with your children; you sit on my right hand and on my left hand, and in like manner the eldest of your children shall sit on his right hand and on his left hand. Come, O ye councillors and officers, let us give [him] your firstborn children, and we shall have two kingdoms; I will rule here with you, and our children shall reign there. And I put my trust in God that a third time He will give me seed, and that a third king will be to me. Now Baltâsôr, the King of Rôm, wishes that I would give my son to his daughter, and to make him with his daughter king over the whole country of Rôm. For besides her he has no other child, and he has sworn that he will only make king a man who is of the seed of David my father. And if we rule there we shall be three kings. And Rehoboam shall reign here over Israel. For thus says the prophecy of David my father: 'The seed of Solomon shall become three heads of kingdoms upon the earth.' . . ."

And the priests, and the officers, and the councillors answered and said to him, "Send your first-born, and we will send our children also according to your wish. Who can resist the commandment of God and the king? They are your servants and the servants of your seed, as you have proclaimed. If you wish, you can sell them and their mothers to be slaves; it is not for us to transgress your command and the command of the Lord your God." And then they made ready to do for them [i.e., their children] what it was right to do, and to send them into the country of Ethiopia, so that they might reign there and dwell there forever, they and their seed from generation to generation.

39. How They Made the Son of Solomon King

And they made ready the ointment of the oil of kingship, and the sounds of the large horn, and the small horn, and the flute and the pipes, and the harp and the drum filled the air; and the city resounded with cries of joy and gladness. And they brought the young man into the Holy of Holies, and he laid hold upon the horns of the altar, and sovereignty was given to him by the mouth of Zadok the priest, and by the mouth of Joas (Benaiah) the priest, the commander of the army of King Solomon, and he anointed him with the holy oil of the ointment of kingship. And he went out from the house of the Lord, and they called his name David, for the name of a king came to him by the law. And they made him to ride upon the mule of King Solomon, and they led him round

about the city, and said, "We have appointed you from this moment"; and then they cried out to him, "Bâh [Long] live the royal father!" And there were some who said, "It is fitting and right that your dominion of Ethiopia shall be from the River of Egypt to the west of the sun [i.e., to the setting sun]; blessed be your seed upon the earth!—and from Shoa to the east of India, for you will please [the people of these lands]. And the Lord God of Israel shall be to you a guide, and the Tabernacle of the Law of God shall be with all that you look upon. And all your enemies and foes shall be overthrown before you, and completion and finish shall be to you and to your seed after you; you shall judge many nations and none shall judge you." And again his father blessed him and said to him, "The blessing of heaven and earth shall be your blessing," and all the congregation of Israel said, "Amen." And his father also said to Zadok the priest, "Make him to know and tell him concerning the judgment and decree of God which he shall observe there" [in Ethiopia].

. . .

44. How It Is Not a Seemly Thing to Revile the King

Now it is not a seemly thing to revile the king, for he is the anointed of God. It is neither seemly nor good. If he does that which is good he will not suffer loss in three kingdoms: First, God shall overthrow for him his enemy, and he shall not be seized by the hand of his enemy. Second, God shall make him reign with Him and with His righteousness, and shall make him to sit on His right hand. Third, God shall make him to reign upon earth with glory and joy, and shall direct his kingdom for him, and shall bring down the nations under his feet. And if he treats God lightly, and does not do that which is good, and does not himself walk in the path of uprightness, God shall work as He pleases against him; on earth He will make his days to be few, and in heaven (sic) his place of abode shall be the habitation of Sheôl with the Devil. And on earth he shall enjoy neither health nor gladness [and he shall live] in fear and terror, without peace and with perturbation. . . .

And Israel from of old reviled their kings and provoked their prophets to wrath, and in later times they crucified their Savior. But believing Christian folk dwell in peace, without sickness and suffering, without hatred and offense, with our king . . . who loves God and who does not remove from his heart the thing of righteousness, and faith in the Churches and in the believers. And his enemies shall be scattered by the might of the Cross of Jesus Christ.

45. How Those Who Were Sent Away Wept and Made a Plan

And the children of the nobles of Israel, who were commanded to depart with the son of the king, took counsel together, saying, "What shall we do? For we have left our country and our birth place, and our kinsfolk and the people of our city. Now, come, let us establish a covenant between us only, of which our kinsfolk shall know nothing, that we will love each other in that country: none shall hasten or tarry here, and we will neither fear nor have any doubt. For God is here, and God is there, and may God's Will be done! And to Him be praise forever and ever! Amen." And Azâryâs and 'Êlmîyâs, sons of the priests, answered, "Let not the other matter—that our kinsfolk hate us—cause us sorrow, but let us sorrow on account of our Lady Zion [i.e., the Tabernacle of the Covenant], because they are making us to leave her. For in her they have committed us to God, and we have served her to this day; and let us be sorrowful because they have made us to leave her. It is because of her and because of this that they have specially made us to weep." And the others answered and said to them, "Truly she is our Lady and our hope, and our object of boasting, and we have grown up under her blessedness. And how is it possible for us to forsake Zion our mistress? For we have been given to her. And what shall we do? If we resist his command the king will kill us, and we are unable to transgress the word of our fathers or the king's command. And what shall we do concerning Zion our Lady?"

And Azâryâs, the son of Zadok the priest, answered and said, "I will counsel you what we shall do. But make a covenant with me to the end

of your lives; and swear to me that ye will not repeat it whether we live or whether we die, or whether we be taken captive or whether we go forth [unhindered]." And they swore an oath to him in the Name of the Lord God of Israel, and by the heavenly Zion, the Tabernacle of the Law of God, and by what God had promised to Abraham, and by the purity and excellence of Isaac, and by His making Jacob to arrive in and inherit a land to which he was a stranger, and his seed after him.

And when they had sworn thus to him, he answered and said to them, "Come now, let us take [with us] our Lady Zion; but how are we to take her? I will show you. And carry out my plan, and if God wills, we shall be able to take our Lady with us. And if they should gain knowledge of our doings and slay us, that shall not trouble us, because we shall die for our Lady Zion." . . .

And Azâryâs said to them, "Do what I tell you, and we shall succeed. Give to me, each of you, ten dîdrachmas, and I will give them to a carpenter so that he will make haste to prepare for me good planks of wood—now because of his love of money he will fasten them together very quickly—of the height, and breadth, and length and size of our Lady [Zion]. And I will give him the dimensions of myself, and I will say to him, 'Prepare for me pieces of wood for a framework (?) so that I may make a raft from them; for we are going to travel over the sea, and in the event of the ship sinking I shall be able to get up on the raft, and we shall be saved from the sea. And I will take the framework without the pieces of wood thereof being fixed together, and I will have them put together in Ethiopia.' And I will set them down in the habitation of Zion, and will drape them with the draperies of Zion, and I will take Zion, and will dig a hole in the ground, and will set Zion there, until we journey and take it away with us thither. And I will not tell the matter to the king until we have traveled far."

And they each gave him ten dîdrachmas, and this money amounted to one hundred and forty dîdrachmas, and he took them and gave them to a carpenter, who straightaway fashioned a good piece of work from the remains of the wood of the sanctuary, and Azâryâs rejoiced and showed it to his brethren.

...

48. How They Carried Away Zion

And behold, the Angel of the Lord appeared again to Azâryâs and he stood up above him like a pillar of fire, and he filled the house with his light. And he raised up Azâryâs and said to him, "Stand up, be strong, and rouse up your brother 'Êlmĕyâs, and 'Abĕsâ, and Mâkarî, and take the pieces of wood and I will open for you the doors of the sanctuary. And take the tabernacle of the Law of God, and you shall carry it without trouble and discomfort. And I, inasmuch as I have been commanded by God to be with it forever, will be your guide when you shall carry it away."

And Azâryâs rose up straightaway, and woke up the three men, his brethren, and they took the pieces of wood, and went into the house of God—now they found all the doors open, both those that were outside and those that were inside—to the actual place where Azâryâs found Zion, the Tabernacle of the Law of God; and it was taken away by them forthwith, in the twinkling of an eye, the Angel of the Lord being present and directing. And had it not been that God willed it Zion could not have been taken away forthwith. And the four of them carried Zion away, and they brought it into the house of Azâryâs, and they went back into the house of God, and they set the pieces of wood on the place where Zion had been, and they covered them over with the covering of Zion, and they shut the doors, and went back to their houses. And they took lamps and set them in the place where [Zion] was hidden, and they sacrificed the sheep thereto, and burned offerings of incense thereto, and they spread purple cloths over it and set it in a secret place for seven days and seven nights.

[*Solomon blesses David, who sets out with the young men for Ethiopia. When they reach Gâzâ, the young men tell David that they have brought the Tabernacle with them.*]

[53]

. . . And King [David] rose up and skipped about like a young sheep and like a kid of the goats

that has sucked milk in abundance from his mother, even as his grandfather David rejoiced before the Tabernacle of the Law of God. He smote the ground with his feet, and rejoiced in his heart, and uttered cries of joy with his mouth. And what shall I say of the great joy and gladness that were in the camp of the King of Ethiopia? One man told his neighbor, and they smote the ground with their feet like young bulls, and they clapped their hands together, and marveled, and stretched out their hands to heaven, and they cast themselves down with their faces to the ground, and they gave thanks to God in their hearts.

[*Meanwhile, Solomon discovers the loss of the Tabernacle and pursues David and his companions.*]

[58]

. . . And the King and his soldiers marched quickly, and they came to Gâzâ. And the King asked the people, saying, "When did my son leave you?" And they answered and said to him, "He left us three days ago. And having loaded their wagons none of them traveled on the ground, but in wagons that were suspended in the air; and they were swifter than the eagles that are in the sky, and all their baggage traveled with them in wagons above the winds. As for us, we thought that you, in your wisdom, had made them to travel in wagons above the winds." And the King said to them, "Was Zion, the Tabernacle of the Law of God, with them?" And they said to him, "We did not see anything."

[*After this the author turns his attention to other topics in the history of Israel and its neighbors, then comes back to the story of the new king of Ethiopia: on completing his journey from Israel, he enters Dabra Mâkĕdâ, the capital city of his mother the queen, who welcomes him with an enormous feast.*]

87. How the Nobles (or Governors) of Ethiopia Took the Oath

And the Queen said to her nobles: "Speak now, and swear by the heavenly Zion that you will not make women queens or set them upon the throne of the kingdom of Ethiopia, and that no one except the male seed of David, the son of Solomon the King, shall ever reign over Ethiopia, and that you will never make women queens." And all the nobles of the king's house swore, and the governors, and the councillors, and the administrators.

And she made 'Êlmĕyâs and Azâryâs the chief of the priests and the chief of the deacons, and they made the kingdom anew, and the sons of the mighty men of Israel performed the Law, together with their King David, in the Tabernacle of Witness, and the kingdom was made anew. And the hearts of the people shone at that sight of Zion, the Tabernacle of the Law of God, and the people of Ethiopia cast aside their idols, and they worshipped their Creator, the God Who had made them. And the men of Ethiopia forsook their works, and loved the righteousness and justice that God loves. They forsook their former fornications, and chose purity in the camp that was in the sight of the heavenly Zion. They forsook divination and magic, and chose repentance and tears for God's sake. They forsook augury by means of birds and the use of omens, and they returned to hearken to God and to make sacrifice to Him. They forsook the pleasures of the gods who were devils, and chose the service and praise of God. The daughters of Jerusalem suffered disgrace, and the daughters of Ethiopia were held in honor; the daughter of Judah was sad, whilst the daughter of Ethiopia rejoiced; the mountains of Ethiopia rejoiced, and the mountains of Lebanon mourned. The people of Ethiopia were chosen [from] among idols and graven images, and the people of Israel were rejected. The daughters of Zion were rejected, and the daughters of Ethiopia were honored; the old men of Israel became objects of contempt, and the old men of Ethiopia were honored. For God accepted the peoples who had been cast away and rejected Israel, for Zion was taken away from them and she came into the country of Ethiopia. For wherever God is pleased for her to dwell, there is her habitation, and where He is not pleased that she should dwell she does not dwell; He is her founder, and Maker, and Builder, the Good God in the temple of His holiness, the habitation of His glory, with His Son and the Holy Spirit, forever and ever. Amen.

And Mâkĕdâ, the Queen of Ethiopia, gave the kingdom to her son David, the son of Solomon, the King of Israel, and she said to him, "Take [the kingdom]. I have given [it] to you. I have made King him whom God has made King, and I have chosen him whom God has chosen as the keeper of His Pavilion. I am well pleased with him whom God has been pleased to make the envoy of the Tabernacle of His Covenant and His Law. I have magnified him whom God has magnified [as] the director of His widows, and I have honored him whom God has honored [as] the giver of food to orphans."

Latin and Byzantine Christianity in the Late Middle Ages

72. Documents by or about Boniface VIII: *Unam Sanctam;* Account of Events at Anagni, 1303

In the bull Unam Sanctam, *issued in 1302 after the French king Philip IV had arrested and imprisoned a bishop against the provisions of canon law, Boniface VIII strongly asserted the papal claim to supreme authority in the world. Philip responded by sending soldiers to confront the pope, as described by an eyewitness below. After Boniface's death in 1303 and the brief reign of his successor Benedict XI, the next pope, Clement V—the first of the succession of popes who would rule from Avignon under the eye of the French kings—issued a mollifying statement in 1306 that* Unam Sanctam *was not to be understood as having made the French king and people "any more subject" to the papacy than they had been before.*

The Bull *Unam Sanctam* (November 1302)

That there is one holy Catholic and apostolic Church we are impelled by our faith to believe and to hold—this we do firmly believe and openly confess—and outside of this there is neither salvation nor remission of sins, as the bridegroom proclaims in Canticles, "My dove, my undefiled is but one; she is the only one of her mother, she is the choice one of her that bare her." The Church represents one mystic body, and of this body Christ is the head; of Christ, indeed, God is the head. In it is one Lord, and one faith, and one baptism. In the time of the flood there was one ark of Noah, prefiguring the one Church, finished in one cubit, having one Noah as steersman and commander. Outside of this all things upon the face of the earth were, as we read, destroyed. This Church we venerate and this alone. . . . It is that seamless coat of the Lord, which was not rent but fell by lot. Therefore, in this one and only Church there is one body and one head—not two heads as if it were a monster—namely, Christ and Christ's vicar, Peter and Peter's successor; for the Lord said to Peter himself, "Feed my sheep." "*My* sheep," he said, using a general term and not designating these or those sheep, so that we must believe that all the sheep were committed to him. If, then, the Greeks, or others, shall say that they were not intrusted to Peter and his successors, they must perforce admit that they are not of Christ's sheep, as the Lord says in John, "there is one fold, and one shepherd."

In this Church and in its power are two swords, to wit, a spiritual and a temporal, and this we are taught by the words of the Gospel; for when the apostles said, "Behold, here are two swords" (in the Church, namely, since the apostles were speaking), the Lord did not reply that it was too

SOURCE: *Readings in European History,* vol. 1, ed. and tr. James Harvey Robinson (Boston: Ginn and Company, 1904), 346-48; and "The Outrage of Anagni" [letter of William Hundleby, September 1303], tr. H. G. J. Beck, *Catholic Historical Review* 32 (1947): 200-205. Used with permission of The Catholic University of America Press.

many, but enough. And surely he who claims that the temporal sword is not in the power of Peter has but ill understood the word of our Lord when he said, "Put up again thy sword into his place." Both the spiritual and the material swords, therefore, are in the power of the Church, the latter indeed to be used for the Church, the former by the Church, the one by the priest, the other by the hand of kings and soldiers, but by the will and sufferance of the priest.

It is fitting, moreover, that one sword should be under the other, and the temporal authority subject to the spiritual power. For when the apostle said, "there is no power but of God: the powers that be are ordained of God," they would not be ordained unless one sword were under the other, and one, as inferior, was brought back by the other to the highest place. For, according to St. Dionysius, the law of divinity is to lead the lowest through the intermediate to the highest. Therefore, according to the law of the universe, things are not reduced to order directly and upon the same footing, but the lowest through the intermediate, and the inferior through the superior. It behooves us, therefore, the more freely to confess that the spiritual power excels in dignity and nobility any form whatsoever of earthly power, as spiritual interests exceed the temporal in importance. All this we see fairly from the giving of tithes, from the benediction and sanctification, from the recognition of this power and the control of these same things.

Hence, the truth bearing witness, it is for the spiritual power to establish the earthly power and judge it, if it be not good. Thus, in the case of the Church and the power of the Church, the prophecy of Jeremiah is fulfilled: "See, I have this day set thee over the nations and over the kingdoms," etc. Therefore, if the earthly power shall err, it shall be judged by the spiritual power; if the lesser spiritual power err, it shall be judged by the higher. But if the supreme power err, it can be judged by God alone, and not by man, the apostles bearing witness, saying, "The spiritual man judges all things, but he himself is judged by no one." Hence this power, although given to man and exercised by man, is not human, but rather a divine power, given by the divine lips to Peter, and

founded on a rock for him and his successors in him (Christ) whom he confessed, the Lord saying to Peter himself, "Whatsoever thou shalt bind," etc.

Whoever, therefore, shall resist this power, ordained by God, resists the ordination of God, unless there should be two beginnings [i.e., principles], as the Manichaean imagines. But this we judge to be false and heretical, since, by the testimony of Moses, not in the *beginnings* but in the *beginning*, God created the heaven and the earth. We, moreover, proclaim, declare, and pronounce that it is altogether necessary to salvation for every human being to be subject to the Roman pontiff.

Given at the Lateran the twelfth day before the Kalends of December, in our eighth year, as a perpetual memorial of this matter.

Letter of William Hundleby, September 1303

Behold, Reverend Father, at dawn of the vigil of the Nativity of the Blessed Mary just past, suddenly and unexpectedly there came upon Anagni a great force of armed men of the party of the King of France and of the two deposed Colonna cardinals. Arriving at the gates of Anagni and finding them open, they entered the town and at once made an assault upon the palace of the Pope and upon that of the Marquis, the Pope's nephew. As the racket echoed throughout the town, men and women got up from their beds and threw open their doors and sought whence it came. They learned that Sciarra, brother of the deposed Colonna cardinals, had made his way into the town with a large troop gotten for him by the King of France and that he intended to seize the Pope and put him to death. Hearing this, the people of Anagni, that is the commune of the town, rang the public bell and gathered at one place; there they discussed the matter as long as time allowed and the commune decreed and chose for itself a captain in Anagni who was to command and govern the whole commune or populace. This captain is the Lord Adenulf; he is the dominant figure of the Campagna and is moreover a mortal enemy of the Pope. To him the officials of the people immediately swore fidelity and obedience and promised to carry out all his commands.

While these affairs were being discussed and arranged by the people of Anagni, the above named Sciarra and his soldiery pushed their attack with vigor upon the palace of the Pope and upon those of the Marquis and three cardinals, namely, the Lord Gentile, papal penitentiary, the Lord Francis, nephew of the Pope, and the Lord [Peter] the Spaniard. Yet so well did the members of the Pope's household within the palace, and the Marquis, the Pope's nephew, and his people in their own stronghold defend themselves, by letting fly missiles in all directions and by hurling stones, that neither the palace of the Pope nor that of the Marquis was breached at all. However the residences of the three cardinals who were looked upon as special friends of the Pope, these three were broken into and all their furnishings carried off, while the cardinals themselves had all they could do to escape with their lives through a latrine at the back of the house.

While this battling was going on, the Lord Adenulf, captain of the town, arrived upon the scene; he had with him the Lord Rainald of Supino, who is of great importance in the Campagna as well as a bitter foe of the Pope, along with two sons of John of Ceccano whose father was at that time held by the Pope in prison. No sooner had the said captain and his companions made contact with Sciarra Colonna and his troops then they joined forces with them, for they were all mortal enemies of the Pope. So strengthened were Sciarra's soldiery through their union with the captain and his band that they felt convinced the Pope and the Marquis his nephew could not possibly hold them off much longer. Knowing this, the Pope asked for a truce. Sciarra granted it to him and to his nephew the Marquis; it was to run until the ninth hour of the same day, which was the vigil of the Blessed Mary's Nativity. This truce commenced, as I said, about the first hour and ran until the ninth.

While the truce held, the Pope sent in secret to the people of Anagni, beseeching them to save his life and promising them that, if they did, he would so reward them that all would enjoy his endless good will. But the townsfolk replied that they had

chosen and commissioned a captain—the aforesaid Lord Adenulf—in whom now resided the full authority of the people; without him they had neither the right nor the intention of making any commitments. Having gotten this answer, the Pope then sent messengers and begged Sciarra that he make known to him, amongst other things, the precise points upon which the Pope had harmed him and his family; in accord with the counsel of the cardinals, the Pope was prepared to give him satisfaction. Sciarra replied, however, that he would never let the Pope off alive unless he were to agree to the three following conditions: first, that he give back or make over to the care of two or three of the senior cardinals of the college all the wealth of the Roman Church; in addition, that the Pope then fully reinstate the Cardinals James and Peter, whom he had deposed, in their temporal and spiritual prerogatives, and along with the cardinals all their relatives; also, thirdly, that the Pope resign the Papacy, upon carrying out this restoration and put himself at the disposition of Sciarra. When the Pope learned these conditions, he groaned: "Alas, this is a hard saying!" So messengers passed back and forth many times over but still no solution was hit upon.

With the approach of the ninth hour, the populace set up the cry: "Ades, ades," which is vernacular and means much the same as our "Aly, ali." The troops pressed home their attack upon the Pope and his nephew only to have the defense continue as stoutly as before. At last, however, because the cathedral of the Blessed Mary at Anagni stood in the way of Sciarra's soldiery getting at the palace of the Pope and of the cardinals, they set fire to the doors of the church, and having destroyed them, broke into the building. Once inside, they pillaged and stripped all the clerics and laymen and merchants who had cutlery and other kinds of merchandise there for sale; thus it was that of all they could lay their hands upon the soldiers missed nothing, even though it were worth as little as a quadrant.

After a time, however, the Marquis, nephew of the Pope, realizing that defense was no longer possible, surrendered to Sciarra and the captain, so that they spared his own life and those of his son and companions. In this fashion were the Marquis and one of his sons taken and thrown into prison, while another son escaped by means of a hidden passage. When the Pope heard this reported, he himself wept bitterly, yet not even the Pope was in a position to hold out longer. Sciarra and his forces broke through the doors and windows of the papal palace at a number of points, and set fire to them at others, till at last the angered soldiery forced their way to the Pope. Many of them heaped insults upon his head and threatened him violently, but to them all the Pope answered not so much as a word. And when they pressed him as to whether he would resign the Papacy, firmly did he refuse— indeed he preferred to lose his head—as he said in his vernacular: "E le col, e le cape!" which means: "Here is my neck and here my head!" Therewith he proclaimed in the presence of them all that as long as life was in him, he would not give up the Papacy. Sciarra, indeed, was quite ready to kill him, but he was held back by the others so that no bodily injury was done the Pope. Cardinal Peter of Spain was with the Pope all through the struggle, though the rest of his retinue had slipped away. Sciarra and the captain appointed guards to keep the Pope in custody after some of the papal doormen had fled and others had been slain. Thus were the Pope and his nephew taken in Anagni on the said vigil of the Blessed Mary at about the hour of vespers, and it is believed that the Lord Pope put in a bad night.

The soldiers, on first breaking in, had pillaged the Pope, his chamber and his treasury of utensils and clothing, fixtures, gold and silver and everything found therein so that the Pope had been made as poor as Job upon receiving word of his misfortune. Moreover, the Pope witnessed all and saw how the wretches divided his garments and carted away his furniture, both large items and small, deciding who would take this and who that, and yet he said no more than: "The Lord gave and the Lord taketh away, etc." And anyone who was in a position to seize or to lay hold upon something, took and seized it and carried it off, while no one then paid any more attention to the person of the Pope than he did to Godfrey Ceco of Lincoln or to Peter Stall.

Truly one finds it hard to believe that all the kings in the world could have disbursed from their treasuries in one year as much as was carried away

from the palaces of the Pope and the Marquis and the three cardinals in one short hour. Besides that, Simon Gerard, the papal banker, was stripped of all that he had and was barely able to get away himself. Thus were the Pope and his nephews held in the custody of some soldiers and other laymen from the vigil of the Blessed Mary's Nativity until the third day following, that is, until Monday, the day after the Nativity.

In the meantime, Sciarra and his party debated whether they should put the Pope to death or hand him over alive to the King of France. But when the people of Anagni, that is the commune of the town, heard that the Pope might be slain, the commune of Anagni summoned a secret meeting without the knowledge of the captain and Sciarra and the other guards of the Pope. This gathering of the commune of Anagni took place on the day after the feast of the Blessed Mary at about the third hour.

Those who came to the meeting said to one another: "Although the Pope has done much evil in his life, still it is not right to kill him in this city, for if he were to be slain amongst us here, men throughout the world would say that we are guilty of his death, and so our town will be interdicted and Mass will not be celebrated here, and all Christendom will rise against us on this score and we shall all be destroyed." And some asked: "What are we to do then?" Others replied: "Let us go together at once to the Pope's palace and free him and his nephew from the guards, and let us ourselves take over their charge and thus shall we save their lives." Thereupon they agreed on oath that should the men assigned by the captain and Sciarra to the guarding of the Pope resist them, not one would get away alive.

Having thus committed themselves, the people of Anagni, that is the commune which is said to number some ten thousand well-armed men, hurried off at once to the Pope's palace where he was held a prisoner. Although they were anxious to get in, they found that the soldiers barred their entrance. But at last, when they had ousted the troops and had killed many of them, the people of Anagni forced their way to the Pope. One of the commune spoke on behalf of the others: "Holy Father, we have come here to save your life, and so we ask that we be allowed to watch over you until this tumult is quieted." Upon the Pope's hearing this, he raised his eyes and his hands to heaven and he gave thanks to God and to the commune for his deliverance from death. In like manner were the nephews of the Pope set at liberty. When the report of these happenings reached Sciarra, he quit the town with his troops, though he was violently angry with the townsfolk of Anagni and swore vengeance upon them. Thus was the Pope given his freedom by the people of Anagni on the day following the Nativity of the Blessed Mary, just after midday.

No sooner was the Pope delivered by the townsfolk of Anagni than they had him brought from his palace to the great piazza before all the people. The Pope preached with tears in his eyes and began by thanking God and the saints and the people of Anagni for his life. All of what he said I cannot narrate here, but part of it ran: "Good men and women, you know indeed how my enemies have fallen upon me and have taken all my belongings and those of the Church and have left me as poor as was Job. I tell you, therefore, that I have nothing to eat or to drink, and at this hour I have not as yet broken my fast. And so if there is any good woman who would like to help me in her kindness with either bread or wine, or, if she has neither bread nor wine, at least with a little water, I shall give her God's blessing and my own. And to all who bring me something for my support, no matter how small it may be, I shall grant absolution from all their sins, both as to punishment and to guilt" And all began to shout: "Vive, Holy Father!" for this is their custom. And behold, those women who had been in the crowd, and many others from the town, hurried off to the Pope's palace and offered him, some of them, wine, some of them, bread, and some of them, water, so that soon his entire chamber was filled with bread, wine, and water. They even had to pour out great quantities of the wine and water in the Pope's courtyard because they could not find enough jars to contain it all. Then were all admitted freely to the Pope, the good with the bad, the little people with the important folk, and all chatted with him just as they would with any other poor person.

In the meantime, when the Pope realized that

he had been set at liberty, he got the consent of his protectors and went out and blessed the people. Again he gave thanks to God and to the townsfolk for having saved his life and he added: "Yesterday I had nothing at all but was badly off as ever Job was. Now, God be praised, I have bread, wine, and water enough for myself and for all of you." Thereupon he absolved the entire commune from both punishment and guilt, exception made, however, for those who had taken the property of the Roman Church or of the cardinals and others of the Curia. These latter he forgave only on condition that within three days they restore such holdings. Nevertheless, the Pope expressly pardoned all who had stolen his own goods, as long as these belonged to him personally and were not of the estate of the Roman Church. With that, the Pope made public his desire to be at peace with the Colonna cardinals and with his other enemies and stated his readiness to reinstate the Colonnas in their temporalities and in their spiritual privileges; this announcement he had proclaimed throughout the town. Thus was the Pope with his nephews in the charge of the commune of Anagni from the day following the Nativity of the Blessed Mary, about the vesper hour, until the next Friday. During that period, indeed, those goods which had been carried off were brought back again, but I would not have you believe that they were restored in their entirety.

On the morning of the Friday after the Nativity of the Blessed Mary, the Pope left Anagni for Rome; he left in haste and rather unexpectedly and with him there went a large party of armed men. Without interrupting his journey, he arrived at the city of Rome on the Wednesday following the octave of the Blessed Mary's Nativity and passed the night at the Lateran. There he remained for two days and, on the third, moved to St. Peter's where he resides at this moment. He seems saddened by the realization that he is safe only at Rome, for he has so many enemies that there is scarcely a city to be found in all Tuscia or the Campagna to defend him against the Colonnas. Unless the Roman people aid and support the Pope, one fears that he may be destroyed. All the Orsini are on the side of the Pope, but many other Romans oppose him and sympathize with the

Colonnas. Thus there are divisions amongst the Romans; on which account, we who are curtisans[1] are badly plagued and live from day to day in fear of being despoiled of all we have. We cannot leave the city for there are thieves on all sides of Rome who lie in wait for travellers, so that even though sixty well-armed men were to fall into their hands, they would not stand against them. Conscious of the danger that constantly hangs over us, the senators of Rome have resigned their authority into the hands of the Roman people; wherefore, there is neither judge nor one to dispense or see to justice in the city, but each man looks to himself for his own protection.

As I have said, the Lord Pope keeps to his palace at St. Peter's in great distress and tries as best he can to win the Roman people to his side, one after another. What the end will be, I know not; only God knows. But would that I were in England and had given to the poor all my goods, even to the last farthing. In these days no one thinks of presenting petitions at the Curia or of pressing cases, for there is no prospect that hearings will recommence within the near future. Be assured that not since Christ was born of the Virgin has one place and one period seen so many great and strange happenings as we have witnessed here. Dated at Rome, on the Friday before the feast of St. Michael, in the year of the Lord 1303.

---

[1] I.e., persons with occupations at the papal court.

73. Gregory Palamas, *Triads*

The Greek theologian Gregory Palamas (ca. 1226-1359) wrote the work known as Triads in Defense of the Holy Hesychasts *between 1338 and 1341 to answer attacks leveled by the monk Barlaam of Calabria on the Orthodox monastic tradition of mystical prayer known as "hesychasm." Against Barlaam's claim that God could be known only indirectly through an understanding of Scripture and the Fathers, Palamas argued that the incarnation of Christ had made direct knowledge of God possible through human experience of both mind and body.*

C. The Hesychast Method of Prayer, and the Transformation of the Body

I.ii

1. My brother, do you not hear the words of the Apostle, "Our bodies are the temple of the Holy Spirit which is in us" (1 Cor. 6:19), and again, "We are the house of God" (cf. Heb. 3:6)? For God Himself says, "I will dwell in them and I will walk in them and I shall be their God" (2 Cor. 6:16). So why should anyone who possesses mind grow indignant at the thought that our mind dwells in that whose nature it is to become the dwelling place of God? How can it be that God at the beginning caused the mind to inhabit the body? Did even He do ill? Rather, brother, such views befit the heretics, who claim that the body is an evil thing, a fabrication of the Wicked One.

Source: Gregory Palamas, *The Triads*, ed. and tr. John Meyendorff (New York: Paulist Press, 1983). Copyright © 1983 by The Missionary Society of St. Paul the Apostle in the State of New York. Used by permission of Paulist Press, Inc., New York/Mahwah, N.J.

As for us, we think the mind becomes evil through dwelling on fleshly thoughts, but that there is nothing bad in the body, since the body is not evil in itself. . . . If the Apostle calls the body "death" (saying, "Who will deliver me from the body of this death?" [Rom. 7:24]), this is because the material and corporeal thought does really have the form of the body. Then, comparing it to spiritual and divine ideas, he justly calls it "body"—yet not simply "body" but "body of death." Further on, he makes it even clearer that what he is attacking is not the body, but the sinful desire that entered in because of the Fall: "I am sold to sin" (Rom. 7:14), he says. But he who is sold is not a slave by nature. And again: "I well know that what is good does not dwell in me, that is, in the flesh" (Rom. 7:18). You note that he does not say the flesh is evil, but what inhabits it. Likewise, there is nothing evil in the fact that the mind indwells the body; what is evil is "the law which is in our members, which fights against the law of the mind" (Rom. 7:23).

2. This is why we set ourselves against this "law of sin," and drive it out of the body, installing in its place the oversight of the mind, and in this way establishing a law appropriate for each power of the soul, and for every member of the body. For the senses we ordain the object and limit of their scope, this work of the law being called "temperance." In the affective part of the soul, we bring about the best state, which bears the name "love." And we improve the rational part by rejecting all that impedes the mind from elevating itself towards God (this part of the law we call "watchfulness"). He who has purified his body by temperance, who by divine love has made an occasion of virtue from his wishes and desires, who has presented to God a mind purified by prayer, acquires and sees in himself the grace promised to those whose hearts have been purified. He can then say with Paul: "God, who has ordered light to shine from darkness, has made His light to shine in our hearts, in order that we may be enlightened by the knowledge of the glory of God, in the face of Jesus Christ" (2 Cor. 4:6); but he adds, "We carry this treasure in earthen vessels" (2 Cor. 4:7). So we carry the Father's light in the face of Jesus Christ in earthen vessels, that is, in our bodies, in order

to know the glory of the Holy Spirit. Shall we be treating the greatness of the mind unworthily if we guard our own mind within the body? What man (I do not say spiritual man) endowed with human intelligence would say that, even if bereft of divine grace?

3. Our soul is a unique reality, yet possessing multiple powers. It uses as an instrument the body, which by nature coexists with it. But as for that power of the soul we call mind, what instruments does that use in its operations? No one has ever supposed that the mind has its seat in the nails or the eyelids, the nostrils or the lips. Everyone is agreed in locating it within us, but there are differences of opinion as to which inner organ serves the mind as primary instrument. Some place the mind in the brain, as in a kind of acropolis; others hold that its vehicle is the very centre of the heart, and that element therein which is purified of the breath of animal soul.

We ourselves know exactly that our rational part is not confined within us as in a container, for it is incorporeal, nor is it outside of us, for it is conjoined to us; but it is in the heart, as in an instrument. We did not learn this from any man, but from Him who moulded man, who showed that "it is not what goes into a man that defiles a man, but what goes out by the mouth," adding "for it is from the heart that evil thoughts come" (Matt. 15:11, 19). And the great Macarius says also, "The heart directs the entire organism, and when grace gains possession of the heart, it reigns over all the thoughts and all the members; for it is there, in the heart, that the mind and all the thoughts of the soul have their seat" (Hom. 15.20).

Thus our heart is the place of the rational faculty, the first rational organ of the body. Consequently, when we seek to keep watch over and correct our reason by a rigorous sobriety, with what are we to keep watch, if we do not gather together our mind, which has been dissipated abroad by the senses, and lead it back again into the interior, to the selfsame heart which is the seat of the thoughts? This is why the justly named Macarius immediately goes on to say, "It is there one must look to see if grace has inscribed the laws of the Spirit" (ibid.). Where but in the heart, the controlling organ, the throne of grace, where the mind and all the thoughts of the soul are to be found?

Can you not see, then, how essential it is that those who have determined to pay attention to themselves in inner quiet should gather together the mind and enclose it in the body, and especially in that "body" most interior to the body, which we call the heart?

4. For if, as the Psalmist says, "all the glory of the king's daughter is within" (Ps. 44:14 LXX), why do we search for it without? And if, according to the Apostle, "God has given His Spirit to cry in our hearts, Abba, Father" (Gal. 4:6), how is it we too do not pray with the Spirit in our hearts? If, as the Lord of the prophets and apostles teaches, "the Kingdom of God is within us" (Luke 17:21), does it not follow that a man will be excluded from the Kingdom if he devotes his energies to making his mind go out from within himself? For the "upright heart," Solomon says, "seeks that sense" (Prov. 27:21) which he elsewhere calls "spiritual and divine" (Prov. 2:5), which the Fathers urge us all to acquire, saying, "The spiritual mind seeks ever to acquire a spiritual sense; let us not cease to seek that sense since it is in us, yet not in us" (John Climacus, *Scala* 26.26).

Do you not see that if one desires to combat sin and acquire virtue, to find the reward of the struggle for virtue, or rather the intellectual sense, earnest of that reward, one must force the mind to return within the body and oneself? On the other hand, to make the mind "go out," not only from fleshly thoughts, but out of the body itself, with the aim of contemplating intelligible visions—that is the greatest of the Hellenic errors, the root and source of all heresies, an invention of demons, a doctrine which engenders folly and is itself the product of madness. This is why those who speak by demonic inspiration become beside themselves, not knowing what they are saying. As for us, we recollect the mind not only within the body and heart, but also within itself.

5. There are, however, those who assert that the mind is not separate from the soul but is interior to it, and who therefore question how it can be recalled within. It would seem such people are unaware that the essence of the mind is one thing, its energy another. Or rather, they are well aware

of this and prefer to range themselves with the deceitful and prevaricate over an ambiguity. "For such men, sharpened to controversy by dialectic, do not accept the simplicity of the spiritual doctrine," as the great Basil says. "They pervert the force of truth by the antitheses of false knowledge, aided by the persuasive arguments of sophistry" (*Hom. XII in Prov.* 7). Such indeed are those who, without being spiritual themselves, consider themselves fit to decide and teach spiritual matters!

Has it not occurred to them that the mind is like the eye, which sees other visible objects but cannot see itself? The mind operates in part according to its function of external observation: This is what the great Denys calls the movement of the mind "along a straight line"; and on the other hand, it returns upon itself, when it beholds itself; this movement the same Father calls "circular" (*De div. nom.* 2.9). This last is the most excellent and most appropriate activity of the mind, by which it comes to transcend itself and be united to God. "For the mind," says St. Basil, "which is not dispersed abroad" (notice how he says "dispersed"? What is dispersed, then, needs to be recollected), "returns to itself, and through itself mounts towards God" (*Ep.* 2.2) as by an infallible road. Denys, that unerring contemplator of intelligible things, says also that this movement of the mind cannot succumb to any error.

6. The Father of Lies is always desiring to lead man towards those errors which he himself promotes; but up to now (as far as we know) he has found no collaborator who has tried to lead others to this goal by good words. But today, if what you tell me is true, it seems he has found accomplices who have even composed treatises towards this end, and who seek to persuade men (even those who have embraced the higher life of hesychasm) that it would be better for them to keep the mind *outside* of the body during prayer. They do not even respect the clear and authoritative words of John, who writes in his *Ladder of Divine Ascent*, "The hesychast is one who seeks to circumscribe the incorporeal in his body" (cf. *Scala* 27).

This is exactly the tradition, and our spiritual Fathers have also handed it down to us, and rightly so. For if the hesychast does not circumscribe the mind in his body, how can he make to enter himself the One who has clothed himself in the body, and Who thus penetrates all organized matter, insofar as He is its natural form? For the external aspect and divisibility of matter are not compatible with the essence of the mind, unless matter itself truly begins to live, having acquired a form of life conformable to the union with Christ.

7. You see, brother, how John teaches us that it is enough to examine the matter in a human (let alone a spiritual) manner, to see that it is absolutely necessary to recall or keep the mind within the body, when one determines to be truly in possession of oneself and to be a monk worthy of the name, according to the inner man.

On the other hand, it is not out of place to teach people, especially beginners, that they should look at themselves and introduce their own mind within themselves through control of breathing. A prudent man will not forbid someone who does not as yet contemplate himself to use certain methods to recall his mind within himself, for those newly approaching this struggle find that their mind, when recollected, continually becomes dispersed again. It is thus necessary for such people constantly to bring it back once more; but in their inexperience, they fail to grasp that nothing in the world is in fact more difficult to contemplate and more mobile and shifting than the mind.

This is why certain masters recommend them to control the movement inwards and outwards of the breath, and to hold it back a little; in this way, they will also be able to control the mind together with the breath—this, at any rate, until such time as they have made progress, with the aid of God, have restrained the intellect from becoming distracted by what surrounds it, have purified it and truly become capable of leading it to a "unified recollection." One can state that this recollection is a spontaneous effect of the attention of the mind, for the to-and-fro movement of the breath becomes quietened during intensive reflection, especially with those who maintain inner quiet in body and soul.

Such men, in effect, practice a spiritual Sabbath, and, as far as is possible, cease from all personal activity. They strip the cognitive powers of the soul of every changing, mobile and diversified operation, of all sense perceptions and, in general, of all corporeal activity that is under our control; as to acts which are not entirely under our control, like breathing, these they restrain as far as possible.

8. In the case of those who have made progress in hesychasm, all this comes to pass without painful effort and without their worrying about it, for the perfect entry of the soul within itself spontaneously produces such inner detachment. But with beginners none of these things comes about without toil; for patience is a fruit of love, "for love bears all" (1 Cor. 13:7), and teaches us to practice patience with all our strength in order to attain love; and this is a case in point.

But why delay over these matters? Everyone who has the experience can only laugh at the contradictions of the inexperienced; for they have learnt not through words but effort, and the experience which indicates the pains they take. It is effort which brings the useful fruits, and challenges the sterile views of the lovers of disputation and ostentation.

One of the great masters teaches, "After the transgression, the inner man naturally is conformed to external forms" (Ps.-Macarius, *Hom.* 16.7). Thus, the man who seeks to make his mind return to itself needs to propel it not only in a straight line but also in the circular motion that is infallible. How should such a one not gain great profit if, instead of letting his eye roam hither and thither, he should fix it on his breast or on his navel, as a point of concentration? For in this way, he will not only gather himself together externally, conforming as far as possible to the inner movement he seeks for his mind; he will also, by disposing his body in such a position, recall into the interior of the heart a power which is ever flowing outwards through the faculty of sight. And if the power of the intelligible animal is situated at the centre of the belly, since there the law of sin exercises its rule and gives it sustenance, why should we not place there "the law of the mind which combats" this power, duly armed with prayer, so that the evil spirit who has been driven away thanks to the "bath of regeneration" may not return to install himself there with seven other spirits even more evil, so that "the latter state becomes worse than the first" (Luke 11:26)?

9. "Pay attention to yourself" (Deut. 15:9), says Moses, meaning, to the whole of yourself, not just a part. How? By the mind, evidently, for by no other instrument is it possible to be attentive to the whole of oneself. Place therefore this guard over your soul and body: It will easily deliver you from the evil passions of the body and soul. Maintain this watch, this attention, this self-control, or rather mount guard, be vigilant, keep watch! For it is thus that you will make the disobedient flesh subject to the Spirit, and "there will no longer be a hidden word in your heart" (Deut. 15:9). "If the spirit of him who dominates"—that is to say, of the evil spirits and passions—"lifts himself up over you," says Scripture, "on no account shift your ground" (Eccles. 10:4); in other words, never leave any part of your soul or any member of your body without surveillance.

In this way, you will become unapproachable to the spirits that attack you from below, and you will be able to present yourself with boldness to "Him who searches the reins and the heart" (Ps. 7:10; Rev. 1:23); and that indeed without His scrutinizing you, for you will have scrutinized yourself. Paul tells us, "If we judge ourselves, we will not be judged" (1 Cor. 11:41). You will then have the blessed experience of David and you will address yourself to God, saying, "The shadows are no longer darkness thanks to you, and the night will be for me as clear as the day, for it is you who have taken possession of my reins" (Ps. 138:12-13). David says in effect, "Not only have you made the passionate part of my soul entirely yours, but if there is a spark of desire in my body, it has returned to its source, and has thereby become elevated and united to you."

For just as those who abandon themselves to sensual and corruptible pleasures fix all the desires of their soul upon the flesh, and indeed become entirely "flesh," so that (as Scripture says) "the Spirit of God cannot dwell in them" (Gen. 6:2), so too, in the case of those who have elevated their minds to God and exalted their souls with divine longing, their flesh also is being transformed and elevated, participating together with the soul in the divine communion, and becoming itself a

dwelling and possession of God; for it is no longer the seat of enmity towards God, and no longer possesses desires contrary to the Spirit.

II. ii

5. When we return to interior reflection, it is necessary to calm the sensations aroused by external activities. But why should one calm those provoked by the dispositions of the soul, the good dispositions? Is there a method of ridding oneself of them, once one has returned into oneself? And indeed, for what reason should one seek to dispose of them, since they in no way impede one, but rather contribute to the greatest possible extent to our integration?

For this body which is united to us has been attached to us as a fellow worker by God, or rather placed under our control. Thus we will repress it, if it is in revolt, and accept it, if it conducts itself as it should. The hearing and sight are more pure and more easily conformed to reason than the touch, but nonetheless one will pay them no attention, nor be disturbed by them in any way, except when what we see or hear affects us disagreeably.

It is the body in particular which suffers as regards sensation, especially when we fast and do not provide it with nourishment from without. For this reason, people recollected within themselves and detached from external things, insofar as they remain undistracted, maintain in a state of inaction those senses which do not operate without external stimulus. As to those sensations which continue active even in the absence of external objects, how should they be disposed to inactivity, especially when they tend towards the end that is prescribed for them? For as all who have experienced ascetical combat, sensation painful to the touch is of greatest benefit to those who practice inner prayer. They have no need here of words, for they know by experience, and do not agree with those who seek such things merely in a theoretical way, for they regard this as "the knowledge that puffs up" (cf. 1 Cor. 8:1).

6. In every case, those who practice true mental prayer must liberate themselves from the passions and reject any contact with objects which obstruct it, for in this way they are able to acquire

undisrupted and pure prayer. As for those not yet arrived at this degree, but who seek to attain it, they must gain the mastery over every sensual pleasure, completely rejecting the passions, for the body's capacity to sin must be mortified; that is, one must be released from domination by the passionate emotions. Similarly the judgment must vanquish the evil passions which move in the world of mind, that is, it must rise above the sensual delights.

For it is the case that if we cannot taste mental prayer, not even as it were with the slightest touch of our lips, and if we are dominated by passionate emotions, then we certainly stand in need of the physical suffering that comes from fasting, vigils and similar things, if we are to apply ourselves to prayer. This suffering alone mortifies the body's inclination to sin, and moderates and weakens the thoughts that provoke violent passions. Moreover, it is this which brings about within us the start of holy compunction, through which both the stain of past faults is done away with and the divine favor especially attracted, and which disposes one towards prayer. For "God will not despise a bruised heart" (Ps. 51:17), as David says; and according to Gregory the Theologian, "God heals in no more certain way than through suffering" (*Hom.* 24.11). This is why the Lord taught us in the Gospels that prayer can do great things when combined with fasting.

7. To become "insensible" is in effect to do away with prayer; the Fathers call this "petrifaction." Was not this man Barlaam the first to . . . criticize those who have real knowledge because they feel physical pain? Indeed, certain of the Fathers have declared that fasting is of the essence of prayer: "Hunger is the stuff of prayer" (John Climacus, *Scala* 14), they say. Others say it is its "quality," for they know that prayer without compunction has no quality.

And what will you reply when you are told, "Thirst and vigils oppressed the heart; and when the heart was oppressed, tears flowed"? And again: "Prayer is the mother of tears, and also their daughter" (ibid., 6.28). Do you see that this physical distress not only causes no obstacle to prayer, but contributes largely to it? And what are those tears whose mother and daughter is prayer? Are they not by nature wretched, bitter and wounding for those who have scarcely tasted "the blessed affliction," but become sweet and inoffensive for those who have the fullness of joy? How is it that prayer does not dispel the bodily motions which produce a sensible joy and pain, or rather, how do these motions engender prayer and are engendered by it? Why does God bestow them as a grace, according to him who says: "If in your prayer, you have obtained tears, then God has touched the eyes of your heart, and you have recovered intellectual sight" (Mark the Monk, *De lege spir.* 12)?

8. Paul was "ravished to the third heaven, and did not know whether he was in the body or out of the body" for he had forgotten all that concerns the body. So, our opponents ask, if someone who strives towards God in prayer has to cease from the perception of corporeal things, how can such things be gifts of God, if he who so strives has to reject them? But it is not only bodily activities which ought to be abandoned by one who strives towards the divine union, but also intellectual ones: "All the divine lights, and every elevation towards all the holy summits must be left behind," as the great Denys says . . . (*De myst. theol.* 1.3). "And how can these things come from grace," asks Barlaam, "when one does not perceive them during the mental prayer that unites man to God? They serve no purpose, whereas all that comes from Him is to some purpose." . . . But do you suppose the divine union surpasses only useless things, and not also things great and necessary? It is obvious that you yourself never elevate yourself above useless things: otherwise, you would realize that union with God surpasses even things that are useful in themselves.

9. . . . This spiritual grace in the heart, alas, you call "fantasy of the imagination, presenting to us a deceptive likeness of the heart." However, those judged worthy of this grace know that it is not a fantasy produced by the imagination, and that it does not originate with us, nor appear only to disappear; but rather, it is a permanent energy produced by grace, united to the soul and rooted in it, a fountain of holy joy that attracts the soul to itself, liberating it from multiform and material images and making it joyfully despise every fleshly

thing. (I call "fleshly thing" that which in our thoughts derives from the pleasures of the body, which attaches itself to our thoughts, appearing as something agreeable to them and dragging them downwards.)

As to that which takes place in the body, yet derives from a soul full of spiritual joy, it is a spiritual reality, even though it does work itself out in the body. When the pleasure originating from the body enters the mind, it conveys to the latter a corporeal aspect, without the body's being itself in any way improved by this communion with a superior reality, but rather giving an inferior quality to the mind, and this is why the whole man is called "flesh," as was said of those overwhelmed by the divine wrath: "My Spirit will not dwell in these men, because they are flesh" (Gen. 6:3). Conversely, the spiritual joy which comes from the mind into the body is in no way corrupted by the communion with the body, but transforms the body and makes it spiritual, because it then rejects all the evil appetites of the body; it no longer drags the soul downwards, but is elevated together with it. Thus it is that the whole man becomes spirit, as it is written: "He who is born of Spirit, is spirit" (John 3:6, 8). All these things, indeed, become clear by experience.

12. Our philosopher brings the further objection: That to love those activities which are common to the passionate part of the soul and to the body serves to nail the soul to the body, and to fill the soul with darkness.

But what pain or pleasure or movement is not a common activity of both body and soul? . . . There are indeed blessed passions and common activities of body and soul, which, far from nailing the spirit to the flesh, serve to draw the flesh to a dignity close to that of the spirit, and persuade it too to tend towards what is above. Such spiritual activities, as we said above, do not enter the mind from the body, but descend into the body from the mind, in order to transform the body into something better and to deify it by these actions and passions.

For just as the divinity of the Word of God incarnate is common to soul and body, since He has deified the flesh through the mediation of the soul to make it also accomplish the works of God; so similarly, in spiritual man, the grace of the Spirit, transmitted to the body through the soul, grants to the body also the experience of things divine, and allows it the same blessed experiences as the soul undergoes.

The soul, since it experiences divine things, doubtless possesses a passionate part, praiseworthy and divine: or rather, there is within us a single passionate aspect which is capable of thus becoming praiseworthy and divine.

When the soul pursues this blessed activity, it deifies the body also; which, being no longer driven by corporeal and material passions—although those who lack experience of this think that it is always so driven—returns to itself and rejects all contact with evil things. Indeed, it inspires its own sanctification and inalienable divinization, as the miracle-working relics of the saints clearly demonstrate.

What of Stephen, the first martyr, whose face, even while he was yet living, shone like the face of an angel? Did not his body also experience divine things? Is not such an experience and the activity allied to it common to soul and body? Far from nailing the soul to terrestrial and corporeal thoughts and filling it with darkness, as the philosopher alleges, such a common experience constitutes an ineffable bond and union with God. It elevates the body itself in a marvelous way, and sets it far apart from evil and earthly passions. For as the Prophet says, "Those whom God has filled with power have been lifted far above the earth."

Such are the realities or mysterious energies brought about in the bodies of those who during their entire life have devoutly embraced holy hesychasm; that which seems to be contrary to reason in them is in fact superior to reason. These things escape and transcend the intellect of one who seeks merely in a theoretical way, and not knowledge of them by practice and the experience that comes through it. Such a man impiously lays hands on the sacred and wickedly rends apart the holy, for he does not approach these things with that faith which alone can attain to the truth that lies above reason.

13. . . . Indeed every man of sense knows well that most of the charisms of the Spirit are granted

to those worthy of them at the time of prayer. "Ask and it shall be given" (Matt. 7:7), the Lord says. This applies not only to being ravished "even to the third heaven," but to all the gifts of the Spirit. The gift of diversity of tongues and their interpretation, which Paul recommends us to acquire by prayer, shows that certain charisms operate through the body. . . . The same is true of the word of instruction, the gift of healing, the performing of miracles, and Paul's laying-on of hands by which he communicated the Holy Spirit.

In the case of the gifts of instruction and of tongues and their interpretation, even though these are acquired by prayer, yet it is possible that they may operate even when prayer is absent from the soul. But healings and miracles never take place unless the soul of the one exercising either gift be in a state of intense mental prayer and his body in perfect tune with his soul.

In short, the transmission of the Spirit is effected not only when prayer is present in the soul, a prayer which mystically accomplishes the union with the perpetual source of these benefits; not only when one is practicing mental prayer, since it is not recorded that the apostles uttered any audible words at the moment of laying on their hands. This communication takes place, then, not only during the mental prayer of the soul, but also at those moments when the body is operating, when for instance the hands through which the Holy Spirit is sent down are touching the man who is being ordained. How can you say that such charisms involving the body are not just as much gifts of God, given for the good of those who pray to possess them, alleging as your reason that those "ravished to the third heaven" must forget what concerns the body?

14. . . . Although God makes those who pray sincerely go out of themselves, rendering them transcendent to their natures and mysteriously ravished away to heaven, yet even in such cases, since they are concentrated within themselves, it is through the mediation of their souls and body that God effects things supernatural, mysterious and incomprehensible to the wise of this world.

When the Holy Spirit visited the apostles in the Temple, where "they were persevering in prayer and supplication," He did not give them ecstasy, did not ravish them to heaven, but endowed them with tongues of fire, making them pronounce *words*—which, according to you, those in ecstasy should forget, since they must be forgetful of themselves. Again, when Moses was silent, God said to him, "Why do you cry to me?" This reference to his voice shows that he was in prayer; but since he prayed while remaining silent, he was clearly engaged in mental prayer. Did he then abandon his senses, not noticing the people, their cries, and the danger hanging over them, nor the staff that was in his visible hand? Why did not God ravish him at that moment, why did He not deliver him from the senses (which you seem to think the sole gift of God to those who pray); but directed his attention towards his visible staff, conferring great power not only on his soul but also on his body and arm—things which according to you, those praying mentally ought to forget? Why, while remaining silent, did he strike the sea with his staff which he was holding in his hand, first to divide the sea, and later, after the crossing, to close it? Had he not in his soul the constant memory of God, was he not sublimely united by mental prayer to Him Who alone could accomplish such things through him? Yet, at the same time, he was engaging in these activities through the body in a sensible manner.

19. . . . Impassibility does not consist in mortifying the passionate part of the soul, but in removing it from evil to good, and directing its energies towards divine things . . . and the impassible man is one who no longer possesses any evil dispositions, but is rich in good ones, who is marked by the virtues, as men of passion are marked by evil pleasures; who has tamed his irascible and concupiscent appetites (which constitute the passionate part of the soul), to the faculties of knowledge, judgment and reason in the soul, just as men of passion subject their reason to the passions. For it is the *misuse* of the powers of the soul which engenders the terrible passions, just as misuse of the knowledge of created things engenders the "wisdom which has become folly."

But if one uses these things properly, then through the knowledge of created things, spiritually understood, one will arrive at knowledge of

God; and through the passionate part of the soul which has been oriented towards the end for which God created it, one will practice the corresponding virtues: with the concupiscent appetite, one will embrace charity, and with the irascible, one will practice patience. It is thus not the man who has killed the passionate part of his soul who has the preeminence, for such a one would have no momentum or activity to acquire a divine state and right dispositions and relationship with God; but rather, the prize goes to him who has put that part of his soul under subjection, so that by its obedience to the mind, which is by nature appointed to rule, it may ever tend towards God, as is right, by the uninterrupted remembrance of Him. Thanks to this remembrance, he will come to possess a divine disposition, and cause the soul to progress towards the highest state of all, the love of God. Through this love, he will accomplish the commandments of Him whom he loves, in accord with Scripture, and will put into practice and acquire a pure and perfect love for his neighbor, something that cannot exist without impassibility.

20. Such is the way which leads through impassibility to perfect love, an excellent way which takes us to the heights. It is most appropriate for those detached from the world, for they are consecrated to God, and this union allows them continually to converse with Him with a pure mind. They easily reject the refuse of the evil passions, and preserve for themselves the treasure of love.

As to those who live in the world, they must force themselves to use the things of this world in conformity with the commandments of God. Will not the passionate part of the soul, as a result of this violence, be also brought to act according to the commandments? Such forcing, by dint of habituation, makes easy our acceptance of God's commandments, and transforms our changeable disposition into a fixed state. This condition brings about a steady hatred towards evil states and dispositions of soul; and hatred of evil duly produces the impassibility which in turn engenders love for the unique Good. Thus one must offer to God the passionate part of the soul, alive and active, that it may be a living sacrifice. As the Apostle said of our bodies, "I exhort you, by the mercy of God, to offer your bodies as a living sacrifice, holy, acceptable to God" (Rom. 12:1). How can this be done?

Our eyes must acquire a gentle glance, attractive to others, and conveying the mercy from on high (for it is written, "He who has a gentle look will receive grace" [Prov. 12:13]). Similarly, our ears must be attentive to the divine instructions, not only to hear them, but (as David says) "to remember the commandments of God . . . in order to perform them" (Ps. 102:18), not becoming "a forgetful hearer, but fixing the gaze on the perfect law of liberty, pressing onwards, and acquiring blessedness in the accomplishment" (Jas. 1:25), as the apostolic brother of God teaches. Our tongues, our hands and feet must likewise be at the service of the Divine Will. Is not such a practice of the commandments of God a common activity of body and soul, and how can such activity darken and blind the soul?

74. Geert Grote, *Letter 29*

Geert Grote, or Groote (1340-1384), a wealthy Dutch layman who had converted at age thirty-five to a life of simplicity and devotion, inspired the movement called the "Modern Devotion," which eventually found expres-

SOURCE: *Devotio Moderna: Basic Writings*, ed. and tr. John H. van Engen (New York: Paulist Press, 1988), 78-83. Copyright © 1988 by John van Engen. Used by permission of Paulist Press, Inc., New York/Mahwah, N.J.

sion in a religious order (that of the canons of Windesheim) and in devout communities unbound by vows, known as "Brothers of the Common Life" and "Sisters of the Common Life." In the following letter, attempting to dissuade a young man from the university studies that would lead to a worldly career, Grote displays the austerity, evangelistic spirit and strict sense of priorities that typified the movement.

Chosen one, once highly loved and still much loved in Christ, whom I strive to win singularly and especially for the greater glory of God and your own salvation, with a zeal granted, I believe, from on high! Would that you might cease singing and walking in the way of iniquity and of worldly deception! Do not proceed in the way of anxiety, sorrow, fear, labor and grief, of which the world is full, but in the way of sincerity, exaltation, certainty, and uprightness; in spiritual joy and in an abundance of things good and true, not false and transient and quickly corrupted, but eternal and lasting. O my beloved soul, yet my very own soul, O Israel, what will be your reward, how great will be your glory and the place of your habitation, if through all this transience you cling permanently and persistently to your Lord! For he who stands firm to the end will be saved (Matt. 24:13)—not he who begins, but he who finishes, not he who wavers, but he who keeps the Word of God he has received; he will gain the reward. For, as the Apostle says, only he who has truly fought the battle will receive the crown (2 Tim. 2:5).

Who enticed you to come so near to a fall? Who drew you away from all good and from Him who is the source of all good, O my beloved, my beloved in the Lord, and led you to the precipice? O treacherous enemy, how many are your spears, how great your force, that you could lead such a devout young man, our John, into such a whirlpool. But you will not, I hope, drown him, suck him under. You have deployed a thousand tricks, but there will be one to free him, I hope, from the fowlers' snare and your deadly word (Ps. 90/91:3). Lord O Lord, heavenly king, our most blessed guardian Mary, together with all the saints and angels of God, come to his aid! Help me to drag him, to drag my most beloved back from the jaws and snares of the abyss that are about to overwhelm him, so that the adversary may not gloat

over him because his feet have slipped (Ps. 37:17/38:16).

See the treachery of the enemy. How forcefully he draws you away from your good intentions under the guise of study so that you turn your face away from the Lord and your own good resolutions and then descend into all manner of carnal, worldly, and vain desires. You sense it, I fear, yourself. I perceive the testimony of your own conscience, which knows that it is being buffeted by all kinds of desires, vacillations, and useless things. Watch out lest you assume the face of a whore and refuse to blush (Jer. 3:3); lest you become hardened in evil, if you once begin; lest you slide even further if you are pushed. For the impious, as the wise man said (cf. Prov. 18:3), when he reaches the depths of evil, becomes contemptuous. Take care lest your heart become hardened, lest you become calloused and insensitive.

Return, return, my beloved. The wound is recent and deep, still curable and responsive to medicine; *resist beginnings*. We all await you, your God and all his saints, your own angel, and also poor me, I who grieve—God alone knows how much—over all the innumerable evils that will overtake you if you turn away from God. Hear the word of the apostle Peter (2 Pet. 2:20-22): "Those who have escaped the corruption of the world by knowing our Lord and Savior Jesus Christ and again become entangled in it are defeated, and they are worse off at the end than they were at the beginning. It would have been better for them not to have known the way of righteousness than to have known it and to turn away from the sacred commandment that was passed on to them. Of them the proverbs are true, "A dog returns to its vomit," and "A washed sow goes back to wallowing in the mud." So too Paul (Heb. 6:6): "Such crucify the Son of God for themselves again and hold him up as a spectacle." Think too, most beloved, of how difficult the same Apostle says your return would be if you were to become hardened in evil, much more difficult than if you had never tasted the sweet goodness of Christ. This is particularly so if you persevere until evil is turned into custom or an excuse, or again until many evil spirits make their way into the paths of your soul, spirits who are much worse for you and seven times more devious in keeping you in evil than they were before your conversion. For according to the Gospel (Luke 11:26), they take seven spirits worse than themselves and enter the house which had formerly been in some sense cleaned and set right, and the latter state of the man, according to Christ, is worse than the former. Those adversaries will keep guard over you so much more forcefully because earlier, by adhering to Christ, you grieved and burdened them. And there is greater joy among the evil angels over one good man turned away than over ninety-nine hardening in their wickedness, just as the Gospel (Luke 15:7) says by contrast that there is greater joy among the angels over one man converted than over ninety-nine righteous.

But I hope that you are not totally turned away. I hope you are still curable, and near to salvation, however sharply and forcefully, yes much too forcefully, tempted. Place before your eyes and remember your coming end. Look out: What would it profit you to win the whole world and suffer the loss of your soul (Matt. 16:26)? Would, my beloved, that you would become wise, come to understanding, and discern what your end will be (Deut. 32:29). Would that you would come to your senses and grieve over yourself the way you once grieved over your father. How you wondered then at your father's blindness and indifference to future dangers. It is indeed unbelievable how much evil can occur when once the will has been turned to evil, for nothing truly and lastingly green remains on the tree once the root of good will is excised.

See now how your eyes wander about, how distracted your heart is, how brazen your face, how laborious the way you have started down. If only you would observe how many evils threaten, how many instruments have been fashioned by diabolic powers to advance your evil and punish-

ment. I ask you to turn your eyes a little toward me, and read the chapter in the *Horologium of Eternal Wisdom* on death and the art of dying. Read it, I ask you, twice or three times. Would that you read it through in a month and by the grace of God were restored to health. Fear, most beloved of my prayers, fear to offend the infinite majesty of God. Do not soothe yourself with thoughts of his mercy as you persist in your sin, for just as he is the father of all mercy and of all consolation (2 Cor. 1:3), so he is also a just judge, strong and fearful to the sons of men. As the Psalmist says (Ps. 89/90:11), who knows the power of his anger and who can tell his anger for fear? For the God of vengeance, just as he gives abundantly of his goodness and does not spare (Jas. 1:5), so, because he gives all to his glory and to that end, requires his honor be upheld in all inner or outer gifts he makes to men. For the honor of the King, as the Psalmist said (Ps. 98/99:4), loves justice. Fear this especially: He will extract everything from us down to the last penny.

Stand in horror, as I said before, of a hard heart through which infinite evil enters a man. Shun the inner darkness that follows upon sin, continuously becoming deeper and denser until at noon you are groping about as in the shadows. Consider how short and transient the time we spend here, and how many of your companions, kin, and forefathers died in sin to receive their just deserts. Against them the whole earth and everything in it now wars and will war into eternity. They say and will say into eternity in effect what is found in Wisdom (5:7-9). "We have grown weary in the way of iniquity, we have walked in difficult ways and do not know the way of the Lord. What use to us are pride and the boasting of riches? All these things pass away as a shadow and a fleeting messenger" and many other such things found in that same passage. A little later (Wis. 6:14-15) the following is added: "Such things they say in hell who sin, since the hope of the ungodly is like dust driven away by the wind or a thin froth blown away by the wind or the memory of a guest passing through for one day." If you consider these things in the depths of your heart, you will certainly return.

Once again, dearest, tremble before an evil will, since your life is so unsure, your death and its hour so uncertain, since the day of the Lord is like a thief that comes in the night (1 Thess. 5:2). When people live in indulgence and vanity, the calamity of death overtakes them in an instant; they die without warning and in a moment go down into hell (cf. Job 21:13). Then Christ, the eternal wisdom, will say to those who refused to heed the warnings in the time of salvation: "I in turn will laugh at your destruction and I will mock when what you feared comes about, when sudden calamity and destruction overtake you like a storm, when distress and anxiety come upon you; then they will call upon me and I will not hear; in the morning they will arise and not find me" (Prov. 1:26-28). There are many other such things in that passage which ought truly to instill an awesome fear.

Consider well, my beloved, and tremble before the last hour of your life lest perhaps you seek an opportunity for repentance and find none—"That day, [*dies irae*] the day of wrath, calamity, and misery," and so on. Who then will free you from those infernal claws and fearful faces coming to devour you? What then of riches, learning, male or female friends will be able to help you when—God forbid—a lion comes to snatch your soul and there is none to rescue it (Ps. 7:3/2)? What of all these things will you be able to bring with you? Everything will suddenly desert you. In an instant your friends and your things will forget you entirely. Only your merits according to your labors and your good or bad conscience will follow you down. Alas, how much fear then in the face of evil! What trembling and tension then! Oh, how they will seek death and not find it (Rev. 9:6)! How good for them if they had never been born (Matt. 26:24)! Tremble, most beloved, before the infinite duration of infernal punishment. What consolation for the damned if such punishment lasted only some countable or conceivable length of time. That fear of the abyss seems to me unspeakable and unimaginable, an infinity of infinite punishment. Consider the variety and bitterness of the punishments, the prick to the conscience, the gnawing worm and a soul near bursting, exceeding all combustion or solidification, and the pain of divine absence which afflicts a soul removed from the body and earthly comforts with unthinkable pains.

Read, I ask you, Ruusbroec's little book *On the Faith*, in which he sets before you the infinite glory of the saints in both body and soul and the punishments and evils of the wicked. Note there what punishments the wicked are exposed to in their sight, their hearing, their touch, their smell, and their taste; what horror, foul corruption, strife, quarrels, remorse, envy, and disturbance will be there; what cold and what heat; what appearance of worms and that deepest of all whirlpools. Tremble before that severe judge, the coming Christ, who was so often mild to you in your prayers. Fear this awful face, fear the sound of the trump calling to judgment, fear the fall and ruin and conflagration of the whole world. Take fright at the dissolving of all things. And especially stand in horror of that irrevocable sentence, that voice saying, "Depart, You who are cursed into the eternal fire" and so on (Matt. 25:41).

Open your eyes, my beloved. See all this lest you remain in eternal blindness. Learn these things: These things are more necessary for you than any worldly learning, to which the devil spurs you on even though you are not up to it. For how could you learn great things when you grasped lesser and boyish things only with difficulty? The adversary says: A priest must know and learn many things. You will know much if you recognize that you are not up to it. I write to you what I know from my own experience: All who come to studies without a good foundation will remain crude asses forever even if they study for a hundred years. Charity is the thing necessary for you; it is never superfluous even if knowledge and learning should cease. For if you do not have charity, which does not exist apart from a good will and a good resolution, you are nothing even if you speak with the tongues of men and of angels and you have all faith, learning, and prophecy with an evil will (1 Cor. 13:1-2, 8). What is knowledge except armed injustice, as it says in the "Politics"? The worst of men is a learned man with an evil will, much worse than a drunk or unfaithful man. Such learning is therefore an impediment for those who possess it. The devil could care less that a man is learned, for he knows that learning puffs up (1 Cor. 8:1). But he takes care, indeed much industry and zeal, to corrupt a good will. It is often to be observed that, through the Adversary and with God's permission, men who were formerly lazy and ignorant suddenly acquire such learning for themselves as far to excel all others in studies.

My beloved, my whole inner being calls out to you. You know that I do not seek anything of yours, which with God's help I regard as dung (Phil. 3:8), but I seek you. Come therefore, beloved, to your lover, who truly loves you and nothing of you except God in you. I ask that you deign to come to me and seek consolation with me, or rather to console me, for I grieve no small amount over you. I lay an oath upon you to come. I swear before heaven and earth and all that is in them that you should come to me, for your sake, for your salvation, and for the glory of God. And I exhort you again to read frequently that chapter on death as well as from Ruusbroec.

My heart, as God gives, nearly bursts for you. Would that it would burst over in true charity for you, and that I dying might have you with me alive in Christ, for Christ, and following Christ. Farewell and may you fare well, be strong and may you become strong in Christ, our sweetest and richest Lord in whom all good and all divinity reside in the flesh (Col. 2:9).

Geert, your servant and humble messenger, most joyously and sweetly acting as a legate to you from Christ.

75. The Council of Constance, *Haec sancta* and *Frequens*

The Great Schism of the West began in 1378, when elections produced two rival papacies, one in Rome and one in Avignon. In 1409, the Council of Pisa exacerbated the schism by electing yet a third pope without being able to remove the others. Finally the Council of Constance (1415-17), supported by all the great European powers, resolved the crisis by replacing all three popes with a single successor, Martin V. The council asserted its "conciliarist" claim to an authority above that of the pope in the decree Haec sancta, *and in* Frequens *it attempted to ensure frequent future councils.*

Haec Sancta

In the name of the holy and undivided Trinity, Father and Son and Holy Spirit, Amen.

This holy synod, constituting the general council of Constance, for the purpose of eradicating the present schism and of bringing about the union and reform of the Church of God in head and in members, lawfully assembled in the Holy Spirit to the praise of Almighty God, ordains, defines, enacts, decrees and declares as follows, in order to achieve more easily, more securely, more completely and freely the union and reform of the Church of God; and, first, it declares that, lawfully assembled in the Holy Spirit, constituting a general council and representing the catholic Church militant, it holds power directly from Christ; and that everyone of whatever estate or dignity he be, even papal, is obliged to obey it in those things which belong to the faith, and to the eradication of the said schism, and to the general reform of the said Church of God in head and in members.

Item, it declares that anyone, of whatever condition, estate or dignity he be, even papal, who

SOURCE: *Unity, Heresy and Reform 1378-1460*, ed. and tr. C. M. D. Crowder (New York: St. Martin's Press, 1977), 83, 128-29. Copyright © C. M. D. Crowder. Reprinted by permission of Palgrave.

should contumaciously disdain to obey the mandates, enactments or ordinances or the precepts of this holy synod, or of any other council whatsoever that is met together according to the law, in respect of the foregoing or matters pertaining to them, done or due to be done, shall be subjected to well-deserved penance, unless he repent, and shall be duly punished, even by having recourse to other supports of the law, if that is necessary.

Frequens

The frequent holding of general councils is a preeminently good way of cultivating the patrimony of Our Lord. It roots out the briars, thorns and thistles of heresies, errors and schisms, corrects excesses, reforms what is deformed, and brings a richly fertile crop to the Lord's vineyard. Neglect of councils, on the other hand, spreads and fosters the foregoing evils. This conclusion is put under our noses by the record of what has happened in the past and by reflections on the present situation. For this reason by a perpetual edict, we establish, enact, decree and ordain that henceforth general councils shall be held so that the first shall take place in five years immediately following on the end of this council, and the second in seven years of that immediately following council; and thereafter they shall take place from ten years to ten years forever. They shall be held in places to be deputed and assigned, within a month before any council ends, by the supreme pontiff with the approval and consent of the council or, in his default, by the council itself. The effect will be that there will always be either a council in being or one awaited at a given term; which term may be shortened, if by chance an emergency arises, by the supreme pontiff with the advice of his brethren, the cardinals of the holy Roman church; but it may not be prorogued for any reason. The place for holding a future council shall not be changed without evident necessity; but if it happens that any reason arises for which it seems necessary to change the site, say, because of a siege, a war, plague or such, then the supreme pontiff, with the consent and written endorsement of his brethren aforesaid, or of two-thirds of them, may substitute another place fairly near to the appointed place and suitable, and at least within the same nation (*nacione*), unless the same or a similar obstacle prevails throughout all that nation (*nacionem*). Then the council can be summoned to some other place suitable for the purpose, fairly near to the place in the former nation (*nacionis*). Thither the prelates and others who are customarily summoned to a council shall be obliged to go, as if it had been the place appointed from the beginning. This change of place or shortening of the interval the supreme pontiff is obliged to publish and announce, with legal solemnity, within a year of the appointed term, so that the prelates may be able to meet and hold the council at the appointed term.

76. The Council of Florence on Church Union, *Laetentur caeli*

This bull of Eugenius IV proclaims the reunion of the Roman Catholic and Greek Orthodox churches agreed upon at the Council of Florence. The Greeks, seeking Western support against the Turks, agreed to recognize papal primacy and the doctrine of the double procession of the Holy Spirit (filioque); but their constituency at home resisted, and in any case after the fall of Constantinople in 1453 the agreement became a dead letter.

SOURCE: *Unity, Heresy and Reform 1378-1460*, ed. and tr. C. M. D. Crowder (New York: St. Martin's Press, 1977), 169-71. Copyright © C. M. D. Crowder. Reprinted by permission of Palgrave.

Definition of the holy, oecumenical synod of Florence.

Eugenius, bishop, servant of the servants of God, for the perpetual record of the matter. With the consent to what is written below of our dearest son, John Palaeologus, famed emperor of the Romaeans, and of the deputies of our venerable brothers, the patriarchs, and of other representatives of the eastern church.

"Let the heavens rejoice (*Laetentur caeli*) and let the earth be glad" (Ps. 96:2; Vulg. 95:2). For the middle wall of partition, which was dividing the eastern and western church, has been taken away and peace and concord have returned, with Christ, the cornerstone, who hath made both one, joining one wall and the other in the strongest bond of charity and peace and tie of perpetual unity, uniting and holding them together. After the long gloom of sadness and the black, ungrateful darkness of lasting discord the bright splendor of the union which has been longed for has shone on all. "And let mother Church be joyful" who sees her sons hitherto disputing with one another, to have returned to union and peace; and let her, who before was weeping most bitterly at their separation, now give thanks to almighty God with unspeakable joy on account of their wonderful concord. Let all faithful people throughout the world show their joy and let anyone who thinks himself a Christian rejoice with his mother, the catholic Church.

For, behold, after a very long period of division and discord the western and eastern fathers have exposed themselves to the dangers of [travel by] sea and land and, refusing no effort, they have met together joyfully and eagerly at this holy oecumenical council, desiring that most sacred union and for the sake of restoring the old bond of charity. And they have not been cheated of their purpose. For after long and laborious enquiry, they have at last accomplished that most holy union, which they so longed for, by the forbearance of the Holy Spirit. Who then suffices to give adequate thanks for the benefits from almighty God? Who is not amazed at the riches of so great a mercy from God? Who is so hard-hearted as not to be softened by the scale of such compassion from above? These truly are the works of God and not the inventions of human frailty; and so they are to be received with immense veneration and to be continued with praises to God. To thee, O Christ, be praise, to thee glory and thanks, O fount of mercies, who has conferred so great a benefit on thy bride, the catholic Church, and in our generation hast demonstrated the miracles of thy mercy, so that everyone may tell thy marvels. God has indeed bestowed on us a great and divine gift. With our eyes have we seen what many before us have been unable to look upon, for all their hearty desire to do so.

For the Latins and the Greeks have met together in holy oecumenical synod and have earnestly applied themselves so that, among other things, that article concerning the godly procession of the Holy Spirit should also be diligently discussed and determinedly examined. But after laying out the evidence of the holy scriptures and the many authorities among the holy doctors of East and West, some saying that the Holy Spirit proceeded from the Father and the Son, and some from the Father through the Son, and all in different words designating the same meaning, the Greeks indeed affirmed that they did not propose the statement that the Holy Spirit proceeds from the Father with the intention of excluding the Son; but because, as they claimed, it seemed to them as if the Latins affirmed that the Holy Spirit proceeded from the Father and the Son as if from two principles and from two origins, so that they were careful not to express it as the Holy Spirit proceeding from the Father and the Son. On the other hand the Latins declared that it was not their intention in saying that the Holy Spirit proceeds from the Father and the Son to exclude the Father from being the source and principle of the whole godhead, that is, the Son and the Holy Spirit, or that the Son does not have from the Father the capacity for the Holy Spirit to proceed from the Son, or that they propose that there are two principles or two origins; but rather in order to affirm that there is only one principle and a unique origin of the Holy Spirit, as they have affirmed hitherto. And since one and the same apprehension of the truth emerges from all of this, they have agreed and consented unanimously to the holy union, pleasing to God, as set out below, in the same sense and with one mind.

Therefore, in the name of the Holy Trinity, Father, Son, and Holy Spirit, with the approval of this holy and universal council of Florence, we define that this truth of the faith be believed and received by all Christians and that all thus make their profession, that the Holy Spirit is eternally from the Father and the Son and that in his being he has his substance and his nature from the Father and the Son together and from both eternally as if proceeding from one principle and from a unique origin, declaring that what the holy doctors and fathers say, that the Holy Spirit proceeds from the Father through the Son, has the meaning that by this it is signified that the Son is, as the Greeks put it, the cause (*causam*) but as the Latins say, the principle (*principium*), of the being of the Holy Spirit, as is the Father also. And since the Father gave all the properties of the Father to his only-begotten Son at his begetting, except to be the Father, the Son has this very thing from the Father eternally, from whom he is also eternally begotten, that the Holy Spirit proceeds from the Son.

In addition we define the explanation of those words "and the Son" (*filioque*) to have been lawfully and reasonably added to the symbol, for the sake of declaring the truth and under the compulsion of necessity.

Item, [we define] that the body of Christ is truly made in unleavened or leavened wheaten bread, and that priests ought to make the very body of the Lord in one of the two, each according to the custom of his church, whether western or eastern.

Item, if any die truly penitent in charity with God, before they have made satisfaction with worthy fruits of repentence for their [faults] of commission or omission, [we define] that their souls are cleansed by the pains of purgatory after death, and that, in order that they may be relieved from pains of this kind, the prayers of the faithful still alive avail them; that is, the sacrifices of the mass, prayers, alms and other pious offices, which it has been the custom for the faithful to undertake on behalf of other faithful [Christians], in accordance with the rules of the Church.

And the souls of those who after receiving baptism have incurred no stain of sin at all; also those souls that after contracting the stain of sin are purged either in their bodies or, divested of the same bodies, as has been said above, [we define] that they are next received into heaven, and clearly behold God himself, threefold and one, as he is, one more perfectly than another, however, according the diversity of their merits. On the other hand, that the souls of those who die in the act of mortal sin or only in original sin subsequently descend into hell to be visited with different punishments.

Item, we define that the holy apostolic see and the Roman pontiff hold the primacy in the whole world, and that the Roman pontiff is the successor of blessed Peter, prince of the apostles, and the true vicar of Christ, the head of the whole Church, and stands out as the father and teacher of all Christians; and to him in blessed Peter has been delivered by our lord, Jesus Christ, the full power of feeding, ruling and governing the universal Church, just as is contained in the acts of oecumenical councils and in the sacred canons. In addition we restate the ranking of the other venerable patriarchs delivered in the canons; the patriarch of Constantinople as second after the most holy Roman pontiff, in third place Alexandria, in fourth Antioch, and Jerusalem fifth in order, that is saving all their rights and privileges.

Index